MOVEMENT SKILL ASSESSMENT

Allen W. Burton, PhD
University of Minnesota

with
Daryl E. Miller

Human Kinetics

> To my parents, Bill and Ruth Burton,
> who have shown me how life should be lived.

Library of Congress Cataloging-in-Publication Data

Burton, Allen William, 1953-
    Movement Skill Assessment / Allen W. Burton with Daryl E. Miller
       p. cm.
    Includes bibliographical references and index.
    ISBN 0-87322-975-4
    1. Motor ability--Testing.   2. Movement disorders--Diagnosis
  I. Title
  QP303.B87   1998
  612.7'6'0287--DC21

                                                      97-21938
                                                        CIP

ISBN: 0-87322-975-4

Acquisitions Editors: Rick Frey and Scott Wikgren; **Developmental Editors:** Holly Gilly and Andy Smith; **Assistant Editors:** Rebecca Crist, Chad Johnson, and John Wentworth; **Editorial Assistants:** Amy Carnes and Jennifer Hemphill; **Copyeditor:** Joyce Sexton; **Proofreader:** Kathy Bennett; **Indexer:** Diana Witt, **Graphic Designer:** Judy Henderson; **Graphic Artists:** Tom Roberts and Angela Snyder; **Photo Editor:** Boyd LaFoon; **Cover Designer:** Jack Davis; **Mac Art Illustrator:** Tom Roberts; **Line Art Illustrator:** Mary Yemma Long; **Printer:** Braun-Brumfield

Printed in the United States of America   10 9 8 7 6 5 4 3 2

Human Kinetics

Web site: http://www.humankinetics.com/

United States: Human Kinetics
P.O. Box 5076
Champaign, IL 61825-5076
1-800-747-4457
e-mail: humank@hkusa.com

Canada: Human Kinetics
475 Devonshire Road, Unit 100
Windsor, ON N8Y 2L5
1-800-465-7301 (in Canada only)
e-mail: humank@hkcanada.com

Europe: Human Kinetics
P.O. Box IW14
Leeds LS16 6TR, United Kingdom
+44 (0)113-278 1708
e-mail: humank@hkeurope.com

Australia: Human Kinetics
57A Price Avenue
Lower Mitcham, South Australia 5062
(08) 82771555
e-mail: liahka@senet.com.au

New Zealand: Human Kinetics
P.O. Box 105-231, Auckland Central
09-523-3462

Contents

Appendixes

Preface

This book is closely modeled after a course I have taught at the University of Minnesota for the past 8 years on movement skill assessment. This course has been designed in particular to provide occupational therapists, physical therapists, physical education teachers, and adapted physical education teachers the skills necessary to successfully carry out their assessment responsibilities. Like the course, the book is intended to be practical and user-friendly, with information on a wide variety of movement skill assessment instruments. However, there are many issues that need to be thoroughly addressed before a practitioner can use any of these instruments. The book probably offers more information on basic issues, such as approaches to movement skill assessment, validity, and reliability, than a teacher or therapist may initially want, but I feel that each chapter provides essential information for a person choosing, administering, and interpreting movement skill assessments.

The book begins with six chapters in part I addressing basic issues in movement skill assessment, including the purposes of movement skill assessment in educational and therapeutic environments (chapter 1), definitions and classifications of movement skills (chapter 3), basic concepts and calculations involved in the measurement of movement skill (chapter 4), various theoretical approaches to movement skill assessment (chapter 5), and validity and reliability (chapter 6). Chapter 2 presents a detailed history of movement skill assessment from before 1850 up to 1974. The great proliferation of tests appearing after 1974 prohibited an in-depth review of them, but many of these tests are mentioned and some are reviewed in subsequent chapters.

Part II is organized around the six levels of the movement skill taxonomy presented in chapter 3: movement skill foundations, motor abilities, early movement milestones, fundamental movement skills, and specialized and functional movement skills. In chapters 7 through 11, I thoroughly consider and explicate these levels of movement skill assessment and present in-depth critiques of eight instruments.

The book concludes in part III with two chapters on the implementation of movement skill assessment (chapters 12-13) and a final chapter on new directions in movement skill assessment (chapter 14). Additional information is provided in a glossary with more than 60 entries and in four appendixes. Appendix A1 categorizes 45 movement skill assessment instruments; these instruments are briefly summarized in appendix A2. Appendix B presents 35 selected standards for test users from the Task Force on

Standards for Measurement in Physical Therapy (1991). Appendix C provides a Z-score table necessary for performing some normative calculations. Thus, specific instruments are considered in three different contexts: (a) more than 150 are identified in the historical review in chapter 2 or briefly mentioned as illustrations of particular assessment concepts or examples of specific types of movement skill assessment instruments in the rest of the book; (b) 45 are categorized and briefly reviewed in appendixes A1 and A2; and (c) 8 are critiqued in depth in chapters 8 through 11. In addition, more than 650 sources are used throughout the book and included in the references.

One of the strengths of this book is its exclusive focus on the assessment of movement skills. My aim was to balance descriptions of specific instruments with presentations of current research related to movement skills at each level of the taxonomy, as well as to include information on basic measurement concepts presented in the context of movement skills. Some texts are available that focus on assessment in particular professional fields, such as adapted physical education or physical therapy, but in this book I sought to go beyond the constraints of professional boundaries and offer a comprehensive view of movement skill assessment that draws on the strengths of many disciplinary and professional perspectives.

Acknowledgments

First, I want to thank Rick Frey for inviting me to write this book while he was director of Human Kinetics' Academic Books Division and for being so patient in waiting for the completed product. I also want to express my appreciation to Scott Wikgren, the acquisitions editor, and Holly Gilly, the developmental editor for this project. There is no question that Holly's insight and skills significantly improved the quality of the final product. The thorough review and helpful suggestions and criticisms by Dale Ulrich from Indiana University also were of great value to me.

Next, I want to acknowledge the contribution of Claudelle Carruthers, a former doctoral student at the University of Minnesota, who assisted with research on the history of movement skill assessment presented in chapter 2. And I want to thank Michael Wade, the director of the School of Kinesiology and Leisure Studies at the University of Minnesota, for his constant support of my work, including this book, and for the fun and friendship he has brought to me and my family over the past 10 years.

My partner from the beginning of this project, Daryl Miller, helped develop the general structure of the book, wrote many of the test reviews, contributed ideas on what to include in the individual chapters, and—as the supervisor of adapted physical education, special education, and related services in a large suburban school district—was able to provide the practitioner's perspective of movement skill assessment. I appreciate Daryl's insight, our discussions about assessment and other aspects of special education services, and his hospitality in opening his home for most of our meetings.

I would be remiss if I did not recognize my wonderful wife, Joanne, for putting up with the presence of a third party in many of our evenings together—my laptop computer. I would rather have Joanne sitting on my lap than my Apple PowerBook, but her patient understanding and encouragement helped me continue to make progress in my writing.

And finally, I want to acknowledge the One who is my strength in all things that I do in my life—Jesus Christ. In my work in academia, I try to remember that "the fear of the Lord is the beginning of knowledge" (Prov. 1:7 New American Standard Bible, 1977).

Part *I*

Basic Issues in Movement Skill Assessment

I N the first section of this book, I devote chapters to laying out basic concepts that a person should understand before attempting to assess movement skills. Chapters 1 to 3 offer information specific to the domain of movement skills: purposes of movement skill assessment, a history of movement skill assessment through 1974, and definitions and classifications of movement skills. The issues addressed in chapters 4 through 6—basic measurement concepts, approaches to assessment, and validity and reliability—are common to all domains of assessment, but are discussed in the context of movement skills.

Chapter *1*

Purposes of Movement Skill Assessment

THE occupational therapist, sensing 5-year-old Heidi's anxiety, began the assessment procedure by asking Heidi what her favorite toys were, and spent several minutes listening to her talk excitedly about her new bicycle. Heidi had been referred for occupational therapy service by her primary-care physician after she had performed poorly on a developmental motor screening test. The purpose of the present assessment was to determine whether she was eligible for occupational therapy service and, if so, what intervention strategies would be appropriate for Heidi's specific movement problems.

> "It is doubtful if all those using tests know what purpose they expect the test to perform. Even when the teacher has a definite purpose in mind it is doubtful, in the case of many tests now used, if the test satisfies the purpose for which it is used.
>
> — *Brace (1924, p. 506)*

Ryan looked up from his math work sheet when the visitor came into his third-grade classroom and spoke to his teacher, Mrs. Nelson. Ryan was surprised when the teacher called his name and told him that he was to go with this person to the gym for a special activity. The visitor was an adapted physical education specialist who was going to assess Ryan's fundamental movement skills. After Mrs. Nelson had noticed Ryan's difficulty in performing basic movement skills such as throwing and skipping during physical education period, she had referred Ryan for this assessment to determine whether he qualified for adapted physical education instruction by a specialist.

John, a 14-year-old boy, sat in a wheelchair waiting for Karen Rasmussen, a physical therapist he had come to know well. They had met over a year earlier, during his initial weeks of recovery from a traumatic brain injury sustained in an accident with his three-wheel all-terrain vehicle. Today, Karen would be working with John to evaluate the status of his strength, range of motion, and coordination in order to determine subsequent steps in his rehabilitation program. John, his parents, his doctor, and Karen hoped that he could succeed in making progress toward independent mobility.

These scenarios briefly describe the context of movement skill assessments of three children by professionals from different disciplines for what would appear to be distinctly different purposes. The assessment of movement skills is not the primary domain of any one professional discipline; on the contrary, movement skill assessment is a critical program component in many disciplines and professions including athletics, geriatrics, neurology, occupational therapy, orthopedics, pediatrics, physical education, physical therapy, recreation, rehabilitation medicine, special education, vocational education, and other areas. Although the specific applications are quite varied, the basic concepts and the general purposes for assessing movement skills are similar across these professional areas.

■ SCOPE OF THE BOOK

The purpose of this book is to offer a comprehensive treatment of the issues related to assessment of movement skills viewed across professional boundaries. The six chapters in part I of the book will address the basic issues in movement skill assessment, with this first chapter focusing on the purposes of assessing movement skills. In part II, I will discuss various levels of movement skill assessment, presenting in-depth reviews of 8 popular movement skill assessment instruments, and also provide summaries of 45 of the assessment instruments most commonly used in the various professional fields. In part III, I will describe the process of movement skill assessment (chapter 12) and present and compare two different approaches for implementing movement skill assessment (chapter 13). In the last chapter, I will discuss the latest trends and developments in this assessment domain.

The term *movement skill* is used to refer to an observable, goal-directed movement pattern. *Movement*, not *motor*, is used as the descriptor of the type of skill because it emphasizes the observable act of moving rather than internal motor processes. In this book, I organize and discuss the assessment of movement skill in relation to the following categories: early movement milestones, fundamental movement skills, specialized movement skills, and functional movement skills. I also include motor abilities as a category because many people confuse motor abilities with movement skills, but abilities are not directly observable—they are inferred from movement performance. I will define these categories in chapter 3 and describe them in detail in individual chapters in part II (chapters 7-11).

Early movement milestones, fundamental movement skills, and even motor abilities consist of a limited set of skills or components that are similar across individuals. Thus I will treat these in a comprehensive manner in chapters 8 through 10. However, because the number of specialized and functional movement skills is great and because the repertoire of these skills is unique to each individual, the single chapter devoted to specialized and functional movement skills (chapter 11) will offer just an overview of assessment in these categories. Note that entire books, such as *Assessing Sport Skills* by Strand and Wilson (1993), are dedicated to specialized movement skill assessment instruments.

I will briefly address the assessment of other aspects of the motor domain, such as cardiovascular functioning, flexibility, or strength, but will treat them in the context of the foundations of movement skill in chapter 7. Again, there are other resources that consider these areas more comprehensively.

■ PURPOSES OF MOVEMENT SKILL ASSESSMENT

Any assessment of movement skill must begin with the question "why?"— not why does a person move in a particular way, but why do we assess movement skill in the first place? The purpose of the assessment must be clearly specified before a test is administered and even before a test is se-lected. Across the professional areas involved in the assessment of move-ment skills, there are at least five major groupings of purposes: (a) to cat-egorize or identify, (b) to plan treatment or instructional strategies, (c) to evaluate change over time, (d) to provide feedback to the performer or to some other concerned party, or (e) to predict.

Categorization or Identification

Perhaps the most common purpose of movement skill assessment is to assign a person to a discrete category related to service delivery. The most basic question related to service delivery is whether or not a person should receive the service. For persons not receiving service at the time of assess-ment, the two categories are *enter* and *not enter;* for persons already receiv-ing service, the two categories are *continue* and *exit*. Assessment to deter-mine need or eligibility for entry may be preceded by a two-choice screening categorization, in which a brief test is administered to identify persons for whom a more complete testing procedure is recommended *(yes* or *no)*. Screening tests also may be used to discriminate between "suspect" and "normal" clients (Hinderer & Hinderer, 1993). The various purposes of as-sessment within the service delivery process are depicted in figure 1.1.

Once it has been found that a person needs or is eligible for service, as-sessment data may be used to determine the type of service or service place-ment for him/her (see figure 1.1). Levels of placement in adapted physical education may be categorized by who is providing the service, such as (a) an adapted physical education specialist working with one student; (b) a specialist working with a small group of students; (c) a specialist team-teaching with a regular physical education teacher, assisting those students who have special needs; or (d) a regular physical educator teaching with no additional assistance. Placement levels in therapy also may be catego-rized by who is providing the service: a therapist, an aide or assistant, or a another clinic or service provided to whom the person is referred. Many movement skill assessments developed and published by physical educa-tors in the early part of this century were designed to divide physical edu-cation classes into discrete, homogeneous units (e.g., Alden, Horton, & Caldwell, 1932; Johnson, 1932). That is, students with the highest skills would be placed in one class, students with moderate skills in another, and students with the lowest skills in yet another. This practice was popular through the 1960s, but now is strongly discouraged on the grounds that it creates a system of bias.

Tests in the motor domain used to assign a person to levels of service are most likely to involve the measurement of movement outcomes or prod-ucts, rather than process. These tests usually yield a single composite or summary score that can be converted to a percentile or a standardized score,

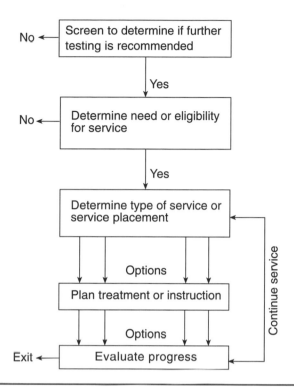

■ **FIGURE 1.1**   The various purposes of assessment within the service delivery process.

allowing for comparison of a person's scores against those of a normative group. These norm-referenced scores then can be applied to a very well-defined set of categorical criteria. For example, entry into adapted physical education may require a score at or below the seventh percentile on a standardized movement skill assessment.

Planning Treatment or Instruction

When a person's need or eligibility for service has been established and the proper type of service or service placement has been chosen, assessment data must be used to plan the actual treatment or instruction. This type of assessment is often referred to in educational contexts as a pretest or present level of performance that, besides providing information on how to plan instruction, also sets a baseline against which progress or change can be measured.

Movement skill assessment to determine treatment or instructional strategies may involve several levels of inquiry. First, the specific skills that are in deficit need to be identified, as do the details of the deficits. For example, the assessment for George, a 12-year-old boy who is not able to throw a ball as far or as accurately as most of his same-age peers, may indicate that he does not rotate his trunk or step with his contralateral foot (opposite to his throwing hand) as he throws. Skills in deficit are usually identified by poor movement outcomes or products, such as distance thrown, while details of the deficits are usually gathered from tests that indicate whether or not specific process criteria are met (i.e., criterion-referenced tests). As chapters 3 and 8 will indicate, motor ability tests cannot provide this type of information.

Next, the context of a performer's limitations or deficits needs to be identified; that is, the specific conditions or situations in which the deficit appears and does not appear need to be documented. To use the throwing example, George may have difficulty throwing a ball for distance when the diameter of the ball is larger than his hand width, but not when it is smaller, and may have difficulty throwing a ball accurately if he is under time pressure in a game but not if allowed to throw when he is ready. This procedure is an important part of the three-step, top-down assessment sequence described in chapter 13 and in the ecological task analysis proposed by Davis and Burton (1991). This type of evaluation usually involves observations recorded on informal or nonstandardized checklists.

Another important step in the planning of treatment or instruction may be identification of the movement skill foundation factors—such as flexibility, muscular strength, knowledge, or motivation—that may limit the person's performance of the skill. George's throwing, for example, may be limited by poor strength and flexibility in both shoulders. Heriza (1991) notes that physical therapists need to look not only at the factors that constrain functional movement, but also at the interaction of these factors. This process, also a key aspect of the three-step, top-down assessment sequence described in chapter 13, is usually assessed with norm-referenced, product-oriented tests. Chapter 7 includes many examples of movement skill foundation tests.

Finally, these planning data should be used to develop measurable treatment or instruction objectives that will allow monitoring of the person's progress. In addition, dates of expected achievement of the objectives may be specified. In adapted physical education, annual goals and short-term instructional objectives, derived from a student's present level of movement performance, must be included in the individualized education program (IEP) as required by federal law (the Individuals With Disabilities Education Act [IDEA], originally enacted as the Education for All Handicapped Children Act in Public Law 94-142 in 1975 and reauthorized as IDEA in Public Law 101-476 in 1990). In physical therapy, Stewart (1993) argues that data collection on the efficacy of treatment procedures and outcomes is pivotal in addressing issues of value in managed care.

Evaluating Change Over Time

Another general purpose of movement assessments is to evaluate change over time. This may include the evaluation of developmental change with no special intervening experiences or, more commonly, the evaluation of change occurring in conjunction with a therapeutic or instructional program. The evaluation of developmental change occurs most typically when one is monitoring children who may be at risk for future problems, following up on individuals once they have exited an intervention program, or conducting longitudinal research programs.

When a treatment or instructional program has been initiated, the effectiveness of the program needs to be monitored. Program effectiveness can be monitored for (a) the individual patient, client, or student, or (b) the entire program. At the individual level, the first and most direct assessment should determine whether the criteria specified in each of the treatment or instruction objectives have been met (i.e., criterion-referenced assessment). In addition, more detailed information can be gathered at each of the levels of inquiry used to plan the program. Together, data on program effectiveness for the individual can be used to help decide whether service should be continued or not and, if it is to be continued, what modifications in the program should be made (see figure 1.1).

The overall effectiveness of a treatment or instruction program can be evaluated in several ways. First, the percentage of persons who achieve their objectives within the specified time frame can be calculated and compared against some predetermined standard of effectiveness, such as 75%. Of course, two factors that could affect this type of assessment are the relative difficulty of the objective and the time allowed to accomplish it.

A second way to evaluate the overall effectiveness of a program is to assess changes in the targeted skills of a group of individuals over time—preferably in terms of movement outcomes or products rather than process—and then determine whether statistically significant improvement has occurred. Problems with this approach are that statistically significant changes may not be functionally meaningful and that a program goal for an individual—for example, a person with muscular dystrophy—may not be to improve performance but to maintain or reduce the rate of loss in a skill.

The third way to evaluate overall program effectiveness, which is also the most objective and most complex, is to randomly assign participants to a standard program group, an alternative program group, and a control group and assess changes in movement outcomes (again, preferred over process data) over time in persons in all groups. Statistical analyses on the difference scores (posttest minus pretest scores) then can be used to examine possible significant differences between the groups. One drawback of this third approach is that it depends upon the willingness of some persons to be randomly assigned to a nontreatment or control group.

Motor ability tests, such as the Bruininks-Oseretsky Test of Motor Proficiency (Bruininks, 1978), are quite popular with occupational therapists, physical therapists, and adapted physical educators and in some situations are used to assess change over time. However, motor abilities—general traits or capacities of an individual that underlie the performance of a variety of movement skills—are relatively stable attributes that are not expected to change much, even after administration of therapeutic or educational interventions. Chapter 8 provides more information on motor ability tests.

Providing Feedback

Sometimes the results of movement skill assessments are used to provide feedback to performers, parents/guardians, or other parties interested in an individual's performance status. In adapted physical education, information concerning all the steps of the assessment process depicted in figure 1.1 are shared with students, parents/guardians, advocates, teachers, therapists, administrators, and others at an IEP meeting. In regular education settings, movement performance scores on health-related fitness tasks, such as sit-ups or the 1-mile run-walk, are sometimes sent home but the actual purpose of the testing is not clearly explained and information needed for proper interpretation of the scores is not provided. More meaningful information regarding performance in physical education for parents, guardians, and students is whether or not the specified objectives in the curriculum were achieved (yes/no) and what the scores were relative to the curriculum standards.

In medical settings, assessment feedback also is provided to patients, parents/guardians, relatives, other health care providers, and reimbursement agencies. As in education settings, the most important information is whether or not the criteria specified in each of the treatment or instruction objectives have been met, and what the scores were relative to the standards. In particular, reimbursement agencies want information about a patient's status relative to functional or disability-related outcomes (Jette, 1995).

In both medical and educational contexts, feedback is usually secondary to the primary purposes, such as planning treatment or instruction or evaluating change, but at times can be the primary purpose. Feedback information may be used to help all interested parties understand the next steps in treatment or instruction, if any are required, and how they might assist the individual. Also, feedback to the performers might be important in motivating them to work toward positive change.

Prediction

The final and perhaps least common purpose of movement skill assessment is prediction. Movement skill assessment data may be used, for example, to predict neurodevelopmental outcomes at a later age, to predict a student's achievement level at the end of a specified instructional period, or to predict resource utilization at rehabilitation facilities. Evidence that future performance or the physical or health status of the performer can be accurately predicted by the assessment of movement skills is somewhat limited (Campbell, 1993b; Piper & Darrah, 1994). However, in a recent paper, Guralnik, Ferrucci, Simonsick, Salive, and Wallace (1995) offer an exception to this general conclusion.

Guralnik et al. (1995) administered a test composed of three performance components to 1,122 persons 65 years and older who reported no disabilities and were able to walk one-half mile and climb stairs without assistance. Three separate scores from 0 to 4 (4 representing highest performance) were assigned for timed performances on three standing balance tasks, normal walking pace, and rising from a chair; then a summary performance score, with a maximum of 12, was created. Four years later, compared to subjects with summary performance scores from 10 to 12, subjects with scores from 4 to 6 were 4.2 times more likely, and those with scores from 7 to 9 were 1.6 times more likely, to have disability in activities of daily living. Guralnik and his colleagues speculated that this simple assessment of lower-extremity function was highly predictive of subsequent disability because "it reflects the effects of chronic disease, coexisting conditions, and physiologic decline that have not yet caused frank disability" (p. 559).

For more information on prediction, see the section on predictive validity in chapter 6.

■ MOVEMENT SKILL ASSESSMENT IN VARIOUS PROFESSIONS

The five general purposes of movement skill assessment—categorization (#1), planning treatment or instruction (#2), evaluating change (#3), providing feedback (#4), and prediction (#5)—are used across various professional areas in relation to movement skill treatment and instruction, albeit with slightly different emphases and approaches. For example, Safrit (1986) lists 10 major purposes of assessment in physical education that fit into the five categories: (a) classification (#1); (b) diagnosis and prescription (#2); (c) assessment of achievement, measurement of improvement, evaluation of a unit of instruction, and evaluation of a program (#3); (d) grading and motivation (#4); and (e) prediction (#5). Similarly, the main purposes of assessment in adapted physical education according to Dunn and Fait (1989) are (a) screening and establishing eligibility for service (#1), (b) developing individualized programs (#2), (c) analysis of progress and reviewing curricular effectiveness (#3), and (d) communication between home and school (#4).

In 1987, Reid reported the results of a survey of 67 occupational therapists in Ontario, Canada, regarding their assessment practices. The assessment purposes therapists mentioned fall into three of the five general categories outlined above: (a) screening (65%), establishing level of function
(94%), and placement (64%) (#1); (b) establishing diagnosis (54%) and program planning (97%) (#2); and (c) monitoring individual progress (86%)
and evaluating the program (74%) (#3). In physical therapy, the Task Force
on Standards for Measurement in Physical Therapy (1991) stated that the
purposes of measurement are "to classify and describe patients, plan treatments, predict outcomes, document the results of treatments, determine
the effectiveness of treatments, and determine when to refer patients to
other practitioners" (p. 592) (#1, #2, #5, #3, and #2, respectively).

In pediatrics, the purposes of screening and surveillance are emphasized.
Vaughan and Litt (1992) argue that "all health personnel having responsibility for the care of children should be familiar with the normal patterns
and milestones of development and be able to recognize deviations from
the norm as early as possible, so that underlying disorders may be promptly
identified and given appropriate attention" (p. 13). With regard to participation in assessment, the pediatrician has an important role as a referral
source or, if more extensive participation is desired, as a member of a
multidisciplinary team (Committee on Children With Disabilities, 1992).

Chapter 2

A History of Movement Skill Assessment

THIS historical review of movement skill assessment is intended to provide a historical context for the in-depth analyses of the specific instruments presented in part II, as well as to point out the historical importance of other instruments that may no longer be commonly used. The review is structured around six periods of history: (a) before 1850, (b) 1850 to 1899, (c) 1900 to 1919, (d) 1920 to 1944, (e) 1945 to 1959, and (f) 1960 to 1974. It ends with 1974 because of the proliferation of assessment instruments appearing after this date. However, I will discuss many of the instruments published after 1974 within various contexts throughout the rest of the book.

For the first two periods, up to 1899, I present information on a broad range of movement assessment in order to provide a perspective of the

> ❝ It is a truism to say that measurement began with the human race, for it has already been pointed out that measurement in a very basic way is associated with the process of thought itself. ❞
>
> — *Massey (1978, p. 16)*

context from which skill assessment emerged. For the last four periods, from 1900 to 1974, I focus exclusively on the assessment of movement skills. In particular, I include the assessment of strength in the periods up to 1899, but not in the later periods.

■ BEFORE 1850

Records of movement assessment tools before the 17th century are very limited, although there is clear evidence that such tools did exist. For example, around 800 B.C. in Sparta, boys were rigorously training for military service and were periodically assessed by state officials to determine their "physical capacity and citizenship" (Van Dalen & Bennett, 1971, p. 45). Similarly, in the centuries just preceding and following the time of Christ, young Chinese men were given special examinations to determine their fitness for serving in the military; the examinations included "the lifting of heavy weights, drawing the long bow, and the drill with the sword" (Laurie, 1904, p. 131). It was not until around 1700, however, that published documentation of movement assessment began to appear.

In 1699 a French scientist, De La Hire, wrote about measuring the strength of men by having them lift weights and carry loads, and compared the strength of men with the strength of horses. The first instrument referred to as a dynamometer was invented by Graham, who was English, and was mentioned in the writings of Desaguliers in 1719 (Bullard, 1886). Desaguliers modified Graham's device and used it to conclude that "five Englishmen were equal in strength to a horse, but only seven Frenchmen or Dutch" (Bullard, 1886, p. 544). However, Graham's and Desaguliers' instruments were too cumbersome and expensive for practical use.

In 1807, a Frenchman, Regnier, developed the first practical dynamometer to measure grip power of the hand, pulling power of the arms, and lifting power of the back. The dynamometer consisted of a metal elliptical spring to which was attached a dial to register the amount of force generated by the hand.

■ FROM 1850 TO 1899

Movement assessment during this era was dominated by neurologists and by physicians affiliated with the emerging field of physical education. Neurologists began to develop objective motor tests around 1850, although they had long been aware that problems in the nervous system often are manifested by abnormal motor behaviors. In his *Manual of Diseases of the Nervous System*, published in 1888, Gowers stated that poor motor coordination or "ataxy" may be revealed by simple observation of natural motor activity, but also proposed more objective motor tests such as having patients attempt to draw a straight line on a sheet of paper, or hold a pencil in contact with a moving surface. Blix (1884, cited by Gowers, 1888) suggested that "incoordination" be measured by "making the patient suddenly try to touch with the point of a pencil a spot on a sheet of paper suspended before him, his eyes being closed at the moment of the attempt" (p. 29). Disturbances in gait were recorded by Gilles de la Tourette in the late 1800s as he applied powder or other coloring medium to patients' feet and had them walk across large sheets of papers (McHenry, 1969).

Gowers (1888) admitted that "our means of measuring defects of muscular power are very imperfect" (p. 28), but mentioned the potential usefulness of the dynamometer, which was first developed in the 18th century. In 1863, the French neurologist, Duchenne, devised two steel spring dynamometers—a powerful one and a sensitive one—that were modifications of the "pocket" dynamometer invented by Burq in 1859 (Bullard, 1886; Gowers, 1888; Poore, 1883). Duchenne (1863, cited by Bullard, 1886) explained:

> The powerful one serves to measure the force of the pressure of the closed hand, that of all movements of parts, and the amount of what I have called nervous excitability, or the degree of exhaustion of this excitability. . . . The sensitive dynamometer . . . is designed to measure in grammes the force of partial movements in persons who suffer from paresis. (pp. 544-545)

Later, Hamilton (1875) developed a pneumatic type of dynamometer that would accommodate patients with extremely weak hands, and Kellogg (1893) originated an elaborate mercurial dynamometer designed to test 42 different muscles or muscle groups. In the latter part of the 1800s, physiologists began to attach recording devices called "dynamographs" to dynamometers to facilitate the data collection process (Grehand, 1891, 1892, 1897; Marey, 1875; all cited in Amar, 1920). Near the turn of the century, Marey designed a "dynamographic stage or gangway" and a track with electric contacts to obtain quantitative data on human locomotion. Marey and Muybridge also began to use "chronophotography" to examine human motion during this same period (Amar, 1920).

In the field of physical education, assessments focused on anthropometric measurement and strength testing from about 1870 to 1900 (Bovard & Cozens, 1930; Van Dalen & Bennett, 1971). Between 1873 and 1878, Sargent began to employ standard procedures at his Hygienic Institute and School of Physical Culture in New York City to assess the strength of muscle groups in the limbs and trunk with dynamometers (Brace, 1931). Sargent was introduced to the dynamometer by Brigham, who brought one to New York from Paris in 1872 (Van Dalen & Bennett, 1971). In 1880, Sargent's test of the strength of the arms, back, legs, and chest was introduced at Harvard University (Krakower, 1937), and in 1897, it was ratified by 15 colleges and universities as the Intercollegiate Strength Tests (Sargent, Seaver, & Savage, 1897).

The assessment of motor achievements also began to appear during this period. In 1890, Gulick constructed the first athletic achievement test of any consequence for the Athletic League of the YMCA (Massey, 1978). Gulick's test consisted of a 100-yd dash, high jump, triple jump, shot put, and rope climb. Nevertheless, public schools or colleges did not begin to use motor achievement tests until after 1900 (Massey, 1978).

Movement assessments were developed in the 1890s for application in various occupations and businesses. At this time, Galton, the famous English scientist, created a method of measuring physical efficiency "from the standpoint of usefulness in the Civil Service and in business" (Meylan, 1905, p. 107). In both the United States and England, many of Galton's tests were used by police and fire departments, railroad corporations, dry goods store firms, and "other large employers of men" (Meylan, 1905, p. 107).

■ FROM 1900 TO 1919

Interest in movement assessment during this period was carried by two primary groups: psychologists and physical educators. The early years of the 20th century brought a strong interest on the part of psychologists in the relationship between cognition and movement. Pillsbury (1911), in his presidential address to the American Psychological Association in 1910, asserted that "the most important advance in psychological theory in recent years is the enhanced value placed upon movement in explaining mental processes" (p. 83). A few years earlier, Bolton (1903) had stated that "mental development and motor power go hand in hand" and concluded that "tests of motor power may be used as measures of intelligence or mental alertness" (p. 353).

The tests of motor ability used by psychologists during this period focused on fine-motor, manual dexterity-type tasks. Bolton (1903) explained that there are various elements of "motor power" but that the only ones that could be reliably measured are rapidity, steadiness, and precision of voluntary control. Thus, the motor tasks that appeared in the psychological literature during the early 1900s were primarily those that could be performed while the person sat at a table, such as tapping with a stylus at various rates, targets, and distances.

In 1930, Bovard and Cozens divided the history of measurement in physical education into five overlapping phases: (a) anthropometric (1860-1880), (b) strength (1880-1915), (c) cardiac functional (1900-1925), (d) physical ability (1904-1930), and (e) single test or index figure (1920-1930). Hence, in the first 20 years of the 20th century, there was a gradual decline in the emphasis on strength testing and an increased interest in motor ability. Van Dalen and Bennett (1971) argued that one factor in this shift in emphasis was the observation that many skilled performers had only mediocre strength scores. In keeping with this view, Meylan (1905) from Columbia University reported a growing feeling among college and university physical directors that the Intercollegiate Strength Tests (IST) was not an adequate measure of "those physical qualifications which represent vitality" (p. 108).

Soon after 1900, tests that measured speed and endurance began to appear. In 1901, Sargent, the creator of the IST, developed a 30-min test composed of six simple exercises. The exercises were continuously performed without rest, with the survivors considered to be physically efficient (Bovard & Cozens, 1930; Sargent, 1913). Meylen (1905) concluded that Sargent's new test of strength, speed, and endurance offered a better measure of an individual's physical efficiency than the IST.

In 1905, Meylan himself devised a system of evaluating physical efficiency, which focused on three factors: health, vitality, and bodily control. The health component was based on a subjective grade of physical condition and score on the IST; the vitality component was based on a repeated jump-and-hang task; and the bodily control component was based on performance of the running high jump, a stunt on rings, and a right and left side vault over a low horizontal bar. Meylan's work reflected his belief that "we should measure those physical qualifications which we endeavor to develop by the instruction we give in physical education" (p. 109).

In 1912, a national athletic fraternity known as Sigma Delta Psi was established. All members were required to meet a minimum scholarship standard and to pass a 12-item movement achievement test, which included a 100-yd dash, 120-yd low hurdles, high jump, long jump, shot put, rope climb, baseball or javelin throw, football punt, 100-yd swim, 1-mi run, tumbling, and posture (Clarke, 1967). Other tests of physical achievement were developed for men at various universities, including the University of California at Berkeley (Kleeberger, 1917, 1918), the University of California at Los Angeles (Cozens, 1928; University of California, Southern Branch, 1922), the University of Illinois (Schuettner, 1919), the University of Oregon (1924), and the Ohio State University (Nichols, 1920). To stimulate interest in physical efficiency, the National Collegiate Athletic Association in 1923 began a competition in which at least 80% of the freshmen at a participating college would need to perform four physical events (McCurdy, 1923).

In 1913, the Playground and Recreation Association of America established the Athletic Badge Tests for Boys and Girls. The items for boys included the pull-up, standing broad jump, 60- or 100-yd dash, running high jump, and 220-yd run (Committee on Tests, 1913a), while the items for girls included a shuttle run, basketball throw, and two balance tasks (Committee on Tests, 1913b). The purpose of the badges was to encourage all children to be "physically efficient."

The appropriateness of modifications of movement assessments made for girls and women was addressed by Schrader in 1913. He argued:

> It is difficult to explain why the girl was not considered in this movement when first it was conceived. With all that we have learnt in recent years from science about woman's superior part in the future of mankind, and furthermore of the insignificant anatomical and structural differences between man and woman, it behooves us to give the girl equal chances by equal means in order that she may make the best of her innate abilities. The tests which have been set aside as efficiency tests for girls are entirely too tame and pedantic. (p. 461)

During this period, other physical ability and efficiency tests, as well as individual scoring systems for athletic events, were developed for children scaled by age, height, and grade (Wayman, 1930). For example, in his textbook *New Rational Athletics for Boys and Girls*, Reilly (1917) described 12 achievement tests for boys and 9 for girls, and Richards (1914) presented percentile data for boys for seven physical efficiency tests. More than 35 anthropometric tests, tests of health and physical fitness, or tests of physical proficiency used for classifying pupils for purposes of instruction were identified in the Proceedings of the Athletic Research Society for 1920-1921 (Brace, 1927b).

In the early years of the 20th century, movement assessment began to make its way into industry. In 1911, Gilbreth, a mechanical engineer, published a book in which he described how to analyze occupational motions and how to use the data generated to identify "standard motions, standard tools, standard conditions, and standard methods of performing the operations of the trades" (pp. 90-91). He advocated the careful examination of every factor that may affect the amount of work produced, including (a) variables of the worker (e.g., brawn, experience, size, skill, and training), (b) variables of the environment (e.g., equipment, clothes, lighting, ventilation, weight of objects manipulated, and union rules), and (c) variables of the motion (e.g., speed and acceleration, automaticity, sequence, path, and amount of work accomplished). He believed that "the arts and trades of human beings should be studied, charted, photographed, and motion-pictured, and every employee, apprentice, and student should be able to receive bulletins of his trade for a sum equal to the cost to a farmer of a bulletin from the Department of Agriculture instructing how to increase the output of cows, hens, and bees" (p. 99). Later, Gilbreth and his wife described how special equipment such as precision clocks, the cinematograph, the cyclegraph, the chronocyclegraph, and the penetrating screen could be used to measure and record movement for the specific purpose of minimizing worker fatigue (Gilbreth & Gilbreth, 1919). Gilbreth's application of his methods to persons with disabilities (e.g., Gilbreth, 1920) led to his election as an honorary member of the National Society for the Promotion of Occupational Therapy at its founding conference in 1917 (Creighton, 1992).

■ FROM 1920 TO 1944

The diversity of motor assessments expanded rapidly between 1920 and 1945. The work in physical education continued to grow, and significant contributions were made by persons in the new field of child development. In addition, interest in movement assessment was shown by people in psychology and the emerging professions of occupational therapy, physical therapy, and neuropsychology.

Physical Education

The motor assessments in physical education that were published during this period can be divided into two general types: (a) tests of motor capacity, efficiency, or ability, usually involving a single index or composite score; and (b) tests of movement skill achievement, with each item interpreted separately.

Tests of Physical Capacity, Efficiency, or Ability. As mentioned in the previous section, Bovard and Cozens (1930) identified the years 1920 to 1930 with the "single test or index figure." At the beginning of this period, Sargent (1921) presented the "physical test of a man," which was calculated by multiplying a person's weight in pounds by vertical jump height in inches, and dividing the product by height in inches. He contended that "the test as a whole may be considered as a momentary try-out of one's strength, speed, energy and dexterity combined" (p. 194). The test was so simple, Sargent (1924) stated, that it could be performed by almost anyone (including "feeble-minded" students), anywhere, at any time.

A test of physical efficiency for women was reported by Wayman in 1923 (see also Wayman, 1930). Her test was based on measures divided into three categories: medical, anthropometric, and motor ability. Subtotal scores for each category could be calculated as well as a total physical efficiency score.

Despite the great interest in the concept of motor ability in the early 20th century, no standardized test of motor ability was published in English until 1927. At this time, Brace (1927a) issued his classic book, *Measuring Motor Ability: A Scale of Motor Ability Tests*. In the Brace Scale of Motor Ability Tests, a single summary score reflected a person's performance of 20 physical stunts (see table 2.1). Brace (1927a) suggested that there were at least four applications of his test: (a) determining an accomplishment quotient for physical education activities, (b) classifying students for physical education participation, (c) diagnosing special performance disabilities, and (d) stimulating other scientific efforts in the field of tests and measurement. One key guiding principle in the development of this work was that "the tests should test native ability rather than acquired ability" (Brace, 1927a, p. 1).

TABLE 2.1 The 20 Items in the Brace Test (Brace, 1927a)

Item number	Movement task description
1	Walk heel to toe, 10 steps.
2	Jump and clap both feet together once while in air.
3	Lie on back with arms folded and legs straight; raise trunk to vertical position.
4	Fold both arms behind back; kneel onto both knees; get up.
5	Perform 3 consecutive push-ups, with back and knees straight.
6	Squat with feet together, knees out, and hands between knees on floor; jump up onto both feet, with arms swung out level with floor and feet about 18 in. apart; perform 3 times rhythmically.
7	Jump and make a full turn to the left.
8	Jump and clap both feet together twice while in air.
9	Stand on right foot, grasping left foot behind right knee; touch left knee to the floor, then stand up.
10	Hold toes of either foot with opposite hand; jump over held foot with free foot.
11	Jump and slap both heels with hand behind back.

TABLE 2.1 *(continued)*

12	Kick right foot up from standing position to at least shoulder level.
13	Stand on left foot; bend forward and place both hands on floor; stretch right leg back in air, and touch head to floor; regain standing position.
14	Squat, reach both arms between knees, behind the ankles, and hold fingers together in front of ankles; hold for 5 s.
15	Jump and make full turn to the right.
16	Kneel onto both knees; extend or plantar-flex both feet out; swing arms and jump to feet.
17	Fold arms across chest and cross feet; sit down cross-legged, then get up.
18	Stand on left foot with right foot inside of left knee, hands on hips, and eyes closed; hold for 10 s.
19	Perform frog stand (squat, place elbows inside knees, lean forward and support entire body with hands only) for 5 s.
20	Stand on left foot with right leg extended forward off the floor; sit down on heel of left foot, then stand up.

During the 1930s and 1940s, many other motor ability tests were developed by persons in physical education. In 1932, Johnson published "Physical Skill Tests for Sectioning Classes into Homogeneous Units," designed to "test native neuro-muscular skill capacity" (p. 128). His test, which was administered to males and females from 11 to 38 years of age, involved the performance of 10 skills on a specially marked gym mat.

The following year, MacCurdy (1933) presented his physical capacity index, which was the product of a force index (sum of pounds of force on dynamometer for legs, back, hands, and arm) and a velocity index (difference between vertical jump and standing height in inches). He stated that his physical capacity index was useful for classifying males from junior high through college level in general physical education according to their physical capacities. MacCurdy cautioned that the physical capacity index should not be used to determine an individual's aptitude in any specific skill.

In 1934, McCloy published his test of general motor capacity, which was based on a weighted sum of four scores: (a) an index of body size and maturity, (b) a vertical jump score, (c) the number of squat-thrusts performed in 10 s, and (d) the score on the Brace Scale of Motor Ability Tests.

Different weightings of the four items were used for younger and older boys and for younger and older girls. A Motor Quotient, analogous to the IQ in the field of mental testing, could be calculated as an estimate of innate motor capacity relative to that of other persons the same age, sex, and size. A General Motor Achievement Quotient also could be calculated as a quantitative statement of the relationship between developed motor ability and innate motor capacity. In addition, McCloy (1937) later published the Iowa Revision of the Brace Test, which was designed to be a test of "motor educability."

In 1942, Carpenter presented several methods similar to McCloy's (1934) for determining general motor capacity for children in Grades 1 to 3. One version used the Brace Scale of Motor Ability Tests along with the Sargent jump, the squat-thrust (Burpee test), and a classification index, while another version substituted the Johnson (1932) test for the Brace Scale of Motor Ability Tests.

During this period, several tests designed to estimate general motor ability of college women were published. The results of these tests were used to create appropriate groupings for physical education. In the tests presented by Alden, Horton, and Caldwell (1932) and Humiston (1937), composite motor ability scores were derived from 14 performance items and 7 performance items, respectively. A little later, Scott (1939) evaluated the validity of using various combinations of two or three motor performance items to estimate the motor ability of college women.

Tests of Movement Skill Achievement. Through the efforts of Hetherington, the California Decathlon Tests were developed by the California State Department of Physical Education to evaluate student achievement in the activities specified in the physical education curricula during the years around 1920 (Bovard & Cozens, 1930; Hjelte, 1922). The tests consisted of 10 items including those related to strength, individual athletic events, and team sport skills. The events varied by student sex and age. Hjelte (1922) stated that the tests "may be used for the purpose of classification of pupils according to capacity and ability and the selection of individuals for special attention and adaptation of exercise" (p. 17).

In 1924, the National Committee on Motor Ability of the American Physical Education Association recommended the development of tests to measure "the fundamental big muscle motor skills" for persons from 6 to 24 years (Committee of the American Physical Education Association, 1924, p. 579). In this preliminary report, tests for three of eight recommended groups of activities were presented. The eight activity groups were (a) free exercises, (b) calisthenics, (c) marching, (d) dancing, (e) track and field athletics, (f) team game activities, (g) apparatus exercises and tumbling, and (h) swimming.

Also in 1924, Barrow presented a six-component test of athletic efficiency. High school boys were rated on a four-level scale on (a) physical condition and posture, (b) gymnastics work and apparatus, (c) swimming, (d) track and field events, (e) minor sports, and (f) major sports. The scores for the last two categories were based on actual participation in school sport activities.

In 1927, Bliss published a study of the development of strength and skill of junior high school boys and girls, with a secondary purpose of formulating a standard motor achievement test. Twelve different items were assessed, including a 50-yd dash, jump and reach, standing broad jump, basketball shooting, and baseball throwing accuracy. Bliss argued that strength is the foundation of skill, but that skill is indicated by speed of movement and by variations of an activity that can be executed.

As a follow-up to the California Decathlon Tests, Cozens and Neilson published four books detailing achievement tests for boys and girls in elementary and junior high schools (Cozens & Neilson, 1934), for boys in secondary schools (Cozens, Trieb, & Neilson, 1936), for men in college (Cozens, 1936), and for girls and women in secondary schools and college (Cozens, Cubberly, & Neilson, 1937). The achievement scales for children in elementary and junior high schools, for example, included information on 33 events for boys and 20 for girls, based on data collected from over 79,000 children in California. A 100-point scale, ranging from –3.00 to +3.00 standard deviations, was presented for each event, with each point representing a change of 0.06 standard deviations. An integral component of these achievement scales was the inclusion of a classification index based on age, height, and weight. Some of these tests also are described in an article in *Research Quarterly* (Neilson & Cozens, 1934).

Later in this period, Gutteridge (1939) presented a 14-point rating scale that could be used to evaluate the quality of movement skill on a wide variety of skills including hopping, jumping, skipping, climbing, tricycling, throwing, and catching (see figure 2.1a). In addition, the test form emphasized the recording of features of the environment that might affect a person's performance, such as weather, location, and social context (see figure 2.1b). Ratings of 1,973 children, 2 to 7 years old, on 1 to 10 different skills also were reported by Gutteridge (1939) in her paper; and when appropriate, multiple ratings for the same skill were presented and task factors such as ball size were systematically manipulated.

Child Development

Gesell, from the Yale Clinic of Child Development, was a pioneer in the study of early childhood development from the early 1900s into the 1950s. In 1918, he began to gather normative data on children 1 to 5 years of age in four areas: motor development, language, adaptive behavior, and personal-social behavior (Gesell, 1924). Gesell first published his developmental norms in 1925 in a book titled *The Mental Growth of the Pre-School*

Gutteridge's (1939) Rating Scale
A Key to Estimate Degree of Motor Skill

Skillful execution with variations in use
 1. Uses skill in larger projects such as dramatic play.
 2. Speeds, races, or competes with self or others.
 3. Combines activity with other skill or skills.
 4. Tests skill by adding difficulties or taking chances.

Basic movements achieved

 5. Evidence of accuracy, poise, and grace.
 6. Easy performance with a display of satisfaction.
 7. Movements coordinated.

Habit in process of formation
 8. In process of refining movements
 9. Is practicing basic movements.
 10. Is progressing but is still using unnecessary movements.
 11. Tries even when not helped or supported, but is inadept.
 12. Attempts activity but seeks help or support.

No attempts made
 13. Makes no approach or attempt but does not withdraw.
 14. Withdraws or retreats when opportunity is given.

Key used in rating the following activities:
Climbing	Tricycling	Throwing balls
Jumping	Hopping	Bouncing balls
Sliding	Galloping	Catching balls
Skipping		

■ **FIGURE 2.1A**   Rating scale from Gutteridge (1939).

Child: A Psychological Outline of Normal Development from Birth to the Sixth Year Including a System of Developmental Diagnosis and continued to publish revisions of his work until 1941. In 1940, he issued developmental schedules for children from 15 months to 6 years in *The First Five Years of Life: A Guide to the Study of the Preschool Child*. The next year, Gesell and Amatruda (1941) produced another book, *Developmental Diagnosis: Normal and Abnormal Child Development*, which was "primarily devoted to methods of diagnosis and to the applications which rest securely on diagnosis" (p. vi) for children from 4 weeks to 60 months of age (see figure 2.2). Colleagues and former students updated and expanded on Gesell's normative contributions until at least 1980 (Knobloch & Pasamanick, 1974; Knobloch, Stevens, & Malone, 1980).

The research and writings of Bayley and Gesell during this period laid the foundation for the assessment of motor skills in infants and young

A STUDY OF THE MOTOR DEVELOPMENT OF YOUNG CHILDREN

(Record of one child during one activity)

Name of child _____   Date _____   Hour _____

Length of child's school experience _____   Type of activity _____

School: Group or grade _____   Nation-ality _____   Date of birth _____   Age of child _____

Address: _____   Weather _____   Sex _____ Height _____ Weight _____

Conditions	EQUIPMENT Give type, number, height, length	Social factors		Details of activity (outline in steps)	Comments	Estimate of skill (see key)
Outdoor			Number of children cooperating			
Roof						
Playground			Number of children in proximity			
Street			Solitary			
Yard			Number of adults active in situation			
Indoor			Changes in grouping or other social factors			
Gymnasium						
Classroom						
Playroom						
Sitting room						
Approx. playing space						
Other Context						

Where desirable to clarify, draw a rough plan of arrangement of equipment below.

Is this activity an indication of child's usual performance? _____   Observer: _____

■ **FIGURE 2.1B**   Score sheet from Gutteridge (1939).

4 weeks or less
  Supine: tonic-neck reflex position predominates.
  Sit: head sags.
  Prone: crawling movements.

16 weeks
  Supine: hands engage.
  Sit: head set forward, steady.
  Prone: rolls to supine.

28 weeks
  Sit: sits erect about one minute.
  Stand: stands hand held.
  Prone: crawls or creep-crawls.

40 weeks
  Rail: cruises, using 2 hands.
  Rail: retrieves toy from floor.
  Rail: lets self down with control.

52 weeks
  Stand: picks up object from floor.
  Walks: rises independently, takes several steps.
  Stairs: creeps up.

18 months
  Stairs: walks down, 1 hand held.
  Large ball: walks into or steps on, demonstration.

24 months
  Jumps: both feet off floor.
  Stands: tries on 1 foot without holding.
  Large ball: kicks on request.

36 months
  Stairs: alternates feet going down.
  Jumps: broad jump.
  Ball: throws overhand.

■ FIGURE 2.2   Sample items from Gesell and Amatruda's (1941) developmental schedules.

children. In 1935, Bayley's California Infant Scale of Motor Development appeared in the *Monographs of the Society for Research in Child Development*. This classic test, which was revised in 1969 and renamed the Bayley Scales of Infant Development, became the criterion against which newer assessments of early motor skills were validated. Bayley, from the Institute of Child Welfare at the University of California, Berkeley, noted that most tests of the mental development of infants included a large percentage of motor coordination items but that up to 1935 there had been relatively few tests devoted to infant motor abilities.

Also during this period, two new motor assessments were developed at the Institute of Child Welfare at Teachers College, Columbia University. In 1924, Andrus completed her dissertation titled "A Tentative Inventory of the Habits of Children from Two to Four Years of Age." One of the four divisions in this inventory was devoted to motor skills, composed of 112 motor items. The two main purposes of this tool were to help teachers more accurately observe the behaviors of preschool children and to allow for evaluation of the abilities of preschool children "with possible diagnostic and prognostic value" (Andrus, 1924, p. 4).

In 1927, Cunningham reported a series of motor tests devised to measure gross motor coordination in children from 12 to 42 months. Over 100 items were divided into six age categories. Among the tests a child was asked to perform were (a) at 12 months, to take a hoop off of her own neck; (b) at 24 months, to climb upon a chair 17.5 in. high; and (c) at 36 months, to jump with two feet from an 8-in. elevation. This work was carried out in collaboration with McGraw, the distinguished motor development researcher.

In 1934, Cowan and Pratt created a motor coordination test for children from 3 to 12 years of age that required them to jump from a standing position over a horizontal pole. Norms for the 10 age groups developed from the highest heights attained were found to be useful for (a) quantifying poor coordination caused by defects of the nervous system, (b) uncovering slight retardations in coordination, and (c) measuring progress during a motor intervention program.

Four years later, McCaskill and Wellman (1938) from the Iowa Child Welfare Research Station presented a set of tests designed to "provide means of discovering the motor development of children from two to six years by utilization of normal activities" (p. 141), including catching, throwing, bouncing, jumping, skipping, and climbing ladders and steps. They calculated the motor age (24-71 months) corresponding to performance at the 50th percentile for 73 levels of the various movement skills.

Psychology

World War II created a surge of interest in individual differences and motor behavior, particularly as they related to the selection of trainees for aircrews (Adams, 1987). As aircrew training was expanding in 1941, the Aviation Psychology Program was established with a strong emphasis on test development and application. During the war, the basic psychomotor test for pilot selection in the Aviation Psychology Program was the Army Air Forces School of Aviation Medicine Complex Coordination Test (Melton, 1947). This test, originally developed by Mashburn (1934) and referred to as the Mashburn Automatic Serial Action Apparatus, required subjects to make successive coordinated movements of hand and foot controls in response to visual signals.

After the war, research on the use of motor tests for selecting pilots was continued by the Air Force in the Perceptual and Motor Skills Research Laboratory (Adams, 1987). Some of the best-known work by this group was published by Fleishman (e.g., 1953, 1956). In 1956, this line of research ended because the Air Force stopped using motor tests to select pilot recruits. The major source of pilot recruits was the Reserve Officer Training Corps units at universities, where printed tests were administered more easily than complex motor tests (Adams, 1987).

Occupational and Physical Therapy

Hall (1921), one of the leaders in the emerging field of occupational therapy, recognized the need for standardization of both the application of therapies and the recording of behaviors. In 1921, he wrote, "It is hoped that the coming year will see perfected a uniform case record . . . which will show at a glance the progression of the patient" (p. 247). Hall suggested that case records focus on common factors of various occupations, such as ability to sustain attention and effort without fatigue.

One of the first assessments of activities of daily life for persons with disabilities, an area of particular interest to occupational therapists, was published by Sheldon, a physical educator, in 1935. Sheldon stated that the purpose of her evaluation tool was to determine "if the physical education work given in our school for crippled children is actually useful to the child in his daily living" and to provide "some accurate standard of judging improvement in the child's activity" (p. 30).

In 1940, Watrous, a physiotherapist, reported the development of the Action Ability Test for children with spastic cerebral palsy. This test was used primarily to determine (a) the ability of children to become independent in their movements and (b) the therapeutic methods that may be helpful in improving movement independence.

Neuropsychology

Early in this period, Oseretsky (1923, cited in Lassner, 1948), a Russian researcher at the Psychoneurological Children's Clinic in Moscow, published "A Metric Scale for Studying the Motor Capacity of Children." This assessment tool, later known as the Oseretsky Tests of Motor Proficiency (Doll, 1946), was designed to measure the degree of clumsiness or awkwardness in children, and was the foundation for future generations of motor ability tests developed as recently as the 1980s (see figure 2.3). Oseretsky's

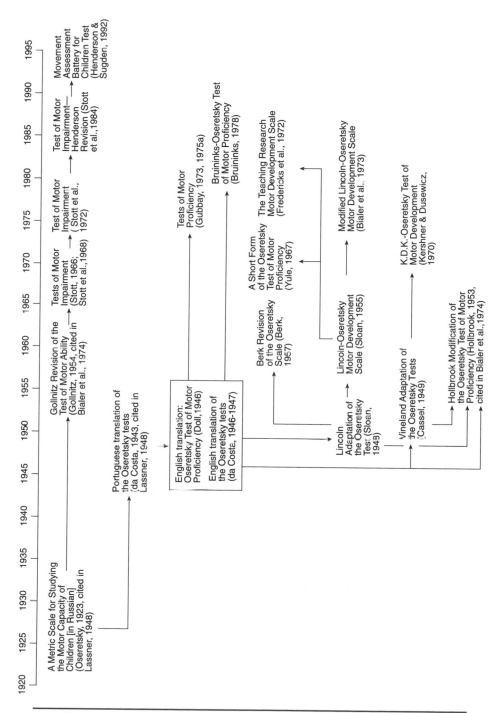

■ FIGURE 2.3 Family tree of motor tests derived from the Oseretsky tests.

original tests contained six groups of items: (a) general static coordination, (b) dynamic coordination of the hands, (c) general dynamic coordination, (d) motor speed, (e) simultaneous voluntary movements, and (f) synkinesia (see table 2.2). During this era, the Oseretsky tests were translated into French, German, Portuguese, and Spanish and were widely used in nine continental European counties (Lassner, 1948).

Another Russian neuropsychologist, Yarmolenko, from the Reflexological State Institute of Brain Research in Leningrad, was interested in correlating measures of motor behaviors of children with neurological and biometric data. He felt that the items in Oseretsky's test were not appropriate for achieving this goal. Thus, as a first step, Yarmolenko (1933) developed an instrument that assessed the speed, strength, and exactness of motor patterns basic to children's life experience. These patterns included walking, jumping, hopping, carrying, balancing, getting

TABLE 2.2   Sample Items From All Six Groupings of the Oseretsky Tests of Motor Proficiency (Doll, 1946) for Three Age Levels

	Age Level		
Item group	4 years	9 years	13-14 years
General static coordination	Remain standing, one foot advanced, eyes closed.	Balance on one leg, eyes closed.	Balance on tip toe, right and left foot.[a]
Dynamic coordination of the hands	Touch nose, eyes closed.	Throw a ball at a target 2.5 m away.[a]	Finger pivot movements, right and left hands.[b]
General dynamic coordination	Hop in place, feet together, 7 times.	Jump in air, clap 3 times.[b]	Jump touching heels with both hands.[a]
Motor speed	Put 20 coins in a box.	Leaf through a book.	Tap 90 times with right and 75 times with left hand in 15 s.[b]
Simultaneous voluntary movements	Make circles with index fingers, arms extended at sides.	Tap feet alternately, tap both index fingers at same time as right foot.	Place 20 coins with left hand and 20 matches with right hand.
Synkinesia	Clasp hand: right, left, both.	Flex and extend the feet while seated.	Close eyes alternately, 5 times.

[a]Item for boys only; another item is specified for girls.
[b]Item for girls only; another item is specified for boys.

up from lying, grasping, throwing, and striking. He felt that his assessment tool could be used to (a) determine a child's level of motor development, (b) diagnose a motor deficiency, and (c) monitor the effect of instructional intervention.

Lassner (1948) stated that the tests developed by Oseretsky (1923; cited in Lassner, 1948) and Yarmolenko (1933), as well as a test of manual ability published in French by a Dutch author (Van Der Lugt, 1939; cited in Lassner, 1948), were stimulated by the work of Homburger, who was German. Homburger (1923, 1925, cited in Lassner, 1948) presented an outline of motor development that "revealed the mechanisms of separate movements" (Lassner, 1948, p. 39).

■ FROM 1945 TO 1959

The era following the end of World War II was marked by the translation of the Oseretsky Test into English, a dramatic decrease in the development of new assessment instruments by physical educators, and a concomitant increase in the development of new assessment instruments by occupational and physical therapists.

Modifications of the Oseretsky Test

The Oseretsky Test was translated from Russian into Portuguese in 1943 and finally from Portuguese into English in 1946. The English translation appeared in four separate issues of *The Training School Bulletin* (da Costa, 1946-1947), and at the same time was published in booklet form (Doll, 1946) and given the title, "The Oseretsky Tests of Motor Proficiency." This assessment instrument captured the attention of many professionals working with children with special needs, and was used as the basis for the development of two new motor ability tests in the late 1940s.

In 1948, Sloan published the Lincoln Adaptation of the Oseretsky Test, and in 1949, Cassel presented the Vineland Adaptation of the Oseretsky Tests. Holbrook, a physical educator, also devised a modification of the Oseretsky tests in his doctoral dissertation in 1953. Sloan revised his original adaptation in 1955, naming it the Lincoln-Oseretsky Motor Development Scale, which became the most widely used adaptation of the Oseretsky tests into the 1970s (Bialer, Doll, & Winsberg, 1973, 1974). In 1978, Bruininks published the still popular Bruininks-Oseretsky Test of Motor Proficiency.

Physical Education

During the era before 1945, researchers in physical education had been highly active in modifying existing motor ability and movement skill assessment tools and developing new ones. From 1945 to 1959, however, the contributions made by physical educators in the area of motor assessment were quite limited. Massey (1978) suggested that the virtual elimination of sport skills from the physical education curriculum during World War II and the subsequent shift toward physical training (with an emphasis on calisthenics, combatives, and running obstacle courses), along with the exposure of thousands of men to rigorous and demanding fitness testing during their military service, led to a general decline of interest in physical education and motor assessments in the postwar years.

In 1954, Kraus and Hirschland's report of the poor fitness of American children as compared to children in Europe was instrumental in the creation of the President's Council on Physical Fitness and the American Association for Health, Physical Education, and Recreation physical fitness test. But movement skill development and the assessment of movement skill continued to be a low priority. During this period, a few new tests of movement skill were reported, but they were very similar to those developed during the previous era.

Also in 1954, Latchaw published modifications of seven established skill tests to accommodate the abilities of fourth-, fifth-, and sixth-grade boys and girls. In her battery of tests, Latchaw carefully examined test-retest reliability and the relationship between performance scores and age, height, and weight.

During the mid-1950s, three tests of general sport skill designed to classify college men into ability groups were presented, two of them in doctoral dissertations. In 1954, Barrow presented a test of motor ability in which a total score was derived from the sum of standardized scores for the standing broad jump, a "zigzag" run, and a medicine ball put. In the same year, Adams (1954) proposed a "sport-type motor educability test" in which weighted values of a wall volley with a volleyball, a tennis ball catch while lying down, a volleyball bounce off a bat, and basketball free throws were combined for a composite score. Two years later, Johnson (1956) reported a similar test of general sport skills, with a total score based on weighted values for basketball dribbling, soccer and volleyball volleying, and softball and football throwing for distance.

Occupational and Physical Therapy

The increased attention to movement assessment in occupational and physical therapy focused on (a) functional movements or activities of daily living and (b) the application of standard motor development assessment methods to children with physical disabilities.

Functional Movements. In 1947, an article on "physical functional analysis" by Griffiths was reprinted from a medical journal in *Occupational*

Therapy and Rehabilitation. In this article, Griffiths presented an outline for a medical report in the form of a functional analysis used by the Ministry of Labour and National Service in England to assist in recommending employment in a particular industry for persons with disabilities. The instructions on this form stated, "It is intended that the ability to perform certain movements with sufficient strength and adequate precision shall be emphasized rather than the various disablements and handicaps involved" (Griffiths, 1947, p. 450). A wide variety of skills were assessed, along with the environmental conditions in which these skills might be performed. In his paper, Griffiths, an engineer, acknowledged the pioneering role of industrial psychologists and motion study experts, such as Gilbreth, in developing this area of research.

At about the same time, in a series of three papers published in the *American Journal of Occupational Therapy,* Brown (1950a, 1950b, 1951) presented (a) a daily activity inventory designed to examine the difficulties persons with disabilities may have in performing 100 activities of daily living, and (b) a corresponding progress record (see table 2.3). In 1953, Brown and Van Der Bogert (1953) presented a similar 100-item inventory for pre-vocational motor skills and, in the same paper, mentioned other instruments developed to estimate motor skill. These other instruments included an elementary motor skill inventory, a grasp and release inventory, and a sitting, posture, and chair evaluation.

The PULSES Profile was used in the 1940s to classify military personnel, but was not published until 1957 (Moskowitz & McCann, 1957). This scale comprised six components, each matching one of the letters in the acronym PULSES: (P) physical condition, (U) upper-limb functions, (L) lower-limb functions, (S) sensory components, (E) excretory functions, and (S) support factors.

Assessing Motor Development in Children With Physical Disabilities.

In the early 1950s, Johnson, Zuck, and Wingate (1951) devised the Motor Age Test to "objectively grade a child's motor age, to record his progress under various forms of therapy, and to compare the progress of different children with one another, regardless of differences in age or severity of motor handicap" (p. 698). They found that the Oseretsky tests (Doll, 1946) were not appropriate for children with severe motor handicaps such as cerebral palsy and thus based their test on Gesell's normative studies. The Motor Age tests yielded an upper-body motor quotient, a lower-body motor quotient, and a total motor age.

In another test created to assess the motor development of children with cerebral palsy, Miller, Stewart, Murphy, and Jantzen (1955) also turned to Gesell's work for their pool of items. This evaluation, designed to be used by occupational therapists, focused only on the upper extremities. Several years later in the *American Journal of Occupational Therapy,* Reuss, Dally,

TABLE 2.3 Summary of the 100 Items in Brown's (1950a,1950b,1951) Daily Activity Inventory

Number of items	Item category
1	Speech
17	Bed maneuvers
4	Bathing and grooming
4	Dressing and undressing
5	Eating
6	Desk actions
22	Wheelchair actions
2	Bathtub maneuvers
4	Appliance (prosthesis or orthosis) manipulation
18	Upright locomotion
15	Standing-to-sitting and sitting-to-standing
2	Traveling upright

and Lis (1959) presented background information on the Gesell Developmental Schedules (Gesell & Amatruda, 1941) and offered suggestions on how to directly use the Schedules with children with physical impairments.

■ FROM 1960 TO 1974

At the end of the period 1960 to 1974, Lewko (1976) surveyed physical educators, occupational therapists, physical therapists, and special educators from 209 institutions in the United States and Canada to ascertain the status of movement assessment. He reported that the respondents used a total of 91 published and 165 unpublished tests. The most frequently used tests were the Denver Developmental Screening Test (Frankenburg & Dodds, 1967), the Purdue Perceptual Motor Survey (Roach & Kephart, 1966), and the Southern California Sensory Integration Test (Ayres, 1972c). Lewko also noted that the respondents were quite critical of the tests they used most frequently, and admitted that they often misused them.

I will discuss the movement assessment instruments developed during this period in the context of four professional areas: (a) physical education,

(b) occupational and physical therapy, (c) special education, and (d) child development and pediatrics.

Physical Education

At the end of the previous period, in 1959, the American Association for Health, Physical Education, and Recreation initiated a sport skills test project to standardize the testing of 15 sport skills (Johnson & Nelson, 1969). This project was headed by Brace, an experienced test developer best known for his motor ability test published in 1927. The work resulted in the publication by 1967 of at least five of these tests (archery, basketball, football, softball, and volleyball).

In 1962, Johnson presented a battery of product-oriented tests of fundamental movement skills for boys and girls in Grades 1 through 6. The skills included running, jumping, throwing, catching, kicking, and batting. The results for each skill were interpreted individually relative to the percentiles provided by Johnson.

In 1967, the Cratty Six-Category Gross Motor Test (described in Cratty, 1969, 1974) was developed to identify children and adults with motor difficulties. The six categories in Cratty's test were balance, body perception, gross agility, locomotor agility, tracking, and throwing. Normative information was provided for children with no mental impairments from 4 to 11 years, persons with mild mental impairments from 5 to 20 years, and persons with moderate mental impairments from 5 to 24 years.

Occupational and Physical Therapy

Movement assessment had been important to occupational and physical therapists in previous periods; but a new emphasis on the part of the medical profession on prevention, and the provision of comprehensive health services in the middle 1960s, forced occupational and physical therapists to work more closely with physicians and other members of the health team and to assume greater responsibility for evaluating the nature of disability and determining the range and level of functioning abilities (West, 1967). This change was reflected in an increase in the number of movement assessments published by professionals in occupational and physical therapy. In the following pages I discuss some of these under the categories of motor development, functional movements, and sensory integration.

Motor Development. Some of the motor development tests developed during the early years of this period were reviewed by Semans (1965), including the Developmental Screening Instrument (Knobloch, 1963), the General Motor Development Test (Footh & Kogan, 1963), and the Cerebral

Palsy Assessment Chart for Basic Motor Control (Semans, Phillips, Romanoli, Miller, & Skillen, 1965). In 1966, Zausmer and Tower published their Quotient for the Evaluation of Motor Development, which was designed to evaluate several areas of normative motor development and to provide a basis for treating identified problem areas. And in 1973, Hoskins and Squires presented a chart for assessing reflex and gross motor development and their inherent relationships. The authors asserted that this test was particularly useful as a treatment planning tool for persons with brain damage.

Functional Movements. By 1965, most occupational and physical therapy programs had instituted some type of assessment of activities of daily living (ADL); many of these were adapted from the original test by Brown (1950a, 1950b, 1951). From a comprehensive review of the rehabilitation literature since 1951, Bruett and Overs (1969) identified 12 different ADL scales. Some of the key ADL instruments developed during this period were the Katz Index of ADL (Katz, Ford, Moskowitz, Jackson, & Jaffe, 1963), the Kenny Self-Care Evaluation (Schoening et al., 1965), and the Barthel Index (Mahoney & Barthel, 1965).

Between 1960 and 1974, at least three instruments devoted to the assessment of function of persons with particular disabilities were published. First, Anderson, Bargowski, and Blodgett (1961) published their Code Method for Evaluating Function in Cerebral Palsy; then Currie (1969) presented an occupational therapy evaluation of function, which focused on play activities with familiar toys performed in a structured environment. Later, Nelson (1974) developed a practical clinical test of locomotor skill called the Functional Ambulation Profile, which could be used to assess the performance of persons with neuromuscular or musculoskeletal disorders.

Sensory Integration. Ayres, an occupational therapist, developed several tests in the 1960s—for example, the Ayres Space Test (1962), the Southern California Motor Accuracy Test (1964), and the Southern California Perceptual-Motor Tests (1968)—that became the basis for the Southern California Sensory Integration Tests (SCSIT), which was published in 1972. The SCSIT was designed to assess the sensory, perceptual, and motor deficits of children between 4 and 8 years of age with learning problems; it was based on the concept that "disordered sensory integration accounts for some aspects of learning disorders and that enhancing sensory integration will make academic learning easier for those children whose problem lies in that domain" (Ayres, 1972b, p. x).

The SCSIT (Ayres, 1972c), a precursor of the Sensory Integration and Praxis Tests (Ayres, 1989), was composed of the following 17 test items standardized on children from 4 to 10 years:

- Space visualization
- Figure-ground perception
- Localization of tactile stimuli
- Double tactile stimulation

- Position in space
- Design copying
- Motor accuracy
- Kinesthesia
- Manual form perception
- Finger identification
- Graphesthesia

- Imitation of postures
- Crossing midline of body
- Bilateral motor coordination
- Right-left discrimination
- Standing balance with eyes open
- Standing balance with eyes closed

The results of a factor analysis study led Ayres to claim that four basic types of sensory integration disorders could be identified from profiles of SCSIT scores. These four disorders were related to (a) form and space perception, (b) praxis, (c) postural and bilateral integration, and (d) tactile defensiveness. Many scholars (e.g., Cratty, 1989; Kavale & Mattson, 1983; Laszlo & Bairstow, 1985) criticized Ayres' (1972c) SCSIT and her contention that academic performance could be improved through sensory integration (Ayres, 1972a); but Laszlo and Bairstow (1985) acknowledged that "more than anyone else in the field of assessment of handicapped children and the design of therapy programmes, she has been a patron of the senses and their role in normal and abnormal motor behaviour" (p. 100).

Special Education

During the period preceding 1960, the volume of motor development research waned, but in the 1960s and 1970s there was a resurgence of research activity in the area of motor development because of an interest in the relationship between academic proficiency and movement skill (Keogh, 1977). Several assessment instruments emerged from this revived interest in motor development, most notably the Purdue Perceptual-Motor Survey (PPMS) (Roach & Kephart, 1966). The main purpose of the PPMS was to "provide the teacher with a tool which can be used to identify those children who do not possess perceptual-motor abilities necessary for acquiring academic skills by the usual instructional methods" (p. iii).

Between 1960 and 1974, further modifications of the Oseretsky tests (Doll, 1946) were published, primarily by persons in special education (see figure 2.3). First, the Test of Motor Impairment (TOMI) was developed in 1966 by Stott, to be revised in 1972 (Stott, Moyes, & Henderson, 1972) and 1984 (Stott, Moyes, & Henderson, 1984). The TOMI later became the Movement Assessment Battery for Children Test (Henderson & Sugden, 1992) (see review in chapter 8). Second, two tests derived from the Lincoln-Oseretsky Motor Development Scale (Sloan, 1955) were published: A Short Form of the Oseretsky Test of Motor Proficiency (Yule, 1967) and the Modified Lincoln-Oseretsky Motor Development Scale (Bialer et al., 1973, 1974). And third, the Vineland Adaptation of the Oseretsky Tests (Cassel, 1949) was modified by Kershner and Dusewicz (1970) to form the K.D.K.-Oseretsky Tests of Motor Development.

Pediatrics/Child Development/Neurology

The Denver Developmental Screening Test (DDST), first presented by Frankenburg and Dodds in 1967 and published in 1969, quickly became the most popular developmental screening instrument in the United States and perhaps the entire world (Meisels, 1989). The DDST was designed to provide an inexpensive and simple means of diagnosing delayed development in children from birth to 6 years in four areas: gross motor, language, fine motor-adaptive, and personal-social. The DDST was revised in 1975 (Frankenburg, Dodds, Fandal, Kazuk, & Cohrs, 1975) and eventually became the Denver II, in 1990 (Frankenburg, Dodds, & Archer, 1990; Frankenburg, Dodds, Archer, Shapiro, & Bresnick, 1992).

In 1969, the Bayley Scales of Infant Development (BSID), with roots extending back to Bayley's California Infant Scale of Motor Development (1935), was published. The BSID (1969) provided normative information on the developmental status of children from 2 to 30 months of age in three test components: the Mental Scale (163 items), the Motor Scale (81 items), and the Infant Behavior Record (30 items). Performance on the Motor Scale can be summarized in terms of a standard score referred to as the Psychomotor Developmental Index. The BSID—designed for depth and thoroughness compared to the simplicity and brevity in the DDST—came to be considered by many scholars and practitioners the premier early movement skill assessment instrument (e.g., Roszkowski, 1989), and in its second edition is known as the Bayley-II (Bayley, 1993). The most common standard used to establish the validity of other tests of early movement milestones has been the BSID, confirming the status of this test.

In 1969, Zdanska-Brincken and Wolanski published their Evaluation of Motor Development in Infants (EMDI). The EMDI consisted of 34 tests corresponding with the stages of motor development leading to infants' ability to assume an upright, bipedal stance. On the basis of longitudinal data collected from a 4-year study of 212 children in Warsaw, the two Polish child development researchers created five grids on which results of the assessment could be plotted (one each for head and trunk movements, the sitting position, the standing position, and locomotion) and one total nomogram. Further information on their graphic method of assessing motor development was reported 4 years later (Wolanski & Zdanska-Brincken, 1973).

About the same time, two Italian neurologists presented a battery of tests designed to assess the developmental status of children with and without mental impairments from birth to 24 months (Milani-Comparetti & Gidoni, 1967). The results of their "routine developmental examination," usually taking no more than 2 to 3 min, were recorded on a developmental chart with two sections: one for early movement milestones (e.g., sitting or walking) and the other for primitive reflexes, and righting, parachute, and tilting reactions. The chart was arranged to depict the relationship between the movement behaviors and the underlying reflexes. This assessment instrument became known as the Milani-Comparetti Motor Development Screening Test in revisions published in 1977 (Trembath, 1977) and 1987 (Stuberg, 1987).

In 1973, Gubbay, another neurologist, developed as his doctoral thesis a test designed to identify children between 8 and 12 years who are "clumsy" or who have "defective" motor skills. His Tests of Motor Proficiency (TMP) was published in a journal article (Gubbay, 1973) and in his book, *Clumsy Children* (Gubbay, 1975a). The TMP, with eight items similar to those in Oseretsky's tests, was standardized on 992 children in Australia. The eight items were

- whistle through pouted lips,
- skip forward five steps,
- roll tennis ball around matchboxes with foot,
- throw, clap hands, then catch tennis ball,
- tie one shoelace with double bow (single knot),
- thread 10 beads,
- pierce 20 pinholes, and
- fit six plastic shapes into appropriate slots.

Using the TMP as a screening instrument, Gubbay (1975b) reported a 6.7% incidence of clumsiness in children in regular schools.

■ 1975 AND BEYOND

In this chapter I have placed approximately 100 movement assessment tools published before 1975 in a historical continuum. Very few of these tests are still in use in their original form. An exception is the Barthel Index (Mahoney & Barthel, 1965), an assessment of activities of daily living. The Bayley Scale of Infant Development (Bayley, 1969) remains very popular, but a second revision referred to as the Bayley-II came out recently (Bayley, 1993).

Since 1975 there has been a plethora of new tests, and I will discuss or cite many of these in the chapters to follow. Many of the tests that continue to be widely used have their roots in tests developed before 1975. For example, the Bruininks-Oseretsky Test of Motor Proficiency (Bruininks, 1978) (see chapter 8) was derived from the Oseretsky Tests of Motor Proficiency (Doll, 1946), and the Denver II (Frankenburg et al., 1990) as well as early versions of the Denver Developmental Screening Test borrowed extensively from Gesell's early tests (Ames, 1989).

Chapter 3

Defining and Classifying Movement Skills

© Terry Wild Studio

AS we saw in the preceding chapter, the assessment of movement skills is a critical program component in many disciplines, including athletics, geriatrics, neurology, occupational therapy, orthopedics, pediatrics, physical education, physical therapy, recreation, rehabilitation medicine, special education, and vocational education. Differences in the knowledge bases, terminology, program emphases, and purposes of movement assessment across the disciplines have led to great variation in

> " Classifications are not passive ordering devices in a world objectively divided into obvious categories. Taxonomies are human decisions imposed upon nature—theories about the causes of nature's order. The chronicle of historical changes in classification provides our finest insight into conceptual revolutions in human thought. Objective nature does exist, but we can converse with her only through the structure of our taxonomic systems. "
>
> —Gould (1996, p. 39)

approaches to movement skill assessment and have limited the cross-disciplinary use of many instruments.

There will continue to be differences in approaches to movement skill assessment by various disciplines; however, at least two strategies may be useful in promoting a better understanding of the diverse assessment options. First, differences in the terminology used by people in various disciplines can be described and explained, and an effort can be made to agree on consistent definitions for key terms. Second, a taxonomy of movement skills can be developed that accommodates the assumptions and knowledge base of each discipline.

The purpose of this chapter is to build a framework for organizing and understanding the foundations of the multitude of available movement skill assessment instruments. To this end the chapter will focus on (a) definitions of common terms related to movement skill and movement performance, (b) information on the classifications or taxonomies of movement skills, and (c) a proposed taxonomy of movement skills that provides a basis for the organization of the review of movement skill assessment instruments in part II of this book.

■ TERMINOLOGY

Consistent definitions of key terms are a prerequisite for discussing and understanding movement skill assessment tools used in different disciplines. Given the variations in interpretation of common terms, the definitions I present here reflect the usages that fit the movement skill taxonomy offered at the end of the chapter. For definitions based on one or more secondary sources, I provide the citations. For a term that authors of specific assessment instruments (described in later chapters) use to convey a meaning other than that given here, I present the alternate meaning in the relevant chapter.

Movement and Motor

The terms *movement* and *motor* are often used synonymously, but in many contexts they refer to distinctly different concepts. *Movement* refers to the observable act of moving, that is, to an observable change in the position of any part of the body (Gallahue & Ozmun, 1995). On the other hand, *motor* refers to the aspects of movement that are not directly observable: neuro-muscular or internal motor processes (Keogh & Sugden, 1985), or the underlying factors that affect movement (Gallahue & Ozmun, 1995). Assuming that these terms have the same meaning may lead to confusion or misinterpretation of important constructs in an assessment instrument.

Movement Performance

Movement performance refers to goal-directed movement that can be described in terms of quantity or quality. Quantitative descriptions of performance focus on products or outcomes relative to the movement goal, such as how fast, how far, or how many. Qualitative descriptions focus on the processes of movement, such as movement form or patterns, or movement kinematics, without regard to the intended goal. The term movement is used in this context, rather than motor, because performance is observable behavior. In this terminology system, then, the terms motor and performance are incompatible.

Motor Abilities and Movement Skill

Motor abilities are general traits or capacities of an individual that underlie the performance of a variety of movement skills (Magill, 1993). These traits are assumed to be not easily modified by practice or experience (Connolly, 1984; Schmidt, 1982) and to be relatively stable across an individual's lifetime (Keogh & Sugden, 1985). Abilities are usually identified through correlational or factor analysis methods. The adjective *motor* is used in this context because abilities are not directly observable but are inferred from performance.

However, there is little evidence that motor abilities exist. Burton and Davis (1992a), in a paper on assessing balance in adapted physical education, presented a brief review of literature addressing the question whether balance is a general ability or is skill specific. They concluded that "there are factor-analytic studies that provide some support for the conceptualization of balance as a general ability, but the bulk of the evidence suggests that balance is specific to the task being performed" (p. 17). Similarly, Henderson (1987) noted that "low correlations have been reported among different skills providing rather little support for the notion of general ability" (p. 514), and Davis (1984) argued that "the overwhelming results of research on the transfer of learning suggests that general motor abilities do not exist" (pp. 128-129).

The term *abilities* also can be interpreted to refer to a person's potential movement competencies as opposed to a person's actual movement performances. The contrast between ability and performance again points to the reality that the results of an assessment procedure indicate only what a person did, not what he or she could do in other circumstances.

Movement skill is used to appropriately refer to two different concepts (Magill, 1993). First, the term movement skill may be used as a qualitative expression of movement performance. For example, an instructor may state that a student has a high level of movement skill. Alternatively, the term movement skill may be used to refer to a specific class of goal-directed movement patterns such as running, throwing, hammering, driving, writing, or even speaking. The classification of movement skills may be quite narrow or quite broad, as table 3.1 shows. Further, the many classes of movement skills are often organized into developmental categories—such as early movement milestones, fundamental movement skills, or specialized movement skills—or other types of categories such as activities of daily living.

Perceptual-Motor, Psychomotor, and Sensorimotor Processes

Terms with hyphenated prefixes added to the root *motor skills*—perceptual-motor skills, psychomotor skills, sensorimotor skills, and others—emphasize the relationship of movement skills to various levels of processing information. Unfortunately, the use of such hybrid terms just increases the potential for confusion in the area of movement skill assessment. The use of the term *motor* is congruent with the emphasis on the internal perceptual, psychological, and sensory processes, but the term *skill* is not. Thus, perceptual-motor, psychomotor, and sensorimotor processes are more appropriately used as descriptors of motor processes rather than movement skills.

Movement Skill Development and Motor Development

The terms *movement skill development* and *motor development* can be defined together as adaptive or functional changes in movement behavior over the life span and the processes or factors that underlie these changes (adapted from Clark & Whitall, 1989b). The first part of the definition specifically refers to movement skill development, or changes in observable movement behaviors, while the last part refers to motor development, or the underlying causes of these changes in actual movement behaviors. The factors

TABLE 3.1   Spectrum of Movement Skill Classifications

General classification	Classification by anatomy	Classlfication by object or function	Classification by component
Throwing	Overhand	Baseball	Backswing
	Underhand	Darts	Elbow extension
	Sidearm	Javelin	Follow-through
	One-hand	Rope	Step
	Two-hand	Shot put	Trunk rotation
	Knuckleball	Softball	Wrist flexion
Walking	Flat-footed	For exercise	Arm swing
	On toes	In formation (march)	Heel strike
	On hands	On forest trail (hike)	Hip flexion
	Pigeon-toed	On police beat	Knee extension
	With limp	Push grocery cart	Toe-off
Driving	With one hand	Automobile	Brake
	With two hands	Golf cart	Control speed
	With no hands	Lawnmower	Shift
	With feet	Motorcycle	Signal
	With thigh	Pickup truck	Steer

within the person that may lead to developmental change in movement behavior include maturation, growth, and experience. Change in movement behavior also may be elicited through modification of the movement task or the movement environment (Davis & Burton, 1991), but these changes are not considered to be developmental.

The generic term *motor development* is usually used to specify both movement skill and motor development; however, an understanding of the distinction between these two terms, as well as their proper use, lessens the chance of misinterpretation in assessment and other contexts.

Movement Tasks and Movement Functions

Each of the terms defined so far focuses on overt movement behavior or on underlying motor processes. Movement tasks or movement functions are included among these key terms because they guide and shape all movement behavior (Reed, 1982). A movement task can be defined by the intention of the performer in moving; in other words, the task is what the performer attempts to accomplish. However, tasks are often externally prescribed and may have little meaning for the performer. The term *movement function* is similar, but it implies goal-directed behavior with both purpose and meaning (Fisher, 1992).

Davis and Burton (1991) suggest that there are five basic categories of functional movement tasks: (a) locomotion, (b) locomotion on an object, (c) propulsion, (d) reception, and (e) orientation, which includes object manipulation. These are listed and explained further in table 3.2, which also includes two additional categories: machine control and play. According to Fisher (1992), occupational therapists view movement function more broadly as the ability to perform the activities of daily living that are needed or wanted, in both work and play.

Movement Product and Movement Process

The measurement of movement is often divided into two general types: movement product and movement process. Movement product is usually viewed as a performance outcome expressed in terms of distance (in inches, feet, yards, miles, centimeters, meters, or kilometers), time (in milliseconds, seconds, minutes, or hours), mass (in pounds or kilograms), energy (in kilocalories), or frequency or number of repetitions. These measures also can be combined to yield other product measures, such as velocity (distance/time) or force (mass $\times$ distance/time^2).

Movement process includes the movement pattern or form used to produce the movement outcome (Sherrill, 1993) as well as the mechanisms that underlie the movement performance (Schmidt, 1982). The movement pattern or form can be considered to be the observable or external aspect of movement process, while the underlying mechanisms can be considered to be the unobservable or internal aspect.

■ CLASSIFICATION OF MOVEMENT SKILLS

A classic book on taxonomies of human performance was written by Fleishman and Quaintance in 1984. The authors addressed some basic issues regarding the classification of tasks performed by humans, and presented many different taxonomies or systems of classification for a wide range of tasks. The following section on the classification of movement skills will begin with an overview of the purposes of classification, based on Fleishman and Quaintance's (1984) work. Next I will present some examples of taxonomies of movement skills.

Purposes of Classification

According to Fleishman and Quaintance (1984), classification involves the arrangement of objects or entities into groups or sets based on the relationships between their observed or inferred properties. The authors argue that

TABLE 3.2   Functional Movment Task Categories and Related Movement Skills

Task categories and definitions	Related movement skills
Locomotion: To move from one place to another	Climb creep/crawl jump/hop/leap roll slide swim walk/run
Locomotion on object: To move on a self-propelled object from one place to another	Propel bicycle propel boat/canoe propel skateboard/scooter propel skates/cross-country skis propel wheelchair
Propulsion: To propel a stationary or moving object or person	Carry drop kick lift pull push strike throw
Reception: To take or receive a (a) stationary, or (b) moving object or person	(a)Grasp (b)catch (b)block
Orientation: (a) To change position of body or body part relative to an object, person, terrain, or event, or (b) to change position of object or person relative to body or body part	(a)Bend (a)lean (a)reach (a)turn (a)twist (b)manipulate

Machine control:
To guide and/or regulate an object that
produces its own operating energy (i.e., a
machine), such as a motorcycle, a power
drill, or a power lawnmower
	Discrete functions
	  Select
	  Turn on/off
	Continuous functions
	  Adjust

Play: Movement not as a means or an end or function, but as an end in itself	May be skills in any other category

Note: Reprinted, by permission, from W.E. Davis and A.W. Burton, 1991, "Eco-logical Task Analysis: Translating Movement Behavior Theory into Practice," *Adapted Physical Activity Quarterly*, Vol. 9(2): 162.

the main purpose of classification is to "describe the structure and relationships of the constituent objects in regard to each other and to similar objects, and to simplify these relationships in such a way that general statements can be made about classes of objects" (p. 23). A taxonomy, then, is such a system of classification.

In the context of movement skill assessment, taxonomies of movement tasks may be useful in describing and categorizing a variety of assessment instruments and in developing new instruments. Moreover, such taxonomies may serve as a bridge between professionals in various disciplines—such as adapted physical education, occupational therapy, and physical therapy—and between researchers and practitioners.

For example, a hierarchically structured taxonomy of assessment tools used in occupational therapy was presented recently by Mathiowetz (1993). The three levels of Mathiowetz' framework for assessment were labeled performance components, occupational performance, and role performance, which were matched with the terms impairment, disability, and handicap, respectively, as defined by the World Health Organization (see figure 3.1). Mathiowetz then used this structure to contrast and compare various movement assessment tools currently employed in occupational therapy practice.

Taxonomies of Motor Abilities and Movement Skills

Over the past 40 years, many taxonomies of movement tasks, motor abilities, and movement skills have been proposed. Taxonomies of movement tasks are the most generic because, as mentioned earlier in this chapter, the task—the intention or purpose in moving—guides and shapes all movement behavior. Moreover, task specification also implies the interaction of the performer and environmental conditions. However, the taxonomies that have had the greatest impact on movement assessment are those that address the structure of motor abilities and the classification of movement skills.

Motor Abilities. Most classification systems of motor abilities have relied on factor analysis methods to identify the general motor factors that underlie the performance of groups of related movement tasks. Factor analysis is a mathematical procedure that isolates common sources of performance variability for a number of tasks. Those tasks with levels of shared or common variance above a set criterion are clustered together as a factor. The factors are subjectively labeled, usually on the basis of the construct or trait that is common to all tasks in the cluster. The general factors that emerge from this type of analysis are limited by the specific tasks initially performed.

For example, a two-dimensional system of motor abilities was proposed by Guilford in 1958. One dimension was assigned to the parts of the body involved in the movement, and the other to basic abilities, including

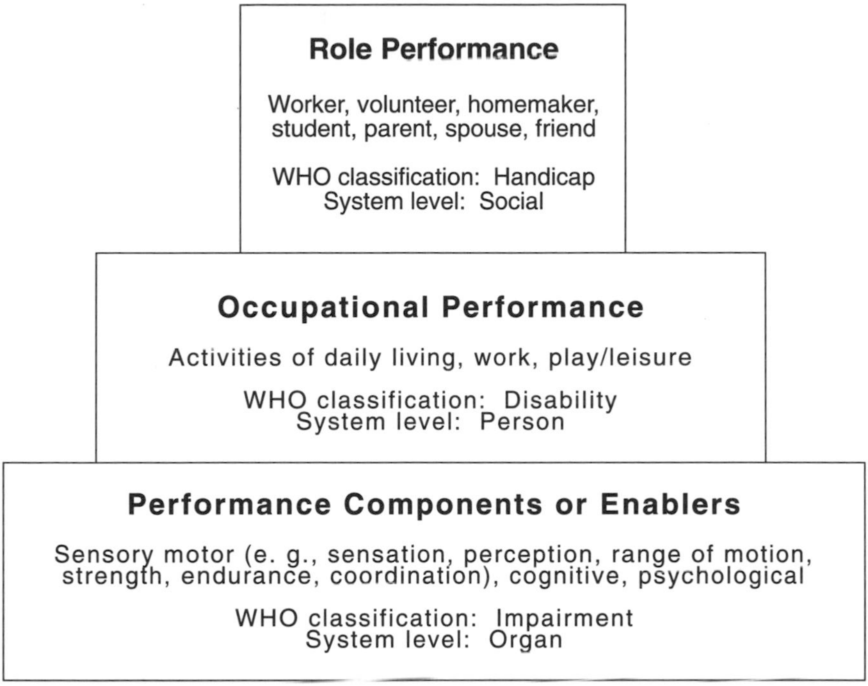

Role Performance

Worker, volunteer, homemaker,
student, parent, spouse, friend

WHO classification: Handicap
System level: Social

Occupational Performance

Activities of daily living, work, play/leisure

WHO classification: Disability
System level: Person

Performance Components or Enablers

Sensory motor (e. g., sensation, perception, range of motion,
strength, endurance, coordination), cognitive, psychological

WHO classification: Impairment
System level: Organ

■ **FIGURE 3.1** Levels of assessment in occupational therapy according to Mathiowetz (1993).

From "Role of Physical Performance Component Evaluations in Occupational Therapy Functional Assessment" by V. Mathiowetz, 1993, *The American Journal of Occuaptional Therapy Association* 47, p. 227. Copyright 1993 by the American Occupational Therapy Association, Inc. Adapted with permission.

strength, impulsion (i.e., the explosive aspect of movement), speed, static precision, dynamic precision, coordination, and flexibility. This system of psychomotor abilities was based on the results of previously published studies using factor analysis methods.

The most widely recognized research on the structure of motor abilities has been carried out by Fleishman and his colleagues. The results of a series of factor-analytic studies led Fleishman to identify nine physical proficiency abilities (Fleishman, 1964) and 11 psychomotor abilities (Fleishman, 1966) that were shown to be the most useful and meaningful in describing performance across a wide variety of tasks. The physical proficiency factors were extent flexibility, dynamic flexibility, explosive strength, static strength, dynamic strength, trunk strength, gross body coordination, gross body equilibrium, and cardiovascular endurance. The psychomotor abilities were control precision, multilimb coordination, response orientation, reaction time, speed of arm movement, rate control, manual dexterity, finger dexterity, arm-hand steadiness, wrist-finger speed, and aiming.

The motor ability structures of boys and girls with and without mental retardation were compared in a large factor-analytic study by Rarick, Dobbins, and Broadhead (1976). For the 145 children who were not mentally retarded, six ability factors emerged from 46 test items, which included both performance and anthropometric measures. These ability factors were strength/power/body size, gross limb-eye coordination, fine visual-motor coordination, fat or dead weight, balance, and leg power and coordination. In addition, this group of researchers identified nine performer types based on clusters of children who demonstrated the same performance profile on five of the ability factors (see figure 3.2). Rarick et al. (1976) concluded that the basic abilities underlying movement performance are highly similar for children with and without mental retardation.

Other motor ability structures have been reported as part of the validation process for separate motor ability assessment instruments. For example, a factor analysis of the 46 movement tasks in the Bruininks-Oseretsky Test of Motor Proficiency (Bruininks, 1978) revealed five ability factors for children between 4 and 14 years old. These factors were labeled general motor ability, upper-limb coordination, balance, strength, and bilateral coordination. More than half of the 46 tasks were clustered under the general motor ability factor, accounting for about 70% of the performance variability between individual children (for more information on the Bruininks-Oseretsky Test, see chapter 8).

Movement Skills.   Taxonomies of motor abilities are based primarily on empirical data and treatments such as factor analysis. Taxonomies of movement skills, on the other hand, have more subjective origins. They are usually derived from the author's interpretation of the relevant body of knowledge, and are designed for particular applications.

In 1962, Smith and Smith proposed three categories of movement skills: postural, travel or locomotor, and manipulative. These movement categories were selected and differentiated in relation to (a) the geometric properties of the environment that support and regulate the movements, (b) the different levels of the brain that control the movements, and (c) the developmental sequence of the movements. Smith and Smith contended that posture is regulated with respect to gravity, locomotion is organized with respect to free space, and manipulation is established with respect to "hard" space.

In 1972, Harrow developed a comprehensive taxonomy of the psychomotor domain based on a careful review of literature in the areas of motor development, physical growth and development, and child psychology. The purpose of this taxonomy was to "assist educators and curriculum developers to categorize relevant movement phenomenon in order to structure educational goals relevant to the needs of children" (Harrow, 1972, p. 9). Harrow classified observable, voluntary actions into six levels of skill, hierarchically organized from low to high. The levels and sublevels of the taxonomy are presented in figure 3.3.

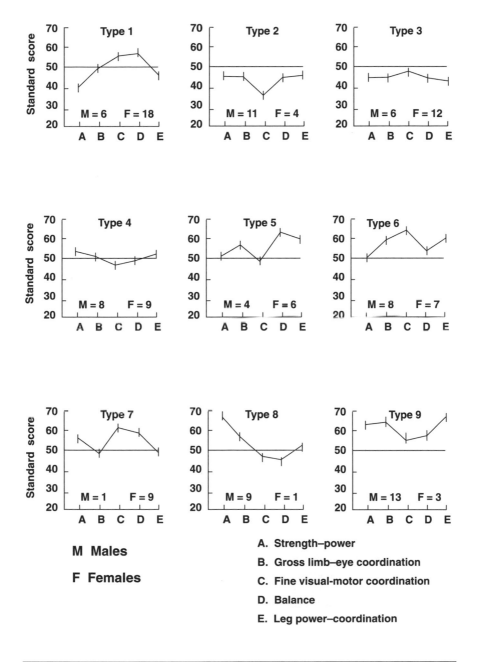

■ FIGURE 3.2 Motor performance typologies for children (from Rarick et al., 1976).

Seefeldt (1980) organized movement skills into a four-level hierarchy. Neonatal reflexes and reactions were at the bottom of the hierarchy, followed by the movement skills acquired during early childhood that are necessary for or fundamental to the performance of more complex sport skills. The fundamental motor skills were subdivided into locomotor (e.g., walk, jump, slide), nonlocomotor (e.g., rock, twist, push), and projection and reception of objects (e.g., catch, throw, strike). The next two levels were identified as transitional motor skills (e.g., rope skipping, diving from the side of a pool) and specific sport skills (e.g., baseball, wrestling) and dances. In his hierarchy of skills, Seefeldt (1980) placed what he called a proficiency barrier between the second and third levels because he felt that mastery of the fundamental motor skills was necessary for the optimal development of the higher-level skills.

Harrow's (1972) Taxonomy of the Psychomotor Domain

Level 1.00 Reflex movements
    1.10   Segmental reflexes
    1.20   Intersegmental reflexes
    1.30   Suprasegmental reflexes

Level 2.00 Basic fundamental movements
    2.10   Locomotor movements
    2.20   Nonlocomotor movements
    2.30   Manipulative movements

Level 3.00 Perceptual abilities
    3.10   Kinesthetic discrimination
    3.20   Visual discrimination
    3.30   Auditory discrimination
    3.40   Tactile discrimination
    3.50   Coordinated abilities

Level 4.00 Physical abilities
    4.10   Endurance
    4.20   Strength
    4.30   Flexibility
    4.40   Agility

Level 5.00 Skilled movements
    5.10   Simple adaptive skill
    5.20   Compound adaptive skill
    5.30   Complex adaptive skill

Level 6.00 Nondiscursive communication
    6.10   Expressive movement
    6.20   Interpretative movement

■ **FIGURE 3.3**   Harrow's (1972) taxonomy of the psychomotor domain.

Gentile (1987) recently presented a 16-category taxonomy of movement skills that was derived from the combination of four task factors with two levels each. Two of the task factors related to the function of the action (body orientation and manipulation), and two related to the environmental context (regulatory conditions during performance and intertrial variability) (see table 3.3). Gentile (1987) suggested that the taxonomy could be used to select functionally appropriate activities for educational or therapeutic purposes, or as a systematic and comprehensive guide for assessment. According to Gentile, applying the taxonomy to assessment allows the teacher or therapist to examine performance deficits in relation to varying environmental constraints on different functional tasks and to track progress in the various performance contexts. Four of the general categories from Gentile's taxonomy have been used to organize the tasks in the Movement Assessment Battery for Children Checklist (Henderson & Sugden, 1992): (a) child stationary—environment stable, (b) child moving—environment stable, (c) child stationary—environment changing, and (d) child moving—environment changing (for more information on the Checklist, see chapter 11).

A taxonomy of movement skills was presented by the American Occupational Therapy Association (Terminology Task Force, 1994a) to delineate and define the terms *occupational performance*, *occupational performance components*, and *performance contexts*. Three main categories of occupational performance, which might be interpreted as categories of movement skills, were identified, including (a) activities of daily living, (b) work and productive activities, and (c) play or leisure activities (see

TABLE 3.3   Gentile's (1987) Taxonomy of 16 Movement Tasks

	Performer			
	Stable		Transport	
Environment	No manipulation	Object manipulation	No manipulation	Object manipulation
Stationary				
Intertrial variability	1	2	3	4
No variability	5	6	7	8
Moving				
Intertrial variability	9	10	11	12
No variability	13	14	15	16

Note: From "Skill Acquisition: Action, Movement, and Neuromotor Processes" by A.M. Gentile, in *Movement science: foundations for physical therapy in rehabilitation* (p. 115) edited by J. H. Carr, R. B. Shepherd, J. Gordon, A.M. Gentile, & J.M. Held, 1987, Rockville, MD: Aspen. Copyright 1987 by Aspen Publishers. Adapted by permission.

figure 3.4 for subcategories). In addition, three categories of occupational performance components that underlie each category of occupational performance were presented: (a) sensorimotor, (b) cognitive and cognitive integration, and (c) psychological and psychosocial skills (see figure 3.4 for subcategories). The Terminology Task Force (1994b) also created a two-dimensional grid with the occupational performance areas on the vertical axis and the performance components on the horizontal axis. The original developers of the grid, Dunn and McGourty (1989), argue that any activity chosen for occupational therapy intervention must fit into a cell on the grid, and that the grid "allows a therapist to systematically identify an individual's deficit and strength areas and to select appropriate activities to address these areas in occupational therapy intervention" (p. 817). Finally, the performance areas and performance components are placed within temporal and environmental contexts.

I. Performance areas
  A. Activites of daily living
    1. Grooming
    2. Oral hygiene
    3. Bathing showering
    4. Toilet hygiene
    5. Personal device care
    6. Dressing
    7. Feeding and eating

---

    8. Medication routine
    9. Performance contexts
    10. Grooming
    11. Functional communication
    12. Functional mobility
    13. Community mobility
    14. Emergency response
    15. Sexual expression
  B. Work and productive activites
    1. Home management
    2. Care of others
    3. Educational activites
    4. Vocational activities
  C. Play or leisure activities
    1. Play or leisure exploration
    2. Play or leisure performance

(continued)

■ **FIGURE 3.4** Taxonomy of occupational therapy performance areas, performance components, and performance contexts (adapted from the Terminology Task Force of the American Occupational Therapy Functional Association 1994a).

II. Performance components
  A. Sensory motor components
    1. Sensory
    2. Neuromusculoskeletal
    3. Motor
  B. Cognitive integration and cognitive components
    1. Level of arousal
    2. Orientation
    3. Recognition
    4. Attention span
    5. Initiation of activity
    6. Termination of activity
    7. Memory
    8. Sequencing
    9. Catagorization
    10. Concept formation
    11. Spatial operations
    12. Problem solving
    13. Learning
    14. Generalization
  C. Psychosocial skills and psychological components
    1. Psychological
    2. Social
    3. Self-management

III. Performance contexts
  A. Temporal aspects
    1. Chronological
    2. Developmental
    3. Life cycle
    4. Disability status
  B. Environment
    1. Physical
    2. Social
    3. Cultural

■ **FIGURE 3.4** *(continued)*

■ A NEW TAXONOMY OF MOVEMENT SKILLS

I devote the rest of this chapter to the presentation of a new taxonomy of movement skills. This taxonomy was constructed specifically (a) to provide a system for categorizing existing movement skill assessment instruments, and consequently promote the understanding of those tools, and (b) to offer a structure that will facilitate the development of valid assessment instruments. After careful examination of existing movement skill assessment tools, I have identified classification levels that minimize the number of tests that could be placed at more than one level.

As depicted in figure 3.5, this taxonomy of movement skills consists of six main levels. The first level includes the foundational components important for all movement skills. The second level, motor abilities, likewise does not include any specific movement skills, but is incorporated into the taxonomy because many tests of movement competency are based on the concept of motor abilities. The next three levels match traditional developmental levels of movement skills: early movement milestones, fundamental movement skills, and specialized movement skills. The top level, functional movement skills, overlaps with the three levels of skills below it, but is set apart as a separate level because of the uniqueness and importance of functional assessment instruments.

I provide detailed information on each of the levels of this taxonomy, including examples of specific assessment tools, in part II (chapters 7-11).

Foundations of Movement Skills

Movement skills emerge from and are supported by the person's various constituent systems. The specific contributions of these underlying foundations of movement skills are often targeted in an assessment of a

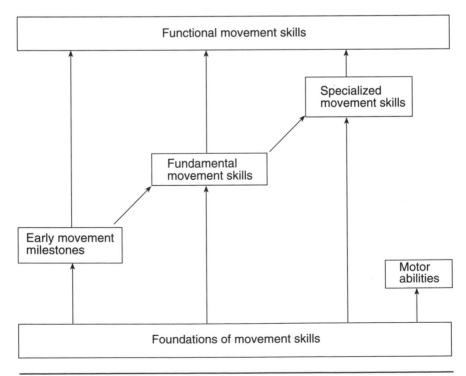

■ **FIGURE 3.5**　Proposed taxonomy of movement skills.

person's movement competency. Table 3.4 lists the foundation areas most commonly assessed. The potential for interaction between persons from different professions is the greatest at this foundational level; indeed, a complete perspective of a person's movement skill foundations can be gained only through the cooperation and collaboration of professionals from various disciplines.

Motor Abilities

Assessment instruments that evaluate motor abilities are composed of a variety of movement tasks grouped into one or more ability areas such as agility, balance, or coordination. The ability areas and the tasks representing the ability areas are usually identified through factor analysis methods. Performance scores for the specific tasks may be summed or combined in various ways to yield a score for each ability area or a total composite score. The purpose of such tests of motor abilities is not to determine proficiency in the performance of certain movement skills, but to measure the general traits or capacities that underlie the performance of a wide variety of motor skills.

For example, the tasks of walking a balance beam and standing on one foot with eyes closed might be used to assess the ability area of balance. Performance on the individual tasks of crossing the beam and standing on one foot, however, is deemphasized and not interpreted directly, while the combined balance score is interpreted to represent balance ability across a larger constellation of skills. Thus, motor ability assessment instruments offer summary or composite scores, but the exact meaning and utility of these scores are often unclear.

Some assessment instruments are organized by categories of movement skills, such as locomotor and object-control skills in the Test of Gross Motor Development (Ulrich, 1985) and locomotor and receipt and propulsion

TABLE 3.4   Eleven Commonly Assessed Movement Skill Foundation Areas

Balance/postural control
Body composition
Body size and morphology
Cardiovascular endurance
Cognition
Flexibility/range of motion
Knowledge
Motivation and affect
Muscular strength and endurance
Neurological functioning/reflexes
Sensations/sensory integration/perception

skills in the Peabody Developmental Motor Scales (Folio & Fewell, 1983). When total scores are derived for these skill categories, primarily for normative purposes, the scores represent the skills as an aggregate. If interpretations of the scores are intended to extend beyond the specific skills included in the test, then the scores assess motor abilities. However, if interpretations of the scores are confined to the specific skills included in the test, then the scores may be thought of as assessing movement skills.

In the taxonomy of movement skills, motor abilities are shown to be influenced by the foundations of movement; but because tests of motor abilities do not directly evaluate movement skills, the box representing motor abilities is isolated from the sequence of true movement skills (see figure 3.5).

Early Movement Milestones

The locomotor and object-control skills that emerge before a child attains upright or bipedal locomotion have been traditionally referred to as early motor milestones. These milestones include rolling over, crawling, creeping, sitting, standing, walking, and object manipulation. The onset of walking, which occurs at an average age of about 12 to 13 months, is often used as a functional marker of the transition from infancy into toddlerhood and is considered to be the last early motor milestone. Because all the milestones are observable skills, the term has been modified in the present context to *early movement milestones*.

The impact of the emergence of these new movement skills on the social, perceptual, and cognitive development of the infant (Bertenthal, Campos, & Barrett, 1984) is reflected in the word *milestone*. The importance of these events makes them attractive candidates for inclusion in assessments designed to evaluate motor development, as well as in those designed to evaluate cognitive and other areas of development.

Fundamental Movement Skills

Fundamental movement skills are the locomotor and object-control skills performed in an upright or bipedal position that are used by persons in all cultures of the world. Fundamental movement skills, as well as early movement milestones, are also referred to as phylogenetic skills because of their universal occurrence. Fundamental locomotor skills include walking, running, jumping, sliding, hopping, and leaping, and the fundamental object-control skills include throwing, catching, striking, bouncing, kicking, pulling, and pushing. These basic movement skills usually emerge between 1 and 7 years of age.

Specialized Movement Skills

Specialized movement skills are defined by Gallahue and Ozmun (1995) as "mature fundamental movement patterns that have been refined and combined to form sport skills and other specific and complex movement skills" (p. 386). Although specialized movement skills involve combinations or variations of one or more early movement milestones and/or fundamental movement skills, they may emerge before all of these basic skills are mastered. Gallahue and Ozmun (1995) assert that fundamental movement skills are generic and that they may be applied in many different task situations, whereas specialized movement skills are specific to particular tasks. Some specialized movement skills are pitching a baseball, spiking a volleyball, shooting a free throw, performing a forward roll or a triple jump, sewing on a button, shooting an arrow from a bow, and hammering a nail. These skills are not performed by persons in all cultures, nor by all persons in any single culture, and thus may be considered ontogenetic skills, or skills unique to individual performers.

Functional Movement Skills

Functional movement skills are movement skills—either early movement milestones, fundamental movement skills, or specialized movement skills—that are performed in their natural and meaningful contexts. In most movement assessment situations, the specified tasks are performed in contrived or unnatural contexts. Because movement behavior can be quite different in contrived or unnatural contexts compared to natural and meaningful contexts, a separate classification level is reserved for functional movement skills.

Functional movement skills can be seen, for example, when an infant sits up in her crib, a young boy throws a snowball at his friend, or a girl shoots free throws during a basketball game. Activities of daily living at home, work, or play also are considered functional movement skills.

Strengths of the Taxonomy

This new taxonomy of movement skills has many features that make it an attractive tool for organizing and classifying movement skill assessment instruments. First, the taxonomy focuses specifically on observable movement skills; however, it also includes motor abilities, but sets them apart from true movement skills. This distinction between skills and abilities is important because assessment instruments in these two categories are appropriate for different types of assessment purposes.

Second, the taxonomy recognizes the interdisciplinary nature of assessing the foundations of movement skills. Input from several professional areas is necessary to generate a complete understanding of the status of a person's movement skills.

Next, three traditional categories of movement skills are used, and they are ordered according to general developmental expectations. However, the direct link of each skill category to movement skill foundations (see figure 3.5) emphasizes that early movement milestones, fundamental movement skills, and specialized movement skills may not develop in a hierarchical fashion. In other words, specialized skills may emerge before all fundamental skills are mastered, and fundamental skills may emerge before all early movement milestones are mastered.

Fourth, the separate classification level for functional movement skills allows one to make a distinction between skills performed in contrived or unnatural contexts and skills performed in natural and meaningful contexts. There has been a recent emphasis on the assessment of functional movement skills, as shown in the occupational therapy assessment taxonomies offered by Mathiowetz (1993) and Smith (1990).

Finally, the overall taxonomy allows for most assessment instruments to be placed into just one category or level, minimizing the overlap and confusion between categories. Moreover, the categories in the taxonomy relate closely to the purposes or uses of movement skills assessment tools. I present more in-depth information on assessment instruments at each classification level in part II, which deals with levels of movement skill assessment. Chapters 7 through 10 are each devoted to one level, from foundations of movement skills to fundamental movement skills, while chapter 11 focuses on specialized and functional movement skills.

Chapter 4

Basic Measurement Concepts

PEOPLE engaged in the process of movement skill assessment must have a solid understanding of basic measurement concepts. The goal of this chapter is to provide an overview of these concepts, with examples and applications related to movement and physical activity. Accordingly, the chapter will begin with definitions and explanations of common terms, followed by descriptions and examples of the four levels of measurement scales. Then I will discuss various calculation procedures,

> 66 Suppose, unbeknownst to you, your camera broke so that the film wouldn't wind. Every picture you took went right on top of all the others. If you had taken pictures of different scenes, you might still be able to make out the individual parts. But suppose you had taken a picture of a high-school graduating class, one person at a time. Each person took a turn sitting in the chair in front of the fixed camera; each smiled; each had a picture taken. Afterward, when you developed the film, you would find just one picture, a composite of all those faces. All the individual records would still be there, but on top of one another, difficult to separate out. You'd have the average high-school graduate. 99
>
> —*Norman (1990, p. 118)*

including indexes of central tendency and variability, the normal distribution, score transformations, correlations, and linear regression procedures. You can find more in-depth treatment of this information, consistent with the approach in this book, in Rothstein and Echternach's (1993) *Primer on Measurement: An Introductory Guide to Measurement Issues.*

■ TERMINOLOGY

Because so many professions are involved in the assessment of movement skills, there may be inconsistencies in the ways people use various terms related to measurement and assessment. This may lead to communication problems that can hinder effective teamwork. In this section, I define and explain the terms *measurement, assessment, evaluation, diagnosis, independent* and *dependent variables,* and *statistics.*

Measurement and Assessment

Measurement and assessment both can be defined as the assignment of numbers to attributes or characteristics of persons, objects, or events according to explicit formulations or rules (Sax, 1989). Consequently, the measurement or assessment of movement skill can be defined as the assignment of numbers to movement-related attributes or characteristics of persons. Scores and data are the numbers assigned, and are usually considered to be synonymous with measurements (Task Force on Standards for Measurement in Physical Therapy [TFSMPT], 1991). For example, movement speed might be measured or assessed by the time taken to run 40 yd as quickly as possible, or skill in throwing might be measured or assessed by assigning a number to the specific pattern used to throw a ball.

A test is a device for obtaining a sample of a person's behavior (Allen & Yen, 1979), in other words, the procedure or set of procedures used to obtain measurements or data (TFSMPT, 1991). Specific tests or sets of tests often are referred to as examinations or as measurement or assessment instruments, tools, or batteries. While a test always requires some type of measurement or assessment, it can consist of just one measured item, such as the time to run an obstacle course as a test of agility.

Evaluation

An evaluation, although often confused with measurement and assessment, is a judgment based on a measurement (TFSMPT, 1991). From a broader perspective, Baumgartner and Jackson (1991) define evaluation as (a) collecting suitable data, (b) judging the value of the data according to some standard, and (c) making decisions based on the judgments. Clearly, the background and training of the person making a judgment from assessment data play a critical role in evaluation.

Diagnosis

In the context of this book, the term *diagnosis* denotes the identification of a potential source of difficulty in the performance of a movement skill. The diagnosis of skill problems is exemplified best in the three-step, top-down assessment sequence I will present in chapter 13. In particular, at Step 3, the main objective is to identify the movement skill foundation areas or systems that limit the individual's performance of particular movement skills.

Several authors have implied that their tests may be used to diagnose motor problems—that is, the ability deficits that may underlie a broad range of skills. These include Ayres (1989) in her Sensory Integration and Praxis Tests, Bruininks (1978) in his Bruininks-Oseretsky Test of Motor Proficiency, and Yarmolenko (1933) in his test of basic movement patterns (see chapters 2 and 8 for descriptions of these tests). Davis (1984) points out that motor ability deficits are often interpreted as reflecting some type of nervous system pathology, but warns that such an interpretation should be avoided because there is not an isomorphic or one-to-one relationship between nervous system function and movement behavior. Given this hazard in interpreting motor ability tests and the other problems with motor ability tests discussed in chapter 3, diagnosis should be limited to identification of the movement skill foundation areas or systems that constrain an individual's performance of specific movement skills. For example, on the basis of some assessments specific to locomotion, a physical therapist may diagnose or identify balance or postural control as a limiting factor for a person struggling to walk independently. However, a therapist cannot appropriately use a poor score on the balance subtest of a motor ability test to diagnose or identify balance as potential source of difficulty for any skill except those actually assessed in the subtest.

Independent and Dependent Variables

Independent variables are those factors that are under the control of and manipulated by the experimenter or examiner. For example, an examiner may have the person being assessed perform the same task under a variety of conditions, such as throwing with balls of different weights, throwing at different distances, or throwing at targets of different sizes. The changes in the movement outcome or movement pattern as one or more factors are varied may offer important insight into the dynamics of the performer's movement behavior. Most of the time, on standardized movement assessment instruments, a person is allowed to perform a specific task under only one set of conditions.

Dependent variables are the actual measurements, assessments, or scores used to document performance under a particular set of constraints. They are referred to as dependent because their values rely upon the conditions specified by the independent variables.

Statistics

When movement performance scores are gathered for a group of persons, the data can be treated in two different ways. First, if the performance of the group is the only concern, then descriptive statistics that represent and summarize the commonality and variability of the group may be used. Later in this chapter I will present and explain descriptive statistics of the central tendency and variability of scores in a group. The interpretation of these statistics, such as mean and standard deviation, requires an understanding of the distribution of scores for the group and the reliability of scores for individual performers.

Second, if the performance of the group is intended to represent and predict the performance of a larger population, then inferential statistics must be used. The same types of indexes of central tendency and variability can be made for inferential statistics, but they must be treated as estimates of the population from the limited sample rather than as exact values. The validity of inferential statistics is based on the assumption that the sample was randomly selected, that is, that each person in the population was equally likely to be included in the sample. A violation of the assumption of random selection may lead to faulty interpretation of the data. Be aware that the formulas for sample statistics utilize symbols different from those used in population statistics—for example, S versus σ for standard deviation—to ensure proper interpretation.

■ LEVELS OF MEASUREMENT

Four levels of measurement are distinguished by the characteristics of the numbers assigned to the attributes being measured or assessed (Stevens, 1946). The four key characteristics that may be used to differentiate between the four levels are (a) distinctiveness, (b) ordering in magnitude, (c) equal intervals, and (d) absolute zero (Allen & Yen, 1979) (see table 4.1). The following questions are used to evaluate the four characteristics:

- *Distinctiveness:* Are different numbers assigned to different values of the given property?
- *Ordering in magnitude:* Do larger numbers represent more of the given property?
- *Equal intervals:* Do equal differences in numbers reflect equal differences in the property being measured?
- *Absolute zero:* Does a measurement of zero indicate the absence of the property being measured?

TABLE 4.1   Characteristics of the Four Levels of Measurement

Characteristics	Level of measurement			
	Nominal	Ordinal	Interval	Ratio
Distinctiveness	yes	yes	yes	yes
Ordering in magnitude	no	yes	yes	yes
Equal intervals	no	no	yes	yes
Absolute zero	no	no	no	yes

Note: From *Introduction to Measurement Theory* by M.J. Allen and W.M.Yen. Copyright (c) 1979, Brooks/Cole Publishing Company, Pacific Grove, CA 93950, a division of International Thomson Publishing Inc. By permission of the publisher.

Nominal Measurement

Nominal measurement is the simplest of the four levels of measurement, with the assigned numbers corresponding to labels or categories that have no particular intrinsic relationship and therefore do not permit logical or arithmetic comparison. In a nominal scale, different numbers are assigned to different values of the same property such that those values with the same number are considered to be equivalent and those with different numbers are not equivalent. Hence, as table 4.1 indicates, distinctiveness is the only characteristic defining nominal measurement. Numbers on players' uniforms, student identification numbers, and insurance policy numbers are just a few examples of the use of nominal numbers to identify people, places, and things.

Ordinal Measurement

Ordinal measurement involves organizing scores in a rank order. Differences in scores are viewed in terms of directional relationships, such as more/less, larger/smaller, faster/slower, or longer/shorter. In an ordinal scale, different numbers are assigned to different values of a given property (distinctiveness), and larger numbers represent more of the property (ordering in magnitude) (see table 4.1). However, the distance between numbers is not known. Merbitz, Morris, and Grip (1989) assert that "ordinal 'numbers' are at best symbols of 'greater than' and 'less than' quantities; we may call them 'nonnumbers'" (p. 309). These characteristics of ordinal numbers, therefore, do not allow them to be meaningfully added or subtracted.

An example of an ordinal scale is the ranking of sport teams. The final standings of the Western Division of the American League in 1987 are presented in table 4.2. The places of the teams in the second column, with numbers ranging from 1 to 6, are based on an ordinal scale, with higher

TABLE 4.2 Final Standings for the Western Division of the American League in1987

Team	Place	Wins	Losses	Games behind
Minnesota Twins	1	85	77	0
Kansas City Royals	2	83	79	2
Oakland Athletics	3	81	81	4
Seattle Mariners	4	78	84	7
Chicago White Sox	5	77	85	8
California Angels	6	75	87	10
Texas Rangers	6	75	87	10

numbers indicating more games behind the best team. Note that the arithmetic differences between place numbers are not equivalent or even proportional to the actual number of games behind.

Even with objective definitions of levels of measurement, there may be some difficulty in categorizing measurement scales. In the Test of Gross Motor Development (Ulrich, 1985), four criteria related to movement form, numbered from 1 to 4, are given for the skill of hopping (see table 4.3). If the numbers are ordered developmentally, such that the average ages at which the criteria are met are older for higher numbers, then the scale is ordinal; however, if the items are not developmentally ordered, then the scale is nominal. In one of the tables in his test manual, Ulrich indicates that Criterion 4 is expected to be met first, followed by Criteria 1, 2, and 3, which leads to the conclusion that these numbers are nominal.

Interval and Ratio Measurements

Interval and ratio measurements possess the basic characteristics of ordinal measurements with the additional characteristic that equal differences in numbers reflect equal differences in the property being measured (see table 4.1). Thus, the addition or subtraction of interval or ratio numbers will yield numbers that accurately reflect the sum or differences of the measured property. The characteristic that differentiates interval and ratio measurements is whether (ratio) or not (interval) a measurement of zero indicates the absence of the property being measured.

In the American League Western Division standings in table 4.2, the numbers of wins, losses, and games behind all appear to be ratio scales, because a zero means that a team has no wins, no losses, or is no games behind. We can accurately state that the World Champion Twins had 2 more wins than the Royals, and that the White Sox were only 1 game behind the Mariners, and that the wins of the Angels and Rangers combined for 150 wins. Ratio numbers also may be multiplied or divided, so the statement that the Athletics were twice as many games behind as the Royals is valid.

TABLE 4.3 Criteria for the Hop in the Test of Gross Motor Development

Criteria number	Performance criteria
1	Foot of nonsupport leg is bent and carried in back of the body.
2	Nonsupport leg swings in pendular fashion to produce force.
3	Arms bent at elbows and swing forward on takeoff.
4	Able to hop on the right and left foot.

Note: From *Test of Gross Motor Development* (p. 20) by D.A. Ulrich, 1985, Austin, TX: PRO-ED. Copyright 1985 by PRO-ED. Reprinted by permission.

However, what *properties* do wins, losses, and games behind represent? If they all represent measures of overall team skill, a team with no wins (something we see more often with football teams because they play fewer games in a season) would be viewed as having absolutely no skill. This, of course, cannot be accepted as true, so the wins and losses should be considered interval scales.

The number of pull-ups a person can perform is often used as an assessment of upper-body strength. On the surface, this appears to be a ratio scale, but because a score of zero does not indicate the absence of strength, it is more accurately classified as an interval scale. Thus, the critical characteristic differentiating interval from ratio measurements—a measurement of zero indicating the absence of the property being measured—can be interpreted on two levels: (a) relative to the actual behavior observed (i.e., the number of pull-ups), or preferably and more accurately, (b) relative to the underlying property or construct (i.e., upper-body strength). Wright and Linacre (1989) take an extreme view in their argument about the seemingly simple concept of zero origins in ratio scales when they state, "However intriguing they may be theoretically, [they] are necessarily unrealizable abstractions" (p. 859). For other comparisons of these two levels of interpretations, see Burton and Davis (1996).

An example of an interval measurement scale at both the observation and construct levels is a sit-and-reach test of flexibility in which a person is asked to sit with knees straight and to reach as far as possible toward or past the toes. A score of zero indicates a reach just to the toes, a negative score indicates a reach short of the toes, and a positive score indicates a reach past the toes. In this test, a score of zero does not indicate the absence of flexibility, but corresponds with a body landmark. Hence, a score of 6 is 8 units better than a score of -2, but a score of 4 is not twice as good as a score of 2.

■ INDEXES OF CENTRAL TENDENCY

The objective of indexes of central tendency is to represent most accurately in a single number the entire set of scores derived from a group. Given this difficult task, any statistic will have some drawbacks. The most commonly used indexes of central tendency are mode, median, and mean. No mathematical rule can indicate which index of central tendency is most appropriate for a given application (Gould, 1996), but proper decisions depend on a solid understanding of the limitations and strengths of each. Gould (1996) warns that it is a serious mistake to view any index of central tendency as the most likely outcome for any single individual, even though most people commit this error all the time.

TABLE 4.4 Final Pitching Results for the 1963 Los Angeles Dodgers

Player	Wins	Losses	Innings pitched	Walks	Strikeouts	Earned run average
Dick Calmus	3	1	44	16	25	2.66
Don Drysdale	19	17	315	57	251	2.63
Sandy Koufax	25	5	311	58	306	1.88
Bob Miller	10	8	187	65	125	2.89
Ron Perranoski	16	3	129	43	75	1.67
Johnny Podres	14	12	198	64	134	3.55
Pete Richert	5	3	78	28	54	4.50
Ed Roebuck	2	4	40	21	26	4.28
Larry Sherry	2	6	80	24	47	3.71

To illustrate these indexes of central tendency, I will use sample calculations based on the final results for the nine pitchers on the 1963 World Champion Los Angeles Dodgers who pitched the most innings that year (see table 4.4).

Mode

The mode of a distribution is the score that occurs most frequently. For example, the mode for wins and losses by 1963 Dodger pitchers was 2 and 3, respectively (see table 4.4). There may be more than one mode (e.g., the distribution can be bimodal or trimodal) if different values that show up an equal number of times match the highest frequency. If all scores are different, as for the number of strikeouts by Dodger pitchers, the mode is all scores, which indicates no pattern of central tendency. The mode can be calculated for all four levels of measurement, including nominal.

Median

The median is the score in the distribution that divides the data into two equal-sized groups. In other words, it is the score that half of the individuals score below and half the individuals score above. If the number of individuals is odd, the median is the score of the person in the middle; if the number of individuals is even, the median is the value midway between the two middle scores. To find the median, arrange the set of scores from low to high, count the total number of scores (N), add 1 $(N + 1)$, divide the sum by 2 $([N + 1] / 2)$, and then find the score that lies that many places up from the lowest score. When there is an even number of scores, an additional step needs to be added because the $(N + 1) / 2$ term will yield a mixed number, a whole number with a fraction. In this case, the median is the value halfway between the scores corresponding to the whole places just above and below the mixed number. For example, the median number of innings pitched by the 1963 Dodgers was 129 because there were 9 pitchers, adding 1 to 9 makes 10, dividing 10 by 2 yields 5, and the pitcher with the fifth least number of innings pitched was Ron Perranoski, who pitched 129 innings.

The median is not affected by extreme scores, and thus it is a more representative measure of central tendency for skewed distributions—or distributions with a single peak that is not at the center—than other measures (Kirk, 1984). Because the median is determined from an ordered sequence, it can be calculated for ordinal, interval, and ratio scales, but not nominal scales.

Mean

The mean is the arithmetic average, which is the sum of all scores divided by the number of scores. The equation for the mean is:

$$\bar{X} = \sum X_i / n. \qquad\qquad 4.1$$

Explanations of the symbols used in Equation 4.1 and in subsequent equations in this chapter are presented in table 4.5. To illustrate, the mean number of losses for the 1963 Dodger pitchers was calculated to be 6.56:

$$\bar{X} = (5 + 17 + 3 + 12 + 8 + 3 + 6 + 1 + 4) / 9 = 59 / 9 = 6.56.$$

The mean is the measure of central tendency used most often for the purpose of statistical description or inference (Kirk, 1984). Unlike the median or mode, the mean takes into account the value of each score, but this makes it vulnerable to dramatic shifts when very large or very small scores are included. Note that the mean number of innings pitched in table 4.6 (154) is considerably larger than the median (129) because the higher values (315 and 311) are further above the median than the lower values are below the median (40 and 44). Because nominal and ordinal numbers cannot be meaningfully added to determine a sum, means can be calculated only for interval and ratio numbers.

Several symbols are used to denote means. First, the Greek letter μ_X (pronounced "mu") is used as a descriptive statistic to represent the mean of an entire population for Variable X. However, a variable letter with a bar over it, such as $\bar{X}$ as in Equation 4.1, is used as an inferential statistic to represent the mean of a sample. Thus, if the Dodgers' data were used as a sample to make inferences about a larger population, such as players on National League teams or Dodger teams of other years, then the symbol $\bar{X}$ would be appropriate; if the only population of concern were the nine pitchers on

TABLE 4.5 Description of Symbols Used in Statistical Equations

Symbol	Description
a	In a linear regression equation, respresents the value at which the regression line crosses the vertical Y axis.
b	In a linear regression equation, respresents the slope of the regression line (i.e., the change in the units of Y for each unit of X).
N	Number of scores or individuals in a total population.
n	Number of scores or individuals in a sample of a population.
S_X	Sample standard deviation of Variable X.
S_X^2	Sample variance of Variable X.
S_{XY}^2	Sample covariance of Variables X and Y.
T	Normalized score with a mean of 50 and a standard deviation of 10.
X	Variable X, in general, or a specific value of Variable X.
X_i	The ith value of Variable X, where i represents the place number within a series of scores (e.g., X_4 is the fourth score of Variable X).
$\bar{X}$	Sample means for Variable X.
Z_X	Standard or Z score for Variable X, with a mean of 0 and a standard deviation of 1.
Σ	Summation sign indicating that the repetitions of the term following a sign should be added together.
μ_X	Population mean for variable X.
μ_X^*	Chosen mean of variable X for population standardized score.
σ_X	Population standard deviation of Variable X.
σ_X^*	Chosen standard deviation of Variable X for population standardized score.
σ_X^2	Population variance of Variable X.

the 1963 Dodgers with the most innings pitched, then the symbol μ_X would be appropriate. The number of subjects or scores in a population is indicated by an N, while the number of subjects or scores in a sample is indicated by an n, as in Equation 4.1.

You can calculate and check the modes, medians, and means for six pitching categories in table 4.4 against the answers provided in table 4.6. A

TABLE 4.6 Sample Central Tendency and Variability Statistics From the Final Pitching Results for the 1963 Los Angeles Dodgers

Player	Wins	Losses	Innings pitched	Walks	Strikeouts	Earned run average
Central Tendency						
Mode	2.0	3.0	*	*	*	*
Median	10.0	5.0	129.0	43.0	75.0	2.89
Mean	10.7	6.6	153.6	41.8	115.9	3.09
Variability						
Range	24.0	17.0	275.0	50.0	282.0	2.83
Variance	69.5	25.8	11,320.8	391.4	10,174.6	0.99
Standard deviation	8.3	5.1	106.4	19.8	100.9	0.99

*All nine scores were different.

fraction of a win or strikeout does not make sense, so all answers are rounded to the smallest meaningful unit.

■ INDEXES OF VARIABILITY

In the assessment of movement behavior, variability often is more important than central tendency, particularly for persons with movement problems (Davis, 1984; Sugden & Keogh, 1990). Gould (1996), a professor of zoology at Harvard and best-selling author, argues that central tendency is an abstraction and variation is the reality. To stay with the baseball theme, Gould points out that

> The enormous variability of individual performance guarantees that even a mediocre player, can for one day of glory, accomplish something never done before, or even dreamed of in baseball's philosophy. . . . Don Larsen was a truly mediocre pitcher for the Yankees, but he achieved baseball's definition of perfection when it mattered most: twenty-seven Dodgers up, twenty-seven Bums down on October 8, 1956, for a perfect game in the World Series (no one before or since had ever thrown a no-hitter of any kind in a World Series game). (p. 131)

Larsen, with a lifetime major league win/loss record of only 81/91, recalls in his book *The Perfect Yankee: The Incredible Story of the Greatest Miracle in Baseball History* (Larsen & Shaw, 1996) that he pitched lousy in Game 2 in the 1956 World Series, lasting only two innings, and was sure that he would not get another chance to pitch in the Series. However, Casey Stengel, the

TABLE 4.7   Final Batting Results for the 1975 Cincinnati Reds

Player	At bats	Runs	Hits	Home runs	Runs batted in	Earned batting average
Johnny Bench	530	83	150	28	110	.283
Dave Concepcion	507	62	139	5	49	.274
Dan Dreisen	210	38	59	7	38	.281
George Foster	463	71	139	23	78	.300
Cesar Geronimo	501	69	129	6	53	.257
Ken Griffey	463	95	141	4	46	.305
Joe Morgan	498	107	163	17	94	.327
Tony Perez	511	74	144	20	109	.282
Merv Rettenmund	188	24	45	2	19	.239
Pete Rose	662	112	210	7	74	.317

Yankees' manager, called on him in Game 5 and Larsen responded with perfection.

There are three commonly used indexes of variability or measures of the distribution of scores: range, variance, and standard deviation. I will use a second set of baseball data, the batting results for the 1975 World Champion Cincinnati Reds, to illustrate the calculation of these statistics (see table 4.7).

Range

The simplest measure of variability—range—is defined differently for discrete and continuous measurements. For discrete numbers, such as frequency, range is the difference between the highest and lowest scores in the distribution plus 1. Thus, the range of the 1975 Reds' runs batted in (a frequency) was 92, from Johnny Bench's 110 to Merv Rettenmund's 19. For continuous numbers, such as distance or time, range is just the difference between highest and lowest scores, without the added 1. The logic of this distinction can be illustrated by the use of only two numbers in a distribution: 0 and 1. If the measurement is discrete with no possible scores between 0 and 1, then a range of 2 (1 − 0 + 1) makes sense because there clearly are two distinct scores. However, if the measurement is continuous such that scores between 0 and 1 are possible (e.g., 0.4), then a range of 1 (1 − 0) makes sense because only one score *unit* is represented. Thus, the range of the 1975 Reds' batting averages (a continuous measurement) was .088, from Joe Morgan's .327 to Merv Rettenmund's .239. The major weakness of using a range is that it does not take into account the dispersion of scores that fall between the two extremes in a set of numbers.

Variance

The variance is an index of the alignment of a set of scores around the mean of the distribution. It can be described as the average squared deviation or variance of the scores from the mean, represented by the equation (using population symbols):

$$\sigma_X^2 = \Sigma \, (X_i - \mu_X)^2 \, / \, N. \qquad\qquad 4.2$$

The population variance of home runs for the 1975 Reds was 76.49, calculated by applying Equation 4.2:

$$
\begin{aligned}
\sigma_X^2 \; = \; & [(28 - 11.9)^2 + (5 - 11.9)^2 + (7 - 11.9)^2 + (23 - 11.9)^2 + (6 - 11.9)^2 + \\
& (4 - 11.9)^2 + (17 - 11.9)^2 + (20 - 11.9)^2 + (2 - 11.9)^2 + (7 - 11.9)^2] \, / \\
& 10 \\[6pt]
= \; & [(16.1)^2 + (-6.9)^2 + (-4.9)^2 + (11.1)^2 + (-5.9)^2 + (-7.9)^2 + (5.1)^2 + \\
& (8.1)^2 + (-9.9)^2 + (-4.9)^2] \, / \, 10 \\[6pt]
= \; & [259.21 + 47.61 + 24.01 + 123.21 + 34.81 + 62.41 + 26.01 + \\
& 65.61 + 98.01 + 24.01] \, / \, 10 \\[6pt]
= \; & 764.9 \, / \, 10 = 76.49.
\end{aligned}
$$

The variance has little value on its own, but is the basis of the very powerful standard deviation and is used to calculate other statistics, such as correlations. Thompson (1942/1992) argues that the "dimension" of this average of the squared differences is wrong, but that "the square root of this average of squares restores the correct dimension, and the result is a useful index of variability, or of deviation which is called σ" (p. 124).

Equation 4.2 can be used to calculate population variance directly, which is symbolized by σ_X^2. To estimate population variance from a sample, symbolized by S_X^2, the N is replaced by $(n - 1)$:

$$S_X^2 = \Sigma \, (X_i - \bar{X})^2 \, / \, (n - 1). \qquad\qquad 4.3$$

Thus, the sample variance will be slightly larger than population variance, 84.99 compared to 76.49 for the Reds' home run example. This adjustment in sample variance is made because of the potential for error in estimating population variance from a limited sample. As the number of subjects in the sample (n) increases, the difference between sample and population variances decreases.

Standard Deviation

The standard deviation is a standardized index of the alignment of a set of scores around the mean of the distribution. It can be described as the square root of the average squared deviation or variance of the scores from the mean, represented by the equation (using population symbols):

$$\sigma_X = \sqrt{\Sigma (X_i - \mu)^2 / N}. \qquad 4.4$$

The standard deviation also can be described more simply as the square root of the variance. Equation 4.4 specifies the population standard deviation, while the sample standard deviation is calculated by replacing the N term with $(n - 1)$.

$$S_X = \sqrt{\Sigma (X_i - \bar{X})^2 / (n - 1)}. \qquad 4.5$$

Accordingly, the population standard deviation of home runs for the 1975 Reds was 8.75, and the sample standard deviation was 9.22. You can see the population central tendency and variability statistics for all batting categories for the 1975 Reds in table 4.8.

■ THE NORMAL DISTRIBUTION

The power of the standard deviation is derived from its application to the standard normal curve, which is a bell-shaped distribution of scores with most scores congregating near the middle and scores becoming progressively fewer at the two extremes. Many variables, such as height, weight, intelligence, and movement skill, follow such a normal distribution. As Thompson (1942/1992), in his classic *On Growth and Form*, explains:

That a "curve of stature" should agree closely with the "normal curve of error" amazed Galton, and (as he said) formed the mainstay of his long and fruitful enquiry into natural inheritance. The curve is a thing

TABLE 4.8 Population Central Tendency and Variability Statistics From the Final Batting Results for the 1975 Cincinnati Reds

Player	At bats	Runs	Hits	Home runs	Runs batted in	Batting average
Central tendency						
Mode	463.0	*	139.0	7.0	*	*
Median	500.0	73.0	140.0	7.0	64.0	.283
Mean	453.3	73.5	131.9	11.9	67.0	.287
Variability						
Range	475.0	89.0	166.0	27.0	92.0	.088
Variance	18,969.2	702.7	2,059.9	76.5	861.8	.0006
Standard deviation	137.7	26.5	45.4	8.7	29.4	.025

*All 10 scores were different.

apart, sui generis. It depicts no course of events, it is no time or vector diagram. It merely deals with the variability, and variation of magnitudes; and by magnitudes we mean anything which can be counted or measured, a regiment of men, a basket of nuts, the florets of a daisy, the stripes of a zebra, the nearness of shots to the bull's eye. It thereby represents one of the most far-reaching, some say one of the most fundamental, of nature's laws. (pp. 119-120)

Figure 4.1 presents the prototypical standard normal curve, with the areas under the curve that match various standard deviation *(SD)* values. The curve is symmetrical, so the mean marks the middle of the curve and is thus equivalent to the median. Other characteristics are that 68% of the total sample or population fall between −1.0 and +1.0 *SD*s, 7% fall below −1.5 *SD*s, and 98% fall below +2.0 *SD*s. You can find the exact proportion of the population lying below or above any standard deviation value in the table of areas under the normal curve, provided in appendix C. Identify the standard deviation in the Z column; then find the proportion below positive Z values (and the proportion above negative Z values) in the second column, and find the proportion above positive Z values (and the proportion below negative Z values) in the last column. For example, the proportion of a population below −1.85 *SD*s is .0322, and the proportion below +0.40 is .6554.

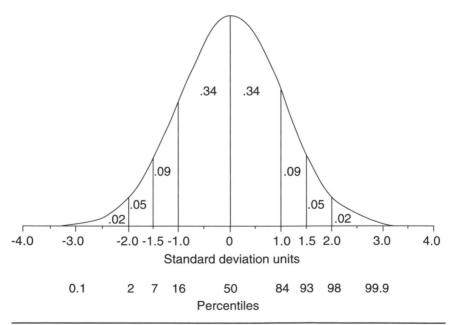

■ **FIGURE 4.1**   The standard normal curve, with areas under the curve and percentiles for various standard deviation values.

A distribution of scores closely resembling a normal curve is the batting averages for the 157 batters in the National League in 1975 who had more than 100 at bats with the same team (see figure 4.2). The mean batting average for this population was .258 with a standard deviation of .039. According to the normal distribution, 68% of the batters should have had batting averages between .219 and .297 (.258 ± .039), 16% should have had them below .219, and 16% should have had them above .297. These are close estimates, as 65% fell within this range, with 17% below .219 and 18% above .297.

■ TRANSFORMATION OF SCORES

Jason, an 8-year-old boy, received a point score of 8.0 on the running speed and agility subtest of the Bruininks-Oseretsky Test of Motor Proficiency (BOT) (Bruininks, 1978), but it is not clear whether this was a

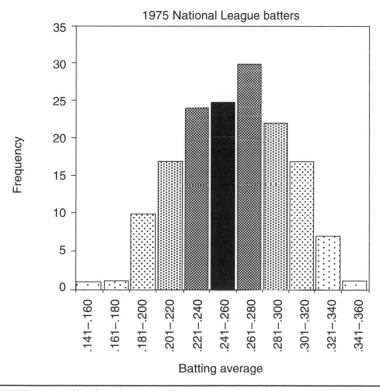

■ **FIGURE 4.2** The distribution of batting averages for the 157 batters in the National League in 1975 who had at least 100 at bats with the same team. The mean of the distribution falls within the darkened bar.

good, average, or poor performance. One solution would be to have an explicit criterion of success, but the criterion may not be appropriate for all individuals. Another solution would be to compare the score to the scores of individuals with similar attributes, such as age, sex, or body size. To minimize the inconvenience of looking up scores from a standardized group from a chart each time we make a comparison, we can convert or transform absolute or raw scores into numbers that carry comparative or relative information. In this section, I describe some common transformations used to increase the meaning of a raw score by providing a comparison to the performances of other persons, including percentiles, standard or Z scores, standardized scores, normalized scores, and age or grade equivalents.

Percentiles

A percentile is the percentage of scores that fall below or are equal to a particular score. This can be calculated by dividing the ordered subject number (from low to high performance) by the number of subjects in the sample or population and then multiplying by 100:

$$\text{percentile} = (\text{subject order} \;/\; N) \times 100. \qquad 4.6$$

For instance, Johnny Podres' 134 strikeouts placed him at the 86th percentile of the National League pitchers in 1963 because only 20 of the 142 pitchers in the National League had the same number or a larger number of strikeouts. His strikeout total placed him at the 86th percentile within his team because teammates Don Drysdale (with 251) and Sandy Koufax (with what was then a major league record of 306!) had more.

League: $(122 \;/\; 142) \times 100 = .859 \times 100 = 86\text{th percentile.}$
Team: $(12 \;/\; 14) \times 100 = .857 \times 100 = 86\text{th percentile.}$

Also, the ordered subject number (from low to high performance) that matches a given percentile can be calculated by dividing the percentile by 100 and then multiplying the product by the number of subjects:

$$\text{Subject order} = (\text{percentile} \;/\; 100) \times N. \qquad 4.7$$

For example, the player in the 30th percentile for the National League pitchers for 1963 would be Player 43, who happened to be Jack Hamilton of the Philadelphia Phillies with 23 strikeouts, because $(30 \;/\; 100) \times 142 = (.30) \times 142 = 43$.

A problem in interpreting percentiles can occur when lower scores indicate better performance, as is the case with the earned run average (ERA). Ordering subjects from low to high in terms of performance, not the actual measurement value, will ensure that higher percentiles always represent higher performance levels. Thus, higher ERAs should be listed first and lower ERAs last.

By definition, the median is always equal to the 50th percentile. Freund and Simon (1992) have described the median as "one of many fractiles which divide data into two or more parts as nearly equal as they can be made. Among them we also find quartiles, deciles and percentiles which are intended to divide data into four, ten and a hundred parts" (p. 53).

Percentiles concern the relative ordering of scores, not the differences between scores in an ordered sequence; thus, they must be considered to be an ordinal scale. Moreover, because the relationships between numbers change in the transformation from raw scores to percentiles, the transformation is nonlinear. Consequently, the arithmetic manipulation of percentiles, such as finding a person's mean or average percentile over a set of five tests, should be discouraged. If a numerical summary is desired, it would be more logical to create a composite score derived from actual performance on the five tests, and then to calculate a percentile based on the relative standings of the subjects on the composite.

Percentiles also can be determined indirectly by using the table of the area under the standard normal curve (see appendix C) and multiplying the proportions by 100. If the standard deviation or Z value is positive, then the percentile is found in the second column; if the standard deviation or Z value is negative, then the percentile is found in the third column. This indirect method of determining percentiles assumes that scores are normally distributed and requires that a raw score be converted into a number expressed in standard deviation units, i.e., standard or Z scores, or standardized scores.

Standard or Z Scores

Raw scores expressed in standard deviation units are referred to as standard or Z scores. Standard scores indicate how many standard deviation units above or below the mean the raw score lies. This linear transformation is accomplished by applying the formula (using population symbols):

$$Z = (X - \mu_X) / \sigma_X. \qquad 4.8$$

To return once more to the 1963 National League pitching data, Johnny Podres' strikeouts can be converted to a standard score of 1.10, a little over 1 SD above the National League mean of 67 strikeouts:

$$Z = (134 - 67) / 61 = 67 / 61 = 1.10.$$

Then, the proportion corresponding to this Z score in the second column of appendix C, multiplied times 100, gives a percentile of 86 (the second column was used instead of the third because the Z score was positive).

This indicates that, assuming a normal distribution, only 14% of the pitchers in the National League had more strikeouts. This result exactly matches the percentile that was calculated directly (the 86th percentile).

Now, Jason's results on the BOT running speed and agility subtest can be given more meaning if we transform his point score of 8.0 into a standard or Z score and then into a percentile. First, the mean and standard deviations for 8-year-old boys are found to be 8.7 and 1.3, respectively, in table 30 in the examiner's manual (Bruininks, 1978). Applying Equation 4.8 yields:

$$Z = (8.0 - 8.7) / 1.3 = -0.7 / 1.3 = -0.54$$

and the corresponding proportion from appendix C in the third column (.2946), multiplied by 100, gives a percentile of 30. This percentile provides a much clearer perspective of Jason's performance than the original point score.

If the question is reversed—that is, if we want to determine a raw score given a particular Z score or corresponding percentile—a few algebraic maneuvers yield the appropriate equation to solve the problem:

$$X = \mu_x + Z(\sigma_x). \qquad\qquad 4.9$$

Thus, if Jason scored in the 30th percentile on the BOT running speed and agility subtest, his point score would be 8.0, because 8.7 + (Z)1.3 = 8.7 + (−0.54)1.3 = 8.0.

With experience, standard or Z scores may become meaningful to a person interpreting a test, but often the matching percentiles need to be looked up. However, you can minimize recourse to the table of areas under the normal curve by memorizing the percentiles matching three key standard deviation values: −1.0 (16th percentile), −1.5 (7th percentile), and −2.0 (2nd percentile). Because the normal curve is symmetrical, the percentiles for positive values of 1.0, 1.5, and 2.0 SDs are easily derived (84th percentile, 93rd percentile, and 98th percentile, respectively) (see figure 4.1). Finally, percentiles of other standard scores can be quickly estimated by extrapolating or interpolating from the known values. An examination of appendix C reveals that the range of Z scores is −4.0 to +4.0, although scores smaller than −2.0 and larger than +2.0 account for less than 5% of the total area.

The transformation of raw scores into standard or Z scores is considered to be linear because the relationships between scores, assuming a normal distribution, remain constant. Thus, if raw scores are interval or ratio measures, then the resulting standard or Z scores can be added or subtracted. Standard or Z scores often are used to convert scores of items that are expressed in different units into equivalent terms by converting them into standard deviation units.

Standardized Scores

A test developer may want the advantages of standard or Z scores but want to avoid certain characteristics, such as having about half the scores transformed into negative numbers or having the mean equal to zero. Negative numbers may increase the chances for errors in mathematical manipulations and may cast a shadow on performances matched with negative numbers. These potential problems can be eliminated with use of standardized scores, which are linear transformations of standard or Z scores to any mean value and to any standard deviation value. The formula for this transformation is (using population symbols):

$$\text{Standardized score} = \sigma_x^* Z + \mu_x^*. \qquad 4.10$$

The term standard score often is used to refer to Z scores as well as these linear transformations of Z scores, but here I use the term *standardized*, as in Allen and Yen's (1979) text, to make a clear distinction between the Z scores and the transformations.

Johnny Podres' strikeouts in 1963 relative to those of other National League pitchers, and Jason's running speed and agility score relative to the normative sample of the BOT, can both be transformed into standardized scores with means of 1,000 and standard deviations of 200. Using the standard or Z scores calculated earlier:

Johnny Podres: $(200)(1.10) + 1,000 = 220 + 1,000 = 1,220.$
Jason: $(200)(-0.54) + 1,000 = -108 + 1,000 = 892.$

These two different types of performances now are expressed in equivalent units.

Any number may be chosen as the mean or standard deviation, but certain numbers often are preferred. For example, the chosen means and standard deviations are 15 and 5 for the BOT subtest standard scores (Bruininks, 1978), 100 and 15 for the Gross Motor Development Quotient of the Test of Gross Motor Development (Ulrich, 1985) and the Developmental Motor Quotients of the Peabody Developmental Motor Scales (Folio & Fewell, 1983), 100 and 16 for the Stanford-Binet IQ Test, and 1,000 and 150 for the Scholastic Achievement Test. The values of various types of score transformations are compared in figure 4.3. Note that some so-called standard scores are actually standardized scores in our terminology.

An understanding of standardized scores may provide insight into why certain scores are set as criterion or landmark values for certain tests. You might wonder why the criterion for mental retardation is an IQ of 68; but if you realize that the standardized mean and standard deviation of the IQ test, such as the Stanford-Binet, are 100 and 16, you should see that the score of 68 is exactly 2 *SD*s below the mean. Further, if you know the

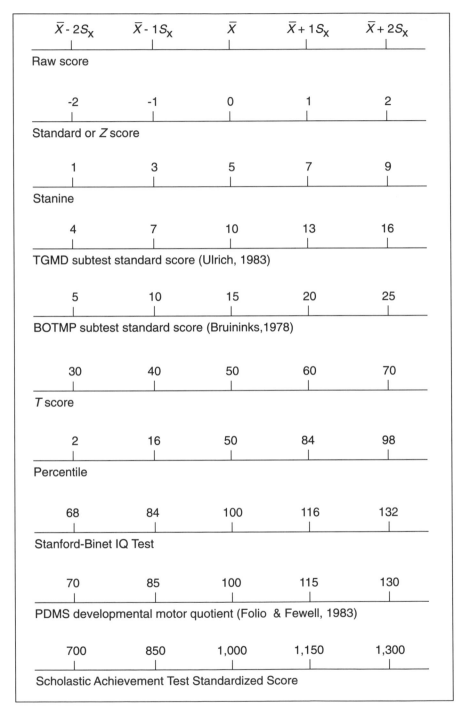

■ FIGURE 4.3   A comparison of various types of score transformations.

percentile values for −1.0, −1.5, and −2.0 SDs, then you can also conclude that a score of 68 is equivalent to the 2nd percentile.

Standardized scores hold information about a performer's standing relative to a normative sample or population, but only if the chosen mean and standard deviation are known. Thus, whenever test users see that an assessment includes standardized scores or standard scores above 4 (Z scores larger than 4 are highly unlikely), they should search the test manual to find the chosen mean and standard deviation. Test users also need to understand that the validity of standard and standardized scores depends upon the assumption of a normal distribution, and that persons with the same raw scores in different age, sex, or physical size groups most likely will have different standard or standardized scores.

Normalized Scores

Raw scores that make up a distribution resembling a normal curve may be transformed into normalized scores to smooth out deviations from normality. This type of transformation may be reasonable if "the test developer feels that the underlying trait has a normal distribution and the nonnormality of the raw-score distribution represents error due to sampling or test construction problems" (Allen & Yen, 1979, p. 164).

Normalization requires at least two steps. Raw scores first need to be directly converted into percentiles using the ([subject order / N] × 100) formula, and then transformed into the standard or Z scores corresponding to the percentiles (proportions) in the table of areas under the standard normal curve. A good candidate for normalization is the distribution of batting averages for National League batters in 1975, which had the basic characteristics of a normal curve (see figure 4.2). When a normal distribution was assumed, Cesar Geronimo's .257 average with the Cincinnati Reds (see table 4.7) was converted to a standard score of −0.03 ($Z = (X − \mu) / \sigma_X$ = (.257 − .258) / .039 = −0.03) and a percentile of 49. However, his actual percentile of 48 ([76 / 157] × 100 = 48) corresponded to a Z score of −0.04, which becomes his normalized score. In a third optional step, a normalized standard or Z score may be converted to a normalized standardized score by applying Equation 4.10. For example, a T score is a normalized standardized score with a mean of 50 and a standard deviation of 10, which for Geronimo's batting average would be 49.6 (10[−0.04] + 50 = −0.4 + 50 = 49.6).

Stanines also are a specific type of normalized score. Instead of raw scores being converted into standard or standardized scores, raw scores are categorized into one of nine ranges of standard scores according to the percentiles matching the standard score ranges. Raw scores are converted into percentiles and then, instead of the percentiles being converted into their corresponding standard or standardized scores, they are assigned a value from 1 to 9 by being matched with a range of standard scores. The middle seven stanines, 2 to 8, represent a Z score range of 0.50, while the 1 and 9 represent Z scores below −1.75 and above +1.75, respectively. The specific standard score and percentile ranges for each stanine are presented in table 4.9. Thus, Jason's point score of 8.0 on the BOT running speed and agility subtest, converted to the 30th percentile, would yield a stanine of 4.

Age or Grade Equivalents

Raw scores also can be transformed into numbers that indicate the level of performance directly in terms of ages or grades. More specifically, in age or grade equivalents, the median raw score for a particular age or grade is converted into the actual age or grade value. For example, if the median maximum throwing distance was 38 ft for second graders, 52 ft for third graders, 62 ft for fourth graders, and 70 ft for fifth graders, then a raw score of 52 would convert to a grade equivalent of 3.0.

To convert raw scores falling between two median scores, some interpolation is required. Interpolation involves two steps: (a) determining the proportional distance a raw score (X) lies between two median raw scores (H = higher score, L = lower score) by dividing the partial distance $(X - L)$ by the total distance $(H - L)$, and (b) adding the lower grade equivalent (L_g) to that proportion of the total distance between grade equivalents $(H_g - L_g)$. In a complete formula:

$$\text{Grade equivalent} = L_g + [(X - L) / (H - L)] [H_g - L_g] \qquad 4.11$$

Thus, a throwing distance of 65 ft would convert to a grade equivalent of 4.38:

$$4 + [(65 - 62) / (70 - 62)] [5 - 4] = 4 + [3 / 8] [1] = 4 + 0.375 = 4.38$$

A score of 65 ft is 0.375 of the way from 62 to 70, so the grade equivalent is 0.375 of the way from 4 to 5, or 4.38.

As with percentiles, the transformation to age and grade equivalents is not linear, and thus only reflects the ordinal relationships between raw scores. Consequently, age and grade equivalents are ordinal measurements and should not be treated with arithmetic operations. Another limitation of age and grade equivalents is that about half of all persons will fall below the score matching their age or grade. Salvia and Ysseldyke (1988) also argue that the use of age or grade equivalents promotes the notion of the average child who does not exist.

■ CORRELATIONS

The statistic most commonly used to depict the magnitude and direction of the relationship between two dependent variables, X and Y, is the Pearson

TABLE 4.9   Standard Score and Percentile Ranges Corresponding to Stanines

Stanine	Standard score range	Percentile range
1	below −1.75	below 04
2	−1.25 to −1.75	04 to 11
3	−0.75 to −1.25	11 to 23
4	−0.25 to −0.70	23 to 40
5	−0.25 to 0.25	40 to 60
6	0.25 to 0.70	60 to 77
7	0.75 to 1.25	77 to 89
8	1.25 to 1.75	89 to 96
9	above 1.75	above 96

product-moment correlation coefficient, symbolized as r_{XY}. The values may range in magnitude from 0 to 1, and the direction may be either positive or negative. Negative correlations indicate an inverse or reciprocal relationship between the two variables. The Pearson product-moment correlation coefficient for a population, often simply referred to as a correlation, can be calculated by (using population symbols):

$$r_{XY} = \frac{\Sigma(X_i - \mu_X)(Y_i - \mu_Y) / N}{\sigma_X \sigma_Y}$$ 4.12

The term in the numerator is very similar to the variance formula presented in Equation 4.2; but instead of multiplying the deviation of the scores from the mean by itself, we multiply the deviations of two different scores from their respective means together. This term is called a covariance and can be represented by σ_{XY}^2. The denominator is simply the product of the standard deviations of the two variables.

Sample correlations can be calculated between pairs of variables from the pitching statistics of the 1963 Los Angeles Dodgers. The correlation between wins and strikeouts was +.91, while the correlation between wins and ERA was −.71 (see the scatter plots in figures 4.4 and 4.5). The directional signs clearly indicate that as the pitchers won more games they had more strikeouts and a lower ERA, but the question remains how to interpret these correlation magnitudes. Interpretation is facilitated by squaring the correlations, because r^2 represents the amount of variance that is in common or is shared between the two dependent variables, or the amount of variance of one variable "determined" by the other (Kerlinger &

Pedhazur, 1973). This common variance is illustrated by the overlapped region between the two circles in figure 4.6.

Thus, the proportion of shared or common variance between wins and strikeouts for the Dodger pitchers was $.91^2 = .828$, and between wins and ERA was $-.72^2 = .518$. The first value is quite high, but the second example shows that variables with correlation magnitudes less than .70 have less than 50% of their variance in common. Squaring other correlation values reveals that correlations with magnitudes less than .30 have less than 10% in common.

A correlation must be interpreted cautiously, because several factors have the potential to markedly change its value. First, if the range of scores for one or both variables is limited or restricted, then the correlation magnitude is likely to be smaller than if there is an unrestricted range of scores. For instance, the correlation between age and maximum throwing distance for a sample of boys from Grades 1 to 12 is likely to be quite high, but the same correlation for boys in Grade 10 exclusively is likely to be much lower because small changes in age probably do not affect throwing much, particularly at that grade level.

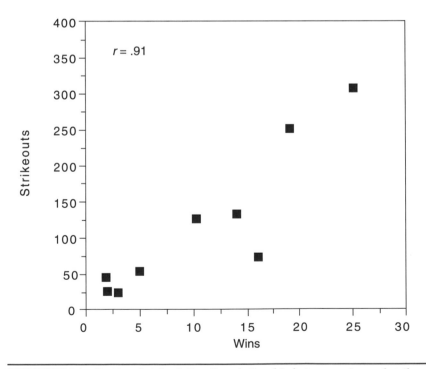

■ **FIGURE 4.4**   Scatter plot depicting the relationship between wins and strikeouts for pitchers on the 1963 Los Angeles Dodgers.

Second, a correlation may be misleading if data for two groups with different characteristics relative to the variables in question are combined. For example, Roche and Malina (1983a) have reported that between the ages of 12 and 18 years the ratio between shoulder and hip widths increases for boys but decreases in girls. Thus, the correlation between age and shoulder-hip ratio would be moderately high and positive for boys and moderately high and negative for girls; but if the groups were combined, the correlation would be near zero because the two trends would be neutralized.

And third, it may be that one measure is highly correlated with another but that the variation in the scores on the one is not caused by the variation in the other. For example, there is a high positive correlation between a player's height and field-goal shooting percentage in the National Basketball Association. The explanation for this relationship cannot be that taller players are better shooters; rather, the relationship is likely caused by a mediating variable, or a third variable that highly correlates with the other two. In this case, shooting distance is the mediating variable, with higher percentages of field goals being achieved from shorter distances and taller

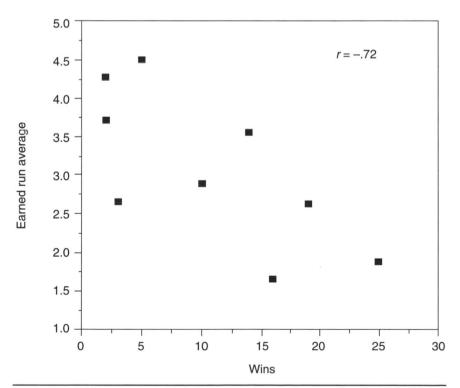

■ **FIGURE 4.5** Scatter plot depicting the relationship between wins and earned run average for the pitchers on the 1963 Los Angeles Dodgers.

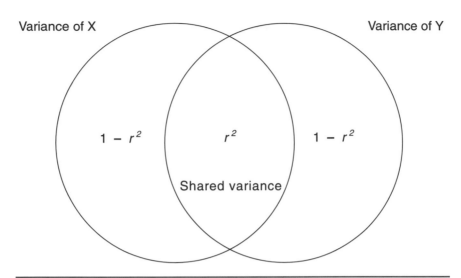

■ **FIGURE 4.6**   A Venn diagram showing the shared variance between paired scores of two variables, X and Y, represented by r^2.

players taking more shots from shorter distances, often very high-percentage slam dunks. The mediating variable in the high correlation between wins and strikeouts shown in figure 4.3 is the number of innings pitched. Kerlinger and Pedhazur (1973) advise that "we need not fear or eschew the word 'cause' . . . we must simply be careful with it" (p. 16).

The relationship between two variables may be appropriately examined with the Pearson product-moment correlation coefficient if both variables have continuous values or many possible values and are at the interval or ratio levels of measurement. If one of the variables is dichotomous, then a point-biserial correlation coefficient (r_{pbis}) should be used; if both variables are dichotomous, then a phi coefficient (ϕ) should be used. If the variables have many possible values and are ordinal, then either the Spearman rank-order correlation coefficient (r_s) or Kendall's tau (τ) should be used. See Allen and Yen (1979) for more information on these alternative measures of association.

■ LINEAR REGRESSION

The letter r, used to indicate a correlation coefficient, represents the word *regression*, which means to return or to go back to the mean. In linear regression, a line is determined for a set of paired values that best represents the scatter of points. This regression line minimizes the squared distance of the points from the line and is described by Equation 4.13:

$$Y = a + bX. \hspace{3cm} 4.13$$

The *a* term indicates where the line crosses the vertical or *Y* variable axis, while the *b* term quantifies the slope of the line by indicating how many units of *Y* the line goes up for every unit of *X*.

In figure 4.7, the regression line is added to the scatter plot for wins and strikeouts for Dodger pitchers in 1963. The equation shows that the line crosses the vertical axis at –1.3, so a pitcher with no wins should have –1.3 strikeouts, which, of course, is impossible. The value of *b* is 11.0, so 11 strikeouts should be added for every win; therefore, at 10 wins, a pitcher should have 108.7 (–1.3 + [11] [10]) strikeouts. The linear regression equation, then, can be used to make predictions about scores on the *Y* variable (e.g., strikeouts) given a value of *X* (e.g., wins). The correlation coefficient (e.g., r_{XY} = .91) provides an indicator of the degree of confidence that should be placed in the predictions derived from the regression equation.

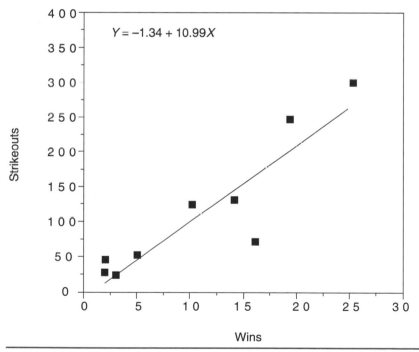

FIGURE 4.7 Scatter plot depicting the relationship between wins and strikeouts for pitchers on the 1963 Los Angeles Dodgers, with regression equation and regression line.

Chapter 5

Approaches to Movement Skill Assessment

MANY different approaches are used in the assessment of movement skills, and there are various ways of conceptualizing or categorizing these approaches. First, we can classify the various approaches according to the level of the movement skills being assessed, using a taxonomy such as the one presented in chapter 3. I will use that taxonomy to organize the review of specific assessment instruments in part II (chapters 7-11). Second, we can classify approaches according to two traditional dichotomies: (a) norm- and criterion-referenced tests and

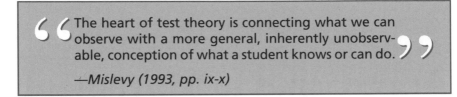

> The heart of test theory is connecting what we can observe with a more general, inherently unobservable, conception of what a student knows or can do.
>
> —Mislevy (1993, pp. ix-x)

(b) formal and informal tests. I will discuss these four categories in the first portion of this chapter. And third, we can classify approaches according to the measurement models or theories underlying the design of the assessment instruments. In the last part of this chapter I will provide an overview of the major measurement models used in movement skill assessment.

■ TRADITIONAL CATEGORIES OF ASSESSMENT

In most treatises on educational, psychological, or movement assessment, a distinction is made between norm-referenced and criterion-referenced tests and between formal and informal tests. In the sections to follow I discuss these four nonexclusive categories separately.

Norm-Referenced Assessment

A norm-referenced test involves the comparison of an individual's performance to the performance of a normative group. Performance scores are usually converted or transformed into relative scores—such as Z scores, standardized scores, or percentiles—by applying means and standard deviations obtained from the group. The normative or reference group is composed of a sample of persons with characteristics similar to those for whom the test was designed (Swanson & Watson, 1989). Norms refer to the tabular data or statistics that summarize the test performance of the group.

Norm-referenced movement skill assessments have their roots in Gesell's work on developmental milestones (Gesell, 1940; Gesell & Amatruda, 1941; Gesell & Thompson, 1934, 1938). In a review of Gesell's career, Thelen and Adolph (1992) observe:

> Like Binet, Gesell was motivated by his concern for providing education that was appropriate for the child's capabilities and for diagnosing delayed development for the purposes of intervention. But somehow within these laudable clinical goals, there was transformation from the typical into the desirable. Gesell elevated the typical child, who of course was no child, into a biological reality with profound consequences for theory and practice. (p. 374)

The contemporary pediatrician and best-selling author, Brazelton, has tried to expand the range of "normality," but still has missed the mark:

> He wrote to combat every parent's excessive fear that one standard of normality exists for a child's growth, and that anything your particular baby does must be judged against this unforgiving protocol. Brazelton used the simple device of designating three perfectly fine pathways, each exemplified by a particular child—one hellion, one in the middle, and one shy baby who, in gentle euphemism, was labeled "slow to warm up." Even three, instead of one, doesn't capture the richness of normal variation. (Gould, 1996, p. 40)

This widely accepted concept of the phantom "normal" child lies at the heart of norm-referenced assessment.

The Bruininks-Oseretsky Test of Motor Proficiency (Bruininks, 1978) is an example of a norm-referenced test. A look at the cover page of the scoring booklet for the test reveals spaces for standard scores, percentiles, and stanines (see figure 5.1). The inclusion of such relative scores confirms the norm-referenced status of any assessment instrument.

Norm-referenced tests allow for the determination of an individual's standing relative to his or her peers. Thus they are most useful for screening, determining eligibility and placement for service or programs, and evaluating programs. Raw performance scores on norm-referenced tests are likely to be product or outcome oriented rather than process oriented. In other words, norm-referenced tests are more likely to focus on time, distance, or number of repetitions resulting from the performance of the skill than on the way the skill was performed.

Despite these advantages, the use of norm-referenced assessment instruments has many disadvantages. First, valid results depend upon appropriateness of the normative group for the individuals being tested. Does the group adequately represent the target ages, geographic locales, races, socioeconomic levels, physical or mental impairments, or other variables? The primary factors used in converting raw scores to relative scores are age and sex, but physical factors such as height, weight, and body composition also are important variables related to movement task performance. For example, would it be valid to compare the performances of a late-maturing boy who is shorter and lighter than his same-age peers, or an early-maturing boy who is taller, heavier, and stronger than his same-age peers, with a normative group defined only by age and sex?

Second, if a norm-referenced assessment is used to identify persons who may need further testing or qualify for certain services, the validity of the critical relative score needs to be established. In many school districts, students are eligible for adapted physical education if they score 1.5 or more standard deviations below the group mean (7 percentile or below). Are this criterion and other similar norm-referenced criteria determined by

TEST SCORE SUMMARY

Complete Battery

SUBTEST	POINT SCORE Maximum Subject's	STANDARD SCORE Test (Table 23)	STANDARD SCORE Composite (Table 24)	PERCENTILE RANK (Table 25)	STANINE (Table 25)	OTHER Age Equiv
GROSS MOTOR SUBTESTS:						
1. Running Speed and Agility ... 15	8	21				7-8
2. Balance 32	16	13				5-2
3. Bilateral Coordination 20	9	23				7-11
4. Strength 42	5	11				4-11
GROSS MOTOR COMPOSITE		*68 SUM	56	72	6	6-5
5. Upper-Limb Coordination ... 21	13	*21				6-11
FINE MOTOR SUBTESTS:						
6. Response Speed 17	5	16				6-2
7. Visual-Motor Control 24	18	23				8-5
8. Upper-Limb Speed and Dexterity............. 72	27	20				6-8
FINE MOTOR COMPOSITE		*59 SUM	64	92	8	6-8
BATTERY COMPOSITE		*148 SUM	63	90	8	6-9

*To obtain Battery Composite: Add Gross Motor Composite, Subtest 5 Standard Score, and Fine Motor Composite. Check result by adding Standard Scores on Subtests 1-8.

Short Form:

	POINT SCORE Maximum Subject's	STANDARD SCORE (Table 27)	PERCENTILE RANK (Table 27)	STANINE (Table 27)
SHORT FORM 98				

■ **FIGURE 5.1** Cover page of the scoring booklet for the Bruininks-Oseretsky Test of Motor Proficiency (Bruininks 1978).

From *Bruininks-Oseretsky Test of Motor Proficiency* by Robert H. Bruininks © 1978, American Guidance Service, Inc., 4201 Woodland Road, Circle Pines, MN 55014-1796. Reproduced with permission of the publisher. All rights reserved.

administrative constraints, as suggested by Broadhead (1985), or by the needs of the students?

Third, when individuals demonstrate poor movement performance on a norm-referenced test, raw product scores or transformed relative scores for individual tasks or relative composite scores may offer little information about why they performed poorly (Davis, 1984). Even if the purpose of the assessment may not have been to gain information for instructional or therapeutic planning, practitioners often use data from norm-referenced tests for purposes beyond their narrow limits, and this practice is often encouraged by misleading statements in test manuals. Bricker (1993) concludes that the value of comparisons with developmental norms for children with disabilities is at best questionable, and argues that it is more important to determine each child's current level of functioning and then work on related skill-specific objectives.

Fourth, variability is perhaps the most common movement skill inadequacy in children (Sugden & Keogh, 1990), yet most norm-referenced assessments rely on mean performance or do not allow for a sufficient number of trials to determine variability. Davis (1984) asserts that "extreme scores represent information about the individual's performance capabilities and should be part of the data recorded and used" (p. 133). However, the additional trials necessary to determine variability require more time; and an objective of designers of norm-referenced tests, consistent with the limited purposes of these tests, is to minimize time.

And fifth, the amount of experience an individual has had with the specific test items may be a possible source of bias in norm-referenced assessments. This type of bias may be random or systematic. Systematic bias may occur, for example, when tasks familiar to persons in a certain cultural group or from a particular geographical location are given to other persons for whom the tasks are relatively novel.

Criterion-Referenced Assessment

A criterion-referenced test involves the comparison of an individual's performance to some predetermined criterion. A score usually represents either a *yes* or a *no*, although an intermediate level also may be used. For example, in the Assessment, Evaluation, and Programming System for Infants and Children Birth to Three Years (AEPS) (Bricker, 1993), the following scoring criteria are applied: 0 = not pass, 1 = pass inconsistently, and 2 = pass consistently. Thus, an individual's performance is interpreted in absolute rather than relative terms, although a criterion-referenced test, such as the Peabody Developmental Motor Scales (Folio & Fewell, 1983), also may be norm referenced when the criterion-referenced scores of a sample population are expressed in terms of means, standard deviations, percentiles, and other types of normative scores.

The concept of criterion-referenced assessment and the distinction between criterion- and norm-referenced assessment were first discussed in a chapter by Glaser and Klaus (1962) and then in a more widely cited article by Glaser (1963). Glaser's concept of criterion-referenced measurement was introduced initially to facilitate the implementation of individualized instructional programs, allowing students to be judged against the intended outcomes of instruction (Hambleton, 1994). Criterion-referenced assessments indicate the content of an individual's "behavioral repertoire" and, because they are historically and functionally rooted in instruction, are primarily used to certify competency, plan instruction or therapy, and evaluate progress (Luftig, 1989; Swanson & Watson, 1989). A common misconception is that the term *criterion* implies a mastery standard (Hambleton, 1994; Linn, 1994). Glaser (1963) discussed the need to specify minimum levels of performance, but he also recognized that an individual's level of achievement falls along a continuum of behaviors.

Three components in movement-related criterion-referenced items are the target movement behavior, the task conditions, and the performance criterion. The items in a criterion-referenced test may be taken directly from a physical education or movement activity curriculum, may be based on a task analysis of a movement skill, or may represent minimum requirements for functional movement in various contexts.

Figure 5.2 presents an example of a criterion-referenced test with items derived from the Minneapolis Public Schools physical education curriculum for second graders (Minneapolis Public Schools, 1991). Fourteen items from eight curriculum areas are assessed on a pass/fail basis. The results may be interpreted in terms of each individual item or a percentage of items that have been passed.

The I CAN program is a resource of performance objectives for many different categories of movement skills. These objectives are organized on score sheets so that they can be used as a criterion-referenced task analysis. An I CAN objective score sheet for the overhand throw (Wessel, 1976) is depicted in figure 5.3. The first four focal points concern the throwing pattern or process, while the last focal point concerns throwing accuracy or product. For each focal point, the behavior, task conditions, and criteria are clearly specified.

The major advantage of criterion-referenced tests is that they accommodate an individualized approach to assessment and intervention (Davis, 1984). They indicate what individuals are able and not able to do, not how their performance stands relative to that of other persons. Furthermore, process-oriented items provide insight into the deficits underlying poor performance.

There also are some negative aspects to criterion-referenced assessment. First, the specific conditions and criteria for the tasks may not exactly match

---

Jump
1. Demonstrate jumping using good form which includes: _____
   a. knees and hips are flexed and arms swing backwards.
   b. swing both arms forward and upward as knees and ankles extend.
   c. land lightly on 2 feet, bending knees and ankles to cushion shock of landing.

(continued)

■ **FIGURE 5.2**   A criterion-referenced test with items derived from the Minneapolis Public Schools physical education curriculum for second graders (Minneapolis Public Schools, 1991).

From *The Learner Outcomes Guide for Physical Education K-10* (pp. 1-35) by Minneapolis Public Schools, 1991, Minneapolis: Minneapolis Public Schools. Copyright 1991 by Minneapolis Public Schools. Reprinted by permission.

2. Jump forward 18 inches using good form. _____

Hop

3. Demonstrate hopping using good form which includes:
    a. spring lightly upward, taking off with ankle extension and landing lightly on ball of the foot.
    b. knees and arms are relaxed.
4. Hop 2 times on right foot, transfer, 2 times on left foot. _____

Skip

5. Demonstrate skipping using good form which includes: _____
    a. the skip is a step hop, the step with a long count and the hop on a short count.
    b. spring from toes and land on ball of the foot.
6. Demonstrate skipping in good form at a slow and fast speed. _____

Slide

7. Demonstrate sliding using good form which includes: _____
    a. a long step is taken to the side on one foot, bringing the other to the first.
    b. spring lightly from toe and land on ball of the foot.
8. Demonstrate sliding at a slow/fast speed and left/right using good form. _____

Bounce

9. Demonstrate bouncing a ball with one hand using good form which includes: _____
    a. wrist flexed, fingers relaxed and spread.
    b. directing ball with slightly cupped hand and fingers spread.

Kick

10. Use a toe kick to propel a ball to a partner 20 feet away. _____

Rope Jump

11. Jump rope using good form which includes: _____
    a. keeping hands below waist level while turning rope.
    b. jumping over rope lightly and close to ground.
    c. continuously turning rope over head on each jump.

Body awareness

12. Correctly identify right and left sides of body and correctly move the body upon command: forward, backward, sideways, right, left, up, and down. _____
13. Demonstrate walking forward and turns on low balance beam. _____
14. Clap to an even and uneven rhythmic beat. _____

TOTAL [X] = _____

Percent [(X/14) × 100] = _____

■ **FIGURE 5.2** *(continued)*

I CAN

CLASS PERFORMANCE SCORE SHEET
PERFORMANCE OBJECTIVE: Overhand Throw

SCORING

Assessment:
X = Achieved
0 = Not achieved

Reassessment:
⊠ = Achieved
Ø = Not achieved

*PRIMARY RESPONSES

N - Nonattending
NR - No Response
UR - Unrelated response
O - Other (specify in comments)

FOCAL POINTS

a Overhand motion
b Ball Release
  a Eyes on Target
  b Overhand motion
    a Arm Exten./Side Orient.
    b Weight Transfer
      c Hip & Spine Rotation
      d Follow through
        e Smooth Integration

STD.

10 ft. distance, 2/3 times
20 ft. target at 15 ft., 2/3 times
2/3 times
age/sex norm., 2/3 times
8 ft. target at 50 ft., 2/3 times

Angle of Release 45°
Accuracy
Primary Responses*

NAME	1 a	1 b	2 a	2 b	3 a	3 b	3 c	3 d	3 e	4	5	COMMENTS
1.												
2.												
3.												
4.												
5.												
6.												
7.												
8.												
9.												
10.												

■ FIGURE 5.3   I CAN objective score sheet for the overhand throw.
From *I Can Fundamental Skills* by J. A. Wessell, 1976, Austin, TX: PRO-ED. Copyright 1976 by PRO-ED. Reprinted with permission.

the desired range of behaviors. Throwing a tennis ball at a 36-in.-diameter target from 10 ft may not adequately represent all throwing behavior. Will comparable performances be found when larger balls, longer distances, or different targets are used, or when no targets are used and maximum throwing force is required?

A second problem concerns the specification of cutoff scores defining mastery or competency (Allen & Yen, 1979), which is not completely consistent with the original concept of criterion-referenced assessment (Hambleton, 1994; Linn, 1994). Often experts may not agree on what level of performance constitutes mastery. A related problem may be that the criteria are based on the faulty assumption that particular movement patterns are optimal for all persons (Burton & Davis, 1992b; Davis, 1984). Persons with physical impairments may be able to successfully perform a specified movement task but use movement patterns considered by some to be abnormal (Latash & Anson, 1996). However, these "abnormal" patterns might optimize these persons' movement behavior in attempting to achieve the task goal (Burton & Davis, 1992b).

Next, the simple *yes/no* or *yes/maybe/no* scores in criterion-referenced tests may not be very sensitive to performance differences between individuals or to performance changes within an individual. Norm-referenced tests are generally more appropriate for determining performance differences between individuals, although the types of scores used (e.g., composites) may not provide the desired information. If a stated purpose of an assessment instrument is to identify performance changes of individuals (changes that may be due to instruction, therapy, or natural developmental processes), the test designer should offer evidence validating that use. Also, the categorical scoring system inherent in criterion-referenced tests involves ordinal measures, which are not amenable to arithmetic manipulations (Merbitz, Morris, & Grip, 1989).

Formal Assessment

Formal assessment instruments are those tests with standardized or uniform conditions and directions. The standardized procedures used in formal tests permit the tests to be repeated by different examiners and allow for consistent comparisons between individuals being assessed, regardless of who administers the test. All norm-referenced tests are also formal tests, while criterion-referenced tests may be either formal or informal. Hence, formal tests, like norm-referenced tests, are particularly useful for screening, making decisions about placement and eligibility, and evaluating programs. These relationships between formal and informal tests and norm- and criterion-referenced tests are depicted in figure 5.4.

When a formal assessment tool is used without adherence to all of the explicit instructions in the manual, it becomes an informal instrument. If the tool used in this situation is also norm referenced, then none of the transformations to relative scores can be meaningfully carried out.

As with the other general categories of assessment, formal tests have several weaknesses. First, there will be aspects of the testing situation that are not addressed in the examiner's manual and thus will not be standardized. For example, while the size and arrangement of the room used for testing, or the sex or age of the examiner may not be specified, these factors may influence the results of the assessment. If physical demonstrations of tasks are allowed, then the skill of the examiner may be a critical variable.

Next, the assessment protocol may require examinees to manipulate equipment that is standardized in size and weight; but the equipment size and weight may be quite different relative to body sizes and weights of different examinees. An 8- to 10-in. ball specified in some items of the Test of Gross Motor Development (Ulrich, 1985) is much larger relative to the hand size of a 3-year-old than to that of a 10-year-old (see Burton, Greer, & Wiese, 1992; Burton, Greer, & Wiese-Bjornstal, 1993). Using equipment in movement assessments that are standardized in terms of body-scaled values is recommended as a solution to this problem (Burton & Davis, 1992b, 1996; Davis & Burton, 1991).

Third, some examiners may have difficulty adhering to explicit procedures, such as the exact instructions to be given or the feedback allowed. If

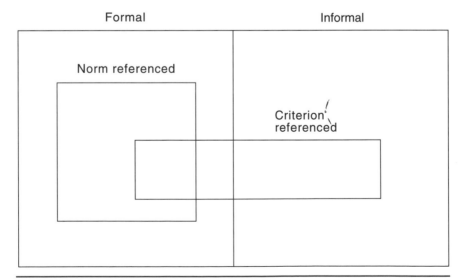

■ **FIGURE 5.4** Relationships between formal and informal tests and norm- and criterion-referenced tests.

the procedures are too detailed, an examiner may not be able to comply; if the procedures are too vague, the variability between examiners may be a confounding factor.

And fourth, formal assessments accommodate the observation and measurement of a person's movement performance on only a limited set of tasks. The exploration of what a person may do in other situations, particularly in more natural movement situations, usually is not allowed. Rowntree (1987) argues that formal tests are "based on specially engineered 'happenings' rather than on experience of how 'honestly' the child behaved in his regular activities" (p. 121).

Informal Assessment

Informal tests are those tests that cannot be categorized as formal; that is, those that do not have standardized or uniform conditions and directions. Luftig (1989) states that there are seven main types of informal assessments: checklists, interviews, inventories, observations, questionnaires, rating scales, and teacher-made tests. Luftig (1989) also organizes informal tests into those based on direct observation and those based on indirect information, and into those that involve the gathering of information with or without a person's awareness (i.e., obtrusive or unobtrusive). Also, as indicated earlier, any formal test that is not administered exactly as specified becomes an informal test.

One of the advantages of informal assessments is that they allow for observations in more natural settings and for an examination of the influence of the environment on movement performance. Davis (1984) asserts:

Assessment, then, is to not only determine and record a level of performance of the individual, but to determine and record the circumstances under which the performance level was obtained. Moreover, these circumstances must be varied (manipulated) to determine the circumstances under which performance varies for each individual. (p. 130)

The lack of standardized constraints in informal assessment offers examiners more flexibility in determining the actual skills of the persons being tested. This allows for sufficient trials to determine performance variability and permits assessment to be more closely integrated into the instructional or therapeutic process. Thus, informal tests are most useful for the planning and monitoring of instruction or therapy.

Nevertheless, informal assessments also have drawbacks. First, the directions for informal tests are intentionally quite general, but they may be too vague for an examiner to administer the test as intended. Also, there is usually not a detailed test manual to refer to when questions arise and, accordingly, usually no information concerning validity and reliability. These potential problems, along with the variable nature of informal tests, increase the difficulty of comparing results across individuals and of comparing results obtained by different examiners.

Another possible disadvantage to using informal tests is the inordinate amount of time that may be necessary to complete the process (Stott, Henderson, & Moyes, 1986). However, if informal assessment becomes more closely integrated with instruction, there may be no need to allocate separate time blocks for assessment (Davis, 1984).

■ MEASUREMENT THEORIES

Measurement theories or models specify the critical assumptions underlying measurement of the traits of interest. An adequate understanding of the measurement theory or model underlying a test is crucial in establishing the validity of a test, choosing an appropriate test for a particular purpose, and interpreting test scores. Here I review three theories of measurement: (a) classical test theory, (b) generalizability theory, and (c) item response theory.

Classical Test Theory

The development of classical test theory was initiated by Charles Spearman in the early 1900s. Also known as classical true-score theory, classical test theory is based on assumptions regarding three types of scores: (a) observed scores (symbolized as X), (b) true scores (symbolized as T), and (c) error scores (symbolized as E). Observed scores are derived directly from an individual's performance; true scores represent the actual ability of an individual but are inferred from observed scores; and error scores are the differences between the observed and true scores. The first assumption of classical test theory summarizes the relationship between these three types of scores in a simple equation:

$$X = T + E. \qquad 5.1$$

The true score T is assumed to be constant, and the observed score X is assumed to rarely exactly match T. Thus, in the examination of individual performances, there is assumed to almost always be some error. If Jane has a true score of 98 but shows an observed score of 104, then her error score equals +6. If Jane is retested and demonstrates an observed score of 96, her true score remains at 98, leaving an error score of –2.

The second assumption of classical test theory states that the expected value of the error score, symbolized by $E(E)$ and determined by a mean of repeated testings, is 0. Hence,

$$E(E) = 0. \qquad\qquad 5.2$$

It follows from this second assumption that the expected value of the observed score, determined by a mean of repeated testings, is the true score, or:

$$E(X) = T. \qquad\qquad 5.3$$

If Jane is tested again and again, the mean of her observed scores is expected to be 98; however, repeated testings are usually impractical and each subsequent testing is likely to be affected by the previous ones, contaminating the observed scores.

The third assumption of classical score theory states that the true scores and error scores obtained from a population of examinees are uncorrelated. Presented in equation form:

$$r_{ET} = 0. \qquad\qquad 5.4$$

This assumption indicates that individuals with higher true scores or greater ability should not have error scores that are systematically higher or lower than those of individuals with lower true scores. This assumption may be violated if persons with lower ability are given more encouragement and feedback than persons with higher ability as they perform the assessment tasks.

These three assumptions constitute the heart of classical test theory, although there are other assumptions that are beyond the scope of this book (see Allen & Yen, 1979). These basic tenets of classical test theory indicate that an observed score provides only an estimate of the true score which is not directly measurable. Consequently, two persons with the same true score or the same actual ability are likely to produce different observed scores. Thus, proper interpretation of observed scores requires an estimate of the error score. I will cover the estimation of error in chapter 6 in the section on reliability and standard error of measurement.

Generalizability Theory

Generalizability theory was introduced by Cronbach, Gleser, Nanda, and Rajaratnam in 1972. In their classic book, Cronbach and his associates showed that total measurement error, the singular E in classical test theory, could be partitioned into a number of individual factors or facets. In generalizability theory (or G theory), the classical test theory concept of reliability is replaced by the broader notion of generalizability. As Shavelson and Webb (1991) explain, "Instead of asking how accurately a set of observed scores reflects their corresponding true scores, G theory asks how accurately a set of observed scores permits us to generalize about a person's behavior in a defined universe of situations" (p. 127).

As a part of the process of developing new assessment instruments, generalizability (G) studies may be carried out to examine the sources of variability in test scores obtained under different conditions or at various levels of the chosen facets (Allen & Yen, 1979) or, in other words, in a particular universe of situations. With use of analysis of variance (ANOVA) procedures, the amount of variance attributed to each facet and interaction is estimated by coefficients of generalizability. G studies are carried out to estimate the magnitude of as many potential sources of error as possible, while decision (D) studies are used to apply information from a G study to design a measurement tool that minimizes error for a particular purpose (Shavelson & Webb, 1991).

An example of a G study, used in the development of the Test of Gross Motor Development (Ulrich, 1985), was reported by Ulrich and Wise (1984). They chose to examine the effect of two facets—raters and occasion—on individual-item and composite scores of 10 children. The percentage of the total variance in the composite scores accounted for by each factor and interaction is presented in table 5.1. As expected and desired, most of the variance in the three composites (between 80.8% and 89.7%) was attributed to differences between subjects (S). The greatest sources of error, from the possible sources identified, were (a) differences between raters (R) and (b) differences between raters but only for certain subjects (RS). Residual or unidentified error (ROS, E) was 3% or less for each composite.

The use of generalizability theory has many advantages. According to Berk (1979), generalizability theory (a) provides a comprehensive analysis of factors or facets related to the reliability of observers by partitioning variance components; (b) can be easily modified to accommodate different numbers of persons, observers, behaviors, intervals, observation periods, settings, and occasions and the assumptions of random- and mixed-effects generalizability models; (c) can be applied to a variety of categorical and quantitative behavioral observation systems; (d) produces estimates of the reliability of a single observation and sets of observations; and (e) yields one or more reliability coefficients using the output from one analysis (p. 464). Morrow (1989) argues that "generalizability theory is perhaps the most appropriate methodology for estimating test reliability available today, because of its ability to identify numerous sources of error variation within a single model" (p. 75).

A excellent source of basic information on generalizability theory is Shavelson and Webb's (1991) recent book, *Generalizability Theory: A Primer.*

Item Response Theory

Inferences from classical test theory and generalizability theory are made only with respect to a particular population and a particular test. Mean

TABLE 5.1 Percent of Total Variance in Test of Gross Motor Development Composite Scores by Components

Components	Locomotor composite	Object control composite	Total composite
Rater (R)	1.5%	4.2%	2.8%
Occasion (O)	1.5%	2.6%	2.4%
Subject (S)	89.7%	80.8%	88.3%
Rater x Occasion (RO)	0.2%	0.3%	0.3%
Rater x Subject (RS)	4.7%	8.8%	4.4%
Occasion x Subject (OS)	0.5%	0.4%	0.4%
Rater x Occasion x Subject Error (ROS,E)	2.0%	3.0%	1.4%
Total	100.1%	100.1%	100.0%

Note: Reprinted, by permission, from Ulrich and Wise, 1984, "Reliability of Scores Obtained with the Objectives-Based Motor Skill Assessment Instrument," *Adapted Physical Activity Quarterly*, Vol. 1(3), 236-237.

scores for individual items and composites vary depending on the population tested and the specific test used. Furthermore, estimates of measurement error are based on group means and thus are assumed to be the same for individuals with differing ability levels or true scores (see Equation 5.4).

In item response theory (IRT), the basic assumptions of classical test theory are neither negated nor contradicted. As Spray (1987) explains:

Additional assumptions are made which facilitate the measurement process at the individual examinee and item level, thereby freeing the generalizations from only a single population and a specific test. In IRT, item characteristics are invariant across tests and populations and individual ability parameters are invariant from one test to another, assuming that the tests measure the same ability. (pp. 204-205)

For example, in the Assessment of Motor and Process Skills (AMPS) (Fisher, 1995), examinees perform 2 or 3 daily life tasks chosen by the examiner and examinee from a set of 56 described in the test manual. The examinee needs to perform only a small subset of tasks because each task is measured on the same scale and thus any set of tasks within the range of the examinee's skills should provide an adequate assessment. It is very important to note that a single, equivalent scale used to represent a person's capacity to perform skills beyond those directly tested, as in the AMPS, is a motor ability scale and takes on all the baggage of motor ability scales as discussed in chapter 8. However, when an IRT scale is applied to specific skills, rather than to persons, to determine the relative difficulty of various items, then the scale may be considered to be skill rather than ability oriented.

One approach to applying IRT was proposed by Rasch (1960/1980). Rasch developed a mathematical model that converts observed ordinal scores, which may be difficult to interpret, into linear interval scores that may be more directly interpreted (Wright & Linacre, 1989). Rasch's model also allows for specification of the extent to which a given conversion matches a hypothetical or empirical function. Haley, Ludlow, and Coster (1993) state that "a primary purpose of Rasch models is to facilitate the construction of measurement scales that define . . . increasingly more difficult functional items along a single dimension . . . leading to an unambiguous interpretation of the summary score" (p. 532). In the AMPS, raw scores for each of the 56 daily activity items, which vary from simple to complex, are collected for 16 aspects of motor skill and 20 aspects of process skill. Then, with use of a Rasch model, raw scores can be converted to an interval scale *(logits)* from less to more able on two dimensions: one for motor skill and the other for process skill. For example, the highest logit value for motor skills was for lifts (0.67) and moves (0.55), and the lowest was for paces (– 0.50) and positions (– 0.63).

Because any task scaled on the chosen dimension(s) may be adequate to determine an individual's ability (not skill!) level, test developers using IRT methods can construct tests tailored to measure specific ability levels (Cole, Wood, & Dunn, 1991). For example, a developer of a screening test or a test to determine eligibility for a special program might choose to select only items closely matching the criterion ability level. Or, an adaptive testing strategy might be developed such that the items presented to an individual are not predetermined but instead, after each response, a new item is chosen by computer to home in on the individual's skill level (Cole et al., 1991). This adaptive testing procedure, because it homes in on a specific skill or difficulty level of a specific skill, is more consistent with a skill-based approach to assessment than other IRT procedures are; but if the resulting score is applied to the performer rather than the skill, as is often the case, then it represents a motor ability.

Some recently developed movement skill assessments that have applied Rasch models of IRT, other than the AMPS, include the Functional Assessment Screening Questionnaire (Granger & Wright, 1993), the Functional Independence Measure (Keith, Granger, Hamilton, & Sherwin, 1987), the

Functional Independence Measure for Children (Msall, DiGaudio, & Duffy, 1993), the Pediatric Evaluation of Disability Inventory (PEDI) (Haley, Coster, Ludlow, Haltiwanger, & Andrellos, 1992), the Test of Gross Motor Development (TGMD) (Zhu & Cole, 1996), and the Tufts Assessment of Motor Performance (Haley & Ludlow, 1992). I present detailed reviews for the TGMD in chapter 10, for the PEDI in chapter 11, and give further information on the AMPS in chapter 11. Also, applications of IRT in physical education assessment have been reported by Safrit, Cohen, and Costa (1989) and Safrit, Zhu, Costa, and Zhang (1992).

Chapter 6

Validity and Reliability

© Connie Springer

AN assessment instrument that is not valid is utterly useless. An assessment instrument that is not reliable cannot be valid. Hence, the utility of an assessment instrument is contingent upon its validity, which in turn is contingent upon its reliability. In this chapter I will discuss the concepts of validity and reliability in terms of general definitions, identified subtypes, and methods of evaluation. I will regularly cite the standards of validity and reliability set by the American Educational Research Association, the American Psychological Association, and the National Council on Measurement in Education (Committee to Develop Standards for Educational and Psychological Testing [CDSEPT], 1985); the American Physical Therapy Association (Task Force on Standards for Measurement in Physical Therapy [TFSMPT], 1991); and the American

> " " If measurement is science and the use of measurements is applied . . . science, the justification and defense of measurement and its validity is and may always be a rhetorical art. " "
>
> —*Messick (1988, p. 43)*

Congress of Rehabilitation Medicine (Johnston, Keith, & Hinderer, 1992). Another excellent source that expands on the validity and reliability issues addressed in this chapter, including the American Physical Therapy Association's Standards for Tests and Measurements in Physical Therapy Practice, is the *Primer on Measurement: An Introductory Guide to Measurement Issues* by Rothstein and Echternach (1993).

■ VALIDITY

Validity is defined as the "appropriateness, meaningfulness, and usefulness of the specific inferences made from test scores," and test validation is defined as "the process of accumulating evidence to support such inferences" in the *Standards for Educational and Psychological Testing* (CDSEPT, 1985, p. 9). The evidence used to validate a test is based on both empirical and theoretical rationale (Messick, 1988). The simple question posed in establishing validity is: Can an assessment instrument be appropriately used for its stated purpose(s)?

These definitions emphasize that validity is established not for the test, but for specific uses of the test or the inferences, decisions, and actions made based on the test scores (Angoff, 1988; CDSEPT, 1985). Earlier versions of standards published by the American Psychological Association in the 1950s, 1960s, and 1970s were titled *Standards for Educational and Psychological Tests*, but in the most recent revision the word *tests* was changed to *testing* (CDSEPT, 1985) to reflect this conceptual shift.

This shift in focus from validating assessment instruments themselves to validating uses of the instruments also changes the issue of who carries the responsibility for establishing validity. Previously, test designers were responsible for validating their tests, but now burden of proof must be assumed to a greater degree by users who claim that certain inferences may be validly drawn from the test scores (Angoff, 1988). This change in perspective requires consumers to possess the skills needed to evaluate the validity of the inferences they want to make from specific movement skill assessment instruments.

The fundamental issue of validity is illustrated in some comments by the Minnesota Vikings player personnel director, Frank Gilliam, on a player picked by the Vikings in the first round of the 1995 National Football League draft:

I've been doing this for 25 years, and I've seen guys who work out extremely well who don't play very well. The name of the game is when we play on Sundays, do you play well? On Sundays, we don't do vertical jumps, we don't do long jumps, and we don't give 40-yard tests. But we do focus on how well you play, and that's what this guy does. (Walters, 1995)

Some of the people responsible for evaluating the skills of prospective professional players have become enamored of measuring the foundations or components of football behavior while paying less attention to the actual playing of the game. Yet if the assessment purpose is to determine how well someone can play football, the most valid measure, as stated by Frank Gilliam, is his productivity on the field. In assessment of other movement skills, this simple principle of validity should be heeded: Assess the targeted skill directly in its natural context (see chapter 11 for further information on assessing functional movement skills).

There are three traditional categories of validity: content validity, criterion-related (or criterion-based) validity, and construct validity. Guion (1980) describes these three types of validity as "something of a holy trinity representing three different roads to psychometric salvation" (p. 386). In the following sections I will explain and discuss each component of this trinity.

Content Validity

Content validity concerns the extent to which a measurement is judged to reflect the meaningful elements of a construct or a domain of content and not any extraneous elements (TFSMPT, 1991). For example, to what extent do the items in the Posture and Fine Motor Assessment of Infants (Case-Smith, 1991) reflect the meaningful elements of posture and fine motor skills in infants, and not any other elements? Content validity is assumed to be greater as more elements within the construct are judged to be assessed by the instrument and as fewer elements outside the construct are included (Sim & Arnell, 1993). These judgments are usually made by persons deemed to be experts in the particular content area. A thorough examination of content validity through the use of experts is provided by Thorn and Deitz (1989).

However, because information regarding the content of a test is not adequate for evaluating uses of the test or inferences made from test scores, it does not qualify as validity evidence according to the contemporary view of validity (Messick, 1988). Thus, the *Standards for Educational and Psychological Testing* published in 1985 uses the term *content-related evidence* instead of content validity to reflect the shift in perspective. Angoff (1988) advocates the terms *content relevance* and *content coverage*. The gathering of content information may not be adequate for establishing validity, but because test content clearly may influence the nature of score inferences supported by other evidence (Messick, 1988), it is an important step in the test development process (Messick, 1975).

A good example of the process of collecting content-related evidence is reported for the Test of Gross Motor Development. Ulrich (1985) selected three experts to judge "whether the specific gross motor skills selected represented skills that are frequently taught to children in preschool and early elementary grades" and "whether the skills were representative of the gross motor skill domain" (p. 30). Three explicit criteria regarding education and experience were used to select the experts. In a more detailed study of the content validity of the Pediatric Evaluation of Disability Inventory (Haley, Coster, Ludlow, Haltiwanger, & Andrellos, 1992), evaluations from 31 experts were used (Haley, Coster, & Faas, 1991).

Face validity, which has been often and inappropriately subsumed under the heading of content validity, concerns the extent to which one or more individuals feel that an assessment instrument appears to measure what it purports to measure (Sim & Arnell, 1993). The judgments involved in face validity are more global than those targeted exclusively on content. Because the judgments may take into account the uses of the test and the inferences made from test scores, they offer stronger evidence of validity than content-related judgments.

Also, the global nature of face validity may allow for the collection of opinions of different stakeholders in the assessment process, including patients, physicians, physical therapists, occupational therapists, social workers, and methodologists. Goldsmith (1993) reported that this type of procedure was used in the development of a quality-of-movement measure for children with cerebral palsy (Boyce et al., 1991). Finally, some aspects of an assessment instrument, such as how much fun it is for children, may be considered in a face validity procedure but completely missed in more technical approaches to establishing validity (Campbell, 1993a).

Criterion-Related Validity

In criterion-related (or criterion-based) validity, inferences based on the results of an assessment instrument are compared against inferences based on a criterion measurement that is accepted as a standard indicator of the targeted construct or trait (Sim & Arnell, 1993; TFSMPT, 1991). For example, inferences about a person's cardiovascular endurance based on distance walked or run in 12 min may be compared with inferences based on an obtained value of maximum oxygen uptake, a universally accepted indicator of cardiovascular endurance. Criterion-related validity is usually categorized into three main types: concurrent, predictive, and prescriptive (TFSMPT, 1991).

Concurrent Validity. To establish concurrent validity, one justifies inferences based on the results of target measurements by comparing these inferences with inferences based on criterion evidence obtained at approximately the same time as the target measurements (TFSMPT, 1991). To illustrate, concurrent validity was estimated for the Posture and Fine Motor Assessment of Infants (PFMAI) (Case-Smith, 1991) by administering the Peabody Developmental Motor Scales (Folio & Fewell, 1983) to 25 healthy full-term infants on the same day or the day after they were given the PFMAI. Correlations then were calculated between scores on the PFMAI and scores on the Peabody Developmental Motor Scales.

Predictive Validity. To establish predictive validity, one justifies inferences regarding future events or conditions based on the results of target measurements by comparing these inferences with inferences based on criterion evidence obtained at a later time than the target measurements (TFSMPT, 1991). Harris et al. (1984) examined the predictive validity of the Movement Assessment of Infants (MAI) (Chandler, Andrews, & Swanson, 1980) by calculating correlations between the risk scores on the MAI at 4 months with scores on the Motor Scale of the Bayley Scales of Infant Development (Bayley, 1969) at 1 and 2 years. In addition, they calculated correlations between risk scores on the MAI at 4 months with pediatricians' ratings of motor development, muscle tone, and degree of handicap at 1 and 2 years.

The predictive validity of tests is often presented in terms of indexes referred to as *sensitivity* and *specificity*. Sensitivity, or the true-positive rate, is the likelihood that a positive test places a person in a disease or impairment category; specificity, or the true-negative rate, is the likelihood that a negative test does not place a person in a disease or impairment category (Sox, 1986). The calculations for these indexes are best illustrated with a 2×2 matrix, in which two levels of test results (positive or negative) are crossed with two levels of actual disease or impairment status (see figure 6.1). Refer to figure 6.1 for the values applied in the formulas that follow.

$$\text{Sensitivity} = \frac{\text{persons with impairment with positive test}}{\text{persons with impairment}}$$

$$= \frac{\text{Cell E}}{\text{Cell B}} = \frac{65}{75.} = 0.87 \qquad\qquad 6.1$$

Actual status

Total persons		Impairment present	Impairment absent
500 (A)		75 (B)	425 (C)

Test results

Test positive		True — positive	False — positive
100 (D)		65 (E)	35 (F)
Test negative		False — negative	True — negative
400 (G)		10 (H)	390 (I)

■ **FIGURE 6.1** Sensitivity and specificity based on two levels of test results and two levels of actual impairment status.

$$\text{Specificity} = \frac{\text{persons without impairment with negative test}}{\text{persons without impairment}}$$

$$= \frac{\text{Cell I}}{\text{Cell C}} = \frac{390}{425.} = 0.92 \qquad\qquad 6.2$$

Further, the probability of disease or impairment if the test is positive can be calculated as

$$\frac{\text{true positive (E)}}{\text{all test positive (D)}} = \frac{65}{100} = 0.65 \qquad\qquad 6.3$$

and the probability of disease or impairment if the test is negative can be calculated as

$$\frac{\text{false negative (H)}}{\text{all test negative (G)}} = \frac{10}{400} = 0.03 \qquad\qquad 6.4$$

Prescriptive Validity. To establish prescriptive validity, one justifies inferences regarding instruction or treatment based on the results of target measurements by comparing these inferences with inferences based on measurements of a successful outcome of the chosen instruction or treatment (TFSMPT, 1991). Although many movement skill assessment instruments are designed to help practitioners plan instruction or treatment, few authors offer evidence of prescriptive validity in their test manuals.

In most cases, the greatest problem in establishing criterion-related validity is identifying an independent criterion or standard for measuring the target entities or traits. Sim and Arnell (1993) reason that "because the criterion used is, in most instances, likely to be less than perfect, any resulting assessment of validity will only be partial" (p. 105). Another problem arises when the subject populations, testing environments, and other variables for the criterion tests are different from those for the tests to be validated (Wood, 1989). Campbell (1993a) argues that practitioners working with children with physical impairments are "wasting time in research efforts to demonstrate criterion-related validity with existing tests of normal maturation when what is important is demonstration of . . . validity for our unique purposes in managing functional limitation to prevent disability" (p. 111).

Construct Validity

According to the TFSMPT (1991), construct validity is defined as the conceptual or theoretical basis for using a measurement to make an inferred interpretation, established through logical argumentation supported by theoretical and research evidence (p. 597). Messick (1980) proclaims that "construct validity is . . . the unifying concept of validity that integrates criterion and content considerations into a common framework for testing rational hypotheses about theoretically relevant relationships" (p. 1015).

The initial exposition of construct validity was published by Cronbach and Meehl in 1955, with the term *construct* (or *hypothetical construct*) defined as "some postulated attribute of people, assumed to be reflected in test performance" (p. 283). The first step in construct validation involves explicitly defining the construct and the test that is purported to measure the construct (Cronbach, Gleser, Nanda, & Rajaratnam, 1972). The construct should be embedded in a conceptual framework that specifies the meaning of the construct, distinguishes it from other constructs, and indicates how measures of the construct should relate to other variables (CDSEPT, 1985).

Factor analysis methods are often used in tests of motor ability to determine (a) how many identifiable factors are included within a construct, (b) which factors account for the most variance in the construct, and (c) which tasks best represent the individual factors (Hughes & Riley, 1981). For the Bruininks-Oseretsky Test of Motor Proficiency (BOT) (Bruininks, 1978), factor analyses did not support the hypothesized structure of motor proficiency. The factor analyses revealed only five factors, with the first factor accounting for about 70% of the performance variability, even though the actual BOT is composed of eight subtests (see table 6.1).

The various presentations of data related to construct validity should be able to be framed in terms of a hypothesis. For example, in the Basic Gross Motor Assessment (Hughes & Riley, 1981), the statistically significant differences in mean scores of children with no identified impairment compared to children receiving special education supported the hypothesis that children with impairments should score lower than children without impairments (see table 6.2).

As in other experimental endeavors, the hypotheses should be directly stated along with rationale for the hypotheses, although this often is not done. An excerpt from the paper describing the Gross Motor Function Measure (Russell et al., 1989) exemplifies this important step:

> Hypothesis three was that non-disabled children under three years of age will show more change than non-disabled children aged three years or older. This reflects both the greater room for change in the younger children and their rapidity of quantitative motor progress. (p. 345)

If a hypothesized result is not supported, there are several options for interpretation and action. First, the conclusion might be made that the assessment is not valid. Second, the rationale for the hypothesis might be carefully examined in light of the results and uses of the test. If the reasoning used to determine the original hypothesis is found to be flawed, then the hypothesis and corresponding rationale might be modified. Third, the assessment itself might be modified to increase the prospect of finding support for the hypothesis.

TABLE 6.1 Subtests in the Bruininks-Oseretsky Test of Motor Proficiency (Bruninks, 1978) Organized According to Identifying Factors

Identifying factors	BOTMP subtests
I. General motor development	1. Running speed and agility
	6. Response speed
	7. Visual-motor control
	8. Upper-limb speed and dexterity
II. Upper-limb coordination	5. Upper-limb coordination
III. Balance	2. Balance
IV. Strength	4. Strength
V. Bilateral coordination	3. Bilateral coordination

TABLE 6.2 Mean Score Differences Between Children Referred From Special Education and Children From Normative Sample on the Basis Gross Motor Assessment (Hughes & Riley, 1981)

Subject group	N	Mean score	t value[a]
6 years			
Special education	11	17.72	−5.19
Norm	11	33.36	
7 years			
Special education	23	27.17	−7.98
Norm	23	47.60	
8 years			
Special education	9	28.77	−7.05
Norm	9	50.22	
9 years			
Special education	7	29.85	−3.83
Norm	7	51.14	
10 years			
Special education	17	34.05	−7.42
Norm	17	52.82	
11 years			
Special education	6	34.66	−4.10
Norm	6	53.16	
12 years			
Special education	8	38.37	−3.46
Norm	8	53.62	

Note: Reprinted from *Physical Therapy*, J. E. Hughes & A. Riley, "Basic Gross Motor Assessment: Tool for use with children having minor motor dysfunction," 1981, *61*, p. 509, with permission of the APTA.
[a]for all values, $p < .01$

The process of establishing construct validity often appears to be vague and complicated, but this is primarily due to the variety of explicit or implicit hypotheses and the overall flexibility in the process (Messick, 1988). Statistical, experimental, rational, and rhetorical sources of evidence, as well as information from content- and criterion-related validation studies, may contribute to inferences related to the construct (CDSEPT, 1985; Messick, 1988).

■ RELIABILITY

Variability is inherent in the assessment process and can be traced to the person taking the test, the test itself, or the administration or scoring of the test (Kubiszyn & Borich, 1987). A professional administering and interpreting a test, then, must know how much variability can be expected from a particular test and whether that amount of variability is acceptable for the purpose of the assessment. The converse of variability is reliability, which can be defined as the degree to which test scores are consistent, dependable, or repeatable, that is, the degree to which they are free of measurement error (CDSEPT, 1985; TFSMPT, 1991). Reliability can be quantified for test consumers in a variety of ways, but one must first understand the theoretical bases of reliability to be able to appropriately use such reliability information.

From the perspective of classical test theory, variability is synonymous with error (E) and is viewed as the difference between observed (X) and true (T) scores:

$$X = T + E, \text{ thus} \qquad\qquad 6.5$$

$$E = X - T \qquad\qquad 6.6$$

Reliability, then, is the degree to which observed scores are free of measurement error (CDSEPT, 1985; TFSMPT, 1991). Or, put another way, reliability is the degree to which observed test scores match true scores. According to Equation 6.6, if $E = 0$, then $X - T = 0$.

Observed score (X), true score (T), and error components also can be expressed as variances (see Equation 6.7), which can be depicted in terms of areas (see figure 6.2).

$$S_X^2 = S_T^2 + S_E^2 \qquad\qquad 6.7$$

The standard psychometric definition of reliability, presented in terms of observed-score and true-score variance components, is the proportion of the observed score that is accounted for by the true score:

$$\text{Reliability} = S_T^2 / S_X^2 \qquad\qquad 6.8$$

Reliability often is estimated in terms of a correlation coefficient (r). Squaring the correlation coefficient allows it to be interpreted in terms of the variance components:

$$r^2 = S_T^2 / S_X^2 \qquad\qquad 6.9$$

Thus, for a correlation coefficient of .76:

$$r^2 = .76^2 = .58 = S_T^2 / S_X^2 \qquad\qquad 6.10$$

which means that about 58% of the observed-score variance is accounted for by the true-score variance, and that about 42% is accounted for by error variance. As the true-score variance accounts for a greater proportion of

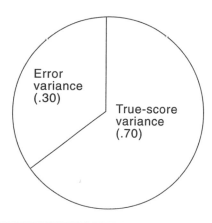

■ **FIGURE 6.2**   Observed score, true score, and error components depicted as variance areas.

the observed-score variance, and as error variance accounts for a smaller proportion, the reliability coefficient will increase (see figure 6.3).

Berk (1979) and others have suggested that reliability should be interpreted only in the context of the standard psychometric definition presented in Equation 6.3. Consequently, Berk (1979) felt that the term reliability is often used inappropriately, and that the term *agreement* provides a more accurate label for the statistics that appear in the literature.

Categories of Reliability

The most general categorization of reliability distinguishes between relative and absolute reliability (Baumgartner, 1989). Absolute reliability indicates the degree to which scores do not change in magnitude or value. Relative reliability indicates the degree to which the same relative positions of scores are maintained between repeated testings, and is usually estimated by using some type of correlation coefficient. Absolute reliability also can be referred to as *agreement* or *consensus,* and relative reliability as *consistency* or *classical reliability* (Ottenbacher, 1995).

Reliability also is categorized into at least five other types: test-retest reliability, intrarater reliability, interrater reliability, parallel-forms reliability, and internal consistency (TFSMPT, 1991).

- *Test-retest reliability:* The consistency or equivalence of repeated performances separated in time measured by the same rater; the consistency between testings; also termed stability.
- *Intrarater reliability:* The consistency or equivalence of the same performance measured at different times by the same rater; the

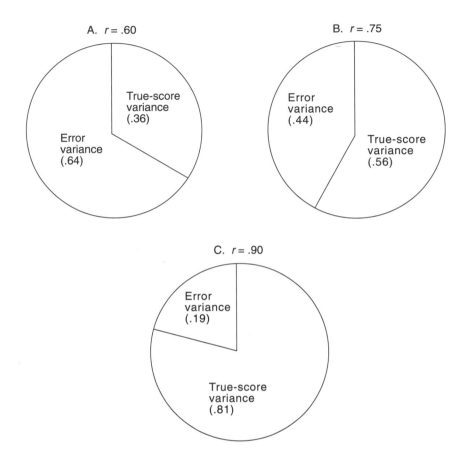

■ FIGURE 6.3　True score and error variance areas shown for three correlation coefficient values.

consistency within a rater. The only way the same performance can be measured at different times by the same rater is by recording the performance on videotape or film.

- *Interrater reliability*: The consistency or equivalence of the same performance measured by different raters; the consistency between raters.
- *Parallel-forms (or alternative-forms) reliability*: The consistency or agreement of performance measurements with different (or alternative) forms of a test by the same rater; indicates whether measurements obtained with different forms of a test can be used interchangeably; the consistency between forms; also termed equivalence.

- *Internal consistency*: The extent to which items or elements that contribute to a measurement reflect one basic phenomenon or dimension.

It is important to emphasize that even though agreement is often thought of as synonymous with reliability, agreement is theoretically different from classical reliability and thus may require different types of indexes or coefficients (Burry-Stock, Shaw, Laurie, & Chissom, 1996).

■ Methods of Estimating Reliability

Many methods of estimating reliability of behavioral observations have been reported in the scientific literature. Berk (1979), in critiquing the procedures used to determine interrater reliability or agreement in studies including persons with disabilities, identified 22 different methods. Ottenbacher and Tomcheck (1993) reviewed and analyzed the methods used in 20 studies examining the reliability of an assessment instrument, published in either the *American Journal of Occupational Therapy* or *Physical Therapy* between 1987 and 1991. They found that the most frequently reported methods of estimating reliability were intraclass correlation coefficients (57%), Pearson product-moment correlation coefficients (15%), kappa values (7%), and percent agreements (7%). Similarly, Ottenbacher (1995) found that the most common statistics in 30 reliability studies in *Developmental Medicine and Child Neurology, Journal of Developmental and Behavioral Pediatrics*, and *Journal of Early Intervention* were Pearson product-moment correlation coefficients (42%), intraclass correlation coefficients (27%), kappa values (13%), and other statistics (18%).

Some methods of estimating reliability are considered by measurement experts to be more suitable than others. Bartko and Carpenter (1976) and Berk (1979) recommend using weighted kappa and intraclass correlation procedures and discourage using percent agreement or product-moment correlation procedures. In the following sections I will describe and discuss these specific methods, along with others.

Percent Agreement. Percent agreement is calculated by dividing the number of exact score agreements between two rating situations (e.g., two raters on the same testing or two testings rated by the same person) by the total number of scores, multiplied by 100 (see Equation 6.11). If the product is not multiplied by 100, it is a proportion of agreement, with a value ranging from 0 to 1.

$$\text{Percent agreement} = (A \; / \; N) \times 100 \qquad \qquad 6.11$$
where: A = number of score agreements, N = total number of scores.

The percent agreement for the interrater reliability data presented in table 6.3 is 78%, found by summing the agreements in bold down the diagonal

(28 + 20 + 17 = 65), dividing by N (65 / 90 = .72), and multiplying by 100 (.72 × 100 = 72%).

Kappa.   The most common criticism of percent agreement is that it ignores chance agreements, which can be relatively high when few rating categories are used. Cohen (1960) proposed kappa (κ) as a coefficient of agreement that corrects for chance agreements. The formula for kappa is:

$$\kappa = (p_o - p_c) / (1 - p_c) \qquad\qquad 6.12$$

where: p_o = observed proportion of agreement and p_c = proportion of agreement expected by chance.

Again if we use the data in table 6.3 for illustration, the actual proportion of agreement (p_o) is .72, as calculated by Equation 6.11. The proportion of chance agreement (p_c) is .34, found by calculating the products of the row and column proportions for each of the three agreement cells (.39 × .37 = .14; .32 × .37 = .12; and .29 × .26 = .08), and then summing the products (.14 + .12 + .08 = .34). Filling these values into Equation 6.12 yields .58 [(.72 − .34) / (1 − .34)]. If chance agreement is higher than actual agreement $(p_c >$ $p_o)$, then a negative value will be obtained.

The weighted kappa (κ_w) was later presented by Cohen (1968) to allow certain cells in the reliability matrix to be weighted more than others. This might be done in situations in which certain disagreements are deemed to be more serious or problematic than others. For example, the assessment portrayed in table 6.3 concerned the judging of movement skill relative to three ordinal levels. If the criterion for eligibility for special services, such as adapted physical education, is a low skill rating, then disagreements between low and medium skill will be more serious than disagreements between medium and high skill. Hence, the low-medium and medium-low disagreement cells might be weighted more than the other disagreement cells. For information on how to calculate weighted kappa, refer to the original source (Cohen, 1968).

TABLE 6.3 Frequency and Proportion of Agreement and Disagreement Between Two Raters Evaluating the Movement Skill of 90 Individuals

	Rater 2			
Rater 1	Low skill	Medium skill	High skill	Total
Low skill	**28 (.31)**	6 (.07)	1 (.01)	35 (.39)
Medium skill	4 (.04)	**20 (.22)**	5 (.06)	29 (.32)
High skill	2 (.02)	7 (.08)	**17 (.19)**	26 (.29)
Total	34 (.37)	33 (.37)	23 (.26)	90 (.100)

Note: Agreement values are in bold print.

For descriptions and formulas for other indexes of agreement, see the recent article by Burry-Stock et al. (1996).

Pearson Product-Moment (or Interclass) Correlation Coefficients.
Pearson product-moment correlation (PPMC) coefficients quantify the relationship between two sets of scores, potentially allowing for an estimate of the proportion of the variance in the observed score that is accounted for by the true score (see Equation 6.8). However, there are at least two major criticisms of the use of PPMC coefficients. First, it may be that two sets of scores have a high degree of association such that one score is high when the other is high and is low when the other is low, but that one set of scores is consistently higher or lower than the other (Bartko & Carpenter, 1976). Pearson product-moment correlation coefficients provide an index of relative differences (i.e., consistency or classical reliability), but are not sensitive to absolute differences (i.e., agreement or consensus). In figure 6.4, both comparisons between Raters 1 and 2 yield correlations of 1.0, even though the absolute differences between the raters on Comparisons 1 and 2 are not the same.

A second criticism of using a PPMC coefficient to estimate reliability is that it is an interclass correlation, a bivariate statistic designed to quantify the relationship between two different variables, not comparisons between repetitions of the same variable (Baumgartner, 1989). Despite these problems, PPMC coefficients are still often used to establish test reliability.

Intraclass Correlation. Of all the methods used to estimate reliability, intraclass correlations most directly express the classical test theory relationship between true- and observed-score variance (Berk, 1979). The

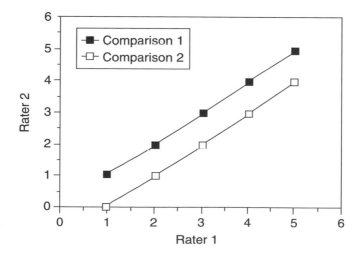

■ **FIGURE 6.4** Raw data for two raters for a correlation of 1.0.

intraclass correlation coefficient *(R)* is determined by running a repeated measures analysis of variance and then creating a ratio including the equivalents of true-score and observed-score variances. Note that because the intraclass correlation is defined in terms of variances, the value does not need to be squared to allow interpretation.

Intraclass correlations are used as generalizability coefficients and thus allow for greater flexibility than other reliability methods in identifying sources of error. Different types of reliability, such as test-retest and interrater reliability, can be examined in a single analysis of variance when they are identified and included as facets in the analysis. In addition, interactions between possible sources of error can be analyzed. Table 5.1 in chapter 5 presents the results from such an analysis of reliability for the Test of Gross Motor Development (Ulrich & Wise, 1984).

■ Standard Error of Measurement

A critical question for practitioners is what reliability coefficient values allow a test to be used with confidence? A general guideline is at least a coefficient of .80, which yields a squared coefficient value of .64; this represents the amount of common or shared variance between the two testing situations (Nunnally, 1978). An argument for a lower coefficient of .70 (Baumgartner & Jackson, 1991) is that it is the minimum value at which the shared variance is at least one-half of the total ($.707^2 = .50$). Thus, for reliability coefficients less than .70, the proportion of variance between the two testing situations accounted for by error exceeds the proportion accounted for by the true score. This should make any test user very nervous.

However, there is a more tangible way of evaluating the confidence that a practitioner may have when using a test with a certain reliability coefficient value. The standard error of measurement (SEM, SE_m, or S_E) allows the test user to calculate the probability that the true score will fall within a certain range of values, specified in terms of raw and/or normative scores. In this case, the acceptability of a certain range of scores for a particular assessment purpose of the test can be evaluated quite directly. I will give an example of how this can be done after describing the standard error of measurement.

A reliability coefficient less than 1.00 indicates that there is some error in the measurement process; in other words, the match between the observed score and the true score is less than perfect. Thus, the practitioner must understand that the true score lies within some range about the observed score. This range is called the confidence interval, which is determined by the standard error of measurement.

The standard error of measurement (SEM, SE_m, or S_E) expresses the variation between an observed score and a true score in terms of a standard deviation from the observed score (see figure 4.3 in chapter 4). If a person has an observed score (X) of 50, and the standard error of measurement is 5, then the confidence interval is indicated by $X \pm SEM$, or 45 to 55. However, there is a specified probability that the true score lies within this range. The standard error of measurement can be interpreted as a standard deviation or Z score, so the probability that the true score lies within 1 SEM of the observed score is 68% (see figure 4.1). Similarly, the probability that the true score lies within 2 $SEMs$ of the true score (50 ± 10) is 96%.

The formula for calculating the standard error of measurement is:

$$SEM = \sigma_X \sqrt{1 - r_{XX'}} \qquad\qquad 6.13$$

where: σ_X = standard deviation and $r_{XX'}$ = reliability coefficient.

The standard error of measure decreases as the standard deviation decreases and the reliability coefficient increases. Then, the formula for the confidence interval is:

$$X - (Z_C)(SEM) \leq T \leq X + (Z_C)(SEM) \qquad\qquad 6.14$$

where: X = observed score, T = true score, and Z_C = Z score corresponding to the specified level of confidence.

This can be simply reduced to $X + (Z_C)(SEM)$. For a confidence interval of 68%, $Z_C = 1.0$; for 86%, $Z_C = 1.5$; and for 96%, $Z_C = 2.0$.

A concrete example may be useful at this point. Assume that an 11-year-old boy is being assessed to determine his eligibility for adapted physical education using the BOT (Bruininks, 1978). His total composite score is 38, which places him at the 12th percentile, just above the eligibility cutoff of the 10th percentile. However, the examiner understands that the observed score of 38 may not match the boy's true score; so she looks in the test manual and finds that for sixth graders, the standard deviation of total composite scores is 10.2 (a standardized score with a chosen mean of 50 and a chosen standard deviation of 10) and the test-retest reliability coefficient is .86. She proceeds to calculate the standard error of measurement, which is equal to 3.8 (she later finds that this result matches the value presented in a standard error of measurement table). Now, the examiner is able to report that there is a 68% probability that the boy's true score lies between 34.2 (6th percentile) and 41.8 (21st percentile) (38 ± 3.8). Because her supervisor wants to increase the level of confidence to 80%, she multiplies the SEM (3.8) by the Z_C value corresponding to 80% (1.28) to get 4.9. The new confidence interval is then 38 ± 4.9, or 33.1 (5th percentile) to 42.9 (24th percentile). Consequently, on the basis of his observed score, the boy does not qualify for adapted physical education; but on the basis of the confidence interval of the true score, there is some question whether he actually does qualify, so he should be examined further with use of other assessment procedures.

By applying the standard error of measurement for a selected confidence level to some sample scores, the test user can evaluate, before actually using a test, whether its reliability is acceptable. If the prospective user comes up with the confidence intervals in the example just presented, he or she may not be willing to use the BOT as a screening tool. You can find additional examples from the BOT and other motor tests, as well as a review of the importance of the standard error of measurement in clinical applications, in a recent article by Amundson and Crowe (1993).

Factors Affecting Reliability

This chapter concludes with an overview of some of the factors that may affect measurement error or reliability. As mentioned at the beginning of the discussion of reliability, error can be traced to three general factors (Kubiszyn & Borich, 1987): (a) the person taking the test, (b) the test itself, and (c) the administration and scoring of the test. A fourth factor that may influence estimated reliability includes the procedures used to standardize the assessment instrument and the method used to establish reliability.

Poor reliability attributed to the performer is most likely related to temporary factors such as fatigue or motivation. However, Baumgartner (1989) warns that age, sex, or experience may affect reliability, concluding that "it is unwise to assume that a test that is reliable for one gender, age, or experience level is automatically reliable for another gender, age, or experience level" (p. 63).

Factors related to the test itself also may affect reliability. In general, as more measures or items are included in a composite score, reliability increases. Also, as test items are measured with more objective scoring systems, reliability usually increases. Moreover, as test items become too easy (a "ceiling" effect) or too difficult (a "floor" effect), reliability tends to decrease. An example of a floor effect might be seen when a boy is unable to perform any pull-ups even though he does have enough upper-body strength to perform other similar tasks. His score of 0 pull-ups will be very consistent regardless of the rater or testing condition and thus would appear to be extremely reliable. However, when reliability is more appropriately viewed as the proportion of the observed score that is accounted for by the true score, then it is shown to be quite poor because the observed score of 0 does not accurately reflect the boy's true upper-body strength very well.

Poor or inconsistent test administration can be responsible for increasing error and decreasing reliability. An examiner's instructions or demonstrations may not be clear or may be incorrect. An examiner's attitude toward individuals may not allow them to demonstrate an optimal performance. The physical environment may be set up improperly or inconsistently. For example, performance on balance tasks such as walking a balance beam or standing on one foot can be influenced by the distance the performers are away from a wall or vertical surface (Burton & Davis, 1992a). As the performers get closer to a wall, the effect of optical flow becomes more powerful. In addition, people can not only make scoring errors, but they can also make miscalculations, make mistakes in transferring numbers, or use the wrong tables for score transformations.

Next, the procedures used to standardize an assessment tool may affect reliability. Baumgartner (1989) and Kubiszyn and Borich (1987) both indicate that a heterogeneous sample usually shows greater reliability because of the larger range of scores. Finally, one method of estimating reliability may produce a different estimate than another method.

Common Reliability Reporting Problems

The former editor-in-chief of *Research Quarterly for Exercise and Sport* and one of his colleagues (Morrow & Jackson, 1993), on the basis of their reviews of many manuscripts including reliability information, offer a list of eight common reliability problems and corresponding suggestions for improvement. The first problem is reporting merely that reliability is based on previous studies. Morrow and Jackson recommend that authors verify the reliability of an instrument for their specific samples and report their methods and results. Second, many authors fail to indicate the type of statistic used to estimate reliability; thus readers are not sure whether the statistic is a proportion of agreement, weighted kappa, interclass correlation, intraclass correlation, or something else. A third problem is that authors who use an intraclass model fail to indicate whether the model is a one- or two-way design. Next, when test-retest reliability is reported, the time lag between administrations is often not given. Fifth and sixth, when multiple trials are performed, authors may not indicate the number of trials on which the reliability is calculated or may base reliability calculations on the mean across trials. Reliability coefficients are often reported as statistically significant, but a statistically significant coefficient (e.g., an interclass correlation coefficient of .20 with $n = 100$ is statistically significant at the $p < .05$ level), is clearly not practically significant. Morrow and Jackson recommend that the obtained reliability should be reported without a statement of statistical significance. Finally, reliabilities are often based on small samples that are assumed to be representative of the results for the defined population. Morrow and Jackson suggest (a) that studies designed to establish the reliability of an assessment instrument include at least 30 performers representative of the target population, and (b) that when small samples are used, authors warn the readers to interpret the reliability information with caution.

Part II

Levels of Movement Skill Assessment

THE next section in this book provides detailed discussions of the six levels of the movement skill taxonomy, including in-depth descriptions and reviews of at least one commonly used instrument at four of the six levels. Reviews of movement skill foundations and specialized movement skills instruments are not included because there are so many different tests at these two levels that just one or two examples would not be very useful. These two levels are addressed in enough depth to allow readers to understand the assessment of movement skills at all levels of the taxonomy, but a thorough treatment would require an entire book for each. In fact, there is a recent book covering many aspects of the assessment of movement skill foundations (*Physiological Assessment of Human Fitness* by Maud and Foster, 1995) and another dedicated to the assessment of specialized movement skills (*Assessing Sport Skills* by Strand and Wilson, 1993).

Movement skill foundations are covered in chapter 7, motor abilities in chapter 8, early movement milestones in chapter 9, fundamental movement skills in chapter 10, and specialized and functional movement skills in chapter 11. A total of eight popular instruments are reviewed:

Chapter 8:   Bruininks-Oseretsky Test of Motor Proficiency (Bruininks, 1978)

Movement Assessment Battery for Children Test (Henderson & Sugden, 1992)

(continued)

Chapter 9:   Peabody Developmental Motor Scales (Folio & Fewell, 1983)

Assessment, Evaluation, and Programming System for Infants and Children Birth to Three Years (Bricker, 1993)

Chapter 10:   Test of Gross Motor Development (Ulrich, 1985)

Top-Down Motor Milestone Test from the Mobility Opportunities Via Education program (Bidabe & Lollar, 1990)

Chapter 11:   Movement Assessment Battery for Children Checklist (Henderson & Sugden, 1992)

Pediatric Evaluation of Disability Inventory (Haley, Coster, Ludlow, Haltiwanger, & Andrellos, 1992)

Chapter 7

Assessing Movement Skill Foundations

© Photophile / Jose Carrillo

I N chapter 3, I introduced foundations of movement skills as the first level of the movement skill taxonomy and described them as constituent systems of the person that contribute to the development of movement skills. To reiterate, movement skill foundations are not movement skills themselves, but are all aspects of a person—physical, mental, and emotional—that facilitate or limit his/her performance of movement skills. But even though movement skill foundations are not movement skills themselves, they are an important part of a complete assessment strategy

> " Performance emerges from a confluence of subsystems within a particular task environment. "
>
> — *Thelen and Smith (1994, p. 84)*

because deficits in one or more of the foundation areas may lead directly to a deficit in one or more movement skills. Clearly, an attempt to modify a movement pattern or outcome by direct instruction of the pattern will be futile if one or more foundation areas are not adequate to allow successful performance of the skill. In chapter 12, I will discuss the role of foundations in two different assessment strategies for movement skill assessment—bottom-up and top-down.

The foundations level in the movement skill taxonomy is very similar to the physical performance component in occupational therapy models. Mathiowetz (1993) explains that physical performance component evaluations include neuromuscular testing (e.g., muscle tone, range of motion, strength) and motor testing (e.g., fine motor dexterity, gross motor coordination, praxis), and argues that selected physical performance component evaluations are necessary to clarify the cause of functional (or occupational performance) deficits and assist in the intervention planning (see figure 3.1, p. 49). Mathiowetz notes further that physical performance evaluations "may be more sensitive to change than occupational performance evaluations" (p. 229). The present notion of movement skills foundation is broader than Mathiowetz' (1993) physical performance component because it extends beyond physical attributes to include mental and emotional attributes.

At a NATO Advanced Study Institute in 1986, Thelen presented and explained the concept of motor development "rate limiters." She argued that movement patterns are specified by "the systems outcomes of interacting components, each with its own developmental course and acting within definite constraints and opportunities afforded by the context" (p. 110). With regard to the development of alternating steps on a treadmill, Thelen and Ulrich (1991) identified six relevant components, whose interaction is depicted for two infants in figure 7.1. The developmental trajectory of each component is different, and certain minima on each, which may vary by individual, are necessary in order for stepping to occur. Just one component below the critical value may keep stepping from emerging. The assessment of movement skills, then, in Thelen's (1986) words, must "identify which components are indeed rate-limiting, that is, which factors constrain the final appearance of the behaviour" (p. 115). Research carried out by Thelen and her colleagues in subsequent years has focused on the notion of how skill may be constrained or hidden by rate-limiting components (Smith & Thelen, 1993; Thelen, 1995; Thelen & Smith, 1994; Thelen & Ulrich, 1991).

Eleven movement skill foundation areas that are among those most commonly assessed by movement professionals, presented in chapter 3, are listed in table 7.1. Note the similarity between these areas and Thelen's (1986) locomotor components. Some of these diverse areas, ranging from cardiovascular endurance to motivation/affect to balance/postural control, may be considered the domain of one particular profession, but most are assessed by persons in various professional areas. For example, neurologists or otolaryngologists are most likely to be the professionals best equipped to assess balance or postural control, but this area also is assessed by adapted physical educators and physical therapists. Clearly, no one profession is best suited to assess all movement skill foundation areas. Hence, a complete perspective of a person's skill foundations can be gained only through multidisciplinary cooperation and collaboration.

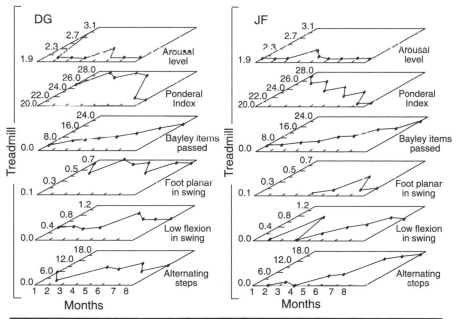

■ **FIGURE 7.1**   The longitudinal development of alternating treadmill steppping, depicted as parallel developmental trajectories of related subsystems, for Subject DG from 1 to 8 months of age and Subject JF from 1 to 9 months.

From "Hidden Skills: A Dynamic Systems Analysis of Treadmill Stepping During the First Year" by E. Thelen and B.D. Ulrich, 1991, *Monographs of the Society for Research in Child Development*, Serial No. 223, 56(1), p. 88. Copyright 1991 by Society for Research in Child Development. Reprinted with permission.

TABLE 7.1   Eleven Commonly Assessed Movement Skill Foundation Areas

Balance/postural control
Body composition
Body size and morphology
Cardiovascular endurance
Cognition
Flexibility/range of motion
Knowledge
Motivation and affect
Muscular strength and endurance
Neurological functioning/reflexes
Sensation/sensory integration/perception

In the rest of this chapter, I will present assessment procedures, strategies, and instruments for 8 of the 11 movement skill foundation areas listed in table 7.1: (a) balance/postural control, (b) body composition, (c) body size and morphology, (d) cardiovascular endurance, (e) flexibility/range of motion, (f) knowledge, (g) motivation and affect, and (h) muscular strength and endurance. The other three areas—cognition, neurological functioning/reflexes, sensation/sensory integration/perception—are very broad in scope and thus are not covered. The following books offer in-depth information on each of the areas not addressed here:

Cognition:

Cognitive Assessment: A Multidisciplinary Perspective edited by Reynolds (1994)

Cognitive Assessment for Clinicians by Hodges (1994)

Cognitively Diagnostic Assessment by Nichols, Chipman, and Brennan (1995)

Neurological functioning/reflexes:

DeJong's The Neurologic Examination by Haerer (1992)

Introduction to the Neurologic Examination by Nolan (1995)

Reflex Testing Methods for Evaluating CNS Development by Fiorentino (1981b)

The Neurological Examination of the Full-Term Newborn Infant by Prechtl and Beintema (1991)

Sensation/sensory integration/perception:

Clinical Tests of Vision by Frisen (1990)

Sensory Evaluation Practices by Stone and Sidel (1993)

Sensory Integration: Theory and Practice by Fisher, Murray, and Bundy (1991)

Visual Perception: A Clinical Orientation by Schwartz (1994)

Another excellent resource with information on five of the eight movement skill foundations elaborated on in this chapter is a recent text edited by Maud and Foster (1995) titled *Physiological Assessment of Human Fitness*, with chapters on body composition (Pollock, Garzarella, & Graves, 1995), body size and morphology (Malina, 1995), cardiovascular fitness (Davis, 1995; Ward, Ebbeling, & Ahlquist, 1995), flexibility/range of motion (Maud & Cortez-Cooper, 1995), and muscular strength and endurance (Kraemer & Fry, 1995).

■ BALANCE/POSTURAL CONTROL

Postural control is defined by Horak (1987) as "the ability to maintain equilibrium in a gravitational field by keeping or returning the center of body mass over its base of support" (p. 1881). A broader perspective is offered by Reed (1989), who argues that postural control involves the controlled and flexible use of all forces acting on the body to achieve the intended outcomes of a particular functional task. Thus, these two synonymous terms—*balance* and *postural control*—should be viewed as a process that "serves to maintain bodily orientation to the environment and its features" (Reed, 1989, p. 1).

The importance of balance as a component of or contributor to movement skill proficiency is reflected in the inclusion of balance items or subtests in many motor ability tests. For example, the Bruininks-Oseretsky Test of Motor Proficiency (Bruininks, 1978) has a separate balance subtest consisting of 8 items (see table 8.1, p. 162), the Movement Assessment Battery for Children Test (Henderson & Sugden, 1992) has three of eight task categories devoted to static and dynamic balance (see table 8.5, p. 173), and the Gross Motor Scale of the Peabody Developmental Motor Scales (Folio & Fewell, 1983) has a balance category with 33 items (see table 9.3, p. 193).

According to Burton and Davis (1992a), the postural control tasks used in motor ability tests or in instruments dedicated exclusively to assessing balance can be organized into five nonexclusive categories. First, there are tasks that involve self-initiated changes in body location, such as walking on a line or a balance beam or stepping over an obstacle (e.g., Henderson & Sugden, 1992). Second, some tasks involve a moving support surface, such as standing on a soft, pliable surface like foam rubber (e.g., Shumway-Cook & Horak, 1986), on a tiltboard (e.g., Horak, 1987), or on an externally controlled moving platform (e.g., Nashner, Shumway-Cook, & Marin, 1983). Other tasks involve changes in the position of extremities, such as the functional reach test in which subjects reach forward as far as possible without moving their feet (Donahoe, Turner, & Worrell, 1994). Fourth, there are tasks that involve reducing the subject's base of support, such as standing on a balance beam or on one foot (e.g., Bruininks, 1978). And fifth, some tasks involve perceptual manipulations, such as having subjects close their eyes or wear a "visual-conflict dome" over the head (e.g., Shumway-Cook & Horak, 1986), or exposing subjects to optical flow patterns (e.g., Ring, Matthews, Nayak, & Isaacs, 1988).

A few tests have been designed to assess balance exclusively. Many clinics in hospitals and research laboratories have balance assessment systems, such as EquiTest (e.g., DiFabio, 1995), which measure a person's body sway and muscle pattern activation as he/she stands on a hydraulically or electronically controlled movable platform. The platform can be moved horizontally or vertically or can be rotated; it can be programmed to rotate in synchrony with body sway to always maintain the ankle angle at 90°, creating a condition in which proprioceptive information is inaccurate; it may be equipped with a visual surround that moves with the platform, creating a condition in which visual information is inaccurate. These systems, based on the apparatus and research reported by Nashner and colleagues (e.g., Nashner et al., 1983), provide accurate information about a person's postural control capabilities and deficits but require more resources than are available to most practitioners.

A field test comparable to testing with the platform systems, now called the Clinical Test for Sensory Interaction in Balance (CTSIB), was developed by Shumway-Cook and Horak (1986), again on the basis of the ideas of Nashner (1982). In the original version, the only materials needed were a blindfold, a visual-conflict dome constructed from a Chinese paper lantern, and a piece of medium-density foam. As subjects stand for 30 s in each of six combinations of three visual conditions (normal, blindfolded, and visual-conflict dome) and two surface conditions (normal, foam), body sway is numerically coded (1 = minimal sway, 2 = mild sway, 3 = moderate sway, 4 = fall). These six combinations, along with the sensory systems compromised, are summarized in table 7.2.

Shumway-Cook and Horak (1986) modified their sensory interaction balance test in the CTSIB by including two stance positions—feet together and heel-to-toe—and measuring amount of sway as well as duration of stance. The CTSIB has been used with adults (e.g., Cohen, Blatchly, & Gombash, 1993) as well as children (e.g., Crowe, Deitz, Richardson, & Atwater, 1990; Deitz, Richardson, Atwater, Crowe, & Odiorne, 1991; Westcott, Crowe, Deitz, & Richardson, 1994). Norms for 6- to 9-year-olds on the Pediatric CTSIB are given in the paper by Deitz et al. (1991). A system of interpreting the results of the CTSIB in relation to four types of specific deficits is offered by Shumway-Cook and Woollacott (1995) (see table 7.2). Note that only two of the six conditions—visual conflict with normal surface and normal vision with foam surface—are required to discriminate between the four types of deficits.

TABLE 7.2   Sensory Systems Compromised in the Six Conditions of the CTSIB (adapted from Deitz et al., 1991) and Balance Deficit Interpretations When Excessive Sway Is Present (marked by X) (adapted from Shumway-Cook & Woollacott, 1995)

Condition	Sensory systems compromised	Deficit interpretation			
		Visual dependent	Surface dependent	Vestibular loss	Sensory selection
Normal vision Normal surface	None				
No vision Normal surface	No vision	X			
Vision conflict Normal surface	Inaccurate vision	X			X
Normal vision Foam surface	Inaccurate proprioception		X		X
No vision Foam surface	No vision Inaccurate proprioception	X	X	X	X
Vision conflict Foam surface	Inaccurate vision Inaccurate proprioception	X	X	X	X

Another popular assessment of balance is the Functional Reach Test (FRT), developed by Duncan, Weiner, Chandler, and Studenski (1990) for an adult population. The FRT measures the maximal distance a person can reach forward beyond arm's length while maintaining a fixed standing position and holding the shoulder at 90° of flexion. Duncan et al. (1990) found that older adults with shorter maximum reaches on the FRT were more likely to experience falls than those with longer reaches. Normative data for the FRT are reported by Duncan et al. for adults from 20 to 87 years and by Donahoe et al. (1994) for children 5 to 15 years.

Balance assessment tests also may emphasize other aspects of postural control. For example, some tests are designed to evaluate postural control as a person performs basic functional tasks such as sitting, standing, getting up, sitting down, turning around, or picking up an object from the floor (e.g., Berg, Wood-Dauphinee, Williams, & Maki, 1992; Mathias, Nayak, & Isaacs, 1986; Tinetti, 1986). Other tests measure postural responses to manipulations of optical flow in a person's visual surround (Lee & Lishman, 1975; Ring et al., 1988; Wade, Lindquist, Taylor, & Treat-Jacobson, 1995). In their motor control textbook, Shumway-Cook and Woollacott (1995) explain a systems approach to postural control assessment, which includes Berg's functional balance scale (Berg, Wood-Dauphinee, & Williams, 1995; Berg et al., 1992; Bogle Thorbahn & Newton, 1996), and provide the form for this systems battery in an appendix.

Clinicians and teachers must be careful in interpreting the results of individual balance items, balance subtests, or tests devoted to balance exclusively. In their review of balance assessment in adapted physical education, Burton and Davis (1992a) point out four common limitations of tasks designed to assess postural control. They caution test users to consider that some tasks or sets of tasks may (a) emphasize conscious control rather than automatic responses; (b) involve contrived movements, not natural actions; (c) focus on feedforward processes only, with no external perturbations requiring feedback-based responses; or (d) include no manipulations that allow for the systematic examination of sensory or perceptual processes. They also argue that subtests or tests that derive composite scores from summed performances on several different balance tasks are based on the questionable assumption that balance is a general ability, not specific to a particular movement skill and context (see also chapter 8).

An excellent reference for more in-depth information on assessing balance and postural control is the recently published *Practical Management of the Balance Disorder Patient* by Shephard and Telian (1996). This book includes separate chapters on neurotologic history and physical examination, electronystragmography evaluation, ocular-motor evaluation, rotational chair testing, postural control evaluation (with force plates and dynamic posturography), integrated management and interpretation of vestibular test results, and diagnostic test selection. The importance of sensory input in balance and postural control, as indicated by the emphases in these chapters, illustrates that the various movement skill foundation areas may overlap with each other.

■ BODY COMPOSITION

Most assessments of body composition are based on the two-compartment model proposed by Brozek, Grande, Anderson, and Keys (1963) and Siri (1961) in the early 1960s. In this model, the body is composed of a fat compartment and a fat-free compartment that includes muscle, bone, and other nonfatty tissues. The methods most commonly used to assess the relative contributions of these two compartments are hydrostatic weighing, water volume displacement, anthropometric techniques, and bioelectric impedance analysis. Other methods have been recently developed to isolate other body components such as bone mineral density and chemical components of fat and fat-free mass, but the expense and complexity of these technologies, and the time involved in their application, presently limit their use (Pollock et al., 1995).

The laboratory procedure most widely used for assessing body composition is hydrostatic weighing (Pollock et al., 1995) (see figure 7.2). The weight of the person is measured in the air and in the water, and is put into a formula to determine body density along with values for residual lung volume and water density. Then body density values are converted to percent body fat values, usually with use of the formulas provided by Brozek et al. (1963) and Siri (1961). Body density also can be determined by measuring the volume of water displaced by the body, but tanks designed for this purpose are less available than underwater weighing facilities.

A second general method of estimating percentage of body fat consists of anthropomorphic techniques, namely the measurement of skinfold thicknesses and segment circumferences. These methods are easy to perform, are relatively inexpensive, and require limited space and little training. Skinfold thicknesses are measured by placing the thumb and index finger about 8 cm apart at the selected body site, drawing the fingers together, and firmly grasping the fold created by two layers of skin. Then the jaws of a caliper are placed around the skinfold and the thickness is read off the caliper scale. Common skinfold sites are pectoral, midaxillary, triceps, subscapular, abdominal, suprailiac, anterior thigh, suprapatellar, medial calf, and biceps. In the circumference method, distances around various body sites, such as shoulders, chest, waist, abdomen, buttocks, thigh, calf, ankle, biceps, forearm, and wrist, are measured with a steel tape.

Once the skinfold or circumference measures have been obtained, the values are put into equations to calculate body density or percent body fat. Pollock et al. (1995) state that although more than 100 equations have been

■ **FIGURE 7.2**   Underwater weighing apparatus.

reported in the literature, the generalized formulas developed by Jackson and Pollock (1978) for men and by Jackson, Pollock, and Ward (1980) for women are the ones most commonly used. The validity of these anthropometric measures is usually established against the "gold standard" criterion of hydrostatic weighing. These equations must be used very cautiously with persons with disabilities or children unless they have been specifically validated for that group. You can find standardized procedures for measuring skinfolds and segment circumferences in the *Anthropometric Standardization Reference Manual* (Lohman, Roche, & Martorell, 1988, 1991).

Another method of assessing body composition is bioelectric impedance analysis (Pollock et al., 1995). In this type of analysis, subjects lie supine on a nonconducting surface, with the legs slightly apart and arms slightly away from the trunk. A pair of electrodes is attached to the ankle and foot and another pair to the wrist and hand, and a low electrical current is passed between the two sets of electrodes. The drop in current as it passes through the body, termed *bioelectric resistance* or *impedance* (R), is known to be inversely related to the amount of fat-free mass within the body. The distance the current has traveled through the body, from foot/ankle to hand/wrist, is estimated by stature (S). These two values are combined to calculate a resistive index, S^2 / R, which has been shown to highly correlate and reasonably predict total body weight and fat-free mass (Lukaski, Johnson, Bolonchuk, & Lykken, 1985). The principles underlying bioelectric impedance analysis and related application techniques are detailed in a review by Baumgartner, Chumlea, and Roche (1990).

■ BODY SIZE AND MORPHOLOGY

The measurement of the size or shape of the body falls within the domain of anthropometry. Body size can be measured in one, two, or three dimensions; that is, the measures may be lengths (length[1]), surface areas (length[2]), or volumes (length[3]). Also, the shape or morphology of the body may be expressed in terms of ratios between these measures, such as the body mass index, or in terms of other unique measures. You can find standardized procedures for making anthropomorphic measurements in *Anthropometric Standardization Reference Manual* (Lohman et al., 1988, 1991).

Lengths, or linear measures, may span the entire body or just a specific segment. The most common linear measure is stature or standing height, encompassing the entire length of the body. Measures of body segments may involve lengths (e.g., sitting height or leg length), breadths or widths (e.g., biacromial or bicristal width), depths (e.g., skinfolds), circumferences or girths (e.g., waist, thigh, or flexed arm), or curvatures or arcs (e.g., the vertebral column, particularly in assessments for conditions such as scoliosis or kyphosis). A linear performance measure, such as standing broad jumping distance or throwing distance, may be scaled to a relevant linear body parameter to more accurately portray an individual's performance relative to his or her own physical constraints (Burton & Davis, 1996; Davis & Burton, 1991). For example, understanding that a girl can horizontally jump 60% of her standing height may be more meaningful than knowing that she can jump 36 in. Thompson (1942/1992), on the basis of his observations of various species of animals (including humans) walking, swimming, and flying, came to the very interesting conclusion that speed or velocity of locomotion tends to vary as the square root of the linear dimensions of the animal.

Surface area, which is the second power of length, perhaps is the least common type of measure. However, some surface area measures may have important implications for movement behavior. For example, the two primary physical factors impacting postural control are height of center of gravity and size of the base of support. The base of support is usually measured as the length of the foot or shoe, but more accurately is the surface area of the foot or shoe (if positioning on one foot) contacting the support surface, or the area between the two feet. Also, wind or water resistance acting against a person is directly related to the surface area of the entire body. Finally, even though it may not be measured directly, the cross-sectional area of a muscle or bone is approximately proportional to the strength of the muscle or bone (Astrand & Rodahl, 1986).

The third power of length yields volume or mass. Total body weight is routinely measured, but other important volume or mass measures relate to movement performance, such as vital capacity of the lungs and stroke volume of the heart. As with some linear measures, some performance measures expressed in terms of volume or mass may be scaled to physical volume or mass measures to clarify the interpretation of the performance. For example, amount of weight lifted or maximum oxygen uptake may be divided by body weight, indicating the percentage of body weight that may be lifted or the amount of oxygen consumed during maximal exercise per unit of body weight.

A fourth type of body measure includes those that quantify the shape or morphology of the whole body or a part of the body. One very general and commonly used measure of body morphology is Quetelet's Index (QI), also known as the body mass index (BMI), proposed by Quetelet in 1835 (Bray, 1994). Quetelet's Index is defined as the ratio between weight (in kilograms) and stature squared (in meters), and has been found to strongly correlate with skinfold measures of body fat, with coefficients between 0.66 and 0.85 (Keys, Fidanza, Karvonen, Kimura, & Taylor, 1972). Garrow and Webster (1985) conclude that QI has been underrated as a measure of obesity in adults and that it provides a measure of fatness just about as accurate as specialized laboratory methods. The ranges of QI associated with various categories of obesity according to Garrow (1988) are presented in table 7.3.

TABLE 7.3   Classification of Ranges of Quetelet Index (QI) Values (Garrow, 1988)

Description	Grade	QI range
Underweight	—	Less than 20.0
Desirable range	0	20.0 - 24.9
Overweight	I	25.0 - 29.9
Obese	II	30.0 - 39.9
Very obese	III	Greater than 40.0

Other types of ratios that quantify body shape or morphology are classified as dimensionless because the units of measure in the two factors are the same and cancel each other out (Burton & Davis, 1996). Some examples are the ratio between bicristal (hip) and biacromial (shoulder) width and the ratio between waist and hip circumference. It has been suggested that the hip-to-shoulder ratio indicates the degree of masculinity in a person's physique (Tanner, 1951), while the waist-to-hip ratio has been used to quantify differences in female body shapes that may be related to fertility and long-term health risk (Singh, 1993).

A unique measure used to quantify physique is the somatotype, meaning body (*soma*) type. Sheldon, Stevens, and Tucker (1940) conceptualized a person's physique as having three components: endomorphy, mesomorphy, and ectomorphy. Endomorphy was characterized by softness and roundness of body contours, mesomorphy by predominance of muscle, bone, and connective tissues, and ectomorphy by linearity and fragility. Each component was rated on a 7-point scale with a 1 representing the least expression of the component, a 4 representing moderate expression, and a 7 representing the greatest expression. Thus, each person's somatotype is represented by three digits, such as 3-6-4 (endo-meso-ecto). Sheldon's method is based primarily on the visual inspection of photographs, but other methods, such as the Heath-Carter method (Carter & Heath, 1990), also incorporate some anthropometric measures. The standard somatotype chart, mapping the digit combinations across three axes of endomorphy, mesomorphy, and ectomorphy, is depicted in figure 7.3. The data in this figure reported by Hebbelinck, Duquet, Borms, and Carter (1995) show the longitudinal changes in somatotypes for two males (a) and two females (b) from 6 to 17 years of age.

An extensive list of publications with normative data on body size and morphology can be found in Malina (1995). Malina comments that the normative data used most often are the growth charts for height and weight for children 2 to 18 years from the Health Examination Survey (Hamill,

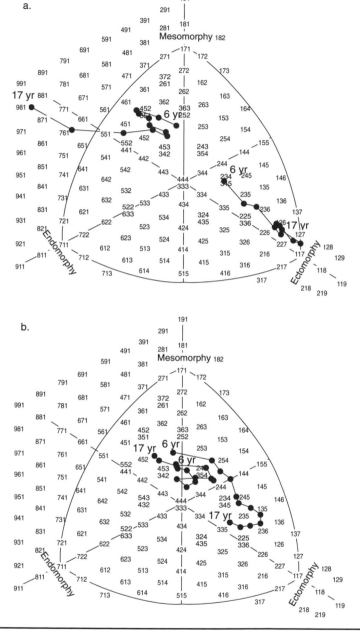

■ **FIGURE 7.3**   Yearly changes in somatotypes for two males (a) and two females (b) from 6 to 17 years of age.

From "Stability of somatypes: A longitudinal study of Belgian children age 6 to 17 years" by M. Hebbelinck, W. Duquet, J. Borms, & J.E.L. Carter, 1995, *American Journal of Human Biology*, 7, pp. 575-588. Copyright © 1995 by Wiley-Liss, Inc. Reprinted by permission of John Wiley and Sons, Inc.

Drizd, Johnson, Reed, & Roche, 1977) and the National Health and Nutrition Examination Survey (Hamill et al., 1979).

■ CARDIOVASCULAR FITNESS

Most exercise physiologists agree that the best index of cardiovascular fitness is maximal oxygen uptake ($\dot{V}O_2$max), as it represents the upper limit of aerobic exercise tolerance or aerobic power (Davis, 1995). Maximal oxygen uptake can be assessed directly by measuring the amount of oxygen consumed during a bout of maximum exercise, but often this is impractical because of the requirement for sophisticated equipment and trained staff, the expense, and the risks associated with exercise at a maximal level (Ward et al., 1995). Consequently some indirect methods of assessing aerobic power have been developed that may be placed into four broad categories: maximal tests, submaximal tests, field tests, and nonexercise procedures (Ward et al., 1995).

Indirect measures of oxygen consumption using maximal or submaximal tests are usually carried out while the subject is walking or running on a treadmill, cycling on an ergometer, or cranking an arm ergometer. The best-validated test for estimating maximum oxygen uptake, and the test most frequently used to diagnose coronary heart disease, is the Bruce protocol on a motor-driven treadmill (Bruce, Kusumi, & Hosmer, 1973). In the Bruce protocol, seven possible 3-min stages are made successively more difficult as the speed and grade of the treadmill are increased (from 1.7 to 6.0 mph and from 10% to 22%). The test is stopped when the subject reaches exhaustion. Then the time duration of the exercise—up to 21 min—is plugged into a population-specific equation to estimate maximum oxygen uptake (e.g., for sedentary men, $\dot{V}O_2$max = 3.778[time in minutes] + 0.19). Other popular protocols for estimating maximal oxygen uptake on a treadmill are modifications of the Balke protocol, which involve a constant walking speed but a 1% to 5% grade increase every 1 to 3 min until exhaustion is reached (e.g., Froelicher & Lancaster, 1974).

Cycle ergometers, which are less expensive and more portable than treadmills, may also be used to determine maximum oxygen uptake, but they yield lower values because they involve smaller muscle mass. In the protocol recommended by the American College of Sports Medicine (1991), subjects pedal at a constant speed while pedal resistance is increased every 2 to 3 min. Then maximum oxygen uptake is calculated from an equation including pedal resistance (mechanical power) and body weight. Similarly, arm-crank ergometers may be used to determine maximum oxygen uptake for persons with lower-limb impairments, but because an even smaller muscle mass is used than in cycling, the values obtained are approximately 20% to 30% lower than with a treadmill (Franklin, 1985).

A second way maximum oxygen uptake may be estimated indirectly is by having subjects perform at submaximal levels on treadmills, cycle ergometers, or arm-crank ergometers. Ebbeling, Ward, Puleo, Widrick, and Rippe (1991) recently developed a single-stage submaximal treadmill test that requires walking at a constant speed at a 5% grade for only 4 min. Heart rate, speed, age, and sex are used in the equation to estimate maximum oxygen uptake. In 1954, Astrand and Rhyming presented their classic nomogram, which graphically predicted maximum oxygen uptake by showing a line between values for heart rate and workload, with subjects performing on a cycle ergometer for 6 min at a constant velocity and constant workload. In the YMCA Cycle Ergometer Test (Golding, Meyers, & Sinning, 1989), heart rate is measured at two or three 3-min submaximal workloads, and maximum workload is extrapolated from these values and age-predicted maximum heart rate (220 – age). Then the maximum oxygen uptake corresponding with the calculated maximum workload is found.

Third, aerobic power may be estimated indirectly by having subjects perform without equipment that controls and measures workload. Compared to the methods just described, these types of tests are more practical for teachers and clinicians working in the field with limited equipment. Perhaps the best-known field test is the 12-min run for distance developed by Cooper (1968). In his initial study, Cooper (1968) found a .90 correlation between distance run in 12 min and maximum oxygen uptake in 115 male subjects with a wide range of fitness levels. Another field test estimates maximum oxygen uptake from an equation including time taken to walk 1 mi, heart rate, body weight, age, and sex (Kline et al., 1987). Step tests are also used in the field to estimate maximum oxygen uptake. For example, in the Queens College Step Test, McArdle, Katch, Pechar, Jacobson, and Ruck (1972) required subjects to step at a constant pace for 3 min and then estimated maximum oxygen uptake from the heart rate between the first 5 and 20 s of recovery.

Some field tests do not provide estimates of maximum oxygen uptake, but offer normative information to assist in assessing cardiovascular fitness. One example is Physical Best, a health-related fitness battery designed for children from 5 to 18 years of age, published by the American Alliance for Health, Physical Education, Recreation and Dance (McSwegin, Pemberton, Petray, & Going, 1989). The basic cardiovascular fitness item is time to run 1 mi, with norms for boys and girls from 5 to 18 years, although norms are also provided for time to run .5 mi (5-9 years) and 1.5 mi (13-18 years) and for distance run in 9 or 12 min (5-18 years). Other items in Physical Best measure skinfolds (body composition), body mass index (body size and morphology), sit and reach (flexibility/range of motion), and sit-ups and pull-ups (muscular strength and endurance). Recently, a handbook was published (Seaman, 1995) that describes and provides standards of alternate test items for individuals who may be unable to perform the regular Physical Best test items.

Some field tests are standardized only for persons with impairments. The Physical Fitness and Motor Skill Levels of Individuals with Mental Retardation project (PFMS) (Eichstaedt, Wang, Polacek, & Dohrmann, 1991) reports normative fitness data on 14 items from 4,448 boys and girls between 6 and 21 years who have mild mental impairments, moderate mental impairments, and Down syndrome. The two cardiovascular endurance items are the 6-min run for distance (for 6- to 11-year-olds) and the 9-min run for distance for (12- to 21-year-olds).

The Kansas Adapted/Special Physical Education Test (KASPET) (Johnson & Lavay, 1988), standardized on 200 children from 5 to 21 years who qualified for adapted physical education services, includes a cardiovascular fitness item in which examinees can move in any manner they choose to reach and maintain a heart rate between 140 and 180 bpm for 12 min after a 6-min warmup. They may run, jog, walk with vigorous arm action, propel a wheelchair, ride an exercise bike, or engage in other activities that raise their heart rates sufficiently. Norms are provided for the number of minutes the heart is maintained within the specified zone, as well as for the sit and reach (flexibility/range of motion), the bench press, holding a push-up position, and sit-ups (muscular strength and endurance). Data for both the PFMS and the KASPET also are available in the text by Eichstaedt and Lavay (1992).

Finally, a method of estimating maximum oxygen uptake without any type of exercise testing has been recently developed by Jackson et al. (1990). A physical activity status rating, along with age, sex, and percent body fat or body mass index, was found to accurately estimate peak oxygen uptake in a wide sample of male and female adults. The accuracy of this nonexercise method was limited in subjects with very high levels of aerobic fitness (top 4%), but overall was shown to be more accurate than submaximal exercise methods.

■ FLEXIBILITY/RANGE OF MOTION

Flexibility is defined as the range of motion of a particular joint (Maud & Cortez-Cooper, 1995). A particular joint is emphasized because flexibility is not a general characteristic of the body but is specific to individual joints (Dickinson, 1968). Thus, range of motion should be assessed for the joints most pertinent for the targeted performance or fitness component.

Flexibility can be measured directly or indirectly. Indirect measurement techniques usually involve the measurement of linear distances from one anatomical reference point to another or to an external object situated in relation to the body (Maud & Cortez-Cooper, 1995). Perhaps the best example of an indirect measurement technique is the sit-and-reach test. In this test, which is purported to assess hamstring and lower-back flexibility, subjects sit on the floor with legs extended and reach forward toward their toes. The measurement is the linear distance from the end of the fingers to the toes. Because indirect assessments of flexibility are measured in terms of linear distances rather than degrees of joint angle, they may be biased by differences in limb and trunk lengths. To control for proportional differences between arm and leg lengths, a modified version of the sit-and-reach test was devised in which a special box with a movable yardstick mounted on the top is placed over the feet (Hoeger, 1987) (see figure 7.4). With subjects sitting with their back and shoulders against a wall and arms extended toward the feet, the zero point on the yardstick is adjusted to the end of the fingers, and subjects then slowly lean forward with their fingers moving along the yardstick.

According to Maud and Cortez-Cooper (1995), three types of instruments are generally used to directly measure joint flexibility: (a) the standard goniometer, (b) the Leighton flexometer, and (c) the inclinometer. The most commonly used instrument, the goniometer, consists of two ruler-like arms joined together with a protractor at the joint to measure the angle between the two arms. The goniometer may have a semicircular or circular protractor marked in increments of 1°, 2°, 5°, or 10° and varies in size to accommodate joints of different shapes and sizes. The American Academy of Orthopaedic Surgeons published a text in 1994, *The Clinical Measurement of Joint Motion* (Greene & Heckman, 1994), which provides methods of measuring

■ **FIGURE 7.4**   Sit-and-reach box.

range of motion and average range of motion data for various joints. Other sources that offer information on measuring range of joint motion with a goniometer have been published by the American Medical Association (1988) and by Norkin and White (1985).

The Leighton flexometer, developed by Leighton in 1955, is composed of a weighted 360° dial and a weighted pointer in a circular case. The dial and the pointer move with gravity independently, but each may be locked at a particular position separately. The flexometer may be strapped to a segment to be measured with the dial locked at 0° at the extreme of the joint's range of motion. Then, after the segment is moved through the entire range of motion, the pointer is locked, giving a reading on the dial of the arc of motion. Specific procedures and normative data for the Leighton flexometer may be found in Leighton's (1987) user's manual; some of these are presented by Maud and Cortez-Cooper (1995). The inclinometer, also known as a clinical goniometer or gravity-and-compass goniometer (Hubley-Kozey, 1990), is essentially the same as the Leighton flexometer except that it is held by hand rather than strapped to a body segment (American Medical Association, 1988).

Direct measures of flexibility are usually applied to identify deficits in ranges of motion of particular joints or to determine alterations in ranges of motion due to chronic conditions, injury, intervention, or rehabilitation. The standard goniometer, the Leighton flexometer, and the inclinometer may give reliable measures of functional flexibility; but when assessing deficits or changes in ranges of motion, clinicians must consider that flexibility is affected by many factors including joint congruence, muscles, tendons, ligaments, fascia, joint capsules, and adipose tissue (Maud & Cortez-Cooper, 1995).

■ KNOWLEDGE/COGNITION

At least two types of knowledge may be applied in movement skill situations: declarative and procedural (Bouffard & Wall, 1990; Thomas & Thomas, 1994; Wall, McClements, Bouffard, Findlay, & Taylor, 1985). Declarative knowledge is factual information stored in memory, such as knowledge of the rules of a game, knowledge of the principles of Newtonian mechanics, or knowledge about how exercise or sport equipment works. Thomas and Thomas (1994) argue that declarative knowledge is "critical to expertise, and in fact, may be necessary before procedural knowledge can develop. However, since high levels of declarative knowledge is [sic] often present in novices, this does not seem to be the limiting factor in the development of expertise" (p. 304).

Procedural knowledge is knowledge of how to do things, such as how to perform a forward roll, how to rollerblade, or which base to throw to in a particular situation (Bouffard & Wall, 1990; Thomas & Thomas, 1994). Thomas and Thomas (1994) further explain that procedural knowledge is "if-then-do" knowledge; that is, when faced with a particular situation, one understands and then carries out the appropriate action.

Declarative knowledge can be assessed with pencil-and-paper tests or interviews, and procedural knowledge can be assessed with pencil-and-paper tests, interviews, or actual physical performance (Thomas & Thomas, 1994). For example, McPherson and Thomas (1989) assessed both declarative and procedural knowledge of tennis players by using pencil-and-paper tests and interviews after each point during a tennis match, and further evaluated procedural knowledge by coding game performance. French and Thomas (1987) used similar procedures to assess declarative and procedural knowledge of basketball players. Most items on written exams in physical education are designed to tap into a student's declarative knowledge base for specific sport or game activities

A unique nonverbal method of assessing declarative knowledge was developed by Reid and Todd (1988). They asked subjects to choose the most mature or most appropriate method of catching from a group of three or four pictures for 10 different aspects of catching, including arm/hand positioning, positioning of feet, and head/eye direction. They found that children who are physically awkward can be quite advanced in declarative knowledge without a corresponding sophistication in procedural knowledge.

■ MOTIVATION AND AFFECT

Many tests have been developed to assess the affective domain of physical activity. In the *Directory of Psychological Tests in the Sport and Exercise Sciences*, Ostrow (1990) lists and summarizes 175 tests, 110 of which relate to affect in sport and physical activity. These tests of affect, most of which were developed and used for research purposes, are related to achievement orientation, aggression, anxiety, attention, attitudes toward exercise and physical activity, attitudes/values toward sport, attributions, confidence, locus of control, and motivation in exercise and sport.

An example of an affect instrument is the Sport Orientation Questionnaire by Gill and Deeter (1988), which assesses the disposition to strive for success in competitive and noncompetitive sport activities. Another example is the Children's Attitudes Toward Physical Activity Inventory (Schutz, Smoll, & Wood, 1981), which assesses the perceived value held for physical activity by children. You can find additional information on the assessment of children's attitudes toward physical activity in Schutz, Smoll, Carre, and Mosher (1985).

Several tests have been designed specifically to assess movement confidence. One such test is the Movement Confidence Inventory (Griffin, Keogh,

& Maybee, 1984), and another is the Activities-specific Balance Confidence Scale (ABC) (Powell & Myers, 1995). The ABC evaluates a subject's fear of falling or confidence in performing 16 different activities, such as reaching on tiptoes or walking on icy sidewalks.

Perhaps the most well-known test of affect in the context of movement is the Ratings of Perceived Exertion (RPE) Scale by Borg (1970, 1982, 1985). In the standard RPE Scale, subjects estimate their own level of exertion in terms of numerical values from 6 to 20, which correspond to phrases like "very light" (9), "somewhat hard" (13), or "very, very hard" (19) (see table 7.4). Research by Borg and others has shown that these numerical responses times 10 estimate heart rate. In general, for a given heart rate, children tend to rate exertion lower than adolescents, and adolescents tend to rate exertion lower than adults (Bar-Or, 1993).

A test not listed in the book by Ostrow (1990) is Ulrich and Collier's (1990) Modified Version of the Pictorial Scale of Perceived Physical Competence, which is based on the physical subscale of the Pictorial Scale of Perceived Competence and Social Acceptance by Harter, Pike, Efron, Chao, and Bierer (1983). In this test, subjects match their self-perception of competence on 10 movement skills (e.g., jumping,, skipping, throwing, shooting a basketball) to pictorial choices.

Motivation or other aspects of affect influence a person's performance in any movement skill assessment situation. A supplementary section focusing on affect can be added to any test to help determine whether the performance was an optimal effort or whether affect appeared to limit the performance. For example, a test behavior inset is provided on the test form of the Denver II (Frankenburg, Dodds, & Archer, 1990). The first item

TABLE 7.4   The Borg Scale of Perceived Exertion

6 -	
7 -	Very, very light
8 -	
9 -	Very light
10 -	
11 -	Fairly light
12 -	
13 -	Somewhat hard
14 -	
15 -	Hard
16 -	
17 -	Very hard
18 -	
19 -	Very, very hard
20 -	

Adapted from Borg (1982).

in the inset asks whether the test performance was typical of the child's usual behavior, and the other four items allow the examiner to judge the child's compliance, interest in surroundings, fearfulness, and attention span.

Another example of a test with a supplementary section focused on affect is the Movement Assessment Battery for Children (MABC) Checklist (Henderson & Sugden, 1992). Four sections of the MABC Checklist are devoted to movement behavior, but a fifth provides information on "Behavioral Problems Related to Motor Difficulties" (also see information in chapters 11 and 12). Examiners rate 12 items, relating to behaviors such as passivity, tenseness, distractibility, overestimation of skill, or lack of persistence, as a 0 (rarely), 1 (occasionally), or 2 (often), but these scores are not summed. Instead, examiners classify the overall contribution of these behaviors to movement difficulties as high, medium, or low. The rater must consider not only whether the behaviors limit a child's movement performance, but also whether they should be taken into account in the development of an intervention program.

■ MUSCULAR STRENGTH AND ENDURANCE

Muscular strength can be defined as the maximal force a muscle or muscle group can generate against external resistance at a specified velocity (Kraemer & Fry, 1995; Malina & Bouchard, 1991). The external resistance may consist simply of gravity as one moves the whole body or one or more body parts, or it may be some additional resistance, such as a stationary or movable object. The velocity may be zero, as in an isometric contraction, or may be greater than zero, as in either shortening (concentric) or lengthening (eccentric) contractions. Muscular endurance can be defined as the ability to repeat or maintain muscular contractions over time (Malina & Bouchard, 1991).

There are five main approaches for testing muscular strength and endurance, with the differences based on how resistance is applied. Resistance may come from (a) body weight only, (b) free weights or other movable objects, (c) immovable objects, (d) exercise machines, or (e) manual pressure from another person. With each of these approaches, one must consider many factors in interpreting a subject's performance on a particular strength or endurance task (Kraemer & Fry, 1995). The factors may be divided into three categories: those related to the task itself, those related to the attributes of the subject, and those related to the surrounding environment. Examples of factors in each of these categories are presented in table 7.5.

The simplest approach to assessing strength is the use of tasks in which body weight alone is moved or held against gravity. Included in this category are calisthenic-type activities such as push-ups, pull-ups/chin-ups, sit-ups, leg lifts, bent-arm hangs, standing broad jumps, and vertical jumps. Normative data for these types of activities are summarized in most motor development texts and may be found in more complete form in resources such as the review chapter by Branta, Haubenstricker, and Seefeldt (1984) and the compilation of physical performance data presented by Roche and Malina (1983b).

Second, muscular strength may be tested by having subjects lift or move free weights or other movable objects. Free weights usually include barbells, dumbbells, Olympic-style weights, and weights attached to wrists or ankles. The purest measure of strength in this category is determined with a single-repetition maximum effort, often referred to as *1-RM*. Higher num-

TABLE 7.5 Examples of Factors That May Affect Performance on Strength or Endurance Tests

Category	Factor
Task	Single maximum effort or multiple repetitions
	Mode of muscle activity (isometric, concentric, or eccentric)
	Joint angle
	Specificity of task to functional behavior
	Movement velocity
	Required technique
	Pretest warmup
	Rest intervals
	Measurement/calculation:
	Reliability
	Units of measure
	Correction for body mass
	Normative data
Performer attributes	Sex
	Age
	Training status
	Joint range of motion
	Muscular balance
	Technique used
	Breathing patterns
	Familiarity with the exercise
	Arousal/motivation
	Ergogenics, or methods or devices used to improve performance
Environment	Temperature and humidity
	Other people present
	Feedback/encouragement

bers of repetitions may be used, but as the number of repetitions increases the task becomes more oriented toward muscular endurance. Objects other than traditional free weights also are used to assess muscular strength and endurance, particularly objects used by people in everyday functional activities. For example, in the New York City Physical Test for Fire Fighters (Andriuolo, 1993), examinees are required to move an 80-lb hose, a 60-lb ladder, and a 145-lb dummy (see figure 11.1, pg. 255). Other functional objects that might be used to assess strength or endurance are gallon containers of milk, 5-lb bags of potatoes, or 40-lb bags of water softener salt.

Next, immovable objects may be used to assess isometric strength and endurance. In this category of tasks, force is usually quantified with dynamometers, cable tensiometers, or force transducers interfaced with a computer (Kraemer & Fry, 1995). Besides maximum force exerted on the measuring device, other dimensions of strength and endurance may be examined. For example, the rate of peak force development as measured by time to peak force may reflect the physiological characteristics of various muscle fiber types (Sale & Norman, 1982); fatigue parameters, such as percentage of initial force after 30 s of effort, may reflect endurance characteristics (Kraemer & Fry, 1995). One of the main advantages of using isometric tasks is that variation in movement velocity is eliminated.

Fourth, movement tasks performed on various types of exercise machines often are used to assess muscular strength and endurance. The machines may be strictly mechanical, involving adjustable weight stacks or plates, or may be more complex, with hydraulic controls or electronic dynamometers interfaced with a computer. Tasks performed on mechanical units such as the Universal weight machines are quite similar to those performed with free weights except that the path of the movements is more constrained. Also, with cable and pulley arrangements, force can be exerted down, as in the "lat" pull, or horizontally, as in the knee flexion pull from a prone position. Other machines—for example, those produced by Nautilus—are equipped with cams that vary the angle of motion throughout the movement.

An important variable in strength testing is movement velocity, which is uncontrolled in most testing situations. However, some machines equipped with appropriate electronic devices, such as those manufactured by Cybex, can control and measure the velocity characteristics of the movements as well as force changes over time. Tests that constrain a lever arm to move at a constant angular velocity are called isokinetic (Sale & Norman, 1992). In the past, isokinetic testing was limited to concentric actions, but now there are units that accommodate eccentric movements. Some machines control movement velocity with hydraulic instruments, but they are not truly isokinetic (Kraemer & Fry, 1995). An extensive review of isokinetic muscle action and assessment has been contributed by Osternig (1986).

The last approach to assessing muscular strength involves subjects performing against pressure exerted manually by the examiner. This approach, widely known as manual muscle testing, is considered by physical therapists and rehabilitation specialists to be an important tool in the diagnosis, prognosis, and treatment of musculoskeletal disorders (Kendall, McCreary, & Provance, 1993). In manual muscle testing, the examiner uses qualitative criteria to judge the ability of a patient to develop muscle tension. Many grading systems have been published over the years, just about all of them based on the original scales by Lovett (1917). Presently, the most commonly used grading systems are those of Hislop and Montgomery (1995) and Kendall et al. (1993). The grading system of Kendall et al. (1993) is depicted in table 7.6. At lower grades (zero, trace), no movement is necessary; then as the grades go up, movement progresses from the horizontal plane (poor), to the vertical plane against gravity (fair), and finally to movement against

TABLE 7.6   Key to Manual Muscle Testing (adapted from Kendall et al., 1993)

Description	Grade	Symbol	Value
No movement			
No contraction felt in muscle.	Zero	0	0
Tendon becomes prominent or feeble contraction felt in the muscle, but no visible movement of the part.	Trace	T	T
Movement			
Moves through partial range of motion in horizontal plane.	Poor–	P–	1
Moves through complete range of motion in horizontal plane.	Poor	P	2
Moves to completion of range against resistance in horizontal plane; or moves to completion of range and holds against pressure; or moves through partial range of motion against gravity.	Poor+	P+	3
Hold test position			
Gradual release from test position.	Fair–	F–	4
Holds test position (no added pressure).	Fair	F	5
Holds test position against slight pressure.	Fair+	F+	6
Holds test position against slight to moderate pressure.	Good–	G–	7
Holds test position against moderate pressure.	Good	G	8
Holds test position against moderate to strong pressure.	Good+	G+	9
Holds test position against strong pressure.	Normal	N	10

manual pressure (fair, good, normal). In 1941, Kendall designed a handheld device that could be used to measure the force applied by the examiner during manual muscle testing (Kendall et al., 1993). Lamb (1985) points out that manual muscle testing grades are relative indexes of muscle tension and not absolute measures of force production, while Hinderer and Hinderer (1996) contend that the manual muscle testing grading scale is a measure too subjective, unreliable, and invalid to survive into the next century as the primary means of assessing muscle function by physical therapists.

Chapter *8*

Assessing Motor Abilities

© CLEO Photography

S defined in chapter 3, motor abilities are general traits or capacities of an individual that underlie the performance of a variety of movement skills. Understanding the differences between motor abilities and movement skills is important in choosing an appropriate assessment instrument and properly interpreting the results of an assessment, as well as in developing new assessment tools.

There are at least four key differences between motor abilities and movement skills. First, motor abilities are general traits underlying the

> ❝ Psychologists are essentially in the position of Plato's dwellers in the cave. They can know ability levels only through the shadows (the observed test scores) cast on the wall at the back of the cave. ❞
>
> — *Gulliksen (1961, p. 101)*

performance of several movement skills, while movement skills are specific, goal-directed movement patterns (Connolly, 1984). To illustrate, balance can be considered either as a motor ability or as a movement skill foundation (as seen in chapter 7). If balance is a motor ability, then a person's balance competence on many different movement tasks—such as walking a balance beam, riding a bicycle, running backwards, or jumping rope—should be essentially the same. But if balance is a movement skill foundation, then a person's balance competence on a variety of movement tasks will be different for each of these tasks, depending primarily on the amount of specific experience on each.

Second, motor abilities are usually identified through correlation or factor analyses, while movement skills are usually categorized by the space-time characteristics of movement patterns and/or the functions of the patterns. Third, the labels for motor abilities are usually subjectively derived from a researcher's speculation about the most salient common feature of the tasks contributing to an identified factor, such as balance or coordination, while the labels for movement skills identify specific classes of movement patterns, such as throwing or writing. And fourth, it is assumed that motor abilities are not easily modified by practice or experience (Connolly, 1984; Schmidt, 1982) and are relatively stable across an individual's lifetime (Keogh & Sugden, 1985), while movement skills are modified and improved through practice and experience, particularly during early stages of learning.

An assessment instrument that produces composite or summary scores for groups of related movement tasks can be considered to be a motor ability test when the interpretations of the scores are intended to extend beyond the specific skills included in the assessment. Performance scores on the specific tasks may be summed or combined in various ways to yield a score for each ability area—such as agility, balance, coordination, or speed—or a total composite score. The Bruininks-Oseretsky Test of Motor Proficiency (Bruininks, 1978), the Basic Gross Motor Assessment (Hughes & Riley, 1981), and the Movement Assessment Battery for Children Test (Henderson & Sugden, 1992) are clear examples of motor ability assessments.

Some assessment instruments organized by categories of movement skills, such as the Test of Gross Motor Development (Ulrich, 1985) and the Peabody Developmental Motor Scales (Folio & Fewell, 1983), also yield composite and summary scores. If interpretations of the scores are intended to extend beyond the specific skills included in the test, then the instrument should be considered a motor ability test. If the interpretations of the scores are confined to the specific skills included in the test, then the instrument should be considered a test of movement skills. One may gain information about specific skills from a motor abilities test if one interprets the scores on individual tasks separately.

This chapter begins with a review of the strengths and weaknesses of motor ability assessment instruments in general. Then I present in-depth reviews for the Bruininks-Oseretsky Test of Motor Proficiency (Bruininks, 1978), which is the motor ability test most commonly used in the United States, and the Movement Assessment Battery for Children Test (Henderson & Sugden, 1992).

■ STRENGTHS AND WEAKNESSES OF MOTOR ABILITY ASSESSMENT INSTRUMENTS

The major strength of motor ability tests is the reduction of information regarding the performance of several different tasks, usually involving several different movement skills, to one score or just a few composite scores. This minimizes the number of test manual tables needed to convert raw composite scores into norm-referenced scores and potentially simplifies scoring procedures for examiners. Also, the use of one score or just a few scores for the purposes of screening or determining eligibility or placement is direct, efficient, and attractive to practitioners and—if the examinees are children—to parents. Moreover, some tests that can be classified as motor ability assessment instruments use standardized scores very similar to the singular IQ, such as the Gross Motor Development Quotient (GMDQ) in the Test of Gross Motor Development (Ulrich, 1985) or the Developmental Motor Quotient (DMQ) in the Peabody Developmental Motor Scales (Folio & Fewell, 1983).

Another strength of motor ability tests is the availability of potential clues into general motor problems that may affect many different skills. For example, the suggestion that a person has a general balance or coordination problem may influence the way deficits in various skills are addressed in an instructional or therapeutic program. However, the validity of both of these identified strengths is contingent upon evidence that motor abilities do exist.

Accordingly, the greatest and perhaps fatal weakness of motor ability assessment instruments is the lack of empirical support for the existence of motor abilities. Many motor behavior researchers, including Adams (1987),

Burton and Davis (1992a), Connolly (1984), Davis (1984), Henderson (1987), Ragsdale and Breckenfeld (1934), and Seashore (1930), have noted this lack of evidence. Magill (1993) concludes that "although theoretical arguments continue about precisely how 'specific' motor abilities are, . . . the value of determining a person's general motor ability or capacity seems to be so limited that the use of such tests appears meaningless and of negligible value" (p. 267).

A related major weakness is that many designers of motor ability tests do not clearly define the constructs identified in their tests. The problem of defining constructs such as balance and speed abilities, fine and gross motor development, and even locomotor and object-control skill is exacerbated by a lack of understanding of what actually are the common features or aspects of the tasks used to assess a particular factor. As discussed in chapter 3, most motor abilities are subjectively labeled by researchers or test developers. Thus, the meaning of a sum of performance scores derived from a set of related movement tasks is usually quite vague and, in effect, uninterpretable. This interpretation problem also exists for tests that are organized in terms of movement skills but that allow for interpretations beyond the specific set of movement skills assessed.

Even when we assume that motor abilities exist, the specific uses may be quite limited. For example, if it is understood that motor abilities are not easily modified by practice or experience (Connolly, 1984; Schmidt, 1982) and that they are relatively stable across an individual's lifetime (Keogh & Sugden, 1985), then tests of motor abilities cannot be very sensitive to changes from instruction or development. There may be improvements or changes in specific movement skills, but these changes may not be reflected in a motor ability test.

■ REVIEW: BRUININKS-OSERETSKY TEST OF MOTOR PROFICIENCY

The Bruininks-Oseretsky Test of Motor Proficiency (BOT) was published in 1978 by Robert Bruininks. This test is one of many revisions of the original Oseretsky Test of Motor Proficiency, which appeared in Russian in 1923, was translated to Portuguese in 1943, and was translated into English from the Portuguese in 1946 (da Costa, 1946-1947) (see general historical review in chapter 2 and figure 2.3, p. 29).

According to Bruininks (1978), the BOT was designed to assess various aspects of fine and gross motor development. The recommended uses include (a) screening, (b) placement, (c) planning of instruction or intervention, (d) evaluation of progress, (e) evaluation of training programs and motor development curricula, (f) diagnosis of various developmental problems, and (g) research.

Bruininks-Oseretsky Test of Motor Proficiency (BOT)

Published by: American Guidance Service

Movement categories tested: motor abilities, fundamental movement skills, specialized movment skills

Uses: (a) make decisions abut educational placement, (b) assess gross and fine motor skills, (c) develop and evaluate motor training programs, (d) screen for special purposes, and (e) assist clinicians and researchers

Time to administer: 45-60 minutes for the long form; 15-20 for the short form

Price: The complete BOT test kit, including the manual, 25 student booklets, 25 individual record forms, and testing equipment, may be purchased for $419.95 (1996 price). The manual can be purchased separately for $67.95, packets of 25 student booklets for $22.95, and packets of 25 individual record forms for $22.95.

Contact: American Guidance Service
                4201 Woodland Road
                P. O. Box 99
                Circle Pines, MN 55014-1796
                (800-328-2560)

Bruininks-Oseretsky Test of Motor Proficiency

INDIVIDUAL RECORD FORM
Complete Battery

Robert H. Bruininks, Ph. D.

NAME _____

SEX: Boy ☐ Girl ☐ GRADE _____

CITY _____ STATE _____

SCHOOL/AGENCY _____

REFERRED BY _____

EXAMINER _____

PURPOSE OF TESTING _____

Arm Preference: (circle one)
    RIGHT   LEFT   MIXED

Leg Preference: (circle one)
    RIGHT   LEFT   MIXED

	Year	Month	Day
Date Tested	___	___	___
Date of Birth	___	___	___
Chronological Age	___	___	___

TEST SCORE SUMMARY

Complete Battery

SUBTEST	POINT SCORE Maximum Subject's	STANDARD SCORE Test Comosite (Table 23) (Table 24)	PERCENTILE RANK (Table 25)	STANINE (Table 25)	OTHER

The BOT is one of the most widely used motor assessments in adapted physical education, occupational therapy, and physical therapy. This is clear from the inclusion of the BOT in most reviews of motor assessment instruments in these three areas. According to a nationwide survey of adapted physical educators by Ulrich in 1985 (cited in Miles, Nierengarten, & Nearing, 1988), the BOT was the standardized motor assessment instrument most commonly used in adapted physical education. This was corroborated by a recent survey of adapted physical education practitioners in Minnesota (Waltman, Folsom-Meek, Bergerson, & Groteluschen, 1996), which indicated that 71% of the surveyed teachers used the BOT to assess students for service eligibility. Also, a survey of occupational therapists working in school settings in five northwestern states showed that they used the BOT more frequently than any other test except the Peabody Developmental Motor Scales (Crowe, 1989).

Test Structure

The long form of the BOT consists of 46 tasks organized into eight subtests. Four of the subtests are categorized under gross motor, three are categorized under fine motor, and the upper-limb coordination subtest stands alone. The short form of the BOT consists of 14 items, including at least 1 item from each of the eight subtests in the long form. The composition of both the long and short forms is depicted in table 8.1. The long form may be administered in about 45 to 60 min, and the short form in about 15 to 20 min.

TABLE 8.1 Structure of the Bruininks-Oseretsky Test of Motor Proficiency

	Number of items	
Area and subtest	Long form	Short form
Gross motor		
Running speed and agility	1	1
Balance	8	2
Bilateral coordination	8	2
Strength	3	1
Gross and fine motor		
Upper-limb coordination	9	2
Fine motor		
Response speed	1	1
Visual-motor control	8	3
Upper-limb speed and dexterity	8	2
Total number of items	46	14

Bruininks (1978) used 11 criteria to create a pool of 100 tasks, 30 from the 60 in the original Oseretsky tests and 70 additional tasks. An item analysis study reduced the items in the long form to 46, including approximately 40% from the Oseretsky tests. However, reviewers have noted that several of the final 46 items fail Bruininks' own criteria, particularly the criterion of measuring skills relevant to everyday tasks (Hattie & Edwards, 1987; Laszlo & Bairstow, 1985).

The complete scoring procedure for the long form involves nine steps (see table 8.2). In the scoring booklet (see figure 8.1), the raw scores (Step 1) are expressed in either time, number of units completed, number of errors, or just pass/fail. The raw scores are converted to point scores (Step 2) to appropriately weight the difficulty of each item. The point score sums for the subtests (Step 3) have maximum values ranging from 15 to 72, and are brought forward to the scoring booklet cover page (see figure 8.2). The subtest point scores are converted to subtest standard scores (Step 4) to equalize the weighting of the eight subtests. Then, the sums of the subtest standard scores (Step 5) are converted to gross motor and fine motor composite standard scores (Step 6) to equalize the weighting of the gross and

TABLE 8.2 Steps in Scoring the Long Form of the Bruininks-Oseretsky Test of Motor Proficiency (Bruininks, 1978)

Step number	Procedure
1	Raw scores recorded.
2	Raw scores converted to point scores and carried to right column.
3	Point scores summed to yield subtest point scores and carried to cover page.
4	Subtest point scores converted to subtest standard scores (M=15, SD=5).
5	Subtest standard scores summed.
6	Standard score sums converted to composite standard scores (M=50, SD = 10), with option for calculating composite standard scores separately for boys and girls.
7	Composite standard scores converted to percentiles and/or stanines.
8	Subtest standard scores converted to subtest age equivalents.
9	Composite age equivalents calculated as median value of subtest age equivalents.

POINT SCORES FOR COMPLETE BATTERY

POINT SCORES FOR SHORT FORM

1. Running Speed and AgilitySF*

Trial 1: _____ seconds   Trial 2: _____ seconds

Raw Scores	Above 11.0	10.9- 11.0	10.5- 10.8	9.9- 10.4	9.5- 9.8	8.9- 9.4	8.5- 8.8	7.9- 8.4	7.5- 7.8	6.9- 7.4	6.7- 6.8	6.3 6.6	6.1- 6.2	5.7- 6.0	5.5- 5.6	Below 5.5
Point Scores	0	1	2	3	4	5	6	7	8	9	10	11	12	13	14	15

SUBTEST 2: Balance

1. Standing on Preferred Leg on Floor *(10 seconds maximum per trial)*

Trial 1: _____ seconds   Trial 2: _____ seconds

Raw Scores	0	1-3	4-5	6-8	9-10
Point Scores	0	1	2	3	4

2. Standing on Preferred Leg on Balance BeamSF *(10 seconds maximum per trial)*

Trial 1: _____ seconds   Trial 2: _____ seconds

Raw Scores	0	1-2	3-4	5-6	7-8	9	10
Point Scores	0	1	2	3	4	5	6

3. Standing on Preferred Leg on Balance Beam — Eyes Closed *(10 seconds maximum per trial)*

Trial 1: _____ seconds   Trial 2: _____ seconds

Raw Scores	0	1-3	4-5	6	7	8	9	10
Point Scores	0	1	2	3	4	5	6	7

4. Walking Forward on Walking Line *(6 steps maximum per trial)*

Trial 1: _____ seconds   Trial 2: _____ seconds

Raw Scores	0	1-3	4-5	6
Point Scores	0	1	2	3

5. Walking Forward on Balance Beam *(6 steps maximum per trial)*

Trial 1: _____ seconds   Trial 2: _____ seconds

Raw Scores	0	1-3	4	5	6
Point Scores	0	1	2	3	4

6. Walking Forward Heel-to-Toe on Walking Line *(6 steps maximum per trial)*

Trial 1: [ ] = _____ seconds   Trial 2: [ ] = _____ seconds

Raw Scores	0	1-3	4-5	6
Point Scores	0	1	2	3

7. Walking Forward Heel-to-Toe on Balance BeamSF *(6 steps maximum per trial)*

Trial 1: [ ] = _____ seconds   Trial 2: [ ] = _____ seconds

Raw Scores	0	1-3	4	5	6
Point Scores	0	1	2	3	4

8. Stepping Over Response Speed Stick on Balance Beam

Trial 1: Fail   Pass   Trial 2: Fail   Pass

Raw Scores	Fail	Pass
Point Scores	0	1

*SF and the box in left-hand margin indicate Short Form items.

POINT SCORE SUBTEST 2 (MAX. 32)

■ **FIGURE 8.1**   One page in the scoring booklet for the Bruininks-Oseretsky Test of Motor Proficiency (Bruininks, 1978).

From *Bruininks-Oseretsky Test of Motor Proficiency* by Robert H. Bruininks © 1978, American Guidance Service, Inc., 4201 Woodland Road, Circle Pines, MN 55014-1796. Reproduced with permission of the publisher. All rights reserved.

TEST SCORE SUMMARY

Complete Battery

SUBTEST	POINT SCORE Maximum	POINT SCORE Subject's	STANDARD SCORE Test (Table 23)	STANDARD SCORE Composite (Table 24)	PERCENTILE RANK (Table 25)	STANINE (Table 25)	OTHER Age Equiv
GROSS MOTOR SUBTESTS:							
1. Running Speed and Agility	15	8	21				7-8
2. Balance	32	16	13				5-2
3. Bilateral Coordination	20	9	23				7-11
4. Strength	42	5	11				4-11
GROSS MOTOR COMPOSITE		68	*SUM	56	72	6	6-5
5. Upper-Limb Coordination ...	21	13	*21				6-11
FINE MOTOR SUBTESTS:							
6. Response Speed	17	5	16				6-2
7. Visual-Motor Control	24	18	23				8-5
8. Upper-Limb Speed and Dexterity...........	72	27	20				6-8
FINE MOTOR COMPOSITE......		59	*SUM	64	92	8	6-8
BATTERY COMPOSITE......		148	*SUM	63	90	8	6-9

*To obtain Battery Composite: Add Gross Motor Composite, Subtest 5 Standard Score, and Fine Motor Composite. Check result by adding Standard Scores on Subtests 1-8.

Short Form:

	POINT SCORE Maximum	POINT SCORE Subject's	STANDARD SCORE (Table 27)	PERCENTILE RANK (Table 27)	STANINE (Table 27)
SHORT FORM........	98				

■ **FIGURE 8.2** Test score summary for the Bruininks-Oseretsky Test of Motor Proficiency (Bruininks, 1978).

From *Bruininks-Oseretsky Test of Motor Proficiency* by Robert H. Bruininks © 1978, American Guidance Service, Inc., 4201 Woodland Road, Circle Pines, MN 55014-1796. Reproduced with permission of the publisher. All rights reserved.

fine motor composites. Finally, the composite standard scores may be converted to percentiles or stanines (Step 7), subtest age equivalents (Step 8), or composite age equivalents (Step 9). The normative data for the BOT were derived from a stratified sample of 765 persons based on the 1970 U.S. census.

Hattie and Edwards (1987) recommend exercising the option to calculate composite standard scores separately for boys and girls (in Step 6). They argue that Broadhead and Bruininks (1982) found sex differences in 11 of the 14 items in the short form and that Edwards (1983, cited in Hattie & Edwards, 1987) reported sex differences across all tests, particularly in running speed (favoring boys) and balance and bilateral coordination (favoring girls).

Reliability

Bruininks (1978) presented information on test-retest reliability and interrater reliability, but the interrater data were given only for the visual-motor control subtest. Test-retest reliability was examined by having 63 second graders and 63 sixth graders take the long form twice within 7 to 12 days. The Pearson product-moment (interclass) correlations for each subtest and composite, as well as the short-form scores, are presented in table 8.3. All except one of the composites and one of the short-form coefficients were .77 or above for both grades, but half of the subtest coefficients across both grades were below .70. Thus, subtest scores should be interpreted very cautiously.

Test-retest reliability information can be more directly evaluated in terms of standard errors of measurement. Table 8.4 shows the standard errors of

TABLE 8.3 Test-Retest Coefficients for the Bruininks-Oseretsky Test of Motor Proficiency

Score	Grade2[a]	Grade 6[a]
Subtests		
Running speed and agility	.66	.87
Balance	.64	.49
Bilateral coordination	.80	.80
Strength	.68	.89
Upper-limb coordination	.81	.29
Response speed	.58	.63
Visual-motor control	.80	.55
Upper-limb speed and dexterity	.89	.82
Composites		
Gross motor	.77	.85
Fine motor	.88	.68
Battery	.89	.86
Short form	.87	.84

Note: Bruininks-Oseretsky Test of Motor Proficiency by Robert H. Bruininks © 1978, American Guidance Service, Inc., 4201 Woodland Road, Circle Pines, MN 55014-1796. Reproduced with permission of the publisher. All rights reserved.
[a]n=63.

measurement for subtest, composite, and short-form standard scores. Given that the mean and standard deviation are 15 and 5 for subtest standard scores and are 50 and 10 for composite and short-form standard scores, the standard errors of measurement appear to cluster at about a half of a standard deviation (2.5 for subtest and 5.0 for composites).

If a sixth-grade girl received a standard score of 10 on the upper-limb coordination subtest (equivalent to the 16th percentile), the 68% confidence interval of her score would be $10 \pm (1)(3.6)$, or 6.4 (4th percentile) to 13.6 (39th percentile). The 96% confidence interval would be $10 \pm (2)(3.6)$, or 2.8 (<1st percentile) to 17.2 (67th percentile). Further, if a second-grade boy received a standard score of 40 on the gross motor composite (16th percentile), the 68% confidence interval of his score would be $40 \pm (1)(5.0)$, or 35 (7th percentile) to 45 (31st percentile). The 96% confidence interval would be $40 \pm (2)(5.0)$, or 30 (2 percentile) to 50 (50th percentile). The BOT should be used only if these or other sample confidence intervals are acceptable to the prospective user.

Validity

Bruininks (1978) stated that "the validity of the B-O Test is based on its ability to assess the construct of motor development or proficiency"

TABLE 8.4 Standard Errors of Measurement for the Bruininks-Oseretsky Test of Motor Proficiency

Score	Grade 2[a]	Grade 6[a]
Subtests		
Running speed and agility	2.9	1.7
Balance	3.0	3.7
Bilateral coordination	2.3	2.1
Strength	2.9	2.0
Upper-limb coordination	2.4	3.6
Response speed	3.2	3.3
Visual-motor control	2.7	2.1
Upper-limb speed and dexterity	2.0	1.9
Composites		
Gross motor	5.0	4.3
Fine motor	4.5	4.9
Battery	4.3	3.8
Short form	4.5	4.6

Note: Bruininks-Oseretsky Test of Motor Proficiency by Robert H. Bruininks © 1978, American Guidance Service, Inc., 4201 Woodland Road, Circle Pines, MN 55014-1796. Reproduced with permission of the publisher. All rights reserved.
[a]$n=63$.

(p. 28). To establish content validity, the eight subtests were compared to aspects of motor performance identified in six published works, such as the *Taxonomy of the Psychomotor Domain* by Harrow (1972), (see figure 3.3, p. 52). There was a reasonable match, but none of these cited works were directly concerned with motor development.

Bruininks (1978) attempted to establish construct validity by examining (a) the relationship of test scores to chronological age, (b) the factor structure of the 46 items, (c) differences in scores between children with and without disabilities, and (d) the intercorrelations between test items. First, subtest scores were expected to positively correlate with increasing age "since motor ability develops with age" (Bruininks, 1978, p. 29). This prediction was supported by Pearson product-moment correlations greater than .70 for both boys and girls on all subtests except balance (.56 for boys, .57 for girls).

Next, a factor analysis of the 46 items in the long form was expected to yield factor clusters matching the eight subtests in the BOT. Only five factors were identified, with one factor—labeled both "general motor development" (Bruininks, 1978) and "general motor ability" (Krus, Bruininks, & Robertson, 1981)—accounting for approximately 70% of the total common factor item variance. The other four factors related to Subtests 2 to 5: balance, bilateral coordination, strength, and upper-limb coordination. The absence of any fine motor factors indicates that the distinction made between gross and fine motor tasks in the test may not be justified (Hattie & Edwards, 1987).

Third, children with mild mental retardation, moderate-to-severe mental retardation, and learning disabilities were expected to score lower than children with no apparent disabilities. As predicted, children with mild (n = 72) and moderate-to-severe (n = 19) mental retardation scored significantly lower than same-aged children without disabilities on each subtest, the three composites, and the short form. Children with learning disabilities (n = 55) also scored significantly lower on each subtest and composite, with the exception of the response speed subtest. Hattie and Edwards (1987) suggest that the BOT be used with caution with children who have mental impairments because "it has not been demonstrated whether their lower performance is because of poor motor ability, lower intellectual performance, or a combination of these factors" (p. 109).

Fourth, the intercorrelations among subtests were expected to decrease with age because previous research suggested that motor abilities tend to become more differentiated with increasing age. This prediction was supported, also indicating that younger children perhaps could be given fewer items on the test than older subjects.

In addition, the use of the short form was validated by high correlations between the short-form and the total-battery (long form) composite standard scores (.80 for 4-year-olds, .93 for 8-year-olds, and .90 for 12-year-olds).

Verderber and Payne (1987) also found high correlations between the short- and long-form standard scores in a sample of 48 children, but reported significantly higher standard scores on the short form than on the long form, particularly for the younger children. As indicated in chapter 6, correlations provide an index of relative differences but are not sensitive to absolute differences (see figure 6.4). Because the short-form scores were taken from the scores for the total battery, the difference in scores could not be attributed to fatigue. Verderber and Payne (1987) concluded that "placement decisions in adapted physical education may vary depending upon which form of the Bruininks-Oseretsky Test of Motor Proficiency is used" (p. 58).

No data and no rationale are provided by Bruininks (1978) to validate uses of the BOT for evaluation of progress or evaluation of training programs and motor development curricula. Wilson, Polatajko, Kaplan, and Faris (1995) provide some information on these issues, and conclude that subtest point scores should be used to evaluate progress instead of standard scores because "standard scores will only reflect change that is faster than typical maturation, which is a rate of progress that few children with mild motor problems are able to achieve" (p. 15).

Summary

The most impressive aspect of the BOT is its great and sustained popularity throughout the United States and Canada. The familiarity of this test has created common ground between persons in different geographic locations and persons from various professional areas who are involved in the assessment of motor abilities and movement skills. However, the popularity of the BOT does not appear to be justified when the validity of its stated purposes is carefully examined.

The evidence supporting use of the BOT for screening or for placement decisions is weak. The most significant problem is the large confidence intervals within which the true score may lie when calculated from the standard errors of measurement. In addition, the bias of the long form for lower scores for younger children as compared to the short form poses a problem.

The BOT is purported to be useful for diagnosing various developmental problems and for planning instruction or intervention, but these are difficult to fulfill because low reliabilities on some subtests do not allow the subtests to be interpreted individually. Moreover, the absence of process data limits the potential for accurate detection of potential performance difficulties and effective program planning. Some of the other problems with attempting to use the test for these two purposes are that (a) the tasks and instructions may be too complex for children with mental disabilities, (b) the tasks do not accommodate children with physical disabilities, and (c) there is no justification for separating gross and fine motor scores (Hattie & Edwards, 1987).

The BOT also is recommended for evaluation of progress and for evaluation of training programs, but these purposes are incongruent with the focus of the test on motor abilities rather than movement skills. Motor abilities are enduring qualities that are resistant to change. A person may improve in the performance of specific skills, but this improvement may be masked by the use of general composite scores. Wilson et al. (1995) argue that subtest point scores are better measures of progress than standard scores, but that retest scores still must exceed the standard error of measurement limits in order for the examiner to be confident that the true score has actually changed.

Hattie and Edwards (1987) summarize their review of the BOT by stating:

> Clearly there is much need to improve many aspects of this test before it can be safely and meaningfully used. It has all the hallmarks of an early research version which is disappointing, given the long heritage of the Oseretsky test. The test has little value in providing dependable scores and any decisions based on the test are suspect. (p. 111)

It is important to note that the BOT, as one of the most popular motor assessment instruments, has been reviewed in many chapters, full-length texts, and articles but has rarely been strongly criticized. Not surprisingly, the article by Hattie and Edwards (1987) in the *British Journal of Educational Psychology*, one of very few papers to denounce the BOT, is hardly ever cited in reviews published after 1987. From the perspective of this book, the greatest problem with the BOT is its focus on phantomlike motor abilities, not real movement skills, a distinction that most persons who use and review these types of tests do not recognize or acknowledge. Ironically, the most attractive feature of the BOT is its neat and tidy quantification of motor proficiency into a single composite and eight ability areas. Until practitioners are convinced that motor abilities are mere specters, the BOT tradition will likely continue.

■ REVIEW: MOVEMENT ASSESSMENT BATTERY FOR CHILDREN TEST

The Movement Assessment Battery for Children (MABC), published in 1992 by Henderson and Sugden, represents the merging of two instruments developed by two independent groups of researchers and clinicians: the MABC Test and the MABC Checklist. In this review I focus on the MABC Test, and later (in chapter 11) I will discuss MABC Checklist in detail.

The MABC Test is rooted in the work of Stott and his colleagues in Canada and Great Britain on the Test of Motor Impairment (TOMI) (see figure 2.3, p. 29), which began with Stott's modification of the Oseretsky tests in the late 1960s (Stott, 1966; Stott, Moyes, & Headridge, 1968). The objective of the original TOMI was "to find a way of diagnosing what might be termed a subclinical spasticity, as found within the general school population" (Stott, 1966, p. 523). A standardized version of the TOMI, which offered reliability and validity data, was published in 1972 (Stott, Moyes, & Henderson). The Henderson Revision (Stott, Moyes, & Henderson, 1984) was standardized in Canada, the United Kingdom, and the United States and included four qualitative checklists. The MABC Test differs from the Henderson Revision only in scoring criteria and in the descriptions of the tasks in the manual.

The two components of the MABC—the Test and the Checklist—are designed to complement each other in the motor assessment process for children 4 to 12 years of age. For screening of children, identification of children for special services, and research purposes, either the Test or the Checklist may be used. For clinical exploration, intervention planning, and program evaluation, use of both the Test and Checklist is recommended.

The MABC Test is categorized under the heading of motor ability tests because of the emphasis on totaling impairment scores on individual items to evaluate the overall degree of motor impairment. Although the Test may be used to informally examine performance on particular items, the reliability and validity analyses are focused almost exclusively on total impairment scores.

The MABC has been available only for a short time and thus has not yet had a chance to become established as an assessment option for professionals interested in evaluating children with movement difficulties. However, the usage of various versions of predecessors to the MABC, in particular the TOMI (Stott, 1966; Stott et al., 1968; Stott et al., 1972, 1984), can be examined. From its inception in 1966, the TOMI has not been widely used in the United States. The TOMI was not mentioned in a survey by Lewko (1976) citing the 9 motor assessment tests most frequently used by occupational and physical therapists, physical educators, and other professionals working with children with disabilities, or in a survey by Ulrich (1984, cited by Miles et al., 1988) listing the top 11 standardized motor assessment instruments used by adapted physical educators. In a survey by Crowe (1989) of the developmental motor assessment instruments most commonly used by school-based occupational therapists in the northwestern United States, the TOMI was listed 12th and was reported to be used frequently by only 20% of the respondents.

Test Structure

The structure of the MABC Test can be conceptualized as an 8×4 matrix, with eight movement task categories crossed with four age bands, yielding a total of 32 age-appropriate tasks (see table 8.5). The eight categories

Movement Assessment Battery for Children Test (MABC Test)

Published by: Therapy Skill Builders

Movement categories tested: motor abilities, fundamental movement skills, specialized movement skills

Uses: MABC Test - (a) screen children for possible movement problems, (b) identify children for special services, and (c) research; MABC Test with the MABC Checklist - (a) clinical exploration, (b) intervention planning, and (c) program evaluation

Time to administer: 20-40 minutes

Price: The 1996 price for the kit, including all materials needed to administer the MABC, is $620. The test manual can be purchased separately for $87.50, and packets of 25 test forms can be purchased for $52.50.

Contact: Therapy Skill Builders
              (a division of The Psychological Corporation)
              555 Academic Court
              San Antonio, TX 78204-2498
              (800-211-8378)

Movement Assessment Battery for Children

Checklist

Compiled by Sheila E. Henderson and David A. Sugden

Name .... Gender .... Date of test ....

Home address .... Date of birth ....

.... Age .... Grade/year.................

School .... Assessed by ....

Section 1	Section 2	Section 3	Section 4	Total	Section 5 L M H (circle one)	Full Movement ABC assessment required	yes no (circle one)
....	+	+	+	=			

Section 1: Child Stationary/Environment Stable

0	1	2	3
Very Well	Just OK	Almost	Not Close

The child can:
1. Put on and take off articles of clothing without assistance (shirt, sweater, socks).
2. Stand on one leg in a stable position (when putting on trousers, skirt).
3. Tie shoelaces, buckle belt, fasten a zipper/buttons.
4. Demonstrate competence in personal hygiene (wash hands, brush/comb hair).
5. Demonstrate good posture when sitting or standing (at a desk/table, on a chair, in line).
6. Hold instruments using proper tension and grasp (scissors/pencil/en/paintbrush).

cover three primary performance areas—manual dexterity, ball skills, and balance—and the ages range from 4 to 12 years. According to the test manual, administration of the eight tasks to an individual takes between 20 to 40 min.

The first step in scoring each item is the recording of the raw performance score, or an F if the child fails to complete the item, an I if the task is inappropriate, or an R if the child does not cooperate. In the second step, the raw score is converted to a scaled score ranging from 0 to 5, with lower scores indicating better performance. The scaled scores match the following percentiles: 0 = 25 to 100, 1 = 15 to 25, 2 = 10 to 15, 3 = 5 to 10, 4 = 2 to 5, and 5 = 0 to 2. An F, I, or R is converted to a 5. In addition, qualitative observations are made about the child's movement performance, behavior, and any physical defects or difficulties.

A total motor impairment score, which can be converted into percentile form, is obtained by summing the eight scaled scores. A total impairment

TABLE 8.5   The 32 Movement Tasks in the Movement Assessment Battery for Children Test (Henderson & Sugden,1992), Organized by Age Band and by Task Category

Task category	Age band			
	4-6 yr	7-8 yr	9-10 yr	11-12 yr
Manual dexterity 1	Posting coins	Placing pegs	Shifting pegs-by-row	Turning pegs
Manual dexterity 2	Threading beads	Threading lace	Threading nuts on bolts	Cutting out elephant
Manual dexterity 3	Bicycle trail	Flower trail	Flower trail	Flower trail
Balls skills 1	Catching beanbag	1-hand bounce and catch	2-hand catch	1-hand catch
Balls skills 2	Rolling ball into goal	Throwing beanbag into box	Throwing beanbag into box	Throwing at wall target
Static balance	One-leg balance	Stork balance	1-board balance	2-board balance
Dynamic balance 1	Jumping over cord	Jumping in squares	Hopping in squares	Jumping and clapping
Dynamic balance 2	Walking heels raised	Heel-to-toe walking	Ball balance	Walking backwards

score of less than 10 is interpreted as "okay," greater than 10 as "motor impairment," and greater than 14 as "serious motor impairment" (Wright & Sugden, 1996). The sums for the three performance areas that match the 5th percentile and the 15th percentile also are given, but the authors suggest that these should be interpreted with caution. Performance differences between boys and girls are reported to be minimal, so only a single set of norms is provided. The behavioral observations are summarized in the question: "Would the behaviors noted have prevented the child from demonstrating his or her true motor competence?"

The examiner can step beyond the standardized procedures of the basic test to gain further information regarding a child's movement skills. Three specific test adaptations are recommended in the manual: (a) testing a child on the items for lower age bands; (b) providing a child with assistance, instruction, or feedback during performance of test items; and (c) modifying the conditions under which the test items were performed.

Reliability

The percentage of agreement on scores on the MABC Test between two testings, separated by 2 weeks, was examined on 92 children in Age Bands 1, 2, and 3, out of a total sample of 1,234 children from the United Kingdom. For the eight task categories, agreement was defined as the two scores falling on the same side of the 15th percentile criterion: above (a score of 0 or 1) or up to the 15 percentile (a score of 2 to 5). Of the 24 percentages calculated for the eight categories across three age bands, 19 were 80% or above, with a low of 66%. For total impairment scores, agreement also was defined in terms of the two scores falling on the same side of the 15th percentile. The percentages were 97% for 5-year-olds, 91% for 7-year-olds, and 73% for 9-year-olds. These results are difficult to judge because (a) percent agreement does not indicate the relationship between error and true scores, (b) corrections in percent agreement values were not made for a 50% rate of chance agreement (e.g., by using kappa), and (c) the proportion of children with expected movement problems included in the sample was not indicated. If a normally distributed sample was used, then 70% would score above the 30th percentile—not even close to the 15th percentile boundary—and would ensure a high agreement percentage.

In addition, test-retest and interrater percentages of agreement for total impairment scores on the Henderson Revision of the TOMI (Stott et al., 1984), for 360 children (60 for each age level) in the United Kingdom, were reported in the MABC Manual, even though the scoring procedures differ slightly from the MABC Test procedures. The agreement percentages were at least .70 between two testers and .75 for testing 1 month apart. Also, percentages of agreement of total impairment scores lying above or at or below the 5th percentile on two testings of 41 five-year-olds was shown to be 90%, with a kappa of .71 (Riggen, Ulrich, & Ozmun, 1990). Agreement percentages for total impairment scores in the .70s, especially when they are not corrected for chance agreement, are lower than expected from a reliable test.

Validity

Research on the validity of the specific purposes of the MABC Test has been limited to three studies. First, the correlation between the MABC Test total impairment score and the BOT (Bruininks, 1978) composite score was found to be −0.53 for 63 American children ranging in age from 4 to 12 years (Henderson & Sugden, 1992). When the children were divided into four groups, ordered according to impairment scores from high to low ($n =$ 14, 16, 18, 15), the group with the highest scores (i.e., poorest performances) had significantly lower BOT scores than the other three groups.

Next, two different groups of children that had been shown to have relatively high rates of movement difficulties were reported to have significantly higher impairment scores than children in control groups. In the test manual, Henderson and Sugden (1992) reported that 5- to 8-year-old, 9- to 10-year-old, and 11- to 12-year-old children with learning disabilities ($n - 139$) had significantly higher impairment scores on the MABC Test than children of the same ages in the United States standardization sample. Similarly, 482 four-year-olds from the United Kingdom whose birth weights were low had higher impairment scores than those specified in the United States norms on each of the eight tasks (Scottish Low Birthweight Study Group, 1992).

Other research addressing the validity of the MABC Test is cited in the manual, but these publications concern the TOMI rather than the MABC Test. With regard to criterion-related validity, correlations from .66 to .79 were reported between scores on the TOMI and the Draw-A-Man Test (Barnett & Henderson, 1992), the Perceptual-Motor Abilities Test (Laszlo, Bairstow, Bartip, & Rolfe, 1988), movement times in a coincident timing task (Henderson, Rose, & Henderson, 1992), and performance on a dressing task (Lam & Henderson, 1987). The agreement between the TOMI and the BOT in placing 5-year-olds above or below the 15th percentile was 88% (Riggen et al., 1990).

There have also been studies that have examined the extent of agreement between TOMI scores and subjective judgments of professionals in identifying children with movement problems. Children identified as having poor motor coordination by teachers (Henderson & Hall, 1982) and therapists (Barnett & Henderson, 1992) demonstrated significantly poorer performances on the TOMI than other children. The correlation between TOMI scores and judgments of teachers using a motor performance checklist for a group of children with learning disabilities was .88 (Lam &

Henderson, 1987); the correlation between TOMI scores and pediatricians' judgments of minor neurological signs for a group of 6-year-olds with low birth weights was .49 (Marlow, Roberts, & Cooke, 1989). After the TOMI was used to identify 16 children who were labeled "clumsy" and 16 controls of the same age and sex, a pediatrician, on the basis of a neurological evaluation of the children, agreed with the group placement of 30 of the 32 children (Henderson & Hall, 1982).

Other studies investigated the ability of the TOMI to differentiate groups of children known to exhibit high incidence of motor impairment. Lam and Henderson (1987) found that TOMI impairment scores of 7- to 10-year-old boys with learning disabilities ($n = 24$) were significantly higher than those of age-matched controls; Sugden and Wann (1987) reported that 36% of a group of children with learning disabilities ($n = 61$) scored below the 15th percentile on the TOMI. Also, 386 nine-year-olds who were diagnosed "at risk" at birth (Lindahl, Michelsson, Helenius, & Parre, 1988) and 58 six-year-olds with low birth weights (Marlow et al., 1989) were shown to perform more poorly on the TOMI than age-matched control groups.

Finally, the sensitivity of the TOMI to the effect of training was examined in two studies. Laszlo et al. (1988) reported that two groups of children with movement difficulties decreased their TOMI impairment scores after 2 weeks of kinesthetic sensitivity training, while two groups that received no training showed no significant improvement. In a doctoral thesis, Schoemaker (1992) identified 18 children with movement difficulties between the ages of 6 and 9 years on the basis of scores on the TOMI and two other instruments. After 3 months of no specific intervention, the children with movement difficulties showed no significant change in their TOMI scores; but after 24 sessions of physical therapy over 12 weeks, their TOMI scores significantly improved (i.e., went down).

Summary

Henderson and Sugden (1992) state that the MABC Test may be used for (a) screening or identifying children for special services and (b) clinical exploration, intervention planning, and program evaluation. I will discuss the usefulness of the MABC Test for these two sets of purposes separately.

First, for screening or identifying children for special services, the reliability of the MABC Test has not been adequately established. The only study cited in the manual included only 92 children, and it used percent agreement (not corrected for chance) for placing children below or above a 15th percentile cutoff. Assuming that a normal population was used, disagreements should have occurred only in about the bottom 30% of the population. Reliability and validity data from earlier versions of the TOMI were included in the manual, but these should not be considered in evaluating the MABC Test. In future reliability studies, the sample should be composed entirely of children who are suspected of having movement problems, and the kappa statistic should be used to correct for chance agreements.

The results of the three studies in which the validity of the MABC Test was examined did not offer adequate support for using the Test to screen children or to identify them for special services. The correlation of the Test with the BOT, although statistically significant, was fairly low (−.53), and the use of the BOT as a criterion test was somewhat questionable (see comments on the BOT earlier in this chapter). Also, even though children with learning disabilities and those with low birth weights scored significantly higher on the Test than other children, the incidence of definite movement problems in these two groups is not high enough to clearly validate the Test. A more convincing approach to establishing the validity of the Test for these purposes would be to compare impairment scores with the judgments of experienced professionals who have observed the children perform different movement tasks in a variety of situations, and to utilize two categories of scores or judgments (e.g., qualifies or does not qualify for special services).

Henderson and Sugden (1992) presented no empirical evidence that the MABC Test is valid for clinical exploration or intervention planning. However, the nonstandardized adaptations of the Test, such as testing at lower age levels, providing instruction or feedback, or modifying task or environmental variables, appear to be very useful for clinical exploration and intervention planning, regardless of the total scores. The manual presented one extensive case study showing how the Test and Checklist can be used to develop an intervention plan, but more information is needed. A starting point for establishing the validity of the Test for clinical exploration and intervention would be to report several case studies including information on how the Test was used to develop an intervention plan and a corresponding evaluation of progress using the Test, the Checklist, and other independent measures.

Earlier I cited evidence regarding the sensitivity of the MABC Test to 2 weeks of kinesthetic training (Laszlo et al., 1988) and 12 weeks of physical therapy (Schoemaker, 1992). These results are surprising given that the Test assesses motor abilities, which are relatively stable over time. Consider that during a period of intervention, a child may move into the next age band and be given a completely different set of movement tasks. Clearly, the usefulness of the Test for evaluating progress needs to be subjected to further study.

In conclusion, the MABC Test suffers from the weaknesses inherent in motor ability tests as well as from insufficient evidence of reliability and validity. However, the MABC Test has several unique features that enhance its usefulness for screening, intervention planning, and clinical exploration—in particular, the nonstandardized adaptations. Also, the Test is just part of an assessment battery which also includes a qualitative checklist.

Chapter 9

Assessing Early Movement Milestones

© Terry Wild Studio

THROUGHOUT this book, I use the term *early movement milestones* to refer to the locomotor and object-control skills that emerge before a child attains upright or bipedal locomotion. These milestones include rolling over, crawling, creeping, sitting, standing, walking, and object manipulation, which are performed in prone, supine, sitting, or hands-and-knees positions. Thus, the onset of walking, which occurs at an average

> " "The parts of our bodies learn to function as levers, beams, columns, and even structures like derricks and bridges as we learn to turn over in our cribs, to sit up, to crawl, to walk, and generally to support the weight of our own bodies as well as what we lift and carry. At first we do these things clumsily, but we learn from our mistakes. Each time the bridge of our body falls down, we build it up again. We pile back on hands and knees to crawl over the river meandering beneath us. We come to master crawling, and we come to elaborate upon it, moving faster and freer and with less and less concern for collapsing all loose in the beams and columns of our back and limbs. We extend our infant theory of structures and hypothesize that we can walk erect, cantilevering our semicircular canals in the stratosphere. We think these words in the Esperanto of babble, and with the arrogance of youth we reach for the stars. With each tottering attempt to walk, our bodies learn from the falls what not to do next time. In time we walk without thinking and think without falling, but it is not so much that we have learned how to walk as we have learned not to fall. " "
>
> — *Petroski (1985, p. 13)*

age of about 12 to 13 months, marks the transition from infancy into toddlerhood, and is considered to be the last early movement milestone and the first fundamental movement skill.

Most well-known assessments of infants' movements have been based on the neuromaturational theory of development as espoused by Gesell (1945) and McGraw (1945) (Piper, 1993). The key assumptions of neuromaturational theory are that (a) movement primarily is reflexive at birth, mediated by lower centers of the central nervous system; (b) with increasing age, the developing cerebral cortex inhibits the lower-level reflexes; and (c) the appearance of early movement milestones follows an invariant sequence (Piper, 1993). The majority of early movement assessment instruments have emphasized either neuromotor aspects, such as muscle tone, primitive reflexes, righting, equilibrium, and protective reactions (e.g., Chandler, Andrews, & Swanson, 1980; DeGangi, Berk, & Valvano, 1983; Fiorentino, 1981a; Milani-Comparetti & Gidoni, 1967), or the acquisition of early movement milestones (e.g., Bayley, 1969; Folio & Fewell, 1983; Gesell & Amatruda, 1941; Griffiths, 1954; Piper & Darrah, 1994).

This chapter focuses on infant assessments devoted primarily to early movement milestones. The first person to develop norms for early movement milestones was Gesell, whose work in this area goes back to 1918 (see the historical review for the years 1920-1945 in chapter 2). Gesell's normative descriptions provided the foundation for most tests of early movement milestones that have followed (Ames, 1989; Scarr, 1984), including the California Infant Scale of Motor Development (Bayley, 1935), the Bayley Scales of Infant Development (Bayley, 1969), the Denver Developmental Screening Test (Frankenburg & Dodds, 1967, 1969; Frankenburg, Dodds, Fandal, Kazuk, & Cohrs, 1975), the Denver II (Frankenburg, Dodds, & Archer, 1990; Frankenburg, Dodds, Archer, Shapiro, & Bresnick, 1992), and the Peabody Developmental Motor Scales (Folio & Fewell, 1983).

In a recent survey of 118 occupational therapists who worked with children from birth to 4 years, Lawlor and Henderson (1989) identified the 10 most commonly used standardized assessment instruments. For the 87 therapists who had used a standardized test in the past 3 months, the top 10 instruments, in order, were the following:

1. Miller Assessment for Preschoolers (Miller, 1988) (40% of the 87)
2. Peabody Developmental Motor Scales (Folio & Fewell, 1983) (36%)
3. Hawaii Early Intervention Profile (Furuno et al., 1985) (29%)
4. Bayley Scales of Infant Development (Bayley, 1969) (29%)
5. Gesell Developmental Scales (Knobloch, Stevens, & Malone, 1980) (23%)
6. Early Infant Developmental Profile (Rogers, D'Eugenio, Brown, Donovan, & Lynch, 1977) (21%)
7. Denver Developmental Screening Test (Frankenburg et al., 1975) (19%)
8. Movement Assessment of Infants (Chandler et al., 1980) (17%)
9. Beery Test of Visual Motor Integration (Beery, 1967) (16%)
10. Learning Accomplishment Profile (Sanford & Zelman, 1981) (13%)

For further information on infant neuromotor assessment, refer to recent reviews of selected instruments by Einarsson-Backes and Stewart (1992) and Palisano (1993a).

■ EARLY MOVEMENT MILESTONES

The most common and most available source of information on early movement milestones is early movement milestone assessment instruments, although other empirical work has been carried out independent of the issue of assessment. This research usually focuses on just one or a very limited number of skills, as opposed to the many skills included in most assessment tools. In the following sections I review recent research on early movement milestones in the areas of locomotion and object control.

Locomotor Milestones

In 1985, Largo, Molinari, Weber, Comenale Pinto, and Duc reported the results of a longitudinal study on the early locomotor milestones of 131 preterm (77 boys and 54 girls) and 111 term (56 boys and 55 girls) infants from Zurich, Switzerland. In the preterm group, 16 boys and 5 girls (16%) were diagnosed with cerebral palsy by the age of 6 months. Figure 9.1 pre-

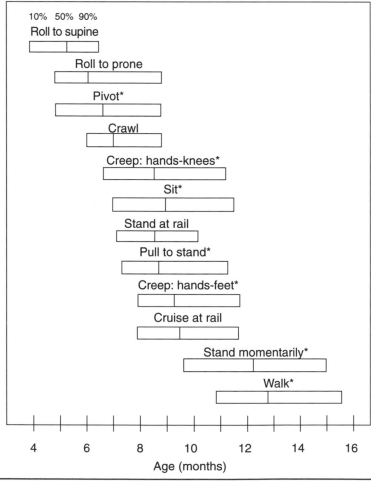

■ **FIGURE 9.1** Ages at which 10% (left vertical line), 50% (middle line), and 90% (right line) of term infants attained 12 milestones, from Largo et al. (1985). The asterisks indicate which milestones were significantly delayed for preterm compared to term infants.

sents the ages at which 10%, 50%, and 90% of the term infants attained 12 milestones.

Most of the milestones listed in figure 9.1 are self-evident, but several may require clarification. First, a pivot is defined as movement in a circular manner by the coordinated actions of arms and legs (Largo et al., 1985). Second, despite disagreement with some sources, crawling refers to prone locomotion with the trunk in contact with the supporting surface, while creeping refers to prone locomotion with the trunk elevated off the supporting surface (Haywood, 1993). Third, creeping on hands and feet is often considered a relatively rare movement pattern and is thus ignored in most motor development textbooks and early movement milestone assessments, but Hrdlicka (1931) has documented hundreds of manifestations of this pattern. And fourth, cruising is the sideways walking that a child does while holding on to a stable object for support (Largo et al., 1985).

In the study by Largo et al. (1985), the ages of achievement were not significantly different between boys and girls in either term or preterm groups for any of the milestones. However, the ages at which 7 of the 12 milestones were attained were significantly delayed for preterm compared to term infants, even when the span of their prematurity was subtracted from their chronological ages (see asterisks in figure 9.1). Surprisingly, achievement age for the preterm infants with cerebral palsy was significantly delayed compared to that of the other preterm infants only for the pivot.

A basic assumption in many early movement milestone assessments is that the sequence of milestone achievement is consistent across children. However, Largo and his colleagues provide some evidence contrary to this view. The various pathways to attaining the upright, bipedal pattern of walking are depicted in figure 9.2. A single pathway accounted for the locomotor sequence of 87% of all term and preterm children, but the variations shown by the other 13% cannot be ignored. Moreover, data from Bottos et al. (1989) indicate that children who demonstrate alternate pathways, such as shuffling only or just standing up and walking, do not show intellectual or language delays any more frequently than children who crawl or creep.

Unique aspects of a child's physical constitution or particular conditions in his or her home may influence this sequencing of early locomotor behaviors. In an early paper on locomotor milestones, Trettien (1900) reported that 30% of a sample of 150 infants used "hitching," or scooting forward on their bottoms, as a primary mode of locomotion. One explanation given by Trettien (1900) for the substitution of the "less natural and less useful" hitching for creeping was the "hampering influence of long skirts and the practice of keeping babies off the floor" (p. 33). The delay of locomotor milestones from restrictive clothing has been noted recently in Japanese infants by Hayashi (1992).

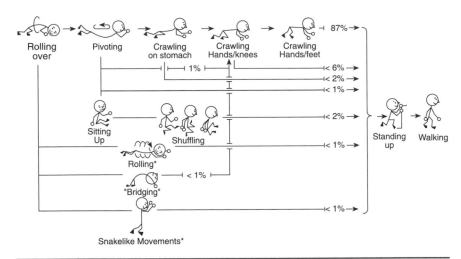

■ FIGURE 9.2 Pathways to locomotion of term and preterm infants, with asterisks indicating infants with cerebral palsy only.

From "Early Development of Locomotion: Significance of Prematurity, Cerebral Palsy and Sex," by R.H. Largo, L. Molinari, M. Weber, L. Comenale Pinto, and G. Duc, 1985, Developmental Medicine and Child Neurology, 27, p. 187. Copyright 1985 by MacKeith Press. Reprinted by permission.

Differences in a child's early experiences dictated by climate changes also may account for variations in locomotor milestones. From a sample of 425 infants in Denver, Colorado, Benson (1993) observed that those born in the summer or fall began to crawl about 3 weeks later than those born in the winter or spring. Perhaps the most compelling explanation for this difference is that infants born in the summer or fall enter the "window of locomotor readiness" from November to April when the weather and other related factors are likely to discourage mobility. Hayashi (1990) also reported a relationship between seasonal temperature changes and the gross motor development of the infant.

Other factors that may potentially affect the timing or sequence of an infant's locomotor milestones include (a) cultural variations in parental care and expectations (Cintas, 1995); (b) limited opportunities to freely explore support surfaces and large objects, as may occur with extensive use of a baby walker (Crouchman, 1986); (c) sensory impairments, such as limited vision (Troster & Brambring, 1993); (d) mental impairments, such as Down syndrome (Chen & Wooley, 1978); and (e) physical impairments, such as cerebral palsy (Bottos, Puato, Vianello, & Facchin, 1995) or spina bifida (Findley et al., 1987). In table 9.1, the effect of cerebral palsy on the use and onset of various locomotor behaviors is shown (compare with the data for other children in figure 9.1).

TABLE 9.1   Locomotor Patterns Preceding Independent Walking of 138 Children
With Cerebral Palsy (from Bottos et al., 1995)

Pattern	Percent	Onset age (months)	Percent achieving walking
Bottom shuffling	8	12-26	100
Bunny hopping[a]	7	24-96	56
Crawling only	8	18-144	0
Creeping only	29	8-42	98
Crawling and creeping	17	13-72	67
Rolling only	5	30-72	0
Walking only	11	14-108	100
No mobility	15	—	0

[a]From prone position on hands and knees, children used a sudden extenstion of the hips to thrust the legs forward.

Object-Control Milestones

The object-control milestones given the most attention in movement assessments are usually reaching and grasping. On the basis of a detailed longitudinal analysis of four infants, Thelen, Corbetta, Kamm, Schneider, and Zernicke (1993) concluded that reaching emerges from a confluence of "the ability to visually locate the toy in space, intention to reach and grab the toy and transport it to the mouth, growing control of the head and trunk, and the increasing ability to modulate the force and compliance of the arms" (p. 1093). The authors suggested further that learning to control the arms to get the hand near the desired object was primarily through haptic and proprioceptive information, not visual information (see also Clifton, Muir, Ashmead, & Clarkson, 1993).

Rochat (1992) observed that when infants first begin to reach for an object or bring an object to the mouth at around 2 months of age, they usually use symmetrical actions of both arms and hands meeting at the midline. As they get older, Rochat found that infants shift primarily to an asymmetrical, lateralized reach. Rochat (1992) argues that infants are not able to utilize the more adaptable lateralized reach until they are able to maintain a sitting posture.

The foundation of our understanding of the development of grasp patterns is Halverson's classic research. In his 1931 paper, Halverson presented a "genetic series" of 10 patterns used to grasp a 1-in. cube, as illustrated in figure 9.3. He felt that the age-related changes in these grasping patterns resulted from the maturation of the neuromuscular system and the growth of the arm, hand, and digits.

No contact (16 months)

Contact only (20 months)

Primitive squeeze (20 months)

Squeeze grasp (24 months)

Hand grasp (28 months)

Palm grasp (28 months)

Superior-palm grasp
(32 months)

Inferior-forefinger grasp
(36 months)

Forefinger grasp (52 months)   Superior-forefinger grasp (50 months)

■ **FIGURE 9.3**   Ten patterns used to grasp a 1-in. cube and the ages at which the patterns are demonstrated.

From Genetic Psychology Monographs, 10, 212-215, 1931. Reprinted with permission of the Helen Dwight Reid Educational Foundation. Published by Heldref Publications, 1319 Eighteenth Street N.W., Washington, DC 20036-1802. Copyright © 1931.

Some recent work by Newell and his colleagues questioning Halverson's interpretations is particularly relevant to the assessment of grasping patterns in young children (Newell, McDonald, & Baillargeon, 1993; Newell, Scully, Tenenbaum, & Hardiman, 1989). Newell et al. (1993) found that infants as young as 5 to 6 months, as well as adults, added more digits to their grasping patterns in a similar manner as object size increased. On the basis of their results, the authors suggested that there are common ratios of object to hand size that define the boundaries of particular grasp configurations for infants through adults. Thus, "the rigidity of the order and regularity in infant grip configurations as proposed in maturational (Halverson, 1931) or cognitive accounts (Connolly & Elliott, 1972) of prehension is as much, if not more, due to the particular constraints imposed by the experimenter on the infant than they are limitations of the infant per se" (Newell et al., 1993, p. 204).

■ PURPOSES OF EARLY MOVEMENT MILESTONE ASSESSMENT INSTRUMENTS

There are a variety of reasons for assessing early movement milestones in infants, including (a) screening for current problems or the prediction of future problems, (b) determining the necessity and/or eligibility for intervention programs, (c) planning an intervention program, and (d) evaluating changes in an infant's movement status over time.

Screening and Prediction

Many tests are available that are designed to identify young children who may have some type of developmental problem or may be at risk for a problem in the future. Several domains of behavior are usually assessed in these tests, including the motor domain. Some examples of screening tests are the Battelle Developmental Inventory Screening Test (Newborg, Stock, Wnek, Guidubaldi, & Svinicki, 1984), the Denver Developmental Screening Test (Frankenburg & Dodds, 1967, 1969), the Developmental Indicators for Assessment of Learning—Revised (Mardell-Czudnowski & Goldenberg, 1983), and the Infant Monitoring System (Bricker & Squires, 1989).

However, the effectiveness of developmental screening tests in identifying current problems or predicting future outcomes has been seriously questioned. Dworkin (1989a) notes that "the failure of research to validate the effectiveness and benefits of developmental screening has resulted in a growing skepticism toward the routine administration of developmental tests" (p. 620). The assessment of "normal" development in infancy is complicated by the range of acceptable variations of behavior and by the dependency of behavior on the particular task context and the state of the infant (Felt & Stancin, 1991). Moreover, Campbell (1993b) states that "the bulk of the literature on assessment in infancy suggests that very little regarding outcome in later years can be successfully predicted for individual children and certainly not from typical developmental assessment scales" (pp. 293-294).

An alternative approach to identifying current problems is developmental surveillance. According to Dworkin (1989b), surveillance is a broader concept than screening, emphasizing the ongoing monitoring of children and identification of the concerns of parents. Surveillance is a flexible process, involving information provided by health professionals, education professionals, parents, and others. The administration of standardized assessments may be included in surveillance but is only one potential component in the process. This shift from screening to surveillance is reflected in the recent revision of the Denver Developmental Screening Test (Frankenburg & Dodds, 1967, 1969). With regard to the new Denver II, Frankenburg et al. (1992) acknowledge that it should be used as part of the surveillance of a child's continuing development, not as a singular, isolated screening test, and that the results should be interpreted in the context of the child's family, community, and cultural contexts.

When dealing with preterm infants, development screening or even the process of surveillance may be muddled further by the decision whether to use chronological age or an age adjusted for prematurity. The use of chronological ages may result in the referral of too many infants for further assessment and in undue parental anxiety, while the use of adjusted ages may lead to an underreferral of children who need special attention. On the basis of his comparison of forty-six 12-, 15-, and 18-month-old preterm and full-term infants on the Peabody Developmental Motor Scales (PDMS) (Folio & Fewell, 1983), Palisano (1986b) recommended that full age adjustments for prematurity should be made at least up to 18 months. After comparing 555 preterm infants with the norms on the standard Dutch neurodevelopmental assessment over a period of 2 years, Den Ouden, Rijken, Brand, Verloove-Vanhorick, and Ruys (1991) concluded that a full correction is justified in the first year but that no correction is necessary in the second year. The adjustment decision may need to be slightly different for each assessment instrument.

Determining Program Eligibility

A second reason for assessing early movement milestones in infants is to determine the necessity and/or eligibility for intervention programs. These decisions may be based only on the results of a screening instrument, but should be based on the results on more comprehensive evaluations of a child's developmental status, such as the Bayley Scales of Infant Development (BSID)

(Bayley, 1969), the newer Bayley-II (Bayley, 1993), or the PDMS. The BSID has been used as the standard against which other early movement milestone assessments are validated, but is not likely to be used as a screening instrument because of the administration time and administration skill requirements.

Intervention Planning

Once an infant has been entered into an intervention program, the goals and objectives of the program must be established. Information from the assessments used to determine program eligibility, such as the BSID or PDMS, sometimes may be used for planning; but instruments focusing on more qualitative aspects of the infant's motor status may be more appropriate for this purpose. The instruments that offer more qualitative information, such as the Movement Assessment of Infants (MAI) (Chandler et al., 1980) and the Posture and Fine Motor Assessment of Infants (PFMAI) (Case-Smith, 1991), emphasize neuromotor items more than movement skill milestones.

Evaluating Progress

Finally, the changes in an infant's movement status over time may need to be assessed to monitor the effect of an intervention program or as a part of developmental surveillance. Again, assessments designed primarily for screening may be used for this purpose, but they are likely to be less sensitive to motor changes than more comprehensive instruments (e.g., the BSID or PDMS) or more qualitative instruments (e.g., the MAI or the PFMAI).

Some early movement milestone assessment instruments have been specifically developed to document change. The Gross Motor Function Measure (GMFM) (Russell et al., 1989; Russell, Rosenbaum, Lane, Gowland, Goldsmith, Boyce, & Plews, 1994), composed of 85 items of which about 90% can be considered early movement milestones, is such an instrument. The ability of the GMFM to detect change in children with cerebral palsy was validated by significant correlations between change in GMFM total scores and changes in parent ratings and physiotherapist ratings.

An alternative to using norm-referenced tests to evaluate change—goal attainment scaling (GAS)—has been used in mental health, rehabilitation, and special education settings since 1968 when it was introduced by Kiresuk and Sherman. In GAS, instead of the usual single behavioral objective, five behavioral outcomes are specified: the expected level of attainment (a score of 0), two more favorable outcomes (+1 and +2), and two less favorable outcomes (–1 and –2). Thus, GAS should be more sensitive to change than traditional behavioral objectives and allow calculation of composite measures of change for more than one goal. However, the responsiveness of GAS depends on the instructor's or therapist's selecting outcomes that represent clinically meaningful change and that are attainable by the student or client (Palisano, 1993b; Palisano, Haley, & Brown, 1992). In comparing the results of this method with results on the PDMS (Folio & Fewell, 1983) for infants with developmental delays, Palisano et al. (1992) found that GAS measured change in specific postures and movements that were directly related to the goals of intervention, while the PDMS provided a more global measure of change in motor development.

■ REVIEW: PEABODY DEVELOPMENTAL MOTOR SCALES

The present version of the PDMS was published in 1983 by Folio and Fewell, although it was preceded by earlier versions dating back to 1973, 1974, and 1979 (Venn, 1986). The scales were developed to "determine the relative developmental skill level of a child, identify skills that were not completely developed or not in the child's repertoire, and then plan an instructional program to develop those skills" (Folio & Fewell, 1983, p. 1). In addition, the PDMS was designed to accommodate children with severe disabilities.

The PDMS is a standardized, norm-referenced test that measures gross and fine motor attributes of children from birth through 6 years 11 months of age. The authors note that the PDMS, consisting of 170 gross motor and 112 fine motor items, also may be used as a criterion-referenced measure of motor patterns and skills. If the PDMS is used as a norm-referenced test, then the resulting composite scores represent motor abilities, because the interpretations of these scores are intended to extend beyond the specific skills included in the assessment (see chapter 8). However, if the PDMS is used as a criterion-referenced test, then it assesses early movement milestones and fundamental movement skills.

Besides the assessment instrument itself, the PDMS includes a set of 282 activity cards to help practitioners set specific movement objectives and identify appropriate intervention strategies. Each card specifies a behavioral objective matching the criterion for one of the 170 gross motor or 112 fine motor test items, as well as several strategies that can be used to help the children achieve the objective.

Folio and Fewell (1983) contend that the PDMS can be used for a variety of purposes, including (a) screening, (b) determining the necessity of and/or eligibility for intervention programs, (c) planning an intervention program, and (d) evaluating changes over time. Eight specific uses, categorized by these purposes, are listed in table 9.2.

Peabody Developmental Motor Scales (PDMS)

Published by: PRO-ED

Movement categories tested: motor abilities, early movement milestones, fundamental movement skills

Uses: (a) identify children whose skills are delayed or aberrant relative to a normative group, (b) determine the necessity and/or eligibility for intervention programs, (c) plan an intervention program, and (d) evaluate changes over time

Time to administer: 20-30 minutes for each scale, for a total of about 45-60 minutes

Price: The PDMS, with 10 of the 34 materials required to administer the test along with the corresponding activity cards, can be purchased for $243. Items that can be purchased separately are the assessment kit without the activity cards ($206), the test manual only ($45), and packets of 15 scoring booklets ($28.50).

Contact: PRO-ED
               8700 Shoal Creek Boulevard
               Austin, TX 78757-6897
               (512-451-3246)

Peabody Developmental Motor Scales
Response/Scoring Booklet

	Yr.	Mo.	Day
Date of Testing			
Date of Birth			
Chronological Age			
Age in months			

Name _____
Educational Program _____
Examiner _____
Examination Center _____

SUMMARY

	Gross Motor	Fine Motor
Basal Age Level		
Ceiling Age Level		
Scaled Score		
Age Equivalant		
Mean Motor Age Equivalant		

GROSS-MOTOR SCALE

	Raw Score	Percentile	z-score T score	Developmental Motor Quotient
Skill A - Reflexes				
Skill B - Balance				
Skill C - Nonlocomotor				

TABLE 9.2 Specific Uses of the Peabody Developmental Motor Scales According to Folio and Fewell (1983), Organized by Categories of Purposes

Purpose	Use
Screening	Identifying children whose gross and fine motor skills are delayed or aberrant relative to normative group.
Program eligibility	Permit an in-depth analysis of a wide range of gross and fine motor skills that may have been identified as questionable by prior screening or by observation.
Program eligibility Intervention planning	Enable the examiner to obtain knowledge about the skills a child has mastered, those currently developing, and those not in the child's repertoire.
Program eligibility Intervention planning	Permit analysis of the characteristics of a gross and/or fine motor problem and a comparison of a child's performance in gross and fine motor skills.
Intervention planning	Enable the examiner to identify a child's unique strengths and deficits and determine ways to use strengths to develop weaker areas.
Intervention planning	Enable the examiner to identify skills that should be included in a child's IEP.
Evaluate progress	Enable the examiner to measure performance across time or before and after intervention.
Evaluate progress	Provide a scoring system that enables the examiner to measure changes that are quite small and thus not likely to be detected using traditional measures expressed in months.

Test Structure

The first version of the PDMS, published in 1973, consisted of a combination of newly developed items and items drawn from a number of existing, validated motor development scales. In the most recent version of the PDMS (1983), 170 items in the Gross Motor (GM) Scale were divided equally across 17 age levels, while 112 items of the Fine Motor (FM) Scale were divided across 16 age levels, with 6 to 8 items at each level. The gross motor and fine motor items were designed to require precise movements of the body's large muscles and small muscles, respectively. The items were organized further into skill categories: five for the GM Scale and four for the FM Scale. The number of items at each age-skill combination is presented in table 9.3 for the GM Scale and in table 9.4 for the FM Scale.

TABLE 9.3 Number of Items in the Gross Motor Scale of the PDMS (Folio & Fewell, 1983) by Age Group and Skill Category

Age (months)	Reflexes	Balance	Non-locomotor	Locomotor	Receipt and propulsion
0-1	7		3		
2-3	3		7		
4-5		3	7		
6-7	1	2	5	2	
8-9	1	1	5	3	
10-11		3	4	3	
12-14		3		5	2
15-17		1		7	2
18-23		2	1	5	2
24-29		3		5	2
30-35		2	1	5	2
36-41		1	7	2	
42-47		3		2	5
48-53		2	2	5	1
54-59		3	2	3	2
60-71		2	2	4	2
72-83		2	3	2	3

TABLE 9.4 Number of Items in the Fine Motor Scale of the PDMS (Folio & Fewell, 1983) by Age Group and Skill Category

Age (months)	Grasping	Hand use	Eye-hand coordination	Manual dexterity
0-1	2	1	3	
2-3	4		4	
4-5	5	2	1	
6-7	3	4	1	
8-9	3	5		
10-11	1	3	3	1
12-14	2	3	2	1
15-17	1	2	5	
18-23		1	4	3
24-29		2	3	1
30-35		1	4	1
36-41		2	2	2
42-47	1		4	1
48-59			4	2
60-71			2	4
72-83			4	2

For each item in the test, a performance criterion is specified. The criteria for five gross motor items at 10 to 11 months and three fine motor items at 36 to 41 months are presented in table 9.5. Each item is scored relative to the performance criterion: A score of 0 indicates that the child cannot or will not attempt the item or that the attempt does not show that the skill is emerging; a score of 1 indicates that the child's performance clearly resembles the criterion, but does not fully meet it; and a score of 2 indicates that the child meets the criterion. Although this 3-point scoring system potentially may be more sensitive to changes in a child's performance than a *yes/no* system, the lack of specific criteria for a score of 1 may lead to inadequate reliability (Hinderer, Richardson, & Atwater, 1989; Palisano, 1993a).

The administration of both scales of the PDMS should begin one age level below the child's expected motor age, which is usually best estimated by the child's chronological age. If the child scores a 0 or 1 on two items at this level, the testing goes down one level. This stepping down continues until the level criterion is achieved. Thus, basal age level is defined as the first level at which a 2 is scored on all items, or the level below the first level at which a 0 or 1 is scored on only one item and a 2 is scored on the remaining items. Then, the testing steps up to the ceiling age level, which is defined as the level at which a 0 or 1 is scored on all items or a 2 is scored on only one item. This procedure, in which each level of the scales from

TABLE 9.5   Criteria for Selected Items in the Gross and Fine Motor Scales of the PDMS (from Folio & Fewell, 1983)

Scale/ item number/ item	Criteria
Gross Motor Scale:	**10-11 months**
52. Sitting up	Raises to sitting position: 1 of 2 trials
54. Pivoting	Pivots around 180° in circular pattern on buttocks: 1 of 2 trials
56. Lowering	Lowers self to sitting position without falling: 1 of 2 trials
58. Standing	Frees hand and body of support and maintains balance in standing position for 3 s: 1 of 2 trials
60. Walking	Takes 4 alternating steps forward
Fine Motor Scale:	**36-41 months**
84. Removing cap	Removes cap within 30 s after bottle is presented
86. Winding toy	Turns key 90° in one turn
88. Copying across	Draws intersecting straight lines within 20° of perpendicular

basal to ceiling is administered completely, takes about 20 to 30 min for each scale, for a total of about 45 to 60 min.

Once the criterion-reference scores have been recorded, the data can be transformed in various ways. The various types of scores that can be determined are indicated in the cover sheet of the PDMS scoring booklet, presented in figure 9.4. First, the raw score for each of the nine skill areas and the fine and gross motor totals can be calculated by adding the cumulative basal score (the total points possible below the basal level) to the score sum from basal to ceiling level. Next, the raw scores can be converted to percentiles by age groups. A sample of one of the tables used for this transformation is shown in table 9.6. Then, Z scores, normalized T scores with a mean of 50 and standard deviation of 10, and standardized developmental motor quotients (DMQs) with a mean of 100 and standard deviation of 15 can be determined for all age groups from the percentiles. Finally, the total raw scores for the GM and FM Scales can be used to identify age equivalents and to obtain normalized scaled scores that are based on an equal interval scale for measuring change in motor development independent of age.

The norm-referenced score transformations were based on data collected from 617 children in 20 states. In each of the 17 age groups there were 25 to 55 children; the proportions of males and females, however, were not specified in the PDMS manual (Folio & Fewell, 1983).

TABLE 9.6   Transformation From Total Raw Scores (TRS) to Percentiles for the PDMS Gross Motor Scale (Folio & Fewell, 1983) for 18-23 Months

TRS	Percentile	TRS	Percentile
0-156	1	181-183	71
157-159	2	184-186	79
160-162	6	187-192	85
163-165	14	193-195	88
166-168	20	196-204	91
169-171	26	205-207	92
172-174	35	208-210	94
175-177	50	211-213	95
178-180	65	214+	98

Peabody Developmental Motor Scales
Response/Scoring Booklet

	Yr.	Mo.	Day
Name _____ Date of Testing	_____	_____	_____
Educational Program _____ Date of Birth	_____	_____	_____
Examiner _____ Chronological Age	_____	_____	_____
Examination Center _____ Age in months	_____		

SUMMARY

	Gross Motor	Fine Motor
Basal Age Level		
Ceiling Age Level		
Scaled Score		
Age Equivalent		
Mean Motor Age Equivalent		

GROSS-MOTOR SCALE

	Raw Score	Percentile	z-score T score	Developmental Motor Quotient
Skill A - Reflexes				
Skill B - Balance				
Skill C - Nonlocomotor				
Skill D - Locomotor				
Skill E - Receipt and Propulsion				
Total Score				

FINE-MOTOR SCALE

	Raw Score	Percentile	z-score T score	Developmental Motor Quotient
Skill A - Grasping				
Skill B - Hand Use				
Skill C - Eye-Hand Coordination				
Skill D - Manual Dexterity				
Total Score				

■ **FIGURE 9.4** Cover page of the Peabody Development Motor Scale (Folio & Fewell, 1983) scoring booklet.

From *Peabody Development Motor Scales and Activity Cards* by M. R. Folio & R.R. Fewell, 1983 Austin, TX: PRO-ED. Copyright 1983 by PRO-ED. Printed by permission.

Reliability

Three types of reliability measures were reported in the PDMS manual (Folio & Fewell, 1983) and in later studies: test-retest, interrater, and standard error of measure. Folio and Fewell (1983) examined test-retest reliability by testing 38 children distributed across all age groups a second time within 1 week. The interclass Pearson product-moment correlation between the total raw scores of the two testings was .999 for the GM Scale and .997 for the FM Scale (the type of reliability coefficient was not mentioned in the manual but was clarified by Stokes, Deitz, & Crowe, 1990). Boulton et al. (1995) tested 12 children with cerebral palsy 2 weeks apart and found the intraclass correlation between total GM Scale raw scores obtained in the two testings to be .98, with correlations for the four individual skill areas ranging from .91 to .97. In a similar study focused on test-retest reliability of the FM Scale, Russell, Ward, and Law (1994) reported the intraclass correlation between total raw scores of 18 children with cerebral palsy on two testings, separated by 1 or 2 weeks, to be .99, with correlations for the four individual skill areas ranging from .96 to .98.

In addition, Folio and Fewell (1983) had the performances of 36 children representing all age groups scored by two persons: the test administrator and an observer. Again, interclass Pearson product-moment correlations between the two sets of total raw scores were very high: .998 for the GM Scale and .996 for the FM Scale. In a recent study, Schmidt, Westcott, and Crowe (1993) evaluated the interrater reliability of the GM Scale by having three therapists rate each of 33 four- to five-year-olds with and without identified delays. The intraclass correlation coefficients for total scores were .94 for the children without delays and .84 and .93 for the two groups of children with delays. Other researchers have found the intraclass correlations between raters to be .98 for the total raw scores on the GM Scale (Boulton et al., 1995) and .99 for the total raw scores on the FM Scale (Gebhard, Ottenbacher, & Lane, 1994), providing further support for the interrater reliability of the PDMS.

The third reliability measure was the standard error of measure for total raw scores, calculated for each age group by dividing the standard deviation by the square root of the number of subjects (this formula is unusual and is considered by Hinderer et al. [1989] to be inappropriate). These values, ranging from 1.10 to 5.39 for the GM Scale and from 0.70 to 2.56 for the FM Scale, are difficult to interpret in themselves, so they need to evaluated in terms of possible ranges of scores that are easily understood, such as percentiles.

For example, the GM standard error of measure for 18- to 23-month-olds is 2.43. For a confidence interval of 86%, which matches a Z score of 1.5, the range of the true total raw score is 7.30 (2.43 × 1.5 = ±3.65) (see Equation 6.12 in chapter 6). An examination of the GM total raw score-to-percentile transformation for this age group in table 9.6 indicates that a range of 7.0 (rounding down to a whole number) in the total raw score could encompass percentile ranges, for example, of 2 to 20, 6 to 26, and 20 to 50. As noted earlier, Hinderer et al. (1989) argue that the standard error of measure formula used by Folio and Fewell (1983) is inappropriate and should be replaced with the more accepted formula given in Equation 6.11, which they show yields even higher standard errors of measure. Thus, despite the high reliability coefficients, ranges of scores representing the confidence interval of the true score, rather than a single score, should be reported, particularly when the PDMS is used for screening or for determining program eligibility.

Intrarater reliability was not addressed in the PDMS manual, but in the study by Boulton et al. (1995), the performances on the GM Scale of 10 children with cerebral palsy were videotaped and rated independently by each of two raters two times, with the second viewing coming 3 to 6 months after the first. The intrarater correlation coefficients between ratings were .99 for both raters, while the correlations for the four individual skill areas ranged from .88 to .99.

Validity

In the test manual, Folio and Fewell (1983) presented information regarding the content validity, criterion-related validity, and construct validity of the PDMS. For content validity, the analysis was limited to a brief description of the relationship of the PDMS to Harrow's (1972) hierarchical taxonomy of the psychomotor domain (see figure 3.3), and was based on the questionable assumption that Harrow's taxonomy is valid. Harrow's taxonomy is suspect because, among other reasons, few neuroscientists still believe that movement is ordered in a strict hierarchy (Shumway-Cook & Woollacott, 1995), and the notion of motor abilities has suffered from a lack of empirical evidence for over 50 years (see chapter 8).

For criterion-related validity, Folio and Fewell (1983) examined the correlations between the PDMS and the mental and psychomotor scores on the BSID (Bayley, 1969) ($n = 43$) and the gross and fine motor scores of the West Haverstraw Motor Development Test (WHMDT) (New York State Rehabilitation Hospital, 1964) ($n = 29$). The choice of these two criterion tests, each with two subtests, allowed the authors to examine the differentiation between the gross and fine motor components in the PDMS. As expected, the correlations of total GM scores were very low with mental scores of the BSID (−.03) and fine motor scores of the WHMDT (.08), but were just moderate with psychomotor scores of the BSID (.37) and gross motor scores of the WHMDT (.55). The correlations of total FM scores were quite high with mental scores of the BSID (.78) and fine motor scores of the WHMDT (.62), and low to moderate with psychomotor scores of the BSID

(.36) and gross motor scores of the WHMDT (.20). These results, although offering some support for the validity of both scales of the PDMS, must be tempered by understanding that (a) the validity of the WHMDT has not been clearly established, and (b) the validity of the specific uses of the PDMS in relation to the uses of the BSID and WHMDT was not explicitly addressed.

Palisano (1986a) also examined the congruence between the PDMS and the BSID by administering both tests to 23 full-term and 21 healthy premature infants at 12, 15, and 18 months of age. The Pearson product-moment correlations between age-equivalent scores on the PDMS GM Scale and the BSID Motor Scale were higher than those reported by Folio and Fewell (1983), ranging from .78 to .95 across the three full-term age groups and from .84 to .96 across the three premature age groups.

Although Folio and Fewell (1983) state that the PDMS allows for measurement of performance across time or before and after intervention, the validity of this prescriptive use has only recently been addressed. Palisano, Kolobe, Haley, Lowes, and Jones (1995) examined the PDMS-GM scores of 124 infants with cerebral palsy, developmental delay—preterm, developmental delay—full term, Down syndrome, hydrocephalus, and other impairments, all of whom were tested three times over a 6-month period as they attended an early intervention program. For the six groups of infants, the mean change in the normalized scaled scores ($\bar{X} = 500$, $S_x = 100$) designed to measure small changes in motor development ranged from 15.0 for infants with cerebral palsy to 33.3 for infants with hydrocephalus. Using the reliable change index (Christiansen & Mendoza, 1986), Palisano, Kolobe, Haley, Lowes, and Jones (1995) reported that the change in raw scores across the 6-month period for 62% of the infants was greater than the change that could be attributed to measurement error ($p < .05$). The authors recommend "using the PDMS-GM to provide a global measure of change in motor development but not as the primary method of evaluating change in infants receiving physical therapy, especially infants with cerebral palsy" (p. 947).

The construct validity of the PDMS was based on the assumptions that

- motor development is orderly and sequential,
- motor performance increases in normal children with increases in chronological age,
- motor development requires lower-level skill acquisition in order to build higher-level skills, and
- handicapping conditions impede or interfere with sequential motor development (Folio & Fewell, 1983, p. 12).

The first and third assumptions were not directly evaluated, but the assumptions themselves might be considered to be invalid: the first in light of the finding of Largo et al. (1985), cited earlier in this chapter, that 13% of the children studied showed a deviation from the usual sequence of early movement milestones, and the third in light of the mounting evidence against strict hierarchical models of motor control (Shumway-Cook & Woollacott, 1995).

The focus of the information presented in the PDMS manual (Folio & Fewell, 1983) was on the second assumption that scores should show improvement as age increased. Support for this assumption was given by (a) correlations of .99 between age and both GM and FM total scores; (b) significant increases ($p < .001$) in both GM and FM total scores at successive age levels (except from 48-53 to 54-59 months for GM scores and from 60-71 to 72-83 for FM scores); and (c) increases in mean individual skill scores at successive age levels (except from 48-53 to 54-59 months for locomotor skills [GM]). Folio and Fewell (1983) argued that "the temporary performance plateau in the GM Scale is not unusual for developmental skills" (p. 110), but this finding still is contrary to the assumption.

The fourth assumption implied that children identified by other tests and/or clinical judgment as having movement skill problems also should score lower on the PDMS than children in the normative group. Indeed, both GM and FM total scores were significantly lower ($p < .05$) for children with identified movement deficits at each age level ($n = 5-12$) except at 0 to 5 months.

Folio and Fewell (1983) examined an additional assumption, that children in the normative sample should show consistent scores for both scales of the PDMS as well as across the skill areas within each scale. These two sets of intercorrelations were very high, with a correlation of .98 between GM and FM totals. However, this result suggests that the skill categories within the two scales can be consolidated with each other, and even that the two scales can be consolidated into one, and supports the contention that the PDMS is an ability-oriented test when it is used as a norm-referenced instrument.

Summary

The PDMS is a popular developmental instrument designed to be used with children from birth to 6 years 11 months of age. In a survey of 293 occupational therapists working in school settings in the northwestern United States, Crowe (1989) reported that the PDMS was used frequently by 83% of the therapists, a higher percentage than for any other developmental test. In another survey of 118 pediatric occupational therapists (Lawlor & Henderson, 1989), the PDMS was the second most commonly used standardized assessment, behind the Miller Assessment for Preschoolers (Miller, 1988). If the PDMS is used as a norm-referenced instrument, it can be categorized as a motor ability test; if it is used as a criterion-referenced instrument, it can be categorized as a test of early movement milestones and fundamental movement skills.

In the rest of this section I will discuss the strengths and weaknesses of the PDMS. You can gain further information from critical reviews by Harris and Heriza (1987), Hinderer et al. (1989), Palisano (1993a), and Palisano and Lydic (1984), whose comments I cite below.

Strengths. Palisano (1993a) concluded that the PDMS offers "the most in-depth assessment of motor development and despite some limitations is recommended over the Bayley Motor Scale and the Gesell Gross Motor and Fine Motor domains for use by physical therapists" (p. 198). The strengths of the PDMS include (a) a focus on movement skills, whereas most developmental motor assessments are embedded within tests including other performance areas, such as the Denver II (Frankenburg et al., 1992); (b) a large number of items across gross and fine motor domains; (c) separate scores for gross and fine motor scales, and scores for performance areas within each scale; (d) a 3-point scoring system; and (e) coverage of a wide age range, including the span from 2.5 to 4.5 years for which there are few test choices (Hinderer et al., 1989; Palisano, 1993a).

Weaknesses. The major weaknesses of the PDMS relate to the issues of (a) developmental sequence, (b) organization of items into skills and scales, (c) scoring and data manipulation, and (d) equipment quality and specifications. With respect to developmental sequence, several reviewers (Harris & Heriza, 1987; Hinderer et al., 1989) have noted that skipping is placed before galloping, at 54-59 months compared to 60-71 months, when most research indicates that galloping precedes skipping (Clark & Whitall, 1989a). Folio and Fewell's (1983) own standardization data show that more 48-53- and 60-71-month-olds are able to gallop than skip. Further, some items are placed at ages at which few children are successful in performance of the item. For example, eight items are placed at ages at which less than 16% of the children met the criterion.

Another set of problems with the PDMS relates to the organization of items into gross and fine motor scales and into skill areas. First, Folio and Fewell (1983) gave no justification, such as results of a factor analysis, for the assignment of items into the two scales or into the nine skill areas (Hinderer et al., 1989). Second, for both the GM and FM Scales, the distribution of items from skill areas across age groups was uneven (Harris & Heriza, 1987; Hinderer et al., 1989) (see tables 9.3 and 9.4). For example, over three consecutive age spans in the GM Scale, the emphasized items shift from locomotor (50%) at 30-35 months, to nonlocomotor (70%) at 36-41 months, to receipt and propulsion (50%) at 42-47 months. Because of the inconsistency in the number of items within a particular skill area that may actually be tested, Hinderer et al. (1989) recommend that caution be used in interpreting skill area scores, particularly for 5- and 6-year-olds. Finally, the high intercorrelations both within and between gross and fine motor skill areas bring into question the utility of dividing the movement tasks into skill areas at all.

The third area of weakness for the PDMS is in its scoring procedures and reliability. The criteria for a successful performance earning a score of 2 are vague for several items, but a more pervasive problem is the lack of clear distinction between scores of 0 and 1 for many items (Harris & Heriza, 1987; Hinderer et al., 1989). Folio and Fewell (1983) explained that "specific item criteria are not provided because examiners in the norming study were found to be highly reliable in scoring . . . when only the criteria for 0 and 2 were specified" (p. 18), but high reliability in scoring individual items may be possible only within examiners (intrarater reliability) or after mutual agreement on exact criteria between examiners (Hinderer et al., 1989). Moreover, although the reported test-retest and interrater reliability coefficients were very high, some confidence intervals of true scores as calculated by standard errors of measure were quite large; this requires test users to interpret actual scores with caution.

The PDMS also has been criticized for poor-quality materials provided with the kit and for vague specifications of necessary equipment not provided with the kit (Hinderer et al., 1989; Palisano, 1993a). Hinderer and her colleagues argue that "the lack of standardized equipment can affect the validity of the PDMS by changing the type of skill being tested and . . . can affect the validity of comparing a given child's score with the normative values" (p. 92).

Although the PDMS is one of the most widely used instruments to assess motor development, its validity for all the uses stated by Folio and Fewell (1983) has not been clearly established. The PDMS was designed to be used as either a norm-referenced or criterion-referenced instrument, but given the authors' emphasis on its normative use, the meaning and interpretation of composite scores (total and individual skills) based on various combinations of movement tasks need to be clarified. Until these issues are resolved, the PDMS is recommended for use as a criterion-referenced assessment of a wide variety of early movement milestones and fundamental movement skills. One can get help with the interpretation of success or failure on individual items by referring to the manual's appendixes for tables (Folio & Fewell, 1983) that present the percentage of the standardization sample passing each of the 282 items by age group.

■ REVIEW: ASSESSMENT, EVALUATION, AND PROGRAMMING SYSTEM FOR INFANTS AND CHILDREN—MEASUREMENT FOR BIRTH TO THREE YEARS

The Assessment, Evaluation, and Programming System for Infants and Children (AEPS) is a comprehensive system for assessing, evaluating, and programming interventions for infants and children. The AEPS for infants and children from birth to 3 years, first commercially published in 1993, included one manual for measurement (Vol. 1: Bricker, 1993) and another manual for curriculum (Vol. 2: Cripe, Slentz, & Bricker, 1993). Recently, the AEPS was expanded to include children from 3 to 6 years, again consisting of two volumes (Vol. 3 on measurement: Bricker & Pretti-Frontczak, 1996; Vol. 4 on curriculum: Bricker & Waddell, 1996). Consistent with the objectives of this chapter, I will address only the measurement component of the AEPS for infants and children from birth to 3 years.

The primary instrument of AEPS measurement for infants and children (Bricker, 1993) is the criterion-referenced AEPS Test, which was designed to be used by direct service personnel and specialists to assess and evaluate the skills and abilities of infants and young children who are at risk or who have disabilities. More specifically, the AEPS Test was structured to examine important behaviors in developmental sequences and then link the results directly to possible intervention activities. Besides the AEPS Test, the measurement component also includes the AEPS Family Report with 64 items, the AEPS Family Interest Survey with 30 items, and the AEPS Child Progress Report.

The seminal ideas for the AEPS came from the Consortium on Adaptive Performance Evaluation, composed of participants from five universities. The group wrote a grant in 1976 and received funding from the Bureau of Education for the Handicapped to lay the conceptual and empirical groundwork for an instrument that would be specifically designed for children ranging from birth to 2 years in developmental age and that would yield educationally relevant outcomes. The first usable tool, called the Adaptive Performance Instrument (API), was the product of a supplemental grant received in 1980. The API had more than 600 items appropriate for infants and children between the developmental ages of birth and 2 years. In 1983 to 1984, the items in the API were rewritten and reduced in number by over one-half, the presentation format was changed, the developmental range was expanded to 3 years, and the system was renamed the Comprehensive Early Evaluation and Programming System. Another extensive revision of the test and the addition of a corresponding curriculum were funded by a 3-year grant from the Office of Special Education Programs. These together became the Evaluation and Programming System: For Infants and Young Children (EPS) (Bricker, Janko, Cripe, Bailey, & Kaminski, 1989). In 1993, the system was published commercially and given its current name: the Assessment, Evaluation, and Programming System (AEPS) for Infants and Children. The specific purposes of this current version of the AEPS are, for children who are at risk or who have disabilities in the developmental period between 1 month and 3 years, to (a) assist in the development of an intervention plan (measurement), (b) provide a set of intervention activities (curriculum), and (c) evaluate progress (measurement).

Assessment, Evaluation, and Programming System for Infants and Children From Birth to Three Years (AEPS)

Published by: Paul H. Brookes Publishing

Movement categories tested: early movement milestones, fundamental movement skills, functional movement skills

Uses: (a) develop intervention programs, (b) evalute progress, and (c) evaluate program

Time to administer: initial assessments of an individual child, 1-2 hours; subsequent assessments, 15-30 minutes

Price: The AEPS measurement (Vol. 1) and curriculum (Vol. 2) manuals for birth to 3 years can be purchased together for $92.50. The Data Recording Forms cost $23 for a pack of 10, the Family Reports cost $17 for a pack of 10, the Family Interest Survey costs $15 for a pack of 30, and the Child Progress Record costs $18 for a pack of 30. The new AEPS measurement (Vol. 3) and curriculum (Vol. 4) manuals for 3-6 years can be purchased together for $96, with the price of the four corresponding packs of forms ranging from $15 to $24.

Contact: Paul H. Brookes Publishing
                P O Box 10624
                Baltimore, MD 21285-0624
                (800-238-3775)

An interesting point is that the royalties from this work did not go to the authors, but were used to fund the extension of the system to developmental ages of 3 to 6 years, which then was published in 1996 (Bricker & Pretti-Frontczak, 1996; Bricker & Waddell, 1996).

Test Structure

The AEPS Test (Bricker, 1993) is organized into four hierarchical levels: domains, strands, goals, and objectives (see table 9.7). First, six curricular domains (fine motor, gross motor, adaptive, cognitive, social-communication, and social) are divided into 23 common behavior categories or strands. These 23 strands give rise to 64 goals and 164 specific objectives. The goals within each strand and the objectives within each goal are organized in

TABLE 9.7 AEPS Test Domains, Strands, and Number of Goals and Objectives in Each Strand

Domain	Strand	No. of goals	No. of objectives
Fine motor	A. Reach, grasp, and release	5	13
	B. Functional use of fine motor skills	4	6
	Total	9	19
Gross motor	A. Movement and locomotion in supine and prone position	3	11
	B. Balance in sitting	2	8
	C. Balance and mobility in standing and walking	3	11
	D. Play skills	5	12
	Total	13	42
Adaptive	A. Feeding	5	13
	B. Personal hygiene	3	4
	C. Undressing	1	6
	Total	9	23
Cognitive	A. Sensory stimuli	1	4
	B. Object permanence	3	6
	C. Causality	2	4
	D. Imitation	2	3
	E. Problem-solving	4	6
	F. Preacademic skills	3	6
	G. Interaction with objects	1	4
	Total	16	33

(continued)

TABLE 9.7   Continued

Social-communicative	A. Prelinguistic communicative interactions	3	5
	B. Transition to words	2	6
	C. Comprehension of words and sentences	2	6
	D. Production of social-communicative signals, words, and sentences	3	15
	Total	10	32
Social	A. Interaction with adults	3	6
	B. Interaction with environment	2	2
	C. Interaction with peers	2	7
	Total	7	15
TEST TOTAL	23 strands	64	164

Note: From *Assessment, Evaluation, and Programming Systems for Infants and children, Vol. 1: AEPS measurement for birth to three years* (p. 499), by D. Bricker (Ed.), 1993, Baltimore: P.H. Brookes, P.O. Box 10624, Baltimore, MD 21285-0624. Adapted with permission.

hierarchical order according to difficulty. Note that the fine and gross motor domains account for 6 strands (26% of the total), 22 goals (34%), and 61 objectives (37%).

A separate recording form is included for each of the six domains with spaces for a criterion score, a score qualifier, and an individualized education plan (IEP)/individualized family service plan (IFSP) check-off for each goal and objective (a total of 228 across all domains), as well as multiple columns accommodating more than one testing (see the recording form for the gross motor domain in figure 9.5). The criterion score, marked in the S (score) column on the form, is based on a 3-point scale, where 0 = not pass, 1 = pass inconsistently, and 2 = pass consistently. The data for this assessment may be collected, in order of preference, from observations of functional activities typical for the child, from direct eliciting of the behavior, or from verbal or written report from others. The functional observations can be made at home or at a center-based setting; for these the AEPS manual provides seven specific Assessment Activity Plans (e.g., water play, snack, books and puzzles) each covering goals and objectives in two to four different domains. The rating qualifier, marked in the Q (qualifier) column, then may be used to indicate that the criterion behavior was directly elicited (D) or reported (R) or that assistance was provided (A), that other behaviors interfered with the criterion behavior (B), or that a modification or adaptation was made in the item (M). If a modification or adaptation was made, the specifics then should be marked in the comments section. If a goal or objective is selected for programming on the child's IEP or IFSP, the box in the IEP column is checked.

The items on the AEPS may be assessed one domain at a time or across domains as they are observed. All goals must be assessed and scored, but if a child's developmental level is clearly above an item, the rater may record a score of 2 (pass consistently) with an R qualifier (reported); conversely, if a child's developmental level is clearly below an item, a score of 0 (not pass) with an R qualifier may be recorded. If a goal item is scored as a 0 or 1, all of the associated objectives also must be scored; if a goal item is scored as a 2, all of the associated objectives are assumed to have been passed and thus also should be scored as 2s.

A child's performance on the individual items can be summarized with several types of scores. First, a raw score can be calculated by summing all goals and objectives within each domain and then also for the total battery. This method is briefly described at the bottom of each domain score sheet (see figure 9.5), but two other types of raw summary scores can be calculated: one in which only scores of 2 are summed, indicating consistent performance, and another in which only scores of 1 are summed, offering an indicator of degree of inconsistency of performance. In addition, all three of the raw summary scores can be converted to percentage scores by dividing domain and battery totals by the total possible scores, and then multiplying by 100 (this final multiplication step is skipped on the score sheets and in the manual). The authors point out that "it is important that children's performances on the test be summarized so progress can be monitored over time" (p. 60).

The initial assessment of a child is estimated to take about 1 to 2 hr, but subsequent assessments should take only 15 to 30 min. To systematically monitor a child's progress in acquiring IEP/IFSP goals and objectives, Bricker (1993) recommends that the AEPS Test be readministered at 3- to 4-month intervals.

Reliability

Interrater and test-retest reliability of the EPS (Bricker et al., 1989), an earlier version of the AEPS, was established in a study by Bricker, Bailey, and Slentz (1990). After five observers were thoroughly trained to score the EPS, two different observers rated 122 children between the ages of 4 months and 6 years, 96 of them at risk or having mild, moderate, or severe disabilities. The Pearson product-moment (interclass) correlations between the two raters for the six domains ranged from .71 (social) to .96 (gross motor), with a correlation of .97 for the total of all domains. The flexible design of the EPS makes it difficult for two observers to observe the same behaviors, so seven activity plans were devised (and carried over to the AEPS) to ensure full coverage of the EPS.

Gross Motor Domain

S = Scoring Key	Q = Qualifying Notes
2 = Pass consistently 1 = Inconsistent performance 0 = Does not pass	A = Assistance provided B = Behavior interfered R = Reported assessment M = Modification/adaptation D = Direct test

Name: _____

Test Period: _____
Test Date: ___/___ ___/___ ___/___ ___/___
Examiner: _____

	IEP	S	Q	S	Q	S	Q	S	Q
A. Movement and locomotion in supine and prone position									
1. Moves body parts independently of each other									
1.1 Turns head past 45°									
1.2 Kicks legs									
1.3 Waves arms									
2. Rolls by turning segmentally									
2.1 Rolls: back to stomach									
2.2 Rolls: stomach to back									
3. Creeps forward using alternating arm and leg movements									
3.1 Rocks in creeping motion									
3.2 Assumes creeping position									
3.3 Crawls forward on stomach									
3.4 Pivots on stomach									
3.5 Bears weight while reaching									
3.6 Lifts head/chest off surface									
B. Balance in sitting									
1. Assumes balanced sitting position									
1.1 Assumes hands and knees position from sitting									
1.2 Regains balanced sitting after reaching									
1.3 Regains balanced sitting after leaning									
1.4 Sits balanced without support									

(continued)

■ **FIGURE 9.5** AEPS data recording form for the gross motor domain.

Gross Motor Domain

	IEP	S	Q	S	Q	S	Q	S	Q
Name: _____ Test Period: _____ Test Date: __/__ __/__ __/__ __/__ Examiner: _____									
1.5 Sits balanced using hands for support									
1.6 Holds head in midline when in supported sitting position									
2. Rolls by turning segmentally									
2.1 Sits down in chair									
2.2 Maintains a sitting position in chair									
C. Balance and mobility in standing and walking									
1. Walks avoiding obstacles									
1.1 Crawls forward on stomach									
1.2 Pivots on stomach									
1.3 Bears weight while reaching									
1.4 Lifts head/chest off surface									
1.5 Cruises									
2. Stoops/recovers without support									
2.1 Rises from sitting to standing									
2.2 Pulls to standing									
2.3 Pulls to kneeling									
3. Walks up and down stairs									
3.1 Walks up and down stairs with two-hand support									
3.2 Moves up and down stairs									
3.3 Gets up and down from low structure									
D. Play skills									
1. Jumps forward									
1.1 Jumps up									
1.2 Jumps from low structure									
2. Pedals and steers tricycle									
2.1 Pushes riding toy with feet while steering									
2.2 Sits on riding toy while adult pushes									

(continued)

Gross Motor Domain

	IEP	S	Q	S	Q	S	Q	S	Q
Name: _____ Test Period: ___ Test Date: __/__ __/__ __/__ __/__ Examiner: ___									
3. Runs avoiding obstacles									
3.1 Runs									
3.2 Walks fast									
4. Catches/kicks/throws/rolls ball									
4.1 Catches ball									
4.2 Kicks ball									
4.3 Throws ball									
4.4 Rolls ball at target									
5. Climbs up and down play equipment									
5.1 Moves up and down inclines									
5.2 Moves under/over/ through obstacle									

A raw score can be computed for the domain by adding all the 2 and 1 scores entered in the S column for a specific test period. To determine the total percent score divide the total score by the total score possible.

RESULTS

Test Date	___	___	___	___
Total Score Possible	110	110	110	110
Total Score	___	___	___	___
Total Percent Score	___	___	___	___

■ **FIGURE 9.5** *(continued)*

From Assessment, Evaluation, and Programming System for Infants and Children. Vol. 1: AEPS measurement for birth to three years (pp. 267-269), by D. Bricker (Ed.), 1993, Baltimore: P. H. Brookes, P.O. Box 10624, Baltimore, MD 21285-0625. Reprinted with permission.

Next, 58 children ranging in age from 2 months to 4 years—38 at risk or with mild, moderate, or severe disabilities—were tested 2 weeks after an initial assessment. The interclass correlations between the two testings for the six domains spanned from .77 (social) to .95 (gross motor), with a correlation of .96 for the total of all domains.

Validity

Studies examining the content, criterion-related, and construct validity of the earlier EPS version of the AEPS (Bricker et al., 1989) have been reported by Bricker et al. (1990) and Notari and Bricker (1990). Bricker et al. (1990) studied content validity by sending questionnaires on the utility of the EPS to 106 interventionists from 23 different sites. According to the 63 questionnaires that were returned, 76% of the sites (the number or percentage of individual responses was not clear in the paper) answered yes to seven of the eight questions related to content (e.g., "Do the results of the EPS accurately reflect the performance of your children?").

Next, to investigate criterion-related validity, Bricker et al. (1990) looked at the relationships between children's scores on the EPS and their scores on the BSID (Bayley, 1969) and the Gesell Developmental Schedule (Knobloch et al., 1980). Bricker et al. reported that the Pearson product-moment correlations between the total scores of 34 children on the EPS and their BSID Mental Age and BSID Motor Age were .93 and .88, respectively. They also reported that the correlation between the total scores of 121 children and their Gesell Maturity Scores was .51.

Construct validity of the EPS was examined in terms of three key sets of assumptions. The first set of assumptions—that scores in individual strands are highly related to summed scores in their respective domains and that summed scores in the domains are highly related to the total score—was supported by evidence from Bricker et al. (1990). They showed that the correlations between the scores in the individual strands and the summed scores in their respective domains ranged from .61 to .95, with a mean of .81 across 22 strands (one strand was missing), and that the correlations between the summed scores in the domains and the total score ranged from .89 (social-communication) to .99 (cognitive). The second assumption—that the long-term goals were ordered in sequence of difficulty—was shown to be true for 81% of the 64 goals from birth to 1 year of age, for 89% of the goals from 1 to 2 years, and for 91% of the goals from 2 to 3 years (Bricker et al., 1990). And the third assumption—that the quality of long-term goals and short-term objectives written by interventionists improves when these are developed from EPS test items rather than from other commonly used assessment instruments—was studied by Notari and Bricker (1990). With their IEP Goals/Objectives Rating Instrument, which examined five aspects of goals and objectives (functionality, generality, instructional context, measurability, hierarchical relationship between goal and objectives), Notari and Bricker evaluated the goals and objectives written by 22 early interventionists who used the EPS with training, 13 who used the EPS with the manual only, and 13 who used other assessment instruments. They found no significant differences between the three groups in their scores on the pretest, but found significant differences between the two groups that used the EPS and the group that used other tests.

Summary

The strengths of the AEPS, at least in relation to the perspectives taken in this book, are many. First, the AEPS is a skill-based test, without composite scores that mix together results from different items. There are summary scores, designed to monitor progress, but they merely indicate how many or what percentage of the total items are passed. Second, the items are sequenced by difficulty, not by age, avoiding stereotyping in terms of which behaviors are appropriate for particular ages. And the items are developed from an explicit curriculum that can be used directly as goals or objectives on an IEP or IFSP. Also, the AEPS is quite flexible in terms of the contexts from which scores can be derived—from observations of functional activities, from direct eliciting of the behavior, or from reports from others—and in terms of the use of qualifier (Q) scores to indicate special circumstances of success. In addition, there are measurement items specifically related to the family in the AEPS Family Report (64 items) and the AEPS Family Interest Survey (30 items). Other strengths are that the domains within the AEPS can be assessed either separately (e.g., the fine motor and gross motor domains) or all together, and that the test was designed to accommodate retestings at regular intervals.

The reliability of a flexible test like the AEPS is hard to establish, but the inclusion of seven Assessment Activity Plans is helpful in creating common contexts for all raters. Nevertheless, raters still have the option of observing natural behaviors, directly eliciting behaviors, or recording reported behaviors from other situations. Given the constraints of the AEPS, the interrater and test-retest reliability coefficients reported by Bricker et al. (1990) are very good, even though (a) the correlations should have been intraclass rather interclass, and (b) it is not clear what the reliability would be between observers if they were not trained as extensively as those in the study.

The first stated use of the AEPS, to assist in the development of an intervention plan, was clearly established by the results of the study by Notari and Bricker (1990). They found that the quality of long-term goals and short-term objectives written by interventionists was better when these were developed from EPS test items than when developed from other commonly used assessment instruments. Further, the IEP Goals/Objectives Rating Instrument created to examine the validity of this first use is an excellent tool for evaluation of any IEP/IFSP goal or objective. However, the validity of the other two stated uses, to provide a set of intervention activities and to evaluate progress, was not explicitly studied.

Thus, the most glaring weakness of the AEPS is the lack of information on its validity for the stated use of evaluating progress. It would perhaps be useful to have a study comparing progress on the AEPS summary scores between a treatment group given specific interventions and a control group given no interventions. There also is no direct validity information on the second stated use, that is, to provide a set of intervention activities; but this is not really a measurement issue, and is covered from a curricular perspective in the book (Vol. 2) corresponding to the AEPS measurement manual (Vol. 1) for birth to 3 years (Cripe et al., 1993).

Other weaknesses are the limitations in the primary reliability study by Bricker et al. (1990), mentioned earlier, and the time necessary for the initial assessment. However, in curriculum-based assessment, the line between assessment and instruction becomes indistinct, and time spent on assessment also can be considered to be time spent on instruction. Overall, the AEPS, particularly with regard to the fine and gross motor domains, offers an excellent model for the development of other skill-oriented, curriculum-based movement skill assessment tools.

Chapter **10**

Assessing Fundamental Movement Skills

© Connie Springer

FUNDAMENTAL movement skills are the locomotor and object-control skills performed in an upright or bipedal position that are used by persons in all cultures of the world. The functional boundary between early movement milestones and fundamental movement skills is the onset of walking. Early movement milestones and fundamental movement skills are both referred to as phylogenetic skills, because of their universal occurrence, and together are commonly viewed as the basic components of all specialized movement skills.

Fundamental movement skills usually emerge between 1 and 7 years of age. Early movement milestones almost always are acquired before

> " "The rapid growth in muscle tissue during the latter part of this period [of early childhood] strongly suggests nature's intent for an ample opportunity for the muscular system to be used. This is further confirmed by a growing neuromuscular restlessness and desire upon the part of the child to turn his energies toward big muscle activity. The challenge to put the physical being into action is so great during this period that no urging is required for the child to run, jump, throw, and climb. The only requirements are space and the opportunity to put the developing motor mechanism into action. " "
>
> —Rarick (1961, p. 48)

fundamental movement skills, but are not prerequisites for the attainment of fundamental movement skills, as represented by the arrow directly pointing from movement skill foundations to fundamental movement skills in figure 10.1. For example, a person with a physical impairment might be able to walk or run but never be able to crawl or creep.

As with early movement milestones, fundamental movement skills traditionally are divided into two main categories: locomotor and object control. Fundamental locomotor skills include walking, running, jumping, sliding, galloping, hopping, and leaping, while fundamental object-control skills include throwing, catching, striking, bouncing, kicking, pulling, and pushing. Skipping usually is considered a fundamental movement skill, although it is not clear whether persons in all cultures perform this skill. According to Seefeldt and Haubenstricker (1982), the general order of emergence is walking, running, jumping, hopping, and skipping for locomotor skills, and throwing, kicking, striking, and catching for object-control skills.

One of the earliest uses of the term *fundamental* to refer to this category of skills was by the National Committee on Motor Ability of the American Physical Education Association, which recommended the development of tests to measure "the fundamental big muscle motor skills" for persons from 6 to 24 years (Committee of the American Physical Education Association, 1924, p. 579). Later this term became part of the title of Wickstrom's (1970) classic book, *Fundamental Motor Patterns*.

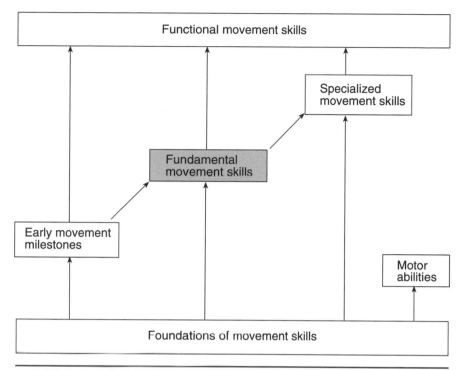

■ **FIGURE 10.1**   Taxonomy of movement skills.

■ APPROACHES TO ASSESSING FUNDAMENTAL MOVEMENT SKILLS

The measurement of what are now commonly known as fundamental movement skills can be traced back at least to 1912, when such an assessment formed part of the Sigma Delta Psi tests (Clarke, 1967). This type of measurement was a key aspect of the movement achievement tests developed in the 1920s and 1930s (see chapter 2). Specific assessment instruments published before 1975 that included fundamental movement skills as significant components were authored by Yarmolenko (1933), Cozens and colleagues (Cozens, 1936; Cozens, Cubberly, & Neilson, 1937; Cozens & Neilson, 1934; Cozens, Trieb, & Neilson, 1936; Neilson & Cozens, 1934), McCaskill and Wellman (1938), Gutteridge (1939), Latchaw (1954), and Johnson (1962). All these assessment instruments, except Gutteridge's (1939) scale for estimating degree of motor skill (see figures 2.1a and 2.1b, pp. 24 and 25), were concerned with the outcome or product of the movement.

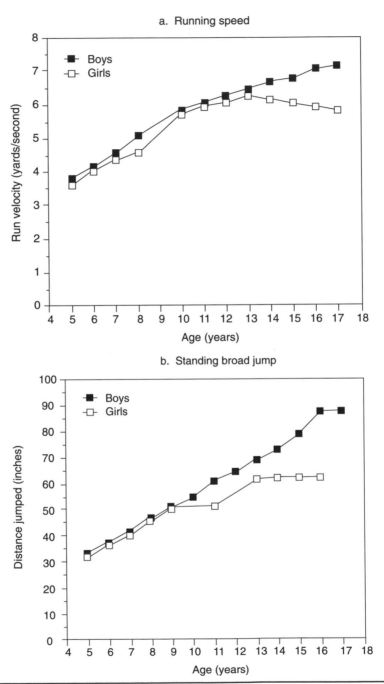

■ FIGURE 10.2 Product data for running speed (a), standing broad jump distance (b), and throwing distance (c, next page) for males and females between the ages of 5 and 17 years based on 18 studies by various researchers dating from 1924 to 1954 (adapted from Espenschade, 1960).

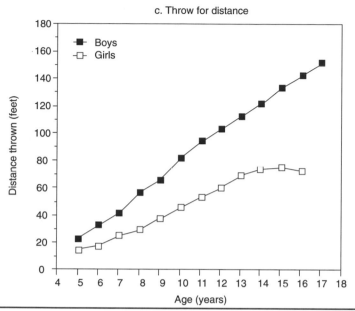

FIGURE 10.2   *(continued)*

Product-Oriented Assessments

Product-oriented assessments are based on the time, distance, or number of successful attempts resulting from the performance of a skill. Examples are the time taken to run 40 yd, the distance jumped, and the number of times a ball is dribbled in 30 s. Product data for running velocity, jumping distance, and throwing distance for males and females between the ages of 5 and 17 years are presented in figure 10.2a-c. The data are based on 18 studies by various researchers dating from 1924 to 1954, as reported by Espenschade (1960). The results of studies published since 1954 have shown similar performance patterns (e.g., Thomas & French, 1985).

Process-Oriented Assessments

Almost all tests of functional movement skills appearing after 1975 were concerned with how the skill was performed, or the process responsible for the performance outcome, rather than the product. The Ohio State University Scale of Intra-Gross Motor Assessment (Loovis & Ersing, 1979), the Test of Gross Motor Development (Ulrich, 1985), and the Motor Skills Inventory (Werder & Bruininks, 1988) are prime examples of these process-oriented tests. The Motor Skills Inventory, for instance, specifies three levels of process performance—rudimentary, functional, and mature—for each of seven locomotor and seven object-control fundamental movement skills.

For kicking, the rudimentary level is kicking a ball with leg movement from the knee, the functional level is kicking a ball with minimal follow-through, and the mature level is walking forward, stopping, and kicking a ball with follow-through (Werder & Bruininks, 1988, p. 96).

Both product and process items are part of the I CAN Fundamental Skills assessment instrument (Wessel, 1976). In the score sheet for the horizontal jump (see figure 10.3), note that process items are used to assess lower levels of jumping skill and that a product item, jumping distance, is used to assess the highest level. Further, jumping distance is expressed in terms of a body-scaled metric (two-thirds of body height) that can be appropriately applied to performers of various ages and sizes. There is a rationale for assessing process first and then product: Inconsistent and poor products may not adequately differentiate between performers at lower levels, while at higher levels, movement processes may not change much but there still may be marked differences in the outcomes produced by similar movement patterns.

The second edition of Wickstrom's (1983) book, *Fundamental Motor Patterns*, is a good resource for "extensive description and discussion of fundamental motor pattern development . . . slanted toward those who are interested in understanding and changing human motor behavior" (p. vii). Wickstrom devotes entire chapters to process and product information on walking, running, jumping, throwing, catching, striking, kicking, and "special skills" such as bouncing/dribbling, rope jumping, and forward rolling.

Early research on changes in movement patterns across age (e.g., Burnside, 1927; Halverson, 1931; Shirley, 1931; Wild, 1938) were founded on the general concept of developmental stages, which implies a universal, invariant sequence of movement skill development that generalizes across similar tasks (Roberton, 1982). In other words, the changes in movement patterns by all individual performers should follow the same sequence and should be the same for similar tasks such as throwing and striking or jumping and hopping. Taking this concept to the extreme, Gesell and Thompson (1938) described up to 58 stages of behaviors for 40 different tasks. However, empirical evidence supporting the validity of the concept of stages for the development of movement skills is limited. To avoid the inappropriate use of this term, Roberton (1982) suggested that levels of developmental skill progressions be referred to as *steps* rather than *stages*.

The validation of developmental stages or steps for specific movement skills requires a longitudinal research design in which changes in the movement patterns of individual performers are monitored. Before one embarks on an extensive longitudinal study, Roberton (1977, 1978) recommends the use of a "prelongitudinal screening" strategy to first determine whether there is movement pattern stability across trials for individuals at a single point in time and, if more than one pattern is observed, whether the patterns are adjacent in the hypothesized ordering of developmental steps.

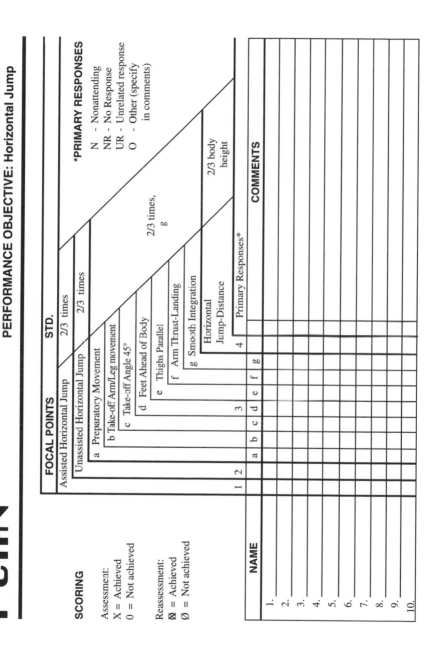

FIGURE 10.3 I CAN objective score sheet for the horizontal jump. From *I CAN Fundamental Skills* by J. A. Wessel, 1976, Austin, TX: PRO-ED. Copyright 1976 PRO-ED. Reprinted with permission.

Positive results of a prelongitudinal screening study for a targeted age group allow researchers to continue a longitudinal study with confidence, while negative results allow them to consider how to adjust their hypotheses before continuing.

For at least the past 20 years, research on fundamental movement skills has been devoted primarily to the study of movement patterns or process. Over these two decades of research, two main approaches to describing movement patterns have emerged: a total body configuration approach and a body component approach.

Total Body Configuration Approach.   The total body configuration approach goes back at least to Wild's (1938) research on changes in the overhand throwing pattern of children with increasing age. Wild described four stages of throwing development, each of which encompassed all relevant body components. For example, Stage 4 was described for a right-handed performer as a "left-foot-step-forward throw with trunk rotation and horizontal adduction of the arm in the forward swing" (p. 22).

The contemporary researchers most closely associated with the total body configuration approach are Seefeldt (now retired), Haubenstricker, and Branta from Michigan State University. These researchers admit that they do not believe that "all of the subroutines within a stage develop as an indivisible unit, or in lock-step fashion," but argue that there is "sufficient cohesion among certain characteristics of a pattern to define those as stages of development" (Branta, Haubenstricker, & Seefeldt, 1984, p. 470). Moreover, they feel that the total body configuration approach is the simplest way to describe a particular developmental task (Seefeldt & Haubenstricker, 1982).

On the basis of data from a longitudinal study begun in 1968 and still continuing, Seefeldt and his colleagues have provided descriptions of the total body configuration stages of a wide range of fundamental movement skills (Seefeldt & Haubenstricker, 1974-1976, 1982). Table 10.1 presents the five stages for the one-hand overhand throw for force from a total body configuration perspective. Complete stage descriptions for 10 skills—catching, galloping, hopping, horizontal jumping, kicking, overarm throwing, punting, running, skipping, and striking with a bat—can be found in the motor development textbook by Payne and Isaacs (1995), while shortened descriptions for 6 skills are given in a chapter by Ulrich and Ulrich (1985).

In 1982, Seefeldt and Haubenstricker reported the ages at which 60% of the children in the longitudinal studies at Michigan State University were able to perform the various developmental levels of eight fundamental movement skills (see figure 10.4). For boys, the highest developmental level was achieved first for running, followed by throwing, skipping, catching, kicking, striking, hopping, and jumping. For girls, the order was similar except that the girls achieved the highest level of hopping earlier, before kicking, and achieved throwing later, after striking. Clark and Whitall (1989a), from their own data and observations, suggest that the

TABLE 10.1 Total Body Configuration Sequence for the One-Hand Overarm Throw for Force (from Seefeldt & Haubenstricker, 1974-1976; cited by Ulrich & Ulrich, 1985)

Stage	Description
1	Arm motion posterior-anterior in direction, feet stationary, force comes from hip flexion, shoulder protraction, and elbow extension.
2	Arm motion is in transverse plane, body rotates as a unit about the vertical axis.
3	Arm begins throw with ball placed above shoulder followed by diagonal throw, ipsilateral step is taken, little or no spine and hip rotation.
4	Arm preparatory movement is vertical and posterior, contralateral step is taken, little trunk rotation.
5	Throwing hand winds up moving in downward and backward arc, contralateral step is taken, sequential rotation and derotation of shoulder, spine, and hip.

developmental ordering of locomotor patterns is walk, run, gallop, hop, and skip, and offer a dynamic system perspective of the changes from one pattern to the next.

Body Component Approach.   The body component approach was conceived by serependipity when Roberton (1977) used two sets of body component categories to describe the overhand throw for force (one for arm action and the other for pelvic-spinal action) and found that development of the two components appeared to occur at different rates. In a subsequent longitudinal study expanded to examine three body components (humerus, forearm, and pelvis-spine), Roberton (1978) reported that from kindergarten to the second grade, 6% of 54 children progressed in all three components, 20% in two, and 39% in only one, while 35% showed no change or regressed in at least one. She concluded that "the issue of 'stages', then, must be confined to the ordering within the components rather than to the total body configuration, although the latter has been a traditional practice in motor development" (Roberton, 1978, p. 174).

In research following Roberton's lead, component sequences have been presented for the fundamental movement skills of forward rolling (Williams, 1980), side rolling (Richter, VanSant, & Newton, 1989), hopping (Halverson & Williams, 1985), horizontal jumping (Clark & Phillips, 1985), overarm striking (Langendorfer, 1987; Messick, 1991), and rising to a stand (VanSant, 1988a, 1988b; VanSant et al., 1988). Roberton also has modified her sequences of overarm throwing to include five components (see table 10.2;

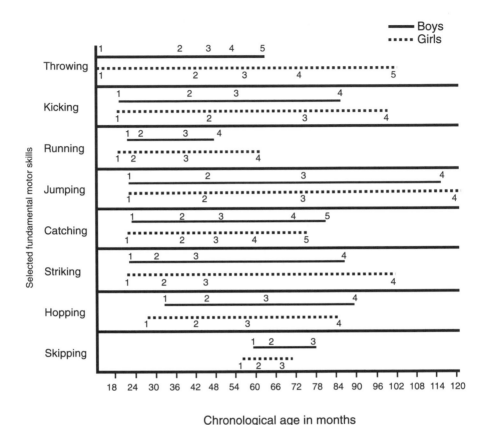

■ **FIGURE 10.4**   The ages at which 60% of the children in the longitudinal studies at Michigan State University were able to perform the various developmental levels of eight fundamental movement skills. The level numbers are presented above the time line for boys and below for girls. From "Patterns, Phases, or Stages: An Analytical Model for the Study of Developmental Movement" by V. Seefeldt and J. Haubenstricker, in *The Development of Movement Control and Co-ordination* (p. 314) edited by J.A.S. Kelso and J.E. Clark, 1982, Chichester, England: John Wiley and Sons. Copyright 1982 John Wiley and Sons, Ltd. Reprinted with permission.

compare with the total body configuration throwing stages in table 10.1). In addition, component sequences have been hypothesized for catching, punting, running, and walking. Some of these component sequences are presented in a chapter by Roberton (1984) and in motor development textbooks by Haywood (1993) and Payne and Isaacs (1995). Detailed observational analyses of gait, or "observational gait analysis" (e.g., Krebs, Edelstein, & Fishman, 1985), also may be considered to utilize a body component approach.

Roberton and Langendorfer (1993) made a bridge between the total body configuration and body component approaches when they examined the

TABLE 10.2 Component Sequences for the One-Hand Overarm Throw for Force (adapted from Roberton, 1984)

Component	Level/description
Backswing	1. No backswing. 2. Ball moves to position behind or alongside head via upward flexion of shoulder and concomitant elbow flexion. 3. Circular, upward backswing with elbow extended, or oblique swing back. 4. Circular, downward backswing that carries hand below waist.
Humerus	1. Humerus oblique to transverse plane. 2. Humerus aligned with transverse plane and, by time shoulders are parallel with frontal plane, has moved ahead of outline of body. 3. Humerus aligned with transverse plane and, when shoulders are parallel with frontal plane, has lagged back within or behind outline of body.
Forearm	1. No forearm lag. 2. Forearm and ball appear to lag (remain stationary or move backward in relation to body), with forward motion begun before shoulders are parallel with frontal plane. 3. Forearm and ball apear to lag, with forward motion begun after shoulders are parallel with frontal plane.
Trunk	1. No trunk action or forward-backward movements (only arm active). 2. Upper trunk rotation or total trunk rotation. 3. Differentiated trunk rotation with pelvic rotation preceding upper-spine rotation.
Feet	1. No step. 2. Step with foot on same side as throwing hand (ipsilateral). 3. Step with foot on opposite side from throwing hand (contralateral). 4. Contralateral step with distance greater than 50% of standing height.

occurrence of all combinations of body component levels for overhand throwing and hopping. Three levels for each of three components for the overhand throw for force yields 27 potential combinations (3 × 3 × 3), but in an 8-year longitudinal study, only 11 of the combinations were observed. Leg (4) and arm (5) components for hopping yield 20 possible combinations, but in a 15-year longitudinal study, subjects demonstrated only 10 of the combinations. From a dynamic systems perspective, Roberton and Langendorfer (1993) referred to the most frequently observed combinations as "attractors" and suggested that proponents of the total body configuration stages "may have been focusing on strong attractor states across body parts to the exclusion of other attractor states and the asymmetrical component development needed to form attractors" (p. S66).

■ SEX DIFFERENCES IN FUNDAMENTAL MOVEMENT SKILLS

Differences between boys and girls in the performance of fundamental movement skills has been confirmed in many studies throughout the 20th century. For example, Seefeldt and Haubenstricker (1982) showed differences between boys and girls in the average ages at which they attain the highest developmental pattern of various fundamental movement skills, as described earlier in this chapter. Perhaps the best summary of the studies documenting sex differences in fundamental movement skill products is the meta-analysis by Thomas and French (1985).

From a comprehensive search of movement performance literature from 1899 to 1983, Thomas and French (1985) selected 64 studies that met task, subject, design, and statistical treatment requirements of the analysis. The 64 studies, written between 1965 and 1982, included more than 30,000 subjects (51% boys, 49% girls) ranging in age from 3 to 20 years. Thomas and French standardized mean differences in performance outcomes between boys and girls across the studies by using *effect size*, which was calculated by dividing mean performance differences by the overall standard deviation. An effect size of 0.2 is considered to reflect small differences; 0.5, medium differences; and 0.8, large differences (Cohen, 1969).

Four fundamental movement skills were included in the meta-analysis: running, jumping, catching, and throwing. The effect sizes for running for maximum speed over short distances and jumping for maximum horizontal distance were about 0.4 to 0.5 until about 12 years, then increased to over 2.0 by 18 years. For catching success, the effect sizes were below 0.4 until about 10 years, then increased up to 1.0 by 13 years. For throwing for maximum distance, the effect sizes were already over 1.0 between 3 and 6 years, and increased beyond 3.5 by 17 years. These results indicated that before puberty, performance differences between boys and girls in these skills (except for throwing) were low to moderate, but that after puberty they were so large that the lowest boys outperformed almost all girls.

Thomas and French (1985) argued that the sex differences in running, jumping, and catching before puberty are primarily environmentally induced, while the rapid increases after puberty are due to both environmental and biological factors. They also contended that the early large differences in throwing are likely caused by biological factors and that the expanding gap in later years is driven by both environment and biology. The importance of biological factors in sex-related throwing differences is confirmed by studies showing that training does little to reduce the disparity (Thomas, Michael, & Gallagher, 1994).

Up to about 1950, separate movement skill tests were often employed for males and females. For example, the items on the Athletic Badge Tests were different for boys (Committee on Tests, 1913a) than for girls (Committee on Tests, 1913b), and Cozens and Neilson's achievement tests were developed separately for males (Cozens, 1936; Cozens et al., 1936) and females (Cozens et al. 1937). In addition, there was the popular "physical test of a man" (Sargent, 1921) as well as a comparable test of physical efficiency for women (Wayman, 1923).

Almost all contemporary movement skill assessments are designed for both males and females, although some may have separate norms for each sex. In the Test of Gross Motor Development (TGMD), one of the most popular tests of fundamental movement skills, Ulrich (1985) found no significant differences between boys and girls in mean performances on locomotor and object-control subtests and consequently used the same conversion tables for both sexes. Langendorfer (1986), in a review of the TGMD, argued that this decision should be questioned because of previous literature showing sex differences in both product and process for some of the skills in the test, such as throwing, striking, hopping, and jumping. However, Ulrich (1985) appears to be justified, because the differences most likely were neutralized as subtest scores were derived by summing across a group of skills. Thus, differences between males and females may be apparent in tests of fundamental movement skills only when norms are available for individual skills.

In the next two sections, I will describe and critique in detail the TGMD and the Top-Down Motor Milestone Test from the Mobility Opportunities Via Education program.

■ REVIEW: TEST OF GROSS MOTOR DEVELOPMENT

Ulrich (1981) originally developed a "criterion-referenced test in fundamental motor and physical fitness skills" as part of his doctoral dissertation at Michigan State University. The fundamental motor skills portion of this work became the Objectives-Based Motor Skill Assessment Instrument (Ulrich, 1982) and was later modified and published as the TGMD (Ulrich, 1985). The TGMD can be described as a criterion- and norm-referenced assessment of fundamental movement skill processes.

The TGMD was designed to evaluate the gross motor skill development of children from 3 to 10 years of age. More specifically, Ulrich (1985) indicates that the TGMD may be used to (a) identify children who are significantly below age norms in gross motor skill development, (b) plan a program to improve gross motor skill development in those children showing delays, (c) assess changes in gross motor skill development as a function of increasing age or experience, or (d) assess changes in gross motor skill development as a function of instruction or intervention. The TGMD can be administered in about 15 to 20 min and involves equipment commonly used in movement activity programs.

Test Structure

The TGMD provides 3 to 4 process criteria for 12 fundamental movement skills, for a total of 45 criteria. The skills are divided into two subtests: locomotor and object control. There are a total of 26 criteria for 7 locomotor skills (gallop, hop, horizontal jump, leap, run, skip, and slide), and a total of 19 criteria for 5 object-control skills (stationary bounce, catch, kick, two-hand strike, and overhand throw). One page from the TGMD scoring booklet, indicating the required equipment, directions, and criteria for 2 locomotor and 2 object-control skills, is presented in figure 10.5.

After observing a child perform the skill three times, the examiner records a 1 for each criterion demonstrated on two or more trials and a 0 for each criterion demonstrated on fewer than two trials. These raw scores are summed across skills for each subtest and are carried forward to the cover sheet of the test booklet (see figure 10.6). The locomotor raw scores then are converted into percentiles and standard (i.e., standardized) scores according to 1-year age intervals. The normative information is based on a stratified sample of 909 children from eight states. Finally, the standard scores, with a mean of 10 and a standard deviation of 3, are summed; they are then converted into a composite standard score, called a Gross Motor Development Quotient (GMDQ), with a mean of 100 and a standard deviation of 15. The summing of the subtest standard scores rather than the raw scores to derive the GMDQ allows the two subtests to be weighted equally even though there are more criteria in the locomotor subtest.

The differences in mean subtest standard scores for boys and girls were not significant at the .01 level, and thus normative information is provided only for the two sexes combined. However, Langendorfer (1986) suggests that there may be some measurement problems inherent in the TGMD that cause it not to be sensitive to previously documented sex differences in both process and product scores of several of the skills (e.g., striking, throwing, hopping, and jumping). Langendorfer's criticism illustrates that the subtest composite scores do not represent any single skill, but rather reflect generalized constructs of "locomotion" and "object control," within which potential sex differences may be washed out.

Besides providing tables for evaluating performance across skills in the locomotor and object-control subtests and across the two subtests, Ulrich (1985) provides tables for evaluating performance on individual criteria. For each criterion, the ages at which 60% and 80% of the standardization

LOCOMOTOR SKILLS

Skill	Equipment	Directions	Performance Criteria	1st	2nd
SKIP	A minimum of 30 feet of clear space, marking device	Mark off two lines 30 feet apart Tell the student to skip from one line to the other three times	1. A rhythmical repetition of the step-hop on alternate feet 2. Foot of nonsupport leg carried near surface during hop 3. Arms alternately moving in opposition to legs at about waist level		
SLIDE	A minimum of 30 feet of clear space, colored tape or other marking device	Mark off two lines 30 feet apart Tell the student to slide from one line to the other three times facing the same direction	1. Body turned sideways to desired direction of travel 2. A step sideways followed by a slide of the trailing foot to a point next to the lead foot 3. A short period where both feet are off the floor 4. Able to slide to the right and to the left side		
LOCOMOTOR SKILLS SUBTEST SCORE					

OBJECT CONTROL SKILLS

Skill	Equipment	Directions	Performance Criteria	1st	2nd
TWO-HAND STRIKE	4-6 inch light-weight ball, plastic bat	Toss the ball softly to the student at about waist level Tell the student to hit the ball hard Only count those tosses that are between the student's waist and shoulders	1. Dominant hand grips bat above nondominant hand 2. Nondominant side of body faces the tosser (feet parallel) 3. Hip and spine rotation 4. Weight is transferred by stepping with front foot		
STATIONARY BOUNCE	8 - 10 inch playground ball hard, flat surface (floor, pavement)	Tell the student to bounce the ball three times using one hand Make sure the ball is not underinflated Repeat 3 separate trials	1. Contact ball with one hand at about hip height 2. Pushes ball with fingers (not a slap) 3. Ball contacts floor in front of (or to the outside of) foot on the side of the hand being used		

■ **FIGURE 10.5** One page from the TGMD scoring booklet.

From *Test of Gross Motor Development* by D. A. Ulrich, 1985, Austin, TX: PRO-ED. Copyright 1985 by PRO-ED. Reprinted by permission.

Name_____

School/Agency_____

Sex: Male_____ Female _____ Grade_____

TGMD

TEST OF
GROSS
MOTOR
DEVELOPMENT

Dale A. Ulrich

TESTING INFORMATION

1ST TESTING

	Year	Month	Day
Date Tested	___	___	___
Date of Birth	___	___	___
Chronological Age	___	___	___

Examiner's Name

Examiner's Title

Purpose of Testing

2ND TESTING

	Year	Month	Day
Date Tested	___	___	___
Date of Birth	___	___	___
Chronological Age	___	___	___

Examiner's Name

Examiner's Title

Purpose of Testing

RECORD OF SCORES

1ST TESTING

Subtests	Raw Scores	%iles	Std. Scores
Locomotor Skills	___	___	___
Object Control Skills	___	___	___

Sum of Standard Scores = _____

Gross Motor Development Quotient (GMDQ) = _____

2ND TESTING

Subtests	Raw Scores	%iles	Std. Scores
Locomotor Skills	___	___	___
Object Control Skills	___	___	___

Sum of Standard Scores = _____

Gross Motor Development Quotient (GMDQ) = _____

COMMENTS / RECOMMENDATIONS

_____

_____

_____

_____

_____

_____

_____

_____

Additional copies of this form (#0552) may be purchased from
PRO-ED, 8700 Shoal Creek Blvd., Austin, Texas 78757, 512/451-3246

■ **FIGURE 10.6** Cover page from the TGMD scoring booklet.
From *Test of Gross Motor Development* by D. A. Ulrich, 1985, Austin, TX: PRO-ED. Copyright 1985 by PRO-ED. Reprinted by permission.

Test of Gross Motor Development (TGMD)

Published by: PRO-ED

Movement categories tested: motor abilities, fundamental movement skills

Uses: (a) identify children who are significantly below age norms in gross motor skill development, (b) plan a progam to improve gross motor skill development in those children showing delays, (c) assess changes in gross motor skill development as a function of increasing age or experience, and (d) assess changes in gross motor skill development as a function of instruction or intervention

Time to administer: about 15-20 minutes

Price: The test manual and a set of 50 student record books for the TGMD can be purchased for $64, or they can be ordered separately for $32 and $34 (1996 prices).

Contact: PRO-ED
               8700 Shoal Creek Boulevard
               Austin, TX 78757-6897
               (512-451-3246)

TGMD   TEST OF GROSS MOTOR DEVELOPMENT

Dale A. Ulrich

Name_____

School/Agency_____

Sex: Male _____ Female _____ Grade_____

TESTING INFORMATION

1ST TESTING

	Year	Month	Day
Date Tested	—	—	—
Date of Birth	—	—	—
Chronological Age			

Examiner's Name

Examiner's Title

Purpose of Testing

2ND TESTING

	Year	Month	Day
Date Tested	—	—	—
Date of Birth	—	—	—
Chronological Age			

Examiner's Name

Examiner's Title

Purpose of Testing

RECORD OF SCORES

1ST TESTING

Subtests	Raw Scores	%iles	Std. Scores
Locomotor Skills	—	—	—
Object Control Skills	—	—	—

2ND TESTING

Subtests	Raw Scores	%iles	Std. Scores
Locomotor Skills	—	—	—
Object Control Skills	—	—	—

sample (909 children representative of the U.S. population based on the 1980 census) were successful are specified and may be used to determine skill mastery. These ages for the hop and kick are shown in table 10.3. Note that the criteria for the skills are not developmentally ordered.

If the subtest scores on the GMDQ are used to make generalizations about skills beyond those 12 included in this test, then the TGMD should be considered an assessment of motor abilities. However, if these scores are interpreted only in relation to the skills in the subtests, or if the scores for the individual skills are interpreted individually, then the TGMD can be considered an assessment of fundamental movement skills. Nevertheless, even if the subtest scores of the GMDQ are interpreted only in relation to the skills in the subtests, the person interpreting these scores must carefully consider what these composite scores actually represent and how they should be used.

Reliability

The reliability of the TGMD for both norm-referenced and criterion-referenced applications was examined in several studies by Ulrich and his colleagues. Two studies addressed reliability of norm-referenced applications from a generalizability perspective (Ulrich, Riggen, Ozmun, Screws, &

TABLE 10.3   Ages at Which 60% and 80% of the TGMD Standardization Sample Met the Performance Criteria for the Hop and Kick

Skill (Subtest)	Performance criteria	60%	80%
Hop (locomotor)	1. Foot of nonsupport leg is bent and carried in back of the body.	5	6
	2. Nonsupport leg swings in pendular fashion to produce force.	7	8
	3. Arms bent at elbows and swing forward on takeoff.	7	10
	4. Able to hop on right and left foot.	4	5
Kick (object control)	1. Rapid continuous approach to ball.	4	4
	2. The trunk is inclined backward during ball contact.	8	9
	3. Forward swing of the arm opposite kicking leg.	8	9
	4. Follow-through by hopping on the nonkicking foot.	10	—[a]

Note: From *Test of Gross Motor Development*, (pp. 17-18), by D.A. Ulrich, 1985, Austin, TX: PRO-ED. Copyright 1985 by PRO-ED. Reprinted with permission.
[a]not achieved by 80% at any age between 3 and 10 years.

Cleland, 1989; Ulrich & Wise, 1984), and two addressed test-retest reliability of criterion-referenced mastery decisions (Chapman, 1984, cited by Ulrich, 1985; Ulrich, 1984). The results of these studies and the standard errors of measurement presented in the test manual indicate that the TGMD has a high level of reliability.

Norm-Referenced Applications.   Ulrich and Wise (1984) carried out a generalizability (G) study by videotaping two administrations of the TGMD, separated by 1 week, to five boys and five girls between 3 and 10 years of age. The two videotaped test performances of each child were scored by 20 undergraduate students, and these scores were analyzed with a 20(rater) × 2(occasion) × 10(subject) analysis of variance. The amount of variance attributed to each facet—rater, occasion, and subject—and their interactions were calculated from the analysis of variance for composite scores (see table 5.1 in chapter 5, p. 105) and for each skill in the locomotor and object-control subtests (see tables 10.4 and 10.5).

As explained in chapter 5 and shown in table 5.1, over 80% of the variance in the three composites was directly attributed to differences between subjects, representing true scores. The greatest source of error from the possible sources identified was Rater × Subject, which indicated that some raters responded differentially to certain subjects or that some subjects were rated differentially by certain raters. Less than 5% of the variance was accounted for by overall differences between raters (interrater) and less than 3% by overall differences between occasions (test-retest). The variance in scores for individual skills attributed to differences between subjects was only 31% for the run and was 58% to 84% for the other skills (see tables 10.4 and 10.5). The low variance by subject for the run was most likely obtained because most subjects passed all four criteria. Again, the greatest source of error was the Rater × Subject interaction (over 20% for the jump, catch, kick, and run), and the contributions of overall differences between raters and occasions were quite low (4% or less).

Ulrich et al. (1989) carried out a second generalizability (G) study by videotaping 20 children with mild mental retardation performing 10 trials of each of three skills on the TGMD: the kick, the horizontal jump, and the overhand throw. The children ranged in age from 5 to 13 years. These 200 trials were rated by graduate students who had trained an average of 18 hr until they reached a specified level of competency or by graduate students who had trained for 3 hr. The variance accounted for by the children only, equivalent to the true score, ranged for the three skills from 64% to 82% for the competency-trained observers and from 50% to 70% for the other observers. Moreover, the variance between competency-trained observers ranged from 0.0% to 0.3% with a residual variance from 4% to 15%, while the variance between the other observers ranged from 0.8% to 4.1% with a residual variance from 13% to 33%.

Ulrich and Wise (1984) showed a high degree of reliability, or a good match between observed and true scores, for the three types of composite scores in the TGMD. However, in both generalizability studies, the reliability for individual skills was considerably lower, indicating a need for caution in interpreting the results for individual skills. Ulrich et al. (1989) also documented the strong effect of the amount or type of training of raters on measurement error, bringing into question the degree of reliability between raters with differing levels of training or experience.

TABLE 10.4 Percent of Total Variance in Locomotor Scores Accounted for by Rater (R), Occasion(O), Subjects (S), and Their Interactions

Variance component	Run	Gallop	Hop	Leap	Jump	Skip	Slide
R	0.9	2.5	0.0	1.8	1.5	0.0	1.7
O	0.0	1.3	1.1	0.7	3.0	0.0	0.0
S	31.0	69.3	78.8	70.9	66.1	74.8	84.4
R×O	0.0	0.1	0.4	0.0	0.0	0.1	0.0
R×S	35.9	19.2	14.1	18.8	20.3	16.8	9.1
O×S	6.7	1.3	0.8	1.0	0.6	1.4	0.2
R×O×S, E (error)	25.5	6.3	4.7	6.7	8.4	6.9	4.6
TOTAL	100.0	100.0	99.9	99.9	99.9	100.0	100.0

Note: Reprinted, by permission, from D.A. Ulrich and S.L. Wise, 1984, "Reliability of Scores Obtained with the Objectives-Based Motor Skill Assessment Instrument," *Adapted Physical Activity Quarterly*, Vol. 1(3), 236-237.

TABLE 10.5 Percent of Total Variance in Object Control Scores Accounted for by Rater (R), Occasion(O), Subjects (S), and Their Interactions

Variance component	Strike	Bounce	Catch	Kick	Throw
R	2.3	0.0	0.0	1.6	4.0
O	0.9	1.8	3.0	1.5	0.3
S	70.4	72.9	57.6	60.8	75.2
R×O	0.1	9.0	0.4	0.2	0.1
R×S	16.5	2.4	26.9	27.6	15.6
O×S	1.7	0.3	1.9	0.0	0.4
R×O×S, E (error)	8.1	13.6	10.1	8.3	4.3
TOTAL	100.0	100.0	99.9	100.0	99.9

Note: Reprinted, by permission, from D.A. Ulrich and S.L. Wise, 1984, "Reliability of Scores Obtained with the Objectives-Based Motor Skill Assessment Instrument," *Adapted Physical Activity Quarterly*, Vol. 1(3), 236-237.

The most tangible reliability statistic for norm-referenced applications is the standard error of measurement *(SEM)* because it is used to create a confidence interval of the true score for performance on a single testing. Standard errors of measurement are specified for both locomotor and object-control subtest raw scores in 1-year intervals from 3 to 10 years, ranging from 0.29 for object control at 10 years to 0.82 for locomotor at 6 years. Hence, if a 6-year-old boy had a raw score of 13 on the locomotor subtest, his score would be equivalent to the 9th percentile. Applying the standard error of measurement of 0.82 at a confidence level of 80% would yield the following raw score confidence interval:

$$X \pm (Z_C)(SEM) = 13 \pm (1.28)(0.82) = 13 \pm 1.05 = 11.95 \text{ to } 14.05.$$

This interval, when converted to percentiles using the actual means and standard deviations for 6-year-olds rather than the conversion table, is from the 6th percentile to the 15th percentile. This relatively small interval supports the contention that the TGMD is a reliable test.

In addition, internal consistency was evaluated by calculating split-half reliability coefficients for the two subtests using data from 200 children across the eight age levels in the standardization sample. The coefficients range from .71 to .93, but as pointed out by Ezzelle and Moutoux (1993), the manual does not indicate how the subtests were divided.

Criterion-Referenced Applications.   The test-retest reliability of certain mastery levels on the TGMD was investigated by Ulrich (1984) and Chapman (1984, cited by Ulrich, 1985). In the first study, the TGMD was administered twice each to 80 children without disabilities and 40 children with moderate mental retardation between the ages of 3 and 10 years. The two testings were separated by 1 week, and the performances were rated by a "university faculty member familiar with the test." The proportion of agreement between the two testings in the classification of the two groups of children, according to mastery criteria of 70% and 85% of the 45 items, ranged from .87 to .93 (kappa values from .62 to .84). Chapman (1984, cited by Ulrich, 1985), using mastery criteria of 45%, 50%, and 60% for children between 3 and 6 years, reported proportions of agreement from .89 to .91 between testings 1 week apart.

Recently Dummer, Haubenstricker, and Stewart (1996) used the TGMD, as well as other tests, to evaluate the movement skills of children who are deaf. Two raters independently evaluated the performances of 195 children who are deaf, ranging in age from 5 to 18 years, from videotape. The percent agreement between the two raters was reported to be 92% on the 45 specific skill criteria and 87% on the mastery of entire skills (correct performance of all criteria for a particular skill).

Validity

Two types of validity of the TGMD have been addressed by Ulrich (1985): content and construct. In the following pages I present information from Ulrich (1985) and other sources regarding these two types of validity.

Content.   Ulrich (1985) established content validity by reporting unanimous agreement among three motor development experts that the gross motor skills in the TGMD represented skills frequently taught to children in preschool and early elementary grades and that the skills were representative of the gross motor skill domain. However, Ezzelle and Moutoux (1993) argue that "the area of gross motor development and function is more than locomotor and object control" and consequently "seriously question whether these two areas adequately represent all aspects of the gross motor domain" (p. 81).

Important in determining the content validity of the TGMD is the operational definition of gross motor development. Ulrich (1985) cites the definition presented by Williams (1983): "The skillful use of the total body in large muscle or gross motor activities that require intricate temporal and spatial coordination of movement of a number of body parts or segments sequentially or simultaneously" (p. 10). However, Langendorfer (1986) points out that this was Williams' (1983) definition of gross motor control, not gross motor development, and asserts that the focus on mature performance levels and the corresponding omission of lower developmental levels "renders the instrument incapable of ascertaining a fundamental aspect of developmental change" (p. 187). Hence, although the responses of three motor development experts offered some tentative validity of the content of the TGMD, others have questioned how well the test items match the purpose of the test.

Construct.   Ulrich (1985) addressed construct validity of the TGMD by examining three key assumptions. First, he evaluated the assumption that "the principal underlying structure of the test would reflect gross motor development" (p. 31) by conducting a factor analysis of the 12 items in the TGMD. He found that 9 of the 12 items loaded on the same factor, accounting for 62% of the common variance. There also were two other factors: one with 6 locomotor items adding 8% variance and another with only the run item contributing an additional 5%. If the first factor is considered to be "general gross-motor development," then what do the other two factors represent? The run does not appear to be related to any of the other skills in this analysis, and perhaps should not have been included in the test. Note that the four criteria for the run are achieved earlier than any other set of criteria and that the run has by far the poorest reliability of any of the 12 skills.

The second assumption was that the TGMD is sensitive to changes due to increasing age and experience as well as instruction. Ulrich (1985) evaluated the age hypothesis by calculating the correlation between age and the subtest total scores and the total composite score. He found that these three correlations were quite high, ranging between .81 and .86. Also, in administering the TGMD to 300 Puerto Rican children, 5 to 7 years old, Aponte, French, and Sherrill (1990) found that TGMD total raw scores were significantly higher for 7-year-olds compared to 6-year-olds and significantly higher for 6-year-olds compared to 5-year-olds.

The correlations between age and individual skills are not provided but, as mentioned earlier, the ages at which 60% and 80% of the standardization sample achieved each of the criteria are presented (see table 10.3). The age at which 60% of the standardization sample achieved success was above 3 years on 39 of the 45 criteria (87%) and above 4 years on 30 of the 45 criteria (67%) across all skills. The 60% cutoff for the object-control subtest also was above 5 and 6 years on 14 (74%) and 11 (58%) of the 19 criteria, respectively. Thus, the TGMD appears to be limited in its ability to identify 3- and 6-year-old children—half of its targeted population—who fall below minimum mastery levels (see Ezzelle & Moutoux, 1993, for a similar criticism).

An application of item response theory to the standardization data of the TGMD, reported by Zhu and Cole (1996), offers further insight into the relationship between age and performance on the TGMD. In this analysis using a Rasch model of item response theory, raw (ordinal) scores were converted to logit (ratio) scores. Hence, these logit scores provided linear representations of skill or ability in which a logit score twice as large as another represented twice the level of movement skill or motor ability. The difficulty of a specific item or skill and the overall motor ability of the

TABLE 10.6   Logit Values for TGMD Skills and Subtests Calculated for the Standardization Sample (adapted from Zhu & Cole, 1996)

Skill/subtest	Logit	Subtest	
		Locomotor	Object control
Run	−0.84	X	
Slide	−0.53	X	
Gallop	−0.44	X	
Catch	−0.10		X
Hop	−0.10	X	
Strike	0.01		X
Jump	0.07	X	
Skip	0.24	X	
Throw	0.31		X
Bounce	0.37		X
Kick	0.46		X
Leap	0.55	X	
Locomotor	−0.04		
Object control	0.04		

subjects were represented in terms of the same linear measurement scale. Zhu and Cole reported that logit scores increased each consecutive year, from –2.77 for 3-year-olds to 2.28 for 10-year-olds, and that the logit scores were higher for males (0.81) than for females (0.65). The logit values for each skill and subtest are presented in table 10.6.

In their paper, Zhu and Cole (1996) provide a new scoring form for the TGMD based on the results of their Rasch analysis (see figure 10.7). This scoring form includes (a) a curve to convert total scores into logits, with a 95% confidence band (on the bottom); (b) a matrix with each skill ordered from easy to difficult on the vertical axis and with the logit values of the individual skill criteria depicted from easy to difficult on the horizontal axis (in the middle); and (c) an evaluation standard by age based on sample statistics. As indicated in the figure, a total raw score of 35 would be equivalent to about 1.7 logits, which would be average for a 7-year-old. Because in this item response theory scoring system all criteria as well as the converted total raw score are on the same interval measurement scale, an examiner is able to clearly identify the easiest items a child did not pass and the most difficult items he or she did pass, and to consider this skill-oriented information in relation to the total ability score in logits.

To examine the sensitivity of the TGMD to instruction, Ulrich and Ulrich (1984) provided formal movement skill instruction to one group of preschoolers three times a week for 10 weeks and compared their pretest and posttest scores on the Objectives-Based Motor Skill Assessment Instrument (Ulrich, 1982), an earlier version of the TGMD, with those of a control group given free play for the same amount of time. When pretest score differences were statistically equalized across the two groups, the instruction group showed significantly greater improvement on the posttest than the control group. Ulrich and Ulrich (1984) therefore concluded that the assessment instrument was sensitive to formal movement skill instruction.

The third key assumption examined by Ulrich was that children with mental retardation would score significantly lower than children of similar chronological age who did not have disabilities. In the examiner's manual, Ulrich (1985) described a study in which the TGMD scores of eighty 4- to 10-year-olds with mild and moderate mental retardation were compared with the scores of children of similar ages without disabilities. He reported that the children without disabilities showed significantly higher scores across the 12 skills in the TGMD than the children with mental retardation. Given some of the apparent limitations of the TGMD with younger children, a lack of statistical significance between the two groups at the lower ages might have been expected, but this possibility was not addressed. Moreover, the results for the individual locomotor and object-control skills also were not offered.

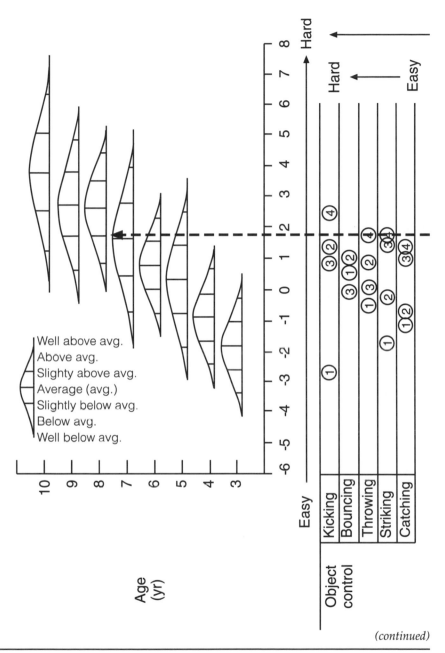

■ **FIGURE 10.7** TGMD scoring form proposed by Zhu and Cole (1996).
From "Many-Faceted Rasch Calibration of a Gross-Motor Instrument" by W. Zhu and E. L.
Cole, 1996, *Research Quarterly for Exercise and Sport*, 67, p. 32. Reproduced with permission
from the American Alliance for Health, Physical Education, Recreation, and Dance.

(continued)

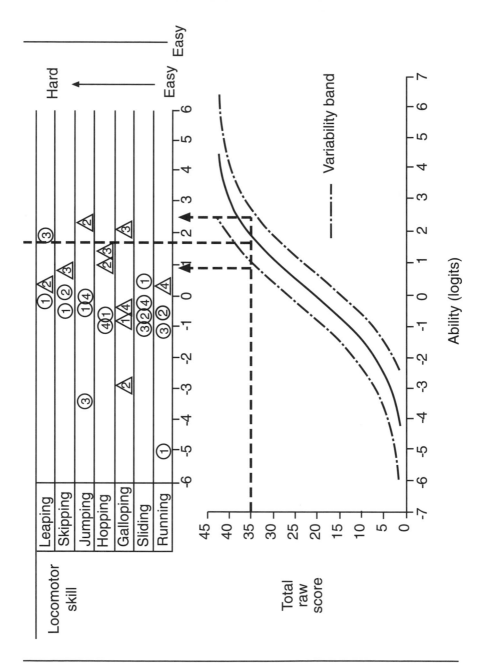

There is considerable empirical evidence that boys and girls within the age range of the TGMD markedly differ in some of the skills included in the TGMD, particularly the overhand throw (Halverson, Roberton, & Langendorfer, 1982; Sakurai & Miyashita, 1983; Thomas & French, 1985). Ulrich (1985) states that differences in the means between boys and girls in the standardization sample were not significant at the .01 level, but does not provide any means or standard deviations for examination or indicate the nature of the statistical analysis. In their study of 5- to 7-year-old Puerto Rican children, Aponte et al. (1990) found that TGMD total raw scores were significantly higher for boys than for girls. If sex differences were shown for these children, then even greater differences should be expected in 8- to 10-year-olds. Langendorfer (1986) argues that "the lack of gender differences inconsistent with the literature suggests that either the .01 significance level was too stringent or there are some measurement problems inherent with the test that render it insensitive to previously detected gender differences" (p. 189).

Summary

The TGMD is a popular criterion- and norm-referenced instrument that assesses the movement process used to perform 12 different movement skills. A just published survey of 225 adapted physical educators in Minnesota showed that 39% of them used the TGMD to assess students for service eligibility (Waltman, Folsom-Meek, Bergerson, & Groteluschen, 1996). The popularity of the TGMD is driven by several clear strengths. First, it has a very specific focus on the movement patterns of locomotor and object-control skills, with good reliability on subtest and composite scores. Next, the examiner's manual is relatively inexpensive, the equipment is easy to acquire and is inexpensive, and the test takes only 15 to 20 min to administer. Third, the test is easy to administer because all instructions are provided directly on each score sheet. And fourth, the TGMD may be used for a variety of purposes, assuming appropriate interpretation of test results. Also, one may modify the TGMD to expand its utility by testing children under a variety of task and environmental conditions, as explained by Ulrich (1988) and in chapter 13 of this book (see figure 13.7, p. 315).

Nevertheless, the TGMD has at least four problem areas that its users should recognize. First, the task of observing and considering all three or four criteria for a particular skill on each of three trials is very difficult. Many examiners adjust the procedures by focusing on just one or two criteria on each of the three trials, rather than meeting the two-out-of-three standard, in order to decide on final scores.

Second, the reliability of some individual skills is questionable, and no data are provided on the reliability of individual criteria. Thus, one should be cautious in using the results on individual skills or criteria to develop intervention programs. Ulrich (1985) states that the TGMD can be used to identify specific gross motor skills strengths and weaknesses; but to validate this use, information on the reliability of mastery decisions for individual skills should be presented. The criterion-related reliability information on mastery decisions reported by Ulrich (1984) and Chapman (1984, cited by Ulrich, 1985) was based only on total raw scores.

Next, although Ulrich (1985) specifies that the TGMD can be used to evaluate the gross motor functioning of children from 3 to 10 years, the test appears to be best suited for children between 5 and 7 years. Most items in the object-control subtest are too difficult for 3- to 4-year-olds, and most items in both subtests are too easy for most 8- to 10-year-olds. For example, a score of 0 on the object-control subtest for 3-year-olds is equivalent to the 5th percentile, and a score of 3 of 19 possible points is equivalent to the 63rd percentile. Furthermore, perfect scores of 26 and 19 on the locomotor and object-control subtests, respectively, are equivalent to the 75th and 84th percentiles for 10-year-olds. In the context of the basic purpose of the test reflected in its title, Langendorfer (1986) points out that the focus on mature performance levels and the corresponding omission of lower developmental levels "renders the instrument incapable of ascertaining a fundamental aspect of developmental change" (p. 187).

And fourth, the combining of data for boys and girls in the normative tables is questionable, particularly for older age groups, in light of existing motor development literature and other studies involving the TGMD (e.g., Aponte et al., 1990). The inclusion of tables with means and standard deviations for boys and girls at each age level at least would allow persons the option of calculating separate norms for each sex.

■ REVIEW: TOP-DOWN MOTOR MILESTONE TEST

The Top-Down Motor Milestone Test (TDMMT) is part of the Mobility Opportunities Via Education (MOVE) curriculum first published in 1990 by Bidabe, a special educator, and Lollar, a physical therapist. Mobility Opportunities Via Education is a top-down, activity-based curriculum designed to teach infants, preschoolers, school-age children, adolescents, and even young adults basic, functional movement skills needed for adult life in home and community environments. The curriculum focuses on three categories of skills—sitting, standing, and walking—and the functional activities derived from these skills. In this program, Bidabe and Lollar assume that just about anyone can sit, stand, and walk, if given enough physical assistance, and can improve these skills if they are taught and practiced in a systematic fashion. In the skill taxonomy used in this book, sitting and standing are early movement milestones and walking is either an early movement milestone or a fundamental movement skill. But because all these skills are likely to be acquired by the target population well after 1 year of age, the TDMMT is included in this chapter on fundamental movement skills. Note also that some of the skills in the TDMMT are evaluated in functional contexts.

The two main purposes of the TDMMT are instructional planning and evaluation of progress. More specifically, with regard to instructional planning, the TDMMT was designed to provide sequences of sitting, standing, and walking skills that (a) are age appropriate and based on a top-down model rather than on sequential skill acquisition of infants, (b) are immediately useful to the participant as well as later in adulthood, and (c) increase the accessibility of community and home environments. With respect to the evaluation of progress, the TDMMT was designed to provide a method of measuring small increments of progress in sitting, standing, and walking skills.

Test Structure

The MOVE program has six steps, beginning with administration of the TDMMT. The other five steps, which I will discuss briefly after giving the details of the TDMMT, include (a) setting goals, (b) task analysis, (c) measuring prompts, (d) reducing prompts, and (e) teaching skills.

The TDMMT is a criterion-referenced instrument composed of 74 skills organized into 16 sitting, standing, and walking skill headings. In addition, the 3 to 11 skills for each of 2 sitting skill headings, 4 standing skill headings, and 10 walking skill headings are sequenced according to four levels of function:

- *Grad Level*—independent mobility in home and minimal assistance in community
- *Level I*—no lifting by caretaker required and a wheelchair needed only for long distances
- *Level II*—minimal lifting by caretaker required and a wheelchair needed for distances longer than 10 ft
- *Level III*—the lowest level that is not used for 5 of the 16 skill headings

The skills and function levels for one skill heading, standing, are presented in figure 10.8, and the summary page for all 16 skill headings (A-P) is shown in figure 10.9. Note in figure 10.9 that some prerequisite skills from other skill headings are included for some skill headings at Levels II and III (e.g., A.7 for B—Moves while sitting; F.3, C.5, and C.6 for K—Turns while walking).

The TDMMT is administered retrospectively by a parent, caregiver, or teacher familiar with the student. For each skill heading (one page in the instrument is devoted to each skill heading), the rater begins with the Grad Level skills and goes down until he or she reaches a skill that the individual has mastered. This is marked with an E for *entry* and the date (see figure 10.8). The items below the entry skill are assumed to be mastered, so they are marked off. If the rater is not sure whether a skill is mastered, the student can be asked to perform the skill. On the summary sheet, all mastered skills also are marked off, but there are no summary or composite scores. The manual indicates that the TDMMT takes about 15 min to complete.

M·O·V·E

STANDING

	GRAD LEVEL	LEVEL I	LEVEL II	LEVEL III
C.1. Can stand in one place without support for a minimum of 60 seconds.	☐ DATE			
C.2. Can stand in one place with one or both hands held for a minimum of five minutes.		☐ DATE		
C.3. Can maintain hip and knee extension to allow weight bearing for a minimum of three minutes while another person keeps participant's body in alignment			☐ DATE	
C.4. Can tolerate weight bearing on feet for a minimum of 45 minutes per day when knees, hips, and trunk are held in alignment by a mobile stander or similiar standing device.			☐ DATE	
C.5. Can tolerate fully prompted extension of hips and knees.				☐ DATE
C.6. Can tolerate being placed in a vertical position.				☐ DATE

■ **FIGURE 10.8** Score sheet for standing, one of 16 skills assessed in the Top-Down Motor Milestone Test from the MOVE program (Bidabe & Lollar, 1992).

M·O·V·E

SUMMARY OF TEST RESULTS

NAME _____

DATE _____

1. Fill in squares representing the current skill levels.
2. Fill in all squares to the right of the current skill levels.
3. Circle skills to be addressed next.

	GRAD LEVEL	LEVEL I	LEVEL II	LEVEL III
A. MAINTAINS A SITTING POSITION	A.1	A.2 A.3	A.4 A.5 A.6	A.7
B. MOVES WHILE SITTING	B.1 B.2	B.3 B.4 B.5 B.6	B.7 B.8 B.9 B.10	B.11 *A.7*
C. STANDS	C.1	C.2	C.3 C.4	*C.5 C.6*
D. TRANSITIONS FROM SITTING TO STANDING	D.1 D.2	D.3 D.4	D.5 D.6	*C.5 C.6 C.7*
E. TRANSITIONS FROM STANDING TO SITTING	E.1 E.2	E.3 E.4	E.5 E.6	*C.5 C.6 C.7*
F. PIVOTS WHILE STANDING	F.1	F.2	F.3	*C.5 C.6*
G. WALKS FORWARD	G.1 G.2	G.3	G.4 G.5	G.6 *C.5 C.6*
H. TRANSITIONS FROM STANDING TO WALKING	H.1	H.2	H.3	*G.6 C.5 C.6*
I. TRANSITIONS FROM WALKING TO STANDING	I.1	I.2	I.3	*G.6 C.5 C.6*
J. WALKS BACKWARD	J.1	J.2	J.3	J.4 *C.5 C.6*
K. TURNS WHILE WALKING	K.1 K.2	K.3 K.4	*E.3*	*C.5 C.6*
L. WALKS UP STEPS	L.1	L.2	L.3 *G.4 C.3*	
M. WALKS DOWN STEPS	M.1	M.2	M.3 *G.4 C.3*	
N. WALKS ON UNEVEN GROUND	N.1	N.2	N.3 *G.4 C.3*	
O. WALKS UP SLOPES	O.1	O.2	O.3 *G.4 C.3*	
P. WALKS DOWN SLOPES	P.1	P.2	P.3 *G.4 C.3*	

PREREQUISITE SKILLS FROM OTHER SECTIONS ARE INDICATED BY ITALICIZED LETTERS AND NUMBERS

■ **FIGURE 10.9**   Summary of Test Results sheet for the Top-Down Motor Milestone Test from the MOVE program (Bidabe & Lollar, 1992).

The two steps of the MOVE program that follow assessment are setting goals and task analysis. First, specific functional activities that the student needs to perform, such as seating self without being lifted, are selected by the parents, caregivers, or teachers. Then the skills that need to be improved for each selected activity are identified and targeted. For example, to seat self without being lifted, skills organized under the following skill headings are needed: walk to chair (G), turn to sit (F), step backward to position self (J), and lower self to chair (E).

The fourth step again involves assessment, this time the measurement of how much help or prompting the student needs to perform the targeted skills. The term *prompts* is used to refer to the amount and type of physical assistance, either by mechanical device or by another person, the individual needs. There are three different prompt assessment sheets that can be used for the 74 skills, one each for (a) static sitting, (b) standing or walking, and (c) hand and arm use in sitting, standing, or walking. Two (hand and arm use), four (sitting), or six (standing or walking) categories of prompts are included; these are rated on a scale from 0 to 5 that is unique for each prompt category. For example, one of the prompt categories for standing or walking is *type of prompt*, with 0 = does not need a physical prompt, 1 = a flexible object needed to maintain balance, 3 = another person's hand needed to maintain balance, and 5 = mechanical or solid prompt needed to maintain balance. If more than one score is appropriate, then the higher number is recorded.

The last two steps in the MOVE curriculum are reducing prompts and teaching the skills. Based on the prompt assessment information, a plan for reducing the prompts is set, including the specification of performance in terms of distance and/or time. Then teaching begins to help the student learn how to reduce the prompts and achieve the target activities. The MOVE manual includes ideas and suggestions for teaching all 74 skills. In addition, an entire chapter is devoted to selecting and using equipment. Bidabe and Lollar (1990) view equipment not as a substitute for teaching, but as an aid that is often necessary to allow instruction to occur. Three pieces of equipment designed by the MOVE staff are now manufactured by and available from Rifton Company: a front-leaning/advancement chair for sitting, a mobile stander, and a front-leaning walker/gait trainer. These were specifically developed to place students in positions to perform functional activities, to allow them to practice skills independently, and to increase the strength of their extensor muscles.

Reliability

No reliability information is mentioned in the MOVE manual. Aspects of the TDMMT pose difficulties in establishing some types of reliability; these need to be acknowledged by the authors, and at least some reliability data need to be collected and reported.

Top-Down Motor Milestone Test (TDMMT)

Published by: MOVE International

Movement categories tested: early movement milestones, fundamental movement skills

Uses: (a) plan instruction, and (b) evaluate progress

Time to administer: about 15 minutes

Price: The MOVE curriculum manual, including all information needed to administer the TDMMT, can be purchased for $89.95. The price of the TDMMT score sheets is not presently available.

Contact: MOVE International
                1300 17th Street - City Centre
                Bakersfield, CA 93301-4533
                (800)397-MOVE or (805)636-4561

M·O·V·E

SUMMARY OF TEST RESULTS

NAMI

DATE

1. Fill in squares representing the current skill levels.
2. Fill in all squares to the right of the current skill levels.
3. Circle skills to be addressed next.

	GRAD LEVEL				LEVEL I			
A. MAINTAINS A SITTING POSITION	A.1				A.2	A.3		
B. MOVES WHILE SITTING	B.1	B.2			B.3	B.4	B.5	B.6
C. STANDS	C.1				C.2			
D. TRANSITIONS FROM SITTING TO STANDING	D.1	D.2			D.3	D.4		
E. TRANSITIONS FROM STANDING TO SITTING	E.1	E.2			E.3	E.4		
F. PIVOTS WHILE STANDING	F.1				F.2			
G. WALKS FORWARD	G.1	G.2			G.3			
H. TRANSITIONS FROM STANDING TO WALKING	H.1				H.2			
I. TRANSITIONS FROM WALKING TO STANDING	I.1				I.2			
J. WALKS BACKWARD	J.1				J.2			
K. TURNS WHILE WALKING	K.1	K.2			K.3	K.4		
L. WALKS UP STEPS	L.1				L.2			
M. WALKS DOWN STEPS	M.1				M.2			
N. WALKS ON UNEVEN GROUND	N.1				N.2			
O. WALKS UP SLOPES	O.1				O.2			
P. WALKS DOWN SLOPES	P.1				P.2			

PREREQUISITE SKILLS FROM OTHER SECTIONS ARE INDICATED BY ITALICIZED LETTERS AND NUMBERS

Validity

The MOVE manual also provides no validity information for the TDMMT. However, some data offered to support the success of the MOVE program can be considered to be related to construct validity. The progress of 15 students on eight performance criteria over a 3-year period is reported, providing some insight into the extent to which the TDMMT can be used to plan instruction and to evaluate progress. The 15 students in this sample ranged in age from 6 to 16 years at program entry, had multiple disabilities (12 with cerebral palsy), scored from 6 to 18 months on Brigance or Gesell developmental scales, and had regressed in their developmental scores as they grew larger. The results showed increases in the number of these students who could perform the following tasks over the 3-year period (the skill number on the TDMMT is indicated in parentheses):

- Sitting (A.2)—from 9 to 12
- Sitting (A.3)—from 9 to 14
- Standing (C.1)—from 6 to 13
- Standing (a skill not on the TDMMT but between C.1 and C.2)—from 0 to 10
- From sitting to standing (D.1)—from 3 to 12
- Walking forward (a skill not on the TDMMT but between G.5 and G.6)—from 5 to 14
- Sitting to standing (D.2), walking forward (G.1), standing to sitting (E.2)—from 0 to 2
- Functional use of upper extremities (not on the TDMMT)—from 6 to 13

The gains shown here indicate the usefulness of the TDMMT in planning successful instruction and monitoring change, but it is not clear how the students would have fared with another program. However, given that all 15 students had been regressing in their developmental scores, the MOVE program appeared to be more effective than no intervention at all.

Summary

The TDMMT is a true skill-oriented instrument designed to plan instruction and monitor progress of individual students, particularly those with delays in sitting, standing, or walking, without summary or composite scores to cloud the interpretation. Other strengths of the TDMMT and the entire MOVE curriculum are that (a) extensive information is provided on how to translate the results of the test into instructional action; (b) a detailed assessment of the prompts or physical assistance needed to perform the targeted skills is included in the MOVE program, which potentially amplifies the information for each of the 74 skills on the TDMMT; and

(c) some empirical support for the effectiveness of the TDMMT in planning instruction and evaluating progress is given, based on data from 15 students over a 3-year intervention period.

The greatest weakness of the TDMMT is the absence of any reliability data. The retrospective nature of this test poses some interesting constraints on the methods used to determine reliability, but reliability is too important to ignore. First, interrater reliability may be hard to establish because the TDMMT is administered for the most part retrospectively by a person who knows the student well, and hence the results may be expected to vary between two raters who do not know the student equally well. Further, this situation precludes using unbiased, independent raters. However, the strategy of examining the reliability between caregivers and teachers used by Haley, Coster, Ludlow, Haltiwanger, and Andrellos (1992) in the Pediatric Evaluation of Disability Inventory (see chapter 11) also may be appropriate here.

Second, intrarater reliability may be almost impossible to examine, again because of the retrospective nature of the test. The exact same "administration" just cannot be repeated. However, the same rater could administer the test for the same student at least two different times, and the proportion of perfect agreement and corresponding kappa value on the highest skill then could be identified for each of the 16 skill headings. This test-retest reliability procedure should include students of different age ranges and with various levels of independent function.

Finally, Bidabe and Lollar need to offer explicit information on the validity of the testing procedures and the overall MOVE program. They provide some data on the success of the program, but these need to be considered in the specific context of validity. The authors obviously developed the skill headings and the specific skills under each heading after careful task analysis of many functional movement activities, and likely adjusted the test as they began to use it, but this information should be reported in a section on content validity. Also, experts in adapted physical education, special education, physical therapy, and rehabilitation medicine could be queried about the validity of the content of the TDMMT and the three prompt assessments in relation to the stated purposes of the test.

Chapter 11

Assessing Specialized and Functional Movement Skills

© Terry Wild Studio

TESTS of specialized skills perhaps are more common than tests in any other category, and a complete review of this category is beyond the scope of this book (for a more in-depth review and many specific examples, see the book by Strand & Wilson, 1993). However, an overview of basic definitions, assumptions, and subcategories of specialized skills is

> 66 The test is the ultimate scholastic invention, a 'decontextualized measure' to be employed in a setting that is itself decontextualized. 99
> — *Gardner (1991, pp. 132-133)*

necessary to understand when assessment at this level of the movement skill taxonomy is appropriate and how assessment at this level coordinates with assessment at the other levels. I do not review any particular tests of specialized movement skills here because the myriad possible tests are so different from one another that one example would not be especially instructive. For example, in *Assessing Sport Skills*, Strand and Wilson mention 21 tests of golf skills, some measuring performance with all types of golf strokes, some focusing on just one stroke (e.g., putting), and some dealing with only one specific club (e.g., the 5-iron).

After giving an overview of specialized movement skill, I will consider the top level of the movement skill taxonomy, functional movement skills. Even though testing at this top level is probably best for most assessment purposes, there are fewer published tests at this level than at any of the other five levels. At the end of the chapter, I will review two specific tests of functional movement skill, the Pediatric Evaluation of Disability Inventory and the Movement Assessment Battery for Children Checklist.

■ SPECIALIZED MOVEMENT SKILLS

Specialized movement skills can be defined as combinations or variations of one or more early movement milestones and/or fundamental movement skills that are used to accomplish specific tasks. Early movement milestones and fundamental movement skills, also referred to as phylogenetic skills, include generic skills used by persons in all cultures of the world to carry out basic tasks such as locomoting, receiving or propelling objects, or orientation. On the other hand, specialized skills, sometimes referred to as ontogenetic skills, are not performed by all persons and are performed in the pursuit of highly specific objectives. The repertoire of early movement milestones and fundamental movement skills is similar for all persons, but the repertoire of specialized movement skills is unique for each person.

As mentioned in chapter 3, among the specialized movement skills are pitching a baseball, spiking a volleyball, shooting a free throw, performing a forward roll or a triple jump, sewing on a button, shooting an arrow from a bow, and hammering a nail. Most of these derive from one or more early movement milestones or fundamental movement skills, adjusted and fine-tuned to match particular task and environmental conditions, while some are completely new skills. Pitching a baseball and shooting a free throw can be considered throwing; spiking a volleyball and hammering a nail can be considered striking; performing a forward roll can be considered rolling; and performing a triple jump combines the fundamental skills of jumping, hopping, and leaping. However, shooting an arrow from a bow and sewing on a button are unique skills.

In hierarchical models or taxonomies of movement skills, specialized movement skills must be preceded by the development of early movement milestones and fundamental movement skills. For example, in his four-level hierarchy of skills, Seefeldt (1980) placed what he called a "proficiency barrier" between the second and third levels because he felt that mastery of the fundamental skills was necessary for optimal development of the higher-level skills. In the present taxonomy (see figures 3.5 and 10.1), there is no proficiency barrier, an acknowledgement that specialized skills may emerge before all early movement milestones or fundamental movement skills are mastered. Indeed, the goal-directed nature of human movement behavior and the diversity of environments in which children live necessitate the development of specialized skills at an early age, but these specialized skills often can be categorized also as early movement milestones or fundamental movement skills. For example, a child may learn a specialized skill such as roller skating or ice skating before the age of 2 years (McGraw, 1935).

Assessing Recreation/Sport Skills

There are many possible categories of specialized movement skills, but the specialized skills that are assessed most often are recreation/sport skills and occupational skills. A recently published book by Strand and Wilson (1993), *Assessing Sport Skills,* is devoted entirely to the description and explanation of sport skills in three categories: individual sports, dual sports, and team sports. Some of the instruments cited in the book assess a broad range of skills, while others assess one very specific skill. For example, the Ellenbrand Gymnastics Skills Test (Ellenbrand, 1973) was designed to evaluate balance beam, floor exercise, uneven parallel bar, and vaulting skills in gymnastics; the Hensley Racquetball Skill Test (Hensley, East, & Stillwell, 1979) was designed to evaluate overall speed and power ability in racquetball; and the American Alliance for Health, Physical Education, Recreation and Dance Basketball Test (AAHPERD, 1984) was designed to evaluate dribbling, passing, shooting, and defensive skills in basketball. In contrast, the Shick-Berg Indoor Golf Test (Shick & Berg, 1983) was designed to evaluate skill in using the 5-iron in golf; the Jones Tennis Serving Test (Jones, 1967) was designed to evaluate tennis service skill; and the Chamberlain

Forehand Bounce Pass (Chamberlain, 1969) was designed to evaluate passing skill in volleyball.

Few assessments of recreation/sport skills are broadly embraced and used; most are constructed directly by the user or modified from other known instruments. Of the six tests from Strand and Wilson's (1993) book just mentioned, three were unpublished master's theses, two were published in a professional journal (*Research Quarterly for Exercise and Sport*), and one was published in a booklet by a professional organization (AAHPERD). Thus, at least half appeared in sources not readily available to practitioners. A reliance on user-developed instruments to assess recreation/sport skills, for whatever reason, creates a situation in which validity and reliability are usually not known and must be considered to be questionable.

Assessing Occupational Skills

The situation is quite different with assessments of occupational skills. For this second category of specialized movement skills, there are certain tests that are endorsed and used by large numbers of groups and individuals. For example, each state in the United States has standard written and movement skill tests for determining who should have licenses to operate various categories of motor vehicles, such as automobiles, motorcycles, buses, or trucks. Special movement skill tests also are used to qualify persons to fly aircraft, pilot boats or ships, or control trains, and there may be different tests for various models or types of aircraft, boats, or trains.

For some occupational skills, people are certified after passing tests designed or endorsed by professional organizations. The American Red Cross, for example, offers training and certification in the specialized movement skills of cardiopulmonary resuscitation and lifesaving in aquatic environments. A welder can be qualified by the American Welding Society by submitting a weldment representing typical production configurations and conditions or by taking a standard weldment test (American Welding Society Committee on Qualification, 1983).

Some organizations have screening tests to determine whether a person should be allowed to receive training for a job requiring specialized movement skills. For example, most cities have movement skills tests that prospective fire fighters must pass before proceeding with extensive fire-fighting training. In the New York City Physical Test for Fire Fighters (Andriuolo, 1993), presented in figure 11.1, the applicant must complete 10 tasks in proper sequence within 7 min or less while wearing about 40 lb of equipment. If Tasks 1 through 3 take longer than 4.5 min, the test is stopped.

Most tests of specialized skills involve the performance of skills in artificial, standardized situations. The situations are designed to simulate the conditions in which the skills will actually be performed, but the match

---

**New York City Physical Test for Fire Fighters
(Andriuolo, 1993)**

Engine Work Simulation
  1. Drag 80 lb hose 50 ft.
  2. Carry folded 46 lb hose up stairs.
  3. Pull a 50 ft length of hose (46 lb) through a simulated window.

Work Transition
        Walk for 100 seconds.

Ladder Work Simulation
  4. Scale 4.5 ft high wall.
  5. Raise a 20-ft, 60-lb ladder
  6. Ascend a ladder 10 ft then descend.
  7. Climb stairs with 15 lb hand weight.
  8. Move 77-lb weighted tire across a 12.5 ft table by striking tire with 8 lb maul as a forcible-entry simulation.
  9. Crawl 25 ft through tunnel (2.5 ft high by 3 ft wide) as a rescue simulation.
  10. Drag 5 ft 5-in., 145-lb dummy 45 ft as a rescue simulation.

■ **FIGURE 11.1**   The 10 tasks in the New York City Physical Test for Fire Fighters Adapted from Andriuolo, 1993.

between standardized and actual conditions is usually less than perfect. An assessment of any movement skill—an early movement milestone, fundamental movement skill, or specialized movement skill—in its actual functional context is considered in the present taxonomy to be an assessment of functional movement skills, which I will discuss in the next section.

■ FUNCTIONAL MOVEMENT SKILLS

The importance of assessing functional movement skills rather than skills in contrived situations is described elegantly by Sacks (1990) in *The Man Who Mistook His Wife for a Hat*:

> When I first saw her—clumsy, uncouth, all-of-a-fumble—I saw her merely, or wholly, as a casualty, a broken creature, whose neurological impairments I could pick out and dissect with precision: a multitude of apraxias and agnosias, a mass of sensorimotor impairments and breakdowns, limitations of intellectual schemata and concepts (by Piaget's criteria) to those of a child of eight. A poor thing, I said to myself, with perhaps a "splinter skill," a freak gift, of speech; a mere mosaic of higher cortical functions, Piagetian schemata—most impaired.

The next time I saw her, it was all very different. I didn't have her in a test situation, "evaluating" her in a clinic. I wandered outside—it was a lovely spring day—with a few minutes in hand before the clinic started, and there I saw Rebecca sitting on a bench, gazing at the April foliage quietly, with obvious delight. Her posture had none of the clumsiness which had so impressed me before. Sitting there, in a light dress, her face calm and slightly smiling, she suddenly brought to mind one of Chekhov's young women--Irene, Anya, Sonya, Nina—seen against the backdrop of a Chekhovian cherry orchard. She could have been any young woman enjoying a beautiful spring day. This was my human, as opposed to my neurological, vision. . . .

She had done appallingly in the testing—which, in a sense was designed, like all neurological and psychological testing, not merely to uncover, to bring out deficits, but to decompose her into functions and deficits. She had come apart, horribly, in formal testing, but now she was mysteriously "together" and composed. . . .

Our tests, our approaches, I thought, as I watched her on the bench—enjoying not just a simple but a sacred view of nature—our approach, our "evaluations," are ridiculously inadequate. They only show us deficits, they do not show us powers; they only show us puzzles and schemata, when we need to see music, narrative, play, a being conducting itself spontaneously in its own natural way. (pp. 180-181)

Assessing movement skills in contrived standardized, idealized, or simulated situations often does not provide an accurate picture of a person's movement behavior. For example, Mathiowetz and Wade (1995) compared the kinematic profiles of persons with multiple sclerosis on the simulated eating and simulated page-turning items of the Jebsen Hand Function Test (Jebsen, Taylor, Trieschmann, Trotter, & Howard, 1969) with the kinematic profiles for actual eating and page-turning, and reported that they were clearly different. Thus, persons involved in the assessment of movement skills must consider assessing skills at the functional level. In the next section, I will present terminology related to functional movement skills and then discuss types of functional movement skill assessments. Then I will review two tests, the Pediatric Evaluation of Disability Inventory (Haley, Coster, Ludlow, Haltiwanger, & Andrellos, 1992) and the Movement Assessment Battery for Children Checklist (Henderson & Sugden, 1992).

Terminology

In chapter 3 I defined functional movement skills as movement skills—either early movement milestones, fundamental movement skills, or specialized movement skills—that are performed in their natural and meaningful contexts. We observe a functional movement skill when an infant creeps across the kitchen floor to get to the family dog, when a college student blocks a ball in a volleyball game, or when a middle-aged man shaves while getting ready for work.

In occupational therapy, the term *movement function* refers to goal-directed behavior with both purpose and meaning (Fisher, 1992). In a recent position statement endorsed by the American Occupational Therapy Association (AOTA) (Commission on Practice, 1993), purposeful activity was defined as goal-directed behaviors or tasks involved in self-maintenance, work, leisure, or play, in which participation is active, voluntary, and directed toward a meaningful goal. The Commission on Practice (1993) points out that persons engaged in purposeful activity direct their attention to achieving a goal rather than to the required motor processes. The subcategories of activities of daily living, work activities, and play or leisure activities, as conceptualized by the Terminology Task Force (1994a) of the AOTA, are presented in figure 3.4 (see chapter 3). In her recent book, *Physical Therapy for Children*, Campbell (1995) observes that functional movements are "self-chosen, self-directed, and, therefore, meaningful in the life of the individual at his or her particular place in the life cycle" (p. 4).

Types of Functional Movement Skill Assessments

Mathiowetz (1993) recently presented a hierarchical taxonomy to organize movement assessment instruments used in occupational therapy. The three-level taxonomy, as depicted in figure 3.1 (see chapter 3), coordinates the occupational therapy concepts of performance components, occupational performance, and role performance with the World Health Organization's (1980) concepts of impairment, disability, and handicap. The second and third levels, concerned with occupational performance and disabilities and role performance and handicaps, respectively, captures the essence of functional movement skills. Thus, in this section, I will classify and discuss various types of functional movement skill assessments according to the three aspects of occupational performance: activities of daily living, work, and leisure and play. I add another category for judgment-based assessments.

Activities of Daily Living Assessments.   Activities of daily living (ADL) have been defined by Pedretti (1990) as tasks of self-care, communication, home management, mobility, and management of environmental hardware and devices that enable an individual to achieve personal independence in his or her environment. A list of skills in each of these five classifications is presented in table 11.1.

There are two main approaches to evaluating ADL: interview with the person being assessed or with a caregiver, and direct observation. The

TABLE 11.1 Examples of Activities of Daily Living Skills Classified Into Five Areas

Classification	Skills
Mobility	Movement in bed Wheelchair mobility and transfers Indoor ambulation with special equipment Outdoor ambulation with special equipment Management of public or private transportation
Self-care	Dressing, feeding, toileting, bathing, grooming
Management of environmental hardware and devices	Ability to use: 　Keys, faucets, light switches, windows, doors, 　scissors, and street control signals
Communication	Ability to: 　Write, operate a personal computer, read, type 　Use a telephone, tape recorder, or special 　　communications systems
Home management	Marketing, meal planning and preparation, 　cleaning, laundry, child care, Operating household appliances, such as vacuum 　cleaners, can openers, ranges, refrigerators, 　electric mixers, and hand-operated utensils

Note: From "Activities of Daily Living" by L.W. Pedretti, in *Occupational Therapy: Practice Skills for Physical Dysfunction* (3rd. ed) (p. 230), 1990, St. Louis, MO: Mosby-Year Book. Copyright 1990 by Mosby-Year Book. Reprinted by permission.

interview approach is more time and cost efficient, but the accuracy of answers to questions about a person's capabilities and limitations may be questionable in some situations (Trombly, 1989). Hence, interviews might be best used for screening to determine the need for further assessment (Pedretti, 1990). The Functional Assessment Screening Questionnaire (Granger & Wright, 1993) is an example of a recently developed interview instrument.

The direct observation approach may be accomplished with nonstandardized checklists, such as the Evaluation of Independent Living/Daily Living Skills (presented by Trombly, 1989), or with standardized instruments such as the Assessment of Motor and Process Skills (Fisher, 1995), the Barthel Index (Mahoney & Barthel, 1965), the Functional Independence Measure (Keith, Granger, Hamilton, & Sherwin, 1987), the Functional Independence Measure for Children (Msall, DiGaudio, & Duffy, 1993), the Katz Index of ADL (Katz, Ford, Moskowitz, Jackson, & Jaffe, 1963), the Kenny Self-Care Evaluation (Schoening et al., 1965), the Klein-Bell ADL Scale (Klein & Bell, 1982), or the Pediatric Evaluation of Disability

Inventory (Haley et al., 1992). Granger and Gresham (1993) note that the Barthel Index has been the most widely used ADL scale in rehabilitation medicine throughout the world and is still preferred by many investigators. The Functional Independence Measure (Keith et al., 1987), created by a joint task force of the American Academy of Physical Medicine and Rehabilitation and the American Congress of Rehabilitation Medicine, was used to start a national patient data system (Uniform Data System for Medical Rehabilitation/Data Management Service).

The observations made in these assessment instruments are usually translated into ordinal scales of measurement, with higher scores for greater degrees of independence. For example, in the Functional Independence Measure for Children (Msall et al., 1993), the scores range from 1 to 7 with 1 = total assistance, 2 = maximal assistance, 3 = moderate assistance, 4 = minimal assistance, 5 = supervision, 6 = modified independence, and 7 = complete independence. It is important to emphasize that the primary focus of ADL assessments is whether a person can accomplish the specified tasks regardless of the quality or efficiency of movement (Campbell, 1991).

One instrument that provides information on process is the unique Assessment of Motor and Process Skills (AMPS) (Fisher, 1995). The AMPS, based on item response theory, includes two instruments composed of five components each. One instrument assesses 16 items related to motor competence, while the other assesses 20 process items related to organizing task operations (see table 11.2). In the AMPS, there is no set task; many different tasks may be used, such as sweeping a floor, folding laundry, making a bed, washing clothes, polishing shoes, or making a fruit salad. More than 50 tasks are included in the test manual. Each item in the two instruments is evaluated on a rating scale of 1 to 4, from deficient to competent, with the quality, impact, and outcome of the task taken into account. The scaling of the motor and process items through the application of a Rasch measurement model, a subtype of item response theory, creates a test that is "sample free" and "test free," that is, a test independent of the individual or populations tested and the tasks used.

Other ADL assessment tools, such as the Functional Assessment Screening Questionnaire (Granger & Wright, 1993) and the Functional Independence Measure for Children (Msall et al., 1993), also are based on a Rasch measurement model. The Functional Independence Measure also has been calibrated recently according to a Rasch measurement model (Linacre, Heinemann, Wright, Granger, & Hamilton, 1994). Fisher (1993) notes that "in response to the increasing awareness of the limitations of traditional psychometric methods, the development of functional assessments based on Rasch measurement models is becoming the preferred method among rehabilitation professionals for constructing tests" (p. 320).

Work Assessments.   In their statement on uniform terminology for occupational therapy, the Terminology Task Force (1994a) of the AOTA

TABLE 11.2   Components and Items in the Motor and Process Parts of the Assessment of Motor and Process Skills (Fisher, 1995)

Skill type	Component	Item
Motor skills	Coordination	Flows Coordinates Manipulates
	Energy	Endures Paces
	Mobility	Bends Reaches Walks
	Posture	Aligns Positions Stabilizes
	Strength and effort	Calibrates Grips Lifts Moves Transports
Process skills	Adaptation	Accommodates Adjusts Benefits Notices and responds
	Energy	Attends Paces
	Space and objects	Gathers Navigates Organizes Restores Searches
	Temporal organization	Continues Initiates Sequences Terminates
	Using knowledge	Chooses Handles Heeds Inquires Uses

specified four categories of work activities: (a) home management, (b) care of others, (c) educational activities, and (d) vocational activities (see figure 3.4). Note that home management can be categorized under ADL or work activities.

Most of these work activities involve the use of movement skills, and many different assessments are used to examine these skills. The majority of these assessments are employer evaluations of a worker's effectiveness and efficiency in producing a required product, such as making hamburgers at a fast food restaurant, painting an automobile on an assembly line, or driving a bus punctually and safely. One assessment instrument, the Vocational Behavior Checklist (Walls, Zane, & Werner, 1978), includes some movement skill items among its 344 employment-related skills. According to the taxonomy used in this text, an assessment based on actual work activity would be classified as an assessment of functional movement skill, while an assessment based on a contrived or simulated task would be classified as an assessment of specialized movement skill.

Leisure and Play Assessments.   "Unlike work and self-care . . . play is a transaction or activity in which we engage only because we want to, not because we feel we must" (Bundy, 1993, p. 217). The control of the participant in leisure and play offers unique opportunities for movement assessment. First, leisure and play may provide a natural context for observing and measuring movement skills, serving as a means to an assessment end. However, leisure and play, which usually include some type of movement behavior, also may be assessed directly as ends in themselves.

A popular instrument that uses play as a setting for the assessment of various areas of development is the Transdisciplinary Play-Based Assessment (TPBA) (Linder, 1993). The TPBA provides guidelines for assessing cognitive, communication and language, sensorimotor, and social-emotional development of children from 6 months to 6 years in free and structured play situations. Eight areas in the sensorimotor domain are addressed:

- General appearance of movement
- Muscle tone, strength, and endurance
- Reactivity to sensory input
- Stationary positions used for play
- Mobility in play
- Other developmental achievements, including jumping, climbing, throwing, catching, and kicking
- Prehension and manipulation
- Motor planning

Some sample observation guidelines under the heading of other developmental achievements are shown in figure 11.2. Persons in a variety of professional areas can use the TPBA to identify service needs, develop intervention plans, and evaluate progress.

Instruments that assess leisure and play directly include the Comprehensive Evaluation in Recreational Therapy—Physical Disabilities (Parker,

VI. Other Developmental Achievements
  A. Jumping
    1. What movements demonstrate the child's ability to project the body in space?
        a. Does the child jump down from bottom step?
        b. Does the child jump up from the floor?
        c. Are the arms in "high guard" during jumping?
        d. Does the child crouch in preparation for jumping?
    2. What variations of jumping are observed (hopping, skipping, galloping, leaping)?
  C-1. Ball Skills — Throwing
    1. What size balls is the child able to throw?
    2. Do the feet remain firmly planted?
    3. Does the foot on the same side of the body as the throwing arm step forward as the ball is thrown?
    4. Does the foot on the opposite side of the body step forward as the ball is thrown?
  C-3. Kicking
    1. Does the child walk into the ball in an attempt to kick it?
    2. Does the kicking leg actually swing in preparation for and follow through the kick?

■ **FIGURE 11.2** Sample observation guidelines for sensorimotor development from the Transdisciplinary Play-Based Assessment.

From *Transdisciplinary play-based assessment: A functional approach to working with young children* (2nd ed., pp. 233-237), by T. W. Linder, 1993, Baltimore: P. H. Brookes, P. O. Box 10624, Baltimore, MD 21285-0624. Adapted with permission.

1988), the Leisure Activities Blank (McKechnie, 1974), the Leisure Diagnostic Battery (Witt & Ellis, 1985), the Minnesota Leisure Time Physical Activities Questionnaire (Taylor et al., 1978), the Leisure Interest Finder (Mirenda, 1973), the Preschool Play Scale (Bledsoe & Shepherd, 1982; Knox, 1974), and the Self-Leisure Interest Profile (McDowell, 1973). In addition, Musselwhite (1986), in his book *Adaptive Play for Special Needs Children*, describes procedures for gathering information during play regarding toy preferences, types and durations of manipulations, appropriateness of manipulations, and independence of activity.

In the second step of the three-step, top-down approach to movement assessment that I describe and advocate in chapter 13, the performer's choice of movement skills (early, fundamental, specialized, or functional) and skill patterns are carefully examined. These movement choices offer insight into how the performer attempts to solve a particular movement problem or complete a particular movement task. Leisure and play, both as a means and as an end in movement skill assessment, take the concept of choice one step further, allowing for the examination of task choices and object preferences. This goes beyond a performer's movement strategies to a performer's desires and intentions.

Judgment-Based Assessment.   Judgment-based assessment (JBA), offering a middle ground between the objective extreme of standardized testing and the subjective extreme of clinical judgment, can be applied to any of the three categories of functional skill assessment we have been considering. I include JBA as a fourth category of functional skill assessment because of its particular relevance to the assessment of skills in naturalistic situations.

Judgment-based evaluation was first defined by Neisworth and Bagnato (1988) in the context of early childhood special education as a process of collecting, structuring, and usually quantifying the impressions of professionals and caregivers about child/environmental characteristics. The most common methods of gathering judgment-based information are through the use of questionnaires, inventories, and ratings scales (Hayes, 1990). Information is provided by those who have a close and continuing knowledge of the more subtle characteristics of the behavior of the person being assessed (Hayes, 1990), and may be based on many samples of present or past behaviors in many different environments or on just one instance (Halcy, Baryza, & Blanchard, 1993). The process of data collection may enhance communication between parents and professionals in different disciplines (Fleischer, Belgredan, Bagnato, & Ogonosky, 1990) and may "bring to light both congruency and discrepancy between individuals' perceptions of a child" (Fleischer et al., 1990, p. 16). Thus, there are many advantages as well as corresponding limitations to using JBAs.

Both the Pediatric Evaluation of Disability Inventory (PEDI) (Haley et al., 1992) and the Movement Assessment Battery for Children (MABC) Checklist (Henderson & Sugden, 1992), to be reviewed in the following sections of this chapter, can be considered JBAs, as they provide a format for the systematic recording of clinical judgments. For example, in the self-care and mobility domains of the PEDI, the examiner is instructed to judge and check off the items that the child can usually do without any physical help. In the MABC Checklist, how a child performs a skill, such as skip or gallop a distance of 15 ft, is judged as "very well," "just OK," "almost," or "not close."

■ REVIEW: PEDIATRIC EVALUATION OF DISABILITY INVENTORY

The PEDI (Haley et al., 1992) is a comprehensive clinical assessment instrument developed to sample functional capabilities and performance of children between 0.5 and 7.5 years of age. One of the three domains assessed is mobility. Haley and his colleagues suggest that the PEDI can be used to (a) detect whether a functional deficit or delay exists, (b) determine the extent and content area of an identified delay or deficit, (c) monitor individual or group progress in pediatric rehabilitation programs, and (d) evaluate pediatric rehabilitation services or therapeutic programs in educational settings.

The PEDI is a new, cutting-edge assessment tool based on a Rasch rating scale model of item response theory, incorporating a judgment-based format. Data may be collected through (a) structured interviews with parents; (b) direct observations of the child by caregivers, teachers, or therapists; or (c) professional judgments by the child's therapists and/or teachers. The specific items in the PEDI, however, have been derived from earlier sources, including the Carolina Curriculum for Handicapped Infants and Infants at Risk (Johnson-Martin, Jens, & Attermeier, 1986); the Functional Independence Measure (Uniform Data System, 1987); the International Classification of Impairments, Disabilities, and Handicaps (World Health Organization, 1980); the Pediatric Assessment of Self-Care Activities (Coley, 1978); the Vineland Adaptive Behavior Scales (Sparrow, Balla, & Cicchetti, 1984); and the Functional Independence Measure for Children (Uniform Data System, 1991).

Structure

Three independent measurement scales can be used to assess functional skills in three domains: self-care, mobility, and social function. The first scale, referred to as the Functional Skills Scale, measures capabilities on 197 tasks, 59 of which are in the mobility domain. The 13 activity sections in the mobility domain, as well as sample items, are presented in table 11.3. The other two domains for the Functional Skills Scale are self-care and social. In the Functional Skills Scale, there are only two possible scores: 0 = unable or limited in capability to perform item in most situations, and 1 = capable of performing item in most situations.

Next, the Caregiver Assistance Scale measures disability in terms of the amount of assistance needed for 20 complex functional activities. Seven of these activities relate to mobility. The following scores may be assigned: 0 = total assistance (caregiver does almost all movement or transfer), 1 = maximal assistance (caregiver does more than half of the movement or transfer), 2 = moderate assistance (caregiver does less than half of the movement or transfer), 3 = minimal assistance (caregiver provides very little assistance), 4 = supervision (caregiver provides no physical help, or is present to set up assistive equipment or for safety reasons), and 5 = independent (caregiver provides no physical help or supervision).

The third section, Modifications, is not really a scale, but instead involves the recording of the frequency of environmental modifications needed by the child for the same 20 complex functional activities. The necessary

TABLE 11.3   Organization of 59 items in the Mobility Domain of the Pediatric Evaluation of Disability Inventory (Haley et al., 1992), With Specific Examples From One Section

Section	Item numbers
A. Toilet transfers	1-5
B. Chair/wheelchair transfers	6-10
C. Car transfers	11-15
D. Bed mobility/ transfers	16-19
E. Tub transfers	20-24

F. Indoor locomotion methods
    25. Rolls, scoots, crawls, creeps on floor
    26. Walks, but holds onto furniture, walls
        caregivers, or uses devices for support
    27. Walks without support
	25-27

G. Indoor locomotion — distance/speed	28-32
H. Indoor locomotion — pulls/carries objects	33-37
I. Outdoor locomotion — methods	38-39
J. Outdoor locomotion — distance/speed	40-44
K. Outdoor surfaces	45-49
L. Up stairs	50-54
M. Down stairs	55-59

modifications are coded by type and extent: N = no modifications, C = child oriented, R = rehabilitation equipment, and E = extensive modifications. These four modification classifications crossed with the three domains yield 12 frequency categories (see summary score sheet in figure 11.3).

The summary score sheet presented in figure 11.3 shows the scores that can be derived from raw scores for the Functional Skills and Caregiver Assistance Scales in each of the three domains. First, the raw scores are the sum of item scores within each domain. Next, the normative T scores, with a mean of 50 and a standard deviation of 10, are calculated for fourteen 6-month age bands from 6 months to 7 years 6 months. If a child is premature, the authors suggest that T scores be calculated for both chronological and gestational age.

Third, the scaled scores are derived from a Rasch measurement model of item response theory, which allows for an evaluation of the hierarchic nature of the items in the PEDI and the generalizability of their sequential development (Haley, Ludlow, & Coster, 1993). The scaled scores, ranging

Pediatric Evaluation of Disability Inventory

Version 1.0

Name CASE 3 (MARK)   Test Date _____   Age 11

ID# _____   Respondent/Interviewer _____

SCORE SUMMARY
Composite Scores

DOMAIN		RAW SCORE	NORMATIVE STANDARD SCORE	STANDARD ERROR	SCALED SCORE	STANDARD ERROR	FIT SCORE*
Self-Care	Functional Skills	29			48.2	1.7	
Mobility	Functional Skills	18			40.3	2.3	
Social Function	Functional Skills	59			59.9	1.3	
Self-Care	Caregiver Assistance	15			49.8	3.7	
Mobility	Caregiver Assistance	10			42.7	4.3	
Social Function	Caregiver Assistance	21			75.3	5.6	

*Obtainable only through use of software program

■ **FIGURE 11.3** Summary score sheet for the Pediatric Evaluation of Disability Inventory.

Reprinted with permission from Haley, SM, Coster, WJ, Ludlow, LJ, et al. *Pediatric Evaluation of Disability Inventory* (PEDI). Boston: New England Medical Center, 1992.

MODIFICATION FREQUENCIES

SELF-CARE (8 ITEMS)				MOBILITY (7 ITEMS)				SOCIAL FUNCTION (5 ITEMS)			
None	Child	Rehab	Exten.	None	Child	Rehab	Exten.	None	Child	Rehab	Exten.
3	2	3	0	2	0	1	4	5	0	0	0

Score Profile

NORMATIVE STANDARD SCORES   SCALED SCORES

DOMAIN

Self-Care	Functional Skills
Mobility	Functional Skills
Social Function	Functional Skills
Self-Care	Caregiver Assistance
Mobility	Caregiver Assistance
Social Function	Caregiver Assistance

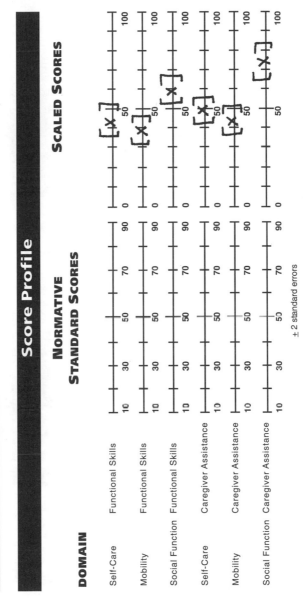

± 2 standard errors

Pediatric Evaluation of Disability Inventory (PEDI)

Published by: PEDI Research Group

Movement categories tested: motor abilities, fundamental movement skills, specialized movement skills, functional movement skills

Uses: (a) detect whether a functional deficit or delay exists, (b) determine the extent and content area of an identified delay or deficit, (c) monitor individual or group progress in pediatric rehabilitation programs, and (d) evaluate pediatric rehabilitation services or therapeutic programs in educational settings

Time to administer: experienced professionals can complete the PEDI for a child with whom they are familiar in 20-30 minutes, while a structured parent interview might take 45-60 minutes

Price: The PEDI test package, including the test manual, scoring software, and a packet of 25 score forms, can be purchased for $185 (1996 price). Also, the manual can be purchased separately for $75, a packet of score forms for $19.95, or the manual and a score form packet for $85. In addition, PEDI scoring software is available for $125.

Contact: PEDI Research Group
               Department of Physical Medicine and
                 Rehabilitation Medicine
               New England Medical Center Hospital
               750 Washington Street, #75 K/R
               Boston, MA 02111-1901
               (617-636-5031)

Pediatric Evaluation of Disability Inventory

Version 1.0

Name _____ Test Date _____ Age _____

ID# _____ Respondent/Interviewer _____

SCORE SUMMARY
Composite Scores

DOMAIN		RAW SCORE	NORMATIVE STANDARD SCORE	STANDARD ERROR	SCALED SCORE	STANDARD ERROR	FIT SCORE*
Self-Care	Functional Skills						
Mobility	Functional Skills						
Social Function	Functional Skills						
Self-Care	Caregiver Assistance						
Mobility	Caregiver Assistance						

from 0 to 100, estimate a child's ability relative to the continuum of items in a particular scale. Because these scores are not related to age, they can be calculated for persons older than 7.5 years. Item maps, as shown for the Functional Skills Scale in the mobility domain in figure 11.4, facilitate the interpretation of scaled scores from a skill perspective by clearly indicating which items a person with a given score should be able to perform.

The last two composite scores listed in the summary score sheet in figure 11.3 are standard errors and fit scores. The standard errors for T scores and scaled scores can be used to establish confidence intervals. The fit scores, more accurately termed goodness-of-fit scores, indicate the degree of discrepancy of a child's pattern of responses from the pattern of responses predicted from the normative data. If a fit score is too high, the examiner should use the other summary scores very cautiously and rely primarily on a direct interpretation of individual items. The goodness-of-fit analyses "help define the meaningfulness and clinical validity of a summary score in relation to the particular hierarchic scale" (Haley, Ludlow, and Coster, 1993, p. 533). Software is available for scoring the PEDI and includes a goodness-of-fit profile.

The PEDI was standardized with a stratified sample of 412 children without disabilities from New England, based on the 1980 U.S. Census. The sample included only children without disabilities because "one of the major goals of the PEDI is to serve as an instrument to discriminate between normal and delayed functional performance" (Haley, Ludlow, and Coster, 1993, p. 531).

Reliability

The results of studies examining the reliability of scoring between interviewers and between interviewers and parents are reported in the PEDI manual (Haley et al., 1992). First, as part of the program in which nurse practitioners were trained to administer the PEDI to children without disabilities in the standardization phase, Caregiver Assistance and Modifications scores given by the practitioners on 29 or 30 interviews were correlated with the scores given by a member of the PEDI research team. The intraclass correlations for the three domains ranged from .96 to .99 for Caregiver Assistance and from .79 to 1.00 for Modifications.

Next, two persons independently completed the Caregiver Assistance Modifications Scales for 12 children with disabilities from interviews with eight parents and four rehabilitation teams (Sundberg, 1992). The intraclass correlations for the three domains and two scales ranged from .93 to 1.00 for the team interviews and from .84 to 1.00 for the parent interviews. Sundberg (1992) also examined the agreement between parents and rehabilitation team members on all three scales for 24 children with disabilities. The intraclass correlations for the three domains ranged from .87 to 96 for

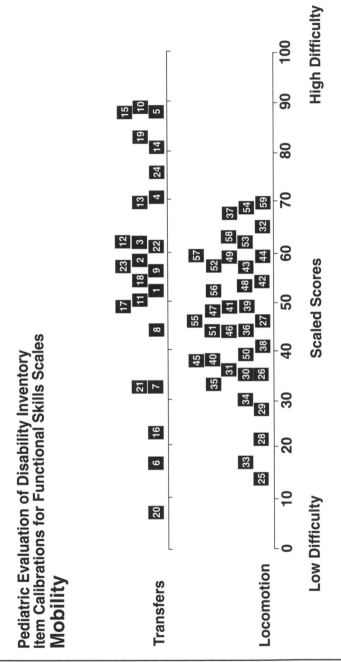

■ **FIGURE 11.4** Item map for the items in the mobility domain for the Pediatric Evaluation of Disability Inventory.

Reprinted with permission from Haley, SM, Coster, WJ, Ludlow, LJ, et al. *Pediatric Evaluation of Disability Inventory* (PEDI). Boston: New England Medical Center, 1992.

Functional Skills, from .74 to .95 for Caregiver Assistance, and from .30 to .88 for Modifications. The .30 correlation for social function modifications was the only correlation below .74.

In 1996, Nichols and Case-Smith studied the intrarater reliability of 23 parents and the interrater reliability for 17 parent-therapist pairs. The intraclass correlations between the repeated parent interviews, separated by 1 week, on the three domains of the Functional Skill Scale were all .98 for raw summary scores, ranged from .88 to .92 for normative standard scores, and ranged from .85 to .89 for scaled scores. The intraclass correlations between parents and therapists on the three domains of the Functional Skill Scale ranged from .80 to .92 for raw summary scores, from .12 (mobility) to .66 (social) to .75 (self-care) for normative standard scores, and from .85 to .89 for scaled scores. Nichols and Case-Smith (1996) note that the greatest discrepancies between parent and therapist responses were in the content areas not likely to be observed in the clinic.

Validity

The PEDI manual (Haley et al., 1992) provides information on three types of validity: content, construct, and criterion related. However, the bottom-line question of any test is: Does it do what the authors claim it will do? Thus, this discussion will be organized according to the types of validity, but will focus on the four purposes of the PEDI as stated at the beginning of this section.

Content Validity. The content validity of a developmental version of the PEDI was examined in a study by Haley, Coster, and Faas (1991). A panel of 31 assessment experts, 25 of whom were in occupational or physical therapy, evaluated seven aspects of the PEDI on a 5-point scale. The ability of the PEDI to measure functional disability, provide a clinically meaningful description of functional status, and measure different dimensions of functional status was rated good (a score of 4) or excellent (a score of 5) by 80% of the panel. The potential of the PEDI to identify clinically meaningful functional change in children was rated good or excellent by 74% of the panel. More than 79% of panel members rated as good or excellent the use of the PEDI as a clinical instrument by therapists, educators, or other professionals, but only 62% rated as good or excellent the use of the PEDI as a parent interview instrument. This study provides a preliminary validation of the functional content of the PEDI, but also indicates some reservations about its sensitivity to change and its use with parents.

The second purpose of the PEDI is to determine the extent and content area of an identified delay or deficit. To address this purpose in their content validity study, Haley, Coster, and Faas (1991) analyzed responses for the overall test battery and for the separate domains. However, because there were four domains of function in the developmental version of the PEDI (self-care, mobility, toileting, and social cognition), content information on individual areas of delay or deficit was difficult to examine. Clearly, more research supporting this purpose is needed.

The third purpose of the PEDI, to monitor individual or group progress in pediatric rehabilitation programs, was judged positively by 74% of the panel for the PEDI overall, but the scores were lower for the individual domains. For example, only 16% of the judges rated social cognition as good or excellent for monitoring progress. Again, this may no longer be relevant, because the domains were reorganized in the newer version of the PEDI. The validity of use of the PEDI to monitor progress is also examined in the context of construct validity.

Construct Validity. Construct validity is defined by the Task Force on Standards for Measurement in Physical Therapy (1991) as the conceptual or theoretical basis for using a measurement to make an inferred interpretation, established through logical argumentation supported by theoretical and research evidence. Construct validity of the PEDI is evaluated in relation to four key assumptions. The first assumption is that change in functional behaviors is age related. This assumption was supported by correlations between age and raw scores for the three domains ranging from .77 to .89 for the Functional Skills Scale and from .78 to .91 for the Caregiver Assistance Scale. However, the age-raw score correlations were much lower for children older than 5 years on both the Functional Skills (.41-.44) and Caregiver Assistance Scales (.09-.36) than across the entire sample, indicating a possible score ceiling for this age group.

Haley and his associates argue that the second assumption—that the Functional Skills and Caregiver Assistance Scales reflect different dimensions of function—is supported by a consistent pattern across domains whereby the highest level of functional skill precedes the attainment of the highest level of independence, as measured in the Caregiver Assistance Scale. An examination of the raw scores reveals this to be true for the self-care domain for all ages, but only for children younger than 2 years for the mobility and social function domains. If the two scales measure different aspects of function, then correlations between function skills and caregiver assistance scores for the same domains should be low. However, the correlations ranged from .93 to .96 for the total standardization sample, from .79 to .91 for children less than 2 years, from .66 to .89 for children 2 to 5 years, and from .11 to .62 for children older than 5 years. Again, the lower correlations for older children can be partially explained by a ceiling effect; thus, contrary to the second assumption, there does appear to be a significant amount of similarity between the two scales across domains and across age.

The third assumption, that the PEDI is able to discriminate between children previously classified as having disabilities and other children, relates directly to the first purpose of the test. According to Feldman, Haley, and

Coryell (1990), the classification of the 412 children in the normative sample and the 102 children with disabilities in the clinical sample was matched better with use of functional skills and modifications raw scores than with caregiver assistance raw scores or scores from the Battelle Developmental Inventory Screening Test (BDIST) (Newborg, Stock, Wnek, Guidubaldi, & Svinicki, 1984). For the mobility domain, 93% of the classifications were correct with use of the Functional Skills Scale, while only 64% were correct with the Caregiver Assistance Scale. Assuming that the method of original classification is valid, the data indicate that caregiver scores should not be used for this purpose until further research is completed.

The last assumption, that the PEDI is sensitive to changes in function, was tested on two different clinical samples (Haley et al., 1992). The analyses for this assumption, which addresses the third purpose of the PEDI, focused on scaled scores because they represent true functional change, not change relative to other persons. In the first sample, 21 children under 6 years, hospitalized at least overnight due to minor trauma, showed significant gains ($p < .05$) in scaled scores of the Functional Skills and Caregiver Assistance Scales for all three domains from 1 to 6 months after discharge.

In the other sample, 23 children between 1 and 9.8 years with severe disabilities in a hospital-based school program showed significant improvement over an 8-month period ($p < .05$) in functional skills and caregiver assistance scaled scores for the mobility domain, but not the self-care or social function domains. A critical question for interpreting this study, one that cannot be answered with the information provided, is whether there were interventions or instruction that would lead to a prediction of functional change in each of the three domains. The conclusion of Haley et al. (1992) that "the PEDI is *selectively* responsive to change in *certain* clinical samples" (italics added) (p. 70) suggests that more research is needed to validate the use of the PEDI to monitor progress.

Criterion-Related Validity. Concurrent validity, a type of criterion-related validity, was investigated in two studies cited in the PEDI manual, although neither of these was concerned with any of the four main purposes of the PEDI. For adequate interpretation of these studies, the content of the criterion tests must be clearly specified, as well as the methods used to validate those other tests.

Feldman et al. (1990) administered a developmental version of the PEDI and the BDIST (Newborg et al., 1984) to 10 children with spina bifida, 10 children with arthritic conditions, and 20 matched children without disabilities. The correlations between the PEDI Functional Skills Scale mobility scores and the BDIST gross motor scores was .77 for the total group, .84 for the children with disabilities, and .34 for the children without disabilities. The correlations between the Caregiver Assistance Scale mobility scores and the BDIST gross motor scores were a bit lower: .65 for the total group, .69 for the children with disabilities, and .09 for the children without disabilities. The low correlations for the children without disabilities may have been caused by a limited range of scores as these children attained near-maximum scores.

In a similar study involving an unspecified number of children with severe disabilities who were enrolled in a hospital-based day school program, Schultz (1992) reported that the correlations between gross motor scores on the BDIST (Newborg et al., 1984) and functional skills and caregiver assistance scores in the mobility domain were .91 and .87, respectively. The correlations between the mobility and locomotion sections of the Functional Independence Measure for Children (Uniform Data System, 1991) and the functional skills and caregiver assistance scores in the mobility domain also were very high, ranging from .89 to .97.

In a recent study that involved 25 children, Nichols and Case-Smith (1996) examined the relationship between the results of the PEDI and the Peabody Developmental Motor Scales (PDMS) (Folio & Fewell, 1983). They calculated Pearson product moment-correlations between the raw scores on the mobility domain of the Functional Performance scale and two sets of raw scores on the PDMS; the correlation with raw scores on four fine motor skill areas in the PDMS ranged from .68 to .77, and that with raw scores on four gross motor skill areas from .79 to .91 (the correlation for reflexes was .24). The correlations between age equivalents from the mobility domain of the Functional Performance Scale and the age equivalents on the Fine and Gross Motor Scales of the PDMS were .94 and .92, respectively. With respect to the first purpose of detecting whether there is a functional deficit or delay, Nichols and Case-Smith found that 12 children scored below the 7th percentile (-1.5 SDs) on the Functional Performance and Caregiver Assistance Scales, but that 8 additional children fell below this normative standard on the Fine Motor Scale and 9 more on the Gross Motor Scale of the PDMS.

The fourth purpose of the PEDI is to evaluate pediatric rehabilitation services or therapeutic programs in educational settings, but no information on the content-, construct-, or criterion-related validity of this purpose was provided in the manual (Haley et al., 1992). Use of the PEDI for program evaluation, therefore, should be discouraged until some rational arguments and empirical evidence are presented.

Summary

The first strength of the PEDI is the structure allowing for various dimensions of function to be assessed. A child's capabilities relative to specific skills (Functional Skills Scale), independence (Caregiver Assistance Scales), and needed modifications (Modifications) are evaluated separately in three domains: self-care, mobility, and social function. However, the high correlations between functional skills and caregiver assistance scores reported by Haley et al. (1992) suggest that there is a significant amount of commonality between the two scales across domains and across age.

The judgment-based format of the PEDI, which allows functional performance in natural settings to be evaluated by professionals as well as parents and caregivers, is a second strength. Some of the reviewers of the content validity of the developmental version of the PEDI questioned its use as a parent interview instrument (Haley, Coster, & Faas, 1991), so further research on the latest version is needed to establish this aspect of the test.

The focus of the PEDI on functional movement outcomes and contexts of performance (such as indoor locomotion, outdoor locomotion, and outdoor surfaces) without specification of the movement process is another strength. However, Reid, Boschen, and Wright (1993) argue that the lack of differentiation between process and methods of performance may be a serious limitation and suggest that process information be incorporated into the PEDI or in a parallel measurement tool. Certainly this additional information may be useful, particularly in evaluating change, but the priorities of the PEDI are properly established.

The scoring flexibility of the PEDI is a strength, but users must consider the assumptions of the various methods. Interpretation of performance on individual tasks is facilitated by figures depicting the ages at which 25%, 50%, and 75% of the normative sample are able to pass each of the 197 functional skills items. This information is skill based, but the standard norm-referenced scores and the scaled scores from the application of a Rasch model of item response theory likely represent abilities. Scaled scores are designed to measure functional performance rather than normative standing (and hence may be used for children older than 7.5 years) but, because these composite-type scores are applied to the performer rather than the task, they represent abilities.

One of the weaknesses of the PEDI is the limited information on reliability provided in the test manual (Haley et al., 1992). Results of studies on the reliability of responses between different raters (interrater) and between professional team members and parents (interresponder) were provided, but these were based on only a small sample of subjects. Therefore there is a need to examine interrater and interresponder reliability further with more subjects and to establish intrarater, interrater, and test-retest reliability on a sample of sufficient size and diversity. The study by Nichols and Case-Smith (1996) provides good support for intrarater reliability, but raises some questions about the reliability between parents and therapists, particularly on the mobility domain of the Functional Performance Scale. The PEDI also suffers from a relatively small and geographically limited standardization sample. A larger national sample stratified according to the 1990 U.S. Census would boost the external validity of the PEDI.

The greatest weakness of the PEDI is a lack of sufficient information validating the use of the test for its intended purposes. Of the four main purposes of the instrument, only the first has some empirical support. With regard to the first purpose, Feldman et al. (1990) showed the effectiveness of using functional skills and modifications scores to detect whether a functional deficit or delay exists, but also revealed the limitations of using caregiver assistance scores. Also, Nichols and Case-Smith (1996) found that about 40% more children were identified as falling below the 7th percentile on the PDMS than on the PEDI mobility domain. However, this is consistent with the understanding that functional skill acquisition of children with developmental disabilities often exceeds their demonstrated developmental milestones (Nichols & Case-Smith, 1996).

The second purpose, to determine the extent and content area of an identified delay or deficit, was addressed in the content validity study by Haley, Coster, and Faas (1991), but the panel's responses were based on the developmental version of the PEDI with four domains, not the three in the current version. The reorganization of content areas makes it very difficult to apply the results from the original study.

The third purpose of monitoring individual or group progress in pediatric rehabilitation programs was considered in the context of both content and construct validity, but the results were not convincing. In particular, it was hard to interpret the finding that children with severe disabilities showed significant change over 8 months in the Functional Skills and Caregiver Scales only for the mobility domain (Haley et al., 1992) because the changes that could be expected were not specified. In addition, an apparent performance ceiling for children between 5 and 7.5 years could hinder the measurement of functional children in this group. And finally, no information was provided concerning the fourth purpose, that of evaluating pediatric rehabilitation services or therapeutic programs in educational settings.

Another critique of the PEDI, even more detailed than the present one, is offered by Reid et al. (1993) in *Physical and Occupational Therapy in Pediatrics*.

■ REVIEW: MOVEMENT ASSESSMENT BATTERY FOR CHILDREN CHECKLIST

The MABC (Henderson & Sugden, 1992) consists of two independent instruments: the MABC Test and the MABC Checklist. The MABC Test is an ability-oriented instrument that I described and critiqued in chapter 8. The focus of the present discussion is the MABC Checklist, which is based on the variety of checklists used by Keogh and his students at the University of California, Los Angeles, to help physical education teachers identify children with movement difficulties (e.g., Keogh, Sugden, Reynard, & Calkins, 1979). The MABC Checklist is a direct derivative of the more recent Motor Competence Checklist reported by Sugden and Sugden (1991).

Some of the information in the qualitative checklists that were included in the Henderson Revision of the Test of Motor Impairment (Stott, Moyes, & Henderson, 1984) is also incorporated into the MABC Checklist.

The two instruments included in the MABC—the Test and the Checklist—are designed to complement each other in the movement assessment process for children 4 to 12 years of age. For screening children, identifying children for special services, and conducting research, either the Test or the Checklist may be used. For clinical exploration, intervention planning, and program evaluation, it is recommended that both the Test and Checklist be used.

Usage of previous versions of the MABC Checklist (e.g., Keogh et al., 1979; Sugden & Sugden, 1991) was quite limited, while the current version has been available only for a short time and thus has not yet had a chance to become established as an assessment option for professionals interested in evaluating children with movement difficulties.

Structure

The MABC Checklist allows teachers, other professionals, or even parents to evaluate a child's movement behaviors in a variety of natural settings over an extended period of time. The Checklist, designed specifically for children between 5 and 11 years of age, contains tasks often encountered in a school environment. The focus on movement in natural settings justifies the classification of the Checklist as a functional movement skill assessment instrument.

The Checklist is divided into five sections, with 12 items in each section. The first four sections, derived from Gentile's (1987) 16-category taxonomy of movement skills (see table 3.3), are labeled as (a) child stationary—environment stable, (b) child moving—environment stable, (c) child stationary—environment changing, and (d) child moving—environment changing. The last section lists behaviors that may interfere with a child's movement performance. Examples of the five sets of tasks are presented in figure 11.5.

The 48 items in the four motor sections are scored on a four-level, ordinal scale: 0 = very well, 1 = just OK, 2 = almost, and 3 = not close. The higher scores for poorer performances reflect the emphasis of this test on motor impairment. The results may be interpreted at three levels. First, the total score may be matched against sums corresponding to the 5th ("movement problems") and 15th ("at risk") percentiles for 6-, 7-, 8-, and 9+-year-olds. Next, the subtotals for each of the four sections may be compared to identify categories of movement tasks that may pose special problems for a child. And third, individual items may be examined for information on the specific tasks that are especially challenging for a child.

Section 1. Child stationary — environment stable
   1.   The child can put on and take off articles of clothing without assistance
        (shirt, sweater, socks).
   8.   The child can form letters, numbers, and basic geometric shapes that are
        accurate and legible.

Section 2. Child moving — environment stable
   2.   The child can carry objects around the classroom/school avoiding a
        collision with stationary objects/persons.
   9.   The child can throw an object (ball, beanbag, ring) into a container using
        an underarm action, while on the move.

Section 3. Child stationary — environment changing
   3.   The child can intercept and stop a moving object (toy train or car, ball) as
        it approaches/enters the field of reach.
  10.   The child can continually bounce a large playground ball while
        standing still.

Section 4. Child moving — environment changing
   4.   The child can push/pull wheeled vehicles such as wagons, library and
        mat trolleys.
  11.   The child can move to enter a turning jump rope.

Section 5. Behavioral problems relating to motor difficulties
   5.   The child is impulsive (starts before instructions/demonstrations are
        complete; impatience of detail).
  12.   The child is apparently unable to get pleasure from success
        (makes no response to feedback; has a blank facial expression).

■ **FIGURE 11.5**   Sample of items from each of the five sections in the MABC Checklist (from Henderson & Sugden, 1992).
Reproduced with permission by The Psychological Corporation LTD © The Psychologoical Corporation LTD 1992, Foots Cray High Street, Sidcup, Kent DA14 SHP, United Kingdom.

The 12 behavior items are scored as 0 (rarely), 1 (occasionally), or 2 (often), but are not summed. Instead, the rater classifies the overall contribution of these behaviors to movement difficulties as high, medium, or low. The rater must consider not only whether the behaviors limit a child's movement performance, but also whether they should be taken into account in developing an intervention program.

Reliability

To examine the test-retest reliability of the MABC Checklist, Henderson and Sugden (1992) asked 41 teachers to complete the Checklist on one child

Movement Assessment Battery for Children Test (MABC Test)

Published by: Therapy Skill Builders

Movement categories tested: motor abilities, fundamental movement skills, specialized movement skills

Uses: MABC Test - (a) screen children for possible movement problems, (b) identify children for special services, and (c) research; MABC Test with the MABC Checklist - (a) clinical exploration, (b) intervention planning, and (c) program evaluation

Time to administer: 20-40 minutes

Price: The 1996 price for the kit, including all materials needed to administer the MABC, is $620. The test manual can be purchased separately for $87.50, and packets of 25 test forms can be purchased for $52.50.

Contact: Therapy Skill Builders
                (a division of The Psychological Corporation)
                555 Academic Court
                San Antonio, TX 78204-2498
                (800-211-8378)

Movement Assessment Battery for Children

Checklist

Compiled by Sheila E. Henderson and David A. Sugden

Name ....

Gender .... Date of test ....

Home address ....

Date of birth ....

Age .... Grade/year ....

Assessed by ....

School ....

Section 1	Section 2	Section 3	Section 4	Total	Section 5 L M H (circle one)	Full Movement ABC assessment required	yes no (circle one)
.... +	.... +	.... +	.... =	....			

Section 1: Child Stationary/Environment Stable

0	1	2	3
Very Well	Just OK	Almost	Not Close

The child can:
1. Put on and take off articles of clothing without assistance (shirt, sweater, socks).
2. Stand on one leg in a stable position (when putting on trousers, skirt).
3. Tie shoelaces, buckle belt, fasten a zipper/buttons.
4. Demonstrate competence in personal hygeine (wash hands, brush/comb hair).
5. Demonstrate good posture when sitting or standing (at a desk/table, on a chair, in line).
6. Hold instruments using proper tension and grasp (scissors/pencil/en/paintbrush).
7. Cut/draw/trace with precision/accuracy.
8. Form letters, numbers and basic geometric shapes that are accurate and legible.

in their classroom two times across a span of 1 month. The Pearson product-moment correlation between the two testings for the total motor score (the first four sections) was .89, while the correlations for the individual sections were .88, .84, .77, and .76, respectively. Although interclass correlations may not be the best way to evaluate test-retest reliability, these values still are quite high given the subjective nature of the Checklist. Information on the reliability of a developmental version of the MABC Checklist, referred to as the Motor Competence Checklist, is described in a paper by Sugden and Sugden (1991).

Validity

The validity of the MABC Checklist was investigated in a study of 6- to 9-year-old children in the United Kingdom (Henderson & Sugden, 1992; see also Sugden & Sugden, 1991). Three boys and three girls were randomly selected from 50 different classes ($n = 298$), as well as the one boy and one girl whom the teachers judged as having the most difficulty with their movement skills ($n = 47$). As expected, scores for the children in the random sample significantly decreased with age; however, the girls' scores were significantly lower than the boys', a result for which an adequate explanation was not given. Also as expected, the scores for Sections 3 and 4 (changing environment) were significantly higher than the scores for Sections 1 and 2 (stable environment), indicating that the Checklist is sensitive to environment demands.

The children identified as having the most difficulty with their movement skills scored significantly higher than the other children on the MABC Checklist, indicating an agreement between the teachers' judgments and the results of the Checklist. Only 72% of the children whom the teachers judged as having the most difficulty with their movement skills scored below the 15th percentile, but it was not determined whether other children who were not selected would have scored lower.

Next, the authors examined the agreement between the MABC Checklist and the MABC Test by comparing the Test scores of the 16 children in the random sample who scored lowest on the Checklist (all below the 5th percentile) with the scores of 16 children who scored above the 15th percentile. Contrary to expectations, 9 of the 16 who scored lowest on the Checklist scored above the 15th percentile on the Test. Henderson and Sugden (1992) explained that the MABC Checklist will always identify more children as having difficulty than the MABC Test because the contexts in which the movement skills are evaluated are much broader. Accordingly, the children with better scores on the Checklist also had significantly lower scores on the Test; but, contradicting the authors' argument, 2 of the 16 (12.5%) scored below the 15th percentile on the Test.

Finally, the summed score in Section 5 of the Checklist (behavioral problems related to motor difficulties) was analyzed in relation to a child's age, sex, and summed score in the four motor sections, even though the summing of scores from the items in Section 5 is not part of the standard Checklist protocol. The Section 5 scores for the group of randomly selected children significantly decreased with increasing age and were significantly lower for girls, matching the patterns for total scores in the four motor sections. Moreover, the correlation between scores in Section 5 and total scores across Sections 1 through 4 was .67, prompting Henderson and Sugden (1992) to conclude that "many children with movement difficulties are hindered by associated behavior problems and that these are evident to the teacher who observes them" (p. 217).

Some further study on the validity of the MABC Checklist has been carried out with children from Singapore. Wright, Sugden, Ng, and Tan (1994) assessed 212 children, 7 and 8 years old, with the MABC Checklist and found that 10.9% fit into the at risk category, between the 5th percentile and 15th percentile, and 4.7% fit into the movement problems category, between the 0 percentile and 5th percentile. These percentages very closely match the expected values of 10% and 5%, respectively. All children at or below the 15th percentile were considered to have a developmental coordination disorder (DCD). In a follow-up study, Wright and Sugden (1996) found similar percentages with a group of 427 Singaporean children ranging in age from 6 to 9 years: 10.1% in the at risk category and 6.1% in the movement problems category. Further, Wright and Sugden (1996) reported that scores from just Section 4 (child moving—environment changing) could be used to correctly classify 81% of the children with DCD; this result, they argued, suggests that these children differed most from their well-coordinated peers when they were required to move in a dynamic environment.

Wright and Sugden (1996) also examined the subtypes of DCD by running a factor analysis on the results for the DCD children only on the first four sections of the MABC Checklist and the eight areas on the MABC Test. They found that Sections 1 and 2 of the MABC Checklist formed one cluster while Sections 2, 3, and 4 formed another, indicating that the distinction between stationary and changing environments is more important than the distinction between a stationary and moving performer and that the MABC Checklist is tapping different movement skill qualities than the MABC Test.

Summary

Henderson and Sugden (1992) state that the MABC Checklist may be used for (a) screening or identifying children for special services and (b) clinical exploration, intervention planning, and program evaluation. I will discuss the usefulness of the MABC Checklist for these two sets of purposes separately.

First, the children who were chosen by teachers as having difficulty with their movement skills did score significantly higher on the Checklist than the other children, but this is not adequate evidence to validate the Checklist for screening or placement purposes. As with the Test, comparisons need to be made in terms of dichotomous categories congruent with the Checklist, not absolute scores. On examination of the agreement between the Checklist and the Test in dichotomous terms, the Checklist was found to have a much higher identification rate, with more than 50% of those who scored at or below the 15th percentile on the Checklist scoring above the 15th percentile on the Test. Also, 12.5% of the children who scored above the 15th percentile on the Checklist scored at or below the 15th percentile on the Test, placing the sensitivity of the Checklist into question. In addition, the reliability of these categorical decisions needs to be established for the Checklist.

Henderson and Sugden (1992) presented no empirical evidence that either the MABC Test or Checklist is valid for clinical exploration or intervention planning. However, the sampling of movement performances in many contexts in the Checklist, as well as related behaviors in Section 5, appears to be very useful for clinical exploration and intervention planning, regardless of the total scores. The manual presented one extensive case study showing how the Test and Checklist can be used to develop an intervention plan. Similar but less detailed case studies would be helpful in establishing the validity of the Checklist for clinical exploration and intervention. The case studies also should include an evaluation of progress using both the Test and the Checklist, as well as other independent measures.

In conclusion, we have insufficient evidence that the MABC Checklist is a reliable and valid instrument. It does, however, have several unique features—in particular, a JBA format focusing on movement behaviors in natural settings—that appear to have potential usefulness for screening, intervention planning, and clinical exploration.

Part III

Implementing Movement Skill Assessment

I N part I of the book, I introduced basic issues in movement skill assessment; in part II, I discussed in detail the levels of the movement skill assessment taxonomy and presented in-depth reviews of sample instruments. In the final section of this book, I apply the information presented in the preceding sections to strategies for accomplishing the goals of movement skill assessment. Chapter 12 provides an overview of the assessment process, from selecting an appropriate measurement tool to collecting and treating data to interpreting results. In chapter 13, I describe two comprehensive assessment strategies—bottom-up and top-down—and discuss their relative advantages and disadvantages. And finally, in chapter 14, I offer insights into new directions in movement skill assessment.

Chapter *12*

The Assessment Process

© Terry Wild Studio

THE assessment process may be considered to include at least five steps:

1. Determining the purpose of the assessment
2. Selecting appropriate assessment instruments
3. Collecting and treating data
4. Interpreting the results
5. Reporting the results

In this chapter, I will identify key issues and recommend general procedures for each of the five steps. In addition, I will especially emphasize some of the pitfalls awaiting users at each of these steps.

> ❝ ❝ In the process of gathering data, theory should pro-
> vide a systematic way of looking for information. ❞ ❞
> — *Kielhofner and Mallinson (1995, p. 191)*

The pitfalls to be discussed, summarized in figure 12.1, are quite insidious because consumers usually fall into them without being aware of the impending peril to the validity of the assessment. The only protection the user has against these along the way is an adequate knowledge and understanding of basic issues in and recommended procedures for assessment, an understanding of the problems that may arise in the assessment process, and the ability to apply this knowledge as specific problems arise. The solution to some of these problems may be simply to recognize and avoid a pitfall; the solution to other more complex problems may be to draw on the information presented in other chapters in this or other books.

A comprehensive list of specific competencies and standards for persons who choose tests, interpret test scores, or make decisions based on test scores is offered in "Standards for Tests and Measurements in Physical Therapy Practice," written by the Task Force on Standards for Measurement in Physical Therapy (TFSMPT) (1991). There are 45 standards for test users as well as separate sets of standards for test developers, test researchers, and test instructors. Appendix B presents some of the standards for test users under five headings (user background, test selection, test administration, test interpretation, and reporting results); I will refer to these throughout the chapter.

■ DETERMINING THE PURPOSE
OF THE ASSESSMENT

As discussed at length in chapter 1, there are many possible reasons for conducting a movement skill assessment. A physical education teacher may want to assess the movement skills of a group of students to assign grades; an adapted physical education specialist may want to assess the movement skills of a particular student to determine whether he qualifies for special services; or a physical therapist may want to assess the movement skills of a patient to identify the best rehabilitation strategies for her. In this critical first step in the assessment process, the purpose must be clearly specified before any instruments are considered for use (Problem #1,

1. The intended purpose of the assessment process may not be clearly specified.
2. The test may not be adequately validated for the intended purpose.
3. The test may be environmentally impractical for the user.
4. The test may not accommodate attributes of the individual being assessed.
5. The examiner may not be competent to administer the assessment instrument.
6. The test may have poor reliability or inadequate standardization procedures.
7. A small change in just one environmental factor may alter the results of a test.
8. The examiner may not have good rapport with the examinee.
9. The test may be administered improperly.
10. Raw scores may be recorded improperly.
11. Calculation errors may be made in manipulating or transforming raw scores.
12. Observed scores may be assumed to be equivalent to true scores.
13. Conclusions may be made about individual items or subtest scores when validity and reliability are established only for composite scores.

■ **FIGURE 12.1**   Common problems in the assessment process.

figure 12.1). An explicit part of the purpose should be a statement of which level or levels of the movement taxonomy are to be included.

■ SELECTING APPROPRIATE ASSESSMENT INSTRUMENTS

Once the specific purpose(s) and the taxonomy level(s) of the assessment process have been identified, then the search for appropriate measurement methods can begin. One must consider three levels of factors in selecting an appropriate assessment tool: (a) the match between the identified purpose and the valid uses of the instrument, (b) the match between the constraints of the examiner and the constraints of the instrument, and (c) the technical adequacy of the instrument.

Beyond consideration of these three levels, other strict standards may be required or recommended. First, the search should be not just for one instrument, but for at least two. Indeed, the evaluation procedures for all special education (including adapted physical education) mandated in the Individuals with Disabilities Education Act of 1990 (Public Law 101-476) specify that no single procedure should be used as the sole criterion for determining an appropriate educational program for a child. And second, the TFSMPT (1991) asserts that test users not only "must be able to justify the selection of tests they use," but "must also be prepared to supply logical arguments to justify the rejection of tests they choose not to use" (p. 614) (see Standard B6 in appendix B).

The Match Between Identified Purpose and Valid Uses of the Instrument

Deficits at any of the three levels may warrant rejection of a tool for possible use, but the first level—the match between the identified purpose and the valid uses of the instrument—must be given primary consideration. At this first level, one must identify assessment tools that may be used for the specified purpose and then carefully scrutinize the validity of these uses. Assessments that at least are intended to be used for the targeted purpose may be identified in a variety of ways. The prospective user can investigate a library of instruments available within a school district or health care facility, examine product catalogues, search the scientific literature via computer, or consult textbooks for summaries of instruments that include stated uses, such as the summary presented in appendix A2. Unfortunately, most movement skill assessment instruments are not available in community or university libraries or bookstores for convenient review. Appendixes A1 and A2 were designed to expose potential users to a wide range of movement skill assessment tools, to offer enough information to enable users to determine the potential value of certain tools for their purposes, and to provide information for further exploring or ordering particular tools.

The stated use of an assessment instrument indicates whether it should be considered, but the validity of the use must be examined closely. A common error that potential consumers make is to accept the uses of a particular test as stated in the test manual without carefully reading the sections of the manual describing the structure, validity, and reliability of the test in light of their specific purpose and needs. This error of blindly accepting the author's interpretation of the relevant data regarding appropriate uses of an assessment instrument then may lead to the problem of using a test that has not been adequately validated (Problem #2, figure 12.1).

For example, the test manual of the Bruininks-Oseretsky Test of Motor Proficiency (BOT) (Bruininks, 1978)—a popular test with adapted physical educators, occupational therapists, physical therapists, and researchers—indicates that it can be used to "assess motor status prior to training so that instruction can meet student needs . . . and assess the effectiveness of training and its transfer to performance outside the instructional program" (p. 15). However, the product-oriented measures on the BOT offer little information about the nature of the problems that need to be addressed in instruction. Also, the eight ability areas assessed in the BOT are traits that should be relatively stable across time and thus are not likely to be sensitive to changes as a result of training. Furthermore, Bruininks does not offer any information to validate this suggested use.

Besides examining details regarding validity in the test manual, potential users must also consider the implicit assumptions of the instruments (Davis, 1984). Neglecting to examine the implicit assumptions of an assessment instrument also may compromise the match between the purpose and the test. For example, the items in the Jebsen Hand Function Test (JHFT) (Jebsen, Taylor, Trieschmann, Trotter, & Howard, 1969) are assumed to be representative of real-life tasks. But a kinematic comparison of the simulated tasks with the actual tasks indicated that there was a poor match between the two (Mathiowetz & Wade, 1995). Thus, the JHFT may be used for the wrong purpose, even though the desired purpose is clearly identified in the test manual.

The Match Between Constraints of the User and Constraints of the Instrument

When one or more assessment tools that are valid for the targeted use have been identified, the match between the constraints of the user and the constraints of each instrument must be taken into account. The constraints of the user can be considered broadly to include three Es: the environment, the examinee, and the examiner (Goldsmith, 1993). Among the environmental constraints placed upon the user may be the cost of the manual, score sheet, test kit, or required equipment; the amount and size of required equipment; and the amount of space needed to administer the test (see Standard B1 in appendix B). The user may not have the resources to purchase expensive test materials, may not be able to store or transport a large volume of equipment, or may not have sufficient physical space to properly administer a test. Thus, a test may be rejected because it is environmentally impractical for the user (Problem #3, figure 12.1).

The user also is limited by the attributes of the examinee. First, the normative aspects of the instrument must be appropriate for the examinee's age, sex, and impairment status. Some instruments may specify a particular age range but not be appropriate at the extremes of the range. For example, the Test of Gross Motor Development (TGMD) (Ulrich, 1985) is designed for children 3 to 10 years of age, but it does not discriminate well at the low skill end for 3-year-olds or at the high skill end for 10-year-olds. Also, the TGMD does not have separate norms for boys and girls even though significant differences in the performances of boys and girls on some individual skills should be expected (Aponte, French, & Sherrill, 1990; Langendorfer, 1986).

Furthermore, the time requirements of the test must accommodate the attention span and energy limits of the examinee, the equipment must be scaled appropriately to the examinee's physical size, and the instructions must be comprehensible to the examinee (see Standard B7 in appendix B). If a test is too long and the examinee shows signs of mental or physical fatigue, an examiner may choose to postpone further testing until another time. However, this practice may have a biasing effect on the norm-referenced results compared to those of examinees who did not have such a break. The examiner is better off choosing a test with a length appropriate for the examinee or one that explicitly allows for long breaks in the testing protocol.

With regard to the equipment scaling issue, Burton and colleagues (Burton, Greer, & Wiese, 1992; Burton, Greer, & Wiese-Bjornstal, 1993) demonstrated that variations in grasping and throwing patterns in children and adults can be driven by just small changes in ball diameters. Even if raw test scores are converted to age norms, equipment that is not appropriately scaled may not allow examinees to fully demonstrate their movement skill.

Complicated instructions for young children or examinees with mental impairments, or instructions in a non-native language, should be avoided to ensure complete understanding of the task instructions. For example, Dunn and Ponticelli (1988) reported that scores on the short form of the BOT (Bruininks, 1978) of 29 children with hearing impairments were significantly higher when the instructions were given in American Sign Language rather than Signed Exact English. A test, then, may be rejected because it does not accommodate attributes of the individual being assessed (Problem #4, figure 12.1).

Finally, users are constrained by their own backgrounds in movement science, motor development, and assessment; by the amount of training they have received to administer, score, and interpret specific tests; and by their own levels of movement skill (see Standards A1-5 in appendix B). Professionals who need to conduct movement skill assessments most likely have extensive backgrounds in movement science and motor development and hold a degree in kinesiology, occupational therapy, physical education, physical therapy, or a related field. However, course work and training in assessment may vary considerably across academic programs, leading to differing levels of understanding of test theory, validity and reliability concepts, the normal distribution, and score transformations. Moreover, passing one or more courses in assessment does not ensure that a person has mastered all principles of measurement. People with more in-depth training in movement science and motor development are likely to be more competent in conducting informal movement skill assessment than those with less training because these types of tests require more subjective judgments and more spontaneous decisions about what manipulations to implement than do formal, standardized assessments.

The amount of training that movement professionals have received for specific tests may vary greatly; one person may have merely skimmed a test manual while another has taken a course focusing on a particular test with a competency examination at the end (see Standard C1 in appendix B). Some publishers of movement skill assessments offer training workshops, particularly for new editions of tests, or training videos. Some tests, such as the Denver II (Frankenburg & Dodds, 1992), have a separate training manual with a competency test at the end. These efforts are attractive features of tests with complex administration and scoring procedures, and may be important considerations in selecting a test.

A final limitation of the examiner may be his or her own movement skill. If the examiner is not able to demonstrate a specified movement properly, the examinee's performance obviously will suffer. Hence, the knowledge and skills of the potential user must match the knowledge and skills required to successfully administer, score, and interpret the selected test (Problem #5, figure 12.1).

The Technical Adequacy of the Instrument

At the third level of factors to be considered in selection of an appropriate assessment instrument are other threats to the validity of the assessment process, including (a) poor reliability and (b) inadequate or inappropriate standardization procedures. First, a test with poor reliability cannot be valid. On the other hand, a test with poorly established validity might be highly reliable, yet such a test would be completely meaningless. Reliability should be established within raters (intrarater), across raters (interrater), and within subjects across time (test-retest). Test users must be aware that a composite score may have high reliability while individual subtest scores have low reliability.

Second, the standardization methods must be appropriate for the specific application of the assessment. The standardization sample must adequately reflect the persons to whom the assessment will be given in terms of age, race/culture, socioeconomic status, and geographical location (see Standard B2 in appendix B). If one plans to use a test with persons who have particular disabilities, the standardization sample should ideally include persons with the same disability, and the assessment should be validated for those persons. If persons with disabilities are not included in the sample, normative-referenced scores will generally underestimate relative movement skill performance. For example, if a person's performance is equivalent to the 7th percentile ($-1.5\ SD$) in a full, normal distribution (see figure 12.2a), then the same performance would be equivalent to the 5th percentile if the performances beyond two standard deviations below the mean (the lowest 2%) were excluded, as illustrated in figure 12.2b. Thus, a test that otherwise appears to meet the needs of the user may be unacceptable because of poor reliability or inadequate standardization procedures (Problem #6, figure 12.1).

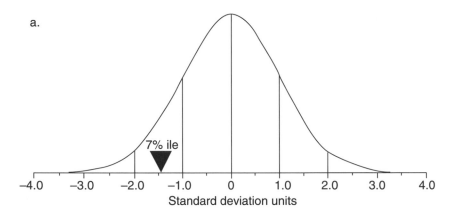

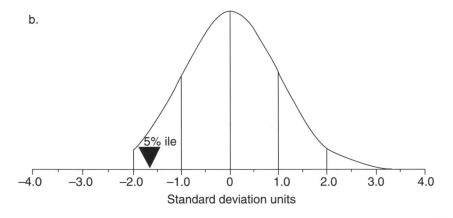

■ **FIGURE 12.2** The relative standing of a person's performance, marked by a triangle, when placed in a full, normal distribution (a) or when placed in a normal distribution excluding performances beyond standard deviations below the mean (b).

■ COLLECTING AND TREATING DATA

The third step in the assessment process involves several substeps: (a) thoroughly reading and understanding the test procedures, (b) properly setting up the testing environment, (c) administering the test, and (d) calculating the results of the test. First, a careful reading through the test procedures is not sufficient; a full understanding is absolutely necessary. If a potential examiner does not feel comfortable with the procedures or does not pass a competency in the training manual, further study is necessary.

An examiner who is not proficient may continue to study the test manual, attend workshops or courses on the particular test if they are available, view a training videotape if one exists, or observe a competent examiner administering the test. The examiner's supervisor is responsible for ensuring the examiner's competency in administering a specific movement skill assessment instrument (Problem #5, figure 12.1).

Second, the examiner must set up the environment according to the directions in the test manual and minimize environmental factors that may negatively impact the performance of the examinee (see Standard C4 in appendix B). Some factors that need to be considered are total space; surface characteristics; lighting; noise level; temperature; time of day; other persons present; arrangement, body scaling, and calibration of equipment; and distracting objects, doorways, or windows. These factors may vary considerably without affecting movement performance, but a small change in just one factor also could alter the results of a test (Problem #7, figure 12.1). An example of a rather subtle factor that may significantly affect a person's movement outcome is the position within a room in which a balance task is performed. Because of the increased optical flow information, a person standing near a patterned or decorated wall should be able to balance longer than if placed near a plain wall or in the middle of a large room (Burton & Davis, 1992a).

Before administering the actual test, the examiner should establish a rapport with the examinee. This may entail briefly introducing oneself and describing the assessment or may require spending extended time with the examinee. Helping examinees feel relaxed and motivated to do their best is important in promoting typical or optimal performance. Time may not be available to establish adequate rapport if the examiner is a stranger to the examinee, but all concerned parties must understand this threat to the validity of the procedure (Problem #8, figure 12.1).

Third, when administering the test, an examiner must follow the stated directions exactly (see Standards C2-3 in appendix B). Deviations from standardized directions in a norm-referenced test may negate the norm-referenced status. Explicit directions are usually given for verbal instructions and physical demonstrations, number of trials or amount of time allowed, number of practice trials or practice time, and type and amount of feedback allowed. Item order should not be changed, and long breaks between items should not be given unless allowed for in the directions. Some assessment tools have summaries of each item, including verbal instructions, printed directly on the score sheet to help the examiner. Unless a person is very familiar with a test, some brief notes on the procedures may help make the administration go more smoothly. In most test administrations, some errors or deviations from the directions will be made. The examiner, then, must decide whether these errors or deviations are sufficient to invalidate the use of norm-referenced scores (Problem #9, figure 12.1).

The tasks presented as part of an assessment will offer differing degrees of challenge to individual examinees. Some may find the test situation inherently rewarding and need no incentive for performing. Others may perform poorly in test situations as a result of performance anxiety or for other reasons unrelated to their movement proficiency. Unless prohibited by standardized directions, examiners may offer encouragement through verbal and nonverbal communication. Positive reinforcement for effort, whether successful or not, generally will provide an incentive for continued participation. Nodding, smiling, words of praise, and tangible rewards are some of the ways of motivating examinees. In addition, giving knowledge of results, particularly to older examinees, may help motivate them.

Mental or physical fatigue can reduce motivation, cooperation, and performance. If allowed by the standardized directions, short breaks between individual items or subtests can help minimize the negative effects of fatigue. Another option may be to administer the test over 2 or more days, but many tests do not allow for this modification.

As the examinee's performance on the test items is observed, raw scores are recorded on a score sheet according to the specified criteria. To free themselves from the score sheet or to increase the accuracy of their scoring, some examiners may choose to record the examinee's performance on videotape or verbally score or describe the performance on audiotape. These modifications must be implemented with caution on standardized tests because of their potential differential impact on scores compared to those obtained with use of the basic procedures. On criterion-referenced tests, the criteria for middle levels of performance—that is, neither yes or no— are often vague and may lead to inconsistent scoring within and between examiners. Thus, another problem may be improper recording of raw scores (Problem #10, figure 12.1).

Even if not specified in the scoring directions, additional written comments about the examinee's performance, recorded during or immediately after the test administration, are strongly encouraged (see Standard D9 in appendix B). Notes on types of errors made, movement patterns demonstrated, comments made by the examinee, or other relevant information may be extremely useful for just about any assessment purpose. Moreover, a brief comment about the examinee's level of motivation and cooperation should help determine whether the scores reflect his or her actual movement skill.

The last substep in data collection and treatment is the calculation of results from raw scores. This may involve simply summing raw scores and calculating percentages in criterion-referenced tests, or converting and transforming raw scores into norm-referenced Z scores, T scores, standardized scores, percentiles, stanines, or age equivalents. Some score transformations involve many steps: transferring scores from one page to another, looking up values on conversion tables, summing scores, or finding median values. For example, the BOT (Bruininks, 1978) requires at least nine score transfers or conversions to determine a gross or fine motor composite percentile or age-equivalent value (see table 8.2). Obviously, increasing the number of conversion steps increases the chance of making a calculation error (Problem #11, figure 12.1).

Test developers can help minimize scoring errors by creating and offering computer software that would require users to enter only examinee data (such as name, test date, and birth date) and raw scores. Then any possible calculation or conversion could be carried out by the computer. Also, help in interpreting the results could be provided and special word-processing forms for reporting the results made available. For example, a software program has been developed for the Pediatric Evaluation of Disability Inventory (Haley, Coster, Ludlow, Haltiwanger, & Andrellos, 1992) for entering data, calculating scores, and generating individual summary score profiles. The examiner's manual provides detailed instructions on how to use this software.

■ INTERPRETING THE RESULTS

When data collection and scoring procedures have been completed, then the question posed by the specified purpose of the assessment can be addressed. Most test manuals provide information on how to interpret assessment results for at least some of the stated uses of the test. The Movement Assessment Battery for Children (MABC) Checklist (Henderson & Sugden, 1992) is a good example. There are five sections in the MABC Checklist: four related to actual movement competency and one related to behavior problems only. The scores across the first four sections are totaled, and there is a table in the interpretation section of the manual for converting total scores into the 5th and 15th percentiles only. The authors assist users in interpreting this score conversion by stating that children whose scores fall at or below the 5th percentile "can confidently be assumed to require more detailed assessment and some form of specialized consideration in terms of a management or remediation program" (pp. 26-27). On the last section focusing on behavior problems only, the interpretation is more direct. Scores across the 12 items are not totaled and quantitatively converted; instead, examiners are instructed to judge, by comparison to other children, whether these behaviors might have prevented the child from demonstrating his/her true capabilities or should be taken into account in future management or remedial programs, and to indicate their judgment level by recording "high," "medium," or "low."

Any interpretation must be confined to the limits of the test and the measurement model on which the test is based (see Standards D1-2 in appendix B). One frequent problem occurs when an observed score, derived from a test based on a classical true-score model (see chapter 5 for elaboration on measurement models), is assumed to directly correspond with a person's "true" ability. The professional interpreting the score may report that the examinee is at a particular percentile for his/her age and sex group, but in fact can only state the probability that his/her true score will fall within a certain percentile range, based on the standard error of measurement (see Standards D7-8 in appendix B). Moreover, even the range determined by the standard error of measurement indicates only what the performer did, not what the performer could do under other circumstances (Problem #12, figure 12.1). When a child performs some tasks unsuccessfully, Stott, Henderson, and Moyes (1986) admit that "we are not justified in assuming that the child is unable to carry out the tasks, only that he or she does not do so" (p. 206).

Another common problem in interpretation involves making conclusions about individual items or subtest scores when test validity or reliability is established for composite scores only (Problem #13, figure 12.1). For example, in the Peabody Developmental Motor Scales (Folio & Fewell, 1983), percentiles can be found for the five gross motor and four fine motor skill areas, which invite interpretation, yet there is no reliability information for these separate skill areas.

One may minimize other errors in the interpretation step by avoiding pitfalls at the previous three steps. In particular, the first problem, that of using test results for inappropriate purposes, can be eliminated if the instrument is carefully matched to the purpose of the assessment and if the user does not modify the purpose of the test. Bundy (1995) argues that another way to minimize interpretation errors is to have the results of an assessment reviewed and interpreted by a team of professionals, not just an individual therapist. Bundy points out that "the notion that others assess the adequacy of our findings and that we can sometimes modify interpretation of our findings is not generally described in therapeutic literature" (p. 75).

■ REPORTING THE RESULTS

The last step in the assessment process is reporting the results. A complete assessment report should include at least five components: (a) information about the examiner or reporter, (b) background information about the examinee, (c) information on the instruments or procedures administered, (d) the actual results, and (e) the recommendations derived from the results.

First, at the beginning or end of the report, the examiner or reporter should include his or her full name, educational titles (e.g., MEd, PhD, OTR/L), and position title (e.g., Adapted Physical Education Specialist, Physical

Therapist). Next one should give pertinent background information on the individual who is being evaluated. This should include giving the person's name, sex, and age (and perhaps grade level if in a school setting); listing relevant anthropometric data, such as height and weight; and pointing out any impairments that may affect movement performance, such as poor visual acuity, low cognitive functioning, or spasticity in one or more limbs.

Third, the instruments and procedures administered need to be briefly described and justified (see Standard E4 in appendix B). The title, purposes, and general content of each test should be provided, as well as the dates on which the tests were administered, and perhaps even the time of day (e.g., morning, afternoon, or evening) and length of the testing period. Any special circumstances in the testing situation should be mentioned, for example, other persons observing the testing, a unique location (e.g., in a school hallway, outdoors on a cold day, or in a small room with a low ceiling), or disturbing or distracting events either preceding or following the testing period. In addition, any variations in a standardized test need to be reported, along with a statement of how the variation may have affected the quality of the measurements (see Standard E2 in appendix B).

Once this prefatory information has been recorded, the results can be presented. The results should be expressed in terms of the scoring systems validated for the specific instruments, such as the motor impairment score in the MABC Test (Henderson & Sugden, 1992) or the Gross Motor Development Quotient in the TGMD (Ulrich, 1985). Scores that laypersons may not understand need to be briefly explained. In addition, descriptions of specific performances that exemplify or contradict summary scores can be very helpful. In its standards, the TFSMPT (1991) emphasizes that in the presentation of results, estimates of error or reliability associated with a measurement and any aspect of a test that may cast doubt on the results must be reported (see Standards E1 and E3, respectively, in appendix B). Also, the behavioral state of the examinee should be described if it appeared to limit his or her movement performance.

The last and most important component of the assessment report is the recommendations for action. The recommendations should evaluate and interpret the test results in relation to the original purpose of the assessment, such as determining whether a person qualifies for a particular service or determining instructional or therapeutic needs. If a recommendation is contingent on the meeting of certain criteria, those criteria need to be explicitly stated in the report (see Standard E5 in appendix B). The recommendations themselves should be as specific as possible. With regard to eligibility for a particular service, for example, they should include suggested level, frequency, and duration of service. Or, with regard to instructional or therapeutic planning, the areas of concern should be identified, measurable objectives listed, and intervention strategies and resources suggested.

Chapter **13**

Two Strategies for Movement Skill Assessment

© Photophile/ Jose Carrillo

AS I have emphasized throughout this book, movement skill assessment instruments should be chosen to match the specific purpose of the assessment. Moving beyond this basic principle, persons engaged in the assessment process need to have a broader perspective of how various purposes of movement skill assessment can be accomplished. In

> **❝ ❝** The job of an NFL scout is to evaluate college play-
> ers. Too often, they over-evaluate. They forget things, **❞ ❞**
> little things, such as whether the kid can play.
> — *Sansevere (1987, p. 1D)*

this chapter, I describe and compare two general strategies for movement skill assessment: a bottom-up approach and a top-down approach. The terms *bottom-up* and *top-down* generally refer to strategies for instruction or intervention, but these concepts also extend to assessment. Ideally, a person's strategy for assessment should be congruent with the strategy for instruction or intervention.

The use of the terms bottom-up and top-down in physical education can be traced back to a textbook by Auxter and Pyfer (1985), or perhaps even earlier. Since 1986, these terms have been used by occupational therapists (e.g., Fisher & Short-DeGraff, 1993; Trombly, 1993), physical therapists (e.g., Bidabe & Lollar, 1990; Long & Cintas, 1995), and other physical educators (e.g., Block, 1994; Burton, 1987; Kelly, 1989). The following descriptions of bottom-up and top-down strategies for assessment will be adapted to the taxonomy of movement skills used throughout this book, but will reflect the views of persons in these various professional areas.

■ BOTTOM-UP STRATEGY FOR ASSESSMENT

In this section I offer several descriptions of bottom-up strategies for assessment and instruction and then discuss the advantages and disadvantages of a bottom-up approach.

Descriptions

In their adapted physical education textbook, Auxter and Pyfer (1985) describe a bottom-up strategy for instruction and assessment as follows:

> Some developmentalists will begin by evaluating each of the sensory input systems and then testing the ability components to determine which deficits are in evidence. Once the deficits are identified, activities that promote functioning of each sensory input system found to be lacking are selected. The rationale is to progress to activities that facilitate development of the ability components. Only after each of these building blocks is in place will the developmentalist attempt to teach the specific sport or functional skills. (p. 44)

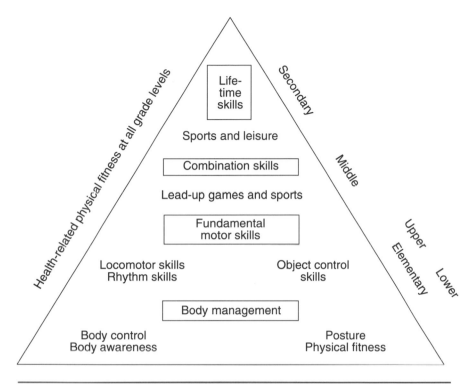

■ **FIGURE 13.1** Physical education curriculum model from Kelly (1989). This figure is reprinted with permission from the *Journal of Physical Education, Recreation & Dance*, volume 60, issue 9, 1989, pages 29-32. JOPERD is a publication of the American Alliance for Health, Physical Education, Recreation and Dance, 1900 Association Drive, Reston, VA 22091.

Similarly, Kelly (1989) portrays a bottom-up curriculum model in physical education as one "designed to provide the students with a broad foundation of fundamental motor skills during the elementary years, which are then combined into games and sports during the middle school years and finally culminate with the attainment of functional lifetime sport and fitness skills in the secondary school years" (p. 29) (see figure 13.1).

An instructional or intervention program should begin with assessment of a person's present level of performance to determine his/her eligibility for service or, if service is already assured, to set appropriate instructional or intervention objectives. From a bottom-up perspective, this initial assessment, in terms of the movement skill taxonomy used in this book, usually focuses on foundations of movement skills, motor abilities, or early movement milestones (see figure 13.2). According to Trombly (1993), a bottom-up approach in occupational therapy begins with the assessment of "the deficits of components of function, such as strength, range of motion,

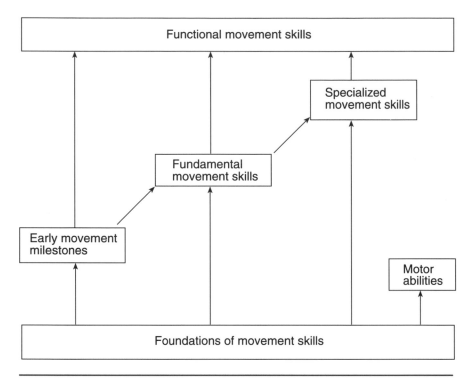

■ **FIGURE 13.2**   Taxonomy of movement skills.

balance, and so on, which are believed to be prerequisites to successful occupational performance or functioning" (p. 253).

An illustration of the concept of bottom-up sequencing is the organization of testing and practice at a football training camp. At the beginning of camp, the movement skill foundations are carefully evaluated and, if necessary, addressed. Players are tested for body weight, body fat percentage, 40-yd-dash time, 2-mi-run time, and bench press weight. As deficiencies are identified, special programming is prescribed. Next, drills on skills specific to particular defensive and offensive positions are begun in isolation. When these skills are tuned, they are performed in limited scrimmages, expanded scrimmages, and finally in actual games. Although the players may not reach complete competency before moving up to the next level, the basic order of events is bottom-up.

A bottom-up sequence may begin with one or more of the many common tests of movement skill foundations used in physical education, occupational therapy, and physical therapy described in chapter 7. In early childhood physical education and pediatric occupational and physical therapy, a bottom-up approach may begin with the use of one or more tests of movement skill foundations, such as the Movement Assessment of Infants (Chandler, Andrews, & Swanson, 1980), or early movement milestones, such as the Peabody Developmental Motor Scales (Folio & Fewell, 1983). In adapted physical education, this bottom-up process is initiated most often with the Bruininks-Oseretsky Test of Motor Proficiency (Bruininks, 1978), an ability-oriented test.

A different description of a bottom-up strategy for instruction in physical education is offered by Vickers (1990). Vickers argues that a bottom-up strategy involves the teacher's breaking down an activity into its components and then having the student progressively reconstruct the activity by working on and adding components in a simple-to-complex order. In this conceptualization, the movement skill assessment would consist of a part-to-whole task analysis of specific skills, most likely based on motions at one or more joints. However, this type of part-to-whole task analysis of specific skills is considered by Auxter and Pyfer (1985) more a top-down than a bottom-up approach, indicating that there is some inconsistency in the use of these terms.

Advantages and Disadvantages

In a classic bottom-up approach, instruction or intervention at higher movement skill levels—fundamental, specialized, or functional—does not occur until competency is gained at the preceding level or, in other words, until lower-level deficits are remediated. The main advantage of a bottom-up approach is that a sound base for learning specialized and functional movement skills is established, allowing individuals to experience success at each step up the skill taxonomy. This approach is best suited for younger children and persons with impairments who have achieved few skills beyond early movement milestones.

Most bottom-up models of instruction are portrayed as triangles or pyramids, with the wide part of the figure encompassing the lower levels of movement function or behavior (see figure 13.1). This hierarchical depiction suggests first that proficiency in lower-level skills or abilities must be attained before higher skills can be achieved. In Seefeldt's (1980) four-level hierarchy of skills described in chapter 3, a distinct proficiency barrier was placed between fundamental motor skills and specific sport skills and dances because Seefeldt thought that mastery of the fundamental motor skills was necessary for optimal development of the higher-level skills. A hierarchical model presented as a triangle or pyramid also implies that there are more competencies to be gained at the lower levels, whereas one of the major contentions and potential advantages of a bottom-up approach is that success in a limited set of foundations, early movement milestones, and fundamental movement skills will lead to success in an unlimited number of specialized and functional movement skills. Thus, a bottom-up model should look more like an inverted triangle or pyramid. Note that the present taxonomy used in this book is not based on a hierarchical model (see figure 13.2).

A bottom-up strategy has several key disadvantages for instruction or intervention. First, a comprehensive bottom-up approach can be very time consuming (Auxter & Pyfer, 1985; Bidabe & Lollar, 1990). The required attainment of competency at an entire level before moving to the next level up may take a very long time for some persons and may be impossible for others. Second, persons who may never be able to move beyond movement skill foundations, motor abilities, or early movement milestones may be deprived of opportunities to learn or at least be exposed to functional skills that they might be able to perform despite their limited skill foundations or lower-level skills. Remember that in the present taxonomy, unlike most other taxonomies, lower-level skills are not prerequisites for higher-level skills. Third, if functional skills are never addressed, the validity or applicability of the instruction or intervention, and thus the assessment strategy, may be seriously questioned. Trombly (1993) argues that an occupational therapist using a bottom-up approach "may not make clear to the client the connection between the component deficit and occupational functioning" (p. 253). Fourth, and perhaps most important, an exclusive emphasis on movement skill foundations, motor abilities, or low-level skills is not very motivating for most students or patients, which may impede progress.

Unfortunately, not all teachers and therapists understand, carefully consider, and make a rational choice of an instructional/assessment approach. In adapted physical education, administrators often require teachers to use a standardized, norm-referenced test to qualify students for special education service. Because most standardized, norm-referenced tests appropriate for adapted physical education assess movement skill foundations or motor abilities, this type of administrative decree may implicitly drive a teacher to implement a bottom-up strategy for assessment and subsequently a bottom-up strategy for instruction.

■ TOP-DOWN STRATEGY FOR ASSESSMENT

My discussion of the top-down approach will consist of (a) general descriptions of top-down approaches in various professional areas, (b) discussion of advantages and disadvantages of top-down approaches, and (c) the presentation of a specific three-step, top-down sequence.

General Descriptions

Auxter and Pyfer (1985) refer to a top-down approach as a task-specific strategy. After targeted skills are selected, they are evaluated for the purpose of identifying any deficiencies. Auxter and Pyfer (1985) explain:

If inefficient movements are found, the teacher investigates the ability components for deficits. If problems are found at the ability level, specific sensory input systems believed to contribute to the deficits at the ability level are tested. When deficiencies are found, activities are selected to promote development at the lowest level first. (p. 43)

The complementary processes of assessment and instruction for each skill continue to step down the skill hierarchy only as necessary to establish competency at the highest level. The highest level in the present taxonomy is functional movement skill. Thus, the primary goal in a top-down strategy for movement skill instruction or intervention is success in performing skills in their natural contexts. Block (1994) argues that a top-down approach forces the teacher to focus on critical skills that a student needs in order to be successful while minimizing attention to less functional items.

In Minnesota public schools, special physical education services for students with disabilities is called developmental/adapted physical education (D/APE). The term *adapted* refers to modifications or adaptations that allow students to participate in functional, age-appropriate physical activities to the maximum extent possible. Adapted physical education focuses on modifying task and/or environmental factors, for instance, adjusting game rules, changing the performance setting, or allowing the use of assistive devices. Developmental physical education, however, focuses on improving the actual skills of the performer. These two perspectives account for all three factors that shape or constrain movement behavior, as proposed by Newell (1986) (see figure 13.3).

Top-down physical education combining both adapted and developmental aspects begins with engaging students in functional activities at the highest level possible. This may involve rolling over to get to a toy (early movement milestones), wheeling a chair or running in a game of tag (fundamental movement skill), or shooting a basketball in a full-court game (specialized movement skill). If a student is unable to succeed at this functional level, the D/APE specialist has two options: (a) modify the task or environment to allow the student to participate in the activity (adapted), and/or (b) help the student improve a specific functional movement skill by stepping down the skill hierarchy only as far as needed (developmental). In the developmental option, if the process extends all the way down to the foundations of movement skill, the foundation areas—such as strength or range or motion—will be addressed only in relation to the targeted skill.

In occupational therapy, a three-level hierarchy is often used, with role performance at the top, occupational performance in the middle, and performance components at the bottom (see figure 3.1). Thus, a top-down strategy for assessment and intervention (Fisher & Short-DeGraff, 1993; Mathiowetz, 1993; Trombly, 1993) first focuses on occupational roles and the purpose of the therapy for the client; it then moves to the

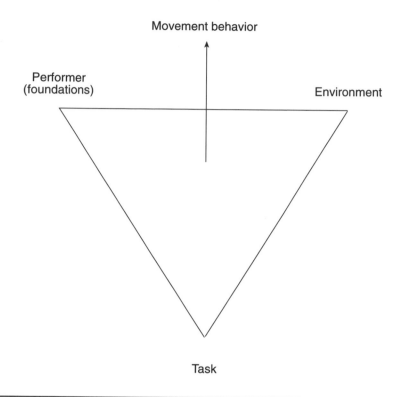

■ FIGURE 13.3 Three interacting categories of constraints on movement behavior (adapted from Newell, 1986).

particular tasks that define each of the roles for the individual. If occupational performance is inadequate, the therapy process would continue down to the performance components.

In the Mobility Opportunities Via Education (MOVE) program (Bidabe & Lollar, 1990), an individual's performance levels on 16 skills on the Top-Down Motor Milestone Test (TDMMT) are first assessed; next, specific functional activities to be addressed (such as walking backwards to seat self without being lifted or going into the community without using a wheelchair) are identified by the person and caregivers. Then the skills necessary to perform the identified activity are chosen from the TDMMT, and goals are set that would allow the person more independence in the activity. These steps in the MOVE program are followed by skill practice, with a focus on reducing the prompts the person needs in order to perform the skills.

Curriculum-based assessment (CBA) also can be considered a top-down approach. This contention is based on the assumption that the curriculum specifies particular functional movement skills to be targeted and achieved.

Bagnato, Neisworth, and Capone (1986) explain that CBA "involves a test-teach-test approach wherein children are assessed on objectives to be learned, provided with instruction, and then assessed on the achievement of these objectives"; the authors argue that CBA "is emerging as the most practical and effective option in educational assessment, showing a rapid growth in conceptual refinement and professional practice" (p. 97). The instruction component of a movement-oriented CBA must include working on movement skill foundations if a student is experiencing continued failure.

Advantages and Disadvantages

There are numerous advantages to a top-down strategy for assessment and instruction or intervention. First, evaluating an individual's movement skills in the highest-level functional context possible at the outset provides a preassessment relative to the ultimate goal of the instruction or intervention. Second, the content validity of the preassessment is clearly established because it is matched exactly to the ultimate goal of the instruction or intervention. Third, such a preassessment should minimize the amount of time spent on skills the individual is already able to perform competently. The preassessment also should help students or patients to see their own needs in light of their own functional performances. And fourth, these advantages should make instruction or intervention not only more efficient, in terms of time, than a broad-based bottom-up approach, but also more motivating to the individual. The participant will work on skills useful in real life, focusing only on the aspects of the skills that still need to be mastered, and will be exposed to the natural reinforcers and consequences unique to functional activities. A top-down approach is most appropriate for persons who have established a minimum repertoire of movement skills in the activity or sport in question.

The most significant disadvantage of the top-down approach is that the specified functional movement skills may be beyond the capabilities of the student or patient and that the initial experience in the functional setting may result in failure and frustration. These negative experiences then may lead to resistance, apathy, or other problems. Unless carefully monitored, the beginning activity also may pose safety hazards for participants.

A Three-Step, Top-Down Assessment Sequence

The three major factors that shape or constrain movement behavior are portrayed in figure 13.3, with the performer node representing movement skill foundation factors. The emergent movement behavior can be described further in terms of movement skills (process), skill patterns (process) and functional movement outcomes (product) (see figure 13.4). These levels of

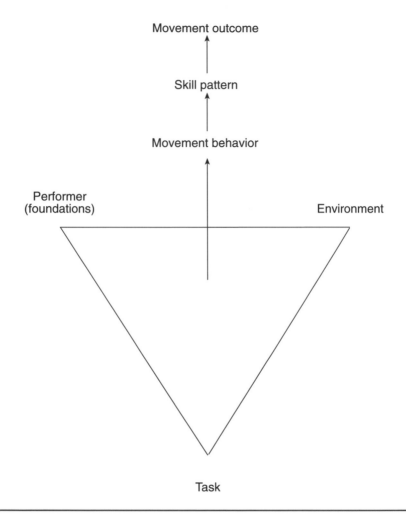

■ FIGURE 13.4 Movement constraints and levels of movement behaviors (adapted from Davis & Burton, 1991).

movement behavior, along with the movement skill foundations of the performer, provide the basis for a three-step, top-down assessment sequence (see figure 13.5). In the following pages I present this sequence and characterize the relationship of the sequence to the categories in the movement skill taxonomy.

Step 1: Functional Movement Outcomes. The first step in this top-down assessment sequence is to identify a functional task goal or outcome and to determine whether the criteria related to functional movement outcomes or products are achieved (see figure 13.5). It is assumed in this step that the specified movement task is functional for and meaningful to the

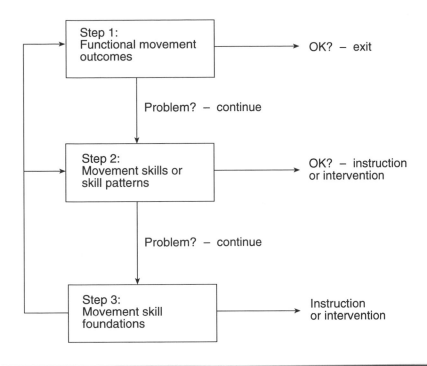

■ FIGURE 13.5 A three-step, top-down assessment sequence.

individual, and that the task is effected through the use of functional movement skills, as defined in the skill taxonomy. In the model of movement behavior presented in figure 13.4, the task is the primary node at the bottom of the triangle because it identifies what needs to be accomplished. Then, the most important question, represented at the top of the model as the functional outcome or product, is whether the task was achieved or completed.

If the criteria are achieved, then the assessment stops here at Step 1; if the criteria are not achieved, the assessment proceeds to Step 2 (see figure 13.5). The decision to stop or proceed may be based on the performance of just one task or a set of tasks. In the case of a set of tasks, the number or percentage of tasks that need to be achieved may be selected to match specific purposes. For example, for students to be eligible for adapted physical education services, they may be required to achieve 50% or fewer of the tasks identified in the functional curriculum for the preceding grade level (third grade for fourth graders). Besides determining program eligibility, criterion-referenced assessment at this functional level may be used for (a) screening, (b) placement, (c) evaluation of progress, or (d) program evaluation.

Some items from the functional movement skill tests described in chapter 11 can serve to illustrate appropriate assessment tasks for Step 1. In the Movement Assessment Battery for Children (MABC) Checklist (Henderson & Sugden, 1992) the following items, judged on a 4-point ordinal scale, specify functional tasks: (a) cut/draw/trace with precision/accuracy, (b) jump across/over obstacles that might be found in the play environment (blocks, low hurdles, ropes), and (c) use skills of striking, kicking, catching and/or throwing to participate in a team game. Two *yes/no* items from the mobility domain of the Pediatric Evaluation of Disability Inventory (PEDI) (Haley, Coster, Ludlow, Haltiwanger, & Andrellos, 1992) are (a) indoor locomotion within a room, able to keep up with peers; and (b) outdoor locomotion 150 ft or more, unable to keep up with peers.

The items in a functional curriculum-based movement assessment also are evaluated in this first step. However, many curriculum-based movement assessments focus on isolated skills not performed in their natural context, because the curriculum specifies criteria for achieving early movement milestones, fundamental movement skills, or specialized skills, not criteria for achieving functional outcomes.

A sample CBA for physical education is shown in chapter 5 (see figure 5.2). This CBA is based on the learner outcomes for Grade 2 physical education in Minneapolis Public Schools (1991). Of the 14 items, 6 specify proper form for fundamental (5) and specialized (1) movement skills, and 4 concern movement products, but none place movement skills in functional contexts. Examples of functional CBA items include (a) in a basketball game, making at least 4 of 10 field goal attempts; and (b) from any infield position in a baseball or softball game, fielding 10 ground balls with three errors or fewer. Although the specific conditions of these tasks are not mentioned, the tasks are scaled by the competition and by the possible modifications of the game (e.g., base length, ball size, or basket height) in which the individual is expected to perform.

The Assessment, Evaluation, and Programming System for Infants and Children Birth to Three Years (AEPS) (Bricker, 1993) also is a CBA instrument, designed specifically for early childhood programs. The AEPS, reviewed in detail in chapter 9, has a separate volume for measurement issues (Vol. 1: Bricker, 1993) and another for curricular issues (Vol. 2: Cripe, Slentz, & Bricker, 1993).

Step 2: Movement Skills and Skill Patterns.   The next step in this top-down assessment sequence has two components: (a) identifying what movement skills and skill patterns are used and (b) examining the effects of task, environmental, and performer variables on these skills and patterns. Skills are defined as in chapter 3 as specific classes of goal-directed movement patterns, such as running, throwing, hammering, driving, writing, or even speaking. Pattern variations within particular skills, such as throwing, can be specified by anatomy (e.g., overhand or two-hand), by object or function (e.g., baseball or shot put), or by component (e.g., downward backswing or forearm lag) (see table 3.1). The main idea of Step 2 is to explore how early movement milestones, fundamental movement skills, and specialized movement skills—the middle categories in the skill taxonomy (see figure 13.2)—are applied to solving a particular movement task. The information is most relevant for instructional or intervention planning, evaluation of progress, or research.

The model in figure 13.4 indicates that the movement skill, or a particular pattern or form of the movement skill that a person uses to complete a specified task, depends upon the interaction between environmental and performer factors. To accomplish the same task, a person may use different skills or patterns if the environment is varied, and different people may use different skills or patterns when the environment is held constant. A key concept here is that there is not just one proper skill or pattern for performing a set task; there may be many effective skills and patterns (Burton & Davis, 1992b; Davis & Burton, 1991). As Burton and Davis (1992b) explain:

> In professional baseball, the batting stances of the best hitters vary considerably from a classic closed stance with the hands positioned at about shoulder height, to an open stance with the front foot barely touching the ground and the hands held over the head; yet the most important consideration for spectators and other players is whether they get on base and score. Similarly, children with physical impairments need to be given the freedom to use the movement skills and skill patterns that are optimal for them, and not be limited by the skills and patterns deemed acceptable by society. (pp. 245-246)

Some of the examples cited from the MABC Checklist (Henderson & Sugden, 1992) and the PEDI (Haley et al., 1992) can serve to illustrate. From Item #1-7 in the MABC Checklist, drawing with accuracy can be accomplished by using various anatomical parts (e.g., hand, foot, or mouth) and various implement grips at each part (e.g., tripod grip or palmar grasp with hand). From the PEDI, indoor and outdoor locomotion can be accomplished in many different ways, including walking, running, galloping, walking with cane or walker, or wheeling in a chair.

Once the movement skill and skill patterns are identified for the original functional task, the effects of task, environmental, and performer variables on these skills and patterns are examined. Some of the factors or dimensions that might be varied are listed in table 13.1. As these factors are scaled up or down, a critical value might be identified at which an abrupt transition to a new pattern or even to a new skill occurs. Note that some performer factors, such as height or strength, might be scaled over a period of weeks, months, or even longer.

This manipulation procedure has been elaborated by Davis and Burton in what they call *ecological task analysis* (ETA) (Balan & Davis, 1993; Burton

TABLE 13.1   Tasks and Environmental Factors That Can be Manipulated in Step 2

Factor	Manipulated attributes
Object or target to be acted on	Shape and volume Weight Texture Speed Trajectory Predictability
Equipment to be used to act on an object	Shape and volume Weight Texture
Support surface	Friction Grade or incline Resiliency Smoothness
Other environmental conditions	Sensory information available Temperature Lighting Observers or spectators
Assistance	From equipment From other person
Task goal	Accuracy Force Distance Frequency Velocity

& Davis, 1996; Davis & Burton, 1991). They recommend that as task, environmental, or performer dimensions are manipulated singly or in combination, the following assessment information be recorded: (a) the specific task; (b) the specific skills and skill patterns used to carry out the task; (c) the absolute dimension value at which a skill or pattern transition occurs; (d) when appropriate, a performer-scaled ratio for the transition point; and (e) the functional outcome relative to the performance criterion. Figure 13.6 provides a sample form for recording these data.

We can convert the absolute dimension value at which a transition is made to a performer-scaled ratio by identifying a relevant performer metric expressed in the same absolute units as the dimension, and dividing the dimension value by the performer value (Davis & Burton, 1991):

$$\text{Performer-scaled ratio} = \frac{\text{absolute dimension value}}{\text{relevant performer value}} \qquad 13.1$$

Ecological Task Analysis Checklist A. Burton University of Minnesota			Movement skills or patterns					
			Throw with 1 hand overhand					
				Throw w/1 hand underhand				
					Throw with 2 hands			
						Roll with 1 hand		
							Roll with 2 hands	
Task	Factor	Factor						Outcome
Propel ball	from 5'	tennis ball			X			10/10
to player on	from 5'	softball			X			10/10
first base,	from 5'	8" playground ball				X		10/10
8/10 times	from 10'	tennis ball			X			7/10
	from 10'	softball			X			5/10
	from 10'	8" playground ball					X	7/10
	from 15'	tennis ball	X					5/10
	from 15'	softball				X		2/10
	from 15'	8" playground ball					X	4/10
	from 20'	tennis ball	X					2/10
	from 20'	softball				X		1/10
	from 20'	8" playground ball					X	3/10

■ **FIGURE 13.6** Sample score sheet for collecting data in Step 2.

For example, for the task of dribbling a ball the length of the court in basketball, the ball diameter at which a change in the dribbling pattern (7.0 in.) occurs can be divided by a relevant performer value, such as hand width (6.6 in.), to yield a performer-scaled ratio of 1.06 (see study by Burton & Welch, 1990).

Davis and Burton (1991) explain that the purpose of ETA is "to gain insight into the dynamics of the movement behavior of students, to provide teachers with clues for developing instructional strategies, and ultimately to promote the success of students in performing the task" (p. 160). More specifically, they assert that ETA procedures provide information for individual performers regarding (a) the set of conditions that affords achievement of the task most efficiently and effectively; (b) the parameter values at which movement skills or skill patterns change; and (c) flexibility or rigidity in the application of various movement solutions (skills and movement patterns) to a range of movement problems (i.e., sets of task conditions).

Unfortunately, in most movement assessment instruments, the skills and patterns are rigidly specified. However, some existing assessment tools may be modified to accommodate the manipulation of task, environmental, and performer variables. For instance, the patterns used as scoring criteria in the Test of Gross Motor Development (Ulrich, 1985) for 12 fundamental movement skills (see chapter 10) can be applied not only to the standard task conditions, but also to other sets of conditions. A form showing how this might be done for the object-control skill of catching is presented in figure 13.7 (see Ulrich, 1988). Also, the MOVE program (Bidabe & Lollar, 1990) includes a system of assessing prompts to indicate the context in which the skills in the TDMMT can be successfully performed. Note that a slight variation on an ecological approach to assessing movement skills can be found in Block's (1994) book.

Step 3: Movement Skill Foundations. If the exploration of movement skills and skill patterns in Step 2 reveals consistent inadequacies relative to the achievement of the task goal in Step 1, then the assessment sequence may continue down to Step 3. In this final step, the main objective is to identify the movement skill foundation areas or systems that limit the individual's performance of particular movement skills or, in Thelen's (1986) terms, to identify the rate limiters. In a bottom-up strategy for assessment, movement skill foundations are evaluated in the context of how they might affect any skill; in this top-down sequence, skill foundations are evaluated in the context of how they might affect specific skills. This strategy for evaluating movement skill foundations is based on the principle of specificity, as explained in chapters 3 and 8.

The procedures in Step 3 may be used for the same purposes as the procedures in Step 2: instructional or intervention planning, evaluation of

Object Control Skill — Catch

Equipment: 6 to 8 inch sponge ball, 15 feet of clear space, tape or other marking device.

Directions: Mark off 2 lines 15 feet apart. Student stands on one line and the tosser on the other. Toss the ball directly to student with a slight arc and tell him/her to "catch it with your hands." Only count those tosses between student's shoulders and waist.

Factors:
ball diameter
ball softness
distance thrown
speed of throw
postural support
support of performer

1. Preparation phase where elbows are flexed and hands are in front of body
2. Arms extended in preparation for ball contact
3. Ball is caught and controlled by hands only
4. Elbows bend to absorb force

TOTAL

■ FIGURE 13.7   Sample score sheet for collecting data on catching, using criteria from the Test of Gross Motor Development.

From *Test of Gross Motor Development* (p. 21) by D.A. Ulrich, 1985, Austin, TX: PRO-ED. Copyright 1985 by PRO-ED. Reprinted with permission.

progress, and research. Using occupational therapy terminology (see figure 3.1), Mathiowetz (1993) argues that evaluations of performance components (i.e., movement skill foundations) "have importance in clarifying the cause of occupational performance deficits and assisting in treatment planning" (p. 226) and "may be more sensitive to change than occupational performance evaluations" (p. 229).

Movement Skill Foundation Checklist

Skill 1			
Skill 2			
Skill 3			

1.	Balance: sudden, jerky movements	O	O	O
2.	Balance: arms in high or middle guard position	O	O	O
3.	Balance: minimal amount of body lean	O	O	O
4.	Balance: stumbles or falls	O	O	O
5.	Flexibility: restricted arm motion	O	O	O
6.	Flexibility: restricted leg motion	O	O	O
7.	Strength: poor arm strength relative to body weight	O	O	O
8.	Strength: poor leg strength relative to body weight	O	O	O
9.	Strength: poor trunk strength relative to body weight	O	O	O
10.	Coordination: when max force required, whole body not used	O	O	O
11.	Control: unable to adjust movement to changing environment	O	O	O
12.	Motivation: passive, lethargic, or tense (under)	O	O	O
13.	Motivation: impulsive, upset by failure or fidgety (over)	O	O	O
14.	Motivation: resistance or lack of effort (negative)	O	O	O
15.	Social: poor interaction with peers	O	O	O
16.	Cognitive: difficulty understanding instructions or strategies	O	O	O
17.	Other	O	O	O

■ **FIGURE 13.8** The Movement Skills Foundation Checklist (Burton, 1993).

To carry out the objective of Step 3, one needs to find or devise some type of checklist or other assessment instrument containing items that can be applied to many different movement skills. An example of such a checklist is offered in figure 13.8. In using the Movement Skill Foundations Checklist (Burton, 1993), the examiner first fills in up to three skills in the blanks at the top of the page. Then the observation clues for each foundation area

Movement Skill Foundation Checklist: Page 2

Skill 1	
Skill 2	
Skill 3	

Specify communication impairments:
1. _____ ○ ○ ○

2. _____ ○ ○ ○

Specify physical impairments:
1. _____ ○ ○ ○

2. _____ ○ ○ ○

Specify sensory impairments:
1. _____ ○ ○ ○

2. _____ ○ ○ ○

Specify other factors which may limit movement performance:
1. _____ ○ ○ ○

2. _____ ○ ○ ○

■ **FIGURE 13.8** *(continued)*

are considered for each skill separately. A foundation area may be adequate for one skill, but not another. For example, a person may show sudden, jerky arm movements when riding a unicycle, so that the circle next to #1 would be checked for that skill, but show smooth arm movements when ice skating. Or a physical impairment such as an arm amputation may pose a problem, and thus a disability, for a person attempting to shoot an arrow with a bow into a stationary target, but not pose a problem for the same person as he or she attempts to pitch and field a baseball (Burton & Davis, 1992b). The judgments for the items on the Checklist may be based on a few or on many trials, or on performances in various situations. The Checklist could be filled out as a direct follow-up to observations made during the assessment procedures in Step 2.

The information gained in a movement skill foundations checklist such as the one presented in figure 13.8 is interpreted and applied to plan an intervention or instructional program item by item and skill by skill. There is no summary score of any kind. The validity of Step 3 evaluations may be established by further testing—for instance, by actually measuring the range of motion of the right arm for the specific actions used in throwing—or by observing the effect of an intervention designed to improve the identified factor on performance of the specific skill.

The top-down assessment procedures that form this three-step sequence can be time consuming. However, in a top-down strategy for assessment and instruction, the boundaries between assessment and instruction become blurred. These procedures need to be considered not just as assessment activities, but also as vital instructional activities.

Chapter 14

New Directions in Movement Skill Assessment

© CLEO Photography

ACROSS the 20th century, the assessment of movement skills has shifted directions several times. In the early 1900s, psychologists examined the relationship between mental abilities and motor abilities, which were represented almost exclusively by fine motor, manual dexterity skills (Bolton, 1903). The 1920s marked the beginning of an emphasis on assessments of motor ability, capacity, or efficiency yielding a single

> 6 6 Testing is a field in the process of being re-created. For half a century, the field has focused on measuring individual differences on major, global proficiencies. The power of this approach has not only defined testing but also inhibited its expansion to the wide range of other important possibilities for which testing technology is useful and needed. 9 9
>
> — Cole (1995, p. 72)

composite score, an emphasis that only in the last 5 years has begun to wane. Some examples of this genre of tests include Sargent's (1921) "physical test of a man," Wayman's (1923) test of physical efficiency for women, Oseretsky's (1923, cited in Lassner, 1948) metric scale of motor capacity in children, Brace's (1927a) motor ability scale, and the many derivatives of da Costa's (1946-1947) translation of Oseretsky's tests, such as the Lincoln-Oseretsky Motor Development Scale (Sloan, 1955), the Modified Lincoln-Oseretsky Motor Development Scale (Bialer, Doll, & Winsberg, 1973, 1974), the Test of Motor Impairment (Stott, 1966; Stott, Moyes, & Henderson, 1972, 1984), the Bruininks-Oseretsky Test of Motor Proficiency (Bruininks, 1978), and the Movement Assessment Battery for Children Test (Henderson & Sugden, 1992).

The more direct measure of movement skills rather than motor abilities was carried out by Gesell (Gesell, 1940; Gesell & Amatruda, 1941) and Bayley (1935), whose norms for the emergence of early movement milestones laid the foundation for future tests, such as the Denver Developmental Screening Test (Frankenburg & Dodds, 1967, 1969), the Bayley Scales of Infant Development (Bayley, 1969), the Peabody Developmental Motor Scales (Folio & Fewell, 1983), the Denver II (Frankenburg, Dodds, & Archer, 1990), the Bayley-II (Bayley, 1993), and the Alberta Infant Motor Scale (Piper & Darrah, 1994). At the same time, Cozens and Neilson published four books detailing movement skill achievement tests for males and females from elementary school to college level (Cozens, 1936; Cozens, Cubberly, & Neilson, 1937; Cozens & Neilson, 1934; Cozens, Trieb, & Neilson, 1936).

From the 1930s to the 1960s, the assessment of fundamental movement skills was dominated by a product-oriented approach as exemplified by the work of Latchaw (1954) and Johnson (1962). In the 1970s, there was a shift to more process-oriented tests of fundamental movement skills, stimulated by Wickstrom's text on fundamental motor patterns and the research of Seefeldt and Haubenstricker (1982) and Roberton (1984). Some of these process-oriented tests are the Ohio State University Scale of Intra-Gross

Motor Assessment (Loovis & Ersing, 1979), the Test of Gross Motor Development (Ulrich, 1985), and the Motor Skills Inventory (Werder & Bruininks, 1988), which are still in common use.

Functional movement skills were the target of assessments of activities of daily living first published in the 1930s and 1940s (Sheldon, 1935; Watrous, 1940). In the 1950s and 1960s, many other tests of activities of daily living appeared and were widely used by occupational and physical therapists (Brown, 1950a, 1950b, 1951; Bruett & Overs, 1969). The assessment of functional movement skills has continued in occupational and physical therapy to the present, but recently has been emphasized more, while the assessment of pathology has been emphasized less (Commission on Practice, 1995). This focus on functional movement skills also has begun to occur in other professional areas, such as adapted physical education and special education (Davis & Burton, 1991), as indicated by the development of the Movement Assessment Battery for Children Checklist (Henderson & Sugden, 1992).

In the future, the prominence of functional movement skills in all professional areas related to movement skill assessment is expected to continue. In this final chapter, I will address several aspects of functional movement skill assessment that we can expect to be emphasized: (a) program outcomes, (b) movement product rather than process, (c) movement skills rather than motor abilities, (d) a dynamic systems approach, and (e) nonstandardized tests. In addition, I will consider the application of technology to movement skill assessment in the future.

■ PROGRAM OUTCOMES

In American society at present, consumers want to know exactly what they are getting for their dollars. The current emphasis on the assessment of program outcomes is driven to a large degree by the demand for accountability—by parents of children in public schools, by patients receiving medical services, and by insurance companies paying for medical services. Relman (1988) has referred to this change in the 1980s and 1990s as the third revolution in the modern age of medicine in the United States, which he calls the Era of Assessment and Accountability. This outcomes movement in medicine represents a shift from the second era focusing on cost containment to a balance between the assessment of gains achieved and an accountability for the cost incurred (Jette, 1995). Wilkerson, Batavia, and DeJong (1992) point out that functional status measures can be used in two general ways to develop a payment system for medical rehabilitation: first, as a means of classifying patients for purposes of determining the applicable payment amount (a "classification payment system") or, second, as a means of justifying that payment is appropriate (a "justification payment system").

There are three key steps in assessing program outcomes: (a) assessing initial competency relative to required performance, (b) specifying measurable program objectives congruent with identified needs, and (c) evaluating progress. It is interesting to note that the concept of criterion-referenced measurement was introduced initially by Glaser (1963) to facilitate the description of the intended outcomes of instruction (Hambleton, 1994).

In physical therapy, assessment traditionally has focused on anatomical or physiological measures (such as range of motion, muscular strength, or pulmonary function) rather than functional skills, such as amount of time or assistance needed to climb a set of stairs or rise from a chair (Jette, 1995). However, therapy reports for clients now must indicate the functional consequences of the medical condition or disease, specify treatment to address functional limitations, and detail the functional outcome of the treatment provided (Swanson, 1993).

Functional performance during and at the end of the intervention can be measured and compared against specified short- and long-term objectives, but improved performance may not necessarily result from the intervention. A step beyond the description of functional performance differences from pretest to posttest is the use of single-subject research designs by pediatric physical therapists to assess the effectiveness of interventions (Palisano, Campbell, & Harris, 1995). Three characteristics of this single-subject research design are (a) a minimum of three baseline data points collected on the outcome behavior before treatment is begun, (b) an intervention sequentially applied and withdrawn, and (c) performance measured at each phase of the study. The intermittent withdrawal of treatment sacrifices some potential progress but more clearly indicates the direct effect of the treatment, providing more complete information on which to base clinical judgments and accountability reports.

In physical education, program objectives for each grade level should be specified in the curriculum. Thus, at the beginning of each unit of instruction, each student's competency relative to the specified objectives should be assessed, the objectives targeted for instruction should be identified for each student, and progress during and at the end of the unit should be evaluated. This approach to program outcomes has been referred to as an achievement-based curriculum (Wessel & Kelly, 1986) or curriculum-based assessment (see chapter 13). One problem with many curricula for physical education is that sport and physical activity units may be identified, along with the appropriate skills, but without any specific, measurable objectives of instruction.

A new document was published in 1995 by the National Association for Sport and Physical Education (NASPE), titled *Moving into the Future—National Physical Education Standards: A Guide to Content and Assessment.* The authors state:

The transformation of assessment programs, especially the day-to-day teacher initiated assessment, is toward performance-based assessments that focus on high-priority objectives and significant outcomes for students. Such performance assessment usually refers to assessment tasks in which students demonstrate skills and competencies rather than

---

A physically educated person:
1. Demonstrates competency in many movement forms and proficiency in a few movement forms.
2. Applies movement concepts and principles to the learning and development of motor skills.
3. Exhibits a physically active lifestyle.
4. Achieves and maintains a health-enhancing level of physical fitness.
5. Demonstrates responsible personal and social behavior in physical activity settings.
6. Demonstrates understanding and respect for differences among people in physical activity settings.
7. Understands that physical activity provides opportunities for enjoyment, challenge, self-expression, and social interaction.

■ **FIGURE 14.1**   Content standards in physical education developed by NASPE (1995).
From *Moving into the Future — National Physical Education Standards: A Guide to Content and Assessment* (p. 1) by the National Association for Sport and Physical Education (NASPE), 1995, St. Louis, MO: Mosby. Copyright by NAPSE 1995. Reprinted by permission.

TABLE 14.1   Assessment Options for Physical Education Standards Suggested by NASPE (1995)

Person responsible	Task
Group	Project
	Role playing
Student	Event task
	Journal
	Log
	Portfolio
	Project
	Role playing
	Self-assessment
Parent	Report
Peer	Observation
Teacher	Interview
	Observation
	Written test

selecting one of several predetermined answers to an exercise. Furthermore, assessments that are "authentic" in nature, that is, designed to take place in a real-life setting rather than in an artificial or contrived setting, are being advocated. (p. vii)

This document begins with seven outcome statements defining a physically educated person (see figure 14.1); then, for each grade level from kindergarten to 12th grade, it describes emphases for the seven outcomes. In addition, some sample benchmarks are listed and many assessment options are defined and described, including those listed in table 14.1. The specific performance criteria for the content standards at each grade level are not yet available, however.

■ MOVEMENT PRODUCT RATHER THAN PROCESS

The Test of Gross Motor Development (TGMD) (Ulrich, 1985) is perhaps the most commonly used assessment of movement skill patterns or process, with no recording of data related to movement product. But now, 10 years after the TGMD first came out, even Ulrich (1995) admits that task achievement is more important than the specific pattern used to achieve the task. A renewed emphasis on movement product is an inherent part of the shift toward the assessment of functional movement skills. Movement function must ultimately be defined by product or outcome rather than process.

Unlike traditional task analyses that focus on the movement pattern or process, the recently developed ecological task analysis (ETA) (Balan & Davis, 1993; Burton & Davis, 1996; Davis & Burton, 1991) emphasizes accomplishing a functional task, specified in terms of a measurable outcome. Ecological task analysis offers information about the set of conditions in which an individual can complete a task, as well as information about an individual's flexibility or rigidity in using various movement patterns to accomplish a range of tasks. An example of a measurable outcome for a functional task might be riding a bicycle 0.1 mile (one city block) in less than 1 min. A person may not be able to successfully perform this task with a standard bicycle with the standard movement pattern; however, ETA procedures may reveal that he or she is able to achieve the task outcome with training wheels mounted on the bicycle, with foot straps on the pedals, or by using a walking pattern while straddling the seat rather than pedaling.

The ETA concept, that there may be many ways to approach the same task, is supported by Latash and Anson (1996), who argue that movement patterns often considered to be abnormal should be viewed as adaptive task solutions and, as such, should not be corrected. For example, standing with the nondominant side of the body facing the pitcher and with feet parallel when preparing to strike a pitched ball is regarded as a "mature" pattern by Ulrich (1985) in the TGMD. However, an open stance with the front of the body facing the pitcher is often used by younger children to help them see and react to the ball better. A recorded score of 0 for this adaptation on the TGMD suggests that this pattern should be corrected, but its use by Hall of Fame baseball players such as Rod Carew (with a lifetime batting average of .328) challenges the validity of this assumption. Indeed, Burton and Davis (1992b) state that "the distinction between normal and abnormal movement patterns, reflexes, and muscle tone, as emphasized in many approaches in adapted physical education, occupational therapy, and physical therapy, may have no functional significance, and attempts to achieve normalcy may divert attention away from the optimization of functional movement behavior" (p. 237).

However, Morris, Matyas, Iansek, and Cunnington (1996) point out that "unless the learning process of the impaired brain are damaged [sic], there is no reason why such learning processes would not also be accessible for optimization of motor action in people with movement disorders" (p. 83). Thus, improvement of skill through practice and feedback, the cardinal principle of motor learning, is likely to hold for just about all people. Movement patterns viewed as abnormal may not need to be corrected, but they also may not be optimal. Walter and Kamm (1996) argue that individuals with movement disorders may choose a movement solution that is appropriate for a particular situation, but then use it in a wide range of other situations, even when it may not be the best solution. Consistent with the tenets of ETA, Walter and Kamm (1996) suggest that these persons may need some structured guidance to explore the "behavioral landscape," nudging the system from locally preferred behavior as a strategy to facilitate optimal learning.

■ MOVEMENT SKILLS RATHER THAN MOTOR ABILITIES

In the future, we can expect the assessment of movement skills to receive more emphasis than the assessment of motor abilities. Motor abilities are considered under the heading of movement skill assessment because this category of tests has dominated our professional fields for many years. However, evidence that motor abilities exist is limited, and even if they did exist, the composite measures of motor abilities are essentially uninterpretable. I outlined these and other disadvantages of motor ability tests in chapter 8. The new emphasis on assessing movement skills directly has been driven partially by a growing understanding of the limitations of motor ability tests, but also by the realization that functional outcomes are

TABLE 14.2　Items Included in the Five Modules of the Motor Skills Inventory (Werder & Bruininks, 1988) and the Relationship of the Items to Categories in the Movement Skill Taxonomy

Module	Taxonomy categories		
	MF[a]	EMM[b]	FMS[c]
Body management			
Body-space awareness	X		
Moving balance			X
Stationary balance			X
Body roll		X	
Agility			X
Locomotor			
Walk			X
Horizontal jump			X
Vertical jump			X
Run			X
Hop			X
Gallop			X
Skip			X
Body fitness			
Arm-shoulder flexibility	X		
Midbody flexibility	X		
Aerobic development	X		
Abdominal strength	X		
Leg-hip flexibility	X		
Arm-shoulder strength	X		
Object movement			
Kick			X
Bounce/dribble			X
Catch			X
Overhand throw			X
Strike			X
Underhand throw			X
Underhand roll			X
Fine motor			
Small-object control		X	
Grasp		X	
Hand strength	X		
Copying a cross			X
Copying a star			X

[a] Foundations of movement skills

[b] Early movement milestones

[c] Fundamental movement skills

produced by a person performing a specific movement skill. Even if motor abilities did exist, they would be more distant from the task outcome than the performance of specific movement skills.

The shift in emphasis from motor abilities to movement skills is illustrated by the publication of Werder and Bruininks' (1988) Motor Skill Inventory (MSI), following Bruininks' (1978) immensely popular Bruininks-Oseretsky Test of Motor Proficiency (BOT). The MSI, part of the Body Skills motor development curriculum, assesses 30 items, including 8 foundations of movement skills, 3 motor abilities, 3 early movement milestones, and 16 fundamental movement skills (see table 14.2). A special feature of the MSI is that a person's results on the motor ability-oriented BOT may be used to predict scores on the specific items on the MSI. Clearly, Werder and Bruininks saw the limitations of the BOT and the need for a test of movement skills with items designed to be interpreted individually, but the procedure used to validate the estimation of MSI scores from the BOT resorts back to using composite scores on the MSI as if it were an ability-oriented test.

■ DYNAMIC SYSTEMS APPROACH

One can hardly address the issue of assessing movement skills without invoking the work of Thelen and her colleagues and the dynamic systems approach to studying motor development (e.g., Smith & Thelen, 1993; Thelen, 1986, 1995; Thelen, Corbetta, Kamm, Schneider, & Zernicke, 1993; Thelen & Smith, 1994; Thelen & Ulrich, 1991). The dynamic systems approach, pioneered by Thelen, marks a shift from the focus on neuromuscular explanations of developmental changes, popularized by Gesell and McGraw (see Bergenn, Dalton, & Lipsitt, 1992; Gesell & Thompson, 1934; McGraw, 1945; Thelen & Adolph, 1992), to a consideration of all systems, even those beyond the person, as potential sources of variation in movement behavior. Thelen (1995) argues that "for infants as well as for adults, movements are always a product of not only the central nervous system but also of the biomechanical and energetic properties of the body, the environmental support, and the specific (and sometimes changing) demands of the particular task" (p. 81).

The term *dynamics* in physics refers to stability and change; thus, the *dynamic systems approach* to studying motor development focuses on periods of developmental stability and the shifts or transitions to qualitatively different behaviors. The most important aspect of the dynamic systems approach is the identification of the system variables—related to the performer, the environment, or the task—that drive transitions from one behavior to another. In their study of the development of alternating steps on a treadmill, Thelen and Ulrich (1991) identified six relevant variables whose interactions are depicted for two infants in figure 7.1. Thelen (1995) suggests that growth or biomechanical factors may be most important in early infancy while experience, practice, or environmental factors may become more important at older ages.

Transitions from one preferred behavior to another—such as from creeping to walking or from using a palmar grip when drawing to using a tripod grip—may be abrupt, but usually are first marked by instabilities in the original behavior. Changing system variables—like increasing strength, decreasing adiposity, or softer locomotor surface—may disrupt the current stable pattern and require the system to explore new behavior options (Thelen, 1995). The similarity of children's movement behavior solutions at certain ages, traditionally viewed as developmental stages genetically determined in the central nervous system, is explained from the dynamic systems perspective as resulting from the anatomical, biomechanical, and environmental constraints common to all humans.

Ecological task analysis (Balan & Davis, 1993; Burton & Davis, 1996; Davis & Burton, 1991), as briefly explained in chapter 13, is based on the principles of the dynamic systems approach to motor development. As task, environmental, or performer dimensions are manipulated singly or in combination, the following assessment information is recorded: (a) the specific task; (b) the specific skills and skill patterns used to carry out the task; (c) the absolute dimension value at which a skill or pattern transition occurs; (d) when appropriate, a performer-scaled ratio for the transition point; and (e) the functional outcome relative to the performance criterion. A sample form for recording these data is presented in figure 13.7.

■ NONSTANDARDIZED TESTS

Nonstandardized tests have been traditionally treated as the backward cousins in a family dominated by standardized, norm-referenced tests. However, practitioners and researchers alike have begun to recognize that these shunned cousins have some virtues beyond their more esteemed relatives. I discussed the advantages and disadvantages of standardized/formal and nonstandardized/informal tests in detail in chapter 5, but perhaps the most salient advantage of nonstandardized assessment is the flexibility allowed for determining the actual skills of the persons being tested. If necessary, additional trials may be given, the environment and task may be manipulated, and feedback or instruction may be offered. Some practitioners argue that they do not have enough time to carry out this type of process, but others now understand that when assessment is integrated with instruction or therapy, time may no longer pose a problem.

In a paper addressing the continuing challenge of functional assessment in rehabilitation, Christianson (1993) asserts:

Traditional standardized approaches can yield misleading information or fail to provide any information about the client's interpretation of events and the meaning of his or her performance deficits. Ethnography, interviews, and document review have been suggested as means by which the therapist can come to know the world of the patient in a richer, more insightful manner. (p. 258)

Perhaps the most powerful untapped source of information regarding an individual's movement skills is parents and caregivers, who have observed the person over an extended period of time and in a great variety of contexts. The Assessment, Evaluation, and Programming System for Infants and Children Birth to Three Years (AEPS) (Bricker, 1993), the Movement Assessment Battery for Children (MABC) Checklist (Henderson & Sugden, 1992), and the Pediatric Evaluation of Disability Inventory (PEDI) (Haley, Coster, Ludlow, Haltiwanger, & Andrellos, 1992) are examples of assessment instruments that take advantage of these rich sources of information (the AEPS is reviewed in chapter 9, and the MABC Checklist and PEDI in chapter 11). The AEPS has three data sheets specifically designed for responses from the family: the Family Report with 64 items, the Family Interest Survey with 30 items, and the Child Progress Report.

■ APPLICATIONS OF TECHNOLOGY

The proliferation of computers in all aspects of our society and the expanding applications of computers for data management, information exchange, and data collection and treatment are sure to significantly affect the assessment of movement skills. First, computers can be used to create databases to keep track of information on students, clients, or patients. Individual teachers or therapists can create and update their own databases, but access to databases may be shared within a school, a school district, a hospital, a health service system, or even nationwide. Palisano, Campbell, and Harris (1995) report that

Developments in the area of monitoring services and tracking outcomes include computerized approaches to creating a database on clients served that may also provide systematic, structured individual patient reports to guarantee uniform reporting of significant information across both therapists and types of patients. . . . Yearly statistics can be rapidly collated, care trends can be monitored across time, and data can be used for prospective or retrospective research. . . . When a database is developed along the lines of the conceptual framework of the disabling process, studies can be undertaken of how impairments or their alleviation affect functional limitations and whether disability in the client's natural environment is reduced by the therapy provided. (p. 199)

For example, the Functional Independence Measure (Keith, Granger, Hamilton, & Sherwin, 1987), created by a joint task force of the American Academy of Physical Medicine and Rehabilitation and the American Congress of Rehabilitation Medicine, was used to start a national patient data system (Uniform Data System for Medical Rehabilitation/Data Management Service). Now clinicians can use both the Functional Independence Measure (Uniform Data System, 1987) and the Functional Independence Measure for Children (Uniform Data System, 1991) to compare progress of their clients with that of clients in other programs.

Computers, particularly laptop models, can also be used in the collection and treatment of data. For example, data collection forms can be displayed on the screen and movement performance information recorded directly into the computer. If any data are missing or are entered incorrectly (e.g., a value is out of the possible range), the computer can signal an error immediately. When data collection is complete, computer programs can perform normative score transformations automatically, saving time and minimizing errors that can occur when one reads multiple tables and transfers numbers from one sheet to another. If the same test has been previously administered to the same person, difference scores can also be calculated in terms of raw and transformed scores. Finally, forms detailing the recommended instruction or therapy, complete with short- and long-term objectives, can be generated directly from the assessment results. Extensive menus can offer sets of objectives, with spaces for specifying level of assistance, environmental context, and expected dates of completion.

The potential of item response theory (IRT) for solving some of the current testing problems in adapted physical education has been hailed by Cole, Wood, and Dunn (1991) (see chapter 5 for a brief explanation of IRT and chapter 10 for an IRT analysis of the TGMD). One application of IRT that would require the examiner to use a computer while administering a test is *adaptive testing*. This procedure first requires an extensive pool of items with a wide range of known difficulties. The testing begins with an item of moderate difficulty relative to the individual's age and other attributes. The computer chooses the next item depending on the performance on the first item. If the first item is passed, a more difficult item will follow; if the first item is not passed, an easier item will follow. The computer continues to adjust and select items most closely matching the examinee's actual skill level until a sufficient number have been given to provide a stable estimate of skill. Adaptive testing may be most useful in reducing the amount of time needed for screening or for determining eligibility for special services (Cole et al., 1991).

However, new applications of IRT to movement skill assessment must be viewed with caution. As mentioned in chapter 5, if a person's performance on a variety of tasks is converted to a single IRT-scaled score, the score must be interpreted as representing motor ability, which poses some theoretical problems for the user. But if the scaled score is used to indicate the relative difficulty of individual items, then it is consistent with a movement skill interpretation.

Clinicians have begun to use laboratory technologies such as videography, infrared movement analysis systems, and kinetic analysis systems more often (Harris & Heriza, 1987; Heriza, 1991), but the expense of the equipment still is prohibitive. Videography involves the digitization of videotaped images of moving joints and limbs and the subsequent calculation of distance, time, velocity, and acceleration of the various body components in two or three dimensions of movement. Graphic displays of the movement can also be produced, including changes in joint angles or limb positions across time (angle-time or displacement-time), changes in one joint angle relative to one or two other joint angles (angle-angle or angle-angle-angle), or changes in the velocity of a joint angle or limb position at various joint angles or limb positions in a movement cycle (phase plane). Infrared movement analysis systems, such as the Selspot or WATSMART systems, are designed to measure and display the same kinematic variables as videography, but the use of infrared markers allows the system to digitize joint and limb positions automatically. In kinetic analysis systems, pads or platforms are equipped with force transducers to measure changes in the amount of force exerted across time. Force platforms often are used to analyze the pattern of force generation between the two feet during quiet stance or when stance is perturbed, or to analyze the distribution of forces generated by the feet during gait. This technology is useful for examining the details of the movement process, but the current emphasis on functional movement outcomes rather than movement process may keep this equipment confined to research laboratories.

■ SUMMARY

This book began with a chapter on the purposes of movement skill assessment and will end with a final admonition that the purpose should direct the entire assessment process. Just about any purpose for assessing movement skills involves a search for better understanding of movement behavior in real-life, functional situations; thus, in most cases, assessment at the functional level of the movement skill taxonomy is optimal.

However, as the summary of movement skill assessment reviews in appendix A1 indicates, few instruments assess skills in functional contexts. This situation leaves practitioners with several choices. First and optimally, they might use one of the few tests of functional movement skills, if the test is appropriate for the desired purpose. Or, if an appropriate functional test cannot be found, practitioners might use a test of early movement milestones, fundamental movement skills, or specialized movement skills, appropriate to the desired purpose.

Another very basic option that has not been discussed much in the literature is for practitioners to rely on their own observations of the movement behavior of an individual or a group of individuals in functional settings without translating their behavior into a numerical system. This would be a judgment-based approach (see chapter 11) in which the observer would directly make a judgment related to a specific purpose based on a few or many observations, but without the assignment of numbers to movement attributes or characteristics. For example, if the purpose is to determine a student's eligibility to receive adapted physical education service, the student's physical education teacher may be able make this *yes/no* judgment based on observations of the student's performance in class over a relatively long period of time. Even though this option does not involve true assessment or measurement, it may be more valid than the application of any assessment strategy.

Ironically, the observations of movement professionals have been used in the criterion-related validation of test instruments (e.g., Hughes & Riley, 1981) but have not been carefully considered as a viable approach in themselves. The strengths and weaknesses of professionals using their observations to make program judgments need to be considered more carefully, and the time is ripe for research and dialogue on this topic.

Finally, I did not include the use of motor ability instruments as an option in this final discussion because of the difficulty in interpreting the results of this category of tests. When performance on a variety of tasks is summarized with a composite score, and the score is intended to represent tasks beyond those actually performed, what does the score really mean? Some motor ability tests can be interpreted as tests of movement skills (see the multiple skill levels in appendix A1), but the use of ability-oriented composites should be avoided.

Purpose should always drive the movement skill assessment process, not the latest or most popular instrument. The primacy of purpose should draw one back to look at previous approaches (see the historical overview in chapter 2), to consider approaches that may seem too simple to be acceptable to others (e.g, the nonassessment approach just described), and to carefully examine current practice.

Appendix A₁

Summary of Movement Skill Assessment Reviews

Movement category code: MF = movement skill foundations; MA = motor abilities; EM = early movement milestones; Fnd = fundamental movement skills; SM = specialized movement skills; Fct = functional movement skills.

Instrument title	MF	MA	EM	Fnd	SM	Fct	Page
Alberta Infant Motor Scale		X	X				335
Assessment, Evaluation, and Programming System for Infants and Children Birth to Three Years		X	X			X	335
Assessment of Motor and Process Skills		X			X	X	336
Basic Gross Motor Assessment		X		X	X		336
Basic Motor Ability Tests-Revised		X		X	X		337
Battelle Developmental Inventory		X	X	X			337
Bayley Scales of Infant Development—Second Edition		X	X	X			337
Brace Scale of Motor Ability Tests		X					338
Brigance Diagnostic Inventory of Early Development	X		X	X	X	X	338
Bruininks-Oseretsky Test of Motor Proficiency		X		X	X		338
Cratty Six-Category Gross Motor Test		X					339
DeGangi-Berk Test of Sensory Integration	X						339
Denver II			X	X			340
Evaluating Movement and Posture Disorganization in Dyspraxic Children				X			340
Evaluation of Motor Development of Infants		X	X				340
Gross Motor Function Measure			X	X			341
Gross Motor Performance Measure			X	X			341
Gutteridge Rating Scale of Motor Skill				X	X		342

(continued)

Instrument title	MF	MA	EM	Fnd	SM	Fct	Page
Harris Infant Neuromotor Test (developmental edition)	X		X				342
I CAN Instructional Management System			X	X	X		342
Los Angeles Unified School District Adapted Physical Education Assessment Scale	X			X			343
Milani-Comparetti Motor Development Screening Test	X						343
Miller Assessment for Preschoolers	X	X	X	X			343
Motor Control Assessment		X	X	X			344
Motor Development Checklist			X				344
Motor Skills Inventory	X			X			345
Movement Assessment Battery for Children Checklist		X	X	X		X	345
Movement Assessment Battery for Children Test		X		X	X		346
Movement Assessment of Infants	X		X				346
Ohio State University Scale of Intra-Gross Motor Assessment				X			346
Peabody Developmental Motor Scales		X	X	X			347
Pediatric Evaluation of Disability Inventory		X		X	X	X	347
Posture and Fine Motor Assessment of Infants	X		X				348
Project ACTIVE Motor Ability Tests	X	X		X			348
Project MOBILITEE	X			X			349
Purdue Perceptual-Motor Survey		X		X	X		349
Quick Neurological Screening Test	X	X		X			349
Sensorimotor Performance Analysis	X	X	X				350
Sensory Integration and Praxis Tests	X						350
Test of Gross Motor Development		X		X			351
Tests of Motor Proficiency		X		X			351
Top-Down Motor Milestone Test			X	X		X	351
Transdisciplinary Play-Based Assessment			X	X			352
Tufts Assessment of Motor Performance		X	X			X	352
Vulpe Assessment Battery	X		X	X			353

Appendix A2

Movement Skill Assessment Reviews

Alberta Infant Motor Scale (AIMS)
Book/journal citation: Piper and Darrah (1994)
Publisher: W.B. Saunders, 6277 Sea Harbor Drive, Orlando, FL 32821 (800-545-2522)
Movement category: Motor abilities, early movement milestones
Description: A criterion-referenced test with a total of 58 items performed in four positions: prone (21 items), supine (9), sitting (12), and standing (16). Points for the four position subscales are summed to give a total score, which may be converted to a percentile.
Stated uses: (a) Identify infants who are delayed or deviant in their motor development and (b) evaluate motor development or maturation over time
Ages: Birth to 18 months
Validity: Content, criterion-related
Reliability: Interrater, test-retest
Standardization: 2,202 infants representative of all infants in Alberta, Canada
Equipment: Age-appropriate toys, bench or chair, examining table, mat
Time required: 20 to 30 min
Assessment, Evaluation, and Programming System for Infants and Children from Birth to Three Years (AEPS)
Book/journal citation: Bricker (1993) (also see Bricker & Pretti-Frontczak, 1996, for AEPS measurement for 3 to 6 years)
Publisher: Paul H. Brookes Publishing, PO Box 10624, Baltimore, MD 21285-0624 (800-701-7868)
Movement category: Early movement milestones, fundamental movement skills, functional movement skills
Description: A criterion-referenced instrument with 164 objectives hierarchically organized into six curricular domains (fine motor, gross motor, adaptive, cognitive, social-communication, social), 23 strands or common behavior categories, and 64 goals. A total raw score and a total percentage score can be calculated for each domain, as well as for the total battery.
Stated uses: (a) Develop intervention programs, (b) evaluate progress, and (c) evaluate programs

Ages: 1 month to 3 years (for 3-6 years, see Bricker & Pretti-Frontczak, 1996)
Validity: Construct, content, criterion-related
Reliability: Interrater, test-retest
Standardization: None
Equipment: Behaviors may be observed in many different environments and with many different sorts of objects and equipment
Time required: Initial assessments of an individual child, 1 to 2 hr; subsequent assessments, 15 to 30 min

Assessment of Motor and Process Skills (AMPS)
Book/journal citation: Fisher (1995)
Publisher: Three Star Press, 4836 Westridge Drive, Fort Collins, Co 80526 (970-226-3178)
Movement category: Motor abilities, specialized movement skills, functional movement skills
Description: Two criterion-referenced assessments designed to evaluate the motor skills and process skills used to perform 2 to 3 domestic or instrumental activities of daily living (IADL) out of a possible set of 56. The motor skills instrument evaluates 16 items related to motor competence, and the process skills instrument evaluates 20 items related to organizing task operations (see table 11.2). Using a Rasch analysis based on item response theory, raw scores from any combination of tasks can be converted to interval-scale ability (logit) scores that take into account the challenge of the tasks performed and the severity of the specific rater's observations.
Stated uses: (a) Determine whether a person has IADL motor or process skill deficits and (b) identify areas of performance deficit that should be targeted for intervention
Ages: Not specified
Validity: Criterion-related, construct
Reliability: Internal consistency, interrater, intrarater, test-retest
Standardization: 4,689 adults from Australia, New Zealand, North America, Scandinavia, and the United Kingdom, used to estimate calibration values contained in the computer scoring program
Equipment: Equipment and environment to perform domestic or instrumental activities of daily living
Time required: 30 to 60 min

Basic Gross Motor Assessment (BGMA)
Book/journal citation: Hughes and Riley (1981)
Publisher: Authors
Movement category: Motor abilities, fundamental movement skills, specialized movement skills
Description: A criterion-referenced test composed of nine gross-motor tasks including balancing, jumping, hopping, skipping, throwing, yo-yoing, and ball handling. Mean and standard deviations by sex and age are given for total raw scores, which allow percentiles or other normative scores to be calculated.
Stated uses: Discriminate between children whose motor aberrations are probably due to experiential lags and those whose performance indicates a need for medical referral, physical therapy evaluation, and possible treatment
Ages: 5.5 to 12.5 years
Validity: Content, criterion-related, construct
Reliability: Internal consistency, interrater, test-retest
Standardization: 1,260 children in Denver, Colorado
Equipment: Balls, beanbags, stopwatch, target, yo-yo
Time required: Not reported

Basic Motor Ability Tests-Revised (BMAT-R)
Book/journal citation: Arnheim and Sinclair (1979)
Publisher: Out of print (complete test in book)
Movement category: Motor abilities, fundamental movement skills, specialized movement skills
Description: A battery of 11 tests, including bead stringing, throwing, marble transfer, flexibility, standing broad jump, rising to stand, and static balance. Raw scores for individual items can be converted to deciles by sex and age (4-12 years).
Stated uses: Evaluate selected motor responses in the areas of eye-hand coordination, finger dexterity, hand speed, flexibility, leg power, agility, static balance, arm strength, and eye-foot coordination
Ages: 4 to 12 years
Validity: Not reported
Reliability: Test-retest
Standardization: 1,563 children of various ethnic, cultural, social, and economic groups
Equipment: Balance board, balls, beads, cones, gym mat, marbles, stopwatch
Time required: 15 to 20 min

Battelle Developmental Inventory (BDI)
Book/journal citation: Newborg, Stock, Wnek, Guidubaldi, and Svinicki (1984)
Publisher: DLM, 1 DLM Park, Allen, TX 75002 (1-800-527-4747)
Movement category: Motor abilities, early movement milestones, fundamental movement skills
Description: A criterion- and norm-referenced test containing 341 items across five developmental domains: personal-social (85 items), adaptive (59), motor (82), communication (59), and cognitive (56). These five domains are divided further into 22 subdomains. The motor subdomains are muscle control, body coordination, locomotion, fine muscle, and perceptual-motor. Standard scores, percentiles, and age equivalents can be calculated from raw scores in each domain and subdomain, as well as for the total raw score across all domains. A shortened version of the BDI, the Screening Test, consists of 96 items, including 20 from the motor domain.
Stated uses: (a) Identify developmental strengths and weaknesses of children with and without disabilities in infant, preschool, and primary programs; (b) via the screening component, screen preschool and kindergarten children at risk for developmental delays
Ages: Birth to 8 years
Validity: Content, criterion-related, construct
Reliability: Internal consistency, interrater, test-retest
Standardization: 800 children without disabilities, stratified by age, sex, and geographic location to represent the U.S. population
Equipment: No special equipment
Time required: 1 to 2 hr for the entire test; 10 to 30 min for the Screening Test

Bayley Scales of Infant Development—Second Edition (Bayley-II)
Book/journal citation: Bayley (1993)
Publisher: Therapy Skill Builders (division of The Psychological Corporation), 555 Academic Court, San Antonio, TX 78204-2498 (800-211-8378)
Movement category: Motor abilities, early movement milestones, fundamental movement skills
Description: A criterion- and norm-referenced test composed of three scales: the Mental Scale (178 items), the Motor Scale (111), and the Behavior Rating Scale (30). The Motor Scale, focusing on body control and fine and gross motor skills, yields a standardized Psychomotor Development Index and an estimated developmental age.

Stated uses: (a) Identify children with developmental delays, (b) design intervention programs, and (c) monitor the effectiveness of intervention programs.

Ages: 1 to 42 months

Validity: Content, criterion-related, construct

Reliability: Internal consistency, interrater, test-retest

Standardization: 1,700 children stratified by age, gender, race, geographic location, and parent education to represent the U.S. population

Equipment: Paper, plastic bags, stairs, stopwatch, test kit, tissues

Time required: 25 to 35 min for children under 15 months; up to 60 min for children 15 months and older

Brace Scale of Motor Ability Tests (BSMAT)

Book/journal citation: Brace (1927a)

Publisher: Out of print (complete test in book)

Movement category: Motor abilities

Description: A criterion-referenced test of 20 physical stunts (see table 2.1) yielding a total raw score that is converted to a *T* scale (each unit is equivalent to one-tenth of the standard deviation). Also, data are provided that allows percentiles to be calculated.

Stated uses: (a) Determine an accomplishment quotient for physical education activities, (b) classify students for physical education participation, (c) diagnose special performance disabilities, and (d) stimulate other scientific efforts in the field of tests and measurement

Ages: 8 to 48 years

Validity: Criterion-related, construct

Reliability: Interrater, parallel forms, test-retest

Standardization: 1,298 persons in New Jersey and New York

Equipment: None

Time required: About 30 min, testing with group of 20 to 30 persons

Brigance Diagnostic Inventory of Early Development (BDI)

Book/journal citation: Brigance (1991)

Publisher: Curriculum Associates, PO Box 2001, North Billerica, MA 01862-0901 (800-225-0248)

Movement category: Movement skill foundations, early movement milestones, fundamental movement skills, specialized movement skills, functional movement skills

Description: A criterion-referenced test of 122 specific skills in 11 areas, including preambulatory motor skills and behaviors, gross motor skills and behaviors, and fine motor skills and behaviors. Items subsumed under each skill are scored on a pass/fail basis and yield a development age for each skill.

Stated uses: (a) Monitor development in specific skill areas, (b) identify and diagnose lags in specific skill areas, and (c) assist in prescribing intervention strategies

Ages: Birth to 7 years

Validity: Content

Reliability: Not reported

Standardization: None (developmental levels of items are based on data from the literature)

Equipment: Balance board, balls, bicycle (with and without training wheels), clay, drawing implements, roller skates, scissors, stairs, tricycle, wagon (for three movement-related areas)

Time required: 1 hr

Bruininks-Oseretsky Test of Motor Proficiency (BOT)

Book/journal citation: Bruininks (1978)

Publisher: American Guidance Service, 4201 Woodland Road, PO Box 99, Circle Pines, MN 55014-1796 (800-328-2560)

Movement category: Motor abilities, fundamental movement skills, specialized movement skills

Description: A norm-referenced, product-oriented test offering two forms: a long form (LF) and a short form. The LF comprises 46 items organized into eight subtests (running speed and agility, balance, bilateral coordination, strength, upper-limb coordination, response speed, visual-motor control, upper-limb speed and dexterity) and yields standardized scores and age equivalents for each subtest, as well as gross motor, fine motor, and overall composite standardized scores, percentiles, stanines, and age equivalents. The SF comprises 14 items (at least 1 from each subtest in the LF) and yields an overall standardized score, percentile, and stanine. See figures 5.1, 8.1, 8.2, and table 8.1.

Stated uses: (a) Make decisions about educational placement, (b) assess gross and fine motor skills, (c) develop and evaluate motor training programs, (d) screen for special purposes, and (e) assist clinicians and researchers

Ages: 4.5 to 14.5 years

Validity: Content, construct

Reliability: Interrater, test-retest

Standardization: 765 children, using a stratified sampling procedure based on the 1970 U.S. Census

Equipment: Chair, stopwatch, table, test kit

Time required: 45 to 60 min for the LF; 15 to 20 min for the SF

Cratty Six-Category Gross Motor Test

Book/journal citations: Cratty (1969, 1974)

Publisher: Cratty (1969)—out of print; Cratty (1974)—Books on Demand, 300 North Zeeb Road, Ann Arbor, MI 48106-1346 (800-521-0600)

Movement category: Motor abilities

Description: Two separate six-item tests (body perception, gross agility, balance, locomotor agility, ball throwing, ball tracking), the first for children with obvious movement problems and the second for children with mild perceptual-motor impairment. Scores (0-5) are totaled across the two tests. Cratty (1969) reports deciles for total scores by age for the three standardization groups, and Cratty (1974) reports means and standard deviations for each item and total scores by age for the three standardization groups.

Stated uses: Identify children with mild to moderate perceptual-motor problems that may limit their ability to participate in playground games (Cratty, 1969)

Ages: 4 to 24 years (see standardization ages)

Validity: Construct (Cratty, 1974)

Reliability: Test-retest (Cratty, 1969)

Standardization: 355 normal children (4-11 years), 38 persons with mild mental impairment (5-20 years), 113 persons with moderate mental impairment (5-24 years) (Cratty, 1974)

Equipment: Balls, specially marked mat, stopwatch

Time required: About 30 min

DeGangi-Berk Test of Sensory Integration

Book/journal citations: DeGangi and Berk (1983a, 1983b)

Publisher: Western Psychological Services, 12031 Wilshire Boulevard, Los Angeles, CA 90025 (800-648-8857)

Movement category: Movement skill foundations

Description: A criterion-referenced test consisting of 36 items organized into three subdomains: postural control (12 items), bilateral integration (16), and reflex integration (8). Scores representing performance from "abnormal" to "normal" can be summed by subdomain or for all items.

Stated uses: (a) Identify sensory integrative dysfunction in preschoolers and (b) facilitate development of intervention programs

Ages: 3 to 5 years

Validity: Construct

Reliability: Interrater, test-retest

Standardization: 101 children without delays and 38 children with developmental delays in the District of Columbia and Indiana

Equipment: Chairs, dowel, paper and pencil, rolling pin, scooter board, stopwatch, table, tape, test kit

Time required: 30 min

Denver II

Book/journal citation: Frankenburg, Dodds, and Archer (1990)

Publisher: Denver Developmental Materials, PO Box 6919, Denver, CO 80206-0919 (303-355-4729)

Movement category: Early movement milestones, fundamental movement skills

Description: A norm-referenced instrument consisting of 125 tasks arranged into four areas of function: personal-social (25 tasks), fine motor-adaptive (29), language (39), and gross motor (32). Performance on individual items can be identified as "advanced," "normal," "caution," or "delayed," and overall results can be interpreted as "normal," "suspect," or "untestable."

Stated uses: (a) Screen asymptomatic children for possible problems; (b) confirm intuitive suspicions; and (c) monitor children at risk for developmental problems, such as those who have experienced perinatal difficulties

Ages: Birth to 6 years

Validity: Content

Reliability: Interrater, test-retest

Standardization: 2,096 children in urban, semi-rural, and rural Colorado

Equipment: Chairs, paper, table, test kit

Time required: 15 to 30 min

Evaluating Movement and Posture Disorganization in Dyspraxic Children

Book/journal citation: Magrun (1989)

Publisher: Therapy Skill Builders (division of The Psychological Corporation), 555 Academic Court, San Antonio, TX 78204-2498 (800-211-8378)

Movement category: Fundamental movement skills

Description: A criterion-referenced test examining 10 skills: supine to stand, supine to flexion hold, prone reach, alternating prone reach, kneel walk forward and back, alternating one-foot kneel, alternating half kneel-stand, one-foot balance, squat pickup, and unilateral/bilateral toss. Each skill is evaluated on two checklists: quality of performance (reflecting standards of adequate performance) and problem performance (detailing subcomponents of movement difficulty). A total quality score and a total problem score can be calculated, as well as a "percent of disorganization" for each skill and for the entire test.

Stated uses: Determine and analyze the normal and disorganized components of movement and posture

Ages: Individuals with learning disabilities 5 years and up (no clear reason is given why this test is limited to children with learning disabilities)

Validity: Not reported

Reliability: Not reported

Standardization: None

Equipment: Gym mat, object to toss

Time required: Not reported

Evaluation of Motor Development of Infants (EMDI)

Book/journal citation: Wolanski and Zdanska-Brincken (1973) (see also Wurth, 1980; Zdanska-Brincken & Wolanski, 1969)

Publisher: Authors (complete test in article)

Movement category: Motor abilities, early movement milestones

Description: A criterion- and norm-referenced test composed of 34 skills from four spheres of movement: head and trunk (6 skills), sitting (9), standing (9), and locomotion (10). Each item has a developmental score given in half-week units. The scores of the highest attained items for each sphere are totaled; this sum then is placed on a percentile grid to determine the development track of the child: 5-15th, 15-35th, 35-65th, 65-85th, or 85-95th percentile. Percentile grids for individual items and spheres are given by Zdanska-Brincken and Wolanski (1969).

Stated uses: Determine the state of a child's motor development relative to that of a normative sample

Ages: 1 month to onset of walking

Validity: Construct

Reliability: Not reported

Standardization: 212 infants in Warsaw, Poland, tested monthly from 1 month to onset of walking

Equipment: No special equipment

Time required: Not reported

Gross Motor Function Measure (GMFM)

Book/journal citations: Russell et al. (1989); Russell, Rosenbaum, Lane, Gowland, Goldsmith, Boyce, & Plews (1994)

Publisher: Department of Pediatrics, Chedoke-McMaster Hospitals, McMaster University, PO Box 2000, Station A, Hamilton, ON, Canada L8N 3Z5

Movement category: Early movement milestones, fundamental movement skills

Description: A criterion-referenced test comprising 88 items divided into five dimensions: lying and rolling (17 items), crawling and kneeling (14), sitting (20), standing (13), and walking, running, and jumping (24). The items are scored on a 4-point scale from 0 (cannot initiate task) to 3 (completes task independently). A raw score and a percentage score can be obtained for each of the five areas as well as the total battery.

Stated uses: (a) Measure the presence or absence of change in the gross motor function of children with cerebral palsy in clinical practice and for research, (b) describe a child's current level of function, (c) determine treatment goals, and (d) evaluate the effectiveness of therapies aimed at improving motor function

Ages: Persons with cerebral palsy under 20 years

Validity: Content, criterion-referenced, construct

Reliability: Interrater, intrarater

Standardization: None

Equipment: Balls, bench, mat, stairs, stick, stopwatch, toys

Time required: Less than 1 hr

Gross Motor Performance Measure (GMPM)

Book/journal citations: Boyce et al. (1991, 1995)

Publisher: Department of Pediatrics, Chedoke-McMaster Hospitals, McMaster University, PO Box 2000, Station A, Hamilton, ON, Canada L8N 3Z5

Movement category: Early movement milestones, fundamental movement skills

Description: A criterion-referenced instrument consisting of 20 items derived from the Gross Motor Function Measure, each matched with five attributes of performance: alignment, stability, coordination, weight shift, or dissociation. Attributes are scored from 1 (severely abnormal) to 5 (consistently normal). Subscale attribute raw scores and the total raw score are expressed as percentages of the maximum possible score relative to the items performed.

Stated uses: (a) Measure the quality of movement in children with cerebral palsy and (b) evaluate changes in movement quality over time

Ages: Persons with cerebral palsy under 20 years

Validity: Criterion-related, construct
Reliability: Interrater, intrarater, test-retest
Standardization: None
Equipment: Balls, bench, mat, stairs, stick, stopwatch, toys
Time required: Less than 1 hr

Gutteridge Rating Scale of Motor Skill
Book/journal citation: Gutteridge (1939)
Publisher: Out of print (complete test in monograph)
Movement category: Fundamental movement skills, specialized movement skills
Description: A 14-level qualitative rating scale that may be applied to just about any movement skill. Medians, means, and standard deviations for 10 skills (hopping, skipping, galloping, jumping, climbing, sliding, tricycling, dribbling, throwing, catching) are given by sex and age (2-6 years in 6-month intervals). See figure 2.1.
Stated uses: Monitor an individual's progress in learning basic habits underlying a variety of movement skills
Ages: 2 to 6 years
Validity: Not reported
Reliability: Interrater
Standardization: 1,851 children in New York
Equipment: Balls, objects to climb, tricycle
Time required: Not reported

Harris Infant Neuromotor Test (developmental edition) (HINT)
Book/journal citation: Harris and Daniels (1996)
Publisher: School of Rehabilitation Sciences, University of British Columbia, c/o 325-2211 Wesbrook Mall, Vancouver, BC, Canada V6T 2B5
Movement category: Movement foundations, early movement milestones
Description: A criterion-referenced instrument consisting of three parts: (a) background information on child and caregiver; (b) subjective, open-ended questions answered by caregiver; and (c) 22 items (including supine lying, transition from supine to prone lying, prone lying, sitting, locomotion skills, posture of hand and feet, frequency and variety of movement, stereotypical behavior, behavioral state, head circumference) scored by observing or physically handling the infant. After calculating a raw score for the third section, the examiner makes summary decisions about the infant's overall neuromotor performance in terms of developmental level and quality of performance.
Stated uses: Identifying early motor deficits and cognitive delays in infants with known risk factors
Ages: 3 to 12 months
Validity: Content, criterion-related
Reliability: Not reported
Standardization: To be provided in the final version of the HINT
Equipment: Materials to elicit movement behaviors
Time required: Less than 30 min

I CAN Instructional Management System
Book/journal citation: Wessel (1976)
Publisher: PRO-ED, 8700 Shoal Creek Boulevard, Austin, TX 78757-6897 (512-451-3246)
Movement category: Early movement milestones, fundamental movement skills, specialized movement skills
Description: A large set of criterion-referenced checklists for many skills, including both process and product items, categorized into Preprimary (28 skills—locomotor, object control, body control, play equipment, play participation, health fitness), Primary (71 skills—fundamental motor, body management, physical fit-

ness, aquatics), and Sport/Leisure/Recreation Skills (64—backyard/neighborhood activities, team sports, outdoor activities, dance and individual sports). See figures 5.3 and 10.3.

Stated uses: The checklist component of the I CAN system is designed to help the practitioner (a) prescribe appropriate movement activities for students and (b) evaluate skill-specific progress

Ages: Not specified

Validity: Not reported

Reliability: Not reported

Standardization: None

Equipment: Specific to individual checklist

Time required: Specific to the individual checklist

Los Angeles Unified School District Adapted Physical Education Assessment Scale (APEAS)

Book/journal citation: Seaman and DePauw (1989)

Publisher: Adapted Physical Education Unit, Los Angeles Unified School District, 6505 Zelzah Avenue, Reseda, CA 91335 (1-818-904-2000)

Movement category: Movement skill foundations, fundamental movements skills

Description: A product-oriented test with 18 items assessing locomotor skills, object-control skills, posture, endurance, balance, abdominal strength, ocular control, and motor planning. Raw scores for individual items can be converted to percentiles by sex and age. Placement recommendations are based on number of items on which the examinee falls below a criterion level, rather than a total composite score.

Stated uses: Determine appropriate placement of students in physical education

Ages: 5 to 12 years

Validity: Construct

Reliability: Not reported

Standardization: More than 2,100 children in California, including 2% with identified disabilities

Equipment: Ball, beanbags, stopwatch, target

Time required: About 20 min

Milani-Comparetti Motor Development Screening Test

Book/journal citation: Stuberg (1987)

Publisher: Meyer Children's Rehabilitation Institute, 444 South 44th Street, University of Nebraska Medical Center, Omaha, NE 68131

Movement category: Movement skill foundations

Description: A criterion-referenced instrument consisting of 27 items in six categories of spontaneous motor behaviors and evoked responses: primitive reflexes (5 items), righting reactions (4), protection reactions (4), equilibrium reactions (5), postural control (7), and active movement (2). Most items are scored as present, absent, or incomplete, while others are scored as just present or absent.

Stated uses: Screen children who may be at risk for neuromotor dysfunction

Ages: Birth to 2 years

Validity: Not reported

Reliability: Interrater, test-retest

Standardization: 312 children

Equipment: Cushion or tiltboard

Time required: 4 to 8 min

Miller Assessment for Preschoolers (MAP)

Book/journal citation: Miller (1988)

Publisher: Therapy Skill Builders (division of The Psychological Corporation), 555 Academic Court, San Antonio, TX 78204-2498 (800-211-8378)

Movement category: Movement skill foundations, motor abilities, early movement milestones, fundamental movement skills

Description: A norm-referenced screening instrument with 27 core indexes scored for five scales: Foundations Index (neuromaturational), Coordination Index (gross, fine, and oral motor), Verbal Index (language), Nonverbal Index (memory, problem-solving, and visual perception), and Complex Tasks Index (combined abilities). Percentile scores can be derived for individual items, each index, and also for the total test score. Three performance ranges—0-5th percentile (refer), 6-25th percentile (watch), and 26-99th percentile (developmentally average)—are emphasized.

Stated uses: (a) Identify developmentally delayed preschool children who need further assessment and (b) determine a child's strengths and weaknesses to guide remedial programming

Ages: 2 years 9 months to 5 years 8 months

Validity: Content, criterion-related, construct

Reliability: Internal consistency, interrater, test-retest

Standardization: 1,204 normal children, stratified to match geographic location, race, sex, community size, and socioeconomic status characteristics of the U.S. population

Equipment: Chairs, table, test kit

Time required: About 30 min

Motor Control Assessment (MCA)

Book/journal citation: Steel, Glover, and Spasoff (1991)

Publisher: Authors

Movement category: Motor abilities, early movement milestones, fundamental movement skills

Description: A criterion-referenced assessment of motor control of children with physical disabilities, consisting of 113 items from five performance areas: supine (11 items), prone (18), sitting (30), kneeling (7), standing and standing up (18), walking (10), and general coordination (14). Each is scored on a 0- to 5-point scale (e.g., 5 = normal, 3 = minimal assistance); then the final Motor Control Assessment score is the average score across all items.

Stated uses: Assess the outcomes of alternate treatment approaches for children with physical disabilities

Ages: Children 2 years and up

Validity: Criterion-related

Reliability: Intrarater, interrater, test-retest

Standardization: None

Equipment: Chair, mat, rope, stairs, stool, table, toys, tricycle

Time required: 30 to 60 min

Motor Development Checklist (MDC)

Book/journal citation: Doudlah (1976) (see also Gevelinger, Ottenbacher, & Tiffany, 1988)

Publisher: Central Wisconsin Center for the Developmentally Disabled, 317 Knutson Drive, Madison, WI 53704 (608-249-2151)

Movement category: Early movement milestones

Description: A criterion-referenced test comprising 35 items organized into five "phases" and "transitions": movement in place (Phase 1), rolling (Transition 1), movement through space in the quadrupedal position (Phase 2), being upright in space (Transition 2), and movement through space in the upright position (Phase 3). Items are interpreted individually and are scored from 0 to 3 (from does not perform task to performs task skillfully).

Stated uses: Record spontaneous motor behavior in persons with severe developmental disabilities

Ages: Not reported
Validity: Not reported
Reliability: Interrater, test-retest
Standardization: None
Equipment: No special equipment
Time required: A minimum of 10 min

Motor Skills Inventory (MSI)

Book/journal citation: Werder and Bruininks (1988)

Publisher: American Guidance Service, 4201 Woodland Road, PO Box 99, Circle Pines, MN 55014-1796 (800-328-2560)

Movement category: Movement skill foundations, fundamental movement skills

Description: A criterion-referenced test comprising 30 items organized into five skill areas: body management (5 items), locomotor (7), body fitness (6), object movement (7), and fine motor (5). Performance scores (rudimentary, functional, or mature) for each item can be placed on a profile that estimates achievement age and placement on an interval measurement scale (W-ability). A scale on the profile also allows scores on the MSI to be estimated from scores on the BOT. The MSI is the assessment component of the Body Skills curriculum. See table 14.2.

Stated uses: (a) Identify skills in the Body Skills curriculum that need attention, (b) monitor individual progress during or following instruction, and (c) evaluate effectiveness of the instructional program

Ages: The Body Skills curriculum—based on the general pattern of motor development of children 2 to 12 years; range of estimated achievement ages on the score profile—3 to 16 years

Validity: Construct

Reliability: Internal consistency, interrater

Standardization: None, but 281 children from 3 to 16 years used to equate the BOT with the MSI

Equipment: Balls, bats, blocks, cones, mat, stopwatch, target

Time required: Not reported

Movement Assessment Battery for Children Checklist (MABC Checklist)

Book/journal citation: Henderson and Sugden (1992)

Publisher: Therapy Skill Builders (division of The Psychological Corporation), 555 Academic Court, San Antonio, TX 78204-2498 (800-211-8378)

Movement category: Motor abilities, fundamental movement skills, specialized movement skills, functional movement skills

Description: A criterion-referenced test composed of 60 process- and product-oriented items organized into five sections with 12 items each: child stationary—environment stable, child moving—environment stable, child stationary—environment changing, child moving—environment changing, and behaviors that may interfere with movement performance (see fig. 11.5). The total scores on the first four sections matching 5th and 15th percentile are given for ages 6 to 9+ years.

Stated uses: MABC Checklist—(a) screen children for possible movement problems, (b) identify children for special services, and (c) research; MABC Checklist with the MABC Test—(a) clinical exploration, (b) intervention planning, and (c) program evaluation.

Ages: 5 to 11 years

Validity: Criterion-related, construct

Reliability: Test-retest

Standardization: 298 children from the United Kingdom

Equipment: Equipment commonly available in an elementary school

Time required: Recommended to be completed over a 1- to 2-week period of observation

Movement Assessment Battery for Children Test (MABC Test)

Book/journal citation: Henderson and Sugden (1992)

Publisher: The Psychological Corporation, Order Service Center, PO Box 839954, San Antonio, TX 78283-3954 (800-211-8378)

Movement category: Motor abilities, fundamental movement skills, specialized movement skills

Description: The MABC Test has 32 items organized into a 4 (age level) × 8 (performance category) matrix, with the eight performance categories covering manual dexterity (3), ball skills (2), and balance (3) (see table 8.5). Product scores are converted into scaled "impairment" scores ranging from 0 to 5, with a higher score indicating poorer performance. Total impairment scores then can be converted into percentiles.

Stated uses: MABC Test—(a) screen children for possible movement problems, (b) identify children for special services, and (c) research; MABC Test with the MABC Checklist—(a) clinical exploration, (b) intervention planning, and (c) program evaluation

Ages: 4 to 12 years

Validity: Criterion-related, construct

Reliability: Test-retest

Standardization: 1,234 children, representing the U.S population according to the 1980 census

Equipment: Stopwatch, test kit

Time required: 20 to 40 min

Movement Assessment of Infants (MAI)

Book/journal citation: Chandler, Andrews, and Swanson (1980)

Publisher: Authors, PO Box 4631, Rolling Bay, WA 98061

Movement category: Movement skill foundations, early movement milestones

Description: A criterion-referenced instrument consisting of 65 items divided into four sections: muscle tone, primitive reflexes, automatic reactions, and volitional movements. Numerical rating scales for each section indicate the expected sequence of development.

Stated uses: (a) Identify motor dysfunction in infants up to 12 months of age, (b) establish the basis for an early intervention program, and (c) monitor the effects of physical therapy on infants and children

Ages: Birth to 12 months

Validity: Criterion-related

Reliability: Interrater, test-retest

Standardization: None

Equipment: No specialized equipment

Time required: 90 min for testing and scoring

Ohio State University Scale of Intra-Gross Motor Assessment (SIGMA)

Book/journal citation: Loovis and Ersing (1979)

Publisher: Tichenor Publishing, PO Box 669, Bloomington, IN 47402-0696 (800-266-5847)

Movement category: Fundamental movement skills

Description: A criterion-referenced instrument assessing qualitative aspects of 11 fundamental movement skills (walking, stair climbing, running, jumping, hopping, skipping, ladder climbing, throwing, catching, striking, kicking). Four levels of development from least to most mature are indicated for each skill, yielding a performance profile across the 11 skills.

Stated uses: Determine the most logical starting point in planning interventions.

Ages: 2.5 to 14 years

Validity: Not reported

Reliability: Interrater, intrarater, test-retest

Standardization: None

Equipment: Balls, bats, ladder, stairs

Time required: Not reported

Peabody Developmental Motor Scales (PDMS)

Book/journal citation: Folio and Fewell (1983)

Publisher: Riverside Publishing Company, 425 Spring Lake Drive, Itasca, IL 60143 (800-767-8378)

Movement category: Motor abilities, early movement milestones, fundamental movement skills

Description: The criterion- and norm-referenced PDMS has two scales: Gross Motor (GM) and Fine Motor (FM). The GM Scale has 12 items divided across five skill areas (reflexes, balance, nonlocomotor, locomotor, receipt and propulsion) for each of 17 age levels for a total of 170 items. The FM Scale has 6 to 8 items divided across four skill areas (grasping, hand use, eye-hand coordination, manual dexterity) for each of 16 age levels for a total of 112 items. For each of the nine skill areas and the GM and FM totals, raw scores can be converted to percentiles, T scores, or a standardized Developmental Motor Quotient. Also, basal and ceiling age levels, scaled scores to measure small changes in performance, and age equivalents can be calculated for both GM and FM, as well as a GM-FM composite mean motor age equivalent. See figure 9.4 and tables 9.2, 9.3, 9.4, and 9.5.

Stated uses: (a) Identify children whose skills are delayed or aberrant relative to those of a normative group, (b) determine the necessity and/or eligibility for intervention programs, (c) plan an intervention program, and (d) evaluate changes over time

Ages: Birth to 6 years 11 months

Validity: Content, criterion-related, construct

Reliability: Interrater, test-retest

Standardization: 617 children, using a stratified procedure to select a sample representative of the U.S. population

Equipment: 10 items are included in the test kit, but 24 other objects, toys, and equipment are needed

Time required: 20 to 30 min for each scale, for a total of about 45 to 60 min

Pediatric Evaluation of Disability Inventory (PEDI)

Book/journal citation: Haley, Coster, Ludlow, Haltiwanger, and Andrellos (1992)

Publisher: PEDI Research Group, Department of Physical Medicine and Rehabilitation Medicine, New England Medical Center Hospital, 750 Washington Street, #75 K/R, Boston, MA 02111-1901 (617-636-5031)

Movement category: Motor abilities, fundamental movement skills, specialized movement skills, functional movement skills

Description: The criterion-referenced PEDI has three parts: (a) 197 functional skill items divided into self-care (73), mobility (59), and social function (65) domains; (b) 20 items evaluating caregiver assistance needed in self-care (8), mobility (7), and social function (5) domains; and (c) a measurement of the modification frequencies for the 20 caregiver assistance items. For the three domains in each of the functional skill and caregiver assistance parts, a Rasch model based on item response theory was applied to generate standardized scores by age and scaled scores (1-100) for children of all ages. See figure 11.3 and table 11.3.

Stated uses: (a) Detect whether a functional deficit or delay exists, (b) determine the extent and content area of an identified delay or deficit, (c) monitor individual or group progress in pediatric rehabilitation programs, and (d) evaluate pediatric rehabilitation services or therapeutic programs in educational settings

Ages: 0.5 to 7.5 years

Validity: Content, criterion-related, construct

Reliability: Between interviewers, between interviewers and parents

Standardization: 412 children without disabilities from New England, based on the 1980 U.S. Census

Equipment: Equipment and environments for activities of daily living

Time required: For experienced professionals testing a child with whom they are familiar, 20 to 30 min; for a structured parent interview, as long as 45 to 60 min

Posture and Fine Motor Assessment of Infants (PFMAI)

Book/journal citation: Case-Smith (1991) (see also Case-Smith, 1992)

Publisher: American Occupational Therapy Association, PO Box 31220, Bethesda, MD 20824-1220 (301-652-2682)

Movement category: Movement skill foundations, early movement milestones

Description: A criterion-referenced test consisting of two sections: one for posture and the other for fine motor. The posture section measures proximal stability and postural control with specific items for the head, shoulder, and pelvic stability and mobility. The fine motor section rates the type and quality of reaching, the grasping pattern, and the quality of isolated arm and hand movements. Each item is assigned a developmentally sequenced score from 1 to 4.

Stated uses: (a) Identify infant's posture and fine motor strengths and limitations, (b) identify the sequential skills to address in therapy, and (c) evaluate the progress made in posture and movement patterns

Ages: 2 to 6 months

Validity: Criterion-related, construct

Reliability: Internal consistency (Case-Smith, 1992), interrater, test-retest

Standardization: None

Equipment: Various toys

Time required: About 45 min

Project ACTIVE Motor Ability Tests

Book/journal citation: Vodola (1978)

Publisher: Out of print

Movement category: Movement skill foundations, motor abilities, fundamental movement skills

Description: A set of four motor performance tests: Levels I, II, III, and Basic Movement Performance Profile (BMPP). The Level II test, designed to be used with "educable mentally retarded learning disabled, or normal" children, is a norm-referenced instrument consisting of 22 items related to gross motor coordination, balance-postural orientation, eye-hand coordination, eye-hand accuracy, and eye-foot accuracy. The Level II test yields subtotal and grand total raw scores, percentiles and stanines for subtotals, and a composite Motor Ability Index. The Level I test, designed for use with "trainable, severely, or profoundly retarded" children, consists of the same 22 items as in the Level II test, but they are evaluated in terms of qualitative criteria rather than quantitative scores. The Level III test, designed for use with "the child who is gifted motorically," is a norm-referenced test focusing on the same areas as the Level II test, but with different items. A composite Motor Ability Index can be calculated from raw scores. The BMPP is designed to evaluate locomotor skills and static and dynamic balance and yields a criterion score for each of 20 items.

Stated uses: (a) Differentiate among student ability levels and (b) assist in diagnosing motor ability deficits and prescribing remedial programming

Ages: 4 to 9 years

Validity: Content

Reliability: Test-retest

Standardization: More than 1,000 children from various states

Equipment: Balls, bat, stairs or steps, target

Time required: About 30 min for each test

Project MOBILITEE

Book/journal citation: Hopewell Special Education Regional Resource Center (1981)

Publisher: Hopewell Special Education Regional Resource Center, 5350 West New Market Road, Hillsboro, OH 45133 (513-393-1904)

Movement category: Movement skill foundations, fundamental movement skills

Description: A criterion-referenced physical education assessment consisting of four parts: Physical/Motor Fitness (7 items), Fundamental Motor Skills (6 items adapted from the Ohio State University Scale of Intra-Gross Motor Assessment), Skills for Participation (8 items), and Motor Pattern Assessments for Low Functioning Students. MOBILITEE stands for Movement Opportunities for Building Independence and Leisure Interests through Training Educators and Exceptional Learners.

Stated uses: (a) Determine present levels of physical and motor fitness, maturity in performing fundamental motor skills, and behaviors and skills for participating in games and sports; (b) identify specific strengths, weaknesses, and areas of need; and (c) provide guidelines for improving specific skills

Ages: 5 to 21 years

Validity: Not reported

Reliability: Not reported

Standardization: Not reported

Equipment: Balls, bat, cone, tape measure

Time required: Not reported

Purdue Perceptual-Motor Survey (PPMS)

Book/journal citation: Roach and Kephart (1966)

Publisher: Out of print (complete test in book)

Movement category: Motor abilities, fundamental movement skills, specialized movement skills

Description: A criterion-referenced test comprising 30 items divided into 11 subtests (walking board, jumping, body part identification, movement imitation, obstacle course, chalkboard, Kraus-Weber, angels-in-the-snow, ocular pursuit, drawing, rhythmic writing) and measured on a 1- to 4-point scale. Items are interpreted separately, with means and standard deviations given for each item for Grades 1 to 4.

Stated uses: (a) Detect errors in perceptual-motor development, (b) designate areas for remediation, and (c) allow the clinician to observe perceptual-motor behavior in a series of behavioral performances

Ages: No age limits, but norms are for first through fourth graders

Validity: Criterion-related, construct

Reliability: Test-retest

Standardization: 297 children in Indiana

Equipment: Balance beam, broom handle, chalkboard, gym mat, penlight

Time required: Not reported

Quick Neurological Screening Test (QNST)

Book/journal citation: Mutti, Sterline, and Spalding (1978)

Publisher: Psychological and Educational Publications, PO Box 520, Hydesville Road, Hydesville, CA 95547-0520 (800-523-5775)

Movement category: Movement skill foundations, motor abilities, fundamental movement skills

Description: A standardized test composed of 15 tasks designed to evaluate a child's maturity in motor development, skill in controlling large and small muscles, motor planning and sequencing, sense of rate and rhythm, spatial orientation, visual and auditory perceptual skill, balance and cerebellar-vestibular function, and attention. The test yields subtest and cumulative scores that place the individual in the normal, suspicious, or high-risk range of performance.

Stated uses: Identify persons with (a) no abnormal neurological signs; (b) distinct differences in sensation, motor control, or control of movement between the two sides of the body, or (c) organic neurological signs in those who do not perform at a level predicted for their age

Ages: 5 years to adult

Validity: Content, construct

Reliability: Interrater, test-retest

Standardization: 2,239 individuals from 6 to 17 years old representing a variety of populations

Equipment: No specialized equipment

Time required: 20 min

Sensorimotor Performance Analysis (SPA)

Book/journal citation: Richter and Montgomery (1989)

Publisher: PDP Press, 12015 North July Avenue, Hugo, MN 55038 (612-439-8865)

Movement category: Movement skill foundations, early movement milestones, fundamental movement skills

Description: A criterion-referenced tool focusing on the underlying sensorimotor components of performance of seven tasks: rolling (8 components), belly crawling (9), bat ball from hands and knees (13), kneeling balance (13), pellets in bottle (14), pencil-and-paper task (16), and scissor task (17). Numerical scores from the Performance Analysis scoring form are transferred to a Scoring Profile.

Stated uses: (a) Plan treatment and (b) evaluate change resulting from intervention

Ages: Children and adults 5 to 21 years who cannot be tested adequately with standardized tests

Validity: Construct

Reliability: Interrater, test-retest

Standardization: None

Equipment: Paper, pellets, pencils, scissors, small bottle, suspended ball, tape, table and chairs, tiltboard

Time required: Less than 30 min

Sensory Integration and Praxis Tests (SIPT)

Book/journal citation: Ayres (1989)

Publisher: Western Psychological Services, 12031 Wilshire Boulevard, Los Angeles, CA 90025 (800-648-8857)

Movement category: Movement skill foundations

Description: A norm-referenced instrument composed of 17 tests designed to assess sensory perception and the processing of the proprioceptive, tactile, vestibular, and visual systems, as well as several aspects of praxis. There is one major score for each test; these are computer weighted, converted to standard scores, and presented as a performance profile. Also, there are 51 partial scores across 15 of the 17 tests.

Stated uses: (a) Evaluate the sensory integrative and praxis abilities of children and (b) guide the treatment of such disorders.

Ages: 4 to 8 years

Validity: Content, criterion-related, construct

Reliability: Interrater, test-retest

Standardization: 1,997 children sampled to represent the U.S. population according to the 1980 census

Equipment: Stopwatch, test kit

Time required: About 2 hr (10 min or less for each of the tests)

Test of Gross Motor Development (TGMD)

Book/journal citation: Ulrich (1985)

Publisher: PRO-ED, 8700 Shoal Creek Boulevard, Austin, TX 78757-6897 (512-451-3246)

Movement category: Motor abilities, fundamental movement skills

Description: A criterion-referenced test on the movement patterns used to perform 12 fundamental movement skills, organized into locomotor (gallop, hop, horizontal jump, leap, run, skip, and slide) and object-control (stationary bounce, catch, kick, two-hand strike, and overhand throw) subtests. Standardized scores and percentiles can be calculated for each of the two subtests, as well as a standardized score (the Gross Motor Development Quotient) for the entire test. See figures 10.5, 10.6, and 10.7.

Stated uses: (a) Identify children who are significantly below age norms in gross motor skill development, (b) plan a program to improve gross motor skill development in those children showing delays, (c) assess changes in gross motor skill development as a function of increasing age or experience, and (d) assess changes in gross motor skill development as a function of instruction or intervention

Ages: 3 to 10 years

Validity: Content, construct

Reliability: Internal consistency, interrater, test-retest

Standardization: 909 children, using a stratified sampling procedure based on the 1980 U.S. Census

Equipment: Equipment commonly used in movement activity programs

Time required: About 15 to 20 min

Tests of Motor Proficiency (TMP)

Book/journal citations: Gubbay (1973, 1975a) (see also Johnston, 1993)

Publisher: Both out of print (complete test in both references)

Movement category: Motor abilities, fundamental movement skills, specialized movement skills

Description: A product-oriented assessment comprising eight fine and gross motor items. Raw scores can be converted to 5th, 10th, 50tth, 90th, and 95th percentiles, which are displayed by age. No total scores or composites are used, but a child may be considered to be below the 5th percentile in motor proficiency if scores on 3 or more items fall below the 10th percentile. Additional norms for 7-year-olds on the TMP (n = 365) are presented by Johnston (1993).

Stated uses: Identify "clumsy" children

Ages: 8 to 12 years

Validity: Criterion-related, construct

Reliability: Not reported

Standardization: 992 children in Australia

Equipment: Beads, hatpin, shoelace, sorting toy, tennis ball

Time required: 2 to 5 min

Top-Down Motor Milestone Test (TDMMT)

Book/journal citation: Bidabe and Lollar (1990)

Publisher: MOVE International, 1300 17th Street—City Centre, Bakersfield, CA 93301-4533 (800-397-MOVE or 805-636-4561)

Movement category: Early movement milestones, fundamental movement skills

Description: A criterion-referenced assessment consisting of 74 skills organized into 16 sitting, standing, and walking skill headings (see fig. 10.9). The TDMMT is part of the Mobility Opportunities Via Education (MOVE) program, which also includes three assessments of prompts or physical assistance needed to perform the 74 skills.

Stated uses: (a) Plan instruction and (b) evaluate progress
Ages: Infants to young adults
Validity: Not reported
Reliability: Not reported
Standardization: None
Equipment: Functional objects and equipment, such as chair, stool, bed, bathtub, mobile stander, or front-leaning walker
Time required: About 15 min

Transdisciplinary Play-Based Assessment (TPBA)
Book/journal citation: Linder (1993)
Publisher: Paul H. Brookes Publishing, PO Box 10624, Baltimore, MD 21285-0624 (800-701-7868)
Movement category: Early movement milestones, fundamental movement skills
Description: A criterion-referenced tool with six phases: I, unstructured facilitation; II, structured facilitation; III, child-child interaction; IV, parent-child interaction; V, motor play; and VI, snack. A developmental age chart is provided with a checklist with criteria for plus or minus scores indicating the presence or absence of age-appropriate skills. Information is collected in the areas of cognitive development, social-emotional development, communication and language development, and sensorimotor development. See figure 11.2.
Stated uses: (a) Identify service needs, (b) develop intervention plans based on individual treatment objectives, and (c) evaluate progress
Ages: Birth to 72 months
Validity: Content, criterion-related, construct
Reliability: Interrater, test-retest
Standardization: None
Equipment: A preschool classroom with typical manipulatives, puzzles, and toys, including a balance beam, barrels, a rocking board, a sand and water table, steps, and a tricycle
Time required: Phase I, 20 to 25 min; II, 10 to 15 min; III, 5 to 10 min; IV, 10 min; V, 10 to 20 min; VI, 5 to 10 min

Tufts Assessment of Motor Performance (TAMP)
Book/journal citation: Gans et al. (1988) (see also Haley & Ludlow, 1992; Haley, Ludlow, Gans, Faas, & Inacio, 1991; Ludlow, Haley, & Gans, 1992)
Publisher: New England Medical Center Hospital, 750 Washington Street, #75 K/R, Boston, MA 02111-1901 (617-636-5031)
Movement category: Motor abilities, early movement milestones, functional movement skills
Description: A criterion-referenced assessment of functional motor status comprising 30 items related to mobility and activities of daily living. Each item is broken down into three to five steps or phases, yielding a total of 91 discrete tasks, which are scored on a scale of 1 to 7 indicating degree of independence. A Rasch model based on item response theory is used to transform total raw scores into an estimate of motor proficiency and to determine estimates of difficulty for each task that are invariant across the subject sample. Then, a person's estimate of proficiency can be matched against estimates of item difficulty.
Stated uses: (a) Assist with treatment planning and (b) describe and identify meaningful clinical change in motor skills
Ages: All ages and all types of disabilities
Validity: Construct (Haley & Ludlow, 1992)
Reliability: Interrater (Gans et al., 1988)
Standardization: 206 children and adults (5-79 years)

Equipment: Materials and equipment to perform tasks related to mobility and activities of daily living

Time required: Less than 1 hr

Vulpe Assessment Battery (VAB)

Book/journal citation: Vulpe (1982)

Publisher: National Institute on Mental Retardation, Kinsmen/NIRNR Building, 4700 Keele Street, North Yorke, ON, Canada M3J 1P3 (416-661-9611)

Movement category: Movement skill foundations, early movement milestones, fundamental movement skills

Description: A criterion-referenced instrument, designed for children with disabilities, composed of over 1,300 items organized into eight subtests (basic senses and functions, gross motor behaviors, fine motor behaviors, language behaviors, cognitive processes, organization of behavior, activities of daily living, and the environment) and five supplemental tests (posture and mobility, reflexes, muscle strength, motor planning, and balance). Performance on each item is evaluated in terms of a seven-level scoring system. This is not a norm-referenced test, but items are grouped by age levels.

Stated uses: (a) Assess whether a child's development is normal, at risk, or impaired; (b) assist in developing program goals and identifying appropriate teaching approaches; (c) evaluate individual progress; and (d) evaluate the program

Ages: Birth to 6 years

Validity: Not reported

Reliability: Not reported

Standardization: None

Equipment: A variety of materials for the many items on the test

Time required: 1 hr

Appendix B

Standards for Test Users

Thirty-five selected standards for test users from the Task Force on Standards for Measurement in Physical Therapy (TFSMPT) (1991) are organized into five sections: user background (A), test selection (B), test administration (C), test interpretation (D), and reporting results (E). Numbers in brackets indicate the TFSMPT standard number. [Reprinted from *Physical Therapy*, Task Force on Standards for Measurement in Physical Therapy, "Standards for tests and measurements in physical therapy practice," 1991, *71*, pp. 613-619, with permission of the APTA.]

A. User Background
1. Test users must have a basic knowledge of the theory and principles of tests and measurements. [U3]
2. Test users who are required to derive or transform measurements must have sufficient training and knowledge to derive or transform those measurements. Test users must have the background information and skills needed to derive measurements or make categorizations necessary for interpretation of their measurements (e.g., how to normalize or standardize a score or how to classify a measurement). [U23]
3. Test users must have background knowledge in basic, applied, and clinical sciences related to the selection, administration, and interpretation of each test they use. [U4]
4. Test users must understand the theoretical bases (construct and content validity) for the tests they use, and they must have knowledge about the attribute (characteristic) being measured. [U5]
5. Test users must have a basic understanding of local, state, and federal laws governing the use of tests in their practice settings. [U2]

B. Test Selection
1. Test users should consider the practicality of the test (e.g., personnel, time, equipment, cost of administration, and impact on the person taking the test) in selecting tests and in planning examination procedures. [U8.2]
2. Test users must be able to describe the population for whom the test was designed. Test users must be able to relate this description to the persons they are testing. [U11]

3. Test users must know the physical settings in which the test should be given and the possible effects of conducting the test in other settings. [U15]

4. Test users, in clinical practice, should avoid the use of tests that were designed solely for research purposes. Such tests, when they are used in the clinical setting, should be identified in all reports as research tests that have not necessarily been shown to be reliable or valid in clinical use. [U38]

5. Test users must be able to determine before they use a test whether they have the ability to administer the test. This determination should be based on an understanding of the test user's own skills and knowledge (competency) as compared with the competencies described by the test purveyor. [U12]

6. Test users must be able to justify the selection of tests they use. Test users must also be prepared to supply logical arguments to justify the rejection of tests they choose not to use. [U8]

7. Test users should select tests based on what is best for the person being tested. Test selection based on considerations of personal benefit to the test user, test purveyor, or the referring practitioner is inappropriate. [U37]

C. Test Administration

1. Test users should not conduct tests unless they have examined all relevant sections of a complete copy of the test manual. [U9.1b]

2. Test users must follow instructions provided by purveyors for all tests they administer. [U13]

3. Test users who deviate from accepted directions for obtaining a measurement should not use published data or documentation relative to reliability and validity to justify their use of the measurement. [U21]

4. Test users must make every effort to control the environment (test setting) in which they test in order to maintain consistent conditions between tests. These efforts are needed to ensure that the validity and reliability of a measurement are not compromised. [U25]

5. Test users must be able to identify any conditions or behaviors in the person being tested that may compromise the reliability or validity of their measurements (e.g., if a modified position must be used in manual muscle testing because of a deformity). Test users who observe such conditions or behaviors should note these observations in their reports of any resultant measurements. Test users who believe that the effect on their measurements could be significant should include a discussion of the implications of these observations in their reports. [U16]

6. Test users have a responsibility to suggest further testing when they have serious concerns about the quality of the measurements they obtain or when they believe that other tests or other personnel can be used to obtain better measurements. [U22]

7. Test users must make every effort when personal information is being obtained to control the environment (test setting) in which they administer tests in order to preserve the privacy of the person taking the test. [U26]

8. Test users are responsible for maintaining confidentiality of test results. Confidentiality of results should be in accordance with standard practices in the institution or community in which the test user obtains the measurements. Results should not be shared with any persons (or organizations) who are known to be unwilling to respect the right of confidentiality of the person who was tested. [U32]

9. Test users have a responsibility to periodically review the test procedures they and their colleagues use in their institutions (practice settings) to ensure that appropriate use of measurements is being made and that the rights of persons tested are being observed. [U42]

D. Test Interpretation

1. Test users must limit their interpretations of measurements to the inferences for which those measurements have been shown to be valid. [U44.1]

2. Test users must avoid overinterpreting the results of their tests. Test users are responsible for understanding both the certainty and the uncertainty with which they can make judgments based on their measurements. [U44.5]

3. Test users must consider the conditions under which they conduct tests and the extent to which results are generalizable to other test situations (e.g., testing in other places or at other times). [U44.7]

4. Test users reporting the results of tests must supply adequate information so that these results can be understood. [U45]

5. Test users must consider whether normative data are available for the measurements they interpret. Test users must consider the sources of the normative data and the extent to which these data are applicable to the measurements they are interpreting. [U44.3]

6. Test users must consider the limitations of their measurements when they classify persons into diagnostic groups based on the presence or absence of a finding (e.g., use of cut scores or tests to determine a positive or negative finding). Test users should use all available data in making their interpretation. [U44.4]

7. Test users must consider the error associated with their measurements when they interpret their test results. Reliability and validity estimates should be considered when the test user makes interpretations of measurements. [U44.2]

8. Test users must consider estimates of reliability and validity when reporting test results. Test users should report estimates of the errors associated with a measurement when they report test results. [U45.5]

9. Test users should report any aspect of the test that may cast doubt on test results (e.g., ways in which the person tested differed from the population for which the test was designed or any observation the test user made during testing). [U45.9]

E. Reporting Results

1. Test users must consider estimates of reliability and validity when reporting test results. Test users should report estimates of the errors associated with a measurement when they report test results. [U45.5]

2. Test users who use a variation of a test must indicate, when they report test results, that a variation was used. The test users must note whether they believe that the variation may have affected the quality of their measurements. Test users who believe the variation had a significant effect on the measurements should discuss this belief in all reports of test results. [U45.8]

3. Test users should report any aspect of the test that may cast doubt on test results (e.g., ways in which the person tested differed from the population for which the test was designed or any observation the test user made during testing). [U45.9]

4. Test users who base their interpretations on the results of a variety of tests should note this fact when they discuss their measurements. Test users should justify their selection of the tests in reporting test results. [U45.14]

5. Test users should note in their reports of test results the specific criteria they use for clinical decisions. When a specific measurement (e.g., cut score) is used for a clinical decision, the test user, in all reports, should justify the use of that specific measurement. [U45.15]

Appendix C

Areas Under the Standard Normal Curve

Z score	Below +	Below –	Z score	Below +	Below –
0.00	.5000	.5000			
0.01	.5040	.4960	0.16	.5636	.4364
0.02	.5080	.4920	0.17	.5675	.4325
0.03	.5120	.4880	0.18	.5714	.4286
0.04	.5160	.4840	0.19	.5753	.4247
0.05	.5199	.4801	0.20	.5793	.4207
0.06	.5239	.4761	0.21	.5832	.4168
0.07	.5279	.4721	0.22	.5871	.4129
0.08	.5319	.4681	0.23	.5910	.4090
0.09	.5359	.4641	0.24	.5948	.4052
0.10	.5398	.4602	0.25	.5987	.4013
0.11	.5438	.4562	0.26	.6026	.3974
0.12	.5478	.4522	0.27	.6064	.3936
0.13	.5517	.4483	0.28	.6103	.3987
0.14	.5557	.4443	0.29	.6141	.3859
0.15	.5596	.4404	0.30	.6179	.3821

(continued)

Z score	Below +	Below −	Z score	Below +	Below −
0.31	.6217	.3783	0.56	.7123	.2877
0.32	.6255	.3745	0.57	.7157	.2843
0.33	.6293	.3707	0.58	.7190	.2810
0.34	.6331	.3669	0.59	.7224	.2776
0.35	.6368	.3632	0.60	.7257	.2743
0.36	.6406	.3594	0.61	.7291	.2709
0.37	.6443	.3557	0.62	.7324	.2676
0.38	.6480	.3520	0.63	.7357	.2643
0.39	.6517	.3483	0.64	.7389	.2611
0.40	.6554	.3446	0.65	.7422	.2578
0.41	.6591	.3409	0.66	.7454	.2546
0.42	.6628	.3372	0.67	.7486	.2514
0.43	.6664	.3336	0.68	.7517	.2483
0.44	.6700	.3300	0.69	.7549	.2451
0.45	.6736	.3264	0.70	.7580	.2420
0.46	.6772	.3228	0.71	.7611	.2389
0.47	.6808	.3192	0.72	.7642	.2358
0.48	.6844	.3156	0.73	.7673	.2327
0.49	.6879	.3121	0.74	.7704	.2296
0.50	.6915	.3085	0.75	.7734	.2266
0.51	.6950	.3050	0.76	.7764	.2236
0.52	.6985	.3015	0.77	.7794	.2206
0.53	.7019	.2981	0.78	.7823	.2177
0.54	.7054	.2946	0.79	.7852	.2148
0.55	.7088	.2922	0.80	.7881	.2119

Z score	Below +	Below–	Z score	Below +	Below –
0.81	.7910	.2090	1.06	.8554	.1446
0.82	.7939	.2061	1.07	.8577	.1423
0.83	.7967	.2033	1.08	.8599	.1401
0.84	.7995	.2005	1.09	.8621	.1379
0.85	.8023	.1977	1.10	.8643	.1357
0.86	.8051	.1949	1.11	.8665	.1335
0.87	.8078	.1922	1.12	.8686	.1314
0.88	.8106	.1894	1.13	.8708	.1292
0.89	.8133	.1867	1.14	.8729	.1271
0.90	.8159	.1841	1.15	.8749	.1251
0.91	.8186	.1814	1.16	.8770	.1230
0.92	.8212	.1788	1.17	.8790	.1210
0.93	.8238	.1762	1.18	.8810	.1190
0.94	.8264	.1736	1.19	.8830	.1170
0.95	.8289	.1711	1.20	.8849	.1151
0.96	.8315	.1685	1.21	.8869	.1131
0.97	.8340	.1660	1.22	.8888	.1112
0.98	.8365	.1635	1.23	.8907	.1093
0.99	.8389	.1611	1.24	.8925	.1075
1.00	.8413	.1587	1.25	.8944	.1056
1.01	.8438	.1562	1.26	.8962	.1038
1.02	.8461	.1539	1.27	.8980	.1020
1.03	.8485	.1515	1.28	.8997	.1003
1.04	.8508	.1492	1.29	.9015	.0985
1.05	.8531	.1469	1.30	.9032	.0968

(continued)

Z score	Below +	Below −	Z score	Below +	Below −
1.31	.9049	.0951	1.56	.9406	.0594
1.32	.9066	.0934	1.57	.9418	.0582
1.33	.9082	.0918	1.58	.9429	.0571
1.34	.9099	.0901	1.59	.9441	.0559
1.35	.9115	.0885	1.60	.9452	.0548
1.36	.9131	.0869	1.61	.9463	.0537
1.37	.9147	.0853	1.62	.9474	.0526
1.38	.9162	.0838	1.63	.9484	.0516
1.39	.9177	.0823	1.64	.9495	.0505
1.40	.9192	.0808	1.65	.9505	.0495
1.41	.9207	.0793	1.66	.9515	.0485
1.42	.9222	.0778	1.67	.9525	.0475
1.43	.9236	.0764	1.68	.9535	.0465
1.44	.9251	.0749	1.69	.9545	.0455
1.45	.9265	.0735	1.70	.9554	.0446
1.46	.9279	.0721	1.71	.9564	.0436
1.47	.9292	.0708	1.72	.9573	.0427
1.48	.9306	.0694	1.73	.9582	.0418
1.49	.9319	.0681	1.74	.9591	.0409
1.50	.9332	.0668	1.75	.9599	.0401
1.51	.9345	.0655	1.76	.9608	.0392
1.52	.9357	.0643	1.77	.9616	.0384
1.53	.9370	.0630	1.78	.9625	.0375
1.54	.9382	.0618	1.79	.9633	.0367
1.55	.9394	.0606	1.80	.9641	.0359

Z score	Below +	Below −	Z score	Below +	Below −
1.81	.9649	.0351	2.06	.9803	.0197
1.82	.9656	.0344	2.07	.9808	.0192
1.83	.9664	.0336	2.08	.9812	.0188
1.84	.9671	.0329	2.09	.9817	.0183
1.85	.9678	.0322	2.10	.9821	.0179
1.86	.9686	.0314	2.11	.9826	.0174
1.87	.9693	.0307	2.12	.9830	.0170
1.88	.9699	.0301	2.13	.9834	.0166
1.89	.9706	.0294	2.14	.9838	.0162
1.90	.9713	.0287	2.15	.9842	.0158
1.91	.9719	.0281	2.16	.9846	.0154
1.92	.9726	.0274	2.17	.9850	.0150
1.93	.9732	.0268	2.18	.9854	.0146
1.94	.9738	.0262	2.19	.9857	.0143
1.95	.9744	.0256	2.20	.9861	.0139
1.96	.9750	.0250	2.21	.9864	.0136
1.97	.9756	.0244	2.22	.9868	.0132
1.98	.9761	.0239	2.23	.9871	.0129
1.99	.9767	.0233	2.24	.9875	.0125
2.00	.9772	.0228	2.25	.9878	.0122
2.01	.9778	.0222	2.26	.9881	.0119
2.02	.9783	.0217	2.27	.9884	.0116
2.03	.9788	.0212	2.28	.9887	.0113
2.04	.9793	.0207	2.29	.9890	.0110
2.05	.9798	.0202	2.30	.9893	.0107

(continued)

Z score	Below +	Below –	Z score	Below +	Below –
2.31	.9896	.0104	2.56	.9948	.0052
2.32	.9898	.0102	2.57	.9949	.0051
2.33	.9901	.0099	2.58	.9951	.0049
2.34	.9904	.0096	2.59	.9952	.0048
2.35	.9906	.0094	2.60	.9953	.0047
2.36	.9909	.0091	2.61	.9955	.0045
2.37	.9911	.0089	2.62	.9956	.0044
2.38	.9913	.0087	2.63	.9957	.0043
2.39	.9916	.0084	2.64	.9959	.0041
2.40	.9918	.0082	2.65	.9960	.0040
2.41	.9920	.0080	2.66	.9961	.0039
2.42	.9922	.0078	2.67	.9962	.0038
2.43	.9925	.0075	2.68	.9963	.0037
2.44	.9927	.0073	2.69	.9964	.0036
2.45	.9929	.0071	2.70	.9965	.0035
2.46	.9931	.0069	2.71	.9966	.0034
2.47	.9932	.0068	2.72	.9967	.0033
2.48	.9934	.0066	2.73	.9968	.0032
2.49	.9936	.0064	2.74	.9969	.0031
2.50	.9938	.0062	2.75	.9970	.0030
2.51	.9940	.0060	2.76	.9971	.0029
2.52	.9941	.0059	2.77	.9972	.0028
2.53	.9943	.0057	2.78	.9973	.0027
2.54	.9945	.0055	2.79	.9974	.0026
2.55	.9946	.0054	2.80	.9974	.0026

Z score	Below +	Below −	Z score	Below +	Below −
2.81	.9975	.0025	3.06	.9989	.0011
2.82	.9976	.0024	3.07	.9989	.0011
2.83	.9977	.0023	3.08	.9990	.0010
2.84	.9977	.0023	3.09	.9990	.0010
2.85	.9978	.0022	3.10	.9990	.0010
2.86	.9979	.0021	3.11	.9991	.0009
2.87	.9979	.0021	3.12	.9991	.0009
2.88	.9980	.0020	3.13	.9991	.0009
2.89	.9981	.0019	3.14	.9992	.0008
2.90	.9981	.0019	3.15	.9992	.0008
2.91	.9982	.0018	3.16	.9992	.0008
2.92	.9982	.0018	3.17	.9992	.0008
2.93	.9983	.0017	3.18	.9993	.0007
2.94	.9984	.0016	3.19	.9993	.0007
2.95	.9984	.0016	3.20	.9993	.0007
2.96	.9985	.0015	3.21	.9993	.0007
2.97	.9985	.0015	3.22	.9994	.0006
2.98	.9986	.0014	3.23	.9994	.0006
2.99	.9986	.0014	3.24	.9994	.0006
3.00	.9987	.0013			
3.01	.9987	.0013	3.30	.9995	.0005
3.02	.9987	.0013	3.40	.9997	.0003
3.03	.9988	.0012	3.50	.9998	.0002
3.04	.9988	.0012	3.60	.9998	.0002
3.05	.9989	.0011	3.70	.9999	.0001

Note: From *Statistical Methods for the Behavioral Sciences* (pp. 490-499) by A. L. Edwards, 1954, New York: Rinehart. Copyright by Allen L. Edwards Living Trust. Adapted by permission.

Glossary

activities of daily living—Tasks of self-care, communication, home management, mobility, and management of environmental hardware and devices that enable an individual to achieve personal independence in his or her environment.

adaptive testing—Items presented to an individual are not predetermined; following each response, a computer selects a new item that most closely matches the examinee's actual skill level, until a sufficient number of items have been administered to provide a stable estimate of skill.

age or grade equivalent—A number in age or grade units that corresponds directly with the median raw score for that age or grade.

assessment—The assignment of numbers to attributes or characteristics of persons, objects, or events according to explicit formulations or rules (same as measurement).

bottom-up—An approach to assessment, instruction, or intervention that begins at the lowest level of the movement skill taxonomy and moves up to higher levels as mastery is broadly established at the targeted level.

classical score theory—A construct based on the premise that an observed score is the sum of a true score (representing the actual ability of the performer) and an error score (representing the mismatch between an observed and true score). It is also known as classical true-score theory.

concurrent validity—A specific type of criterion-related validity that involves justifying inferences from the results of target measurements by comparing them with inferences from criterion evidence obtained at approximately the same time as the target measurements.

confidence interval—The range of observed scores within which the tester is confident that the true score lies. It is calculated with the standard error of measurement and a Z score corresponding to the selected probability or confidence level.

construct validity—The conceptual or theoretical basis for using a measurement to make an inferred interpretation, established through logical argumentation supported by theoretical and research evidence.

content validity—The extent to which a measurement is judged to reflect the meaningful elements of a construct or a domain of content and not any extraneous elements.

correlation—A depiction of the magnitude and direction of the relationship between two dependent variables.

criterion-referenced test—A test that compares an individual's performance to some predetermined criterion.

criterion-related validity—The extent to which the inferences from the results of an assessment instrument match the inferences from a criterion measurement that is accepted as a standard indicator of the targeted construct or trait.

data—The numbers assigned to attributes or characteristics of persons, objects, or events according to explicit formulations or rules (same as scores).

dependent variable—The actual measurement, assessment, or score used to document performance under a particular set of constraints.

diagnosis—The identification of a potential source of difficulty in performing a movement skill.

364

dynamic systems—Stability and change in movement product or process, focusing on the system variables—related to the performer, the environment, or the task—that drive transitions from one behavior to another.

early movement milestones—The locomotor and object-control skills that emerge before a child attains upright or bipedal locomotion, including rolling over, crawling, creeping, sitting, standing, walking, and object manipulation.

ecological perception—A shortened reference to Gibson's (1979) ecological approach to visual perception. It is founded on the concept of an affordance, which can be defined as the usefulness of an object, event, or environmental feature for the perceiver.

ecological task analysis—An approach to assessment, instruction, and intervention that is based on the fundamental tenets of dynamic systems and ecological perception. It has been developed and advocated by Davis and Burton (Burton & Davis, 1996; Davis & Burton, 1991).

evaluation—A judgment based on a measurement.

factor analysis—A mathematical procedure that isolates common sources of performance variability for a number of tasks. Those tasks with levels of shared or common variance above a set criterion are clustered together as a factor. Factors are subjectively labeled, usually on the basis of the construct or trait that is common to all tasks in the cluster.

fine motor skills—Ability to perform movements with smaller muscles, usually involving precise manipulation of small objects with the hands and fingers.

formal test—A test with standardized or uniform conditions and directions; also referred to as a standardized test.

functional movement skills—Movement skills, either early movement milestones, fundamental movement skills, or specialized movement skills, performed in their natural and meaningful contexts.

fundamental movement skills—The locomotor and object-control skills performed in an upright or bipedal position that are used by persons in all cultures of the world. These, as well as early movement milestones, are also referred to as phylogenetic skills because of their universal occurrence.

generalizability theory—A construct in which measurement error is partitioned into a number of individual factors or facets, rather than just a single error term as in classical test theory.

gross motor skills—Ability to perform movements with larger muscles, usually involving movement of the body through space or manipulation of larger objects.

independent variable—A factor that is under the control of and is manipulated by the experimenter or examiner.

informal test—A test that cannot be categorized as formal; that is, a test that does not have standardized or uniform conditions and directions. Also referred to as a nonstandardized test.

interclass correlation—A bivariate statistic, such as the Pearson product-moment correlation coefficient, designed to quantify the relationship between two different variables, not comparisons between repetitions of the same variable.

internal consistency—The extent to which items or elements that contribute to a measurement reflect one basic phenomenon or dimension.

interrater reliability—The consistency or equivalence of the same performance measured by different raters; the consistency between raters.

interval measurement—A level of measurement involving different numbers assigned to different values of a given property (distinctiveness), larger numbers representing more of the property (ordering in magnitude), and equal differences in numbers reflecting equal differences in the property being measured (equal intervals).

intraclass correlation—A relational statistic determined by running a repeated measures analysis of variance and then creating a ratio including the equivalents of true-score and observed-score variances.

intrarater reliability—The consistency or equivalence of the same performance measured at different times by the same rater; the consistency within a rater. The only way the same performance can be measured at different times by the same rater is by recording the performance on videotape or film.

item response theory—A construct in which the characteristics of test items are invariant across different tests and different populations, assuming that the tests measure the same general ability. In most cases, a person's performance on several items is used to determine where the individual lies on a single scale of item difficulty. It is then assumed that the person should be able to successfully perform items lower on the scale and to have difficulty with items higher on the scale.

judgment-based evaluation—A process of collecting, structuring, and usually quantifying the impressions of professionals and caregivers about characteristics of the performer and the given environment. The most common methods of gathering information are questionnaires, inventories, and ratings scales.

kappa—A coefficient of agreement that corrects for chance agreements.

linear regression—A line that best represents the scatter of points for a set of paired dependent variables. It can be used to make predictions about one variable, given a score on the other, with the correlation coefficient indicating the degree of confidence that should be placed in the predictions.

logit—A ratio score derived from a Rasch model of item response theory.

mean—The arithmetic average, which is the sum of all scores divided by the number of scores.

measurement—The assignment of numbers to attributes or characteristics of persons, objects, or events according to explicit formulations or rules (same as assessment).

median—The score in the distribution that divides the data into two equal-sized groups.

mode—The score that occurs most frequently in a distribution.

motor—Aspects of movement that are not directly observable: neuromuscular or internal motor processes or the underlying factors that affect movement.

motor abilities—General traits or capacities of an individual that underlie the performance of a variety of movement skills. These traits are assumed to not be easily modified by practice or experience and to be relatively stable across an individual's lifetime. The term also can refer to a person's potential movement competencies as opposed to a person's actual movement performances.

motor development—Adaptive or functional changes in movement behavior over the life span and the processes or factors that underlie these changes (same as movement skill development).

movement—The observable act of moving; that is, an observable change in the position of any part of the body.

movement function—Similar to movement task (the intention of the performer in moving; what the performer attempts to accomplish), but implying goal-directed behavior with both purpose and meaning.

movement performance—Goal-directed movement that can be described in terms of product or process.

movement process—The movement pattern or form used to produce the movement outcome, as well as the mechanisms that underlie the movement performance.

movement product—As usually viewed, a performance outcome expressed in terms of metrics of distance (in inches, feet, yards, miles, centimeters, meters, or kilometers), time (in milliseconds, seconds, minutes, or hours), mass (in pounds or kilograms), energy (in kilocalories), or frequency or number of repetitions.

movement skill—A qualitative expression of movement performance, or a specific class of goal-directed movement patterns, such as running, throwing, hammering, driving, writing, or speaking.

movement skill assessment—The assignment of numbers to movement-related attributes or characteristics of persons.

movement skill development—Adaptive or functional changes in movement behavior over the life span and the processes or factors that underlie these changes (same as motor development).

movement skill foundations—Not movement skills themselves, but all aspects of a person—physical, mental, and emotional—that facilitate or limit his/her performance of movement skills.

movement task—The intention of the performer in moving; in other words, what the performer attempts to accomplish.

nominal measurement—A level of measurement having only the property of distinctiveness. That is, different numbers are assigned to different values of the same property in such a way that those with the same number are considered to be equivalent and those with different numbers are not equivalent.

norm-referenced test—A test that compares an individual's performance to the performance of a normative group.

normal curve—A bell-shaped distribution of scores with most scores congregating near the middle and scores becoming progressively fewer at the two extremes. The curve is symmetrical, so the mean marks the middle of the curve and is thus equivalent to the median.

normalized score—A score created when raw scores are transformed to smooth out deviations from normality. A stanine is a specific type of normalized score.

ontogenetic skills—Movement skills that are not universal but are unique for each person. In this book, these are called specialized movement skills.

ordinal measurement—A level of measurement involving different numbers assigned to different values of a given property (distinctiveness), with larger numbers representing more of the property (ordering in magnitude).

parallel-forms reliability—The consistency or agreement of performance measurements with different (or alternative) forms of a test by the same rater; indicates whether measurements obtained with different forms of a test can be used interchangeably; the consistency between forms; also termed equivalence.

percent agreement—A calculation obtained by dividing the number of exact score agreements between two rating situations (e.g., two raters on the same testing or two testings rated by the same person) by the total number of scores, multiplied by 100.

percentile—The percentage of scores that fall below or are equal to a particular score.

phylogenetic skills—Movement abilities that are universal, or found in almost all humans, referred to in this book as early movement milestones and fundamental movement skills.

predictive validity—A specific type of criterion-related validity that involves justifying inferences regarding future events or conditions from the results of target measurements by comparing them with inferences from criterion evidence obtained at a later time than the target measurements.

prescriptive validity—A specific type of criterion-related validity that involves justifying inferences regarding instruction or treatment from the results of target measurements by comparing them with inferences from measurements of a successful outcome of the chosen instruction or treatment.

range—For discrete numbers, such as frequency, the difference between the highest and lowest scores in the distribution plus 1; for continuous numbers, such as distance or time, just the difference between highest and lowest scores, without the added 1.

ratio measurement—A level of measurement involving different numbers assigned to different values of a given property (distinctiveness), with larger numbers representing more of the property (ordering in magnitude), equal differences in numbers reflecting equal differences in the property being measured (equal intervals), and a measurement of zero indicating the absence of the property being measured (absolute zero).

reliability—The degree to which test scores are consistent, dependable, or repeatable; that is, the degree to which they are free of measurement error.

score—A number assigned to an attribute or characteristic of persons, objects, or events according to explicit formulations or rules (same as data).

score transformation—The conversion (transformation) of absolute raw scores into numbers that carry comparative or relative information, such as percentiles; standard, or Z, scores; standardized scores; normalized scores; and age or grade equivalents.

sensitivity—The likelihood that a positive test results in accurately predicting a person with disease or impairment, or the true-positive rate.

specialized movement skills—Combinations or variations of one or more early movement milestones and/or fundamental movement skills that are specific to particular tasks. These skills are not performed by persons in all cultures, nor by all persons in any single culture, and thus may be considered to be ontogenetic skills.

specificity—The likelihood that a negative test results in accurately predicting a person without disease or impairment, or the true-negative rate.

standard or Z score—A raw score converted to or expressed in standard deviation units.

standard deviation—A standardized index of the alignment of a set of scores around the mean of the distribution, described specifically as the square root of the average squared deviation or variance of the scores from the mean.

standard error of measurement—An expression of the variation between an observed score and a true score in terms of a standard deviation from the observed score, allowing the test user to calculate the probability that the true score will fall within a certain range of values, specified in terms of raw and/or normative scores.

standardized score—A linear transformation of a standard or Z score to any mean value and to any standard deviation value.

stanine—A specific type of normalized score, with values from 1 to 9, each corresponding to a particular range of standard scores.

taxonomy—A system of classification involving the arrangement of objects or entities into groups or sets based on the relationships between their observed or inferred properties.

test—A device for obtaining a sample of a person's behavior or the procedure or set of procedures that is used to obtain measurements or data.

test-retest reliability—The consistency or equivalence of repeated performances separated in time measured by the same rater; the consistency between testings; also termed stability.

top-down—Characterizing an approach to assessment, instruction, or intervention that begins at the highest level possible in the movement skill taxonomy and moves down to lower levels only as deficits in specific skills are revealed.

validity—The appropriateness, meaningfulness, and usefulness of the specific inferences made from test scores.

variance—An index of the alignment of a set of scores around the mean of the distribution, described specifically as the average squared deviation or variance of the scores from the mean.

References

Adams, A.R. (1954). *A test construction study of sport-type motor educability test for college men.* Unpublished doctoral dissertation, Louisiana State University, Baton Rouge.

Adams, J.A. (1987). Historical review and appraisal of research on the learning, retention, and transfer of human motor skills. *Psychological Bulletin, 101,* 41-74.

Alden, F.D., Horton, M.O., & Caldwell, G.M. (1932). A motor ability test for university women for the classification of entering students into homogeneous groups. *Research Quarterly, 3,* 85-120.

Allen, M.J., & Yen, W.M. (1979). *Introduction to measurement theory.* Monterey, CA: Brooks/Cole.

Amar, J. (1920). *The human motor.* London: Routledge & Sons.

American Alliance for Health, Physical Education, Recreation and Dance. (1984). *AAHPERD skills test manual: Basketball for boys and girls.* Reston, VA: Author.

American College of Sports Medicine. (1991). *Guidelines for exercise testing and prescription* (4th ed.). Philadelphia: Lea & Febiger.

American Medical Association. (1988). *Guides to the evaluation of permanent impairment* (3rd ed.). Chicago: Author.

American Welding Society Committee on Qualification. (1983). *Standard for welding procedure and performance qualification.* Miami, FL: American Welding Society.

Ames, L.B. (1989). *Arnold Gesell—themes of his work.* New York: Human Sciences Press.

Amundson, S.J.C., & Crowe, T.K. (1993). Clinical applications of the standard error of measurement for occupational and physical therapists. *Physical and Occupational Therapy in Pediatrics, 12,* 57-71.

Anderson, R., Bargowski, E., & Blodgett, W.H. (1961). *A code method for evaluating function in cerebral palsy.* Detroit: Detroit Orthopaedic Clinic.

Andriuolo, R. (1993). *Firefighter* (10th ed.). New York: Prentice Hall.

Andrus, R. (1924). *A tentative inventory of the habits of children from two to four years of age* (Columbia University, Teachers College, Contributions to Education, No. 160). New York: Columbia University, Teachers College.

Angoff, W.H. (1988). Validity: An evolving concept. In H. Wainer & H.I. Braun (Eds.), *Test validity* (pp. 19-32). Hillsdale, NJ: Erlbaum.

Aponte, R., French, R., & Sherrill, C. (1990). Motor development of Puerto Rican children: Cross-cultural perspectives. *Perceptual and Motor Skills, 71,* 1200-1202.

Arnheim, D.D., & Sinclair, W.A. (1979). The clumsy child: A program of motor therapy (2nd ed.). St. Louis: Mosby.

Astrand, P.-O., & Rhyming, I. (1954). A nomogram for calculation of aerobic capacity (physical fitness) from pulse rate during submaximal work. *Journal of Applied Physiology, 7,* 218-221.

Astrand, P.-O., & Rodahl, K. (1986). *Textbook of work physiology: Physiological bases of exercise* (3rd ed.). New York: McGraw-Hill.

Auxter, D., & Pyfer, J. (1985). *Principles and methods of adapted physical education and recreation* (5th ed.). St. Louis: Times Mirror/Mosby.

Ayres, A.J. (1962). *The Ayres Space Test.* Los Angeles: Western Psychological Services.

Ayres, A.J. (1964). *Southern California Motor Accuracy Test.* Los Angeles: Western Psychological Services.

Ayres, A.J. (1968). *Southern California Perceptual-Motor Tests.* Los Angeles: Western Psychological Services.

Ayres, A.J. (1972a). Improving academic scores through sensory integration. *Journal of Learning Disabilities, 5,* 339-343.

Ayres, A.J. (1972b). *Sensory integration and learning disorders.* Los Angeles: Western Psychological Services.

Ayres, A.J. (1972c). *Southern California Sensory Integration Tests.* Los Angeles: Western Psychological Services.

Ayres, A.J. (1989). *Sensory Integration and Praxis Tests.* Los Angeles: Western Psychological Services.

Bagnato, S.J., Neisworth, J.T., & Capone, A. (1986). Curriculum-based assessment for the young exceptional child: Rationale and review. *Topics in Early Childhood Special Education, 6*(2), 97-110.

Balan, C.M., & Davis, W.E. (1993). Ecological task analysis—an approach to teaching physical education. *Journal of Physical Education, Recreation & Dance, 64*(9), 54-61.

Barnett, A., & Henderson, S.E. (1992). Some observations on the figure drawings of clumsy children. *British Journal of Educational Psychology, 62,* 341-355.

Bar-Or, O. (1993). Importance of differences between children and adults for exercise testing and exercise prescription. In J.S. Skinner (Ed.), *Exercise testing and exercise prescription for special cases* (pp. 57-74). Philadelphia: Lea & Febiger.

Barrow, H.M. (1924). A general athletic ability test. *American Physical Education Review, 29,* 506-510.

Barrow, H.M. (1954). Test of motor ability for college men. *Research Quarterly, 25,* 253-260.

Bartko, J.J., & Carpenter, W.T. (1976). On the methods and theory of reliability. *Journal of Nervous and Mental Disease, 163,* 307-317.

Baumgartner, R.N., Chumlea, W.C., & Roche, A.F. (1990). Bioelectrical impedance for body composition. *Exercise and Sport Sciences Reviews, 18,* 193-224.

Baumgartner, T.A. (1989). Norm-referenced measurement: Reliability. In M.J. Safrit & T.M. Wood (Eds.), *Measurement concepts in physical education and exercise science* (pp. 45-72). Champaign, IL: Human Kinetics.

Baumgartner, T.A., & Jackson, A.S. (1991). *Measurement for evaluation in physical education and exercise science* (4th ed.). Dubuque, IA: Brown.

Bayley, N. (1935). The development of motor abilities during the first three years. *Monographs of the Society for Research in Child Development, 1*(1), 1-26.

Bayley, N. (1969). *Bayley Scales of Infant Development.* New York: Psychological Corporation.

Bayley, N. (1993). *Bayley Scales of Infant Development* (2nd ed.). San Antonio: Therapy Skill Builders.

Beery, K.E. (1967). *Developmental Test of Visual-Motor Integration administration and scoring manual.* Chicago: Follett.

Benson, J.B. (1993). Season of birth and onset of locomotion: Theoretical and methodological implications. *Infant Behavior and Development, 16,* 69-81.

Berg, K., Wood-Dauphinee, S., & Williams, J. (1995). The Balance Scale: Reliability assessment with elderly residents and patients with acute stroke. *Scandinavian Journal of Rehabilitation Medicine, 27,* 27-36.

Berg, K. ,Wood-Dauphinee, S., Williams, J., & Maki, B. (1992). Measuring balance in the elderly: Validation of an instrument. *Canadian Journal of Public Health, 83,* S7-S11.

Bergenn, V.W., Dalton, T.C., & Lipsitt, L.P. (1992). Myrtle B. McGraw: A growth scientist. *Developmental Psychology, 28,* 381-395.

Berk, R.A. (1979). Generalizability of behavioral observations: A clarification of interobserver agreement and interobserver reliability. *American Journal of Mental Deficiency, 83,* 460-472.

Berk, R.I. (1957). A comparison of performance of subnormal, normal, and gifted children on the Oseretsky Tests of Motor Proficiency. *Dissertation Abstracts, 17*, 1947-1948.

Bertenthal, B.I., Campos, J.J., & Barrett, K.C. (1984). Self-produced locomotion: An organizer of emotional, cognitive, and social development in infancy. In R.N. Emde & R.J. Harmon (Eds.), *Continuities and discontinuities in development* (pp. 175-210). New York: Plenum Press.

Bialer, I., Doll, L., & Winsberg, B.G. (1973). *Modified Lincoln-Oseretsky Motor Development Scale.* New York: New York State Department of Mental Hygiene.

Bialer, I., Doll, L., & Winsberg, B.G. (1974). A Modified Lincoln-Oseretsky Motor Development Scale: Provisional standardization. *Perceptual and Motor Skills, 38*, 599-614.

Bidabe, L., & Lollar, J.M. (1990). *Mobility opportunities via education.* Bakersfield, CA: Office of Kern County Superintendent of Schools.

Bledsoe, N.P., & Shepherd, J.T. (1982). A study of reliability and validity of a pre-school play scale. *American Journal of Occupational Therapy, 36*, 783-788.

Bliss, J.G. (1927). A study of progression based on age, sex and individual differences in strength and skill. *American Physical Education Review, 32*, 11-21, 85-99.

Block, M.E. (1994). *A teacher's guide to including students with disabilities in regular physical education.* Baltimore: Brookes.

Bogle Thorbahn, L.D., & Newton, R.A. (1996). Use of the Berg Balance Test to predict falls in elderly persons. *Physical Therapy, 76*, 576-583.

Bolton, T.L. (1903). The relation of motor power to intelligence. *American Journal of Psychology, 14*, 351-367.

Borg, G. (1970). Perceived exertion as an indicator of somatic stress. *Scandinavian Journal of Rehabilitation Medicine, 2*, 92-98.

Borg, G. (1982). Psychophysical bases of perceived exertion. *Medicine and Science in Sports and Exercise, 14*, 377-381.

Borg, G. (1985). *An introduction to Borg's RPE scale.* Ithaca, NY: Mouvement.

Bottos, M., Dalla Barba, B., Stefani, D., Pettena, G., Tonin, C., & D'Este, A. (1989). Locomotor strategies preceding independent walking: Prospective study of neurological and language development in 424 cases. *Developmental Medicine and Child Neurology, 31*, 25-34.

Bottos, M., Puato, M.L., Vianello, A., & Facchin, P. (1995). Locomotion patterns in cerebral palsy syndromes. *Developmental Medicine and Child Neurology, 37*, 883-899.

Bouffard, M., & Wall, A.E. (1990). A problem solving approach to movement skill acquisition: Implications for special populations. In G. Reid (Ed.), *Problems in movement control* (pp. 107-131). Amsterdam: North-Holland.

Boulton, J.E., Kirsch, S.E., Chipman, M., Etele, E., White, A.M., & Pape, K.E. (1995). Reliability of the Peabody Developmental Gross Motor Scale in children with cerebral palsy. *Physical and Occupational Therapy in Pediatrics, 15*, 35-51.

Bovard, J.F., & Cozens, F.W. (1930). *Tests and measurements in physical education.* Philadelphia: Saunders.

Boyce, W.F., Gowland, C., Hardy, S., Rosenbaum, P.L., Lane, M., Plews, N., Goldsmith, C., & Russell, D.J. (1991). Development of a quality-of-movement measure for children with cerebral palsy. *Physical Therapy, 71*, 820-832.

Boyce, W.F., Gowland, C., Rosenbaum, P.L., Lane, M., Plews, N., Goldsmith, C.H., Russell, D.J., Wright, V., Potter, S., & Harding, D. (1995). The Gross Motor Performance Measure: Validity and responsiveness of a measure of quality of movement. *Physical Therapy, 75*, 603-613.

Brace, D.K. (1924). Possibilities of tests in physical education. *American Physical Education Review, 29*, 506-513.

Brace, D.K. (1926). The classification of tests in physical education. *American Physical Education Review, 31,* 1113-1118.

Brace, D.K. (1927a). *Measuring motor ability: A scale of motor ability tests.* New York: Barnes.

Brace, D.K. (1927b). Possibilities of tests in physical education. *American Physical Education Review, 32,* 506-513.

Brace, D.K. (1931). The development of measures of pupil achievement in physical education. *Research Quarterly, 2,* 32-37.

Branta, C., Haubenstricker, J., & Seefeldt, V. (1984). Age changes in motor skills during childhood and adolescence. *Exercise and Sport Sciences Reviews, 12,* 467-520.

Bray, G.A. (1994). Commentary on classics in obesity 1. Quetelet: Quantitative medicine. *Obesity Research, 2,* 68-71.

Bricker, D. (Ed.). (1993). *Assessment, Evaluation, and Programming System for Infants and Children. Vol. 1: AEPS measurement for birth to three years.* Baltimore: Brookes.

Bricker, D., Bailey, E., & Slentz, K. (1990). Reliability, validity and utility of the Evaluation and Programming System: For Infants and Young Children (EPS-I). *Journal of Early Intervention, 14,* 147-160.

Bricker, D., Janko, S., Cripe, J., Bailey, E., & Kaminski, R. (1989). *Evaluation and Programming System: For Infants and Young Children.* Eugene, OR: University of Oregon, Center for Human Development.

Bricker, D., & Pretti-Frontczak, K. (Eds.). (1996). *Assessment, Evaluation, and Programming System for Infants and Children. Vol. 3: AEPS measurement for three to six years.* Baltimore: Brookes.

Bricker, D., & Squires, J. (1989). *Infant Monitoring System.* Eugene, OR: University of Oregon, Center for Human Development.

Bricker, D., & Waddell, M. (Eds.). (1996). *Assessment, Evaluation, and Programming System for Infants and Children. Vol. 4: AEPS curriculum for three to six years.* Baltimore: Brookes.

Brigance, A.H. (1991). *Revised Brigance Diagnostic Inventory of Early Development.* North Billerica, MA: Curriculum Associates.

Broadhead, G.D. (1985). Placement of mildly handicapped children in mainstream physical education. *Adapted Physical Activity Quarterly, 2,* 307-313.

Broadhead, G.D., & Bruininks, R.H. (1982). Childhood motor performance traits on the short-form of the Bruininks-Oseretsky test. *The Physical Educator, 39,* 149-155.

Brown, M.E. (1950a). Daily activity inventory and progress record for those with atypical movement: Part 1. *American Journal of Occupational Therapy, 4,* 195-204.

Brown, M.E. (1950b). Daily activity inventory and progress record for those with atypical movement: Part 2. *American Journal of Occupational Therapy, 4,* 261-272.

Brown, M.E. (1951). Daily activity inventory and progress record for those with atypical movement: Part 3. *American Journal of Occupational Therapy, 5,* 23-29, 38.

Brown, M.E., & Van Der Bogert, M. (1953). Pre-vocational motor skill inventory: Preliminary report. *American Journal of Occupational Therapy, 7,* 153-163, 188.

Brozek, J., Grande, J., Anderson, T., & Keys, A. (1963). Densitometric analysis of body composition: A review of some quantitative assumptions. *Annals of the New York Academy of Sciences, 110,* 113-140.

Bruce, R.A., Kusumi, F., & Hosmer, D. (1973). Maximal oxygen intake and nomographic assessment of functional aerobic impairment in cardiovascular disease. *American Heart Journal, 85,* 545-562.

Bruett, T.L., & Overs, R.P. (1969). A critical review of 12 ADL scales. *Physical Therapy, 49,* 857-862.

Bruininks, R.H. (1978). *Bruininks-Oseretsky test of motor proficiency examiner's manual.* Circle Pines, MN: American Guidance Service.

Bullard, W.N. (1886). Dynamometer. In A.H. Buck (Ed.), *A reference handbook of the medical sciences* (Vol. 2) (pp. 544-546). New York: Wood.

Bundy, A.C. (1993). Assessment of play and leisure: Delineation of the problem. *American Journal of Occupational Therapy, 47,* 217-222.

Bundy, A.C. (1995). Assessment and intervention in school-based practice: Answering questions and minimizing discrepancies. *Physical and Occupational Therapy in Pediatrics, 15,* 69-88.

Burnside, L. (1927). Coordination in the locomotion of infants. *Genetic Psychology Monographs, 2,* 283-372.

Burry-Stock, J.A., Shaw, D.G., Laurie, C., & Chissom, B. (1996). Rater agreement indexes for performance assessment. *Educational and Psychological Measurement, 56,* 251-262.

Burton, A.W. (1987). Confronting the interaction between perception and movement in adapted physical education. *Adapted Physical Activity Quarterly, 4,* 257-267.

Burton, A.W. (1993). *Movement Skill Foundations Checklist.* Unpublished checklist, University of Minnesota, Minneapolis.

Burton, A.W., & Davis, W.E. (1992a). Assessing balance in adapted physical education: Fundamental concepts and applications. *Adapted Physical Activity Quarterly, 9,* 14-46.

Burton, A.W., & Davis, W.E. (1992b). Optimizing the involvement and performance of children with physical impairments in movement activities. *Pediatric Exercise Science, 4,* 236-248.

Burton, A.W., & Davis, W.E. (1996). Ecological task analysis: Theoretical and empirical foundations. *Human Movement Science, 15,* 285-314.

Burton, A.W., Greer, N.L., & Wiese, D.M. (1992). Changes in overhand throwing patterns as a function of ball size. *Pediatric Exercise Science, 4,* 50-67.

Burton, A.W., Greer, N.L., & Wiese-Bjornstal, D.M. (1993). Variations in grasping and throwing patterns as a function of ball size. *Pediatric Exercise Science, 5,* 25-41.

Burton, A.W., & Welch, B.A. (1990). Dribbling performance in first-grade children: Effect of ball and hand size and ball-size preferences. *The Physical Educator, 47,* 48-51.

Campbell, S.K. (1991). Framework for the measurement of neurologic impairment and disability. In M.J. Lister (Ed.), *Contemporary management of motor control problems* (pp. 143-153). Alexandria, VA: Foundation for Physical Therapy.

Campbell, S.K. (1993a). Commentary on: Measurement validity in physical therapy research. *Physical Therapy, 73,* 110-113.

Campbell, S.K. (1993b). Future directions for physical therapy assessment in early infancy. In I.J. Wilhelm (Ed.), *Physical therapy assessment in early infancy* (pp. 293-308). New York: Churchill Livingstone.

Campbell, S.K. (1995). The child's development of functional movement. In S.K. Campbell (Ed.), *Physical therapy for children* (pp. 3-37). Philadelphia: Saunders.

Carpenter, A. (1942). The measurement of general motor capacity and general motor ability in the first three grades. *Research Quarterly, 13,* 444-465.

Carter, J.E.L., & Heath, B.H. (1990). *Somatotyping—development and applications.* New York: Cambridge University Press.

Case-Smith, J. (1991). *Posture and fine motor assessment of infants.* Rockville, MD: American Occupational Therapy Foundation.

Case-Smith, J. (1992). A validity study of the Posture and Fine Motor Assessment of Infants. *American Journal of Occupational Therapy, 46,* 597-605.

Cassel, R.H. (1949). The Vineland Adaptation of the Oseretsky Tests. *Training School Bulletin,* Monograph Suppl., No. 1, 1-32.

Chamberlain, D. (1969). *Determination of validity and reliability of a skill test for the bounce pass in volleyball.* Unpublished master's thesis, Brigham Young University, Provo, UT.

Chandler, L.S., Andrews, M.S., & Swanson, M.W. (1980). *Movement Assessment of Infants: A manual.* Rolling Bay, WA: Authors.

Chen, H., & Wooley, P.V. (1978). A developmental assessment chart for non-institutionalized Down syndrome children. *Growth, 42,* 157-165.

Christiansen, L., & Mendoza, J.L. (1986). A method of assessing change in a single subject: An alteration of the RC index. *Behavior Therapy, 17,* 305-308.

Christianson, C. (1993). Continuing challenges of functional assessment in rehabilitation: Recommended changes. *American Journal of Occupational Therapy, 47,* 258-259.

Cintas, H.L. (1995). Cross-cultural similarities and differences in development and the impact of parental expectations on motor behavior. *Pediatric Physical Therapy, 7,* 103-111.

Clark, J.E., & Phillips, S.J. (1985). A developmental sequence of the standing long jump. In J.E. Clark & J.H. Humphrey (Eds.), *Motor development: Current selected research* (Vol. 1) (pp. 73-85). Princeton, NJ: Princeton Book.

Clark, J.E., & Whitall, J. (1989a). Changing patterns of locomotion: From walking to skipping. In M.H. Woollacott & A. Shumway-Cook (Eds.), *Development of posture and gait across the lifespan* (pp. 128-151). Columbia, SC: University of South Carolina Press.

Clark, J.E., & Whitall, J. (1989b). What is motor development: The lessons of history. *Quest, 41,* 183-202.

Clarke, H.H. (1967). *Application of measurement to health and physical education* (4th ed.). Englewood Cliffs, NJ: Prentice Hall.

Clifton, R.K., Muir, D.W., Ashmead, D.H., & Clarkson, M.G. (1993). Is visually guided reaching in early infancy a myth? *Child Development, 64,* 1099-1110.

Cohen, H., Blatchly, C.A., & Gombash, L.L. (1993). A study of the Clinical Test of Sensory Interaction and Balance. *Physical Therapy, 73,* 346-354.

Cohen, J. (1960). A coefficient of agreement for nominal scales. *Educational and Psychological Measurement, 20,* 37-46.

Cohen, J. (1968). Weighted kappa: Nominal scale agreement with provision for scaled disagreement or partial credit. *Psychological Bulletin, 70,* 213-220.

Cohen, J. (1969). *Statistical power analysis for the behavioral sciences.* New York: Academic Press.

Cole, E., Wood, T.M., & Dunn, J.M. (1991). Item response theory: A useful test theory for adapted physical education. *Adapted Physical Activity Quarterly, 8,* 317-332.

Cole, N.S. (1995). Comments on Chapters 1-3. In N. Frederiksen, R.J. Mislevy, & I.I. Bejar (Eds.), *Test theory for a new generation of tests* (pp. 72-77). Hillsdale, NJ: Erlbaum.

Coley, I.L. (1978). *Pediatric Assessment of Self-Care Activities.* St. Louis: Mosby.

Commission on Practice. (1993). Position paper: Purposeful activity. *American Journal of Occupational Therapy, 47,* 1081-1082.

Commission on Practice. (1995). Position paper: Occupational performance: Occupational therapy's definition of function. *American Journal of Occupational Therapy, 49,* 1019-1029.

Committee of the American Physical Education Association. (1924). Motor ability tests. *American Physical Education Review, 29*, 579-590.

Committee on Children with Disabilities. (1992) Pediatrician's role in the development and implementation of an Individual Education Plan (IEP) and/or an Individual Family Service Plan (IFSP). *Pediatrics, 89*, 340-342.

Committee on Tests. (1913a). The Athletic Badge for Boys. *The Playground, 7*, 33-37.

Committee on Tests. (1913b). The Athletic Badge for Girls. *The Playground, 7*, 57-60.

Committee to Develop Standards for Educational and Psychological Testing of the American Educational Research Association, the American Psychological Association, and the National Council on Measurement in Education. (1985). *Standards for educational and psychological testing.* Washington, DC: American Psychological Association.

Connolly, K.J. (1984). The assessment of motor performance in children. In J. Brozek, & B. Schurch (Eds.), *Malnutrition and behavior: Critical assessment of key issues* (pp. 230-259). Lausanne, Switzerland: Nestle Foundation.

Connolly, K.J., & Elliott, J.M. (1972). The evolution and ontogeny of hand function. In N. Blurton-Jones (Ed.), *Ethological studies of child behaviour* (pp. 329-383). Cambridge, England: Cambridge University Press.

Cooper, K.H. (1968). A means of assessing maximal oxygen intake. *Journal of the American Medical Association, 203*, 135-138.

Cowan, E.A., & Pratt, B.M. (1934). The hurdle jump as a developmental and diagnostic test of motor coordination for children from three to twelve years of age. *Child Development, 5*, 107-121.

Cozens, F.W. (1928). The measurement of general athletic ability in college men. *American Physical Education Review, 33*, 634-638.

Cozens, F.W. (1936). *Achievement scales in physical education activities for college men.* Philadelphia: Lea & Febiger.

Cozens, F.W., Cubberly, H.J., & Neilson, N.P. (1937). *Achievement scales in physical education activities for secondary school girls and college women.* New York: Barnes.

Cozens, F.W., & Neilson, N.P. (1934). *Achievement scales in physical education activities for boys and girls in elementary and junior high schools.* New York: Barnes.

Cozens, F.W., Trieb, M.H., & Neilson, N.P. (1936). *Achievement scales in physical education activities for boys in secondary schools.* New York: Barnes.

Cratty, B.J. (1969). *Perceptual-motor behavior and educational processes.* Springfield, IL: Charles C. Thomas.

Cratty, B.J. (1974). *Motor activity and the education of retardates.* Philadelphia: Lea & Febiger.

Cratty, B.J. (1989). *Adapted physical education in the mainstream* (2nd ed.). Denver: Love.

Creighton, C. (1992). The origin and evaluation of activity analysis. *American Journal of Occupational Therapy, 46*, 45-48.

Cripe, J., Slentz, K., & Bricker, D. (Eds.) (1993). *Assessment, Evaluation, and Programming System for Infants and Children. Vol. 2: AEPS curriculum for birth to three years.* Baltimore: Brookes.

Cronbach, L.J., Gleser, G.C., Nanda, H., & Rajaratnam, N. (1972). *The dependability of behavioral measurements: Theory of generalizability for scores and profiles.* New York: Wiley.

Cronbach, L.J., & Meehl, P.E. (1955). Construct validity in psychological tests. *Psychological Bulletin, 52*, 281-302.

Crouchman, M. (1986). The effects of babywalkers on early locomotor development. *Developmental Medicine and Child Neurology, 28*, 757-761.

Crowe, T.K. (1989). Pediatric assessments: A survey of their use by occupational therapists in northwestern school systems. *Occupational Therapy Journal of Research, 9,* 273-286.

Crowe, T.K., Deitz, J.C., Richardson, P.K., & Atwater, S.W. (1990). Interrater reliability of the Pediatric Clinical Test of Sensory Interaction for Balance. *Physical and Occupational Therapy in Pediatrics, 10,* 1-27.

Cunningham, B.V. (1927). An experiment in measuring gross motor development of infants and young children. *Journal of Educational Psychology, 18,* 458-464.

Currie, C. (1969). Evaluating function of mentally retarded children through the use of toys and play activities. *American Journal of Occupational Therapy, 23,* 35-42.

da Costa, M.I.L. (1946-1947). The Ozeretzky Tests: Method, value and results (Portuguese adaptation). *Training School Bulletin, 43,* 1-13, 27-38, 50-59, 62-74.

Davis, J.A. (1995). Direct determination of aerobic power. In P.J. Maud & C. Foster (Eds.), *Physiological assessment of human fitness* (pp. 9-17). Champaign, IL: Human Kinetics.

Davis, W.E. (1984). Motor ability assessment of populations with handicapping conditions: Challenging basic assumptions. *Adapted Physical Activity Quarterly, 1,* 125-140.

Davis, W.E., & Burton, A.W. (1991). Ecological task analysis: Translating movement behavior theory into practice. *Adapted Physical Activity Quarterly, 8,* 154-177.

DeGangi, G.A., & Berk, R.A. (1983a). *DeGangi-Berk Test of Sensory Integration.* Los Angeles: Western Psychological Services.

DeGangi, G.A., & Berk, R.A. (1983b). Psychometric analysis of the Test of Sensory Integration. *Physical and Occupational Therapy in Pediatrics, 3*(2), 43-60.

DeGangi, G.A., Berk, R.A., & Valvano, J. (1983). Test of motor and neurological functions in high-risk infants: Preliminary findings. *Journal of Developmental and Behavioral Pediatrics, 4,* 182-189.

Deitz, J.C., Richardson, P., Atwater, S.W., Crowe, T.K., & Odiorne, M. (1991). Performance of normal children on the Pediatric Clinical Test of Sensory Interaction for Balance. *Occupational Therapy Journal of Research, 11,* 336-356.

De La Hire, M. (1699). Examen de la force de l'homme. *Memoires de l'Academie Royale des Sciences, 12,* 153-162.

Den Ouden, L., Rijken, M., Brand, R., Verloove-Vanhorick, S.P., & Ruys, J.H. (1991). Is it correct to correct? Developmental milestones in 555 "normal" preterm infants compared with term infants. *Journal of Pediatrics, 118,* 399-404.

Dickinson, R.V. (1968). The specificity of flexibility. *Research Quarterly, 38,* 729-794.

DiFabio, R.P. (1995). Sensitivity and specificity of platform posturography for identifying patients with vestibular dysfunction. *Physical Therapy, 75,* 290-305.

Doll, E.A. (Ed.). (1946). *The Oseretsky Tests of Motor Proficiency: A translation from the Portuguese translation.* Circle Pines, MN: American Guidance Service.

Donahoe, B., Turner, D., & Worrell, T. (1994). The use of functional reach as a measurement of balance in boys and girls without disabilities ages 5 to 15 years. *Pediatric Physical Therapy, 6,* 189-193.

Doudlah, A. (1976). *A motor development checklist.* Madison, WI: Central Wisconsin Center for the Developmentally Disabled.

Dummer, G.M., Haubenstricker, J.L., & Stewart, D.A. (1996). Motor skill performances of children who are deaf. *Adapted Physical Activity Quarterly, 13,* 400-414.

Duncan, P.W., Weiner, D.K., Chandler, J., & Studenski, S. (1990). Functional reach: A new measure of balance. *Journals of Gerontology, 45,* M192-M197.

Dunn, J., & Fait, H. (1989). *Special physical education: Adapted, individualized, developmental* (6th ed.). Dubuque, IA: Brown.

Dunn, J.M., & Ponticelli, J. (1988, April). *The effect of two different communication modes on motor performance test scores of hearing impaired children.* Presentation at the American Alliance for Health, Physical Education, Recreation and Dance Convention, Kansas City, MO.

Dunn, W., & McGourty, L. (1989). Application of uniform terminology to practice. *American Journal of Occupational Therapy, 43,* 817-831.

Dworkin, P.H. (1989a).Developmental screening—expecting the impossible? *Pediatrics, 83,* 619-622.

Dworkin, P.H. (1989b). British and American recommendations for developmental monitoring: The role of surveillance. *Pediatrics, 84,* 1000-1010.

Ebbeling, C.B., Ward, A., Puleo, E.M., Widrick, J., & Rippe, J.M. (1991). Development of a single-stage submaximal treadmill walking test. *Medicine and Science in Sports and Exercise, 23,* 966-973.

Edwards, A.L. (1954). *Statistical methods for the behavioral sciences.* New York: Holt.

Eichstaedt, C., & Lavay, B. (1992). *Physical activity for individuals with mental retardation: Infant to adult.* Champaign, IL: Human Kinetics.

Eichstaedt, C., Wang, P., Polacek, J., & Dohrmann, P. (1991). *Physical fitness and motor skill levels of individuals with mental retardation: Mild, moderate, and individuals with Down syndrome: Ages 6-21.* Normal, IL: Illinois State University Printing Services.

Einarsson-Backes, L.M., & Stewart, K.B. (1992). Infant neuromotor assessments: A review and preview of selected instruments. *American Journal of Occupational Therapy, 46,* 224-232.

Ellenbrand, D.A. (1973). *Gymnastics skills test for college women.* Unpublished master's thesis, Indiana University, Bloomington.

Espenschade, A. (1960). Motor development. In W.R. Johnson (Ed.), *Science and medicine of exercise and sports* (pp. 419-439). New York: Harper & Brothers.

Ezzelle, L., & Moutoux, M. (1993). Critical review of the Test of Gross Motor Development. *Physical and Occupational Therapy in Pediatrics, 12,* 73-87.

Feldman, A.B., Haley, S.B., & Coryell, J. (1990). Concurrent and construct validity of the Pediatric Evaluation of Disability Inventory. *Physical Therapy, 70,* 602-610.

Felt, B., & Stancin, T. (1991). Letters to the editor: A comparative review of developmental screening tests. *Pediatrics, 88,* 180-182.

Findley, T.W., Agre, J.C., Habeck, R.V., Schmalz, R., Birkebak, R.R., & McNally, M.C. (1987). Ambulation in the adolescent with myelomeningocele. I: Early childhood predictors. *Archives of Physical Medicine and Rehabilitation, 68,* 518-522.

Fiorentino, M.R. (1981a). *A basis for sensorimotor development: Normal and abnormal.* Springfield, IL: Charles C. Thomas.

Fiorentino, M.R. (1981b). *Reflex testing methods for evaluating CNS development* (2nd ed.). Springfield, IL: Charles C Thomas.

Fisher, A.G. (1992). Functional measures, Part 1: What is function, what should we measure, and how should we measure it? *American Journal of Occupational Therapy, 46,* 183-185.

Fisher, A.G. (1993). The assessment of IADL motor skills: An application of many-faceted Rasch analysis. *American Journal of Occupational Therapy, 47,* 319-329.

Fisher, A.G. (1995). *Assessment of Motor and Process Skills.* Fort Collins, CO: Three Star Press.

Fisher, A.G., Murray, E.A., & Bundy, A.C. (1991). *Sensory integration: Theory and practice.* Philadelphia: Davis.

Fisher, A.G., & Short-DeGraff, M. (1993). Improving functional assessment in occupational therapy: Recommendations and philosophy for change. *American Journal of Occupational Therapy, 47*, 199-201.

Fleischer, K.H., Belgredan, J.H., Bagnato, S.J., & Ogonosky, A.B. (1990). An overview of judgment-based assessment. *Topics in Early Childhood Special Education, 10*(3), 13-23.

Fleishman, E.A. (1953). Testing for psychomotor abilities by means of apparatus tests. *Psychological Bulletin, 50*, 243-262.

Fleishman, E.A. (1956). Psychomotor selection tests: Research and application in the United States Air Force. *Personnel Psychology, 9*, 449-467.

Fleishman, E.A. (1964). *The structure and measurement of physical fitness.* Englewood Cliffs, NJ: Prentice Hall.

Fleishman, E.A. (1966). Human abilities and the acquisition of skill. In E.A. Bilodeau (Ed.), *Acquisition of skill* (pp. 147-167). New York: Academic Press.

Fleishman, E.A., & Quaintance, M.K. (1984). *Taxonomies of human performance.* Orlando, FL: Academic Press.

Folio, M.R., & Fewell, R.R. (1983). *Peabody Developmental Motor Scales and Activity Cards.* Austin, TX: PRO-ED.

Footh, W.K., & Kogan, K.L. (1963). Measuring the effectiveness of physical therapy in the treatment of cerebral palsy. *Journal of the American Physical Therapy Association, 43*, 867-873.

Forssberg, H., & Nashner, L.M. (1982). Ontogenetic development of postural control in man: Adaptation to altered support and visual conditions during stance. *Journal of Neuroscience, 2*, 545-552.

Frankenburg, W.K., & Dodds, J.B. (1967). The Denver Developmental Screening Test. *Journal of Pediatrics, 71*, 181-191.

Frankenburg, W.K., & Dodds, J.B. (1969). *The Denver Developmental Screening Test.* Denver: University of Colorado Medical Center.

Frankenburg, W.K., & Dodds, J.B. (1992). *Denver II training manual* (2nd ed.). Denver: Denver Developmental Materials.

Frankenburg, W.K., Dodds, J.B., & Archer, P. (1990). *Denver II technical manual.* Denver: Denver Developmental Materials.

Frankenburg, W.K., Dodds, J., Archer, P., Shapiro, H., & Bresnick, B. (1992). The Denver II: A major revision and restandardization of the Denver Developmental Screening Test. *Pediatrics, 89*, 91-97.

Frankenburg, W.K., Dodds, J.B., Fandal, A.W., Kazuk, E., & Cohrs, M. (1975). *The Denver Developmental Screening Test* (Rev. ed.). Denver: University of Colorado Medical Center.

Franklin, B.A. (1985). Exercise testing, training and arm ergometry. *Sports Medicine, 2*, 100-199.

Fredericks, H.D.B., Baldwin, V.L., Doughty, P., & Walter, L.J. (1972). *The Teaching Research Motor Development Scale.* Springfield, IL: Charles C. Thomas.

French, K.E., & Thomas, J.R. (1987). The relation of knowledge development to children's basketball performance. *Journal of Sport Psychology, 9*, 15-32.

Freund, J.E., & Simon, G. (1992). *Modern elementary statistics* (8th ed.). Englewood Cliffs, NJ: Prentice Hall.

Frisen, L. (1990). *Clinical tests of vision.* New York: Lippincott-Raven.

Froelicher, V.F., & Lancaster, M.C. (1974). The prediction of maximal oxygen consumption from a continuous exercise treadmill protocol. *American Heart Journal, 87*, 445-450.

Furuno, S., O'Reilly, K.A., Hosaka, C.M., Inatsuka, T.T., Allman, T.L., & Zeisloft, B. (1985). *Hawaii Early Learning Profile—activity guide.* Palo Alto, CA: VORT.

Gallahue, D.L., & Ozmun, J.C. (1995). *Understanding motor development: Infants, children, adolescents, adults* (3rd ed.). Madison, WI: Brown & Benchmark.

Gans, B.M., Haley, S.M., Hallenborg, S.C., Mann, N., Inacio, C.A., & Faas, R.M. (1988). Description and interobserver reliability of the Tufts Assessment of Motor Performance. *American Journal of Physical Medicine and Rehabilitation, 67*, 202-210.

Gardner, H. (1991). *The unschooled mind: How children think and how schools should teach.* New York: Basic Books.

Garrow, J.S. (1988). *Obesity and related diseases.* Edinburgh: Churchill Livingstone.

Garrow, J.S., & Webster, J.D. (1985). Quetelet's Index (W/H^2) as a measure of fatness. *International Journal of Obesity, 9*, 147-153.

Gebhard, A.R., Ottenbacher, K.J., & Lane, S.J. (1994). Interrater reliability of the Peabody Developmental Motor Scales: Fine motor scale. *American Journal of Occupational Therapy, 48*, 976-981.

Gentile, A.M. (1987). Skill acquisition: Action, movement, and neuromotor processes. In J.H. Carr, R.B. Shepherd, J. Gordon, A.M. Gentile, & J.M. Held (Eds.), *Movement science: Foundations for physical therapy in rehabilitation* (pp. 93-154). Rockville, MD: Aspen.

Gesell, A. (1924). The nursery school movement. *School and Society, 20*, 644-652.

Gesell, A. (1925). *The mental growth of the preschool child: A psychological outline of normal development from birth to the sixth year, including a system of developmental diagnosis.* New York: Macmillan.

Gesell, A. (Ed.). (1940). *The first five years of life: A guide to the study of the preschool child.* New York: Harper & Brothers.

Gesell, A. (1945). *The embryology of behavior: The beginnings of the human mind.* Philadelphia: Lippincott.

Gesell, A., & Amatruda, C.S. (1941). *Developmental diagnosis: Normal and abnormal child development.* New York: Hoeber.

Gesell, A., & Thompson, H. (1934). *Infant behavior: Its genesis and growth.* New York: Macmillan.

Gesell, A., & Thompson, H. (1938). *The psychology of early growth, including norms of infant behavior and a method of genetic analysis.* New York: Macmillan.

Gevelinger, M., Ottenbacher, K.J., & Tiffany, T. (1988). The reliability of the Motor Development Checklist. *American Journal of Occupational Therapy, 42*, 81-86.

Gibson, J.J. (1979). *The ecological approach to visual perception.* Boston: Houghton Mifflin.

Gilbreth, F.B. (1911). *Motion study: A method for increasing the efficiency of the workman.* New York: Van Nostrand.

Gilbreth, F.B. (1920). *Motion study for the handicapped.* London: Routledge & Sons.

Gilbreth, F.B., & Gilbreth, L.M. (1919). *Fatigue study.* New York: Macmillan.

Gill, D.L., & Deeter, T.E. (1988). Development of the Sport Orientation Questionnaire. *Research Quarterly for Exercise and Sport, 59*, 191-202.

Glaser, R. (1963). Instructional technology and the measurement of learning outcomes: Some questions. *American Psychologist, 18*, 519-521.

Glaser, R., & Klaus, D.J. (1962). Proficiency measurement: Assessing human performance. In R. Gagne (Ed.), *Psychological principles in system development* (pp. 419-474). New York: Holt, Rinehart & Winston.

Golding, L.A., Meyers, C.R., & Sinning, W.E. (1989). *Y's way to physical fitness: The complete guide to fitness testing and instruction* (3rd ed.). Champaign, IL: Human Kinetics.

Goldsmith, C.H. (1993). Commentary on: Measurement validity in physical therapy research. *Physical Therapy, 73*, 113-114.

Gould, S.J. (1996). *Full house: The spread of excellence from Plato to Darwin*. New York: Harmony Books.

Gowers, W.R. (1888). *A manual of diseases of the nervous system*. Philadelphia: P. Blakiston, Son & Co.

Granger, C.V., & Gresham, G.E. (1993). Functional assessment in rehabilitation medicine: Introduction and brief background. *Physical Medicine and Rehabilitation Clinics of North America, 4*(3), 417-423.

Granger, C.V., & Wright, B.D. (1993). Looking ahead to the use of functional assessment in ambulatory physiatric and primary care: The Functional Assessment Screening Questionnaire. *Physical Medicine and Rehabilitation Clinics of North America, 4*(3), 595-605.

Greene, W.B., & Heckman, J.D. (1994). *The clinical measurement of joint motion*. Rosemont, IL: American Academy of Orthopaedic Surgeons.

Griffin, N.S., Keogh, J.F., & Maybee, R. (1984). Performer perceptions of movement confidence. *Journal of Sport Psychology, 6*, 395-407.

Griffiths, H.E. (1947). Analysis of function. *Occupational Therapy and Rehabilitation, 26*, 440-454.

Griffiths, R. (1954). *The abilities of babies: A study in mental measurement*. London: University of London.

Gubbay, S.S. (1973). A standardized test battery for the assessment of clumsy children. *Proceedings of the Australian Association of Neurologists, 10*, 19-25.

Gubbay, S.S. (1975a). *The clumsy child: A study of developmental apraxic and agnosic ataxia*. London: Saunders.

Gubbay, S.S. (1975b). Clumsy children in normal schools. *Medical Journal of Australia, 1*, 233-236.

Guilford, J.P. (1958). A system of the psychomotor abilities. *American Journal of Psychology, 71*, 164-174.

Guion, R.M. (1980). On trinitarian doctrines of validity. *Professional Psychology, 11*, 385-398.

Gulliksen, H. (1961). Measurement of learning and mental abilities. *Psychometrika, 26*, 93-107.

Guralnik, J.M., Ferrucci, L., Simonsick, E.M., Salive, M.E., & Wallace, R.B. (1995). Lower-extremity function in persons over the age of 70 years as a predictor of subsequent disability. *New England Journal of Medicine, 332*, 556-561.

Gutteridge, M.V. (1939). A study of motor achievements of young children. *Archives of Psychology*, No. 244, 1-178.

Haerer, A.F. (Ed.). (1992). *DeJong's The neurologic examination* (5th ed.). Philadelphia: Lippincott.

Haley, S.M., Baryza, M.J., & Blanchard, Y. (1993). Functional and naturalistic frameworks in assessing physical and motor disablement. In I.J. Wilhelm (Ed.), *Physical therapy in early infancy* (pp. 225-256). New York: Churchill Livingstone.

Haley, S.M., Coster, W.J., & Faas, R.M. (1991). A content validity study of the Pediatric Evaluation of Disability Inventory. *Pediatric Physical Therapy, 3*, 177-184.

Haley, S.M., Coster, W.J., Ludlow, L.H., Haltiwanger, J., & Andrellos, P.J. (1992). *Pediatric Evaluation of Disability Inventory*. Boston: New England Medical Center Hospitals.

Haley, S.M., & Ludlow, L.H. (1992). Applicability of the hierarchical scales of the Tufts assessment of motor performance for school-aged children and adults with disabilities. *Physical Therapy, 72*, 191-206.

Haley, S.M., Ludlow, L.H., & Coster, W.J. (1993). Pediatric Evaluation of Disability Inventory: Clinical interpretation of summary scores using Rasch rating scale methodology. *Physical Medicine and Rehabilitation Clinics of North America, 4*(3), 529-540.

Haley, S.M., Ludlow, L.H., Gans, B.M., Faas, R.M., & Inacio, C.A. (1991). Tufts Assessment of Motor Performance: An empirical approach to identifying motor performance categories. *Archives of Physical Medicine and Rehabilitation, 72,* 359-366.

Hall, H.J. (1921). Forward steps in occupational therapy during 1920. *The Modern Hospital, 16,* 245-247.

Halverson, H.M. (1931). An experimental study of prehension in infants by means of systematic cinema records. *Genetic Psychology Monographs, 10,* 107-286.

Halverson, L.E., Roberton, M.A., & Langendorfer, S. (1982). Development of the overarm throw: Movement and ball velocity changes by seventh grade. *Research Quarterly for Exercise and Sport, 53,* 198-205.

Halverson, L.E., & Williams, K. (1985). Developmental sequences for hopping over distance: A prelongitudinal screening. *Research Quarterly for Exercise and Sport, 56,* 37-44.

Hambleton, R.K. (1994). The rise and fall of criterion-referenced measurement? *Educational Measurement: Issues and Practice, 13*(1), 21-26.

Hamill, P.V.V., Drizd, T.A., Johnson, C.L., Reed, R.B., & Roche, A.F. (1977). NCHS growth curves for children birth - 18 years. *Vital and Health Statistics,* Series 11, No. 165.

Hamill, P.V.V., Drizd, T.A., Johnson, C.L., Reed, R.B., Roche, A.F., & Moore, W.M. (1979). Physical growth. National Center for Health Statistics percentiles. *American Journal of Clinical Nutrition, 32,* 607-629.

Hamilton, A.L. (1875). A new dynamometer. *The Psychological and Medico-Legal Journal, 2,* 255-256.

Harris, S.R., & Daniels, L.E. (1996). Content validity of the Harris Infant Neuromotor Test. *Physical Therapy, 76,* 727-737.

Harris, S.R., & Heriza, C.B. (1987). Measuring infant movement: Clinical and technological assessment techniques. *Physical Therapy, 67,* 1877-1880.

Harris, S.R., Swanson, M.W., Andrews, M.S., Sells, C.J., Robinson, N.M., Bennett, F.C., & Chandler, L.S. (1984). Predictive validity of the "Movement Assessment of Infants." *Developmental and Behavioral Pediatrics, 5,* 336-342.

Harrow, A.J. (1972). *Taxonomy of the psychomotor domain: A guide for developing behavioral objectives.* New York: David McKay.

Harter, S., Pike, R., Efron, C., Chao, C., & Bierer, B. (1983). *Pictorial Scale of Perceived Competence and Social Acceptance for Young Children.* Denver: University of Denver.

Hattie, J., & Edwards, H. (1987). A review of the Bruininks-Oseretsky Test of Motor Proficiency. *British Journal of Educational Psychology, 57,* 104-113.

Hayashi, K. (1990). Letter: Correlation between temperature and infants' gross motor development. *Developmental Medicine and Child Neurology, 32,* 832-834.

Hayashi, K. (1992). Letter: The influence of clothes and bedclothes on infants' gross motor development. *Developmental Medicine and Child Neurology, 34,* 556-559.

Hayes, A. (1990). The context and future of judgment-based assessment. *Topics in Early Childhood Special Education, 10*(3), 1-12.

Haywood, K.M. (1993). *Life span motor development* (2nd ed.). Champaign, IL: Human Kinetics.

Hebbelinck, M., Duquet, W., Borms, J., & Carter, J.E.L. (1995). Stability of somatotypes: A longitudinal study of Belgian children age 6 to 17 years. *American Journal of Human Biology, 7,* 575-588.

Henderson, L., Rose, P., & Henderson, S. (1992). Reaction time and movement time in children with a developmental coordination disorder. *Journal of Child Psychology and Psychiatry, 33,* 895-905.

Henderson, S.E. (1987). The assessment of "clumsy" children: Old and new approaches. *Journal of Child Psychology and Psychiatry, 28,* 511-527.

Henderson, S.E., & Hall, D. (1982). Concomitants of clumsiness in young children. *Developmental Medicine and Child Neurology, 24,* 448-460.

Henderson, S.E., & Sugden, D.A. (1992). *Movement Assessment Battery for Children.* Sidcup, Kent, England: Therapy Skill Builders.

Hensley, J.E., East, W.B., & Stillwell, J.L. (1979). A racquetball skills test. *Research Quarterly, 50,* 114-119.

Heriza, C. (1991). Motor development: Traditional and contemporary theories. In M. Lister (Ed.), *Contemporary management of motor control problems* (pp. 99-126). Alexandria, VA: Foundation for Physical Therapy.

Hinderer, S.R., & Hinderer, K.A. (1993). Quantitative methods of evaluation. In J.A. DeLisa (Ed.), *Rehabilitation medicine: Principles and practice* (2nd ed.) (pp. 96-121). Philadelphia: Lippincott.

Hinderer, K.A., & Hinderer, S.R. (1996, June). *Manual muscle testing versus myometry: Should manual muscle testing survive into the 21st century?* Presentation at the American Physical Therapy Association Scientific Meeting and Exposition, Minneapolis, MN.

Hinderer, K.A., Richardson, P.K., & Atwater, S.W. (1989). Clinical implications of the Peabody Developmental Motor Scales: A constructive review. *Physical and Occupational Therapy in Pediatrics, 9,* 81-106.

Hislop, H.J., & Montgomery, J. (1995). *Daniels and Worthingham's muscle testing: Techniques of manual examination* (6th ed.). Philadelphia: Saunders.

Hjelte, G. (1922). California Decathlon Tests and their relation to educational tests and measurements. *American Physical Education Review, 27,* 15-17.

Hodges, J.R. (1994). *Cognitive assessment for clinicians.* New York: Oxford University Press.

Hoeger, W.K. (1987). *The complete guide for the development and implementation of health promotion programs.* Englewood, CO: Morton.

Hopewell Special Education Regional Resource Center. (1981). Project MOBILITEE: Movement Opportunities for Building Independence and Leisure Interests through Training Educators and Exceptional learners. Hillsboro, OH: Author.

Horak, F.B. (1987). Clinical measurement of postural control in adults. *Physical Therapy, 67,* 1881-1885.

Hoskins, T.A., & Squires, J.E. (1973). Developmental assessment: A test for gross motor and reflex development. *Physical Therapy, 53,* 117-126.

Hrdlicka, A. (1931). *Children who run on all fours.* New York: Whittlesey House.

Hubley-Kozey, C.L. (1990). Testing flexibility. In J.D. MacDougall, H.A. Wenger, & H.J. Green (Eds.), *Physiological testing of the high-performance athlete* (pp. 309-359). Champaign, IL: Human Kinetics.

Hughes, J.E., & Riley, A. (1981). Basic Gross Motor Assessment: Tool for use with children having minor motor dysfunction. *Physical Therapy, 61,* 503-511.

Humiston, D. (1937). A measurement of motor ability in college women. *Research Quarterly, 8,* 181-185.

Jackson, A.S., Blair, S.N., Mahar, M.T., Wier, L.T., Ross, M., & Stuteville, J.E. (1990). Prediction of functional aerobic capacity without exercise testing. *Medicine and Science in Sports and Exercise, 22,* 863-870.

Jackson, A.S., & Pollock, M.L. (1978). Generalized equations for predicting body density of men. *British Journal of Nutrition, 40,* 497-504.

Jackson, A.S., Pollock, M.L., & Ward, A. (1980). Generalized equations for predicting body density of women. *Medicine and Science in Sports and Exercise, 12,* 175-182.

Jebsen, R.H., Taylor, N., Trieschmann, R.B., Trotter, M.J., & Howard, L.A. (1969). An objective and standardized test of hand function. *Archives of Physical Medicine and Rehabilitation, 50,* 311-319.

Jette, A.M. (1995). Outcomes research: Shifting the dominant research paradigm in physical therapy. *Physical Therapy, 75,* 965-970.

Johnson, B.L., & Nelson, J.K. (1969). *Practical measurements for evaluation in physical education.* Minneapolis: Burgess.

Johnson, G.B. (1932). Physical skill tests for sectioning classes into homogeneous units. *Research Quarterly, 3,* 128-134.

Johnson, K.P. (1956). *A measure of general sports skill of college men.* Unpublished doctoral dissertation, Indiana University, Bloomington.

Johnson, M.K., Zuck, F.N., & Wingate, K. (1951). The Motor Age Test: Measurement of motor handicaps in children with neuromuscular disorders such as cerebral palsy. *Journal of Bone and Joint Surgery, 33-A,* 698-707.

Johnson, R.D. (1962). Measurements of achievement in fundamental skills of elementary school children. *Research Quarterly, 33,* 94-103.

Johnson, R.E., & Lavay, B. (1988). *Kansas Adapted/Special Physical Education Test manual.* Topeka, KS: Kansas Department of Education.

Johnson-Martin, N., Jens, K.G., & Attermeier, S.M. (1986). *The Carolina Curriculum for Handicapped Infants at Risk.* Baltimore: Brookes.

Johnston, M.V., Keith, R.A., & Hinderer, S.R. (1992). Measurement standards for interdisciplinary medical rehabilitation. *Archives of Physical Medicine and Rehabilitation, 73,* S3-S23l.

Johnston, O. (1993). Gubbay screening test. *Journal of Paediatrics and Child Health, 29,* 319.

Jones, S.K. (1967). *A measure of tennis serving ability.* Unpublished master's thesis, University of California, Los Angeles.

Katz, S., Ford, A.B., Moskowitz, R.W., Jackson, B.A., & Jaffe, M.W. (1963). Studies of illness in the aged. The Index of ADL: A standardized measure of biological and psychosocial function. *Journal of the American Medical Association, 185,* 914-919.

Kavale, K., & Mattson, P.D. (1983). "One jumped off the balance beam:" Meta-analysis of perceptual-motor training. *Journal of Learning Disabilities, 16,* 165-173.

Keith, R.A., Granger, C.V., Hamilton, B.B., & Sherwin, F.S. (1987). The Functional Independence Measure: A new tool for rehabilitation. In M.G. Eisenberg & R.C. Grzesiak (Eds.), *Advances in clinical rehabilitation* (Vol. 1) (pp. 6-18). New York: Springer.

Kellogg, J.H. (1893). A new dynamometer for use in anthropometry. *Modern Medicine and Bacteriological World, 2,* 269-275.

Kelly, L.E. (1989). Instructional time: The overlooked factor in PE curriculum development. *Journal of Physical Education, Recreation & Dance, 60*(6), 29-32.

Kendall, F.P., McCreary, E.K., & Provance, P.G. (1993). *Muscles: Testing and function* (4th ed.). Baltimore: Williams & Wilkins.

Keogh, J.F. (1977). The study of movement skill development. *Quest,* Monograph 28, 76-88.

Keogh, J., & Sugden, D. (1985). *Movement skill development.* New York: Macmillan.

Keogh, J.F., Sugden, D.A., Reynard, C.L., & Calkins, J.A. (1979). Identification of clumsy children: Comparisons and comments. *Journal of Human Movement Studies, 5,* 32-41.

Kerlinger, F.N., & Pedhazur, E.J. (1973). *Multiple regression in behavioral research.* New York: Holt, Rinehart & Winston.

Kershner, K.M., & Dusewicz, R.A. (1970). K.D.K.-Oseretsky Tests of Motor Development. *Perceptual and Motor Skills, 30,* 202.

Keys, A., Fidanza, F., Karvonen, M.J., Kimura, N., & Taylor, H.L. (1972). Indices of relative weight and obesity. *Journal of Chronic Diseases, 25,* 329-343.

Kielhofner, G., & Mallinson, T. (1995). Application of the model in practice: Case illustrations. In G. Kielhofner (Ed.), *A model of human occupation: Theory and application* (pp. 271-342). Baltimore: Williams & Wilkins.

Kiresuk, T., & Sherman, R. (1968). Goal attainment scaling: A general method of evaluating comprehensive mental health programs. *Community Mental Health Journal, 4,* 443-453.

Kirk, R.E. (1984). *Elementary statistics* (2nd ed.). Monterey, CA: Brooks/Cole.

Kleeberger, F.L. (1917). Physical efficiency tests as a practical method of popularizing physical education at the University of California. *American Physical Education Review, 22,* 551-554.

Kleeberger, F.L. (1918). Physical efficiency tests as a practical method of popularizing physical education at the University of California (concluded). *American Physical Education Review, 23,* 27-33.

Klein, R.M., & Bell, B. (1982). Self-care skills: Behavioral measurement with Klein-Bell ADL Scale. *Archives of Physical Medicine and Rehabilitation, 63,* 335-338.

Kline, G.M., Porcari, J.P., Hintermeister, R., Freedson, P.S., Ward, A., McCarron, R.F., Ross, J., & Rippe, J.M. (1987). Estimation of VO_2max from a one-mile track walk, gender, age, and body weight. *Medicine and Science in Sports and Exercise, 19,* 253-259.

Knobloch, H. (1963). *Developmental Screening Instrument.* Columbus, OH: Children's Hospital, Child Development Service.

Knobloch, H., & Pasamanick, B. (1974). *Gesell and Amatruda's developmental diagnosis: The evaluation and management of normal and abnormal neuropsychologic development in infancy and early childhood* (3rd ed.). Hagerstown, MD: Harper & Row.

Knobloch, H., Stevens, F., & Malone, A.F. (1980). *Manual of developmental diagnosis.* New York: Harper & Row.

Knox, S. (1974). A play scale. In M. Reilly (Ed.), *Play as exploratory learning* (pp. 247-266). Beverly Hills, CA: Sage.

Kraemer, W.J., & Fry, A.C. (1995). Strength testing: Development and evaluation of methodology. In P.J. Maud & C. Foster (Eds.), *Physiological assessment of human fitness* (pp. 115-138). Champaign, IL: Human Kinetics.

Krakower, H. (1937). Testing in physical education. *Research Quarterly, 8,* 54-67.

Kraus, H., & Hirschland, R.P. (1954). Minimum muscular fitness tests in children. *Research Quarterly, 25,* 178-188.

Krebs, D.E., Edelstein, J.E., & Fishman, S. (1985). Reliability of observational kinematic gait analysis. *Physical Therapy, 65,* 1027-1033.

Krus, P.H., Bruininks, R.H., & Robertson, G. (1981). Structure of motor abilities in children. *Perceptual and Motor Skills, 52,* 119-129.

Kubiszyn, T., & Borich, G. (1987). *Educational testing and measurement: Classroom application and practice* (2nd ed.). Glenview, IL: Scott, Foresman.

Lam, Y.Y., & Henderson, S.E. (1987). Some applications of the Henderson Revision of the Test of Motor Impairment. *British Journal of Experimental Psychology, 57,* 389-400.

Lamb, R.L. (1985). Manual muscle testing. In J.M. Rothstein (Ed.), *Measurement in physical therapy* (pp. 47-55). New York: Churchill Livingstone.

Langendorfer, S. (1986). Review of the Test of Gross Motor Development. *Adapted Physical Activity Quarterly, 3,* 186-190.

Langendorfer, S. (1987). Prelongitudinal screening of overarm striking development performed under two environmental conditions. In J.E. Clark & J.H.

Humphrey (Eds.), *Advances in motor development research* (Vol. 1) (pp. 17-47). New York: AMS Press.

Largo, R.H., Molinari, L., Weber, M., Comenale Pinto, L., & Duc, G. (1985). Early development of locomotion: Significance of prematurity, cerebral palsy and sex. *Developmental Medicine and Child Neurology, 27,* 183-191.

Lassner, R. (1948). Annotated bibliography on the Oseretsky Tests of Motor Proficiency. *Journal of Consulting Psychology, 12,* 37-47.

Laszlo, J.I., & Bairstow, P.J. (1985). *Perceptual-motor behaviour: Developmental assessment and therapy.* New York: Praeger.

Laszlo, J.I., Bairstow, P.J., Bartip, J., & Rolfe, U. (1988). Clumsiness of perceptuomotor dysfunction. In A. Colley & J.R. Beech (Eds.), *Cognition and action in skilled behaviour* (pp. 293-309). Amsterdam: Elsevier.

Larsen, D., & Shaw, M. (1996). *The perfect Yankee: The incredible story of the greatest miracle in baseball history.* Champaign, IL: Sagamore.

Latash, M.L., & Anson, J.G. (1996). What are "normal movements" in atypical populations? *Behavioral and Brain Sciences, 19,* 55-106.

Latchaw, M. (1954). Measuring selected motor skills in fourth, fifth, and sixth grades. *Research Quarterly, 25,* 439-449.

Laurie, S.S. (1904). *Historical survey of pre-Christian education* (2nd ed). New York: Longmans.

Lawlor, M.C., & Henderson, A. (1989). A descriptive study of the clinical practice patterns of occupational therapists working with infants and young children. *American Journal of Occupational Therapy, 43,* 755-764.

Lee, D.N., & Lishman, J.R. (1975). Visual proprioceptive control of stance. *Journal of Human Movement Studies, 1,* 87-95.

Leighton, J.R. (1955). An instrument and technique for the measurement and range of joint movement. *Archives of Physical Medicine and Rehabilitation, 36,* 24-28.

Leighton, J.R. (1987). *Manual of instruction for Leighton flexometer.* Author.

Lewko, J.H. (1976). Current practices in evaluating motor behavior of disabled children. *American Journal of Occupational Therapy, 30,* 413-419.

Linacre, J.M., Heinemann, A.W., Wright, B.D., Granger, C.V., & Hamilton, B.B. (1994). The structure and stability of the Functional Independence Measure. *Archives of Physical Medicine and Rehabilitation, 75,* 127-132.

Lindahl, E., Michelsson, K., Helenius, M., & Parre, M. (1988). Neonatal risk factors and later neurodevelopmental disturbances. *Developmental Medicine and Child Neurology, 30,* 571-589.

Linder, T.W. (1993). *Transdisciplinary play-based assessment: A functional approach to working with young children* (2nd ed.). Baltimore: Brookes.

Linn, R.L. (1994). Criterion-referenced measurement: A valuable perspective clouded by surplus meaning. *Educational Measurement: Issues and Practice, 13*(1), 12-14.

Lohman, T.G., Roche, A.F., & Martorell, R. (Eds.). (1988). *Anthropometric standardization reference manual.* Champaign, IL: Human Kinetics.

Lohman, T.G., Roche, A.F., & Martorell, R. (Eds.). (1991). *Anthropometric standardization reference manual* (Abridged ed.). Champaign, IL: Human Kinetics.

Long, T.M., & Cintas, H.L. (1995). *Handbook of pediatric physical therapy.* Baltimore: Williams & Wilkins.

Loovis, E.M., & Ersing, W.F. (1979). *Assessing and programming gross motor development for children* (2nd ed.). Bloomington, IN: Tichenor.

Lovett, R.W. (1917). *The treatment of infantile paralysis* (2nd ed.). Philadelphia: P. Blakiston's Son.

Ludlow, L.H., Haley, S.M., & Gans, B.M. (1992). A hierarchical model of functional performance in rehabilitation medicine: The Tufts Assessment of Motor Performance. *Evaluation and the Health Professions, 15,* 59-74.

Luftig, R.L. (1989). *Assessment of learners with special needs.* Boston: Allyn & Bacon.

Lukaski, H.C., Johnson, P.E., Bolonchuk, W.W., & Lykken, G.I. (1985). Assessment of fat-free mass using bioelectrical impedance measurements of the human body. *American Journal of Clinical Nutrition, 41*, 810-817.

MacCurdy, H.L. (1933). *A test for measuring the physical capacity of secondary school boys.* New York: Author.

Magill, R.A. (1993). *Motor learning: Concepts and applications* (4th ed.). Dubuque, IA: Brown & Benchmark.

Magrun, W.M. (1989). *Evaluating movement and posture disorganization in dyspraxic children.* Tucson, AZ: Therapy Skill Builders.

Mahoney, F.I., & Barthel, D.W. (1965). Functional evaluation: The Barthel Index. *Maryland Medical Journal, 14*, 61-65.

Malina, R.M. (1995). Anthropometry. In P.J. Maud & C. Foster (Eds.), *Physiological assessment of human fitness* (pp. 205-219). Champaign, IL: Human Kinetics.

Malina, R.M., & Bouchard, C. (1991). *Growth, maturation, and physical activity.* Champaign, IL: Human Kinetics.

Mardell-Czudnowski, C., & Goldenberg, D. (1983). *Developmental Indicators for the Assessment of Learning—Revised.* Edison, NJ: Childcraft Education.

Marlow, N., Roberts, B.L., & Cooke, R.W.I. (1989). Motor skills in extremely low birthweight children at the age of 6 years. *Archives of Disease in Childhood, 64*, 839-847.

Mashburn, N.C. (1934). Mashburn automatic serial action apparatus for detecting flying aptitude. *Journal of Aviation Medicine, 5*, 155-160.

Massey, B.H. (1978). Measurement: Historical review. In H.J. Montoye (Ed.), *An introduction to measurement in physical education* (pp. 16-24). Boston: Allyn & Bacon.

Mathias, S., Nayak, U., & Isaacs, B. (1986). Balance in elderly patients: The "Get-up and Go" test. *Archives of Physical Medicine and Rehabilitation, 67*, 387-389.

Mathiowetz, V. (1993). Role of physical performance component evaluations in occupational therapy functional assessment. *American Journal of Occupational Therapy, 47*, 225-230.

Mathiowetz, V.G., & Wade, M.G. (1995). Task constraints and functional motor performance of individuals with and without multiple sclerosis. *Ecological Psychology, 7*, 99-123.

Maud, P.J., & Cortez-Cooper, M.Y. (1995). Static techniques for the evaluation of joint range of motion. In P.J. Maud & C. Foster (Eds.), *Physiological assessment of human fitness* (pp. 221-243). Champaign, IL: Human Kinetics.

Maud, P.J., & Foster, C. (Eds.). (1995). *Physiological assessment of human fitness.* Champaign, IL: Human Kinetics.

McArdle, W.D., Katch, F.I., Pechar, G.S., Jacobson, L., & Ruck, S. (1972). Reliability and interrelationships between maximal oxygen intake, physical work capacity and step-test scores in college women. *Medicine and Science in Sports, 4*, 182-186.

McCaskill, C.L., & Wellman, B.L. (1938). A study of common motor achievements at the preschool ages. *Child Development, 9*, 141-150.

McCloy, C.H. (1934). The measurement of general motor capacity and general motor ability. *Research Quarterly, 5*(Suppl.), 46-61.

McCloy, C.H. (1937). An analytical study of the stunt type test as a measure of motor educability. *Research Quarterly, 8*, 46-55.

McCurdy, J.H. (1923). Physical efficiency standards. *American Physical Education Review, 28*, 109-110.

McDowell, C.P. (1973). *Approaching leisure counseling with the Self-Leisure Interest Profile.* Salt Lake City: Educational Support Systems.

McGraw, M.B. (1935). *Growth: A study of Johnny and Jimmy.* New York: Appleton-Century.

McGraw, M.B. (1945). *The neuromuscular maturation of the human infant.* New York: Hafner Press.

McHenry, L.C., Jr. (1969). *Garrison's history of neurology* (Rev. ed.). Springfield, IL: Charles C Thomas.

McKechnie, G.E. (1974). *Leisure Activities Blank booklet.* Palo Alto, CA: Consulting Psychologists Press.

McPherson, S.L., & Thomas, J.R. (1989). Relation of knowledge and performance in boy's tennis: Age and expertise. *Journal of Experimental Child Psychology, 48,* 190-211.

McSwegin, P., Pemberton, C., Petray, C., & Going, S. (1989). *Physical Best: The AAHPERD guide to physical fitness education and assessment.* Reston, VA: American Alliance for Health, Physical Education, Recreation and Dance.

Meisels, S.J. (1989). Can developmental screening tests identify children who are developmentally at risk? *Pediatrics, 83,* 578-585.

Melton, A.W. (1947). *Apparatus reports* (Army Air Forces Aviation Psychology Program Research Report No. 4). Washington, DC: U.S. Government Printing Office.

Merbitz, C., Morris, J., & Grip, J.C. (1989). Ordinal scales and foundations of misinference. *Archives of Physical Medicine and Rehabilitation, 70,* 308-312.

Messick, J.A. (1991). Prelongitudinal screening of hypothesized developmental sequences for the overhead tennis serve in experienced tennis players 9-19 years of age. *Research Quarterly for Exercise and Sport, 62,* 249-256.

Messick, S. (1975). The standard problem: Meaning and values in measurement and evaluation. *American Psychologist, 30,* 955-966.

Messick, S. (1980). Test validity and the ethics of assessment. *American Psychologist, 35,* 1012-1027.

Messick, S. (1988). The once and future issues of validity: Assessing the meaning and consequences of measurement. In H. Wainer & H.I. Braun (Eds.), *Test validity* (pp. 33-45). Hillsdale, NJ: Erlbaum.

Meylan, G.L. (1905). Marks for physical efficiency. *American Physical Education Review, 10,* 106-112.

Milani-Comparetti, A., & Gidoni, E.A. (1967). Routine developmental examination in normal and retarded children. *Developmental Medicine and Child Neurology, 9,* 631-638.

Miles, B.H., Nierengarten, M.E., & Nearing, R.J. (1988). A review of the eleven most cited assessment instruments used in adapted physical education. *Clinical Kinesiology, 42,* 33-41.

Miller, A.S., Stewart, M.D., Murphy, M.-A., & Jantzen, A.C. (1955). An evaluation method for cerebral palsy. *American Journal of Occupational Therapy, 9,* 105-111.

Miller, L.J. (1988). *Miller Assessment for Preschoolers.* San Antonio: Therapy Skill Builders.

Miller, L.J., & Roid, G.H. (1994). *The T.I.M.E. Toddler and Infant Motor Evaluation.* San Antonio: Therapy Skill Builders.

Minneapolis Public Schools. (1991). *The learner outcomes guide for physical education K-10.* Minneapolis: Author.

Mirenda, J.J. (1973). *Leisure Interest Finder.* Washington, DC: American Association of Health, Physical Education, and Recreation.

Mislevy, R.J. (1993). Introduction. In N. Frederiksen, R.J. Mislevy, & I.I. Bejar (Eds.), *Test theory for a new generation of tests* (pp. ix-xii). Hillsdale, NJ: Erlbaum.

Morris, M., Matyas, T., Iansek, R., & Cunnington, R. (1996). Rehabilitation promotes functional movement in atypical populations. *Behavioral and Brain Sciences, 19,* 82-83.

Morrow, J.R., Jr. (1989). Generalizability theory. In M.J. Safrit & T.M. Wood (Eds.), *Measurement concepts in physical education and exercise science* (pp. 73-96). Champaign, IL: Human Kinetics.

Morrow, J.R., Jr., & Jackson, A.W. (1993). How "significant" is your reliability? *Research Quarterly for Exercise and Sport, 64,* 352-355.

Moskowitz, E., & McCann, C.B. (1957). Classification of disability in the chronically ill and aging. *Journal of Chronic Diseases, 5,* 342-346.

Msall, M.E., DiGaudio, K.M., & Duffy, L.C. (1993). Use of functional assessment in children with developmental disabilities. *Physical Medicine and Rehabilitation Clinics of North America, 4*(3), 517-527.

Musselwhite, C.R. (1986). *Adaptive play for special needs children.* San Diego: College-Hill Press.

Mutti, M., Sterline, H., Spalding, N.V. (1978). *Quick Neurological Screening Test.* Burlingame, CA: Psychological and Educational Publications.

Nashner, L.M. (1982). Adaptation of human movement to altered environments. *Trends in Neuroscience, 5,* 358-361.

Nashner, L.M., Black, F.O., & Wall, C. (1982). Adaptation to altered support and visual conditions during stance: Patients with vestibular deficits. *Journal of Neuroscience, 2,* 536-544.

Nashner, L.M., Shumway-Cook, A., & Marin, O. (1983). Stance posture control in select groups of children with cerebral palsy: Deficits in sensory organization and muscular coordination. *Experimental Brain Research, 49,* 393-409.

National Association for Sport and Physical Education. (1995). *Moving into the future—national physical education standards: A guide to content and assessment.* St. Louis: Mosby.

Neilson, N.P., & Cozens, F.W. (1934). Achievement scales in physical education activities for boys and girls in elementary and junior high schools. *Research Quarterly, 5,* 3-13.

Neisworth, J.T., & Bagnato, S.J. (1988). Assessment in early childhood special education. In S.L. Odom & M.B. Karnes (Eds.), *Early intervention for infants and children with handicaps* (pp. 23-49). Baltimore: Brookes.

Nelson, A.J. (1974). Functional Ambulation Profile. *Physical Therapy, 54,* 1059-1065.

Newborg, J., Stock, J.R., & Wnek, L., Guidubaldi, J., & Svinicki, J. (1984). *Battelle Developmental Inventory.* Allen, TX: DLM Teaching Resources.

Newell, K.M. (1986). Constraints on the development of coordination. In M.G. Wade & H.T.A. Whiting (Eds.), *Motor development in children: Aspects of coordination and control* (pp. 341-360). Dordrecht, Netherlands: Nijhoff.

Newell, K.M., McDonald, P.V., & Baillargeon, R. (1993). Body scale and infant grip configurations. *Developmental Psychobiology, 26,* 195-205.

Newell, K.M., Scully, D.M., McDonald, P.V., & Baillargeon, R. (1989). Task constraints and infant grip configurations. *Developmental Psychobiology, 22,* 817-832.

Newell, K.M., Scully, D.M., Tenenbaum, F., & Hardiman, S. (1989). Body scale and the development of prehension. *Developmental Psychobiology, 22,* 1-13.

New York State Rehabilitation Hospital. (1964). *West Haverstraw Motor Development Test.* West Haverstraw, NY: Author.

Nichols, D.S., & Case-Smith, J. (1996). Reliability and validity of the Pediatric Evaluation of Disability Inventory. *Pediatric Physical Therapy, 8,* 15-24.

Nichols, J.H. (1920). Ohio State University physical efficiency tests. *American Physical Education Review, 25*, 212.

Nichols, P.D., Chipman, S.F., & Brennan, R.L. (1995). *Cognitively diagnostic assessment*. Hillsdale, NJ: Erlbaum.

Nolan, M.F. (1995). *Introduction to the neurologic examination*. Philadelphia: Davis.

Norkin, C.C., & White, D.J. (1985). *Measurement of joint motion: A guide to goniometry*. Philadelphia: Davis.

Norman, D.A. (1990). *The design of everyday things*. New York: Doubleday/Currency.

Notari, A.R., & Bricker, D.D. (1990). The utility of a curriculum-based assessment instrument in the development of individualized education plans for infants and young children. *Journal of Early Intervention, 14*, 117-132.

Nunnally, J.C. (1978). *Psychometric theory*. Reading, MA: Addison-Wesley.

Osternig, L.R. (1986). Isokinetic dynamometry: Implications for muscle testing and rehabilitation. *Exercise and Sport Sciences Reviews, 14*, 45-104.

Ostrow, A.C. (Ed.), (1990). *Directory of psychological tests in the sport and exercise sciences*. Morgantown, WV: Fitness Information Technology.

Ottenbacher, K.J. (1995). An examination of reliability in developmental research. *Journal of Developmental and Behavioral Pediatrics, 16*, 177-182.

Ottenbacher, K.J., & Tomchek, S.D. (1993). Reliability analysis in therapeutic research: Practice and procedures. *American Journal of Occupational Therapy, 47*, 10-16.

Palisano, R.J. (1986a). Concurrent and predictive validities of the Bayley Motor Scale and the Peabody Developmental Motor Scales. *Physical Therapy, 66*, 1714-1719.

Palisano, R.J. (1986b). Use of chronological and adjusted ages to compare motor development of healthy preterm and fullterm infants. *Developmental Medicine and Child Neurology, 28*, 180-187.

Palisano, R.J. (1993a). Neuromotor and developmental assessment. In I.J. Wilhelm (Ed.), *Physical therapy assessment in early infancy* (pp. 173-224). New York: Churchill Livingstone.

Palisano, R.J. (1993b). Validity of goal attainment scaling in infants with motor delays. *Physical Therapy, 73*, 651-658, 659-660.

Palisano, R.J., Campbell, S.K., & Harris, S.R. (1995). Clinical decision-making in pediatric physical therapy. In S.K. Campbell (Ed.), *Physical therapy for children* (pp. 183-204). Philadelphia: Saunders.

Palisano, R.J., Haley, S.M., & Brown, D.A. (1992). Goal attainment scaling as a measure of change in infants with motor delays. *Physical Therapy, 72*, 432-437.

Palisano, R.J., Kolobe, T.H., Haley, S.M., Lowes, L.P., & Jones, S.L. (1995). Validity of the Peabody Developmental Gross Motor Scale as an evaluative measure of infants receiving physical therapy. *Physical Therapy, 75*, 939-951.

Palisano, R.J., & Lydic, J.S. (1984). The Peabody Developmental Motor Scales: An analysis. *Physical and Occupational Therapy in Pediatrics, 4*, 69-75.

Parker, R. (1988). *Comprehensive evaluation in recreational therapy—physical disabilities*. Ravensdale, WA: Idyll Arbor.

Payne, V.G., & Isaacs, L.D. (1995). *Human motor development: A lifespan approach* (3rd ed.). Mountain View, CA: Mayfield.

Pedretti, L.W. (1990). Activities of daily living. In L.W. Pedretti & B. Zoltan (Eds.), *Occupational therapy: Practice skills for physical dysfunction* (3rd ed.) (pp. 230-271). St. Louis: Mosby-Year Book.

Petroski, H. (1985). *To engineer is human: The role of failure in successful design*. New York: St. Martin's Press.

Pillsbury, W.B. (1911). The place of movement in consciousness. *Psychological Review, 18*, 83-99.

Piper, M.C. (1993). Theoretical foundations for physical therapy assessment in early infancy. In I.J. Wilhelm (Ed.), *Physical therapy assessment in early infancy* (pp. 1-11). New York: Churchill Livingstone.

Piper, M.C., & Darrah, J. (1994). *Motor assessment of the developing infant.* Philadelphia: Saunders.

Pollock, M.L., Garzarella, L., & Graves, J.E. (1995). The measurement of body composition. In P.J. Maud & C. Foster (Eds.), *Physiological assessment of human fitness* (pp. 167-204). Champaign, IL: Human Kinetics.

Poore, G.V. (1883). *Selections from the clinical works of Dr. Duchenne.* London: New Sydenham Society.

Powell, L.E., & Myers, A.M. (1995). The Activities-specific Balance Confidence (ABC) Scale. *Journal of Gerontology: Medical Sciences, 50A,* M28-M34.

Prechtl, H.F., & Beintema, D. (1991). *The neurological examination of the full-term newborn infant* (2nd ed.). New York: Cambridge University Press.

Ragsdale, C.E., & Breckenfeld, I.J. (1934). The organization of physical and motor traits in junior high school boys. *Research Quarterly, 5*(3), 47-55.

Rarick, G.L. (1961). *Motor development during infancy and childhood* (Rev. ed.). Madison, WI: College Printing & Typing.

Rarick, G.L., Dobbins, D.A., & Broadhead, G.D. (1976). *The motor domain and its correlates in educationally handicapped children.* Englewood Cliffs, NJ: Prentice Hall.

Rasch, G. (1960/1980). *Probabilistic models for some intelligence and attainment tests.* Copenhagen: Danish Institute for Educational Research/Chicago: University of Chicago Press.

Reed, E.S. (1982). An outline of a theory of actions systems. *Journal of Motor Behavior, 14,* 98-134.

Reed, E.S. (1989). Changing theories of postural development. In M.H. Woollacott & A. Shumway-Cook (Eds.), *Development of posture and gait across the life span* (pp. 3-24). Columbia, SC: University of South Carolina Press.

Reid, D. (1987). Occupational therapists' assessment practices with handicapped children in Ontario. *Canadian Journal of Occupational Therapy, 54,* 181-188.

Reid, D.T., Boschen, K., & Wright, V. (1993). Critique of the Pediatric Evaluation of Disability Inventory. *Physical and Occupational Therapy in Pediatrics, 13*(4), 57-87.

Reid, G., & Todd, T. (1988). *Declarative knowledge about catching by physically awkward and nonawkward children.* Paper presented at the North American Society for the Psychology of Sport and Physical Activity, Knoxville, TN.

Reilly, F.J. (1917). *New rational athletics for boys and girls.* New York: Heath.

Relman, A. (1988). Assessment and accountability: The third revolution in medical care. *New England Journal of Medicine, 319,* 1220-1222.

Reuss, A.L., Dally, A., & Lis, E.F. (1959). The Gesell Developmental Schedules and the physically handicapped child. *American Journal of Occupational Therapy, 13,* 117-124, 135.

Reynolds, C.R. (Ed.). (1994). *Cognitive assessment: A multidisciplinary perspective.* New York: Plenum Press.

Richards, J.N. (1914). Physical education efficiency tests for grade schools. *American Physical Education Review, 19,* 637-646.

Richter, E., & Montgomery, P.C. (1989). *Sensorimotor Performance Analysis.* Hugo, MN: PDP Press.

Richter, R.R., VanSant, A.F., & Newton, R.A. (1989). Description of adult rolling movements and hypothesis of developmental sequences. *Physical Therapy, 69,* 63-71.

Riggen, K.J., Ulrich, D.A., & Ozmun, J.C. (1990). Reliability and concurrent validity of the Test of Motor Impairment—Henderson Revision. *Adapted Physical Activity Quarterly, 7,* 249-258.

Ring, C., Matthews, R., Nayak, U.S.L., & Isaacs, B. (1988). Visual push: A sensitive measure of dynamic balance in man. *Archives of Physical Medicine and Rehabilitation, 69*, 256-260.

Roach, E.G., & Kephart, N.C. (1966). *The Purdue Perceptual-Motor Survey*. Columbus, OH: Merrill.

Roberton, M.A. (1977). Stability of stage categorizations across trials: Implications for the "stage theory" of overarm throw development. *Journal of Human Movement Studies, 3*, 49-59.

Roberton, M.A. (1978). Longitudinal evidence for developmental stages in the forceful overarm throw. *Journal of Human Movement Studies, 4*, 167-175.

Roberton, M.A. (1982). Describing "stages" within and across motor tasks. In J.A.S. Kelso & J.E. Clark (Eds.), *The development of movement control and co-ordination* (pp. 293-308). New York: Wiley.

Roberton, M.A. (1984). Changing motor patterns during childhood. In J.R. Thomas (Ed.), *Motor development during childhood and adolescence* (pp. 48-90). Minneapolis: Burgess.

Roberton, M.A., & Langendorfer, S. (1993). Developmental profiles: Evidence for constraints on action. *Journal of Sport and Exercise Psychology, 15*(Suppl.), S66.

Rochat, P. (1992). Self-sitting and reaching in 5- to 8-month-old infants: The impact of posture and its development on early eye-hand coordination. *Journal of Motor Behavior, 24*, 210-220.

Roche, A.F., & Malina, R.M. (1983a). *Manual of physical status and performance in childhood* (Vol. 1). New York: Plenum Press.

Roche, A.F., & Malina, R.M. (1983b). *Manual of physical status and performance in childhood* (Vol. 2). New York: Plenum Press.

Rogers, S.J., D'Eugenio, D.B., Brown, S.L., Donovan, C.M., & Lynch, E.W. (1977). *Early Intervention Development Profile*. Ann Arbor, MI: University of Michigan Press.

Roszkowski, M.J. (1989). Review of the Bayley Scales of Infant Development. In J.C. Conoley & J.J. Kramer (Eds.), *The tenth mental measurements yearbook* (pp. 74-82). Lincoln, NE: University of Nebraska Press.

Rothstein, J.M., & Echternach, J.L. (1993). *Primer on measurement: An introductory guide to measurement issues*. Alexandria, VA: American Physical Therapy Association.

Rowntree, D. (1987). *Assessing students: How shall we know them?* (Rev. ed.). London: Kogan Page.

Russell, D.J., Rosenbaum, P.L., Cadman, D.T., Gowland, C., Hardy, S., & Jarvis, S. (1989). The Gross Motor Function Measure: A means to evaluate the effects of physical therapy. *Developmental Medicine and Child Neurology, 31*, 341-352.

Russell, D.J., Rosenbaum, P.L., Lane, M., Gowland, C., Goldsmith, C.H., Boyce, W.F., & Plews, N. (1994). Training users in the Gross Motor Function Measure: Methodological and practical issues. *Physical Therapy, 74*, 630-636.

Russell, D.J., Ward, M., & Law, M. (1994). Test-retest of the Fine Motor Scale of the Peabody Developmental Motor Scales in children with cerebral palsy. *Occupational Therapy Journal of Research, 14*, 178-182.

Sacks, O. (1990). *The man who mistook his wife for a hat*. New York: Harper Collins.

Safrit, M.J. (1986). *Introduction of measurement in physical education and exercise science*. St. Louis: Times Mirror/Times College.

Safrit, M.J. (1989). An overview of measurement. In M.J. Safrit & T.M. Wood (Eds.), *Measurement concepts in physical education and exercise science* (pp. 3-20). Champaign, IL: Human Kinetics.

Safrit, M.J., Cohen, A.S., & Costa, M.G. (1989). Item response theory and the measurement of motor behavior. *Research Quarterly for Exercise and Sport, 60,* 325-335.

Safrit, M.J., Zhu, W., Costa, M.G., & Zhang, L. (1992). The difficulty of sit-ups tests: An empirical investigation. *Research Quarterly for Exercise and Sport, 63,* 277-283.

Sakurai, S., & Miyashita, M. (1983). Developmental aspects of overarm throwing related to age and sex. *Human Movement Science, 2,* 67-76.

Sale, D.G., & Norman, R.W. (1982). Testing strength and power. In J.D. MacDaugall, H.A. Wenger, & H.J. Green (Eds.), *Physiological testing of the elite athlete* (pp. 7-37). Ithaca, NY: Mouvement.

Salvia, J., & Ysseldyke, J. (1988). *Assessment in special and remedial education* (4th ed.). Dallas: Houghton Mifflin.

Sanford, A.R., & Zelman, J.G. (1981). *Learning Accomplishment Profile.* Winston-Salem, NC: Kaplan Press.

Sansevere, B. (1987, April 27). It's inevitable: Somebody will mess up in the NFL draft. *Minneapolis Star and Tribune,* pp. 1D, 4D.

Sargent, D.A. (1913). Twenty years' progress in efficiency tests. *American Physical Education Review, 18,* 452-456.

Sargent, D.A. (1921). The physical test of a man. *American Physical Education Review, 26,* 188-194.

Sargent, D.A. (1924). Some observations on the Sargent Test of Neuromuscular Efficiency. *American Physical Education Review, 29,* 47-56.

Sargent, D.A., Seaver, J.W., & Savage, W.L. (1897). Intercollegiate Strength-Tests. *American Physical Education Review, 2,* 216-220.

Sax, G. (1989). *Principles of educational and psychological measurement and evaluation* (3rd ed.). Belmont, CA: Wadsworth.

Scarr, S. (1984). *Mother care, other care.* New York: Basic Books.

Schmidt, L.S., Westcott, S.L., & Crowe, T.K. (1993). Interrater reliability of the Gross Motor Scale of the Peabody Developmental Motor Scales with 4- and 5-year-old children. *Pediatric Physical Therapy, 5,* 69-175.

Schmidt, R.A. (1982). *Motor control and learning: A behavioral emphasis.* Champaign, IL: Human Kinetics.

Schoemaker, M.M. (1992). *Evaluation of the effects of physiotherapy in children with a developmental coordination disorder.* Unpublished doctoral thesis, State University of Groningen, Netherlands.

Schoening, H.A., Anderegg, L., Bergstrom, D., Fonda, M., Steinke, N., & Ulrich, P. (1965). Numerical scoring of self-care status of patients. *Archives of Physical Medicine and Rehabilitation, 46,* 689-697.

Schrader, C.L. (1913). How may efficiency tests be made generally efficient? *American Physical Education Review, 18,* 457-462.

Schuettner, A.J. (1919, April 14). The University of Illinois plan to stimulate interest in physical education for men. *University of Illinois Bulletin, 16,* No. 33.

Schultz, C.I. (1992). *Concurrent validity of the Pediatric Evaluation of Disability Inventory.* Unpublished master's thesis, Tufts University, Medford, MA.

Schutz, R.W., Smoll, F.L., Carre, F.A., & Mosher, R.E. (1985). Inventories and norms for children's attitudes toward physical activity. *Research Quarterly for Exercise and Sport, 56,* 256-265.

Schutz, R.W., Smoll, F.L., & Wood, T.M. (1981). A psychometric analysis of an inventory for assessing children's attitudes toward physical activity. *Journal of Sport Psychology, 3,* 321-344.

Schwartz, S.H. (1994). *Visual perception: A clinical orientation.* Stamford, CT: Appleton & Lange.

Scott, M.G. (1939). The assessment of motor abilities of college women through objective tests. *Research Quarterly, 10,* 63-83.

Scottish Low Birthweight Study Group. (1992). The Scottish Low Birth Weight Study: Outcome at 4 1/2 years in a geographically defined population of children weighing less than 1750 grams at birth. I. Survival, growth, neuromotor and sensory impairment. *Archives of Diseases of Childhood, 67,* 675-681.

Seaman, J.A. (Ed.). (1995). *Physical Best and individuals with disabilities: A handbook for inclusion in fitness programs.* Reston, VA: American Alliance for Health, Physical Education, and Recreation.

Seaman, J.A., & DePauw, K.P. (1989). *The new adapted physical education: A developmental approach* (2nd ed.). Mountain View, CA: Mayfield.

Seashore, R.H. (1930). Individual differences in motor skills. *Journal of General Psychology, 3,* 38-65.

Seefeldt, V. (1980). Developmental motor patterns: Implications for elementary school physical education. In K. Newell, G. Roberts, W. Halliwell, & G. Nadeau (Eds.), *Psychology of motor behavior and sport—1979* (pp. 314-323). Champaign, IL: Human Kinetics.

Seefeldt, V., & Haubenstricker, J. (1974-1976). *Developmental sequences of fundamental motor skills.* Unpublished manuscripts, Michigan State University, East Lansing.

Seefeldt, V., & Haubenstricker, J. (1982). Patterns, phases, or stages: An analytical model for the study of developmental movement. In J.A.S. Kelso & J.E. Clark (Eds.), *The development of movement control and co-ordination* (pp. 309-318). Chichester, England: Wiley.

Semans, S. (1965). Specific tests and evaluation tools for the child with central nervous system deficit. *Journal of the American Physical Therapy Association, 45,* 456-462.

Semans, S., Phillips, R., Romanoli, M., Miller, R., & Skillen, M. (1965). A cerebral palsy assessment chart. *Journal of the American Physical Therapy Association, 45,* 463-468.

Shavelson, R.J., & Webb, N.M. (1991). *Generalizability theory: A primer.* Newbury Park, CA: Sage.

Sheldon, M.P. (1935). A physical achievement record for use with crippled children. *Journal of Health and Physical Education, 6*(5), 30-31, 60.

Sheldon, W.H., Stevens, S.S., & Tucker, W.B. (1940). *The varieties of human physique.* New York: Harper & Brothers.

Shephard, N.T., & Telian, S.A. (1996). *Practical management of the balance disorder patient.* San Diego: Singular.

Sherrill, C. (1993). *Adapted physical activity, recreation and sport: Crossdisciplinary and lifespan* (4th ed.). Dubuque, IA: Brown & Benchmark.

Shick, J., & Berg, N.G. (1983). Indoor golf skill test for junior high school boys. *Research Quarterly for Exercise and Sport, 54,* 75-78.

Shirley, M. (1931). *The first two years, a study of twenty-five babies.* Minneapolis: University of Minnesota Press.

Shumway-Cook, A., & Horak, F.B. (1986). Assessing the influence of sensory interaction on balance. *Physical Therapy, 66,* 1548-1550.

Shumway-Cook, A., & Woollacott, M.H. (1995). *Motor control: Theory and practical applications.* Baltimore: Williams & Wilkins.

Sim, J., & Arnell, P. (1993). Measurement validity in physical therapy research. *Physical Therapy, 73,* 102-110.

Singh, D. (1993). Adaptive significance of female attractiveness: Role of waist-to-hip ratio. *Journal of Personality and Social Psychology, 65,* 293-307.

Siri, W.E. (1961). Body composition from fluid spaces and density. In J. Brozek & A. Henschel (Eds.), *Techniques for measuring body composition* (pp. 223-244). Washington, DC: National Academy of Science.

Sloan, W. (1948). *The Lincoln Adaptation of the Oseretsky Test.* Lincoln, IL: Lincoln State School.

Sloan, W. (1955). The Lincoln-Oseretsky Motor Development Scale. *Genetic Psychology Monographs, 51,* 183-252.

Smith, K.U., & Smith, W.H. (1962). *Perception and motion.* Philadelphia: Saunders.

Smith, L.B., & Thelen, E. (1993). *A dynamic systems approach to development: Applications.* Cambridge, MA: MIT Press.

Smith, R.O. (1990). *Occupational Therapy Functional Assessment Compilation Tool (OT FACT).* Rockville, MD: American Occupational Therapy Association.

Sox, H.C., Jr. (1986). Probability theory in the use of diagnostic tests. *Annals of Internal Medicine, 104,* 60-66.

Sparrow, S.S., Balla, D.A., & Cicchetti, D.V. (1984). *Vineland Adaptive Behavior Scales.* Circle Pines, MN: American Guidance Service.

Spray, J.A. (1987). Recent developments in measurement and possible applications to the measurement of psychomotor behavior. *Research Quarterly for Exercise and Sport, 58,* 203-209.

Steel, K.O., Glover, J.E., & Spasoff, R.A. (1991). The Motor Control Assessment: An instrument to measure motor control in physically disabled children. *Archives of Physical Medicine and Rehabilitation, 72,* 549-553.

Stevens, S.S. (1946). On the theory of scales of measurement. *Science, 103,* 677-680.

Stewart, D.L. (1993). Health care delivery system. In D.L. Stewart & S.H. Abeln (Eds.), *Documenting functional outcomes in physical therapy* (pp. 1-31). St. Louis: Mosby.

Stokes, N.A., Deitz, J.L., & Crowe, T.K. (1990). The Peabody Developmental Fine Motor Scale: An interrater reliability study. *American Journal of Occupational Therapy, 44,* 334-340.

Stone, H., & Sidel, J.L. (1993). *Sensory evaluation practices* (2nd ed.). San Diego: Academic Press.

Stott, D.H. (1966). A general test of motor impairment for children. *Developmental Medicine and Child Neurology, 8,* 523-531.

Stott, D.H., Henderson. S.E., & Moyes, F.A. (1986). The Henderson Revision of the Test of Motor Impairment: A comprehensive approach to assessment. *Adapted Physical Activity Quarterly, 3,* 204-216.

Stott, D.H., Moyes, F.A., & Headridge, S.E. (1968). *Test of Motor Impairment.* Guelph, Ontario, Canada: University of Guelph, Department of Psychology.

Stott, D.H., Moyes, F.A., & Henderson, S.E. (1972). *Test of Motor Impairment.* Guelph, Ontario, Canada: Brook Educational.

Stott, D.H., Moyes, F.A., & Henderson, S.E. (1984). *The Test of Motor Impairment—Henderson Revision.* San Antonio: Psychological Corporation.

Strand, B.N., & Wilson, R. (1993). *Assessing sport skills.* Champaign, IL: Human Kinetics.

Stuberg, W. (Ed.). (1987). *Milani-Comparetti Motor Development Screening Test.* Omaha: Meyer Children's Rehabilitation Institute.

Sugden, D.A., & Keogh, J.F. (1990). *Problems in movement skill development.* Columbia, SC: University of South Carolina Press.

Sugden, D., & Sugden, L. (1991). The assessment of movement skill problems in 7- and 9-year-old children. *British Journal of Educational Psychology, 61,* 329-345.

Sugden, D.A., & Wann, C. (1987). Kinaesthesis and motor impairment in children with moderate learning difficulties. *British Journal of Educational Psychology, 57,* 225-236.

Sundberg, K.B. (1992). *Inter-rater reliability of the Pediatric Evaluation of Disability Inventory.* Unpublished master's thesis, Boston University, Boston, MA.

Swanson, G. (1993). Functional outcome report: The next generation in physical therapy reporting. In D.L. Stewart & S.H. Abeln (Eds.), *Documenting functional outcomes in physical therapy* (pp. 101-134). St. Louis: Mosby.

Swanson, H.L., & Watson, B.L. (1989). *Educational and psychological assessment of exceptional children* (2nd ed.). Columbus, OH: Merrill.

Tanner, J.M. (1951). Photogrammetric anthropometry and an androgyny scale. *Lancet, 1*, 574-579.

Task Force on Standards for Measurement in Physical Therapy. (1991). Standards for tests and measurements in physical therapy practice. *Physical Therapy, 71*, 589-622.

Taylor, H.L., Jacobs, D.R., Jr., Schucker, B., Knudsen, J., Leon, A.S., & Debacker, G. (1978). A questionnaire for the assessment of leisure time physical activities. *Journal of Chronic Diseases, 31*, 741-755.

Terminology Task Force. (1994a). Uniform terminology for occupational therapy—third edition. *American Journal of Occupational Therapy, 48*, 1047-1054.

Terminology Task Force. (1994b). Uniform terminology—third edition: Application to practice. *American Journal of Occupational Therapy, 48*, 1055-1059.

Thelen, E. (1986). Development of coordinated movement: Implications for early human development. In M.G. Wade & H.T.A. Whiting (Eds.), *Motor development in children: Aspects of coordination and control* (pp. 107-124). Dordrecht, Netherlands: Nijhoff.

Thelen, E. (1995). Motor development: A new synthesis. *American Psychologist, 50*, 79-95.

Thelen, E., & Adolph, K.E. (1992). Arnold L. Gesell: The paradox of nature and nurture. *Developmental Psychology, 28*, 368-380.

Thelen, E., Corbetta, D., Kamm, K., Schneider, K., & Zernicke, R.F. (1993). The transition to reaching: Mapping intention and intrinsic dynamics. *Child Development, 64*, 1058-1098.

Thelen, E., & Smith, L.B. (1994). *A dynamic systems approach to the development of cognition and action.* Cambridge, MA: MIT Press.

Thelen, E., & Ulrich, B.D. (1991). Hidden skills: A dynamic systems analysis of treadmill stepping during the first year. *Monographs of the Society for Research in Child Development*, Serial No. 223, 56(1).

Thomas, J.R., & French, K.E. (1985). Gender differences across age in motor performance: A meta-analysis. *Psychological Bulletin, 98*, 260-282.

Thomas, J.R., Michael, D., & Gallagher, J.D. (1994). Effects of training on gender differences in overhand throwing: A brief quantitative literature analysis. *Research Quarterly for Exercise and Sport, 65*, 67-71.

Thomas, K.T., & Thomas, J.T. (1994). Developing expertise in sport: The relation of knowledge and performance. *International Journal of Sport Psychology, 25*, 295-312.

Thompson, D.W. (1992). *On growth and form* (Complete rev. ed.). New York: Dover. (Original work published 1942)

Thorn, D.W., & Deitz, J.C. (1989). Examining content validity through the use of content experts. *Occupational Therapy Journal of Research, 9*, 334-346.

Tinetti, M.E. (1986). Performance-oriented assessment of mobility problems in elderly patients. *Journal of the American Geriatrics Society, 34*, 119-126.

Trembath, J. (Ed.). (1977). *Milani-Comparetti Motor Development Screening Test.* Omaha: Meyer Children's Rehabilitation Institute.

Trettien, A.W. (1900). Creeping and walking. *American Journal of Psychology, 12*, 1-57.

Trombly, C. (1993). Anticipating the future: Assessment of occupational function. *American Journal of Occupational Therapy, 47*, 253-257.

Trombly, C.A. (1989). Evaluation of occupational performance tasks. In C.A. Trombly (Ed.), *Occupational therapy for physical dysfunction* (pp. 377-384). Baltimore: Williams & Wilkins.

Troster, H., & Brambring, M. (1993). Early motor development in blind infants. *Journal of Applied Developmental Psychology, 14*, 83-106.

Ulrich, B.D., & Ulrich, D.A. (1985). The role of balancing ability in performance of fundamental motor skills in 3-, 4-, and 5-year-old children. In J.E. Clark & J.H. Humphrey (Eds.), *Motor development: Current selected research* (Vol. 1) (pp. 87-97). Princeton, NJ: Princeton Book.

Ulrich, D.A. (1981). The standardization of a criterion-referenced test in fundamental motor and physical fitness skills. *Dissertation Abstracts International, 43*, 146A-147A.

Ulrich, D.A. (1982). *The Objectives-Based Motor Skill Assessment Instrument.* Unpublished manuscript, Southern Illinois University, Carbondale, IL.

Ulrich, D.A. (1984). The reliability of classification decisions made with the Objectives-Based Motor Skill Assessment Instrument. *Adapted Physical Activity Quarterly, 1*, 52-60.

Ulrich, D.A. (1985). *Test of Gross Motor Development.* Austin, TX: PRO-ED.

Ulrich, D.A. (1988). Children with special needs—assessing the quality of movement competence. *Journal of Health, Physical Education, Recreation & Dance, 59*(1), 43-47.

Ulrich, D.A. (1995, October). *A new test of fundamental motor skills.* Presentation at the Motor Development Research Consortium, DeKalb, IL.

Ulrich, D.A., & Collier, D.H. (1990). Perceived physical competence in children with mental retardation: Modification of a pictorial scale. *Adapted Physical Activity Quarterly, 7*, 338-354.

Ulrich, D.A., Riggen, K.J., Ozmun, J.C., Screws, D.P., & Cleland, F.E. (1989). Assessing movement control in children with mental retardation: A generalizability analysis of observers. *American Journal of Mental Retardation, 94*, 170-176.

Ulrich, D.A., & Ulrich, B.D. (1984). The Objectives-Based Motor-Skill Assessment Instrument: Validation of instructional sensitivity. *Perceptual and Motor Skills, 59*, 175-179.

Ulrich, D.A., & Wise, S.L. (1984). Reliability of scores obtained with the Objectives-Based Motor Skill Assessment Instrument. *Adapted Physical Activity Quarterly, 1*, 230-239.

Uniform Data System, State University of New York at Buffalo. (1987). *Guide for the Functional Independence Measure.* Amherst, NY: University Research Foundation.

Uniform Data System, State University of New York at Buffalo. (1991). *Guide for the Functional Independence Measure for Children* (Version 1.5). Amherst, NY: University Research Foundation.

University of California, Southern Branch. (1922). Organization of tests—Department of Physical Education for Men. *American Physical Education Review, 27*, 442, 444-445.

University of Oregon. (1924). The Pentathalon, a physical ability test. *American Physical Education Review, 29*, 30, 32, 88, 90-94.

Van Dalen, D.B., & Bennett, B.L. (1971). *A world history of physical education: Cultural, philosophical, comparative* (2nd ed.). Englewood Cliffs, NJ: Prentice Hall.

VanSant, A.F. (1988a). Age differences in movement patterns used by children to rise from a supine position to erect stance. *Physical Therapy, 68*, 1330-1338.

VanSant, A.F. (1988b). Rising from a supine position to erect stance: Description of adult movement and a developmental hypothesis. *Physical Therapy, 68,* 185-192.

VanSant, A.F., Cromwell, S., Deo, A., Ford-Smith, C., O'Neil, J., & Wrisley, D. (1988). Rising to stand from supine: A study of middle adulthood. *Physical Therapy, 68,* 830.

Vaughan, V.C., III, & Litt, I.F. (1992). Growth and development: Introduction. In R.E. Behrman (Ed.), *Nelson textbook of pediatrics* (14th ed.) (pp. 13-43). Philadelphia: Saunders.

Venn, J.J. (1986). Review: Peabody Developmental Motor Scales and Activity Cards. In D.J. Keyser & R.C. Sweetland (Eds.), *Test critiques* (Vol. 5) (pp. 310-313). Kansas City, MO: Test Corporation of America.

Verderber, J.M.S., & Payne, V.G. (1987). A comparison of the long and short forms of the Bruininks-Oseretsky Test of Motor Proficiency. *Adapted Physical Activity Quarterly, 4,* 51-59.

Vickers, J.N. (1990). *Instructional design for teaching physical activities: A knowledge structures approach.* Champaign, IL: Human Kinetics.

Vodola, T. (1978). *Project ACTIVE Motor Ability Tests.* Bloomfield, NJ: Wood.

Vulpe, S.G. (1982). *Vulpe Assessment Battery.* Downsview, Ontario, Canada: National Institute on Mental Retardation.

Wade, M.G., Lindquist, R., Taylor, J.R, & Treat-Jacobson, D. (1995). Optical flow, spatial orientation, and the control of posture in the elderly. *Journals of Gerontology, 50B,* P51-P58.

Wall, A.E., McClements, J., Bouffard, M., Findlay, H., & Taylor, M.J. (1985). A knowledge-based approach to motor development: Implications for the physically awkward. *Adapted Physical Activity Quarterly, 2,* 21-42.

Walls, R.T., Zane, T., & Werner, T.J. (1978). *The Vocational Behavior Checklist.* Dunbar, WV: Research and Training Center.

Walter, C.B., & Kamm, K. (1996). Optimal search strategies for optimal motor solutions: Self-determination or informed guidance? *Behavioral and Brain Sciences, 19,* 91-92.

Walters, C. (1995, April 23). Alexander, Stringer won't come cheaply. *St. Paul Pioneer Press,* p. 2C.

Waltman, M., Folsom-Meek, S., Bergerson, M., & Groteluschen, W. (1996, September). *Survey of physical education services for students with disabilities in Minnesota.* Mankato, MN: Mankato State University, Department of Human Performance.

Ward, A., Ebbeling, C.B., & Ahlquist, L.E. (1995). Indirect methods for estimation of aerobic power. In P.J. Maud & C. Foster (Eds.), *Physiological assessment of human fitness* (pp. 37-56). Champaign, IL: Human Kinetics.

Watrous, M. (1940). An action ability test for the spastic patient. *Physiotherapy Review, 20,* 140-145.

Wayman, A.R. (1923). A scheme for testing and scoring the physical efficiency of college girls. *American Physical Education Review, 28,* 415-420.

Wayman, A.R. (1930). Testing and scoring the physical efficiency of college women. *Research Quarterly, 1,* 74-86.

Werder, J.K., & Bruininks, R.H. (1988). *Body Skills: A motor development curriculum for children.* Circle Pines, MN: American Guidance Service.

Wessel, J.A. (1976). *I CAN Fundamental Skills.* Austin, TX: PRO-ED.

Wessel, J.A., & Kelly, L. (1986). *Achievement-based curriculum development in physical education.* Philadelphia: Lea & Febiger.

West, W.L. (1967). The occupational therapist's changing responsibility to the community. *American Journal of Occupational Therapy, 11,* 312-316.

Westcott, S.L., Crowe, T.K., Deitz, J.C., & Richardson, P. (1994). Test-retest reliability of the Pediatric Clinical Test of Sensory Interaction for Balance (P-CTSIB). *Physical and Occupational Therapy in Pediatrics, 14*, 1-22.

Wickstrom, R.L. (1970). *Fundamental motor patterns.* Philadelphia: Lea & Febiger.

Wickstrom, R.L. (1983). *Fundamental motor patterns* (3rd ed.). Philadelphia: Lea & Febiger.

Wild, M.R. (1938). The behavior pattern of throwing and some observations concerning its course of development in children. *Research Quarterly, 9*(3), 20-24.

Wilkerson, L., Batavia, A.I., & DeJong, G. (1992). Use of functional status measures for payment of medical rehabilitation services. *Archives of Physical Medicine and Rehabilitation, 73*, 111-120.

Williams, H.G. (1983). *Perceptual and motor development.* Englewood Cliffs, NJ: Prentice Hall.

Williams, K. (1980). The developmental characteristics of a forward roll. *Research Quarterly for Exercise and Sport, 51*, 703-713.

Wilson, B.N., Polatajko, H.J., Kaplan, B.J., & Faris, P. (1995). Use of the Bruininks-Oseretsky Test of Motor Proficiency in occupational therapy. *American Journal of Occupational Therapy, 49*, 8-17.

Witt, P., & Ellis, G. (1985). *Leisure Diagnostic Battery.* State College, PA: Venture.

Wolanski, N., & Zdanska-Brincken, M. (1973). A new method for the evaluation of motor development of infants. *Polish Psychological Bulletin, 4*, 43-53.

Wood, T.M. (1989). The changing nature of norm-referenced validity. In M.J. Safrit & T.M. Wood (Eds.), *Measurement concepts in physical education and exercise science* (pp. 23-44). Champaign, IL: Human Kinetics.

World Health Organization. (1980). *International classification of impairments, disabilities, and handicaps.* Geneva: World Health Organization.

Wright, B.D., & Linacre, J.M. (1989). Observations are always ordinal; measurements, however, must be interval. *Archives of Physical Medicine and Rehabilitation, 70*, 857-860.

Wright, H.C., & Sugden, D.A. (1996). The nature of developmental coordination disorder: Inter- and intragroup differences. *Adapted Physical Activity Quarterly, 13*, 357-371.

Wright, H.C., Sugden, D.A., Ng, R., & Tan, J. (1994). Identification of children with movement problems in Singapore: Usefulness of the Movement ABC Checklist. *Adapted Physical Activity Quarterly, 11*, 150-157.

Wurth, B.H. (1980). Review of the Wolanski Gross Motor Evaluation. *Physical and Occupational Therapy in Pediatrics, 1*, 63-70.

Yarmolenko, A. (1933). The motor sphere of school-age children. *Pedagogical Seminary and Journal of Genetic Psychology, 42*, 298-318.

Yule, W. (1967). A Short Form of the Oseretsky Test of Motor Proficiency. *Bulletin of the British Psychological Society, 20*, 29A-30A.

Zausmer, E., & Tower, G. (1966). A quotient for the evaluation of motor development. *Journal of the American Physical Therapy Association, 46*, 725-727.

Zdanska-Brincken, M., & Wolanski, N. (1969). A graphic method for the evaluation of motor development in infants. *Developmental Medicine and Child Neurology, 11*, 228-241.

Zhu, W., & Cole, E. L. (1996). Many-faceted Rasch calibration of a gross-motor instrument. *Research Quarterly for Exercise and Sport, 67*, 24-34.

Index

About the Authors

Allen Burton is an associate professor in the School of Kinesiology and Leisure Studies at the University of Minnesota. Since 1986, he has taught a successful graduate-level course that directly addresses issues related to movement skill assessment. He has also made many workshop presentations and written numerous articles on the topic of movement skill assessment.

One of two associate editors for *Adapted Physical Activity Quarterly*, Burton is a member of the American Alliance for Health, Physical Education, Recreation and Dance and the North American Society for the Psychology of Sport and Physical Activity. Honors he has received include the Award for Distinguished Teaching from the University of Minnesota's College of Education (1991) and the Joseph P. Kennedy Foundation Research Scientist Award in Mental Retardation (1988-89).

Burton earned his doctorate in physical education and human movement studies from the University of Oregon.

Daryl Miller, a special education administrator for a large suburban school district in Minnesota, has more than 25 years' combined experience as a therapist, teacher, and coach. Miller developed assessment guidelines and procedures at the local and state levels and was a founding member of state organizations for allied health professionals and adapted physical education specialists. He earned his specialist certificate in educational administration from the University of Minnesota.

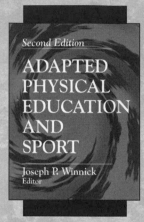

ANDREW MARR

A short book about painting

quadrille

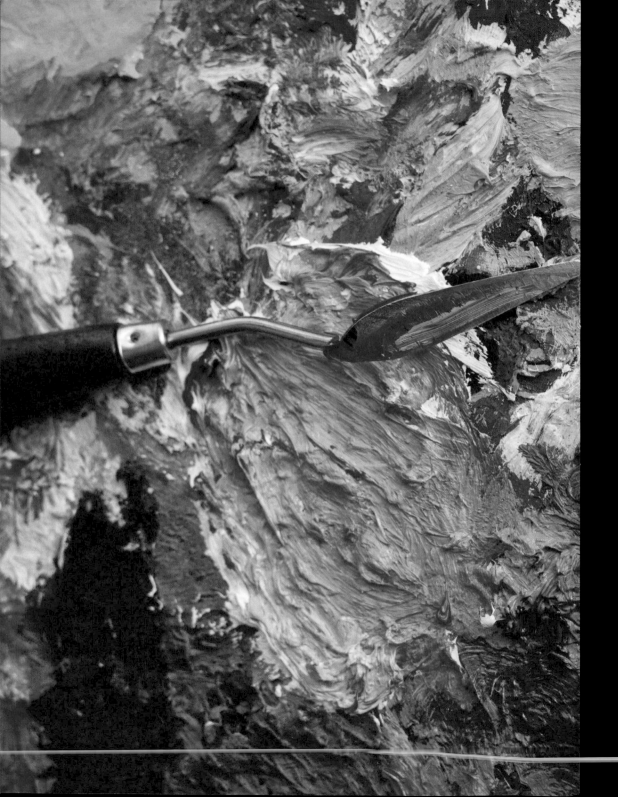

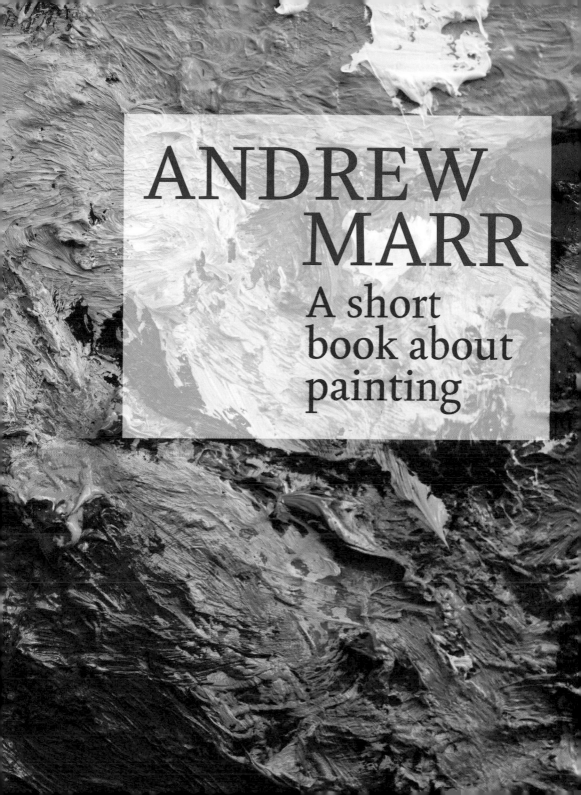

ANDREW MARR

A short book about painting

Publishing director: Sarah Lavelle
Creative director: Helen Lewis
Project editor: Jinny Johnson
Designer: Gemma Wilson
Picture researcher: Liz Boyd
Proofreader: Mary-Jane Wilkins
Production director: Vincent Smith
Production controller: Tom Moore

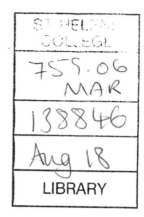
First published in 2017 by
Quadrille Publishing Ltd
Pentagon House
52-54 Southwark Street
London SE1 1UN
www.quadrille.com

Quadrille is an imprint of Hardie Grant
www.hardiegrant.com

Cataloguing in Publication Data: a catalogue record for this
book is available from the British Library.

978 1 84949 993 4

Printed in China

CONTENTS

INTRODUCTION

What is this book and who is it for? To begin with, here is what it isn't: it isn't a painting primer, any kind of manual or a "how-to" book. If that's what you're after, there are hundreds to choose from. Neither is it a book about the history of painting, nor a collection of essays on art. Again, you may have come across one or two of those already.

This is a book for people who enjoy looking at paintings, and for people who paint. As someone who does both, I realised that the problems of looking at paintings – and I'm thinking mostly about contemporary paintings – and making paintings are intimately connected.

Why do I like this picture? And why do I think that one's a failure? Why do some compositions hold attractively together, and others collapse? Why do I feel an emotional response to one combination of colours, while another leaves me cold?

Looking at modern painting is both popular and quite difficult. The exhibitions of modern masters swarm with art lovers, who have mostly paid for tickets and travel. If you look at their faces you will see concentrated, rapt expressions. Why, really, are they there? What do they want from the experience?

Whatever they're doing, they are making judgements about hard problems. They are making sense of canvases painted in a single colour, with no motifs; they may be engaging emotionally with entirely abstract shapes; they are responding to the material presence of something that's a long way away from being a photograph. And as they look, they are thinking about, and perhaps resolving, issues that practising painters struggle with every day.

My only advantage in writing about all this is that because I paint, I can talk about colour, composition, ambition and failure without libelling anybody else. I hope I can get close to the mystery of what happens in the studio when a painter is thinking about what to do – though I don't think I have resolved that mystery. In general, when it

*comes to painting, we talk perhaps too easily and
triumphantly about success and we don't think
enough about the failures from which lessons are
learned and on which success is built.*

*I have structured this short book as follows: after
an introductory chapter which dives straight into
questions about what painting, or indeed any art, is
for, I deal with changing taste; with colour; and with
the problem of shape, or motif. I then try to describe
what happens in the studio, and the materials art
is made from and why they matter. On the way,
I express heartfelt hostility to aspects of the art
market and contemporary taste.*

*So this is a book about the most enjoyable,
difficult, serious thing I have so far found to spend
time on. If it makes you look at pictures even slightly
differently, or if it encourages you in the making of
your own pictures, then it will have done its job.*

Andrew Marr, *Primrose Hill, March 2017*

1 LOSING MY RELIGION

What is painting for?
Our time in this world is very beautiful, and very
brief. To properly grasp this, every day, we need
perspective, a view of it. The appropriate word is
transcendence, meaning to climb above, or climb
out of, the everyday. Up there, reflecting, we may
be better able to appreciate the world's beauty and
its brevity.

Transcendence is what we hope for from art
whether it be through the slow movement of a
Beethoven string quartet, a soliloquy in a Samuel
Beckett play, or the shapes and colours of a late
Matisse. These are simply different routes – different
fixes, different needles – to achieve the same end,
which is, I repeat, a better perspective on this

business of being alive. Most of the time in day-to-day life there is no such perspective. And in trying to discover it, much art fails.

Our world is beautiful; but also very boring. I am writing this in Florida, once an untamed tract of mangroves and marshy rainforest, full of wildness and surprising beauty, but now a huge, bleak grid of turnpikes and motorways, endlessly scored across with lines of concrete and wire. Unlovely barrack-like buildings and a tangle of advertising signs offer a rare splash of colour. The roads are congested; as cars dawdle alongside you, you see angry and frustrated faces flinching at the red lights ahead. Everybody is on the move. Everybody, it seems, is anxious to be somewhere else. Time is sliced into harried segments.

That is one person's impression of life in one place, but there is a more general point. Almost wherever we are, our experience of life is often of boredom and frustration. We are glued into time, the fourth dimension, and yet there is never nearly enough of it. And this, for me, is the point of art. Art helps us to stop off and remind ourselves that we are making but a brief visit to a beautiful world. Remembering this regularly is probably a way to be happy.

Painting is a system of communication with only one message, the sensation of being alive more intensely than normal.

Some people will say this is not true. Or at least, not completely true. And yes, painting can be sardonic, sarcastic, ironic – many things. And yes, we live in a profoundly sarcastic, ironic and even cruel culture. The inaptly described "social media" produces a vortex of fear, mockery and hatred. More of our films are about violence and destruction than any other subject. Our mainstream media relates a ceaseless narrative of failure and greed, disaster and cowardice. I'm part of it; I hate that. And some paintings, like many pieces of music, theatrical performances and other art forms, fall woefully short: they add to the general boredom.

But of course we are much more interesting than this, and we know it, at least some of the time. We want to climb out of the grey filth; we are desperate for transcendence.

Many people achieve transcendence through religion or a quasi-religious practice – prayer, meditation, praise. But religion's rival for transcendence, for a better perspective on the brief and surprising glory of being alive, is art.

Looking or listening?

If that is true, how does visual art differ from, for instance, the arts of poetry or music? Is the difference trivial or fundamental? These are questions not just for those who make art but also for all of us who experience it. And there is no doubt that the materials or forms used to create an artwork affect its possibilities. A poem, composed of words, necessarily involves different parts of the brain from a painting. The poem carries with it the

A SHORT BOOK ABOUT PAINTING

whole complex history and structure of daily language, echoes, expectations, and the underlying logic of syntax. The mind is scurrying to make sense, even as it is being seduced by the music. A successful poem might be said to occur at the point when the reader ceases to be aware of the words as words, and the poem appears to become life itself. But a poem that tries to leave behind the literal meaning of the packets of syllables, their everyday significance, generally falls into obscurity and fails.

Music, originating deep in our prehistoric past, and fired by the human need for communal movement and rhythm, works differently. It has its logic, of course, and its highly sophisticated language, which can be written out just like English, German or Mandarin. But it stands further away from mundane communication. It works by seducing our natural love for harmonies and regular rhythms, and then overturning or subverting our expectations – thus time is given added drama.

To enjoy a poem or a piece of good music you need to concentrate while emptying your mind of the surrounding clutter. If you are thinking about the school pickup, or an unpaid bill, you aren't going to be pulled in by T S Eliot or by Beethoven. You are going to get your transcendence – you're going to climb that ladder and look at life afresh – only if you focus hard on the lines or the sounds.

In a poem, that most intense and unstable of art forms, we naturally enjoy assonance, wit and rhythm, as we follow the logic of the words. In a

piece of music, we seem to have a natural liking
for certain harmonies, and we yearn for harmonic
resolution even as we enjoy being wrong-footed. In
painting, certain shapes and colour combinations
mean a great deal to us, probably because of our
evolutionary history – more on this later. Yellows
and blues, greens and reds, sit naturally together.
A horizontal horizon line, particularly if we are
looking down at it towards the bottom of the picture
frame, brings a feeling of calm and security. Slanted
lines, particularly zigzags, produce disquiet. A range
of soft to aquamarine blues, redolent of a warm
sky, appeal to almost everyone. And as in music or
poetry, we look for harmony and balance – we like
shapes to be echoed, though not monotonously,
and we expect the energy of the picture to be
resolved inside it, not to fly off on to the wall
over one side or another.

In all of the arts, we understand when they
are having an impact on us, physically. Our blood
pressure rises. We breathe slightly faster and more
deeply. And we feel a nervous concentration that
isn't sexual (far from it) and yet is parallel. These
are the bodily evidences of the better perspective
on life that we are looking for.

The deal; and a little autobiography

But in all the arts, this only happens through a
contract between the artist and the reader, listener or
watcher. It's a two-way deal. If you aren't open to the
experience, it won't come to you. The problem with

painting is that it can be glanced at. You don't buy
a ticket, and promise to stand looking for x amount
of time. Just as you can skim a poem, not properly
reading it, or half-hear a piece of music, treating it
as muzak, so you can walk past a picture and get the
impression that you've seen it, rather than *actually*
seeing it. You need a lot of time, looking hard, before
a painting really releases its energy and its message.

For around 40 years, from my early teenage years
to the age of 53, I painted like this: I would take a
small box or a grimy bag of tubes of gouache or oil
paint, a foldaway easel and a pre-prepared board to
a hillside or a flat rock or to the side of the road.
Then I would sketch out roughly what I saw in front
of me, and paint it in colours. I would do this when
I had a holiday or over a few free days – not very
often. Over time and not surprisingly I became
slightly more skilled, learned a few tricks and
became, therefore, more artful. Then I had a stroke,
which paralysed the left-hand side of my body, and
I had to give all that up.

I now recognise that I've been telling a deceitful
story about what happened next. I've said that
because of the practical difficulties of being unable
to paint outside, I was forced to start again in a
studio, where I could control my environment.
There, I was obliged to find a new way of painting
because I didn't want to do still lifes of flowers or
oranges, or indeed nudes.

Though all of that is true enough, it leaves out the
most important thing. After coming close to losing

my life, I had a more intense sense of how little time I had left – the "shortness of life" thing, running alongside the "beauty of life" thing. I realised that, more than anything else, I'd always wanted to paint well, but that I'd put it off because I was frightened of not being good enough. Now I thought to myself: Andrew, you're in danger of running out of time. How would you feel if you found yourself too old and simply too frail to paint – and you'd never tried, not seriously? You'd never risked it?

I knew I would feel mightily hacked off – a coward – miserable. So I told myself to *get on with it*. Try to paint properly. That's what I have been doing, and it isn't really much to do with physical disability. And I have never enjoyed myself more.

Well, enjoyed? Sometimes, with my back aching and after several hours of intense concentration, I find myself weeping with frustration. Why don't I have that innate understanding of shape and form that Kandinsky had? Why, after years of trying, can't I draw a single line with the honesty of Matisse? There are no answers beyond the vagaries of differently distributed human skills and characters. But at least I know where the gaps are.

I had originally decided to call this book *How to Paint Badly* because that is mostly what I do. And indeed, I think that very many painters, maybe most, paint badly and then rescue failed marks and designs at the last minute, wresting the roses of success from the ashes of disaster, like those white-bearded scientists in *Chitty Chitty Bang Bang*. But then I decided that, apart from giving every critic too easy an introductory paragraph, such a title would be fundamentally dishonest. It's a kind of joke, made against myself. It sounds offhand, maybe cynical. But for me, nothing here is a joke.

What do I mean by painting "well"? I don't, I hope, have exaggerated ideas of my own talent but I want to make pictures that express how deeply I feel about the world, and aren't simply copies of how other people feel. And I want to make images that are alive and self-confident enough to hold their place on a wall. This, I have found, is surprisingly difficult.

The market problem

One of the reasons it's difficult here and now is that painting is enclosed by a loud and distracting art market. The shapers of taste and price are dauntingly grand. In the normal way, you wouldn't want to rub up against them. You have them and their favoured artists on the one hand, and a mutinous, deeply sceptical public on the other. And nobody, it seems just now, much wants to use words like transcendence or beauty.

We must be more knowing, apparently. We should be less naive. The art market is, like most markets, fast and efficient – but it's also hard-boiled and cynical. Entrepreneurs, investors and their experts dominate it. A chilly knowingness prevails; artists are bullied and bribed into producing predictable chunks of value that can be easily sold on.

The artist and the dealer need a brand. But the brands also need to keep changing – for why else would people keep buying? To maintain high prices in the market, to keep the buyer and media interest hot, relentless innovation is needed. *Yesterday's* new idea is deader than dead. To dwell on what is over is fatal – pathetic. Nothing is more dangerous in the bustle and press of the contemporary art market than nostalgia. As in financial markets, smoking-hot news is the only currency.

Well, that's how things are in our accelerating world. The danger is that through this process, art becomes like everything else – as ugly, as cynical and as pointless as much of the rest of contemporary culture. Dull as a traffic jam. And yet art that's being made right now all around the world by relatively unknown people can still grab us by the throat and take us out of ourselves, overthrowing our petty egotism.

This process is hard won, however. Successful art engages the intellect as well as emotion. It makes us concentrate. It quickens our breathing. It sharpens our attention. It cleans our spectacles, and it teaches us new ways of concentrating. It is so powerful – so very powerful – that it is triumphantly surviving its own snobby, cynical globalised market.

I've called this chapter "Losing my Religion", the title of the famous REM song. Apparently, it's simply Texan slang for becoming infuriated – as in "losing it". But art is the nearest thing I have to a religion and I do fear losing it because of the cynicism and condescension of the modern art world. If you talk to intelligent, thoughtful gallery owners, and indeed to some artists, you find plenty of people just as worried.

But I'm trying *not* to lose my religion. When I'm tired, when I'm lonely, when I'm despairing, I go into a gallery and see a picture for the first time, perhaps by a 20-year-old from round the corner, perhaps by a Venetian who has been dead for four centuries, and I come alive again.

Dead art and alive art: yet another problem
Making "alive" art is hard even for the hugely talented and the closely observant. A painting by a famous and gifted artist, who has given it all his attention and accumulated skill, can suddenly, and dramatically, lose its life. It can become just another sticky "thing" rather than something that urgently communicates. I want to use this short book to try to explain what seems to me to be the key problem: what separates a dead failure from a living and inspiring artwork? This is something that confronts us surprisingly often.

Think of going into a chain hotel in any big city. There will be pictures, probably prints, scattered along the corridors and in the bedrooms. They will have been made by trained artists, who will have sold the rights to the images to the corporation that owns the hotel. These artists will be serious and perhaps committed people, certainly not cynical: and yet, 99 times out of a hundred, the art on the walls will be dead. You will walk past it and you will feel entirely unchanged. Go into a big department store and you will find, in the bedroom furniture department, glossy, gold-leafed modern art works guaranteed to make you feel bored. Click on one of the popular image-based websites such as Pinterest, and you will quickly find more of the same.

And the point is that these are nearly quite good pictures. The gap between an abstract painting by Mark Rothko, which should bring you to the edge of tears, and a picture by one of his hundreds of talented imitators, which will bring you only tears of ennui, is a very tiny, thin and hard-to-describe line.

To complicate things further, plenty of dead art is made by famous and expensive artists. Jeff Koons is about as lauded as it gets. He specialises in fabricated sculptures of wood, steel or porcelain, on the most banal of subjects; they're a kind of running critique, presumably, of our trivial and commercialised world. But as commerce, they certainly work. In 2013 one of his "balloon dog" sculptures was sold by Christie's in New York for US$58.4 million, becoming the most expensive work by a living artist sold at auction.

Koons's work is knowing and glossy. Much of it is fabricated by others. If it is meant satirically, then nobody loves it more than the materialist super-rich at whom it is presumably aimed. (In which case, you might say, the aiming isn't so good.) For me, at least, it is utterly dead – banal and closer to appeasement than satire.

Genuinely alive art – whether it's a quick sketch of a mineral water bottle by David Hockney, or an assemblage of leaves pinned together with thorns by an environmental artist – depends first of all upon fresh looking. The artist may well be aware of the hundreds and thousands of years of art-making, but will have resisted the temptation to look at the world through spectacles borrowed from the dead. The contemporary artist must bring information that our restless eyes and memories have not already made stale.

Easy to say. So many brilliant people have worked so hard for so many centuries, deploying new techniques, new materials and new ideas, that it can seem hard to find something fresh to say. Jean-Michel Basquiat was an untrained Haitian-American artist from Brooklyn who died of a heroin overdose at the age of 27. But he had an eye and a sense of colour and line that meant that he could make explosive pictures which are brimming with life and like nothing else that had ever been made before.

All around the world every day, artists do exactly that. If you take the trouble to visit small galleries and hunt out the work, you will be thrilled and constantly surprised by what is being done near you, wherever you are, right now. But that art won't be all in one style, or mode, and it may differ shockingly. The question is – is it alive or is it dead? To begin to try to answer this, I want to turn in the next chapter to the very slippery, but inescapably important, question of taste. Before we do that, however, we have to deal with an even more obvious question, the apparent division in modern painting between representational or "that's what it looks like" art and so-called abstract art.

PYRO, 1984 (ACRYLIC AND MIXED MEDIA ON CANVAS)
Jean-Michel Basquiat

What are paintings of?

People who look at paintings properly would surely agree that the old firebreak between representational or "proper" paintings and "abstract" paintings is now completely useless. All paintings are representational – just of different things. What really matters is the quality of the representation, the thought that's gone into it. Because painting is a form of knowledge, it should not be cut off from other kinds of knowledge. Our understanding of the world around us is changing fast; and it is natural that painting should also be changing.

Take something simple – a picture of a field. Overleaf is a picture I made a few years ago in South Devon, and I think that in terms of composition – the way the curves meet, the role of the land, the use of curving dykes to tie the picture together, and so forth – it works OK. The soft reddish-browns and sharp greens fairly represent the mixed arable and grazing farming of the Otter Valley.

It isn't a great piece of painting – the brushstrokes are rather crude, it was done hurriedly and so on – but it's OK. Isn't it? No it isn't, not really. It's a sentimental, lazy, second-hand piece of work.

What is a field? It's a stretch of topsoil – seething,

living, infinitely complex, a mulch of microorganisms, including many bacteria, fragments of shell and stone, decaying vegetable matter, water, feathers, bones – that allows the regular seeding and growth of plants, which in turn keep us alive. It changes colour and shape almost by the week. Anyone who drives past fields must see how quickly the farmer's work, as well as seasonal shifts of water and wind, alters them. So fields are moving.

For a painting of fields to be alive, the quality of looking must be much better than it is in this example. It's all about information. The Scottish poet Hugh MacDiarmid argued that to really see landscape, you need an understanding of its farming history, its economics and its biology – a knowing countryman's eye. In one of a series of poems with the Gaelic title *Direadh*, which means "act of surmounting" – quite close to transcendence, therefore – he describes the borderlands of Dunbar, whose soil and shape aren't so different from those in South Devon:

This is the cream of the country – probably
The cream of the earth, the famous Dunbar red lands.
These red loams combine a maximum of fertility
With friable easy-working qualities of unequalled perfection.
Potatoes, a level sea of lusty shaws and flowery tops
From a fence to fence in summer-time,
Then wheat, going to eight quarters an acre,
And then the swedes and turnips
Flickering strong and lusty...

happy day. 29·8·07

This is as far away from traditional nature writing as modern painting should be from traditional landscape. Somehow, we need painting that's aware of the fast changes, the decay and rebirth – the hidden dramas – in the most humdrum field. But I think the best painters have always been aware

HAPPY DAY, 29.8.2007
Andrew Marr

LOSING MY RELIGION

of this. At the birth of modern painting, Claude Monet was working more politically, and even polemically, than perhaps many of his modern admirers have noticed. In an important exhibition in 1990 from the Museum of Fine Arts in Boston, *Monet in the 90s*, Paul Hayes Tucker showed that Monet's apparently innocuous subjects, from the grain stacks behind his house to a stand of poplar trees which he bought to prevent them being cut down while he was working, had much to say about the agricultural market, and indeed the state of rural France, in his time. Monet talked with local peasants and tradesmen: he knew exactly what he was painting. It was very far from being a blur of pretty colours.

A decent picture of something as simple as a field can't be merely nostalgic, static, or made without knowledge. While travelling with David Hockney as he was drawing and painting in the East Yorkshire landscape around Bridlington, I was struck by how he felt he was relearning knowledge of the changing shapes of leaves, plants and landscapes, and the common sense of the farmers who have now vanished from the scene; knowledge that needs to be reabsorbed by a painter looking intently.

But as knowledge moves forward, the painter's problems increase. The Russian Jewish sculptor Naum Gabo, who influenced many modern British artists, pointed out that a tree trunk is not what it appears. It is "a mass of seething particles which do not even keep within the bounds of its apparent skin,

POPLARS ON THE EPTE, 1891
Claude Monet

A SHORT BOOK ABOUT PAINTING

but fly out and mingle with adjacent matter."[1] That's modern physics talking. Under the most apparently static surfaces, matter is in constant, buzzing movement. How can painters begin to represent these things without falling back on the literalist numerical or symbolic scientific means? They can't. The job of the painter is to find other ways, not to mimic scientists. It isn't hard to see a version of the underlying instability of the world in the work of artists such as Paul Klee, Kandinsky, the Cubists or Jackson Pollock. But they have found other ways of describing truths, miles away from scientific diagrams. In the end, the painter produces a painting which must work in its own right. It must have its own bulk and identity, stand on its own feet and be the thing itself, not something "about" something else.

That isn't simply what I think. It's what the most eloquent and some of the best recent painters think as well. John Hoyland, a very successful non-representational painter throughout the second half of the 20th century and into this one said, "Painting is making form out of chaos. You can't end with chaos." Patrick Heron, another wonderful painter, said: "I hate all symbols in painting: I love, instead, all images."

One answer is what has been called abstract painting, which is merely image and colour working outside the obvious boundaries of mimesis. Bridget Riley, whose complex paintings of stripes have made her internationally famous, says that she tries to

1 Quoted by Patrick Heron in his catalogue for a Zurich exhibition, 1963

2 Bridget Riley, *The Eye's Mind*, Ridinghouse, 2010

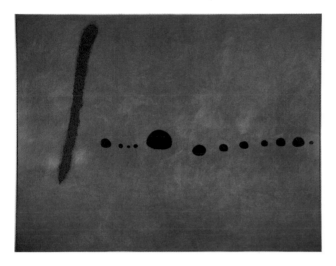

realise "visual and emotional energies" at the same time… "Such things as fast and slow movements, warm and cold colour, vocal and open space, repetition opposed to 'event', increase and decrease, static and active, black opposed to white, greys as sequences harmonising those polarities…"[2] If Bridget Riley chose to paint a field in Devon, she would get much closer to the underlying realities than I did.

In the end, painters are not little gods but human beings, living inside nature. So we all return to the natural envelope in which we live for our art, whatever it looks like. John Hoyland, whose paintings can seem entirely "abstract" tells an interesting story about his own art, and that of the renowned Catalan painter Joan Miró.

At the time, Hoyland was friends with Robert Motherwell, the great American painter. Hoyland tells us: "I thought I could invent and invent and invent. And Bob Motherwell gave me this book on Miró. I'd always thought that Miró had the greatest imagination of any artist in the 20th century, and then I found out that he went down to the beach every day and picked up bits and pieces, anything that he thought would give him a kick-start. And I realised that unless you're going to produce sterile geometric painting you have got to have some form of external inspiration. You can't live in a vacuum."[3]

So you go back to the world around you, whether or not you produce something that "looks like" that world. Clare Woods, a contemporary British painter, makes landscapes with poured and worked-over oil on aluminium, using masking tape and a cutter to give her hard black lines. She uses photographs, blown-up images, the sculpture of other artists; anything to – as Hoyland said of Miró – kick-start her pictures. Her landscapes are places of decay, darkness and menace – much closer to the reality of soil and nature than a sun-drenched "pretty" picture. To me they are modern, in the way that the poetry of Hugh MacDiarmid is modern.

Another way of dealing with fields, bringing new information and new looking to an old subject, came from the Cornish artist Peter Lanyon. After making dark, clotted, grimy pictures, which literally dug down below the surface of the Cornish landscape, Lanyon took up gliding. This didn't just let him see what had been familiar from many different perspectives, hanging from above, at the same time. It also allowed him to introduce the moving air that's

**DEAD SPRING, 2011
(OIL ON ALUMINIUM)**
Clare Woods

3 John Hoyland,
Unmistakable Identity, Alan Wheatley Art, 2009. Quoted in the introductory essay by John McEwen

all around us and which we are so often unconscious of, into the body of his art. This introduced completely different perspectives – exuberant, perhaps "abstract" and yet entirely representational of Cornwall. Just as Monet made pictures which have changed forever the way the ordinary person sees French landscape, or the River Thames, so Peter Lanyon made pictures that have changed the way any thinking person sees Cornwall.

Now, of course, almost all judgements about art have a strong element of individual prejudice. I find the work of Woods, Hoyland, Lanyon and Riley speaks to me more about the experience of living in the world than does more conventional representational painting. But many people would disagree. Why, they would ask, should the insights into representation hard won by the Impressionists in the 19th century be cast aside?

Why can't they be used to describe the modern world as it is, just as Monet or Manet described the fast-moving Paris of their day? Well, there are painters doing exactly that and although they aren't entirely to my taste, these are formidable and honourable artists.

Two examples are Ken Howard and Pete Brown. Howard is hugely popular and many of his paintings are of completely predictable things – vases of flowers in a window, cornfields, Venice. But he also turns his skill to modern London street scenes, harbours filled with powerboats, or beaches covered in sun umbrellas and loungers. His composition and his brushwork would have been wholly familiar to a painter starting out in 1910. His subjects, though, would be less so.

Similar points could be made about Pete Brown. His handling of paint is looser, perhaps more in the way of John Constable and the English tradition, but again he produces scenes which, in their colouring

OLD BROMPTON ROAD LOOKING EAST, MORNING LIGHT, 2016
Ken Howard

and composition, could have been made at almost any point in the past 200 years. But in other moods, Brown confronts the realities of modern urban life with great power. During the London riots of August 2011 he painted the aftermath and the burned-out shops, including Carpetright, in Tottenham High Road.

There is an old tradition of this as well, of course: Turner painted a vivid watercolour in 1792 of the old Pantheon Theatre just after it had been burned down. Still, if anyone in the future wants to know what London in 2011 could feel like, Brown's traditional representational painting is a good place to begin.

I don't want in any way to denigrate these two extremely fine and talented painters, but for me, the problem is that if you paint like Camille Pissarro or John Constable, even if your subject is defiantly and unmistakably contemporary, your picture will be like a Pissarro or a Constable several centuries after the event. You can't avoid that backward-looking, nostalgic atmosphere because it's deeply imprinted already on the minds of the viewer. You find yourself quoting – even if you are painting an ambulance or a set of traffic lights.

What's wrong with that? These are men making objects in the modern world which are a hundred times more worth having and enjoying than most of what is produced. But they don't – for me – lock into that sense of excitement and hard thinking, the feeling of being slightly off-balance and struggling

A SHORT BOOK ABOUT PAINTING

**SONNING LOCK,
LUNCHTIME, 2011**
Pete Brown

to understand things, that work by Bridget Riley or Clare Woods gives me.

At this point it would be dishonest of me not to mention that I have struggled with the same problem of what to paint. One way of dealing with change and decay in a landscape – movement, different perspectives – is to layer the work, scraping off and revealing different episodes in the same painting. The painting overleaf is of wet and boggy peat country in Wester Ross, Scotland, painted in London. Very thin paint and very thick paint are used to convey my memories of squelch and aromatic instability. It's better than the careful representational landscape on page 25.

There's not much more I want to say about it. The ice-blues, the yellows, reds, oranges and sludge-greens can be found in any patch of apparently dull moorland; the black lines relate to the insecurity of any path, track or direction. It's a simple picture, but I can smell and hear the memories it evokes. But if there's one thing evidently wrong with it, it's that it quotes too obviously from the long tradition of Scottish landscape painting. And that you could say, in 2017, is bad taste.

Changing taste, and what is good taste and what is bad taste, is such a knotty problem that it needs a chapter of its own.

**TOTTENHAM HIGH ROAD:
THE JEWELLER, THE
HAIRDRESSER AND THE
POST OFFICE, 2011**
Pete Brown

A SHORT BOOK ABOUT PAINTING

**WALKING NEAR
GREENSTONE**
Andrew Marr

2 TASTE

On failure

Here is a picture I made which, while it has energy, is in thoroughly bad taste. It's both a still life and a celebration of summer – a kind of outdoorsy, picnic-like explosion of exuberance. But it's also gauche – look at the crudity, albeit deliberate, of the drawing. And the nuzzling together of the jug and the semi-abstract biomorphic shapes on either side of it breaks a basic rule of painting, which is that there must be coherence. You can't just stick a bit of one kind of painting into another kind of painting, and hope the whole thing coheres. When I first made this I was cheerily pleased with it. Now I see it as a failure.

But what's wrong with failure? In the evergreen words of Samuel Beckett: "Ever tried. Ever failed.

SUMMER PICNIC
Andrew Marr

No matter. Try again. Fail again. Fail better."
Several times a week, I struggle with very basic
problems of colour combination, balance, texture,
meaning and so forth. And fail again.

But what follows is not intended to be a
perverse celebration of failure, still less to praise
poor painting. This is a book about learning.
As we fail, we learn. Time and again, I find colour
combinations that don't work, basic structures that
fall apart, and imagery that is too obvious, banal or
second-hand. The centre of the picture starts, swiftly
and mysteriously, to collapse; or the edges press in
to devour it, or they themselves slide off into
oblivion. I can see the catastrophe taking place
under my fingers but, however much I sit and stare,
I am helpless to prevent it.

Kind people who say, "painting must be so
relaxing for you" don't understand what painting
is. As I swear and kick things and paint over the
latest failures I am conscious that all the time
I am learning.

By indirections, we seek directions out. And it
struck me that there isn't – at least so far as I can
discover – a book about failure in art, and how
we writhe and sweat and crawl our way towards
working a little more effectively. So, if you really
knew how to paint badly – if you had accumulated
in your head and hands experience of all the
possible mistakes – then, one way or another, you
would be well on your way to knowing how to paint
well, or at any rate to paint better.

"It was a kind of so-so love"
Marc Almond, Soft Cell

There is a vast trove of copycat, timid painting
clogging up many local art society exhibitions:
lovingly if stiffly rendered domestic animals; gory
sunsets over jagged coasts, and sub-Impressionist
renderings of back gardens, with too much blue in
the shadows. You see these, too, strung along the
railings of parks in central London, or exhibited on
easels in Montmartre and "artistic" small French
towns and they will not detain us here.

So-so art is inherently dull. You look at it. Your
attention flickers for a second: "Ah yes, I know that
sort of thing, I recognise what's going on." Then you
move on. That's why it is so-so.

Dedicated followers of fashion

As I mentioned in the previous chapter, this is also
about taste. The art world is various, jumbled and
fragmented. All around Britain there are art dealers
catering for people who want something nice and
cheerful to put on the wall. There are probably
hundreds of galleries – often in coastal towns, or
prettier county towns – selling perfectly well-made
and perfectly predictable pictures of flowers in vases,
sunlit high streets, or boats bobbing in the sea. Some
of them are entirely representational. Many others
are the kind of degraded offspring of modern art –
cutesily naive, splashy, and a very long way after Paul
Klee or Nicholson. There's a hierarchy of snobbery
involved. Aunt Louise is proud of a pastel of roses by

the retired lady next door in the local art class. But Cousin George is prouder because his flower painting is wilder, and done with a palette knife by a student. But I'm on the top of the tree: my painting of flowers was made by a member of the modern Edinburgh school, whose use of pinks and yellows has made her at least locally famous.

In other words, contemporary taste seems to require at least a nod to the mainstream of modern painting. Most people wouldn't want the full energy and extremity of a major modern painter inside their homes. They wouldn't want a Frank Auerbach of a claggy, filthy London excavation, the paint hanging off the wood, or a gigantic, bejewelled Chris Ofili of African faces and a rather obvious huge penis, complete with balls of elephant dung. Er, too much, chaps.

Yet it turns out that what very many people want is something by somebody who has learned from the way Auerbach puts paint on, and the way he has thought deeply about painting; or work by a younger artist, perhaps, who has learned from Ofili's subversive exuberance. Most people, candidly, prefer the gentler followers to the pioneers. Behind the pioneers, there always seems to be a second group who learned the lessons but then dilute, simplify and prettify. The history of Cubism shows precisely this. So does the history of the so-called Fauve painters of 1905–6.

A good parallel is fashion. The haute couture collections, eagerly followed by glossy magazines and

newspapers, are, to most people, largely ridiculous – models used as coat hangers for the most extreme fantasies of couturiers and hat designers. Few of us are actually going to walk along the street in shredded PVC, with pink knitted undergarments and faces painted blue. Yet the great names of haute couture are changing styles and expectations in ways that will arrive on the high street very quickly – again, the commercial rag trade dilutes, simplifies and

**BUILDING SITE,
EARL'S COURT ROAD,
WINTER 1953**
Frank Auerbach

prettifies the propositions the pioneers have made.

Perhaps there the parallel breaks down, because there are of course people who have paintings by Chris Ofili, or Peter Doig or Frank Auerbach in their houses. By doing so they are not only advertising their understanding and appreciation of contemporary painting – their grip on contemporary taste – but also nodding to their fabulous wealth.

Quentin Bell, that child of the Bloomsbury group who survived into our own times, wrote a useful book, which he bluntly called *Bad Art*, in 1989. One of the things Bell demonstrates is that because taste constantly changes, one generation's view of what is "bad" can be overturned by the next, which sees undiscovered virtues. Bell himself dislikes Pre-Raphaelite Victorian painting, which is now very much back in favour. The art of the curator is also a voyage of perpetual rediscovery, fine-tuning and reassessing old reputations.

If you go into the opening rooms of the Scottish National Gallery in Edinburgh, you will find huge pictures, which not that long ago might have risked being banished to some dusty basement. Two American examples tell us a lot about changing taste. Benjamin West's 1786 monster, *Alexander III of Scotland Rescued from the Fury of a Stag by the Intrepidity of Colin Fitzgerald*, is everything we recently thought we hated. The subject, for one thing: here is a noble wild beast being slaughtered by a gang of frenzied men with dogs, observed by four terrified horses. Then there's the treatment – the gestures not just Mannerist but highly mannered and thoroughly implausible; stock, frozen faces, and too much muddy, brownish and slightly sloppy brushwork.

A second picture nearby by Frederic Edwin Church is about as big, but different in every other way. It's a huge painting of Niagara Falls, painted with an attention to detail – tiny brushstrokes over a vast canvas – that now seems borderline insane. But it reminds us that before the invention of photography, one of the crucial functions of painting was simply to show people what they otherwise

ALEXANDER III OF SCOTLAND RESCUED FROM THE FURY OF A STAG BY THE INTREPIDITY OF COLIN FITZGERALD, 1786 (OIL ON CANVAS)
Benjamin West

couldn't see themselves – landscapes from far parts of the world, portraits of great men and women, views of central Rome, Jerusalem or other iconic sites. Accuracy and scale were what the public wanted, and queued up to enjoy in huge numbers.

Both these paintings, which would not have been much admired at the height of modernism, take centre stage in the museum because we have learned to admire them once more, but in new ways. After some 60 years in which the traditional skills of realistic landscape painting have not been taught in art colleges, we can again gape at Church's sheer skill. And with the Benjamin West example, a renewed interest in Scottish history comes together with a greater admiration for the complex mathematics involved in creating work this big and this bonkers. There's nobody alive today who could do it.

So good taste, and bad taste, are slippery concepts. We can be reasonably sure that the values of today – our detestation of racism, for instance – affect the way we see art made under different ideologies. The sheer cruelty in many old paintings of fox-hunting or bear-baiting put them outside the circle of modern taste. But we can never be sure that any art is dead forever.

Quentin Bell's most useful distinction is sincerity. For him, the good artist describes the world full on, as he or she sees it directly, whereas the bad artist relies on what he calls "social beauty" or a second-hand common market of ideas. In every art movement of the past hundred years, he says,

NIAGARA FALLS, FROM THE AMERICAN SIDE, 1867 (OIL ON CANVAS)
Frederic Edwin Church

"the good artist has fought against the popular conception of beauty, the bad artist has accepted it at once or after a brief struggle." This, says Bell, explains why paintings by artists such as Landseer and Millais make him cringe. They "had completely accepted the opinion of their age as to what constituted a beautiful picture, and, having done so, addressed themselves to the beautiful with horrifying success." I would add Jeff Koons as an excellent contemporary example.

This understanding that versatility simply makes bad taste horrifying can be applied more widely today. Go online and look at the vast range of digitally drawn fantasy art easily available on the website Pinterest: imaginary space landscapes populated by pneumatic heroines; thick, ribbed woods with Gothic castles and muscle-bunny heroes; rusting space cruisers with cool punk chicks astride them... Here is an entire visual world of second-hand and half-digested images stolen from Hollywood films and pulp fiction, all the worse because so meticulously achieved. This has been done by artists who have completely accepted the opinion of their age... with horrifying success.

Bad taste comes from a lazy, slick readiness to slot into the expectations of the here and now. Thus, in our time, bad taste must be intimately linked to the digital revolution. We live surrounded by a multicoloured, vivid, sexualised and glassy hyper-reality. It's easy for technically competent artists to use digital drawing tools, or even simply acrylic

**TRIAL BY JURY, OR
LAYING DOWN THE LAW,
c.1840 (OIL ON CANVAS)**
Edwin Landseer

paint, to produce glossy, smooth and apparently provocative art which has made its diabolical pact with the modern world.

Again, Quentin Bell, here describing Victorian taste, offers a sidelight on the 21st century. Our stuff is different, of course – digital rather than material – but doesn't the following ring a bell or two? "No other age… clamoured for beauty as a child clamours for sweets; it produced beauty by the ton and by the square mile, it applied beauty with reckless profusion

MERMAID
Jason Heeley

to every available space in the form of frills and flounces, stucco and gutta-percha mouldings, buttons, beading and Berlin wool, Lincrusta, papier mâché and Britannia metal, crockets, buttresses, cherubs, scroll work, arabesques and foliage…"[1] Think of our buildings, clothing, malls and screens too. Trump art.

So here, at last, is the case for good painting. Modern digital culture is changing much of what we have been living with for thousands of years – birdsong, the smell of rotting foliage, a world of torn clouds and watery paths, the erotic and the tragic, the cold and brightness and the deep, deep dark. Living through screens drives away the reality of what it has been like to be alive on this planet.

Reality, by contrast, resists us. It is cussed and surprising, with sharp edges and inexplicable patches, so it must be pursued with visual curiosity and exactness. The talented artist with the pleasing manner – the bad artist – is the artist pretending that reality easily conforms, and moulds itself, to pre-loaded human expectations. But if we "already know "what a beautiful human face looks like, or a "satisfying" landscape, why bang on? Why copy out yet another example?

Good painting is surprising because it returns us, with a jolt, to realities we too often evade. The eye can't slide across it and move easily on. And that's about hard-won technique and skill. The painter Patrick Heron once said that Rembrandt's beauty "was not in the old man's face (which is like many faces you may see anywhere) but in the abstract

1 Quentin Bell *Bad Art*, Chatto & Windus, 1989

crystals of Rembrandt's paint surface (which is only found in a Rembrandt)…"

Compared to slick art, I am more interested in heroic failures – art which was done by someone at full stretch, with sincerity and seriousness, some degree of skill, and yet which falls flat on its nose. There is a gallery in Venice, the Ca' Rezzonico on the Grand Canal – a lovely, cool, welcoming place, which specialises in the art and furniture of the Venetian 18th century. So it tells us what happened to Venetian painting after all the greats – and their immediate successors who had learned from them – had died. We know of Titian, Veronese, Tintoretto

JUDITH
Giulia Lama

A SHORT BOOK ABOUT PAINTING

and Giorgione; and art scholars know quite a lot about their pupils and those who copied from them across Europe. But what happened next? After the golden age of Venetian art, and then the silver age, what follows? Giulia Lama, that's what.

Art history is obsessively eloquent about the growth and development of schools and styles, but largely silent when it comes to declines and falls. The Ca' Rezzonico is full of competently brushed, carefully drawn and achingly sincere monstrosities – fat, ugly angels doing nothing in particular, constipated monks, unpleasing random butchery and so forth. It's absolutely fascinating.

Then, to jump forward in time, it's not the case that every great artist carries on developing and getting better. To take one example, the French Fauve painter André Derain was at first an absolute hero, breaking barriers and boundaries, shoulder to shoulder with Matisse, Dufy, Braque and Vlaminck. Then he somehow, mysteriously, "lost it" and produced dun-coloured faux-classical pictures for the rest of his life. You can see them in some French collections and you always think, "Gosh. That's rather dull. Wonder why they've hung it? Oh! It's by Derain…"

Taste is complex when it comes to modern art. But that doesn't mean it doesn't exist – or that there aren't any objective hierarchies. Shows by the greatest modern painters may be easy or difficult but they attract vast crowds who carry on paying the entrance fee and coming back, day after day.

The David Hockney retrospective at Tate Britain in early 2017 broke all records for pre-ordered tickets. Rooms of video art, charcoal drawings and what the artist himself described as gay propaganda, were choked with people who had travelled from all over the UK and beyond. At the same time, an exhibition of portraits, mostly highly non-representative, by the late Howard Hodgkin, was buzzing – people were laughing and talking loudly about almost every picture.

There was something in those rooms that many thousands of people felt they needed and wanted and would make a great effort to see. The brutal competitive questions of what people revere and what they don't challenge all contemporary art curators, and they are real ones. Stepping into a minefield, I would propose the following few simple thoughts.

First, people are attracted still to very strong colour combinations and to coherent composition – as Hoyland said, you can't end up with chaos. Second, the subject of art remains important. The subject doesn't have to be literally present – Clare Woods paints about decay and fear, Gillian Ayres about the exhilaration of being alive. But it may be literal: Kiefer's art deals directly with Germany's modern history and the possibility of imminent environmental collapse; Auerbach describes modern urban living, with its confusions and collisions. If there isn't something in the subject to get your teeth into – if it's all floral arrangements or beach scenes – the public reaction will be tepid.

Third, and perhaps most important, art must look somehow fresh, novel, of the now and not of the then. If it does, the "now" can last, however. Go to see an exhibition of Rauschenberg or Jackson Pollock paintings from the 1950s and their freshness bursts from the walls. People don't want imitations of the past, certainly if they're spending good money on going to an exhibition.

Finally, modern taste seems to prefer paintings that look like paintings. Surrounded by a glossy sheen of digital imagery – on your tablet, your computer, iPhone or television screen – you don't want cold, glassy, smooth surfaces from living paintings. You want the marks to be visible, the hand and the eye to be still somehow present. You want to live in the here and the now.

You may think that these principles are so obvious as to be banal and useless. But I need to start somewhere. So let's try at least to remember them as we dig a little deeper, heading on next to the problem (if it is a problem) of colour.

3 COLOUR

What is colour?

The modern, scientific answer could be summarised thus: it is the brain's apprehension of the energy of the cosmos.

The colours of the spectrum are different wavelengths of light energy, electromagnetic radiation, ranging from red in the least frequent waves, to purple in the most frequent. The wavelengths enter the human eye and are noted by the six million receptor cells on the retina, organised in three kinds of rod and cone cell. Different cells are more or less receptive to different wavelengths – that is, different colours. Rod cells in particular are incredibly sensitive, tracking differences in frequency of as little as one nanometre, that is one billionth of a metre. These cones contain opsins, or photo pigments.

The information then passes from the retinal ganglion cells along the optic nerve from each eye. They cross over, and then the optic tracts continue the journey to the thalamus, deep in the centre of the brain, and thus to the visual cortex, the main processing area at the back of the brain. (The common phrase "eyes in the back of your head" is rooted in neuroscience.)

There, colour-processing cells are arranged in blobs concentrating on red-green and blue-yellow "flavours". The rods and cones in the eye only pick up certain wavelengths – in a sense the information they are sending back is pretty crude – and it is here, in the visual cortex, that the brain finally makes "sense" of our complex multicoloured world.

I am brutally summarising a much more complicated picture and I'm sure neurologists would suck their teeth. But in a book on painting, we don't need much more information than that. The important thing to remember is that "colour" is wavelength, part of the electromagnetic energy of the world we live in. More specifically, colour is how the brain processes the wavelength information. With our vision, we suck in the energy of the cosmos and break it down to understand what's around us.

This at once raises fascinating questions. Since every human is different, it's perfectly possible that our visual cortexes are not quite the same, and that therefore every one of us apprehends, say, dark red slightly differently. Ethnologists tell us that different human groups have evolved more or less sophisticated colour awareness depending on their environment – for instance, the Inuit apprehend snow with special subtlety, and Amazon tribes similarly have a special sensitivity to different greens.

Since the artist is trying to communicate with as wide an audience as possible, this information isn't particularly useful and is slightly unsettling. If my bright yellow is different from your bright yellow, there is damn all I can do about it. The condition of synaesthesia, in which perceptions are mixed up, so that some people can hear the sounds of colour, or taste sound, reminds us that this is a fluidly subjective matter.

Science certainly shows that different species have different quantities of cone and rod receptors, so see colour differently. It would be bad news for a painter to be reincarnated as a cat or a dog since, like many other mammals, they have two, not three kinds of receptor and therefore presumably apprehend less colour than we do. Worse would be to come back as a seal or a whale, since they have only one kind. On the other hand, since many birds and fish have more than three kinds of cone cell their world is probably more coloured than ours. It has been suggested that pigeons and butterflies have five. I hope that if Titian was reincarnated, he returned as a turtledove or a red admiral. It would have been a short second life, but a merry one.

More seriously, what I take away from this is that colour is a profound register of reality, of the constantly moving and dynamic world around us; it is also, literally, deeply rooted in our brains, and therefore our imaginations and emotions. To talk about the power of colour is anything but arty-farty.

Pigmentation

For a painter, however, this is just the very start. The colour we use, whether it comes in a metal tube, a bucket or a spray can, has been plundered from nature to give us more intensity. Pigment is the visual sibling of spice; and it's interesting that the most expensive pigments, such as ultramarine, traditionally had a price that was only rivalled by the cost of the most expensive tastes and smells, such as nutmeg or frankincense. The lusts of the brain accept no parsimony.

Pigments are the finely ground substances which, mixed with liquid – oils, water or synthetic media – pass on their colour without fading or decaying. The search for and use of these pigments is almost as old as the human story itself and they can come from minerals, plants and animals. Lapis lazuli, for instance, is a semi-precious stone found in Iran and Afghanistan, and also in China. When separated from the surrounding greyish rock, it produces an intense and long-lasting blue which has been valued for centuries. The Babylonians used it for decoration and European painters were shelling out vast amounts of money for it throughout the Middle Ages and into the Renaissance. These days, it has mostly been replaced by artificial ultramarine pigments.

Cinnabar, a bright vermilion red, came from Spanish mines. Ralph Mayer's *The Artist's Handbook of Materials and Techniques* contains some wonderfully laconic descriptions of other pigments. Indian yellow, for instance, is "an obsolete lake of euxanthic acid made in India by heating the urine of cows fed on mango leaves." Tyrian purple was "prepared from the shellfish *Murex trunculus* and *Murex brandaris*." Of Vandyke brown he says, "Native earth, composed of clay, iron oxide, decomposed vegetation (humus), and bitumen. Fairly transparent. Deep-toned and less chalky than umbers in mixtures. One of the worst dryers in oil…"

These days almost all artists obtain their colours from commercial suppliers who produce them synthetically, allowing for reliable results. We don't have to grind up bugs, steep vegetation in urine or clamber up mountains with pickaxes. But the origins of pigment really matter. Painting was from the first a physical activity rooted in the world of nature around painters – the insects, the barks, the herbs. A painting was a material object composed (for instance) of oils from seeds and ground-up soil and rock. It might look like a madonna or a dragon, but what it was, was dust and pith and juice on wood or vegetable fibres.

This materiality is worth recalling and valuing in a world becoming ever-faster a virtual one. It is, I suggest, a virtue: if colour is electromagnetic energy, sorted inside the wet organic electrics

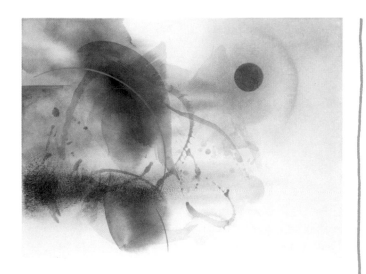

**THE WATERING PLACE,
2013**
William Tillyer

of the brain, the stuff of painting also roots us in nature. The best painters know this. I have a friend called Adrian Hemming, whose landscapes require a special blue he has made up for him, and grinds meticulously with a knife. For watercolours of nature, the very fine painter William Tillyer uses pigments created from the same North Yorkshire soils and plants he is describing.

This is not, in any sense, to advocate some kind of ruralist reaction, a literal back-to-the-soil movement away from the modern world; Tillyer famously uses industrial materials, handles, plastics and the latest acrylics as well. But it is to say that colour is both constant movement, and entirely material; which is, in short, why painting, far from being a dead or dying tradition, is still exciting and thoroughly part of contemporary life.

Colour language

Writing in 1962, the painter and critic Patrick Heron declared that colour was the only way forward for modern artists: "Colour is both the subject and the means; the form and the content; the image and the meaning, in my painting today. It is obvious that colour is now the only direction in which painting can travel today."[1]

This caused some offence at the time but Heron, whose paintings had indeed banished any forms more complicated than a rough circle or a rough line between colours, wasn't so much attacking all representation as archaic, but making a case for the emotional impact of pure colour in a dissatisfying world. "One reels at the colour possibilities now: the varied and contrasting intensities, opacities, transparencies; the seeming intensity and weight, warmth, coolness, vibrancy; all this superbly inert 'dull' colour – such as the marvellously uneventful expanses of the surface of an old green door in the sunlight. Or the terrific zing of a violet vibration... I can get a tremendous thrill from suddenly seeing two colours juxtaposed."

Here, I think we are coming close to the heart of the matter. We all absorb our colour palette from the world around us. This gives colour fundamental meanings that artists can't really escape. Green is chlorophyll, grass, growth, fecundity – but dark green evokes shadows, dank and dismal places, even poison. Red is the colour of blood, fire, sunset and heat. Yellow is the sun's colour, but also the colour

1 Zurich catalogue, quoted in Heron, op cit

JANUARY 1973: 13
1973
Patrick Heron

of sickly skin, of disease. White is cold, frost, snow, ice, the north, logic, intellect. Blues, which are always cold, are the colours of the skies and seas.

We can't get away from these thoughts, any more than a poet who is interested in the sound of language can get away from the literal meanings of the words he deploys – although some, like Swinburne, tried very hard. These correspondences slide and jar; we can subvert and reject them, but they burrow back and snap at our fingers. In a series of *White Stones* pictures (see page 67) I've been making of underwater themes, where the colours are heightened but also blurred, there is a whole family of blues, ranging from threatening indigos to softly benign light purples and turquoises, closer to the sun. The yellows, greens and reds towards the bottom third seem to me to represent organic life and danger.

There is a long and interesting tradition of writing about colour combinations and contrasts. Why do some colours simply seem to go well together – blue and yellow, red and green? These harmonies seem to belong more to music than to vision and yet they are very powerful. Partly it's about what sits where on the spectrum, and which primaries combine to make secondary colours. But I also think there is a simple, primal sense in which the yellow of the sun and the blue of the sky have sat alongside one another forever until they are deep inside our understanding; and red earth and green growth likewise. One aspect of the job of a painter, as above, is to take and reshape these expectations.

Cleaning Windows – the title comes from the Van Morrison song I was listening to as I finished it – is "about" a windy, hot, summer afternoon, and the colours refer to bright clashes and unexpected juxtapositions as the glass swings, and indoor becomes outdoor, and vice versa.

Just as composers can hear and emotionally respond to chords of greater complexity than most of us are able to apprehend, so painters have the same emotional responses to colour combinations as the rest of us – but more so. Ever since I was a small boy I have had very strong responses to colours. The golden-yellows and red-browns of a Perthshire autumn, streaked with violet undershadows; and the throbbing turquoise, green and dark blue combinations of the Atlantic seen from the Scottish Highlands run through me still, in my dreams and

right
**THE WHITE STONE AND
THE BATTLE AT SEA
MARCH**
Andrew Marr

below
CLEANING WINDOWS
Andrew Marr

daydreams. Colours, even divorced from discernible shapes, make me happy and sad, energetic and depressed and this seems to be common to painters.

In a beautiful essay Bridget Riley argued, "I don't paint light. I present a colour situation which releases light as you look at it." She goes on to ask where this comes from: "Long before I ever saw a major painting... I had been fortunate enough to discover what 'looking' can be... I spent my childhood in Cornwall, which of course was an ideal place to make such discoveries... Swimming through the oval, saucer-like reflections, dipping and flashing on the sea surface, one traced the colours back to the origins of those reflections. Some came directly from the sky and differently coloured clouds, some from the golden greens of the vegetation growing on the cliffs, some from the red-orange of the seaweed on the blues and violets of adjacent rocks, and, all between, the actual use of the water, according to its various depths and over what it was passing. The entire, elusive, unstable, flicking complex subject to the changing qualities of the light itself..."[2]

This returns us to colour theory, the attempt to explain or codify the emotional impact of different colours, and different colours in combinations. I mentioned this in the previous chapter briefly, in regard to Kandinsky and it's something painters tend to think about quite a lot.

Patrick Heron wisely suggested that there is a limit to how much we can understand about this verbally. Words, he pointed out, are not paint:

2 Bridget Riley, *The Eye's Mind, Collected Writings 1965-2009*, Ridinghouse, 2010

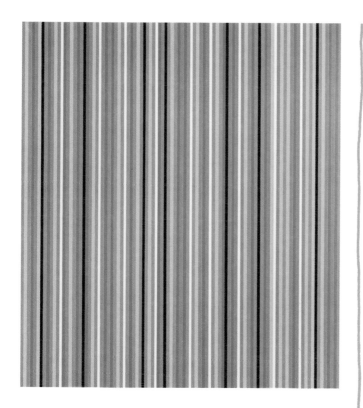

**WINTER PALACE, 1981
(OIL ON LINEN)**
Bridget Riley

"I have always found that it takes at least twenty times as long to describe in words any specific feature of a painting of mine – a colour-area of cadmium scarlet scribbled, delineated, filled out by brush-marks or brush-weavings of this nature or that."[3] But some basic points can be made.

We start with the hierarchy of primary colours – red, blue and yellow – from which other colours can be mixed, but which cannot be produced themselves by other colours. This does seem to relate directly to the three different receptor cells on the retina.

3 1978 E. William Doty Lecture, *The Colour of Colour*, op cit

Further, as I mentioned earlier, the human brain does appear to find that some colours go well together or complement one another – blue and yellow, red and green. I have not yet read a compelling account of why this should be so, though I've already made my amateurish stab at it earlier in the chapter. As we've seen other colours can clash almost painfully – an acid green against a bright pink.

But what, finally, of the emotional effect of colour? Is there anything secure we can say? With due caution about the individual perception problem, most people recognise a contrast between hot or warm colours, the reds, oranges and yellows; and the cooler blues, greens and whites. If you doubt this, consider why "cold orange" or "hot green" don't, to most of us, make much sense. We feel it on the body. I'm surer than ever that these distinctions emerged early from our perceptions of the world around us – the warmth of the rising sun, the glow of burning wood, or cold, misty blue winter days – and that they have become somehow rooted or innate.

A final example here is a picture referring to a card or board game, in which several overexcited players jealously compete. The colours are – almost – all. Oddly, if the motifs were less crudely painted, this picture wouldn't work.

A SHORT BOOK ABOUT PAINTING

4 MOTIF

I have argued that powerful contemporary painting must have a subject. By that I don't mean that it must look like something directly, but more that it must have a point, a meaning. That can be, by and of itself, colour – and the emotions summoned by colour – or the texture and the doing of the artwork itself. Or the simplest compositions can summon existential thoughts. It isn't "pseudy" or unusual for people standing in front of paintings by Rothko to feel that they confront death and obliteration, and even to be made dizzy by them. Kazimir Malevich's famous black square – it is what it says it is – summons up a different kind of confrontation, the world-ending despair of global war and revolution. Barnett Newman's so-called "zip" paintings –

ADAM, 1951–2
Barnett Newman

thin vertical lines of colour against a different coloured backdrop – nevertheless managed to summon up heroic Jewish mythologies.

Malevich was painting both within and against the tradition of Russian icon painting, which can be notably stark, while Newman was responding to the almost inhumanly large figures of the age of prophets. Both found that almost entirely motif-less canvases could bear the weight of substantial meaning. For other artists, intense colour can replace the need for complex imagery. Robert Motherwell's famous series of elegies for the Spanish Republic, with their boulder-like black ovals and blocks, depend upon the harsh yellows and occasional bright gleams of red, alongside the ominous black shadows, to make the viewer think about the bloodthirsty political tragedy that preceded the second global war. So "must have a subject" doesn't mean "must have a human figure in it" or "must show a tree".

Circles and wiggles

So far, so comparatively easy. But anything more complex than a square or a straight line is likely to summon up some representational response in the viewer. If we see a wobbling horizontal line a third or two-thirds up a canvas then we will think, "horizon". We can't help it. The painter can't help it. If we see a circle, we think sun or moon. The most vestigial scrawl can automatically find itself translated into something such as a tree, running figure or rabbit. That's simply how our minds, tuned to make sense of the world at huge speed, work. So a painter who doesn't want to represent, primarily, a line of hills in the distance or a rabbit or a church, but is trying to show something else, something more complex, has to work pretty hard at the problem of the motif. There will be something – there must be something – of shapes in the paint. Where will these shapes come from? From the world around the painter. The contemporary painter – remember Joan Miró scouring around on the beach – is likely to be forced back into nature to be kick-started. And yet, when the painter comes back to the studio, he or she doesn't want motifs that can be misunderstood as traditional representation. It's a hard problem.

Yet, like so many hard problems, clever people have found ways to deal with it. Bridget Riley, by slashing the world into thin ribbons which may intersect and dance with one another, created a whole way of representing things which is complicated, subtle and yet avoids the problem of motif.

Gillian Ayres, another hugely important painter of the same generation, made her earlier works using very rough circles and oblongs of thick, smeared paint, so much so that visible shapes virtually obliterated one another and the viewer was forced to think differently. There were motifs there; but there weren't. In her later paintings, she devised simple motifs – triangles encasing squares, long patterned tendrils, diamonds and Matisse-like leaf formations – which could be read as organic shapes, stars or whatever. And yet she kept them so simple in outline

and so blazingly powerful in colour that the shapes
ceased to be terribly important. They were the hooks
on which she hung meditations about being alive,
about energy and light, rather than visualised objects
in their own right.

Another approach to the same problem has
evolved in the art of Fiona Rae, now one of the most
popular members of the Royal Academy in London.
She crashes different kinds of motif or image into
one another on the same picture surface. You might

find little Japanese figures, of the kind that populate computer games, cohabiting with thickly worked or smeared gobbets of paint; neatly stencilled circles which might have emerged from a book on mathematics; butterfly shapes and Day-Glo explosions. Fiona Rae gives us so many kinds of motifs, so many layers of meaning, that we are almost forced to shrug them aside and to think about the painting as a painting – about its complexity and its energy.

All these artists are dealing with the same conundrum – that we want something for the eye to hang on to without trying to fool the viewer that they are seeing a copied representation of real objects. Painters as various as Jackson Pollock and Mondrian ended up with motifs that, whether they wished them to be or not, could be "read" as references to the real world. The wiry arterial dances of Pollock's paint refer to the movement of his own body and the energies inside it; the grid of a Mondrian abstract appears to be a map of urban traffic. The problem simply won't go away. Many 20th-century painters shrugged and accepted that there will be motifs. Paul Klee played with them – sea monsters and birds, traffic-directing arrows and the cupolas of Mediterranean cities dance through his essentially non-representational art. The great Kandinsky refers to riders, horses, angels and alpine landscapes in his networks of coloured lines.

Quite quickly, we realise that there is no such thing as abstract art, assuming that abstract means divorced from the world of signs and things. A painting by Ad Reinhardt – flat, barely inflected pigment on canvas – is nevertheless an Ad Reinhardt, a thing, a sign, which means "a lot of money", or "part of the history of New York abstract painting". These are just as much signs as a ruff painted by Nicholas Hilliard, or Carel Fabritius's *The Goldfinch*.

Vision evolved not to give us artistic pleasure but to keep us alive – to enable us to hunt food, avoid danger and so forth. We are unable to see without reading messages and decoding them, without using signs all the time. Artists who attempt to keep us focused on, for instance, the material surface of the picture plane, or thinking about the act of painting, or the simple effects of different colour combinations, will all end up having to accept that image decoding cannot be divorced from the present business of looking. Perhaps the best thing is to accept this, and to use motifs deliberately but as simply as possible.

This is difficult, however, and to show why, here is a series of pictures I made when I had decided that *the studio* itself would be as plain a motif as I could use. These would be pictures about starting to make pictures again. I wanted a light source coming from the top or back of the room; a very plain rectangle represents the easel and canvas; and around that basic blocks of colour represent walls, outdoors and so forth (a, overleaf). I wanted to keep the thing as scumbled and loosely painted as I could in order to emphasise the lack of a "real" studio. And, because I was interested in overpainting older work, I wanted a target image from an earlier picture to be still dimly present in this one.

So far, so good. I went on – further adventures in the studio – to heighten some of the colours, emphasising the shadows more strongly and playing with the idea of being inside and outside at the same time (b) – for the studio is both a lightbox and a window. Again, these are very traditional thoughts and I continued keeping the paintwork deliberately loose and obvious. But already I am in trouble. Forget, for a second, that the yellow and the cheesy red in the background go unpleasantly together. It's a different time of year and the light is artificial. The problem is that the "motif" is now a little too strong to be a motif. It has become an upended object with a shadow uneasily placed between a landscape and a room. In short, it is neither one thing nor the other – it is not a representation nor a well thought-through dance of attractive colours. In pushing forward, I am falling back.

The motif, then, has a life of its own. A studio contains an artist (otherwise it wouldn't be a studio) and a model or at least a subject. And so I moved innocently ahead, representing the artist in various guises as, for instance, an open eye and a palette; while a model to the right of the picture appeared variously as a buffoonish Gauguin caryatid or a series of stripped-down geometric colours (c).

By now, as you can see, I am making a right mess. The great golden swathe of light falling diagonally across the picture plane is pleasing enough, or at

a

b

c

d

least it is to my eye, but the caryatid on the right
has vanished into a semicircle and triangle; and
representing the artist by an eye is something
Picasso might have got away with, but I haven't.
By including some painting materials on a table,
I have slipped in the direction of representation.
If I'm trying to represent a real studio, why not
paint it properly? The motifs have taken over and
made a fool of me. One answer to this is to return

to simplifying everything and knocking back representation (d, page 81). I wanted to keep the sense of light, of inside and outside jousting against each other; and also of the materiality of the room, which included floorboards. The artist and his model have now completely retreated to triangles, circles and leaf shapes.

This works better; at least there is a satisfying sense of balance and harmony, alongside the energy of the light. But it's all a little too balanced and calm, and by now quite a long way away from the original studio idea.

So I changed direction again and this time, after all those failures, I began to paint a little better. The energy of the light, I realised, comes from strong colour contrasts, not from diagonals or cones. I could keep both the artist and model, radically simplified, and use the floorboards to give a sense of the outside world pushing in. I emphasised the central canvas, which had rather vanished, and brought in a sun from outside, to flame away and keep me warm – all this was painted during the winter.

You may well disagree but *Winter in the Studio III* seems to me a better picture than any of the previous ones, and one that could only be arrived at by struggling with the problem of the motif. It's rough and it's crude but it has movement, energy, and it does reflect for me the experience of working and painting in a particular room at a particular time of year.

In more detail: a study of failure

Some time after I had finished the "studio" pictures,
I began to make a series of pictures with a different
theme – going for a walk. I used semicircles moving
from the right towards the left to give me a basic
structure, with dark triangles for their shadows, and
diagonal black lines, sometimes with circles, to mark
out the rest of the picture plane. They had to be the
size of a single rotation of the wrist. What I was
trying to do was to give a visual shorthand for
movement through different landscapes, using

**WINTER IN THE STUDIO
III**
Andrew Marr

varied thicknesses of paint for air quality and energy.
So these were not, properly speaking, abstract
pictures and indeed each one, as it developed,
represented the memory of a particular place and
walk for me. I didn't set out with this in mind, but as
the pictures formed that's what happened. Here is
the first of them (a). As you can see, I was interested
particularly in texture, and in this case the effect of
dropping raw pigment on to wet paint as part
of the process.

That first picture was about a walk in
Cambridgeshire in the late autumn, with a lot of
cold light, and yet the warm crackling colours
of decaying farm foliage. The next picture, again
with a firm stride from right to left, was about
walking just outside Dundee, where I was born
(b and detail). Although in many ways the pictures
are similar, I hope you can see that the added cold
blue and white produce something very different.

At this point I felt I was on to something –
pictures whose motifs represented something real
and felt, with the structure that was my own, not
borrowed from anyone else. In the first sketches,
such as (c, overleaf), there are vague memories of
Russian constructivist painting but they aren't so
obvious as to get in the way. What makes these
pictures a bit more interesting in the flesh than they
are on the page is that there is a deliberate dance
or conversation between thick, impasto paint,
sometimes scattered with pigment, and much
more loosely painted areas. For me this is a way

A SHORT BOOK ABOUT PAINTING

of portraying physical experience and breathing, though I can't quite explain why.

At any rate, things were chugging along nicely and I had that dangerous sense of overconfidence that comes when you are on a roll. Each picture started with a very simple piece of drawing – about as simple as one can imagine.

And on that structure I could hang an ever-greater variety of colours and shapes and textures, always referring to a specific event.

c

d

A SHORT BOOK ABOUT PAINTING

Problems started to emerge as I introduced what might be called biomorphic forms – vague references to foliage or the shape of hillsides (d). The problem here is bastardy, introducing different modes of painting which don't belong together into the same picture. So here you can see me making a basic mistake even at the time of drawing (e).

I think I more or less saved this particular picture by thinking very hard about deep winter colours in North London. In fact, the end product, using a lot

of white paint, and vivid reds, composed both of pre-prepared cheap paint and thrown pigment, worked well (f). But that, frankly, was the kind of luck that happens sometimes in the studio.

Now I come to the heart of this particular story – why a painting, despite a lot of hard work and close attention, can go spectacularly wrong. I was still thinking about these walking pictures and was starting to make a much bigger one, set in Camden, North London where I live, and reflecting on the disruption and the damage to the fine structure of the place likely to be caused by the tunnelling for the new high-speed rail link to Birmingham. I wanted a very strong and tense underlying structure (g).

The moving, or striding semicircles, with their own clear rhythm, are confronted by the botched circles on the left, and the plane is divided three ways by the diving triangle: diagonals always tend to produce a sense of insecurity in a picture. Using "urban" purples and blues I hastily filled in some of the right-hand side of the picture (h).

But, given the subject and the mood I wanted, this already seemed a little gentle, and so I added jagged dark shadows or triangles at the bottom of the lower curve, which immediately changed the mood (i).

But what of the all-important centre of the picture? I wanted to represent the strength of electric light, the energy and the intricate beauty of urban streets, and did so using pastel crayons overpainted with linseed oil – a deliberate contrast to the flat painting on the right.

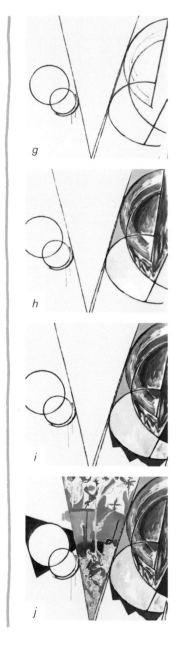

g

h

i

j

I wanted the colour and mood of the streets, not their literal representation, but as I worked, the shapes became far too specific, and as I hope you can see, the overall effect was revolting (j). Realising I was in trouble, I completed the rest of the picture using dark urban browns, reds and greys – I think relatively effectively.

k

There are, I hope, interesting passages of painting in this version (k). The maroons and greys and the deliberately unfinished, sketchy circles on the left, and the original pushing blues, purples and whites on the right get more or less exactly to the theme of the picture and the motif I wanted. But the centre is an abomination. Why? It's not just that the colours are unappealing: they are meant to be – they are there to describe something jangling and essentially disturbing. It's more that the shapes that have emerged virtually by themselves are, again, neither one thing nor the other – not simply representations of paint in paint, or yet drawings of anything in particular. I have stupidly mingled different ways of seeing on the same picture plane and at this point there is no way forward but to start wiping poor work out, and beginning again.

In the studio, a lot of what happens is obliteration and repair. In this case the first thing I had to do was wipe out the overemphatic shapes in the central V. I did this by over-painting with white, while leaving flashes and fragments of the original painting still visible. Second, I somehow had to ground the picture – there were too many lines and

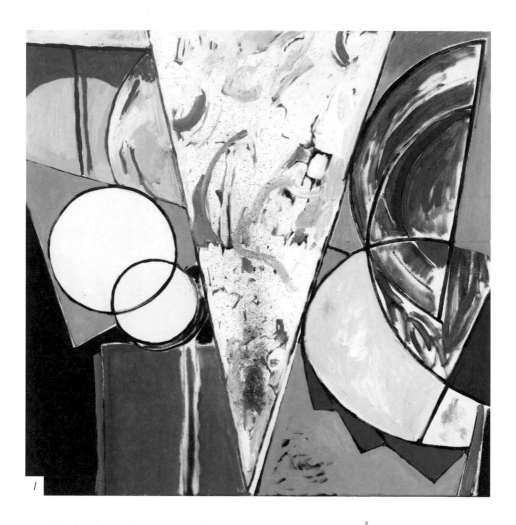

/

semicircles jumping around in too many directions.
So I introduced an icy blue, tying together the left
and right of the picture behind the centre (l). And
in this way I saved it.

Or at least, I think so. But it's worth noting
that the picture has become a rather different one.

It's still about the experience of walking through Camden during the winter of 2016–17. But the centre of the picture, instead of representing urban grime, now has a feeling of warmth and human colour. And the blue relates to one of those invigorating, vivid, very cold days we had so many of at that time. It has become a more optimistic picture, and a different picture.

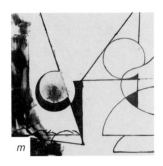

m

Here is one final example from the same series, shown because it presented me with some hard problems, and again, problems essentially of motif (m). I wanted to paint about a walk in Cornwall over the New Year, when the greens and browns were particularly vivid, the sea was lashing and the sky was menacingly white. As with the previous picture, I started off with a pretty simple piece of underpainting.

n

There was a landscape feel to this, clearly – the parabolas on the right were no longer simply about moving across the surface but referred to, however simplified, the shapes of fields and hills (n). On the dark left-hand side of the drawing you can see a rock coastline below a moon. The central part had to serve for the ominous, white yet menacing sky. I set to work pretty fast, essentially doing a colouring-in exercise, though trying to keep different textures of paint visible as I went.

There are some good passages of painting in this, from the central, scored sea to the purplish clouds above it. But there are problems of motif and composition that I hope are obvious. The giant circle to the centre right is too dominating, too flat, perhaps too big. And, worse, given that I have used naturalistic muddied greens and browns and purples for the fields, what is the relationship between an abstract red circle and what lies below it? Is that a horizon line towards the bottom of the picture? And what is the second circle really doing on the left? In the drawing, it's clearly there for balance, and to remove any sense of the red circle being a direct representation of the setting sun – in other words to fool the eye. But now the colours have been worked in, it doesn't fool the eye; it just irritates it.

The problem here is that I'm not sure whether I am painting a picture about the experience of going for a walk or whether it's really a stylised landscape. It can't be both. In the end, it came down more to the first. This is the final version (o). At least for now. The suns have become telescopic holes, punched through the landscape, and the unresolved gloom on the far left-hand side has been painted out with blues to answer the blues on the right. And I'm not at all sure whether I've improved it, or ruined it.

Over to you: but at least I hope I've given an honest account of what goes on in the place we're visiting next, the studio.

o

5 IN THE STUDIO

In all of the books I have read about painting and painters, there is almost nothing about what, to me, is the big reality and mystery – *what happens in the studio when a picture is being made.*

I don't mean gossip. I don't mean whether or not somebody else is mixing colour or cleaning brushes, if there is music playing, or the artist has had a drink. There is a certain amount of studio gossip, just as there is gossip about what happens backstage in a theatre.

But what we are talking about here is eerier – what is going on in the mind of the picture-maker, as he or she confronts an empty surface, then an increasingly busy surface, and tries to work out what marks to make.

It isn't movement. Gillian Ayres says that she spends a huge amount of time simply sitting and staring, rather than actually applying paint. Howard Hodgkin, according to rare film of him at work, is in the same boat and I suspect that, in fact, for most painters the real work gets done mentally – just looking and thinking. David Hockney speaks about "eyeballing", the swift movement of eye up and down from a subject, before the hand starts work. But non-figurative painters do something similar. So what are they looking for, and why?

What's actually going on in the mind at this point? With the obvious apologies for not being a "real" or professional painter, all I can say is that as I'm looking, I'm almost deliberately losing focus, choosing to let my consciousness go skittering helplessly around... until I hear myself thinking: "That whole upper third must be painted out with light blue" or, "There needs to be a thick black line running down the red on the right-hand side".

These thoughts, dredged up from the subconscious, seem instantly obvious and necessary, and propel me back towards the painting. Sometimes, I see much later, they were absolutely wrong. There is nothing infallible about the unconscious. But I think there are some innate feelings about colour, which I have discussed already, and motif (ditto), and composition. In other words, I think that most of us share under-discussed ideas about which paintings work and which don't.

Shape and structure

I'm now talking about something different from
personal taste or fashion in art: I'm talking about
substructure. At this point, most art manuals start
to talk about "the rule of thirds" or the golden mean.
The mathematical formula is: "a plus b is to a, as a
is to b". In practice, as used by Mondrian and other
modern artists, this deploys crucial lines on the
picture plane slightly more than a third away from
any particular edge; throughout art, painters have
used hidden triangles, rectangles and pentagrams to
express this allegedly beautiful ratio. Mathematicians
from Pythagoras onwards have been fascinated by
the golden mean, or golden ratio, which does indeed
recur frequently in nature, in the foldings of leaves,
for instance, or the arrangements of branches. But
it's easy to be carried away by something so neat,
and studies of a huge range of paintings suggest that
most artists don't actually follow the golden mean at
all. They probably work by instinct, and quite often
come somewhere close.

And that in itself is interesting. There are very
many paintings which simply have an object or
motif right at the centre, and leave it at that –
how many portraits are composed that way, for
instance? But in a less representational picture,
or in a landscape, for some reason the eye revolts
against neat bisection. I have in my hand a book of
Monet landscapes, and very rarely is there a strong
vertical or horizontal right at the centre of the
picture. Where there is, the composition feels

uncharacteristically lumpish and unattractive (sorry Claude).

Mostly Monet pushes the horizon line or the central division – which might be vertical, in a scene of trees – to not-quite-exactly a third of the way up or along; and almost everybody does the same. What is it about this proportion that is so very satisfying?

Could it be that as vertical bipeds we are used to constantly moving our heads? We must scan the landscape in front of us for signs of danger or food, while periodically checking the sky (particularly if we live in northern Europe). Sometimes, as the day is ending or beginning, or some important weather system is moving in, we are concentrating above the horizon, rather than below it. It's about the tilt of the skull on the spine – two-thirds, one third; one third, two-thirds. Could it really be as simple as that? I don't know but I haven't so far heard a better explanation.

Like all rules, it is there to be broken. One of the most sophisticated and witty masters of composition was Henri Matisse. In his famous *The Piano Lesson* of 1916, which is for me one of the most beautiful things ever painted, he put a bold light-blue vertical line almost (not quite but almost) down the centre of the painting. But by connecting it to a thicker vertical blue and then to a light orange, he jerks it towards the right of the picture and the golden mean. Further, by concentrating much of the action – the piano-playing boy and the attentive, slightly forbidding, seated woman – on the right, leaving left of the plane emptier, he achieves a completely satisfying composition. The flurry of the vertical lines towards the bottom of the picture plane – the blacks on pink and the blues on green – all converge around the golden mean, or something like it. Matisse is playing with us – playing with our expectations about composition – very successfully.

THE PIANO LESSON. ISSY-LES-MOULINEAUX, LATE SUMMER 1916
Henri Matisse

A SHORT BOOK ABOUT PAINTING

Another way of subverting the "rule of thirds" is to ensure that one part of the canvas is so thickly painted that we frankly don't care exactly where the division appears. Joan Eardley, the 20th-century Scottish painter, made a series of pictures of the sea off the north-east coast, some of which are indeed divided – horizontally – about halfway up. But the frenzied brushstrokes and loaded paint of the bottom half so dominate the more thinly painted skies that she gets away with it.

Very much the same was done by Robert Rauschenberg at about the same time in his picture *Rebus*. Painted on three panels, it is dominated by a horizontal composed of small vertical colour swatches, as if from a paint manufacturer's catalogue. But almost all the action of the picture – including clippings from comics, slashes of white paint and dripping slabs of maroon – is hunched above the line, most, but not all the way to the top, because that would be too blatant a division. Below the line are only the thinnest of scribblings, dripping paint and blank grey-brown space. It's a brilliant example of the use of thirds.

Of course, there is much more to composition than this. The picture plane is a limited surface and the eye will naturally speed towards its centre. To make sure that the viewer doesn't simply look all in one place, the painter needs to aim away, but subtly. Centre, but not dead centre. In front of an interesting picture, the eye will keep moving. But this means, in turn, that the edges of the picture will become a zone of anxiety – is

everything falling away towards them? Where is the coherence? This is about colour as much as shape. And again – just because he seems to me the most important painter since Pablo Picasso – overleaf is another Rauschenberg example, this time from an oil and silkscreen print he made in 1963.

Note, first, how he deals with the centre of the picture. The teetering white building, central to its theme of city chaos and near collapse, pulls over to the right. But the picture remains centred because

REBUS, 1955
Robert Rauschenberg

of the savage slashes of red and yellow around the "stop" sign just to its left. Above it, the remains of a street lamp divides the picture vertically almost a third, not quite two-thirds, as the eye likes. Rauschenberg only bothers with a little bit of this and lets the viewer complete the line internally.

Now let's focus on his use of colour. The reds and yellows, which are dominant, run from small blocks in the top right down to the bottom left in a rough diagonal line. Diagonals tend to signal danger or uncertainty, and this is part of the meaning of the image. If New York is an estate, it's one in very poor order. But had he left that diagonal as the only colour theme, the whole picture would have felt very unbalanced. So, alongside the strips of blackish screen-printed images of buildings running down the right-hand side of the picture, and then along the bottom (and ending with the Statue of Liberty seen from below), he has used patches of cobalt and ultramarine blue. The effect is to create a reversed L shape, which literally underpins and holds the rest of the picture together. It is so strong that Rauschenberg can allow the left-hand side of the picture to dissolve in kaleidoscopic patches of yellow, white and grey. He has perfectly resolved both the problem of the edges and of the centre; but I bet he did so almost unconsciously.

There are many other ways, clearly, of composing a picture surface. Richard Wright is a Glasgow-based artist who in 2009 won the Turner prize. Although he has produced "traditional" abstract paintings,

he is now best known for painting directly on to walls in different locations, making art that is designed to be scrubbed off again or to decay – deliberately ephemeral work. It's an interesting response to the ruthless commercialisation of the modern art world. Wright says: "It's not so easy for the work to be absorbed into the market... The work is not for the future, it's for now." His painting, which can be small in scale or very large, involves elaborate rococo patterns, meshes, the repetitions of lozenges and dashes in intricate, often gold, very beautiful forms. Because it's not made on a board or canvas which can be moved around, but on walls or ceilings, or behind bookcases, Wright doesn't have to worry about the problems of centring or edges, or not nearly so much. His composition is much closer to that of traditional textiles – Moroccan carpets for instance – than to composition as Matisse or Rauschenberg would have understood it.

What Wright proposes is that we could think about painting completely differently, getting away from the easel and the canvas. He is not alone. Richard Long, the British environmental artist, has made ephemeral spiral pictures using mud handprints on gallery walls. We will return to this later, looking at the big problem of the art market today. But all that needs to be said here is that composition is one of those things any conventional oil painter will be thinking about relentlessly while sitting in the studio, staring, apparently vacantly, at an empty canvas or a failing one.

The help that's at hand

If struggling artists are looking for specific help,
of course, there is plenty at hand, though much
of it turns out to be just selling by another name.
An excellent magazine, *The Artist*, is one of many
that offer practising painters monthly advice about
which crayons to try, how to cope with shadows
quickly in watercolour, how to represent a fast-
moving crowd, waves breaking, or whatever. The art
industry constantly presses upon practising painters
new sets of colour sticks, new brushes, new surfaces,
all with endless handbooks. Websites like that of
Keiko Tanabe, a popular watercolourist, constantly
update painting enthusiasts with tips and ideas. We
are surrounded by affable, self-deprecating gurus of
the sable brush.

But what these sources don't help with, in my
experience, is the fundamental problem: what should
a painting be? They tend to assume that mouth-
meltingly beautiful views of the Venetian canals,
street scenes in Nice, or the Appalachian hills, are
what's needed. Yes, really: yet more of all that. We
can all admire the virtuoso technique of a top-rate
conventional portraitist, or the photorealist who uses
tiny airbrushes to make an image of a chain fence
around an abandoned mid-American gas station, so
accurate that you initially assume it's a photograph.
I'm not knocking this stuff, which is all around us.
It just doesn't bring the heart into the mouth, or
make the hairs stand up on the nape of the neck.
Or not my heart, mouth, hairs and neck, anyway.

Almost all amateur painters want to improve, and that's a good thing. They may start off making badly drawn and implausibly coloured images of Devon cottages, and be determined to work and learn their way to doing the same thing much more proficiently – so that we "believe" the shadows on windows, and nod with recognition at the shape of trees and the yellowish crud on the bottom of November clouds. This is all fine.

This is what an influential section of the art industry wants us all to do – a patient upgrading of skills and observation that raises really bad painters into perfectly acceptable, house-trained image-makers who do no harm. But, although "do no harm" is a good starting point for a doctor or nurse, and a lot better than the alternative, it's not really good enough for painting.

It suggests that painting is like baking or knitting and that with enough practice and dexterity and close attention to process, you will be able to produce a good picture of the Thames at sunset, just as you will eventually, after a lot of smoke and cursing, learn to produce an almost perfect Victoria sponge. It will be harmoniously balanced with convincingly falling shadows, composed of mixtures of ultramarine and umber (the Thames, not the sponge); the horizon line in exactly the right place; and the details of buildings and shipping indicated, but not drawn in with irritating and confusing detail. You will have learned your lessons, and learned them well.

I'm aware that by now I will have infuriated quite a lot of readers, who will be thinking, "and what the hell is wrong with that?" Nothing. Learning to look really closely is good in itself. You cease to take the beauties of the world for granted and you sharpen your intelligence. Just as learning to listen to complex music is good for the brain, I am sure that learning to look closely is an incontrovertible good.

Similarly, as a craftsman, learning how to use, clean and exploit your materials is a damned sight better than bodging. I'd rather go around a local art show whose members understand oil paint and linseed oil, than one whose members thwack on the acrylic and can't draw.

Better is better. But I come back to the problem that only a few paintings or painters actually rock you, change the way you think, make you see and think about the world afresh. Competent, conventional art may be good for the artist but it doesn't much help the keen-eyed and avid art lover.

To say that isn't being elitist. Think again about the huge crowds that force their way into towns to come and look at work by the big names of today – Gillian Ayres, Bridget Riley, Howard Hodgkin, Anselm Kiefer, Frank Auerbach, Georg Baselitz, Gerhard Richter. These are not, by and large, "easy" painters who have worked their way up through magazines and websites. But they have all asked fundamental questions about what pictures should look like now, and why, and as a result they have set aflame the imaginations of millions of fellow humans and – a really trivial point for which I apologise in advance – set new records for the prices of their work. Interesting new painting compels attention. Even if hundreds of thousands of hard-working, attentive people learn to paint the light on a Venice canal not quite as well as John Singer Sargent managed to do in 1904 – and that is a very high bar – they won't change our imaginations a jot.

Humankind absorbed those pictures long ago, swallowed them down, digested them. They lack the one thing that all great painting requires, fresh freshness. The argument of this book is that to get there, you can't travel via the conventional high road of good painting. You have to push away the easy messages, the solutions that have emerged from centuries of practice, and work and think harder. Inevitably, most of the time, you will be making mistakes. Sometimes, they will turn out to be the right mistakes, and take you through a door you didn't know existed.

But if only it was as easy as that.

Every time I set up a blank canvas or a blank piece of paper, I experience the same feeling – queasiness, something approaching panic, and a profound lack of self-belief. There are a limitless number of marks that could be made, and almost all of them will be mistakes. That is, they will set up a logic which will lead the picture towards banality or pointless mimicry. For every mark implies another. Will that circle be repeated or answered by a different shape? Will it be a sun,

a plate, a face? That stuttering horizontal line –
it's the sea isn't it? Or if it's not, you'd better
work hard and fast to make that clear. And so on.

One of the reasons painters tend to develop a
signature style and stick to it is that this helps answer
the original panic. Some people will always begin
with an image at the centre of the picture plane. It
seems that Picasso mostly does this – a face, a bird,
a group of figures, will shoulder themselves out of
the centre, and the lines will press away towards
the edges of the paper or canvas. Other painters
think very hard about the edges, and work inwards.
Oddly, because his pictures mostly involve a central
shimmering block of colours, I think Mark Rothko
probably painted that way. But an initial, bold
decision about how to break up the picture surface,
and – to put it banally – what will go where, helps
any painter get going. And once you have a way in,
you are likely to use it again and again; and that way
in will hugely influence what's going to happen next.

The final thing I'm always thinking about when
I'm staring at a possible picture is balance. You
want the eye to move around the picture surface,
and that means it's better to set up echoes, or
correspondences, in shape and colour that encourage
the eye to keep moving. But if there's too much
balance, like a perfectly matched tug-of-war contest,
the picture becomes static. On the next page is a
little picture of a seaside garden, partly in homage to
Patrick Heron, who at the end of his life loved the
combination of yellow and violet I use on the far left.

The different systems of balance are, I hope, pretty obvious. You have the vertical violet and yellow columns down the left, answered by orange and green columns on the right – not too balanced and therefore differently sized. The axe shapes on the left are met by the primitive boat-like orange eruption on the right. The brown/dull blue diagonal below the shark fin or boat is matched by the sky blue diagonal above it; the violet circle and the blurred orange circle observe each other.

HIGHLAND GARDEN
Andrew Marr

A SHORT BOOK ABOUT PAINTING

I don't claim that this is a particularly profound painting, and its subject is only the emotional experiences of being outside on a particular day surrounded by vague thoughts of ancient days that I couldn't write down in words. But it's a good example of the problems of composition: if you took away a single one of the elements I have listed, the whole thing would collapse and be nothing but an incoherent mess. It holds together. Just. It nearly didn't. And that's what goes on in the studio.

6 PAINTING NOW

What are paintings made from, and why?
The artist Antony Gormley has said that all art is made for the future. By that he might mean simply that innovative art is often not understood during the era when it's being made. It takes time for people to get used to changes of direction and fully appreciate their point. But I guess that Gormley meant something subtler – that art is a message, thrown from the present into the future – *hello, you, this is how it felt for us.*

Proper art is about wrestling with the here and now, more than it is consciously pitched forward; but authentic accounts of any kind will be interesting when the artists involved are long gone. Art that is in any way serious will reflect the conditions in which it is made.

So what, in the teenage years of the 21st century, are those conditions? We live in a pessimistic age, and one of accelerating change, in which we are expected to be scared about climate change, terrorism, growing inequality, shrinking biodiversity and much more besides. Art which reflected that would be angry and pessimistic, and carry within it some sense of things careering out of control: and from Jake and Dinos Chapman, to Gilbert and George, to some of the work of Damien Hirst, there are indeed plenty of examples of this kind of art.

But we also live in what you might call *the age of new toys*. We are digitally informed, digitally entertained and often digitally employed generations. We are drunk on virtual reality and we are hooked on contemporary technologies – even if we are also

HELL, 1998–2000
Jake and Dinos Chapman

uneasily aware that the robots may be coming for our jobs. And our increasingly omnipresent digital surroundings also have a direct effect on contemporary art. They are part of the times we live in, reflected in the increasing use of digital film and computer drawing, including by artists such as Michael Craig-Martin.

Nothing very new there, you might say. Some of the biggest changes in art have been in response to technological innovation. David Hockney has written passionately about the impact of better lenses, better grinding and photographic boxes on the work of artists as diverse as Caravaggio, Vermeer and Ingres. More recently, during the late 19th and early 20th centuries when chemical photographs arrived to challenge original, handmade art, artists reacted by trying to make their work as little like any possible reproductions as they could.

The "eat me" stippled and blurred brushwork of the Impressionists and Fauvists showed the importance of breaking away from the smooth surfaces of academic painters – photography could do smooth surfaces and brushless effects far better than they could. Next, the Cubists and later the Abstract Expressionists, responded to photography by making images that broke further away from immediate, easily apprehended reality – images that photography couldn't have imagined.

Today's digital revolution takes this old argument much, much further. First, digital manipulation means that photography has chased after the artists

UNTITLED (GROUP I), 2017
(ACRYLIC ON ALUMINIUM)
Michael Craig-Martin

and caught them pretty easily. It allows endless "effects" – copies, variations, improvements, blurrings, stipplings. A relatively simple computer program can be used to turn an image of a Tokyo street, or your neighbour, into a "Van Gogh"; Picasso's distortions can be mimicked by a child in a bedroom with a touchpad or a mouse.

But second, the digital world is global and almost seamlessly interconnected. It obliterates the local. Contemporary artists are responding to both things. They have been concentrating on the material fabric of their art, creating "real-world" pictures and sculptures that are a conscious rebuke to digitalisation – art made from mud, wood, fabric, lead and ice. Third, in the midst of economic and cultural globalisation, the most interesting art has been defiantly local or national – today's great German painters are very Germanic, while the

BOTTLE OF RUM AND NEWSPAPER, 1913–4
Juan Gris

LILBURN TOWER, DUNSTANBURGH CASTLE, NORTHUMBERLAND,
Ross Armstrong

art of Tokyo and London is at least as far apart in tone and feel as it was in 1870.

In short, there is an artistic counter-revolution going on which, because of the fashionable nature of the art world itself, has not perhaps been properly understood.

Let's start with the material fabric of contemporary art. Robert Rauschenberg was one of the great American originals, a man whose interests and ambitions flared in many directions, and whose influence on today's art has been underestimated. As I suggested earlier, I think he may be the most important painter since Pablo Picasso.

Most of his work is the opposite of a glossy, smooth digital surface, though he did make screen-prints. In any exhibition or museum, the labels traditionally give the viewer the same basic, essential information – the name of the artist and the piece, its date of creation, and what it is made of. "John Fuller, *Portrait of a Man*, 1948, oil on canvas" – that kind of thing. Well, here is the equivalent from the Tate exhibition for Rauschenberg's 1955–59 work *Monogram*: "oil, paper, fabric, printed reproductions, metal, wood, rubber shoe-heel, and tennis ball on two conjoined canvases with oil on taxidermy Angora goat with brass plaque and rubber tire on wood platform, mounted on four casters..."

That is an extreme example but other more conventional-looking works involve, we are told, "cut-out compartment containing four Coca-Cola bottles... And unidentified debris" or "glass, mirror, tin, caulk, a pair of the artist's socks and painted leather shoes, dried grass and taxidermied Plymouth Rock hen", or "oil, pencil, toothpaste, and red fingernail polish on pillow, quilt... and bed sheet mounted on wood supports."

This sounds just the kind of thing that haters of modern art love to laugh at – typical London metropolitan 21st-century rubbish. So the first thing to be said is that these are works made quite a long time ago, in the mid-1950s; and the second, is that they are all extremely beautiful. Rauschenberg had an almost uncanny ability to scatter shapes and colours across the surface in a way that forces you to stare, and finally makes you grin with delight. So why was he importing taxidermy, articles of clothing, pieces of metal and rubbish into his paintings? In part, he was interested in making art in three dimensions out of the debris of contemporary New York, where he was then living.

But he was also making pieces that are impossible to reproduce, because they depend upon "real stuff". The result is that you absolutely have to go and see them in person to understand what he was doing. He can't be understood from books. Or, indeed, from computer screens. He ditched canvases in favour of wooden supports because he could nail or drill through them to introduce foreign objects to make them thicker and more complex. These are pictures which, despite the high quality of the art catalogue that came with the show, are completely impossible to reproduce. They are much more, almost defiantly, themselves than 99 per cent of modern painting.

There is virtually no such thing as a completely new idea in art and Rauschenberg learned a lot from the German artist Kurt Schwitters.

One of the modern artists hated by Hitler, Schwitters fled Nazi Germany to work in Holland, then in an internment camp on the Isle of Man, before at last ending up in the English Lake District. A true original, he experimented early on with collages composed of torn pieces of scrap, matchboxes, bus tickets and discarded fragments of painted wood and glass. Some of his experiments were more successful than others: sculptures made in the Isle of Man from porridge quickly turned to foul-smelling mould. But the bulk of his collages, many of them three-dimensional, are breathtakingly beautiful. They are some of the most gorgeous objects ever made by a modern artist. Schwitters always regarded himself as a painter, though one who "nails his paintings together"; he called his technique *Merz*, a made-up name which came from a fragment of paper used in a 1918 work which had the German word "Commerz" printed on it.

His work has survived not because of what he made it from, but because of his innate feeling for colour and composition. But the way Schwitters made pictures has been hugely influential. First of all, if you have a slight three-dimensionality on the picture plane, then it constantly changes, as the light source shifts. It can't be entirely static. Subtle

above
**KURT SCHWITTERS,
DURING RECITAL OF HIS
"URSONATE", LONDON
1944**

right
**MERZBILD ROSSFETT,
1918–19**
Kurt Schwitters

shadows alter the composition at different times of day: in the age of film, art was moving away from the notion that a picture is always the same thing once it has been made.

Second, his use of scrap and found materials was itself a challenge to the pomposities of high art – Marcel Duchamp was the other great innovator here, though I think the lesser artist. Finally, because the found materials came from popular culture, these were pictures that helplessly carried the impress of the place and time of their making. They include Berlin bus tickets, or adverts for chocolate peppermints in 1940s Britain, or a fragment of a label advertising a long-forgotten exhibition. Schwitters might have been a transient, international artist, but he lived and created very much in his here and now.

A much more famous German artist shows the power but also the limitations of these ways of working. Joseph Beuys was born under the Nazis and fought in the Second World War as the gunner in a Stuka dive-bomber. When his plane crashed in the Crimea in 1944, Beuys survived – he said, because he had been found in the snow by Tatar tribesmen who wrapped him in animal fat and felt as part of the healing process. Records suggest that in fact Beuys had a much more humdrum rescue and was discovered by a German rescue party, there being no tribesmen in the area. Even so, he used this memory, or fantasy, throughout his life in art, deploying rolls of felt, sticks, pieces of basalt rock, sledges and much more to create a kind of epic spiritual story. He inserted himself as a kind of shaman in the modern art story.

Beuys's position is paradoxical. He was undoubtedly one of the most influential artists of the second half of the 20th century, famous in every major city and exhibited all around the world. His ponderous self-importance and rather grim style have been copied by hundreds, probably thousands, of lesser figures. And yet, in terms of public affection and a living, vital tradition, his art has not taken off. Animal fat and felt are admirable materials, but art is more than stories. Without a sense of beauty, and skill as a communicator in shape and colour, even the most ambitious innovator is bound to fail. Today, Schwitters is more alive than Beuys.

His work has great relevance for painters in the teenage years of this new century because it insists not only that art can be made out of anything – not only that it must be material and specific – but also that it must grab you by the throat. What cannot be devoured by the digital revolution? The smudgy, aromatic nature of charcoal. The random clagginess of heavy oil paint. Sticks. Stones. Broken bones. Dust. Stink. In short, the materiality of life. But what must art also be? That unfashionable but essential thing – beautiful.

Many of the most interesting contemporary artists feel the same. In an interview published by the Royal Academy magazine in the winter of 2016, the painter Aimée Parrott, in conversation with Basil Beattie, defended what she called the directness of painting made by hand and without new technology. She liked, she said, the "material presence of a painting, its fragility and yet density – its sense of layered time which benefits from a long slow look in order to unfold – in contrast to the slipperiness of the sanitised, disembodied image on a screen hastily scrolled through. I think this makes painting seem out of step, makes it stick out and sets up a very interesting tension between two very different modes of looking and experiencing..."

The issue could hardly be put more clearly. Beattie agreed with her, pointing out that work made by hand involves trial and error, emotion and happenstance – all, of course, part of being alive. He told a story about a group of American painters being asked by a critic what it was like when they went into the studio. One of them, Philip Guston, answered by quoting the composer John Cage: "The studio is full of other people, and as you begin to paint, the people begin to leave, one by one. And if you're really lucky, you'll leave." This sense of awe, and delight in the contingent, is pure Kurt Schwitters.

Rauschenberg said of Schwitters that he felt he had made everything "just for me" and many other artists have felt the same delighted recognition when encountering the art of this genial, modest German genius. In 1967, the Italian art critic Germano Celant coined the term "Arte Povera" for a wave of radical Italian art making. Celant himself made sculptures out of wire and human hair. Others in the movement used logs, sticks, ropes, mounds of old clothes and discarded industrial rubbish – and even, in one notorious case, the artist's own excrement, carefully encased in metal tins. In all this, we are getting a long way from painting, the subject of this book, and towards assemblage, performance art and conceptualism. But the basic point is that by using objects from the real world, contemporary artists can defend themselves against the overwhelming wave of digital imagery.

We see this still, running riot in contemporary Britain, from the "YBAs" or young British artists (though they no longer are young) through to environmental artists. Think of Hirst with his cabinets, his pickled shark and his flies emerging from rotten meat only to be electrocuted. Think of the satirical-erotic work of Sarah Lucas, with her buckets, fried eggs, stuffed stockings and suggestive fruit.

Think of the work of Richard Wright, the ephemeral, delicate painting on walls, destined to be scrubbed off again, or Richard Long and his mud paintings. Think of Andy Goldsworthy, who makes exquisite sculptures out of fragments of ice, brightly coloured autumn leaves pinned together with thorns, teetering assemblages of stones, or wall-pictures from mud.

Of course, there is a paradox in much of this art. Sarah Lucas, defiant fag hanging from her mouth, found that most of the work had to be photographed to be disseminated. She couldn't sit forever with her fried eggs on her chest, so the work is known now entirely from reproductions.

Goldsworthy's art melts, decays or is blown over – that is in the nature of what he does. Very few people can experience a Goldsworthy sculpture in the flesh (and the snow, and the woods, and the puddles). Though I find it very fine and moving, this art too can only be understood generally in reproductions in art books or occasional gallery shows, again often as photographs of the original work.

So does this mean that the breakthroughs established by Kurt Schwitters must disintegrate and vanish as well? That, in the age of digital reproduction, art made out of the crumbling materials of life itself, as a response to technology and a global market, can only be enjoyed through digital reproduction?

Well hold on. What about the art of Schwitters himself? You can still see that. You can walk into galleries all around the world and enjoy his assemblages, paintings and drawings still as bright and fresh and immediate as on the day they were made. The best response to the cold digital present is painting, that old and simple practice.

The country that has dominated contemporary painting more than any other over the past couple of decades is not the United States but Germany, and among the best-loved German artists is Anselm Kiefer. Younger than Beuys or Schwitters, Kiefer was born right at the end of the Nazi era. His work confronts German history much more directly than either of theirs does but, like Rauschenberg, his kind of oil paintings had never been seen before.

SELF-PORTRAIT WITH FRIED EGGS, 1996
Sarah Lucas

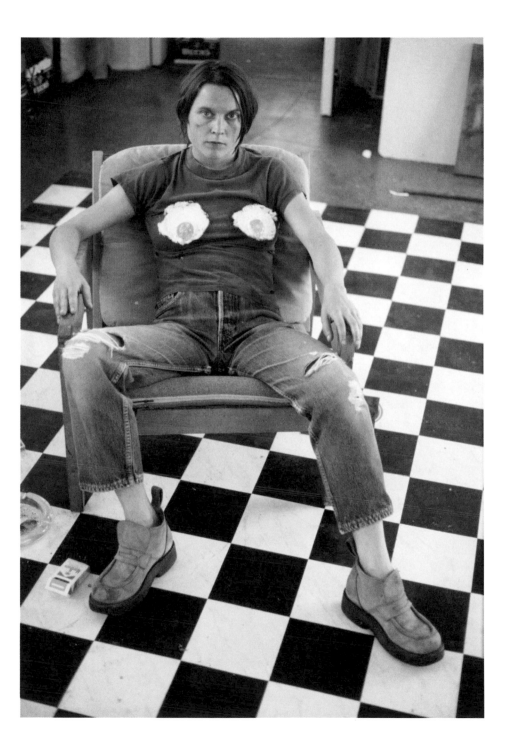

He isn't only a painter. He has made massive, wood-bound books, huge metal sculptures, stark, gigantic woodcuts, fantastic works of architecture, and vitrines that hold dresses, fragments of trees and feathers. But it's the paintings that hold the viewer most directly. Whether his subject is the ancient cities of Mesopotamia, with their brick ruins and messages about power and civilisation; or the endless German plains; or wartime dogfights; or dragon-haunted Teutonic forests; or the optimistic uplift of sunflowers and cornfields, Kiefer's paintings are big in every direction.

They sprawl across gallery walls, forcing the viewer to keep walking backwards to see them properly. But then you are tugged closer to them again, to stare at the thickness of the paint almost falling off the backing, and the savage, scored lines through the paint. This is not paint that represents bricks, or the rutted surface of a field. It is, apparently, paint that has *become* bricks, or mud, or human flesh. As with Rauschenberg's work, there are objects inserted into the surface of the picture – they might be model ships made out of lead, or real pieces of corn, or industrial diamonds. Some paintings include glass cases, so that woodland might be both painted and represented by real twigs and sticks.

Again, as with Rauschenberg, it is possible to take photographs of Anselm Kiefer's paintings and reproduce them but they are really nothing like the real thing. You have to go and see them.

LET A THOUSAND FLOWERS BLOOM, 2000
Anselm Kiefer

In the course of this short chapter I find that I have chosen artists – Schwitters, Rauschenberg and now Kiefer – who have been the subject of recent exhibitions in London. There is nothing surprising about that. Good art can't be enjoyed at second hand, even in the most lavishly produced catalogue, and that becomes more true, not less, as artists rough up the surface of their work. The surface records the making, not just the subject.

Because Jackson Pollock's action paintings were a record of Jackson Pollock's balletic body movements, recording the size and shape of his arms, legs and torso, they were a record of something that couldn't be mimicked by machines. Scroll towards 2017 and the argument has become more urgent, not less so. The best art doesn't present a smooth, lucent shine to the world. It almost assaults the physical viewer.

Potent influence doesn't simply bounce from one genius to the next, like a ball being thrown. It ripples out and eddies and is found in unexpected corners, repeatedly and all over the place. Concentration on the material nature of painting, and leaving in the marks as a record of what was done to the surface, and an interest in the humble as against the expensive or elite – these are traits found almost everywhere.

Jason Martin is a London based painter whose work consists of a very thick pigment, in oil bound with poppy seed oil, or sometimes acrylic, slewed on to an aluminium base using a metal or plastic slider, so that the subject of the picture is the richly enfolded paint itself and incredibly sensuous. Even

UNTITLED (DAVY'S GREY/ TITANIUM WHITE/RAW UMBER), 2016
OIL ON ALUMINIUM
220 x 178CM
Jason Martin

when he is restricting himself to grey and white, this is painting which, when you meet it, you want to eat it.

Another painter, a friend of mine, Adrian Hemming, demonstrates how this interest in the surface and the texture of paint can produce landscapes which are both recognisable and unlike anything done before. He grinds and mixes his own pigments and uses a wide variety of fixatives to get effects that again – I am glad to say – cannot quite be reproduced and have to be seen in the flesh.

So, I hope I've convinced you that one of the most important aspects of good contemporary painting is that it should react against the omnipresent, glassy, digital effect of most modern culture – that it insists on being itself. And a second, perhaps less obvious, quality is that it often derives from local circumstances, rather than from some nebulous, abstract globalised culture. In short, it is *real* and it is *local*.

But also, it ought to be fresh, even unique. I've listed a great many influential contemporary artists here, and this raises another question that everyone who tries to paint must confront: what is acceptable learning from the masters and mistresses, and what is merely plagiarism? There are so many examples of painting all around us, so many different kinds of experimentation running in so many different directions, that it's increasingly hard for an artist to respond to that simple-seeming injunction: be yourself.

WATER SLIDE, 2010
Adrian Hemming

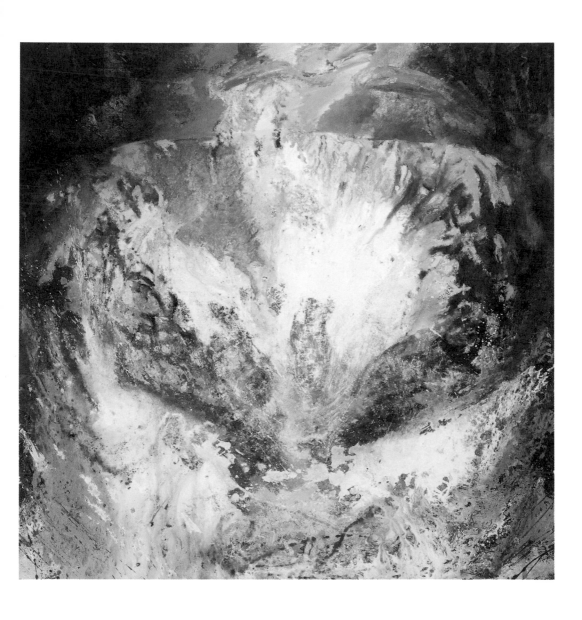

My answer is that no artist owns a technique, whether or not he or she invented it. Ways of laying on paint, unexpected mediums to mix with paint, the use of scalpels, masking tape, aluminium bases, or plastic boxes inserted on to the painting surface – all these techniques, or tricks, are available to anyone who wants to try them. I spend a lot of time ambling around looking at other people's pictures and trying to learn from them. Declining to try something out yourself because it has been done first by another person would be as logical as a guitarist declining to use newly invented pedals, or a film-maker rejecting a new camera. And artists tend to be magpies in other ways too. Including aspects of photorealism alongside much rougher painting was a trick used by almost all the great pop artists. As soon as Caravaggio demonstrated the powerful, visceral effects of a harsh overhead light source on the wrinkled, battered faces of the street, everybody was trying it. So far, so much virtuous learning.

But once an artist has painfully won through to find a unique way of drawing the world, swiping *that* for yourself is simply theft. The one thing you cannot appropriate is the vision. To make your own pictures using Roy Lichtenstein's cartoon spots technique would – rightly – invite ridicule. Other artists have copied David Hockney's sophisticated coloured pencil drawing technique from the 1970s. But it still belongs to him, and nobody else.

Somehow or another, it is the obligation of any proper painter to eventually make images which belong to them, which aren't quite like pictures made by anybody else before, and which represent their own individual human view of the world. It's incredibly difficult. But it's also incredibly important because only then, and not before then, do you have the right to call the work your own.

And intellectual property matters, in turn, because of the bloody, grinding-down and increasingly depressing problem of art economics.

Following the money

Art materials have never been more handily available, probably never cheaper. The trouble is that images have never been cheaper and easier to obtain, either. In the Victorian period, an artist like Turner knew that there was an insatiable demand for coloured representations, big and impressive, to hang in the homes of the wealthy. But even when demand from the Earl of Oatcake and Lord and Lady Porridge was lagging a bit, Turner and his contemporaries could sell engravings in huge quantities – either to illustrate books or to hang in the houses of the less wealthy middle classes. Even in the 1930s, artists such as the East London group, painting smallish oil pictures of the streets and landscapes around them, could rely on a steady flow of customers wanting to decorate their lives.

But today you can get an excellent reproduction of almost any of the world's greatest art to hang wherever you want it. Only the super-rich still buy art as a form of investment and showing off. There aren't many of them. Economically, the biggest shifts in past decades have seen wealth and power cluster around a small number of super-winners – look at the change in the distribution curve of income in the United States or the UK, for instance, over the past decade.

It's a common perception that in many fields, the gap between the hyper-successful minority and the unsuccessful majority has grown wider. Whether you are a Premier League footballer, a tennis player, a worker in banking or indeed a journalist, a very small number of people are now paid far more, proportionally, than they would have been in the 1950s or 1970s, while the majority find their real incomes are worth a lot less. Analysis of the average wages in major companies, compared to the earnings of the CEOs (Chief Executive Officers – or top knobs) suggests that in business at least this pervasive feeling is not merely a rumour. According to *Fortune* magazine, in a 2015 article reporting on an independent survey, "In between 1978 and 2014, inflation-adjusted CEO pay increased by almost 1000%...Meanwhile, typical workers in the US saw a pay raise of just 11% during that same period."

While I have no statistical evidence for this, my strong impression is that in art making as well, the gap between those earning fabulous fortunes and those just chugging along has also grown substantially. In early 2012, the American journalist Joy Yoon attempted to list the world's most wealthy living artists. Many of the names are indeed world-famous. David Hockney, Antony Gormley, Anish Kapoor and

Damien Hirst, who was the world's richest artist at the time, were all on it. So too were much less well-known artists who simply had the luck of having very rich patrons. Yoon argued that Hirst was worth around $1 billion, while Hockney, like the German artist Gerhard Richter, was worth $40 million.

The details, frankly, don't matter and are probably as much to do with shrewd financial decisions taken by successful artists as the original price tags of their work. Artists who are particularly interested in wealth understand that making prints, for instance, is an excellent way to boost their income: one well-known name told me recently that he could make more than half a million dollars very quickly by doing a print edition, and it was far more sensible economics than labouring away making original works.

If I compare this with the lives of professional painters I know who try to make a living by producing oblong canvases of representational or abstract work in oil, watercolour or acrylic, then it's frankly a different world.

These days, relatively few professional people – by which I mean doctors, teachers, entrepreneurs, office managers and the like – would think of spending several thousand pounds on an original artwork to hang in the lounge. Yet, to earn a decent living from painting, you need to sell works at several thousand pounds apiece, and you need to sell them relatively frequently. Price something at a few hundred pounds, and the world will take you at your very low self-estimation; you will have no chance of living on that.

A lot of this is about salesmanship and luck – finding an individual keen enough on what you do to keep coming back for more – as well as original talent. But if I didn't already have a full-time job as a broadcaster and writer, there is no way that I could afford to rent my own studio and spend so much time making paintings. I feel a little guilty about it at times: young professional artists must feel plagued by the lively and cut-price market in pictures by amateurs. If a computer programmer enjoys making delicate watercolours of city streets and sells them as a hobby for, say, £700 apiece, that may be disastrous news for the woman around the corner hoping to live from her paintings of similar scenes.

Of course, the artist starving in a garret is a stock cultural cliche; and painters as great as Van Gogh and Claude Monet lived at times in utter penury. But that was often because the starving artist was trying to make new, surprising and unfashionable art. There were plenty of ordinary, dull, fat artists as well. During the late 19th and early 20th centuries, artists could rely on a prosperous bourgeoisie to make a real market. That market is now smaller, not only because the prosperous bourgeoisie is proportionally smaller, but because of the disruptive effect of technology. Pictures are cheap. The super-rich compete for the works of a tiny number of globally famous, instantly recognisable art-makers, jostling one another in an obscure competition. Everybody else is scrabbling for coppers.

So what?

So what? That is the proper, emotionally mature response of proper, grown-up artists. Most full-time artists can think of doing nothing else and regard every hour they spend in a studio as a stroke of luck, time stolen from pointlessness. Painting has always been involved in the politics of power and money, from the high princes of the Renaissance, to the industrial barons of Boston and Minnesota. Painters have always been in trouble. But painting, proper painting, turns out to be as defiantly resilient as live music or poetry – an ancient art that revives itself in every human season. We have looked at the surrounding circumstances of contemporary art in different ways, from problems of technology and geography, to problems of money. It's time now, at the end, to ask again – what's it really all about?

7 IMMORTALITY

My wife and children ask me that. They find it odd
and, I'm afraid, slightly irritating when I trail off,
yet again, to the painting studio round the corner.
I should be doing something more normal, like
watching television, or eating buttered toast.
"What are you doing it for?" they want to know.

What is this compulsion to leave something
behind? What is this rather pathetic reaching
for some sort of immortality? The interrogative
banter starts to have an edge to it. Painting might
be a reasonable thing to do if you are a lifelong,
full-time and professional painter who can actually
earn a living by making pictures that people want.
For somebody like me, who has a perfectly good job
doing something else, it seems to smell of delusions

of grandeur. What *do* I do it for?

It's a reasonable question. It deserves an answer at the end of this short book. I am not completely deluded. I don't think I am Camden's Caravaggio, or the Picasso of Primrose Hill. I can tell the difference between great paintings and the rest and I know perfectly well that the pictures I make will never change the course of anything and may well be quickly forgotten just as soon as I shut up about them. I started on this journey far, far too late in life. There *are* important painters. I am not, and to my eternal regret, will never be.

Yet there is something inside that seems to have to fight its way out. What it feels like to be me and alive now is something I want to explain, and I can do so only through paint. I'm in my late 50s, not particularly well, and time is running out.

And I know enough to see that sometimes the pictures are successful as communication and sometimes they aren't. The ones that work are postcards. They are messages sent outside my immediate circle of friends and family, and even into the future. And all I really want is that they stay alive. I certainly don't want them to be inflated carriers of wealth – paint and canvas investments the price of which spirals ever upwards.

I want them to be conversationalists, smiling, gregarious yet silent talkers on the walls of private flats and houses, and perhaps public spaces such as schools, nursing homes and hospitals. I want them to speak to people I have never met and never will. That is, I hope people will stop in front of them and find something that catches their attention, and provokes questions and a musing half-smile.

For mysteriously, the thought and passion and work that goes into an oil painting can be caught on its dried surface – and then released, time and time again, as energy to the viewer. If I go and look at a picture by Peter Doig or Patrick Heron, something of what they poured into it in remote places or long ago, floods into me. Immortality, importance, a place in art history are all, no doubt, wonderful things, but the real point is a transfer of energy.

Often it doesn't happen. Paintings don't all live. On Monday, you can be putting your everything into a picture, thinking hard, working hard, and leaving the studio feeling that you have made something that earns its place, that's alive. And then you come in feeling chirpy on Tuesday… and the poor beast has died in the night. Yes, there are just the same colours in just the same places, but it's a dry corpse. If you hung it on a wall, you couldn't keep coming back to look again, except with mounting distaste and horror.

The line between this dead picture and another picture which, against all the odds, despite some terrible bodging and moments of despair, seems to stay alive, is a tiny, flickering thing. It isn't a line you can touch with your finger. But it's the fatal division between transcendence and boredom. It's the only thing that matters.

Acknowledgments

I'd like to thank the hugely professional Quadrille team, Sarah Lavelle, Helen Lewis and Liz Boyd; my excellent editor Jinny Johnson and talented designer Gemma Wilson; the late, great Ed Victor, my agent; my invaluable life-boss Mary Greenham; and Nic Corke of the Nic Corke Gallery in Liverpool, who took the huge risk of mounting my first solo show in the summer of 2017.

PICTURE CREDITS

The images used within this book are the copyright of the author, unless stated otherwise.
The publisher would like to thank the following artists, photographers, agencies, galleries and organisations for their kind permission to reproduce the photographs in this book:

p2-3, p5 and p7 Andy Sewell; p23 Private Collection/James Goodman Gallery, New York, USA/ Bridgeman Images © The Estate of Jean-Michel Basquiat / ADAGP, Paris and DACS, London; p27 © Tate, London 2017; p29 2017©Photo Josse/Scala, Florence. © Successió Miró / ADAGP, Paris and DACS London 2017; p31 Courtesy of the artist and Simon Lee Gallery London/Hong Kong; p33 Private Collection, UK. Photograph courtesy of Richard Green Gallery, London; p34-35 David Messum Fine Art; p37 David Messum Fine Art; p45 © Frank Auerbach, courtesy Marlborough Fine Art; p47 National Galleries of Scotland, Edinburgh/Bridgeman Images; p49 National Galleries of Scotland, Edinburgh / Bridgeman Images; p51 Collection of the Duke of Devonshire, Chatsworth House, UK/© Devonshire Collection, Chatsworth/Reproduced by permission of Chatsworth Settlement Trustees/Bridgeman Images; p52 Mermaid, Jason Heeley; p54 ©2017. Photo Scala, Florence – courtesy of the Ministero Beni e Att. Culturali; p63 courtesy of the artist and Bernard Jacobson Gallery; p65 © Tate, London 2017 © The Estate of Patrick Heron. All rights reserved, DACS 2017; p69 Leeds Museums and Galleries (Leeds Art Galllery) U.K./ Bridgeman Images © Bridget Riley 2017. All rights reserved; p73 © Tate, London 2017. © The Barnett Newman Foundation, New York / DACS, London 2017; p76 Wonderland (oil, acrylic and glitter on canvas, 2004) © Fiona Rae. All rights reserved, DACS 2017; p77 Anthony and Cleopatra, 1983, Gillian Ayres OBE (b. 1930), purchased by Tate 1982. © Tate, London 2017; p97 Brooklyn Museum of Art, New York, USA/Gift of A. Augustus Healy/Bridgeman Images; p99 © 2017. Digital image, The Museum of Modern Art, New York/Scala, Florence. © Succession H. Matisse/DACS 2017; p101 © 2017. Digital image, The Museum of Modern Art, New York/Scala, Florence © Robert Rauschenberg Foundation/DACS, London/VAGA, New York; p103 © 2017. Photo, The Philadelphia Museum of Art/Art Resource/Scala, Florence © Robert Rauschenberg Foundation/DACS, London/ VAGA, New York; p113 © Jake and Dinos Chapman. Courtesy of the Saatchi Gallery, London; p115 © Michael Craig-Martin. Courtesy the artist and Gagosian. Photo: Mike Bruce; p116 Ross Armstrong; p117 © Tate, London 2017; p120 bpk/Sprengel Museum Hannover/Ernst Schwitters © DACS 2017; p121 © 2017. White Images/Scala, Florence © DACS 2017; p127 copyright the artist, courtesy Sadie Coles HQ, London; p129 © Anselm Kiefer. © Tate, London 2017; p131 © Jason Martin; Courtesy Lisson Gallery. Photography: Jack Hems; p133 © Adrian Hemming.

Andrew Marr's paintings photographed by A C Cooper.

The publisher has made every effort to trace the copyright holders. We apologise in advance for any unintentional omissions and would be pleased to insert the appropriate acknowledgement in any subsequent edition.